Synchronization Algorithms and Concurrent Programming

Visit the *Synchronization Algorithms and Concurrent Programming* Companion Website at **www.pearsoned.co.uk/taubenfeld** to find valuable **student** learning material including:

- Multiple choice questions
- PowerPoint slides
- All figures from the book
- Programming assignments
- Errata

PEARSON
Education

Synchronization Algorithms and Concurrent Programming

Gadi Taubenfeld

Harlow, England • London • New York • Boston • San Francisco • Toronto
Sydney • Tokyo • Singapore • Hong Kong • Seoul • Taipei • New Delhi
Cape Town • Madrid • Mexico City • Amsterdam • Munich • Paris • Milan

Pearson Education Limited
Edinburgh Gate
Harlow
Essex CM20 2JE
England

and Associated Companies throughout the world

Visit us on the World Wide Web at:
www.pearsoned.co.uk

First published 2006

ISBN: 978-0-13-197259-9

British Library Cataloguing-in-Publication Data
A catalogue record for this book is available from the British Library

Library of Congress Cataloging-in-Publication Data

Taubenfeld, Gadi.
Synchronization algorithms and concurrent programming / Gadi Taubenfeld.
p. cm.
Includes bibliographical references and index.
ISBN 0-13-197259-6
1. Electronic data processing—Distributed processing. 2. Parallel programming (Computer science) 3. Computer algorithms. I. Title.
QA76.9.D5.T38 2006
004'.35—dc22

2006040785

10 9 8 7 6 5 4 3 2
10 09

Typeset in 10/12pt Sabon by 71
Printed in Great Britain by Henry Ling Ltd., at the Dorset Press, Dorchester, Dorset

The publisher's policy is to use paper manufactured from sustainable forests.

For my parents,
Hana and Arie Taubenfeld

Contents

Supporting resources

Visit **www.pearsoned.co.uk/taubenfeld** to find valuable online resources

Companion Website for students

- Multiple choice questions
- PowerPoint slides
- All figures from the book
- Programming assignments
- Errata

For instructors

- Instructor's Manual with solutions
- All figures from the book

For more information please contact your local Pearson Education sales representative or visit **www.pearsoned.co.uk/taubenfeld**

Preface

Synchronization is a fundamental problem in computer science. It is fast becoming a major performance and design issue for concurrent programming on modern architectures, and for the design of distributed systems.

The focus of this book is on interactions between processes that involve synchronization. Two types of synchronization are considered: contention and cooperation. The contention problem is, how to resolve conflicts that result from several processes trying to use shared resources. Put another way, how to allocate shared resources to competing processes. A special case of a general resource allocation problem, which we study in detail, is the mutual exclusion problem where only a single resource is available. Cooperation (or coordination) is characterized by the fact that an action by one process may enable an action by another process. Hence, processes may need to coordinate their actions.

The book covers various research results motivated by problems of synchronization which arise from building systems. This includes concurrent algorithms, lower and upper bounds, and impossibility results. Emphasis is placed on realistic models of computation and realistic fault assumptions. We concentrate mainly on asynchronous systems. That is, systems that do not run off a single clock, where there is no assumption regarding the relative speed of the processors, or where an operation can be delayed for arbitrarily long time. We cover both fault-free and fault-tolerant solutions. We focus on deterministic solutions but will also discuss randomized solutions.

The book is meant to be used as a textbook for an upper level undergraduate, or graduate course. The expected prerequisite knowledge is courses in analysis of (sequential) algorithms and data structures. Otherwise, the book is self-contained. No reliance on previous knowledge is made beyond the general background discussed above. Another main purpose is to bring together much of the research conducted in recent years on synchronization concepts, so that it can be used as a tool for relating to past research and to stimulate further research.

Each chapter ends with a section that contains problems about the material of the chapter. In my opinion, this section is the most interesting section of the chapter and the reader is encouraged to read it as part of the text. The problems are divided into six categories according to their difficulty. Some of problems introduce new results and topics, while others introduce open problems–problems that, as far as I know, have not been solved yet. A bibliographic notes section gives historical perspective, references, and places the chapter within a broader field.

Contact information: Please feel free to contact me with any criticism or comments which might help to improve any future version of this book. I would be glad to hear from you! I can be reached by electronic mail at `tgadi@idc.ac.il` or by sending hardcopy mail to: Prof. Gadi Taubenfeld, The Interdisciplinary Center, P.O. Box 167, Herzliya 46150, Israel.

Acknowledgments: I would like to thank the following colleagues for joint work and the influence they had on my work, and therefore on this book (in alphabetic order): Yehuda Afek, Rajeev Alur, Yoah Bar-David, Michael Fischer, Nissim Francez, Eli Gafni, David Greenberg, Shmuel Katz, Dahlia Malkhi, Michael Merritt, Shlomo Moran, Omer Reingold, Michael Reiter, Frank Stomp, Dan Touitou, Da-Wei Wang, and Rebecca Wright. Special thanks go to Michael Merritt for his influence on my thinking in this area. I am grateful to Andrea Shustarich, from Pearson Education, for her continuing encouragement and support.

Most importantly, I thank my family. It would have taken me even longer to finish this book, were it not for the love and support of my wife Miki, my sons Amir and Assaf, and my daughter Tamar.

Gadi Taubenfeld
Israel, 2006

Key Features

- The book is directed at a wide audience, including students, programmers, system designers, and researchers. It familiarizes readers with important problems and algorithms, and provides a coherent view of the area of synchronization algorithms and concurrent programming, highlighting common themes and basic techniques.
- The book extends the coverage of synchronization algorithms beyond its limited treatment in books on operating systems, distributed computing, distributed systems, and concurrent programming.
- The book covers in detail many synchronization problems including, mutual exclusion, concurrent data structures, barrier synchronization, ℓ-exclusion, dining philosophers, producer–consumer, reader and writers, consensus, and more.
- The book covers fundamental concepts including, adaptivity and scalability, local spinning, wait-free and nonblocking synchronization, fault tolerance, self-stabilization, contention and cooperation, deadlock avoidance and prevention, fairness, the relative power synchronization primitives, and universality.
- The book contains the most significant algorithms and lower bounds in the area. Dozens of algorithms, that were discovered during the last forty years, are presented and their complexity is analyzed according to precisely defined complexity measures.
- The book covers important synchronization primitive and constructs including, atomic registers, test-and-set bits, fetch-and-add, swap, compare-and-swap, read-modify-write, semaphores and monitors.
- The book incorporates contemporary research topics in an accessible manner, focusing on fundamental concepts rather than optimizations. It includes over 300 annotated references to books and papers published on synchronization algorithms and concurrent programming.
- Each section concludes with a set of self review question and solutions. Each chapter includes many end-of-chapter exercises and bibliographic notes.
- The companion website contains PowerPoint presentations, and other teaching aids; `http://www.pearsoned.co.uk/taubenfeld/`

Introduction

1.1 Concurrent and Distributed Computing

A concurrent system is a collection of processors that communicate by reading and writing from a shared memory. A distributed system is a collection of processors that communicate by sending messages over some communication network. Such systems are used for various reasons: to allow a large number of processors to solve a problem together much faster than any processor can do alone, to allow the distribution of data in several locations, to allow different processors to share resources such as printers or discs, or simply to enable users to send electronic mail. Reasoning about such systems does not come naturally, although it can be learned.

Many applications of large scale concurrent or distributed systems require a high level of reliability, for example, an air traffic control system, spacecraft navigation systems, or an integrated corporate management system. As the system size increases, so does the need to design fault-tolerant algorithms, for the probability that the entire system functions correctly at any given time rapidly approaches zero. Such algorithms enable the system as a whole to continue to function despite the failure of a limited number of components.

1.1.1 Data Communication and Synchronization

A *process* corresponds to a given computation. That is, given some program, its execution is a process. Sometimes, for convenience, we will refer to the program code itself as a process. A process runs on a *processor*, which is the physical hardware. Several processes can run on the same processor although in such a case only one of them may be active at any given time. Real concurrency is achieved when several processes are running simultaneously on several processors. Interactions between processes or processors – we shall use the terms interchangeably – are of two types: *data communication* and *synchronization*.

Data communication is the exchange of data, either by sending messages or by reading and writing of shared memory. Sending electronic mail, or getting information from a remote database is usually considered data communication.

Synchronization relates the executions of several processes, by exchanging control information (that is, information about the location of the processes). Synchronization is required when operations of various processes need to obey some order restrictions. Such a restriction might be that no two processes are doing some predefined action at a given time; or that an action by one process must take place only after some action by some other process, etc. For example, if two processes want to print on the same printer then they should be synchronized so that they will not print at the same time.

1.1.2 Contention, Cooperation, and Resource Allocation

Synchronization between processes can be further classified as either *contention* or *cooperation*.

Contention is characterized by the fact that an action by one process may disable a possible action by another process. Hence, processes may need to contend on the permission of taking some action. However, a process should be able to take an action, if all of its possible contenders have failed or are not interested in competing. Contention arises when several processes compete for exclusive use of shared resources, such as data items, files, discs, printers, etc. For example, the integrity of the data may be destroyed if two processes update a common file at the same time, and as a result, deposits and withdrawals could be lost, confirmed reservations might have disappeared, etc. In such cases it is sometimes essential to allow at most one process to use a given resource at any given time.

Cooperation is characterized by the fact that an action by one process may enable an action by another process. Hence, processes may need to coordinate their actions. In this case, unlike in the contention case, one process may block another process by simply not taking some action. That is, the progress of a process may depend upon the progress of another. A typical problem is the *producer-consumer* problem in which the producers produce items which the consumers then consume. The simplest case is the *bounded buffer* problem, in which the interface between the consumer and the producer is a bounded size queue. The producer inserts items into the queue, and the consumer consumes items from the queue.

Resource allocation is about interactions between processes that involve contention. The problem is, how to resolve conflicts resulting when several processes are trying to use shared resources. Put another way, how to allocate shared resources to competing processes. A special case of a general resource allocation problem, which we study in detail, is the mutual exclusion problem where only a single resource is available.

1.2 Synchronization: Two Examples

Many of our daily interactions with other people involve synchronization. You and your spouse may have to synchronize on who will buy the groceries, empty the garbage can, take the kids to school, which one of you will be the first to take a shower (assuming you only have one shower at home), will take the car, or use the single computer you have. Assume that you have a cat and your neighbor has a dog and you and your neighbor are sharing a yard, then you and your neighbor might want to coordinate to make sure that both pets are never in the yard at the same time.

In these examples, synchronization is used to ensure that only one participant (and not both) will take a certain action at a given time. Another type of synchronization has to do with cooperation. You and your spouse might need to move a heavy table together to its new location (it is too heavy for just one person). A classical example of cooperation is for two camps of the same army to decide on the exact time for a coordinated attack on the enemy camp.[1]

1.2.1 Why is Synchronization Difficult?

The examples for synchronization between people have corresponding examples for synchronization between computers. Synchronization is needed in all systems and environments where several processors (or processes or threads) can be active at the same time. As we have already mentioned, without proper synchronization, the integrity of the data may be destroyed if two computers update a common file at the same time, and as a result, deposits and withdrawals could be lost, confirmed reservations might have disappeared, etc. However, while achieving synchronization between humans is relatively easy, achieving synchronization between computers is challenging and difficult. The reason is that computers communicate with each other in a very restricted way.

While humans can see and hear each other, computers can only read and write. So, one computer can write a note (or send a message) that the other computer

[1] The use of the term *synchronization* in computer science is slightly more general than its use in standard English. The following quote from the Oxford dictionary explains this point, "The use of *synchronize* to mean *coordinate* or *combine* as in '*We must synchronize our efforts*' is considered incorrect by some people and should be avoided in standard English". In computer science, synchronization also means coordination.

will later read, but they cannot see each other. To understand the difficulty with this type of restricted communication, let us first examine two simple two-person interactions where communication is restricted either to writing and reading of notes or to sending messages. In the first example below, the two people involved, let's call them Alice and Bob, can not see each other and they communicate only by writing and reading of notes. In particular, Alice can not see that Bob is reading a note that she has written to him earlier.

Time	Alice	Bob
5:00	Arrive home	
5:05	Look in fridge; no milk	
5:10	Leave for grocery	
5:15		Arrive home
5:20		Look in fridge; no milk
5:25	Buy milk	Leave for grocery
5:30	Arrive home; put milk in fridge	
5:40		Buy milk
5:45		Arrive home; oh no!

Figure 1.1 Too much milk: a possible scenario without synchronization.

1.2.2 Too Much Milk

We use the *too much milk* problem to demonstrate the difficulty involved in synchronization. In this example Alice and Bob are sharing an apartment. Alice arrives home in the afternoon, looks in the fridge and finds that there is no milk. So, she leaves for the grocery to buy milk. After she leaves, Bob arrives, he also finds that there is no milk and goes to buy milk. At the end they both buy milk and end up with too much milk. This scenario is described in Figure 1.1. So, Alice and Bob are looking for a solution to ensure that:

1. Only one person buys milk, when there is no milk.
2. Someone always buys milk, when there is no milk.

Notice that a solution in which only Bob is responsible for buying milk would not work. In such a solution, there is a scenario where Alice arrives home and finds that there is no milk, and waits forever for Bob to show up. Alice and Bob have discussed the situation and agreed that in order to synchronize their actions, they will communicate by leaving (signed) notes on the door of the fridge. More specifically, they came up with the following solution:

Solution 1: *If you find that there is no milk and there is no note on the door of the fridge, then leave a note on the fridge's door, go and buy milk, put the milk in the fridge, and remove your note. The code is as follows:*

PROGRAM FOR ALICE:

```
if (no note) then
    if (no milk) then
        leave note
        buy milk
        remove note
    fi
fi
```

PROGRAM FOR BOB:

```
if (no note) then
    if (no milk) then
        leave note
        buy milk
        remove note
    fi
fi
```

Well, the problem with this solution is that again both of them might buy milk. To see that, assume that they arrive home at the same time and recall that they can not see each other (they can only read and write notes). Now Alice finds that there is no milk and that there is no note, so she writes a note and *before* she leaves her note, Bob checks and sees that there is no milk and no note. Thus, both will put their notes and will go to buy milk ending up with "too much milk". To resolve this problem they slightly modified their previous solution.

Solution 2: *As soon as you arrive home, you leave a note on the fridge's door. Only then you check, and if you find that there is no milk and there is no note (other than yours), then you go and buy milk, put the milk in the fridge and remove your note. The code is as follows:*

PROGRAM FOR ALICE:

```
leave note Alice
if (no note Bob) then
    if (no milk) then
        buy milk
    fi
fi
remove note Alice
```

PROGRAM FOR BOB:

```
leave note Bob
if (no note Alice) then
    if (no milk) then
        buy milk
    fi
fi
remove note Bob
```

Well, this time Alice and Bob might end up with no milk at all! To see that, assume that they arrive home at the same time. Since it is assumed that they can not see each other, each one writes a note and leaves it on the fridge's door. Then, each one finds the note of the other, and no one goes to buy milk. Next, we present an "almost" correct solution. It works only if we make a timing assumption about the relative *speed* of Alice and Bob.

Solution 3:

Alice: *When Alice arrives home, she leaves a note on the fridge's door. Then, if she finds that there is no milk and that there is no note (signed by Bob), she buys milk, puts the milk in the fridge and removes her note. Otherwise, if Bob left a note then she removes her note, and does nothing.*

Bob: *When Bob arrives home, he leaves a note on the fridge's door. Then if he finds that there is a note signed by Alice, he checks the fridge's door over and over again waiting for Alice to remove her note. Once Bob finds that Alice's note has been removed, he checks if there is milk. If there is no milk, he buys milk, puts the milk in the fridge and removes his note. Otherwise, if there is milk, he removes his note without buying milk.*

PROGRAM FOR ALICE:

```
leave note Alice
if (no note Bob) then
      if (no milk) then
            buy milk
      fi
fi
remove note Alice
```

PROGRAM FOR BOB:

```
leave note Bob
while (note Alice) do skip od
      if (no milk) then
            buy milk
      fi

remove note Bob
```

For Solution 3 to be correct, an assumption must be made about Bob's speed. Let's assume that Bob is waiting for Alice to remove her note. Then, we should assume that, between the time Alice removes her note, and the time she leaves a new note the day after, Bob must find out that Alice's note has been removed. Without this assumption, Alice and Bob might never buy milk.

Next we present a correct solution. Unlike (the incorrect) Solution 3, this solution is symmetric: Alice and Bob behave similarly and hence have the same chance to go and buy milk. For this solution, four labelled notes are used. Alice uses notes *A1* and *A2*, while Bob uses notes *B1* and *B2* (see Figure 1.2). At any point, as illustrated in Figure 1.3, if Alice (Bob) finds that there is no note labelled *B1* (*A1*) on the fridge's door, then it is Alice (Bob) responsibility to buy milk.

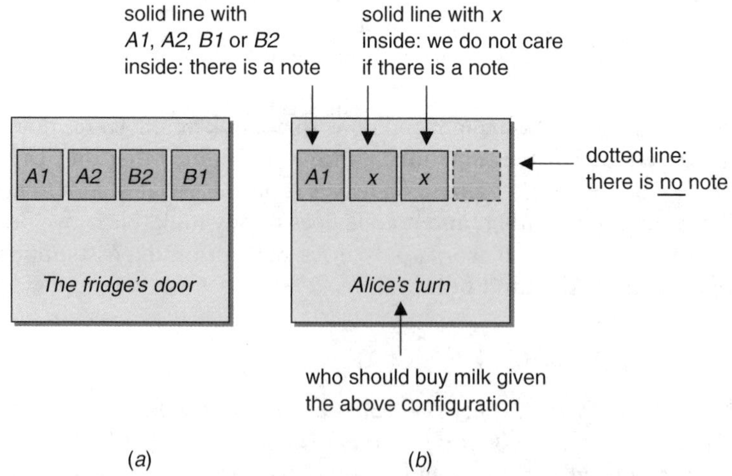

Figure 1.2 (*a*) The fridge's door with all the four notes. Assume that the position of each one of the notes on the fridge's door is fixed. (*b*) Notations used in Figure 1.3.

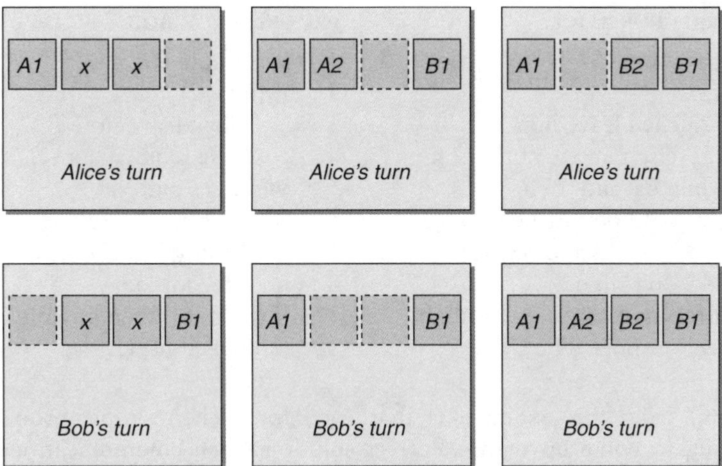

Figure 1.3 The six possible configurations of the notes on the fridge's door.

Otherwise, when both *A1* and *B1* are present, a decision is made according to the notes *A2* and *B2*. If both *A2* and *B2* are present or if neither of them is present than it is Bob's responsibility to by milk, otherwise it is Alice's responsibility.

Solution 4:

Alice: *When Alice arrives home, she does the following:*

- *First, she leaves a note labelled A1 on the fridge's door. Then, if there is a note labelled B2, she leaves a note labelled A2, otherwise she removes A2. By doing so Alice gives priority to Bob in buying milk.*
- *Then, she checks the fridge's door over and over again as long as the following two conditions hold: (1) there is a note labelled B1, and (2) either both A2 and B2 are present or neither of them is present.*
- *Once Alice finds that one of these two conditions is not satisfied, she checks if there is milk. If there is no milk, she buys milk and puts it in the fridge. Finally, she removes A1.*

Bob: *When Bob arrives home, he does the following:*

- *First, he leaves a note labelled B1 on the fridge's door. Then, if there is no note labelled A2, he leaves a note labelled B2, otherwise he removes B2. By doing so Bob gives priority to Alice in buying milk.*
- *Then, he checks the fridge's door over and over again as long as the following two conditions hold: (1) there is a note labelled A1, and (2) either A2 or B2 are present (but not both).*
- *Once Bob finds that one of these two conditions is not satisfied, he checks if there is milk. If there is no milk, he buys milk and puts it in the fridge. Finally, he removes B1.*

PROGRAM FOR ALICE:

```
leave note A1
if B2
      then leave note A2
      else remove note A2 fi
while B1 and
      ((A2 and B2) or
       (no A2 and no B2))
      do skip od
if (no milk) then buy milk fi
remove note A1
```

PROGRAM FOR BOB:

```
leave note B1
if (no A2)
      then leave note B2
      else remove note B2 fi
while A1 and
      ((A2 and no B2) or
       (no A2 and B2))
      do skip od
if (no milk) then buy milk fi
remove note A1
```

The moral from this example is that even for such a simple problem it is challenging to come up with a correct solution when communication is done by reading and writing of notes (i.e., Alice and Bob can not see each other). Solution 4 is rather complicated and it is not trivial to formally verify that it is correct. This solution is based on Kessels' algorithm (1982) which in turn is based on Peterson's algorithm (1981). These two algorithms are presented in Section 2.1 (page 31) together with a formal correctness proof.

To see the corresponding synchronization problem for computers, replace *milk* in the above example with *file*, and let Alice and Bob be the names of two computers that are trying to avoid updating a shared file at the same time. In the book we will present and systematically solve much more difficult synchronization problems which arise from building systems, assuming there are many participants (not just Alice and Bob), many resources, and under various assumption and requirements.

1.2.3 The Coordinated Attack Problem

The problem is for two camps of the same army to decide on the exact time for a coordinated attack on the enemy camp. The problem, which again involves two-person interactions, demonstrates the difficulty of reaching agreement when communication is restricted to sending and receiving messages. The problem, which is illustrated in Figure 1.4, was invented by Jim Gray (1978) who has described it as follows:

> "There are two generals on campaign. They have an objective (a hill) that they want to capture. If they simultaneously march on the objective they are assured of success. If only one marches, he will be annihilated.
>
> The generals are encamped only a short distance apart, but due to technical difficulties, they can communicate only via runners. These messengers have a flaw, every time they venture out of camp they stand some chance of getting lost (they are not very smart).
>
> The problem is to find some protocol that allows the generals to march together even though some messengers get lost."

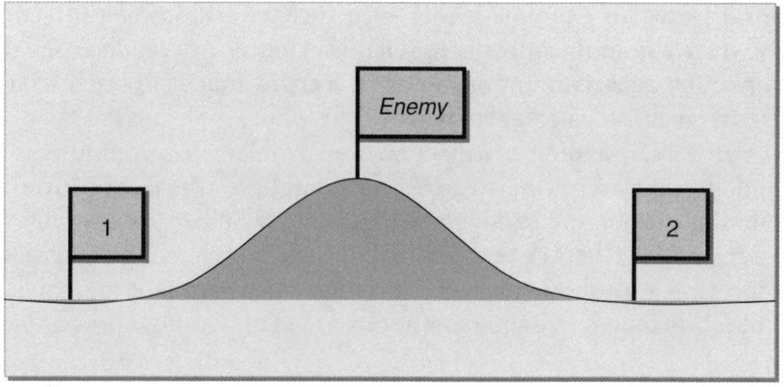

Figure 1.4 The coordinated attack problem. The army wins only if both camps attack simultaneously. The problem is to design an algorithm to ensure that both camps attack simultaneously.

Thus, neither general will decide to attack unless he is sure that the other will attack with him. Let's assume that everything goes smoothly and the messengers do not get lost. How long does it take the two generals to coordinate an attack?

If one of the generals, say general A, decides to attack at a certain moment in the future, he can send a messenger to alert the other general. Would this be enough? As the messenger could be lost on his way, general A can not be sure that the other will attack with him and hence will not attack. Thus the other general, call him general B, in his turn has to send another messenger back to inform A that the message has been delivered. Would this be enough for them to attack? Well, now B needs to know whether his message has been delivered, to make sure that he will not attack alone. Hence B will not attack until his message is acknowledged.

To solve this problem A, when he gets the message from B, has to send another messenger back to inform B that the message has been delivered, and so on. This scenario will never bring enough information to the generals, and hence we reach the following surprising conclusion:

There is no solution to the coordinated attack problem.

Here is a simple proof of this result. Assume that a solution to the coordinated attack problem exists. Among all such possible solutions, let P be a solution that, in scenarios where no messenger is lost, sends the minimum number of messages. Now, suppose the last messenger in P gets lost. Then either this messenger is useless or one of the generals does not get a needed message. By the minimality of P, the last message is not useless so one of the generals does not attack if the last message is lost. This means that P does not solve the problem as assumed. This contradiction proves that there is no solution to the coordinated attack problem.

The moral from this example is that even such a very simple problem can not be solved when communication is unreliable. Hence, in certain cases there is a need to make stronger assumptions about the environment in order to be able to solve various synchronization problems.

To see the corresponding synchronization problem for computers, consider two computers that are trying to perform a database transaction over an unreliable communication line, and need to decide whether to commit or abort the transaction. In Chapter 9 we will consider a related problem, the *consensus* problem, and show that this problem also can not be solved in the presence of faults unless strong assumptions are made on how processes communicate.

Self Review

1. Does it matter if we replace the order of statement 1 and the if statement (lines 2–4) in Solution 4?
2. Is the coordinated attack problem solvable if both generals are required to attack but not necessarily simultaneously?

Answers: (1) With such a replacement, it is possible that both Alice and Bob will buy milk at the same time. (2) No.

1.3 The Mutual Exclusion Problem

The *mutual exclusion* problem is the guarantee of mutually exclusive access to a single shared resource when there are several competing processes. The problem arises in operating systems, database systems, parallel supercomputers, and computer networks, where it is necessary to resolve conflicts resulting when several processes are trying to use shared resources, such as data items, files, discs, printers, etc. For example, the integrity of the data may be destroyed if two processes update a common file at the same time, and as a result, deposits and withdrawals could be lost, confirmed reservations might disappear, etc. In such cases it is sometime essential to allow at most one process to use a given resource at any given time. The problem is of great significance, since it lies at the heart of much concurrent process synchronization.

Situations as described above, where several processes may access the same resource and the final result depends on which process runs when, are called *race conditions*. The mutual exclusion problem is essentially how to avoid race conditions. Numerous solutions for the problem have been proposed, since it was first introduced by Edsger W. Dijkstra in 1965. Because of its importance and as a result of new hardware and software developments, new solutions to the problem are being designed all the time.

We describe here some of the most interesting results. By doing so we will introduce the reader to the inherent difficulty of writing distributed algorithms and verifying their correctness, even when the algorithms are very short – only 10 or 15 lines long.

1.3.1 The Problem

The problem is defined as follows: it is assumed that each process is executing a sequence of instructions in an infinite loop. The instructions are divided into four continuous sections of code: the *remainder*, *entry*, *critical section*, and *exit*. Thus, the structure of a mutual exclusion solution looks as follows:

loop forever
  remainder code;
  entry code;
  critical section;
  exit code
end loop

A process starts by executing the remainder code. At some point the process might need to execute some code in its critical section. In order to access its critical section a process has to go through an entry code which guarantees that while it is executing its critical section, no other process is allowed to execute its critical section. In addition, once a process finishes its critical section, the process executes its exit code in which it notifies other processes that it is no longer in its critical section. After executing the exit code the process returns to the remainder. See Figure 1.5.

The mutual exclusion problem is to write the code for the *entry code* and the *exit code* in such a way that the following two basic requirements are satisfied.

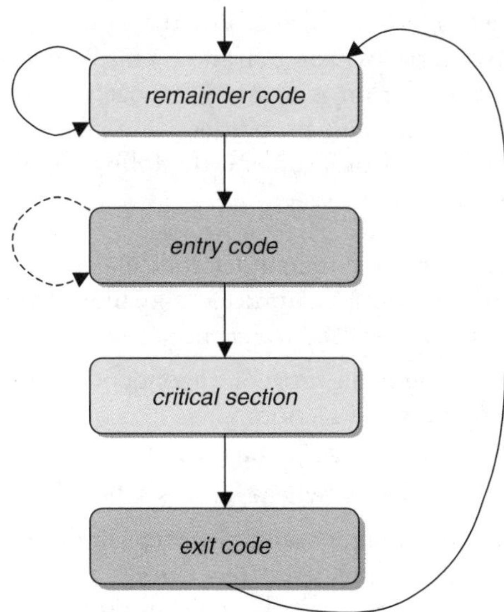

Figure 1.5 The mutual exclusion problem is to design the entry code and the exit code in a way which guarantees that the mutual exclusion and deadlock-freedom properties are satisfied.

Mutual exclusion: *No two processes are in their critical section at the same time.*

Deadlock-freedom: *If a process is trying to enter its critical section, then some process, not necessarily the same one, eventually enters its critical section.*

The deadlock-freedom property, which is sometime referred to as the global progress property, guarantees that the system as a whole can always continue to make progress. It guarantees that in the absence of contention for the critical section, if a single process enters its entry code then eventually it will succeed to enter its critical section. However, deadlock-freedom may still allow "starvation" of individual processes. That is, a process that is trying to enter its critical section, may never get to enter its critical section, and wait forever in its entry code. Later, we will examine also solutions which do not allow starvation, which is defined as follows:

Starvation-freedom: *If a process is trying to enter its critical section, then this process must eventually enter its critical section.*

Although starvation-freedom is strictly stronger than deadlock-freedom, it still allows processes to execute their critical sections arbitrarily many times before some trying process can execute its critical section. Stronger requirements which prevent such a behavior are presented in Section 2.4 (page 47).

The first two properties, mutual exclusion and deadlock-freedom, were required in the original statement of the problem by Dijkstra, while starvation-freedom was not required. They are the minimal requirements that one might want to impose.

Requirements or properties of algorithms are usually divided into two classes. The first are the *safety properties* which ensure that nothing bad will happen. The second are *liveness properties* which guarantee that something good eventually happens. Thus, mutual exclusion is a safety property, while deadlock-freedom and starvation-freedom are liveness properties.

In solving the mutual exclusion problem, the following assumptions are made about the behavior of the processes:

1. Nothing is assumed about the remainder code except that it can not influence the behavior of other processes. A process may loop there forever, it may halt or it may, at some point, proceed to its entry code.
2. Shared objects appearing in an entry or an exit code may not be referred to in a remainder code or a critical section.
3. A process can not fail (i.e., stop) while executing the entry code, critical section, and exit code. That is, whenever it is scheduled it must take a step.
4. A process can take only a finite number of steps in its critical section and exit code. That is, the exit code is *wait-free*: once a process starts executing its critical section and exit code, it always finishes them regardless of the activity of the other processes.
5. While the collection of processes is concurrent, individual processes are sequential.

Of all the problems in interprocess synchronization, the mutual exclusion problem is the one studied most extensively. This is a deceptive problem, and at first glance it seems very simple to solve. The only way to understand its tricky nature is by trying to solve it. For that reason we suggest that readers stop at this point and try themselves to solve the problem, assuming that there are only two processes which communicate by reading and writing shared registers. The reader may want to answer first the simple problems for this section (on page 25).

Throughout the book we assume that there may be up to n processes potentially contending to enter their critical sections. Each of the n potentially contending processes is assigned a unique identification number which, for simplicity, is assumed to be a positive integer taken from the set $\{1, \ldots, n\}$. In all chapters, except Chapter 10, it is assumed that the processes are completely asynchronous. That is, no assumption is made about the relative speed of the processes. This assumption about asynchrony reflects the situation of most modern multi-processor (and also uni-processor) architectures, where process delays are unpredictable as a result of cache misses, page faults, or scheduling decisions. In Chapter 10, we will leave the complete asynchrony assumption and assume that there is an upper bound on the speed of the processes which can be used for the design of efficient algorithms.

To simplify the presentation, when the code for a mutual exclusion algorithm is presented, only the entry code and exit code are described, and the remainder code and the infinite loop within which these codes reside are omitted.

Self Review

Let A and B be two algorithms which were designed to solve the mutual exclusion problem, and let C be the algorithm obtained by replacing the critical section of A with the algorithm B. That is, the code of C is:

loop forever
    remainder code (of C);
    entry code of A;
    entry code of B;
    critical section;
    exit code of B;
    exit code of A
end loop

Assume that the registers of A are different from the registers of B. Are the following statements correct?

1. If both A and B are deadlock-free then C is deadlock-free.
2. If both A and B are starvation-free then C is starvation-free.
3. If either A or B satisfies mutual exclusion then C satisfies mutual exclusion.

4. If A is deadlock-free and B is starvation-free then C is starvation-free.
5. If A is starvation-free and B is deadlock-free then C is starvation-free.

Answers: True, true, true, false, false.

1.4 Complexity Measures

The time efficiency of a synchronous algorithm is often of crucial importance. However, it is difficult to find the appropriate definition of time complexity, for systems where nothing is assumed about the speed of the processes. There are two approaches for measuring time: one is to count steps and the other is to assume that a step takes at most one time unit. We will use both approaches.

1.4.1 Counting Steps

While deadlock-freedom seems to be an essential requirement, the stronger starvation-freedom, which guarantees that every process that is trying to enter its critical section eventually enters its critical section, is not always essential. This is so because contention for a critical section should be rare in well designed systems. Hence, since in most cases processes do not have to compete in order to enter their critical sections, a most desired property of a solution is that in the absence of contention a process can enter its critical section fast. We say that an algorithm is *fast* if it satisfies this desired property. Namely, that the number of accesses to the shared memory in order to enter a critical section in the absence of contention, is a small constant. This leads us to our first definition of time complexity.

Contention-free time complexity: *The maximum number of times (i.e., steps) a process may need to access the shared memory in its entry code in order to enter a critical section in the absence of contention, plus the maximum number of accesses to the shared memory in its exit code.*

It is also important to try (when possible) to minimize the time it takes to enter the critical section when there is contention. The simple step counting, used in the above definition, is natural where there is no interaction among processes. To take into account the interactions among processes, two complementary definitions are proposed.

Process time complexity: *The maximum number of times (i.e., steps) a winning process (the process that gets to enter its critical section) may need to access the shared memory in its entry code and exit code, since the last time some process released its critical section.*

The above definition does not always capture the actual running time of an algorithm, for if one process is in a loop waiting for another to complete some action, then the faster it goes, the more time it will go around the loop. But making the first process go faster does not necessarily degrade the total system performance, although it certainly increases the amount of "wasted" effort by the first process. This leads to the following alternative definition.

1.4.2 Counting Time Units

Assume that a computation is taking place through time and that every step of every process in its entry code or its exit code takes some amount in the interval (0,1]. That is, there is an upper bound 1 for step time but no lower bound. Thus, for example, if during some period of time, where two processes are in their entry or exit code, one process takes 100 steps while the other takes five steps, then the total time that has elapsed is at most five time units (also for the process which took 100 steps).

System response time: *The longest time interval where some process is in its entry code while no process is in its critical section, assuming there is an upper bound of one time unit for step time in the entry or exit code and no lower bound.*

Notice that the maximum time is not necessarily achieved when every step takes a full unit of time; achieving a "bad" interleaving of steps may only be possible if certain steps happen very quickly. It is sometimes difficult to analyze algorithms with this measure. Also, we notice that if the steps one process is taking, while it is in a loop waiting for another to complete some action, are counted as just one step, then the definitions of process time complexity and system response time become very similar. The system response time is bounded from below by the contention-free time complexity.

Instead of measuring the time since a critical section was last released, one can measure the maximum number of time units that it takes for a process to enter its critical section since it started trying. More formally:

Process response time: *The longest time interval where some process is in its entry code to the time that this process finishes its exit code, assuming there is an upper bound of one time unit for step time in the entry or exit code and no lower bound, and assuming that the time for which a process is in the critical section is ignored.*

While a process is trying to enter its critical section, many other processes can enter and exit their critical sections. Hence, for the above definition to make sense, it is assumed that the time in the critical section is ignored. Because of this problematic assumption on the time in a critical section, in most cases we will use in this book the notion of *system response time.*

There are some variants of the above definitions. For example, amortized time complexity can also be defined based on the above definitions. The definitions of time complexity given here are appropriate for asynchronous systems where no assumption is made about the relative speed of the processes and the processes have no access to a clock. Later in Section 10.1, we will also consider systems where timing assumptions are made about the speed of the processes, and hence modify the definition.

1.4.3 Counting Remote Memory Accesses

For certain shared memory systems, it makes sense to distinguish between *remote* and *local* access to shared memory. Shared registers may be locally-accessible as a result of coherent caching, or when using distributed shared memory where shared memory is physically distributed among the processors. That is, instead of having the "shared memory" in one central location, each process "owns" part of the shared memory and keeps it in its own local memory. These different shared memory models are illustrated in Figure 1.6.

Remote access: *We define a remote access by process p as an attempt to access a memory location that does not physically reside on p's local memory. The remote memory location can either reside in a central shared memory or in some other process' memory.*

Next, we define when remote access causes *communication.*

Communication: *Two models are possible:*

1. Distributed Shared Memory (DSM) model: *Any remote access causes communication;*
2. Coherent Caching (CC) model: *A remote access to register r causes communication if (the value of) r is not (the same as the value) in the cache. That is, communication is caused only by a remote write access that overwrites a different process' value or by the first remote read access by a process that detects a value written by a different process.*

Next we define time complexity when counting remote memory accesses. This complexity measure is defined with respect to either the DSM model or the CC model, and whenever it is used, we will say explicitly which model is assumed.

Time complexity in the CC model or the DSM model: *The maximum number of remote accesses which cause communication that a process, say p, may need to*

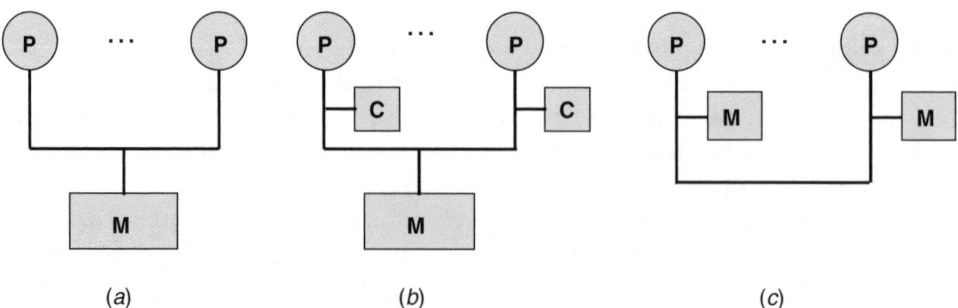

Figure 1.6 Shared memory models. (*a*) Central shared memory. (*b*) Cache Coherent (CC) model. (*c*) Distributed Shared Memory (DSM) model. P denotes processor, C denotes cache, and M denotes shared memory.

perform in its entry and exit sections in order to enter and exit its critical section since p started executing the code of its entry section.

An alternative definition would be to count the maximum number of remote accesses which cause communication that a process may need to perform in its entry code and exit code in order to enter and exit its critical section since the *last* time some process released its critical section.

We discuss and use the notions of time complexity in the CC and DSM models in much detail, when we define the notion of *local spinning* in Section 3.1 (page 97).

1.4.4 Space Complexity

Finally, it is also desirable to minimize the space complexity, which is defined as follows:

Space complexity: *The number and size of the shared memory objects used in the solution.*

Self Review

1. What is the relation between contention-free time complexity and system response time?
2. Assume that algorithm A satisfies mutual exclusion and deadlock-freedom. Is it the case that the contention-free time complexity of A is bounded by some integer k.
3. Is it correct that spinning on a remote variable is counted only as one remote operation that causes communication in the CC model.

Answers: (1) Contention-free time complexity is never greater than system response time. (2) No, for example, the number of steps may depend on the value of some register and this value may change over time. (3) Only if the value of the variable does not change while spinning.

1.5 Processes, Threads and Scheduling

We briefly discuss a few basic technical issue regarding processes, threads, and scheduling.

1.5.1 Processes

A process is a program in execution and, as illustrated in Figure 1.7, it can be in one of five states:

- *New*: The process is being created;
- *Running*: Using the CPU at that instance;
- *Ready*: Temporarily stopped to let another process use the CPU;

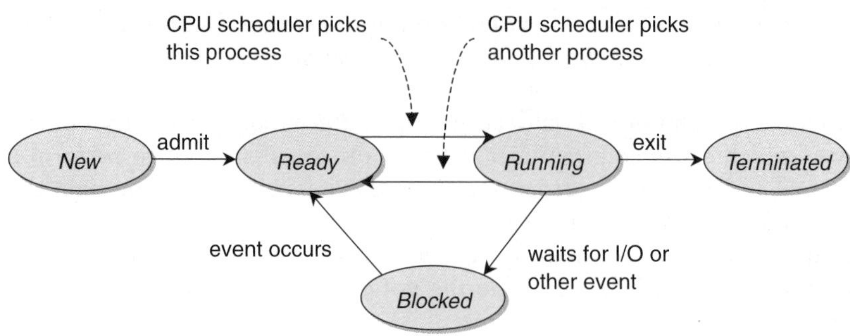

Figure 1.7 The five possible states a process can be in.

- *Blocked*: Unable to run until some external event (such as, an input/output event) happens;
- *Terminated*: The process has finished its execution.

The principal events that cause process creation are: system initialization, execution of a process creation system call, or a user request to create a new process. A *parent* process may create (using a system call) a *child* process, and a child process may create its own child processes. These processes form a *process hierarchy*. The UNIX operating system calls this hierarchy a "process group". The Windows operating system has no concept of process hierarchy, and assumes that "all processes are created equal".

When a process is created, all the information associated with this process is kept by the operating system in a structure called the Process Control Block (PCB). Thus each process has its own PCB. This information includes: the process state, its program counter, CPU registers, CPU scheduling information, memory-management information, I/O status information, and more.

Conditions which terminate processes are: normal exit (voluntary by the process itself), error exit (voluntary), fatal error (involuntary), or the process is killed by another process (involuntary).

At any give time only one process can use a given CPU. When a CPU switches from one process to another process, the operating system must save the state of the old process (in its PCB) and load the saved state for the new process. Context-switch time is overhead: the system does no useful work while switching.

Switching a process happens as a result of either: (1) Interrupts: for example, clock interrupt which indicates that the current running process has executed a full time-slice, or an I/O interrupt. (2) Memory fault: memory address is in virtual memory. (3) Control is returned to the operating system as a result of a system call or as a result of an error that has occurred during the process execution.

1.5.2 Threads

A process may be composed of several *threads*. For example, a process that corresponds to the execution of some game may be composed of three threads: the first controls the keyboard, the second is for doing the computations, and the third is responsible for doing I/O. A thread is sometimes called a lightweight process. Items that are shared by all the threads which belong to the same process are: address space, open files, program code, global variables and data, child processes (and more). Items that are private to each thread are: program counter, registers, and stack. Thus, since all the threads share the address space of the process, they can communicate by reading and writing from the shared memory.

Threads can be implemented as either user-level threads or as kernel-level threads. In the case of user-level threads, all thread management is done by the process to which the threads belong (i.e., by the application); the (operating system) kernel is not aware of the existence of the user-level threads (only of processes); thread context-switching does not require kernel mode privileges, and scheduling is done internally by the process without involving the operating system. However, system calls by a single user-level thread may block the whole process (i.e., it may block all the other threads in that process).

In the case of kernel-level threads, the kernel maintains context information for both the process and the threads, and hence blocking a thread does not have to block the process. One disadvantage is that switching between kernel-level threads requires the involvement of the operating system in the switch. To prevent confusion we note that: kernel-level threads are managed by the kernel but run in user space. There is also the notion of *kernel threads* which are threads that are managed by the kernel and run in kernel space.

Some of the benefits of using threads are: it takes less time to create a new thread than a new process, it takes less time to terminate a thread than a process, it takes less time to switch between two threads within the same process than to switch between processes (and it is faster to switch between user-level threads than between kernel-level threads), threads within the same process share memory and files and hence they can communicate without invoking the kernel. For the rest of the book, we will use only the notion of a process; however, all the results in the book apply to both processes and threads.

1.5.3 Scheduling

When the number of processes that are ready to run is bigger than the number of CPUs, a decision has to be made which of the processes, that are ready to run, will get a chance to use the CPU and which will have to wait. This decision is made by an operating system module called the (CPU) scheduler algorithm. We notice that the scheduler is not responsible for process' synchronization. In order to be synchronized, the processes must communicate between themselves. We informally list below some of the scheduling algorithm goals:

- *Fairness*: Give each process a fair share of the CPU;
- *Balance*: Keep all parts of the system (like I/O devices) busy;
- *Maximize throughput*: Maximize the number of processes that can properly terminate per unit of time;
- *Minimize turnaround time*: Minimize time between the submission and (proper) termination of a process;

- *Maximize CPU utilization*: Keep the CPU (or CPUs) busy all the time;
- *Minimize response time*: Enable processes to respond to (users) requests quickly.

A process execution can be described as bursts of CPU usage alternating with periods of I/O wait. A process can be described as either (1) an I/O-bound process, meaning the process spends more time doing I/O than computations, and thus it has many *short* CPU bursts; or (2) a CPU-bound process, meaning the process spends more time doing computations, and thus it has few *long* CPU bursts. In order to keep all parts of the system busy, the scheduler will usually favor I/O-bound processes over CPU-bound processes.

Scheduling decisions may take place when a process either, (1) switches from running to waiting (blocking) state; (2) switches from running to ready state; (3) switches from waiting to ready; or (4) terminates. A restricted scheduling in which decisions are allowed to take place only in the first and the fourth cases is called *non-preemptive*. Scheduling in which decisions are allowed to take place in all the above four cases is called *preemptive*. Thus, a preemptive scheduler can interrupt a running process, while a non-preemptive scheduler can not.

Even with a preemptive scheduler it is sometimes necessary to guarantee that a running process will not be preempted. This can be achieved by *disabling interrupts*. An interrupt is a signal that a device can send to the CPU when an event happens. When an interrupt occurs, usually the operating system is invoked to determine how to respond. For example, a process may be preempted as a result of a clock interrupt when its quantum expired. On a uni-processor, where there is no true concurrency and at most one process (or thread) can run at any give time, there is a simple way to guarantee mutual exclusion by disabling interrupts. Disabling interrupts has lots of drawbacks and hence it is usually avoided. For example, a process that enters an infinite loop or makes a blocking I/O request in its critical section after disabling interrupts leads to a situation where the whole system is unable to proceed, since the process can not be preempted. However, the operating system itself sometimes disables interrupts when it needs exclusive access to resources for a short period of time.

There are many scheduling algorithms, a few of which are mentioned below. The simplest one is First-Come, First-Served (FCFS) scheduling, which schedules the processes in the order they become ready to use the CPU.

Shortest-Job-First (SJF) scheduling associates with each process the length of its next CPU burst, and uses these lengths to schedule the process with the shortest time. In the non-preemptive version, once a CPU is given to the process it can not be preempted until the process completes its CPU burst. In the preemptive version, if a new process arrives with a CPU burst length less than the remaining time of the current running process the running process is preempted.

Priority scheduling. A priority number (integer) is associated with each process, and the CPU is allocated to the process with the highest priority. Again there is a preemptive version and a non-preemptive version. SJF scheduling is a priority scheduling where priority is the predicted next CPU burst time. One problem is that low priority processes may never execute. A common solution to this problem, called *aging*, is to increase the priority of the process as time progresses.

Another problem with priority scheduling is the *priority inversion problem*. Consider the following situation. There are two processes, p_1 which has high priority and p_2 which has low priority. There is only one CPU and it is required that the high priority process p_1 will be immediately scheduled once it is ready to run. Initially p_1 is not ready (it is blocked for some reason) and only p_2 is ready. Thus p_2 is scheduled and let us assume that p_2 enters its critical section. While p_2 is in its critical section, p_1 becomes ready. So, the scheduler suspends p_2 (i.e., there is a context switch) and schedules p_1 instead. Now, when p_1 tries to enters its critical section, it has to wait for p_2 to release its critical section first. However, since p_2 has lower priority it will not be scheduled again and p_1 will busy-wait forever. This situation is called the priority inversion problem.

Round Robin (RR) scheduling. Each process gets a small unit of CPU time (time quantum), and after this time has elapsed, the process is preempted and another process is executed. Many other possibilities exist.

Finally, *mutual exclusion scheduling* is the problem of scheduling unit-time processes non-preemptively on m processors subject to constraints, represented by a graph G, so that processes represented by adjacent vertices in G must run in disjoint time intervals. Minimizing the completion time is NP-hard even if either the number of processors or the completion time is fixed but greater than two. However, polynomial time is sufficient to produce optimal schedules for forests, and simple heuristics perform well on certain classes of graphs.

Self Review

1. Is the following statement true or false? When a user-level thread makes a blocking system call, only the thread that makes the system call is blocked.
2. Is the following statement true or false? An I/O-bounded process will be more likely to be favored by the CPU-scheduler over a CPU-bounded process.
3. Consider the following two processes, A and B, to be run concurrently in a shared memory (all variables are shared between the two processes).

```
PROCESS A:
for i := 1 to 5 do
    x := x + 1
od
```

```
PROCESS B:
for i := 1 to 5 do
    x := x + 1
od
```

Assume that load (read) and store (write) of the single shared register x are atomic, x is initialized to 0, and x must be loaded into a register before being incremented. What are all the possible values for x after both processes have terminated?

Answers: (1) False. (2) True. (3) The values 2 through 10 inclusive.

1.6 Bibliographic Notes

1.1 & 1.2 & 1.3

In 1968 Edsger Wybe Dijkstra published his famous paper "Co-operating sequential processes" [107], that originated the field of concurrent programming. The mutual exclusion problem was first stated and solved by Dijkstra in [106]. The first solution for two processes is due to Dekker (page 77), whose algorithm is described and proved correct by Dijkstra [107]. The first solution for n processes is due to Dijkstra (page 81), and has appeared in [106]. In [43], various aspects of Dijkstra's life are discussed, including sections about his scientific career, scientific contributions, working style, opinions, lifestyle, and legacy.

An interesting description of the mutual exclusion problem can be found in [220]. Raynal's book [294], is a collection of some early algorithms for mutual exclusion (see [32] for a survey of more recent algorithms). Another short book by Raynal and Helary focuses on synchronization algorithms for message passing systems [296]. Books on distributed computing [55, 245], operating systems [57, 145, 308, 310, 313, 321], concurrent and multithreading programming [40, 41, 66, 67, 311], distributed systems [98, 102, 322], and (concurrency control in) database systems [67, 275] usually discuss the mutual exclusion problem and/or other synchronization problems and present few representative solutions.

The *too much milk problem* has been used in the past as an example for teaching process synchronization. The correct solution we have presented for this problem, Solution 4 (page 7), is an adaptation of an algorithm that was developed by J.L.K. Kessels for the mutual exclusion problem [200] (Kessels' algorithm appears on page 35). Kessels' algorithm itself is an adaptation of a mutual exclusion algorithm due to G. Peterson (Peterson's algorithm appears on page 32).

The *coordinated attack problem* was first described by Jim Gray who called this problem *the generals paradox* and *the two generals problem* [151]. The proof that there is no solution to the coordinated attack problem is also from [151]. An alternative (and more complex) proof appears in [159].

1.4

The importance of the notion of contention-free time complexity (page 14) was first pointed out in [224], and was further studied in [23, 24]. In [287], it was pointed out that the definition of (worst-case) process time complexity (page 14) does not always capture the real time complexity of an algorithm, which leads the authors (of [287]) to suggest the notion of system response time (page 15) as an alternative definition.

Our definitions of time complexity (page 14) do not take into account the contention level – the number of processes that may access the same shared memory simultaneously. Some formal frameworks to model contention have been proposed. In [121], modeling contention at a shared object with the help of *stall* operations is suggested. In the case of simultaneous accesses to a single memory location, only one operation succeeds, and other pending operations must stall. The measure of contention is simply the worst-case number of stalls that can be induced by an adversary scheduler. In [147], the authors proposed the Queue-Read Queue-Write PRAM model, in which the time to execute a read or a write on a shared register is a linear function of the number of processes accessing the same register concurrently.

The work in [39, 150, 254] on local spinning, has motivated the proposal to distinguish between *remote* and *local* access to shared memory. Shared registers may be locally accessible as a result of coherent caching, or when using distributed shared memory where memory is physically distributed among the processors. The definition of a remote access is very delicate and depends on specific architectural details of a given system. For more details see Section 3.1.

1.5

We briefly only discussed a few basic technical issues regarding processes and threads. A more detailed discussion appears in operating systems textbooks such as [57, 308, 313, 321]. The problem of mutual exclusion scheduling is discussed in [58].

1.7 Problems

The problems are divided into several categories. Problems with a single circle (◦) are the easiest and should be solved within five minutes, on average. They are meant to draw the attention of the reader to something that might have been overlooked otherwise. Problems with two circles (◦◦) are easy to solve and should take 5–30 minutes, after reading the appropriate section. Problems with a circle followed by a bullet (◦•) are still not too difficult to solve but may consume more time, and should take 10–120 minutes. Problems with a bullet followed by a circle (•◦) are difficult, and may take several hours to solve. Problems with two bullets (••) are very challenging, and may take several days to solve. Some of the harder problems introduce new material.

Problems marked with a question mark (?) are open problems – problems that, as far as I know, have not been solved yet. Some of them are probably easy, some are very hard. Most of these problems have been invented while writing this book and have not been studied before.

Problems based on Section 1.2

◦ 1.1 Consider the following two processes, *A* and *B*, to be run concurrently in a shared memory (all variables are shared between the two processes).

PROCESS A:	PROCESS B:
1 **for** $i := 1$ **to** 5 **do**	1 $x := 2x$
2 $\quad x := x + 1$	
3 **od**	

Assume that load (read) and store (write) of the single shared register x are atomic, x is initialized to 0, and x must be loaded into a register before being incremented. What are all the possible values for x after both processes have terminated?

◦ 1.2 Consider the following two processes, A and B, to be run concurrently in a shared memory (all variables are shared between the two processes).

PROCESS A:	PROCESS B:
$x := 2x;$	$x := 1;$
$x := 2x$	$x := x + 1$

Assume that load (read) and store (write) of the single shared register x are atomic, x is initialized to 0, and x must be loaded into a register before being incremented. What are all the possible values for x after both processes have terminated?

◦ 1.3 Consider the following three processes, A, B, and C, to be run concurrently in a shared memory (all variables are shared between the two processes).

PROCESS A:	PROCESS B:	PROCESS C:
$x := x + 1;$	$x := x + 1;$	$x := 10$
$x := x + 1$	$x := x + 1$	

Assume that load (read) and store (write) of the single shared register x are atomic, x is initialized to 0, and x must be loaded into a register before being incremented. What are all the possible values for x after the three processes have terminated?

◦◦ 1.4 Consider the following three processes, A, B, and C, to be run concurrently in a shared memory (all variables are shared between the two processes).

PROCESS A:	PROCESS B:	PROCESS C:
$x := 2x;$	$x := 2x;$	$x = 1$
$x := 2x$	$x := 2x$	$x := x + 1$

Assume that load (read) and store (write) of the single shared register x are atomic, x is initialized to 0, and x must be loaded into a register before being incremented. What are all the possible values for x after the three processes have terminated?

◦◦ 1.5 We have noticed that Solution 3 (page 5) is correct, only if a timing assumption is made about Bob's speed. Modify Solution 3, so that it is correct without such an assumption.

◦◦ 1.6 Assume that Alice and Bob have a daughter, and modify Solution 4 so that it will work for all the three of them.

◦◦ 1.7 In Solution 4, Bob checks the fridge's door over and over again as long as the following two conditions hold: (1) there is a note labelled *A1*, and (2) either *A2* or *B2* are present (but not both). Why can Bob not simply check these two conditions only once, and if both hold, conclude that Alice will buy milk and go to sleep?

∘∘ 1.8 Mention three different models in which the coordinated attack problem is solvable.

Problems based on Section 1.3

∘ 1.9 Mention one more case where mutual exclusion is needed.

∘ 1.10 Does starvation-freedom imply deadlock-freedom?

∘ 1.11 Are there any restrictions on the time a process can spend in its exit code? Can it stay there forever?

∘ 1.12 Show that any finite execution of a mutual exclusion algorithm has an extension in which all the processes are in their remainder codes.

∘ 1.13 Explain why mutual exclusion is a safety property, while deadlock-freedom and starvation-freedom are liveness properties.

∘ 1.14 Do the following two definitions have the same meaning as the original definitions on page 12?

Deadlock-freedom: *If some process never completes its trying code, then there is an infinite sequence of critical sections being executed by other processes.*

Starvation-freedom: *Every execution of a trying code eventually terminates.*

∘∘ 1.15 Let A and B be mutual exclusion algorithms, and let C be the algorithm obtained by replacing the critical section of A with the algorithm B. That is, the code of C is:

```
loop forever
   remainder code (of C);
   entry code of A;
   entry code of B;
   critical section;
   exit code of B;
   exit code of A
end loop
```

Assume that the registers of A are different from the registers of B. Are the following statements correct?

1. If either A or B are starvation-free then C is deadlock-free.
2. If both A and B satisfy mutual exclusion and B is starvation-free then C is starvation-free.
3. If both A and B satisfy mutual exclusion and A is deadlock-free then C is deadlock-free.
4. If A is deadlock-free, B is starvation-free, and B satisfies mutual exclusion then C is starvation-free.

5. If C is starvation-free then both A and B are starvation-free.
6. If C is deadlock-free then both A and B are deadlock-free.
7. If C satisfies mutual exclusion then both A and B satisfy mutual exclusion.

○○ 1.16 Explain why the following algorithm is not deadlock-free. The algorithm is for two processes with identifiers 0 and 1, and it makes use of a shared bit called *turn*. In the code of the algorithm, the statement **await** *condition* is used as an abbreviation for **while** ¬*condition* **do** *skip*. (The symbol ¬ means negation.)

INCORRECT ALGORITHM NUMBER 1.

Initially: $turn = 0$.

PROGRAM FOR PROCESS 0

```
await turn = 0;
critical section of process 0;
turn := 1;
```

PROGRAM FOR PROCESS 1

```
await turn = 1;
critical section of process 1;
turn := 0;
```

Does the algorithm satisfy mutual exclusion?

○○ 1.17 Explain why the following algorithm does not satisfy mutual exclusion. The algorithm is for two processes. It makes use of one shared boolean bit called *lock*, which both processes can read and write. The processes follow the same program.

INCORRECT ALGORITHM NUMBER 2.

Initially: $lock = 0$.

PROGRAM FOR BOTH PROCESSES

```
await lock = 0;
lock := 1;
critical section;
lock := 0;
```

Does the algorithm satisfy deadlock-freedom?

○○ 1.18 Explain why the following algorithm does not satisfy mutual exclusion. The algorithm is for two processes with identifiers 0 and 1, and it makes use of two shared boolean bits called *flag*[0] and *flag*[1]. Both processes can read the two shared bits but only process 0 can update *flag*[0] and only process 1 can update *flag*[1].

INCORRECT ALGORITHM NUMBER 3.

Initially: *flag*[0] = *false* and *flag*[1] = *false*.

PROGRAM FOR PROCESS 0

```
1  await flag[1] = false;
2  flag[0] := true;
3  critical section of process 0;
4  flag[0] := false;
```

PROGRAM FOR PROCESS 1

```
1  await flag[0] = false;
2  flag[1] := true;
3  critical section of process 1;
4  flag[1] := false;
```

Does the algorithm satisfy deadlock-freedom? Show that changing the order of statements 1 and 2 does not make the algorithm correct. That is, after the change the algorithm satisfies mutual exclusion but does not satisfy deadlock-freedom.

∘∘ 1.19 Explain why the following algorithm is not deadlock-free. The algorithm is for two processes with identifiers 0 and 1, and it makes use of two shared boolean bits called *flag*[0] and *flag*[1]. Both processes can read the two shared bits but only process 0 can update *flag*[0] and only process 1 can update *flag*[1].

INCORRECT ALGORITHM NUMBER 4.

Initially: *flag*[0] = *false* and *flag*[1] = *false*.

PROGRAM FOR PROCESS 0

```
flag[0] := true;
while flag[1] do flag[0] := false;
                 await flag[1] = false;
                 flag[0] := true od;
critical section of process 0;
flag[0] := false;
```

PROGRAM FOR PROCESS 1

```
flag[1] := true;
while flag[0] do flag[1] := false;
                 await flag[0] = false;
                 flag[1] := true od;
critical section of process 1;
flag[1] := false;
```

Does the algorithm satisfy mutual exclusion?

∘∘ 1.20 Let *A* be an arbitrary deadlock-free mutual exclusion algorithm that does not satisfy requirement 4 on page 12, that is, the number of steps in the exit code depends on the activity of the other processes. In the following,

A is modified, so that the new algorithm satisfies requirement 4. One additional shared bit, called *flag*, is used.

Initially: *flag* = *false*.

```
Former entry code of A;
while flag do skip od;
flag := true;
Former exit code of A;
critical section;
flag := false;
```

Does the modified algorithm satisfy deadlock-freedom and/or mutual exclusion (for any A)? Assuming that A satisfies also starvation-freedom, does the modified algorithm satisfy starvation-freedom?

Problems based on Section 1.4

○ 1.21 A *virtual clock* (also called logical clock) is a clock that ticks before the first step, and then ticks before a step, only if every active process executed at least one step since the last tick. The sequence of steps between two clock ticks is called a *round*. The *round complexity* of an algorithm is the largest number of ticks (or rounds) possible where some process is in its entry code while no process is in its critical section. What is the relationship between the notions of round complexity and system response time?

○○ 1.22 Is there a connection between process time complexity and space complexity?

○○ 1.23 Consider the following time complexity measure:

Process step complexity: *The maximum number of steps a process may need to take (in its entry code and exit code), from the moment it starts trying to enter its critical section until it finishes its exit code, assuming that the time for which a process is in its critical section is ignored. (Only steps in which a process accesses the shared memory are counted.)*

What is the relation between *process step complexity* and all the other time complexity measures defined in Section 1.4?

Problems based on Section 1.5

○○ 1.24 Which of the following statements is true and which is false? An important difference between user-level threads and kernel-level threads is:

1. Switching between user-level threads which belong to the same process is faster than switching between kernel-level threads.
2. User-level threads are independent of each other, whereas kernel-level threads share their memory space.
3. User-level threads which belong to the same process have a shared stack, whereas each kernel-level thread has its own stack.

○○ 1.25 Circle the correct answer. In round-robin CPU scheduling algorithm, using very large time-slices (quantum) degenerates into:

1. Non-preemptive SJF.
2. Preemptive SJF.
3. FCFS.
4. Non-preemptive priority.
5. None of the above.

Mutual Exclusion Using Atomic Registers: Basic Topics

2.1 Algorithms for Two Processes

In this section we describe two algorithms that solve the mutual exclusion problem for two processes. The algorithms are simple and in addition to being deadlock-free they are also starvation-free. As mentioned, the only atomic operations on the shared registers are reads and writes. Below is a quote from a paper where Dijkstra has first introduced this problem.

> "In considering two sequential processes, *process 1* and *process 2*, they can for our purpose be regarded as cyclic. In each cycle a so-called *critical section* occurs, critical in the sense that at any moment at most one of two processes is allowed to be engaged in its critical section. In order to effectuate this mutual exclusion, the two processes have access to a number of common variables. We postulate that inspecting the present value of such a common variable and assigning a new value to such a common variable are to be regarded as indivisible, non-interfering actions, i.e. when the two processes assign a new value to the same common variable *simultaneously*, then the assignments are to be regarded as done the one after the other, the final value of the variable will be one of the two values assigned, but never a *mixture* of the two. Similarly,

when one process inspects the value of a common variable *simultaneously* with the assignment to it by the other one, then the former process will find either the old or the new value, but never a mixture." (*E. W. Dijkstra*, 1968 [107])

We will use the statement **await** *condition* as an abbreviation for **while** ¬*condition* **do** *skip*. (The symbol ¬ means negation.) We emphasize that the boolean condition in the await statement is *not* evaluated atomically. That is, when the evaluation of the condition requires more than one register to be read, the registers are not read in one atomic step, but rather read sequentially one after the other.

The terms *busy-waiting* and *spinning* are often used to describe a situation of using an await statement to wait for a condition to become *true*. Busy-waiting can be implemented by any modern operating system without hardware support. Although busy-waiting is less efficient when all processes execute on the same processor (CPU), it is efficient when each process executes on a different processor. Multi-processors are common in large high-performance computers and are becoming common even in personal computers. Busy-waiting is especially useful in two situations: if the critical section is small so that the expected wait is less than the cost of blocking and resuming a process, or when no other work is available.

2.1.1 Peterson's Algorithm

The algorithm was developed by Gary L. Peterson (1981). The programs for process 0 and process 1 are symmetric, that is, they are identical except for the way the identifiers are used. The algorithm makes use of a register called *turn* which can take the values 0 and 1 (i.e., the two possible identifiers), and two boolean registers $b[0]$ and $b[1]$. Both processes can read and write the register *turn*, both processes can read the two boolean registers, but only process 0 can write $b[0]$ and only process 1 can write $b[1]$. The algorithm is defined formally below.

PETERSON'S ALGORITHM FOR TWO PROCESSES:

Initially: $b[0] = \mathit{false}$, $b[1] = \mathit{false}$, the initial value of *turn* is immaterial.

PROGRAM FOR PROCESS 0:

$b[0] := \mathit{true}$;
turn := 0;
await ($b[1] = \mathit{false}$ **or** $\mathit{turn} = 1$);
critical section;
$b[0] := \mathit{false}$;

PROGRAM FOR PROCESS 1:

$b[1] := \mathit{true}$;
turn := 1;
await ($b[0] = \mathit{false}$ **or** $\mathit{turn} = 0$);
critical section;
$b[1] := \mathit{false}$;

In line 1, process $i \in \{0, 1\}$ indicates that it is contending for the critical section by setting $b[i]$ to *true*. Then it sets *turn* to i so that later it is possible to observe whether it or the other process was the first to write to *turn*. Next, it checks the values of the other b bit, if the value is *false* it means that the other process is not contending and process i can start executing its critical section. Otherwise when there is contention, the *first* process to write into *turn* wins and enters its critical section.

Figure 2.1, illustrates the structure of the algorithm and emphasizes that the register *turn* is used to determine which of the two processes is the first to arrive at the await statement, that is, which of the two processes is the first to assign a value to *turn*. This fact is then used to choose a winner in the case of contention. Note that in this algorithm, the first process which writes to *turn* "knows" that it is the first, by observing that the value of *turn* is not the value it has written to it. However, the last process which writes to *turn* does not know that it is the last since it does not know whether the other process is about to write to *turn* or has already done so.

Properties of Peterson's Algorithm:

- Satisfies mutual exclusion and starvation-freedom.
- The contention-free time complexity (i.e., in the absence of contention) is only four accesses to the shared memory – three accesses in the entry code and one in the exit code.

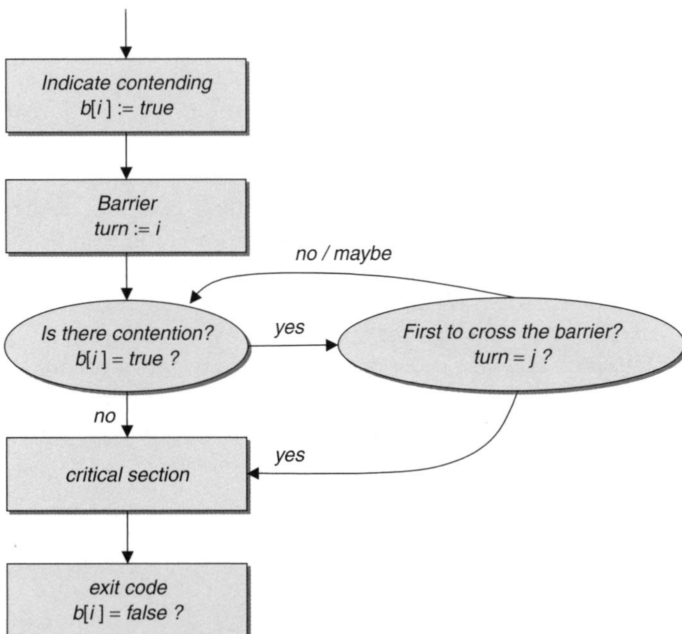

Figure 2.1 Schematic for Peterson's mutual exclusion algorithm. The first process to cross the barrier is the one which gets to enter the critical section. When there is no contention a process can enter the critical section immediately.

- *Process time complexity is unbounded*: the winner may need to busy-wait (spin) until the other process finishes its assignment to *turn* (and there is no bound on how much time this may take).
- *System response time*: (at least) five time units.
- Three shared registers are used.

The following is an example of a run in which the system response time is five time units. That is, it includes an interval where some process is in its entry code while no process is in its critical section, which takes five time units to execute, assuming there is an upper bound of one time unit for step time in the entry or exit code and no lower bound. The run starts with both processes in their remainders and proceeds as follows:

1. Process 0 executes $b[0] := true$;
2. Process 0 executes $turn := 0$;
3. Process 1 executes $b[1] := true$; process 0 performs the test $b[1] = false$; process 0 performs the test $turn = 1$;
4. Process 1 executes $turn := 1$; process 0 performs the test $b[1] = false$;
5. Process 1 performs the test $b[0] = false$; process 0 performs the test $turn = 1$;
6. Process 1 performs the test $turn = 0$; at this point, after five time units have passed, process 0 which found that indeed $turn = 1$ is in its critical section.

We next prove the correctness of the algorithm, showing that it satisfies mutual exclusion and starvation-freedom.

Theorem 2.1 *The algorithm satisfies mutual exclusion.*

Proof: Assume to the contrary that the two processes can be in their critical sections at the same time. If this is the case then their last tests of the condition in the await statement could not have been at the same time since the value of *turn* would have given priority to only one of them, and the other part of the test would have failed for both processes because the values of both $b[0]$ and $b[1]$ should have been *true*. Thus, the second process to pass the test did at least one assignment since the first process passed its test, and must have seen *turn* favorable to itself. However, this is not possible: the last assignment before testing sets *turn* to an unfavorable value, and hence the second process could not have passed the test, a contradiction. ∎

Theorem 2.2 *The algorithm is starvation-free.*

Proof: Again we assume to the contrary that the algorithm is not starvation-free and show how this assumption leads to a contradiction. Assuming that the algorithm is not starvation-free means that one of the processes, say process 0, is forced to remain in its entry code forever. This implies that at some later point process 1 will do one of the following three things: (1) stay in its remainder forever, or (2) stay in its entry code forever, not succeeding in proceeding into its critical section, or (3) repeatedly enter and exit its critical section. In the first case $b[1] = \mathit{false}$, and hence process 0 can proceed. The second case is impossible since *turn* is either 0 or 1, and hence it always enables at least one of the processes to proceed. In the third case, when process 1 exits its critical section and then tries to enter its critical section again, it will set *turn* to 1 and will never change it back to 0, enabling process 0 to proceed. Thus, we have shown that each of the three possible cases leads to a contradiction. ∎

These two theorems establish the correctness of the algorithm.

Peterson's algorithm is built around the idea of letting the processes know who is the *first* to assign a new value to some register, a fact which makes it difficult to extend the algorithm to work for more than two processes. The idea in the algorithm of Section 2.3, which works also for more than two processes, is to enable the processes to know who is the *last* process to assign a value to some register, and to choose this last process as the winner.

A simple generalization of Peterson's algorithm, which works also for more than two processes, is mentioned in Problem 2.63. The two process solution is used repeatedly in $n - 1$ levels to eliminate at least one process per level until only one remains. This generalization is not efficient in both time and space. Yet another generalization of Peterson's algorithm is presented in Problem 2.65.

2.1.2 Kessels' Single-writer Algorithm

Peterson's algorithm makes use of a register *turn* which both processes have to be able to read and write. Below is a simple modification of the algorithm where each register can be written by exactly one process. Algorithms that use only single-writer registers can be easily implemented in a message passing network. The algorithm was developed by J. L. W. Kessels (1982).

The algorithm makes use of two registers called $turn[0]$ and $turn[1]$ which can take the values 0 and 1 (i.e., the two possible identifiers), and two boolean registers $b[0]$ and $b[1]$. Process 0 can write the registers $turn[0]$ and $b[0]$ and read the registers $turn[1]$ and $b[1]$, while process 1 can write the registers $turn[1]$ and $b[1]$ and read the registers $turn[0]$ and $b[0]$.

The idea is to encode the register *turn* of Peterson's algorithm using the registers $turn[0]$ and $turn[1]$ as follows:

$$turn = 0 \text{ if and only if } turn[0] = turn[1],$$
$$turn = 1 \text{ if and only if } turn[0] \neq turn[1].$$

Using this encoding, it is possible to modify Peterson's algorithm. The registers $local[0]$ and $local[1]$ are local to processes 0 and 1, respectively.

Kessels' Algorithm for Two Processes:

Initially: $b[0] = \mathit{false}$, $b[1] = \mathit{false}$, the initial values of $turn[0]$ and $turn[1]$ are immaterial.

PROGRAM FOR PROCESS 0:

```
b[0] := true;
local[0] := turn[1];
turn[0] := local[0];
await (b[1] = false or local[0] ≠ turn[1]);
critical section;
b[0] := false;
```

PROGRAM FOR PROCESS 1:

```
b[1] := true;
local[1] := 1 − turn[0];
turn[1] := local[1];
await (b[0] = false or local[1] = turn[0]);
critical section;
b[1] := false;
```

Recall that the boolean condition in the await statement is *not* evaluated atomically. That is, when the evaluation of the condition requires more than one register to be read, the registers are not read in one atomic step, but rather read sequentially one after the other. Also, notice that the await statement in the code of process $i \in \{0, 1\}$ can be written as: **await** ($b[i] = \mathit{false}$ **or** $\mathit{local}[i] \neq (\mathit{turn}[1-i] + i) \bmod 2$).

It is easy to see that the algorithm is starvation-free. First observe that both processes can not stick in their await statements, since either $\mathit{turn}[0] = \mathit{turn}[1]$ or $\mathit{turn}[0] \neq \mathit{turn}[1]$, which means that the algorithm is deadlock-free. If one process is waiting and the other process is in its critical section then the other process will eventually enter its remainder. If this process remains in its remainder then its b bit will stay *false*, which will enable the first process to enter its critical section. If instead this process enters its entry code, it will change the value of its *turn* register and hence will allow the first process to proceed.

The fact that the *turn* register of Peterson's algorithm is implemented using two shared registers which can not be read together in one atomic step makes the correctness proof slightly harder, and this is left as an exercise. Finally, we point out that Kessels' algorithm satisfies an interesting property called *local spinning* (defined in Section 3.1), which is not satisfied by Peterson's algorithm.

Self Review

1. Does it matter if we replace the order of line 1 and line 2 in Peterson's algorithm (page 32)?
2. Consider a variant of Peterson's algorithm, where the statement: *turn* := 0; is added at the end of the code of both process 0 and process 1. Does the modified algorithm satisfy mutual exclusion and starvation-freedom?
3. Consider a variant of Peterson's algorithm, where the statement: **await** ($b[1] = \mathit{false}$); is added at the end of the code of process 0. Does the modified algorithm

satisfy deadlock-freedom and/or starvation-freedom? (Once you solve this problem, have a second look at Problem 1.20)

Answers: (1) With such a change the algorithm would not satisfy mutual exclusion. (2) Yes. (3) It satisfies deadlock-freedom but not starvation-freedom.

2.2 Tournament Algorithms

In this section we introduce a simple method, due to Gary L. Peterson and Michael J. Fischer (1977), which enables the construction an algorithm for n processes from any given algorithm for two processes.

The solution for n processes is built up inductively using a divide-and-conquer strategy. It is obtained by splitting the n processes into two groups of $n/2$ processes each. In each group, the processes compete to enter the critical section using recursively the solution for $n/2$ processes. That is, each group of $n/2$ processes is divided into two subgroups of $n/4$ processes each, etc. The "winners" of each of the two groups (of $n/2$ processes) use the given solution for two processes to determine which is the one allowed to enter the top-level critical section.

Another way to view this idea is to consider the competition between the processes as a competition in a tournament, as illustrated by the tree structure in Figure 2.2. Each process is progressing from a leaf to the root, where at each level of the tree it participates in a two process mutual exclusion algorithm, competing against at most one process in its neighbor's subtree. As a process advances towards the root, it plays the role of process 0 when it arrives from the left subtree, or of process 1 when it arrives from the right subtree. The winner

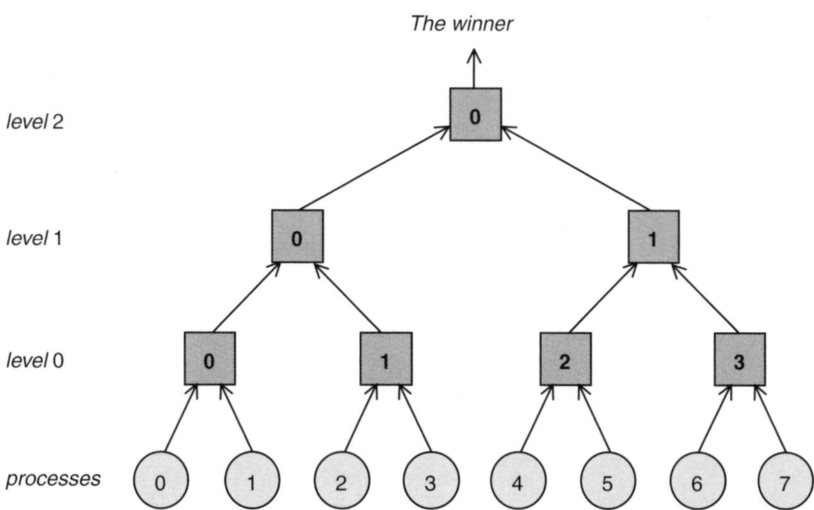

Figure 2.2 The tournament tree for 8 processes. At each level the nodes are numbered from left to right starting from 0. Thus, each node of the tree is uniquely identified by its level and node number.

of the top level is allowed to enter its critical section. Upon exiting its critical section, the winner traverses the reverse path (from the root to the leaf) executing the exit code at each level.

2.2.1 A Solution Based on Peterson's Algorithm

We will show how to construct a tournament algorithm for n processes, by placing Peterson's two process mutual exclusion algorithm (page 32) at each node of the tree. By doing so we get a time efficient algorithm, since a process that reaches an internal node only needs to know whether it arrives from the left subtree or from the right subtree. However, it does not need to know the identity of the process with which it has to compete.

For simplicity, it is assumed that the number of processes n is a power of two. When n is not a power of two, it is always possible to add a few more "dummy" processes which never do anything. The processes are numbered 0 through $n-1$.

A tournament tree has $\log n$ levels numbered 0 through $\log(n-1)$, and at each level the nodes are numbered from left to right starting from 0. Thus, each node of the tree is uniquely identified by its level and node number. Let *level* and *node* be the level and node number of some node v. With each node v, we associate three shared registers: $b[level, 2 \cdot node]$, $b[level, 2 \cdot node + 1]$, and $turn[level, node]$. These registers are used to implement Peterson's two process mutual exclusion algorithm which is associated with this node.

The registers *level*, *node*, and *id* are local to each process. The *level* and *node* registers together identify the node of the tree at which the process is competing, while the *id* register indicates whether the process arrived at the node from the left subtree (and hence plays the role of process 0), or from the right subtree.

A TOURNAMENT ALGORITHM: `process i's program.`

Initially: all the b registers are *false*, and the initial values of the *turn* registers and the local registers are immaterial.

```
node := i;
for level := 0 to log n − 1 do
     id := node mod 2;
     node := ⌊node/2⌋;
     b[level, 2 · node + id] := true;
     turn[level, node] := id;
     await (b[level, 2 · node + 1 − id] = false or
                    turn[level, node] = 1 − id)
od;
critical section;
for level := log n − 1 downto 0 do
     node := ⌊i/2^(level+1)⌋;
     b[level, node] := false
od;
```

At each level the value of the local register *id*, as computed in statement 3, determines whether process i competes like process 0 or like process 1 in Peterson's two process algorithm. Notice that at level k the value of *id* is the same as the value of the $k+1$ least significant bit of the binary representation on i. The possible opponents of i at level k are those processes whose numbers in binary begin with the same bits as i, up to the $k+1$ (least significant) bit which differs from the $k+1$ bit of i.

Properties of the Algorithm:

- Satisfies mutual exclusion and starvation-freedom.
- Contention-free time complexity is $4 \log n$ accesses.
- Process time complexity is unbounded.
- System response time is of order $\log n$ time units.
- $3 \cdot (n-1)$ shared registers are used, three for each node.
- One process can enter its critical section arbitrarily many times ahead of another.

We now prove the correctness of the algorithm. The proof should also work with minor modifications for tournament algorithms based on other two process algorithms.

Theorem 2.3 *The tournament algorithm satisfies mutual exclusion.*

Proof: Assume to the contrary that there exists a run in which two processes are in their critical sections at the same time. Since each process has to progress from a leaf to the root, before entering its critical section, there is at least one node in the run which has been visited by two processes, and both processes got past this node at the same time. Among all such nodes, let k be a node at the lowest level. Since the two processes succeeded to the next level beyond k, it means that there is a point in time where both are the winners in Peterson's algorithm which is associated with k. Furthermore, since k is at the lowest level, no other process was at k together with the other two processes. This contradicts the fact that Peterson's algorithm satisfies mutual exclusion, which is proven in Theorem 2.1. ∎

Theorem 2.4 *The tournament algorithm is starvation-free.*

Proof: Assume to the contrary that one or more processes is stuck, that is, they can not proceed to a higher level. Among these processes, let process p be stuck at the highest level. Then, it must be the case that p waits for some process, say q, which is either at the same level or higher. If p and q are at the same level then the value of *turn* (in this node) is favorable to q. In either case, q is not stuck, and will eventually enter its critical section, and later will return to its remainder. From the structure of Peterson's algorithm, once q exits its critical section, no other process can bypass p, and hence p must be able to advance to the next level, which contradicts the assumption that p is stuck. Thus, no process is stuck forever. ∎

We notice that process response time is of order n time units. The proof is as follows: Let $T(\ell)$ be the maximum number of time units for a process to go ℓ levels away from the root to its critical section and through its exit code. Notice that each process starts its entry code $\log n$ levels away from the root. A process p at level ℓ that loses to its competitor, say q, has to wait first for q to go through $\ell - 1$ levels. After q executes its exit code, p can advance to level $\ell - 1$. This implies, $T(0) = 0$; $T(\ell) = 2T(\ell - 1) + O(1)$. Thus, for $\log n$ levels we get $T(\log n) = O(2^{\log n}) = O(n)$.

As already mentioned, the tournament algorithm has the property that one process can enter its critical section more than once ahead of another. This is possible because nothing is assumed about the relative speed of the processes. Assume that a slow process p is waiting for some condition to become *true*. Suppose that later this condition becomes *true*, but p is slow to advance. In such a case, if another process from the other subtree is fast enough, it can re-enter its critical section an arbitrary number of times before p succeeds to enter its critical section.

2.2.2 A Solution Based on Kessels' Algorithm

The following tournament algorithm for n processes is due to Kessels (1982). The algorithm is constructed by placing Kessels' two process algorithm (page 35) at each node of the tree. For simplicity, it is assumed that the number of processes n is a power of two. The processes are numbered 0 through $n - 1$.

Kessels used the following numbering scheme for the nodes of the tree: the root is numbered 1, and for each node v, the left child of v is numbered $2 \cdot v$, while the right child is numbered $2 \cdot v + 1$ (see Figure 2.3). Each node of a tournament tree

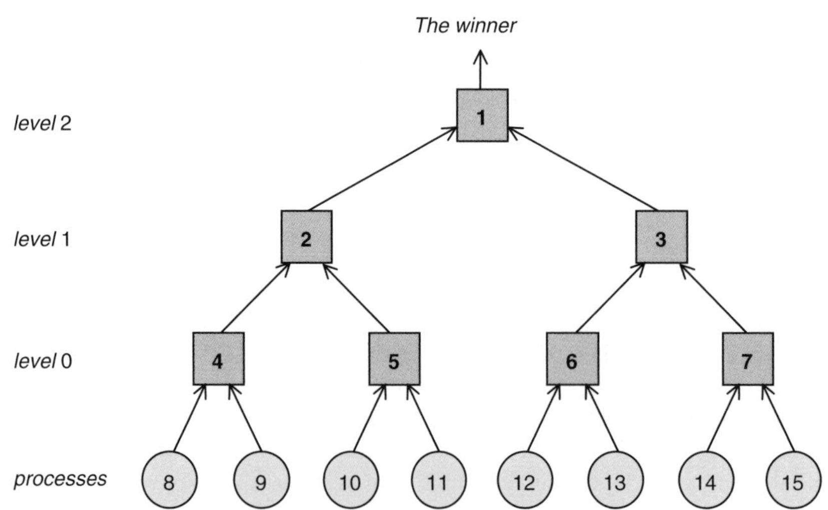

Figure 2.3 The numbering scheme in Kessels' algorithm: the root is numbered 1, for each node v, its left child is numbered $2 \cdot v$, while its right child is numbered $2 \cdot v + 1$. The leaf number of process i is $n + i$.

is uniquely identified by its node number. This numbering scheme allows a simple derivation of the number of the parent from the number of any child node.

In such a balanced tree, the leaf number of process i is $n + i$. In order to simplify the reversed traversal in the exit code, each internal node $v \in \{1, \ldots, n-1\}$ is provided with a binary variable $edge[v]$ which indicates the subtree from which the winner at v arrived. In addition, node v is provided with four shared registers: $b[v,0]$, $b[v,1]$, $turn[v,0]$, and $turn[v,1]$. These registers are used to implement Kessels' two process mutual exclusion algorithm which is associated with v.

The registers *node*, *id*, and *local* are local to each process. The *node* register identifies the node of the tree at which the process is competing, while the *id* register indicates whether the process arrived at the node from the left subtree (and hence plays the role of process 0), or from the right subtree.

KESSELS' TOURNAMENT ALGORITHM: `process i's program.`

Initially: all the b registers are *false*, and the initial values of the *turn* registers and all the other registers are immaterial.

```
node := i + n;
while node > 1 do
      id := node mod 2;
      node := ⌊node/2⌋;
      b[node, id] := true;
      local := (turn[node, 1 − id] + id) mod 2;
      turn[node, id] := local;
      await (b[node, 1 − id] = false or
                local ≠ (turn[node, 1 − id] + id) mod 2)
      edge[node] := id;
od;
critical section;
node := 1;
while node < n do
      b[node, edge[node]] := false;
      node := 2 · node + edge[node];
od;
```

Notice that, while the two process solution uses only single-writer registers, the solution for n processes does not. Shared registers may be modified by more than one process, though by one at most at any given time. The properties and correctness proof of Kessels' algorithm are similar to those of the tournament algorithm from the previous example.

Self Review

1. Does a tournament algorithm, which is based on a starvation-free mutual exclusion algorithm for two processes, always satisfy starvation-freedom?
2. Does it matter if we replace the exit code in the first tournament algorithm (lines 10–13, page 38) with the following exit code:

```
for level := 0 to log n − 1 do
      node := ⌊i/2^(level+1)⌋;
      b[level, node] := false
od;
```

Answers: (1) In such a case, a tournament algorithm would always satisfy starvation-freedom. (2) Yes, it matters.

2.3 A Fast Mutual Exclusion Algorithm

In this section, we describe an algorithm for n processes, due to Leslie Lamport (1987), which has the following two properties:

- Only five accesses to the shared memory are needed in order to enter a critical section in the absence of contention, and just two accesses are needed in the exit code.
- In the presence of contention, the winning process may have to check the status of all other n processes before it is allowed to enter its critical section.

While the first property is very important, and makes the algorithm useful in practice, the second property is a drawback of the algorithm. (In Section 3.2.2, we discuss how this drawback can be overcome.)

2.3.1 Lamport's Fast Algorithm

The algorithm was developed by Lamport (1987). The algorithm is defined formally below and is illustrated in Figure 2.4. The only atomic operations on the shared registers are reads and writes. That is, it is assumed that any two operations to a single shared register occur in some definite order. The algorithm makes use of two registers x and y which are long enough to store a process identifier, and a boolean array b. All the processes can read and write the registers x and y, the processes can read the boolean registers $b[i]$, but only process i can write $b[i]$. The processes are numbered 1 through n.

LAMPORT'S FAST DEADLOCK-FREE ALGORITHM: `process i's program.`

Initially: $y = 0$, and $b[i] = false$.

```
start: b[i] := true;
       x := i;
       if y ≠ 0 then b[i] := false;
                     await y = 0;
                     goto start fi;
       y := i;
       if x ≠ i then b[i] := false;
                     for j := 1 to n do await ¬b[j] od;
                     if y ≠ i then await y = 0;
```

```
10                goto start fi fi;
11      critical section;
12      y := 0;
13      b[i] := false
```

In line 1, process i indicates that it is contending for the critical section by setting its bit to *true*, and then it sets x to i so that it can later observe if there is contention. In lines 3–5, if $y \neq 0$ then there is contention or the critical section is occupied. In that case the process indicates that it is no longer contending, and waits until some process exits its critical section. In line 6, the process sets y to i. The last process to execute this line is the one to become the winner. Now, in line 7, a process checks x. If process i finds out at this point that $x = i$, it means that no other process, say process j, that is about to change y will find later that $x = j$, and hence process i can safely enter its critical section. Otherwise process i waits, by executing line 8, until it is clear that no other process will change y. Then, in line 9, it checks whether it was the last to change y. If so, it enters its critical section, otherwise it waits until y is released.

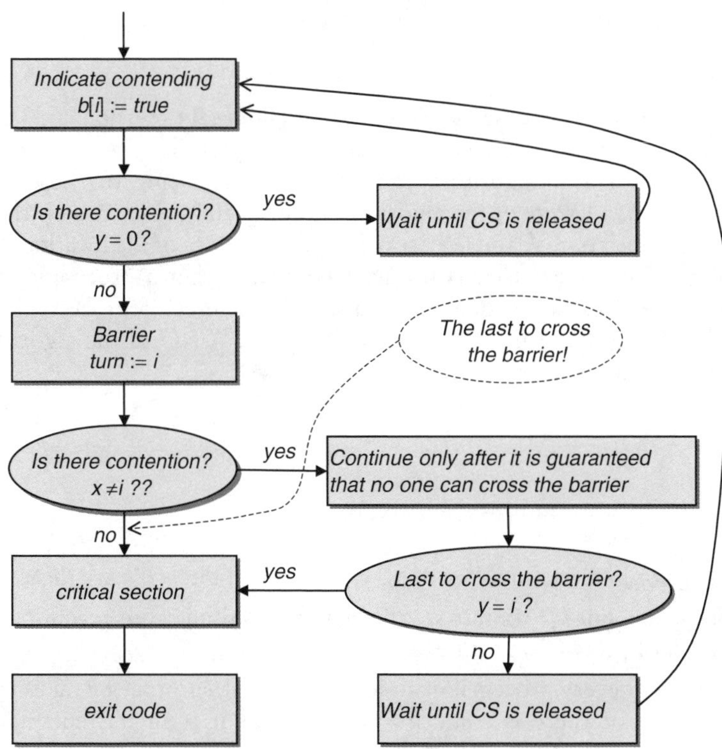

Figure 2.4 Schematic for fast mutual exclusion. The last process to cross the barrier is the one which gets to enter the critical section. When there is no contention a process can enter the critical section immediately after the second test and does not have to execute a code which guarantees that it is the last to cross the barrier.

Properties of the Fast Mutual Exclusion Algorithm:

- Satisfies mutual exclusion and deadlock-freedom.
- Starvation of individual processes is possible.
- *Fast access*: in absence of contention time complexity is constant, only seven accesses to the shared memory (five in the entry code and two in the exit code).
- *Process time complexity is unbounded*: even if only two processes contend, the winner may need to check and busy-wait on all the shared registers.
- System response time is of order n time units.
- $n+2$ shared registers are used.

Lamport's algorithm provides fast access in the absence of contention; however, in the presence of contention, however small, the winning process may have to check the status of all other n processes before it is allowed to enter its critical section. Recall that the statement **await** *condition* is an abbreviation for **while** $\neg$*condition* **do** *skip*, and hence may involve many accesses to the shared memory. Even if we assume that an *await* statement costs only one access, whenever two processes are contending, the winning process may need to access the shared memory more than n times. The properties of fast access in the absence of contention and unbounded process time complexity are obvious.

Correctness Proof

We turn now to prove that the algorithm satisfies mutual exclusion and deadlock-freedom. First we define a few notions that we use later.

The behavior of our algorithm can be formalized using the model of *fair transition systems*. A *state* of the algorithm is completely described by the values of the shared registers x, y, and the array b, and the values of the location counters of all the processes (i.e., what is the next command that a process is about to execute). We will use ℓ_i to denote the location counter of process i. Thus, ℓ_i ranges over the set 0..13 (0 is the remainder code). A *run* of the algorithm is a finite or an infinite sequence

$$\sigma \;=\; s_0 \xrightarrow{e_1} s_1 \xrightarrow{e_2} \cdots$$

of states s_i and process indices e_i satisfying

1. *Initialization*: In the initial state s_0, $y = 0$ and all the $b[i]$'s are *false*.
2. *Consecution*: For $i \geq 0$, state s_{i+1} is the state resulting from executing a single transition of process e_i in state s_i.
3. *Fairness*: For every process i, in an infinite run, either process i takes infinitely many steps, or there is some $k \geq 0$ such that it is in its remainder code (ℓ_i equals 0) in all states $s_{k'}$ with $k' \geq k$.

We want to prove that for any run, in any state no two processes are at their critical section, and that if a process is in its entry code then some process eventually enters its critical section.

Theorem 2.5 *The fast mutual exclusion algorithm satisfies mutual exclusion.*

Proof: In the algorithm, process i first sets x to i, and then checks the value of y. When it finds $y = 0$, it sets y to i and then checks the value of x. Let us say that process i enters its critical section along path α if it finds $x = i$ at this step. At most one process can enter its critical section along path α. If a process finds $x \neq i$ then it delays itself by looping until it sees that all the bits in the array b are false. Checking these n bits plays three roles:

1. Say that process i enters its critical section along path β if it finds $y = i$ after exiting the for loop. A consequence of having observed all the bits to be *false* is that the value of y will not be changed thereafter until process i leaves the critical section. This follows because every other contending process either reads $y \neq 0$ in the third line and is looping in the first three statements, or reads $y = 0$ and then finished the assignment $y := j$ in the sixth line before setting $b[j]$ to *false*. Hence, once process i finds $y = i$ after the loop, no other process can change the value of y until process i sets y to 0 in its exit code. It follows that at most one process can enter along path β.
2. The for loop ensures that if a process enters the critical section along path α, then any other process is prevented from entering along path β. To see this, observe that when a process j enters its critical section along path α, its bit $b[j]$ remains *true*. Thus, if another process tries to enter along path β it will find that $b[j] = true$ and will have to wait until process j exits its critical section and sets $b[j]$ to *false*.
3. The for loop also ensures that if a process enters the critical section along path β, then any other process is prevented from entering along path α. To see this, observe that when a process j enters its critical section along path β, it finds that all the bits in the array b are *false* and that $y = i$. Thus, if another process tries to enter along path α it will find $y \neq 0$ and will wait until process j exits its critical section and sets y to 0. ∎

Theorem 2.6 *The fast mutual exclusion algorithm is deadlock-free.*

Proof: We want to prove that if some process starts executing its algorithm then some process eventually enters its critical section.

Consider a run $\sigma = s_0, s_1, \ldots$ of the algorithm. We will prove that the deadlock-freedom property holds for this run. The proof is by contradiction. Suppose it does not. The following sequence of assertions leads to the desired contradiction. In the following sequence, each assertion is followed by a brief justification.

1. *There exists k such that $\ell_i \in 1..10$ in s_k for some i, and $\ell_j \neq 11$ for all j in all states $s_{k'}$ with $k' \geq k$.*

   This is because the run σ violates deadlock-freedom by assumption.
2. *There exists m such that $\ell_i \in 1..10$ in s_m for some process i, and in all states $s_{m'}$ with $m' \geq m$, $\ell_j \notin 11..13$ for all processes j.*

Since the run is fair, starting from state s_k (assertion 1) every process eventually leaves the locations 11..13, and from this, and assertion 1, assertion 2 follows.

3. *There is some state* s_p, $p \geq m$, *with* $y \neq 0$.

   As long as $y = 0$ a process j can be blocked only by busy-waiting for one of the $b[i]$'s to become *false*, and at this point its bit $b[j]$ is *false*. This means that not all the processes can be blocked at the same time. Hence, some process will eventually return to location 1 (since by assertion 1 it can not enter its critical section), and then, if y stays 0 it will eventually execute the assignment at location 6.

4. *In all states* $s_{p'}$ *with* $p' \geq p$, y *is non-zero.*

   Following the state s_p, no process is ever at location 12, which is the only place where y is reset.

5. *There exists* $q \geq p$ *and process* j *such that* $y = j$ *and* $b[i] = false$ *for all* $i \neq j$, *in all the states* $s_{q'}$ *with* $q' \geq q$.

   From assertion 5, it follows that for process j, if $\ell_j \neq 6$ in s_p, then in all the following states also $\ell_j \neq 6$ (no process can get past the await statement at location 4). Consequently, after all the processes at location 6 in state s_p execute the assignment, the value of y can not change. Assume without loss of generality that at this point $y = j$. Each process $i \neq j$, which is in its entry code, will eventually find that $y \neq i$ and will set its bit $b[i]$ to *false* and then busy-wait forever in one of the await statements.

6. From assertion 5, since process j can not be blocked on any await statement, there exists $r \geq q$ such that process j is in its critical section. This is a contradiction to assertion 1. ∎

2.3.2 A Simple Observation

Lamport's fast algorithm uses $n + 2$ shared registers, two of which are not single-writer registers. It is easy to see that a fast algorithm must use at least one shared register which is not a single-writer register.

Proposition 2.7 *In any deadlock-free mutual exclusion algorithm for n processes, which uses only single-writer registers, the number of different shared registers a process has to access in its entry code in order to enter its critical section in the absence of contention is at least n.*

Proof: Before entering its critical section a process must write at least once, otherwise other processes may not know that the process is in its critical section and another process may enter its critical section violating mutual exclusion. Each process must also read at least one register owned by every other process (a total of $n - 1$ reads). To see this, assume that process p, when run alone, never reads a register owned by process q. We can have a scenario where q runs alone and enters its critical section, then p is activated, and since it never reads registers owned by q, it will also enter its critical section violating mutual exclusion. ∎

Proposition 2.7 implies an $n+1$ lower bound on the *contention-free time complexity* of any such algorithm (the extra 1 is for the exit code).

Self Review

1. Does it matter if we change the order of the last two statements of Lamport's fast mutual exclusion algorithm (lines 12 and 13)?
2. Is Lamport's algorithm correct if we remove the statement "**await**($y = 0$)" in line 4?
3. Is Lamport's algorithm correct if we remove the statement "**await**($y = 0$)" in line 9?
4. Would Lamport's fast algorithm still be correct if the statement: "$y := 0$" in line 12, is replaced with: "**if** $y = i$ **then** $y := 0$ **fi**"?

Answers: (1) The algorithm would not satisfy mutual exclusion with such a change. (2) It will not satisfy deadlock-freedom. A process can loop keeping its b flag *true* any time another process checks it. (3) The algorithm is correct with such a change. (4) The algorithm is also correct with this change.

2.4 Starvation-free Algorithms

There are various ways to specify how contention can be resolved. The deadlock-freedom requirement, which guarantees that some process eventually gets into its critical section, is one way to do it. Although, in many cases it is a sufficient requirement, for some applications it might be a too weak requirement. For example, in cases where a process needs to stay in its critical section for a long time, a fact that might suspend other processes, there could be a higher level of contention.

Many of the papers about mutual exclusion focus on designing algorithms which are fair in the sense that a process does not have to wait too long while other processes are entering their critical sections many times. We repeat here the definition from page 12, of a requirement which guarantees that a process will not "be starved" (stay in its entry code forever).

Starvation-freedom: *If a process is trying to enter its critical section, then this process must eventually enter its critical section.*

The starvation-freedom requirement was first considered by Donald E. Knuth in May 1966. Knuth's algorithm, the first algorithm which satisfies starvation-freedom, is described in Problem 2.52. As already pointed out, in many practical systems, starvation-freedom is not necessary since contention is rare, and hence if a process tries long enough eventually it will get to access its critical section. The term *lockout-freedom* or *weak fairness* is sometimes used in the literature instead of starvation-freedom (with the same meaning).

Although starvation-freedom is strictly stronger than deadlock-freedom, it still allows processes to execute their critical sections arbitrarily many times before some trying process can execute its critical section. Such a behavior is prevented by the requirements defined in the next section.

2.4.1 Basic Definitions

In the definitions below, by *waiting process* we mean that the process is *busy-waiting* on some condition in its entry code. That is, it is waiting for some other process to do something that will enable it to proceed. The code before the waiting statement, and the last statement before the waiting statement, are sometimes called the *doorway*. More formally, we assume that the entry code consists of two parts. The first part, which is called the doorway, is *wait-free*: its execution requires only a bounded number of atomic steps and hence always terminates; the second part is a *waiting* statement (a loop that includes one or more statements). Thus, a *waiting process* in the above definition simply refers to a process that has finished the doorway code and reached a waiting part in its entry code. This is illustrated in Figure 2.5.

r**-bounded-waiting:** *A waiting process will be able to enter its critical section before each of the other processes is able to enter its critical section* $r + 1$ *times.*

Bounded-waiting: *There exists a positive integer* r *for which the algorithm is* r*-bounded-waiting. That is, if a given process is in its entry code, then there is a bound on the number of times any other process is able to enter its critical section before the given process does so.*

We notice that r-bounded-waiting and bounded-waiting do not imply deadlock-freedom.

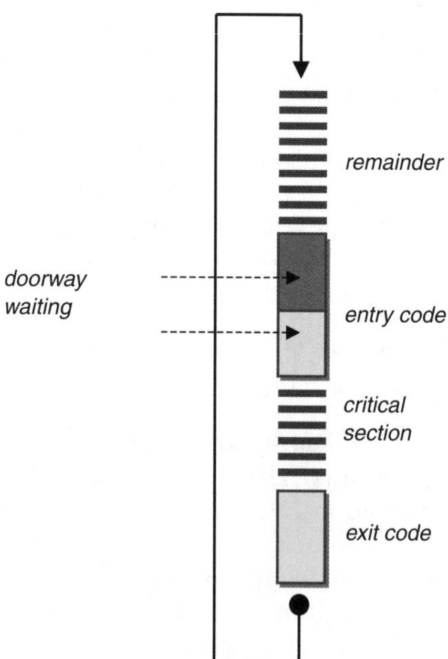

Figure 2.5 FIFO fairness. The doorway is wait-free: its execution requires only bounded number of atomic steps and hence always terminates; it is followed by a *waiting* statement (a loop that includes one or more statements).

Linear-waiting: *The term linear-waiting is sometimes used in the literature for 1-bounded-waiting. Thus, linear-waiting ensures that no process can execute its critical section twice while some other process is kept waiting.*

First-in-first-out: *The terms first-in-first-out (FIFO), and first-come-first-served (FCFS), are used in the literature for 0-bounded-waiting. Thus, first-in-first-out guarantees that: no beginning process can pass an already waiting process (i.e., a process that has already passed through its doorway).*

Sometimes it is more convenient to actually count the *total* number of times a waiting process may be passed by other processes before it can enter its own critical section, which leads us to the following definition.

r-fairness: *A waiting process will be able to enter its critical section before all the other processes collectively are able to enter their critical section $r + 1$ times.*

Notice that r-fairness does not imply deadlock-freedom. The r-fairness requirement does imply r-bounded-waiting, while r-bounded-waiting implies $((n-1) \cdot r)$-fairness, where n is the number of processes.

In Section 2.2, we have already introduced starvation-free algorithms. However, tournament algorithms do not satisfy r-fairness, for any finite integer r. That is, one process can enter its critical section arbitrarily many times ahead of another. They are also not fast in the absence of contention.

We first present the Bakery algorithm which is a classical solution to the mutual exclusion problem. The Bakery algorithm satisfies the *FIFO* requirement and has the additional interesting property that it works correctly even when it is allowed for reads which are concurrent with writes to return an arbitrary value. The Bakery algorithm uses only single-writer registers and hence, by Proposition 2.7, it is not fast. We complete this section by presenting a bounded space version of the Bakery algorithm called the Black-White Bakery algorithm.

At this point, we suggest that readers solve Problem 2.34 (page 82) before they continue reading.

2.4.2 The Bakery Algorithm

The Bakery algorithm is based on the policy that is sometime used in a bakery. Upon entering the bakery a customer gets a number which is greater than the numbers of other customers that are waiting for service. The holder of the lowest number is the next to be served. It is assumed that there may be up to n processes potentially contending to enter the critical section. Each of n potentially contending processes has a unique identifier which is a positive integer taken from the set $\{1, \ldots, n\}$, and the only atomic operations on the shared registers are reads and writes.

The algorithm makes use of a boolean array *choosing*[1..n], and of an integer array *number*[1..n]. The entries *choosing*[i] and *number*[i] can be read by all the processes but can be written only by process i. The relation $<$ used in the algorithm on ordered pairs of integers is called the *lexicographic order* relation and is defined by $(a, b) < (c, d)$ if $a < c$, or if $a = c$ and $b < d$. The algorithm is defined formally below.

THE BAKERY ALGORITHM: `process i's program.`

Initially: all entries in *choosing* and *number* are *false* and 0, respectively.

```
1   choosing[i] := true;
2   number[i] := 1 + maximum(number[1], ..., number[n]);
3   choosing[i] := false;
4   for j = 1 to n do
5           await choosing[j] = false;
6           await (number[j] = 0 or (number[j], j) ≥ (number[i], i))
7   od;
8   critical section;
9   number[i] := 0;
```

In line 1, process i indicates that it is contending for the critical section by setting its bit to *true*, and then it takes a number which is greater than the numbers of the ones that are waiting. Then, in the loop in lines 4–7, it waits until it has the lowest number and then it enters the critical section. If two processes have the same number then line 6 guarantees that the process with the smaller identifier enters first. An execution of the Bakery algorithm is illustrated in Figure 2.6.

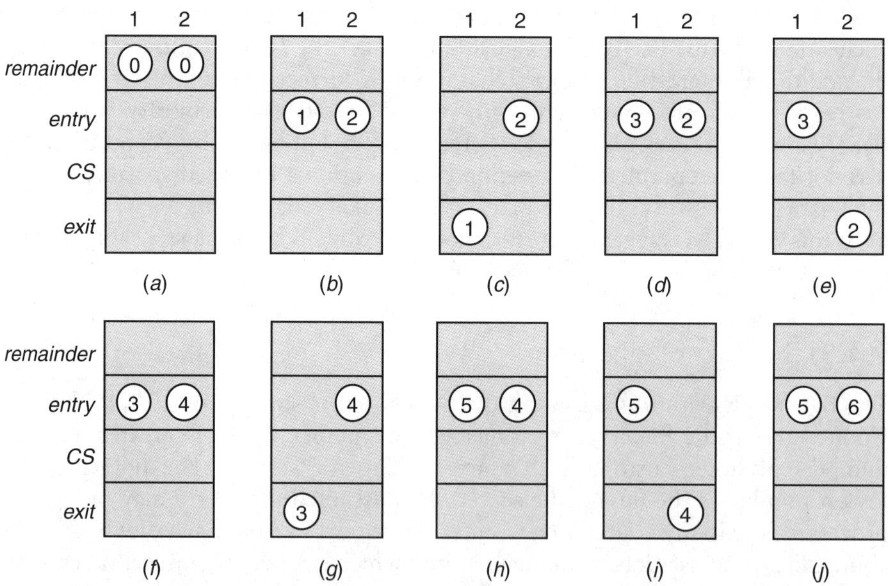

Figure 2.6 An execution of the Bakery algorithm. (*a*) Both processes start with ticket number 0; (*b*) process 1 moves first takes #1 and process 2 takes #2; (*c*)–(*d*) process 1 exits, reenters and takes #3; (*e*)–(*f*) process 2 exits, reenters and takes #4; (*g*)–(*j*) the processes repeat steps (*c*)–(*f*). It should be clear from this example why the size of the registers must be unbounded.

Computing the Maximum
As Lamport has pointed out, the correctness of the Bakery algorithm depends on an implicit assumption on the implementation of computing the maximum (line 2). Next, we give two implementations. The Bakery algorithm is correct with the first one, but is incorrect with the second. For each process, three additional *local* registers are used. They are named $local_1$, $local_2$, and $local_3$, and their initial values are immaterial.

CORRECT COMPUTATION OF THE MAXIMUM: `process i's program.`

```
local1 := 0;
for local2 := 1 to n do
    local3 := number[local2];
    if local1 < local3 then local1 := local3 fi
od;
number[i] := 1 + local1;
```

The above implementation is the first that comes to mind when thinking about how to compute the maximum. It is easy to prove that it satisfies the following property.

Lemma 2.8 *If the value of number*[k] *does not change while process i is computing the maximum (using the above implementation), then number*[i] *will be set to a value greater than the value of number*[k].

The second implementation, below, would be fine if it appeared in a sequential algorithm, but is incorrect in a concurrent algorithm.

INCORRECT COMPUTATION OF THE MAXIMUM: `process i's program.`

```
1  local1 := i;
2  for local2 := 1 to n do
3      if number[local1] < number[local2] then local1 := local2 fi
4  od;
5  number[i] := 1 + number[local1];
```

The proof that the above implementation is incorrect is somewhat tricky and we suggest that readers first try to prove it by themselves.

Theorem 2.9 *The Bakery algorithm does not satisfy the mutual exclusion property when the second implementation for computing the maximum is used.*

Proof: We construct a run in which three processes, 1, 2, and 3, participate and where both process 1 and process 3 are at their critical sections at the same time. We first let process 2 and process 3 run in lock steps, until they set both *number*[2] and *number*[3] to 1. Now, we let them proceed until process 2 enters its critical section, while process 3 is awaiting (in statement 6) for process 2 to exit its critical section. At this point, we activate process 1, and let it run until it reaches statement 5 in the procedure for computing the maximum (at which point $local_1 = 2$). We let process 2 exit its critical section, setting *number*[2] to 0, and let process 3 continue until it enters its critical section. Finally, we let process 1 set *number*[1] to 1, and then run without interruption until it also enters its critical section. ∎

Notice that the proof breaks, when "$<$" is replaced with "$\leq$" in statement 3 (Problem 2.39).

For the rest of the section we assume that the first (correct) implementation for computing the maximum is used.

Properties of the Bakery Algorithm:

- Satisfies mutual exclusion and first-come-first-served.
- *The algorithm is not fast*: even in the absence of contention it requires a process to access the shared memory $3 \cdot (n - 1)$ times. Hence, also the system response time is (at least) of order n time units.
- *The size of number*[*i*] *is unbounded*: in practice this is not a problem assuming that contention is rare. Thirty-two bits registers will give us ticket numbers which can grow up to 2^{32}, a number that in practice is unlikely to be reached. In the next subsection we will show how, using only one additional shared bit, the ticket numbers can be easily bounded.
- It uses only $2 \cdot n$ shared registers (but can trivially be modified to use only n shared registers).
- *Fault-tolerance*: the algorithm works correctly even when a *finite* number of processes may fail. By a failure of process i, we mean that the process program counter is set to point to the beginning of its remainder code and that the values of *choosing*[*i*] and *number*[*i*] are set to *false* and 0, respectively. The process may then resume its execution; however, if a process keeps failing infinitely often, then it may prevent other processes from entering their critical section. For more on the subject of fault tolerance see Section 3.3.
- *Non-atomic registers*: it is enough to assume that the registers are *safe* registers. That is, there is no need to assume that operations on the same memory location occur in some definite order; it works correctly even when it is allowed for reads which are concurrent with writes to return an arbitrary value.

As we have pointed out, the size of the registers *number*[*i*] in the Bakery algorithm must be unbounded. To see that, construct a run in which the numbers taken grow without a bound, as follows: Run p_1 until it enters its critical section with *number*[1] $= 1$; run p_2 until it chooses *number*[2] $= 2$; let p_1 exit its critical section and p_2 enter its critical section; run p_1 until it chooses *number*[1] $= 3$; let p_2 exit its critical section and p_1 enter its critical section; run p_2 until it chooses *number*[2] $= 4$, and so on. Clearly, the numbers taken by processes p_1 and p_2 in such a run grow without a bound.

Since the registers *choosing*[*i*] and *number*[*i*] can be written only by process i, it is possible to combine them and use only one register. By doing so we get an algorithm for n processes which uses only n registers and hence matches the lower bound on the *number* of registers as proven in Section 2.5.1. Notice that while the Bakery algorithm is starvation-free, the One-bit algorithm in Section 2.5.2 is not. However, the One-bit algorithm provides tight upper bound on both the number and the *size* of registers needed for deadlock-free algorithms.

Correctness Proof

We prove that the Bakery algorithm satisfies the mutual exclusion, 0-bounded-waiting (FIFO) and deadlock-freedom properties. We assume that the registers are atomic registers, and that processes do not fail. The proofs can be easily modified to show that the algorithm is correct even when assuming non-atomic registers (i.e., registers that can be written and read concurrently), and when a finite number of faults occur.

We will be using the following definitions. Process i is said to be in the *doorway* while executing statements 1–3 (i.e., while $choosing[i] = true$), and it is said to be *in the bakery* while executing statements 4–8 (i.e., from the time it sets $choosing[i]$ to *false* until it leaves its critical section). The following lemmas follow immediately from Lemma 2.8.

Lemma 2.10 *If process i and process k are in the bakery and i entered the bakery before k entered the doorway, then* $number[i] < number[k]$.

Lemma 2.11 *If process i is in its critical section, and process j is in the bakery then* $(number[i], i) < (number[k], k)$.

Proof: Let T^i_5 be the last time at which process i read $choosing[k]$ (which happened during its last execution of statement 5, for $j = k$). Let T^i_6 be the last time at which i began executing statement 6, for $j = k$. Thus:

$$T^i_5 < T^i_6.$$

For process k, let T^k_1 be the time at which it last executed statement 1 (entered the doorway), let T^k_3 be the time at which it last executed statement 3 (left the doorway), and let T^k_2 be the time at which it has finished writing the current value of $number[k]$. Thus:

$$T^k_1 < T^k_2 < T^k_3.$$

Since $choosing[k]$ was equal to *false* at time T^i_5, and $choosing[k]$ was equal to *true* at the time interval $[T^k_1, T^k_3]$, it is either the case that, $T^i_5 < T^k_1$ or $T^k_3 < T^i_5$.

In the first case, it follows from Lemma 2.10 that $number[i] < number[k]$, and we are done. In the second case, we have that

$$T^k_2 < T^k_3 < T^i_5 < T^i_6.$$

Thus, when process i executed statement 6, at time T^i_6, it read the current value of $number[k]$ (which was written at the time T^k_2). Since process i has continued to its critical section after executing statement 6, it must have found $(number[i], i) < (number[k], k)$. ∎

Theorem 2.12 *The Bakery algorithm satisfies mutual exclusion, first-come-first-served fairness, and is deadlock-free.*

Proof: The fact that no two processes can be at their critical sections at the same time follows from Lemma 2.11. From Lemmas 2.10 and 2.11, it follows that processes enter their critical sections on a first-come-first-served basis.

To prove that the algorithm is deadlock-free, assume to the contrary that from some point on, no process ever enters its critical section and that some process is in the bakery. Then, there is some time after which no more processes enter or leave the bakery. At this time, let process i be with the minimum value of $(number[i], i)$, among all the processes in the bakery. Then process i must eventually complete the loop of statement 4, and enter its critical section, a contradiction. ∎

A Simple Variant of the Bakery Algorithm

A shorter and simpler version of the Bakery algorithm is described below. In this version, for each process i, the $number[i]$ register is never decreased, and thus the correctness proof is much simpler than that of the original algorithm. However, this is the main drawback of this algorithm: in *every* run the values chosen by the processes grow without bound.

As before, the algorithm makes use of a boolean array $choosing[1..n]$, and of an integer array $number[1..n]$. The entries $choosing[i]$ and $number[i]$ can be read by all the processes but can be written only by process i. The relation $<$ used in the algorithm on ordered pairs of integers is called the *lexicographic order* relation and is defined by $(a, b) < (c, d)$ if $a < c$, or if $a = c$ and $b < d$. The algorithm is defined formally below.

THE MODIFIED BAKERY ALGORITHM: `process i's program.`

Initially: all entries in *choosing* and *number* are *false* and 0, respectively.

```
1  choosing[i] := true;
2  number[i] := 1 + maximum(number[1], ..., number[n]);
3  for j = 1 to n do
4          await (choosing[j] = false or (number[j], j) ≥ (number[i], i));
5  od;
6  critical section;
7  choosing[i] := false;
```

In line 1, process i indicates that it is contending for the critical section by setting its choosing bit to *true*, and then it takes a number which is greater than the numbers of all the other processes. Then, it waits until it has a lower number than any other active process. If two active processes have the same number then line 4 guarantees that the process with the smaller identifier enters first. (More details are discussed in Problem 2.43.)

As we have pointed out, the Bakery algorithm uses *unbound* size registers. Using only one additional shared bit, we bound the amount of space required in the Bakery algorithm, by *coloring* the tickets taken in the Bakery algorithm with the colors black and white. The resulting Black-White Bakery algorithm, due to G. Taubenfeld (2004), preserves the simplicity and elegance of the original algorithm, and has the following two desired properties, (1) it satisfies FIFO: processes are served in the order they arrive, and (2) it uses finite number of bounded size registers: the numbers taken by waiting processes can grow only up to n, where n is the number of processes.

The first thing that process i does in its entry section is to take a colored ticket $ticket_i = (mycolor_i, number_i)$, as follows: i first reads the shared bit *color*, and sets its ticket's color to the value read. Then, it takes a number which is greater than the numbers of the tickets which have the same color as the color of its own ticket. Once i has a ticket, it waits until its colored ticket is the *lowest* and then it enters its critical section. The order between colored tickets is defined as follows: If two tickets have different colors, the ticket whose color is *different* from the value of the shared bit *color* is smaller. If two tickets have the same color, the ticket with the smaller number is smaller. If tickets of two processes have the same color and the same number then the process with the smaller identifier enters its critical section first. Next, we explain when the shared *color* bit is written. The first thing that process i does when it leaves its critical section (i.e., its first step in the exit section) is to set the *color* bit to a value which is different from the color of its ticket. This way, i gives priority to waiting processes that hold tickets with the same color as the color of i's ticket.

Until the value of the *color* bit is first changed, all the tickets have the same color, say white. The first process to enter its critical section flips the value of the *color* bit (i.e., changes it to black), and hence the color of all the new tickets taken thereafter (until the color bit is modified again) is black. Next, *all* the processes which hold white colored tickets enter and then exit their critical sections one at a time until there are no processes holding white tickets in the system. Only then the process with the lowest black ticket is allowed to enter its critical section, and when it exits it changes to white the value of the *color* bit, which gives priority to the processes with black tickets, and so on. An execution of the Black-White Bakery algorithm is illustrated in Figure 2.7.

Three data structures are used: (1) a single shared bit named *color*, (2) a boolean array *choosing*[1..n], and (3) an array with n entries where each entry is a colored ticket which ranges over $\{black, white\} \times \{0, \ldots, n\}$. We use $mycolor_i$ and $number_i$ to designate the first and second components, respectively, of the ordered pair stored in the ith entry. (To improve readability, we use below subscripts to index entries in an array.)

THE BLACK-WHITE BAKERY ALGORITHM: `process i's code.`

shared
  color: a bit of type $\{black, white\}$
  choosing[1..n]: boolean array

$(mycolor, number)[1..n]$: array of type $\{black, white\} \times \{0, \ldots, n\}$
Initially $\forall i : 1 \leq i \leq n : choosing_i = false$ and $number_i = 0$,
the initial values of all the other variables are immaterial.

```
choosing_i := true                                   /* beginning of doorway */
mycolor_i := color
number_i := 1 + max({number_j | (1 ≤ j ≤ n) ∧ (mycolor_j = mycolor_i)})
choosing_i := false                                  /* end of doorway */
for j = 1 to n do
     await choosing_j = false
     if mycolor_j = mycolor_i
     then await  (number_j = 0) ∨ ([number_j, j] ≥ [number_i, i]) ∨
                 (mycolor_j ≠ mycolor_i)
     else await  (number_j = 0) ∨ (mycolor_i ≠ color) ∨
                 (mycolor_j = mycolor_i) fi
od
critical section
if mycolor_i = black then color := white else color := black fi
number_i := 0
```

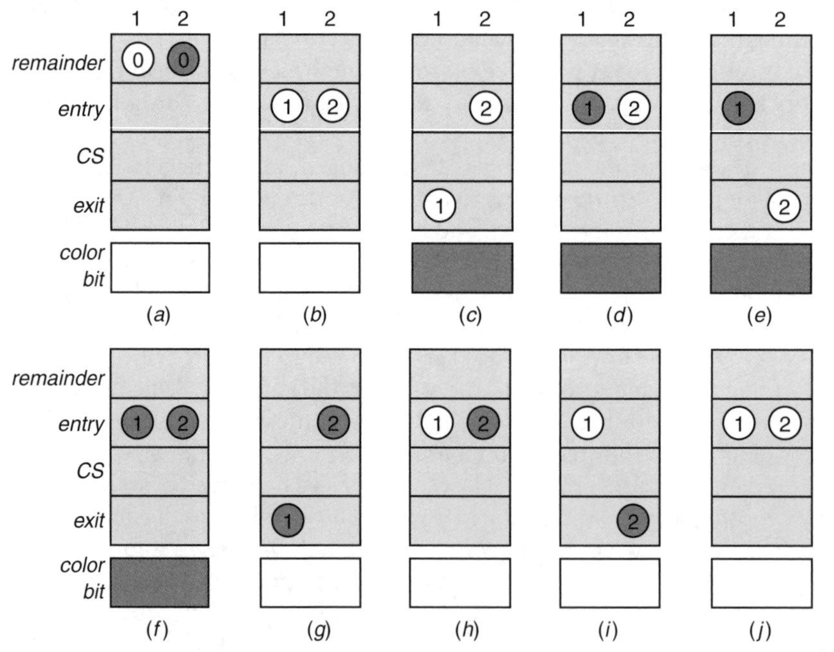

Figure 2.7 An execution of the Black-White Bakery algorithm. (*a*) Both processes start with ticket number 0; (*b*) process 1 moves first and takes white ticket #1 and process 2 takes white ticket #2; (*c*)–(*d*) process 1 sets the color bit to black and exits, reenters and takes black ticket #1; (*e*)–(*f*) process 2 sets the color bit to black (i.e., no change) and exits, reenters and takes black ticket #2; (*g*)–(*j*) the processes repeat steps (*c*)–(*f*) using black tickets instead of white. Notice that states (*b*) and (*j*) are the same.

In line 1, process i indicates that it is contending for the critical section by setting its *choosing* bit to *true*. Then it takes a colored ticket by first "taking" a color (step 2) and then taking a number which is greater by one than the numbers of the tickets with the same color as its own (step 3). For computing the maximum, we assume a simple implementation in which a process first reads into local memory all the n tickets, one at a time atomically, and then computes the maximum over numbers of the tickets with the same color as its own.

After passing the doorway, process i waits in the for loop (lines 5–10), until it has the lowest colored ticket and then it enters its critical section. We notice that each one of the three terms in each of the two await statements is evaluated separately. In the case where processes i and j have tickets of the same color (line 8), i waits until it notices that either (1) j is not competing any more, (2) i has a smaller number, or (3) j has re-entered its entry section. (If two processes have the same number then the process with the smaller identifier enters first.) In the case where processes i and j have tickets with different colors (line 9), i waits until it notices that either (1) j is not competing any more, (2) i has priority over j because i's color is *different* than the value of the color bit, or (3) j has re-entered its entry section.

In the exit code (line 12), i sets the *color* bit to a value which is different than the color of its ticket, and sets its ticket number to 0 (line 13). The algorithm is also correct if we replace the order of lines 11 and 12, allowing process i to write the *color* bit immediately before it enters its critical section. We observe that the order of lines 12 and 13 is crucial for correctness; and that without the third clause in the await statement in line 9 the algorithm can deadlock. Although the *color* bit is not a purely single-writer register, there is at most one write operation pending on it at any time.

We point out that the *color* bit can be easily implemented using n single-writer atomic bits. To change the color, process i changes the value of the i-th bit. *Black* corresponds to the case where the number of bits which are set to 1 is even, while *white* corresponds to the case where the number of bits which are set to 1 is odd (Problem 2.51).

We observe that the Black-White Bakery algorithm is not deadlock-free if the third clause in the await statement in line 9 is removed. To see that consider the following run: Assume that you have two processes in their entry sections–one holds a white ticket (call it the white process) and the other process holds a black ticket (the black process). Also, assume that the value of the shared *color* bit is white. Hence the black process has priority over the white process. Now run the processes so that the black process enters its critical section while the white process waits in line 9. Next, the black process exits its critical section, and immediately re-enters its entry section (now with a white ticket). Notice that when this happens the value of the *color* bit *does not* change (the *color* bit must have been already changed before by another black process). The only way for the white process waiting in line 9 to find out that it is its turn is using clause 3. Without clause 3 the white process will spin forever in line 9 and the other process will eventually spin forever in line 8.

Notes About Correctness

Since a full correctness proof was already given for the Bakery algorithm, to prevent repetitions, we only state below the lemma which captures the effect of the tickets' colors on the order in which processes enter their critical sections.

Lemma 2.13 *Assume that at time t, the value of the color bit is $c \in \{black, white\}$. Then, any process which at time t is in its entry section and holds a ticket with a color different than c must enter its critical section before any process with a ticket of color c can enter its critical section.*

For example, if the value of the *color* bit is white, then no process with a white ticket can enter its critical section until all the processes which hold black tickets enter their critical sections. The following corollary follows immediately from Lemma 2.13.

Corollary 2.14 *Assume that at time t, the value of the color bit has changed from $c \in \{black, white\}$ to the other value. Then, at time t, every process that is in its entry section has a ticket of color c.*

The following theorem states the main properties of the algorithm.

Theorem 2.15 *The Black-White Bakery algorithm satisfies mutual exclusion, deadlock-freedom, FIFO, and uses finite number of bounded size registers each of size one bit or* $\log(2n + 2)$ *bits.*

Self Review

1. Does *FIFO* imply *deadlock-freedom*?
2. Why is the Bakery algorithm not correct when lines 1, 3, and 5 (which refer to the *choosing* array) are omitted?
3. Would the Black-White Bakery algorithm be correct if we replace the order of lines 11 and 12, allowing process i to write the *color* bit *before* it enters its critical section?
4. Does it matter if we change the order of the last two statements (in the exit code) of the Black-White Bakery algorithm? Justify your answer.

Answers: (1) No. (2) No. (3) Without these three lines the algorithm would not satisfy mutual exclusion. (4) The algorithm would still be correct with such a change. (5) Yes, it matters.

2.5 Tight Space Bounds

We show that for n processes, n shared bits are necessary and sufficient for solving the mutual exclusion problem, assuming that the only atomic operations are reads and writes, and the processes are asynchronous. The algorithm (upper bound) is interesting since it is space optimal; however, it is not fast in the absence of contention.

The result presented in this section was first proved by James E. Burns and Nancy A. Lynch in 1980. We show that when only atomic reads and writes are possible, it is necessary to use at least one shared register per process, regardless of how large the register is. This implies that in a situation where all the memory space has to be allocated in advance, it is not possible to design a mutual exclusion algorithm without knowing in advance the number of processes. In the sequel, it is assumed that $n \geq 2$, where n is the number of processes.

Theorem 2.16 *Any deadlock-free mutual exclusion algorithm for n processes must use at least n shared registers.*

All the lemmas and definitions below refer to one arbitrary deadlock-free mutual exclusion algorithm for n processes. To prove the result, it is shown that any algorithm has a run in which at least n registers are accessed.

On page 44 we have defined a run as a sequence of alternating states and events (also referred to as steps). For the purpose of this proof, it is more convenient to define a run as a sequence of events omitting all the states except the initial state. Since the states in a run are uniquely determined by the events and the initial state, no information is lost by omitting the states.

Each event in a run is associated with a specific process that is *involved* in the event. We will use x, y, and z to denote runs. When x is a prefix of y, we denote by $(y - x)$ the suffix of y obtained by removing x from y. Also, we denote by x; *seq* the sequence obtained by extending x with the sequence of events *seq*. We will often use statements like "in run x process p is in its remainder", and implicitly assume that there is a function which for any run and process lets us know whether a process is in its remainder, entry code, critical section, or exit code. Also, saying that an extension y of x involves only process p, means that all events in $(y - x)$ involve only process p. Finally, by a run we always mean a finite run, and by a register we mean a shared register.

Our first definition captures when two runs are indistinguishable to a given process.

Definition 2.1 *Run x looks like run y to process p, if the subsequence of all events by p in x is the same as in y, and the values of all the registers in x are the same as in y.*

Notice that the looks like relation is an equivalence relation. The next step by a given process always depends on the previous step taken by the process and the current values of the registers. The previous steps uniquely determine whether the next step is a read or a write. The current values of the registers determine what value is going to be read in case of a read step. It should be clear that if two runs look alike to a given process then the next step by this process in both runs is the same.

Lemma 2.17 *Let x be a run which looks like run y to every process in a set P. If z is an extension of x which involves only processes in P then y; $(z - x)$ is a run.*

Proof: By a simple induction on k – the number of events in $(z - x)$. The basis when $k = 0$ holds trivially. We assume that the lemma holds for $k \geq 0$ and prove for $k + 1$. Assume that the number of events in $(z - x)$ is $k + 1$. For some event e, it is the case that $z = z'; e$. Since the number of events in $(z' - x)$ is k, by the induction hypothesis $y' = y; (z' - x)$ is a run. Let $p \in P$ be the process which is involved in e. Then, from the construction, the runs z' and y' look alike to p, which implies that the next step by p in both runs is the same. Thus, since $z = z'; e$ is a run, also $y'; e = y; (z - x)$ is a run. ∎

We next define the notion of a hidden process. Intuitively, a process is hidden in a given run, if all the steps it has taken since the last time it has been in its remainder communicate no information to the other processes. We say that a write event e_1 is *overwritten* by event e_2 in a given run r if e_2 is a write event which happens after e_1 in r, and both e_1 and e_2 are write events to the same register.

Definition 2.2 *For process p and run z, let z' be the longest prefix of z such that p is in its remainder in z'. Process p is hidden in run z if each event which p is involved in $(z - z')$ is either: a read event, or a write event that is overwritten (in z) before any other process has read the value written.*

We notice that a process is not hidden if it is involved in a write event which is not later overwritten, even if the write does not change the current value of a register. Also, if a process is in its remainder in z then it is hidden in z, and thus initially all the processes are hidden. A hidden process looks just like a process halted in its remainder, and hence no process can wait until a hidden process takes a step.

Lemma 2.18 *If a process p is in its critical section in run z then p is not hidden in z.*

Proof: Assume to the contrary that process p is hidden and is in its critical section in run z. Let z' be the longest prefix of z such that p is in its remainder in z'. Since p is *hidden* in run z, it is possible to remove from z all the events in which p is involved in $(z - z')$ and get a new run y.

The run y looks like z to all processes other than p, and p is in its remainder in y. By the deadlock-freedom property, there is an extension of y which does not involve p in which some process $q \neq p$ enters its critical section.

Since y looks like z to all processes other than p, by Lemma 2.17, a similar extension exists starting from z. That is, q can enter its critical section in an extension of z, while p is still in its critical section. However, this violates the mutual exclusion property. ∎

Lemma 2.19 *Let x be a run in which all the processes are hidden. Then, for any process p, there exists a run y which looks like x to p, where all processes except maybe p are in their remainders.*

Proof: Let k_q be the number of steps of process $q \neq p$ in run x since q was last in its remainder during x. The proof is by induction on k, defined as:

$$k = \sum_{q \neq p} k_q.$$

The basis when $k = 0$ holds trivially, since it means that all processes other than p are in their remainders in x and hence $y = x$ satisfies the requirements.

We assume that the claim holds for $k \geq 0$ and prove for $k + 1$. Let e be the *last* event which involves a process other than p in x. Since it is assumed that all the processes are hidden in x, the process that is involved in e is hidden in x. Thus, e is either: a read event, or a write event that is overwritten before any process has read the value written.

Clearly, by removing e from x we get another run, say x'. We next show that in x', all processes are still hidden. If e is a read event then no write after e will be effected, and hence, clearly, in x' all processes are still hidden. Suppose that e is a write event. Let e' be the event in x that has overwritten e before any process has read the value written by e. If in x, the event e has overwritten some write event, then this event is now overwritten by e' in x' before any other process has read the value written. Hence, again, in x' all processes are still hidden.

By the induction hypothesis, there exists a run y which looks like x' to p, where all processes except maybe p are in their remainders. Since x' looks like x to p, then (since "look like" is an equivalence relation) also y looks like x to p. Thus, the run y is as required in the lemma. ▮

Definition 2.3 *Process p covers register r in run x, if x can be extended by an event in which p writes to r.*

Notice that if process p covers register r in run x then p covers r in any extension of x which does not involve p.

Lemma 2.20 *Let x be a run in which all the processes are hidden. Then, for any process p, there is an extension z of x which involves only p in which p covers some register that is not covered by any other process.*

Proof: By Lemma 2.19, there exists a run y which looks like x to all processes except maybe p, where all processes except maybe p are in their remainders.

By the deadlock-freedom property, starting from y process p is able to enter its critical section on its own. Since y looks like x to p, by Lemma 2.17, p should be able to do the same starting from x. That is, p can enter its critical section on its own starting from x. Suppose p only writes registers covered by other processes before entering its critical section. Then when all the covered registers are written one after the other we get a run in which p is hidden and is in its critical section. However, by Lemma 2.18, this is not possible. Thus, p writes some register which is not covered by any other process before entering its critical section. The extension of x where p is stopped just before it writes this register is as required in the lemma. ∎

Theorem 2.16 follows immediately from the following lemma, which implies that there is a run in which n distinct registers are covered.

Lemma 2.21 *Let x be a run in which all the processes are in their remainders. Then, for every set of processes P there is an extension z of x which involves only processes in P, in which the processes in P are hidden and cover $|P|$ distinct registers.*

Proof: The proof is by induction on k–the size of P. The basis when $k = 0$ is trivial. We assume that the lemma holds for $k \geq 0$ and prove that it also holds for $k + 1$. Let P be an arbitrary set of k processes and let p be a process not in P. We need to show that there is an extension z of x which involves only p and the processes in P, in which these $k + 1$ processes are hidden and cover $k + 1$ distinct registers.

By the induction hypothesis, there is an extension y_1 of x which involves only the processes in P in which the processes in P are hidden and cover k distinct registers. Let W_1 be the set of these k registers. Notice that all the processes which are not involved in y_1 are still in their remainders.

Let y_2 be an extension of y_1 defined as follows: first let each process in P take one step (and hence all registers in W_1 are overwritten), then repeat in round-robin fashion (i.e., one after the other) until one process goes to its remainder – this must happen by the deadlock-freedom property. Repeat this procedure with the processes not in their remainders, until all processes are in their remainders. By the induction hypothesis, there is an extension y_2 of this run which involves only processes in P where the processes in P are hidden and cover k distinct registers. Let W_2 be the set of these k registers. (Notice that when $|P| = 0$, $y_1 = y_2$.)

This construction can be repeated *ad infinitum*, finding successive extensions $y_3, y_4, \ldots$ and sets $W_3, W_4, \ldots$ such that for all i, only the processes in P are involved in $(y_i - x)$, and these processes are hidden and cover k distinct registers in y_i. W_i is the set of k registers covered by P in y_i. (See Figure 2.8.)

Next we bring process $p \notin P$ into the picture. By Lemma 2.20, for every i, y_i has an extension which involves only p, in which p writes some register which is not covered by any process in P. Let z_i be the shortest such extension. Thus, in z_i process p covers some register $w_i \notin W_i$, and any register that p writes in $(z_i - y_i)$ is in W_i. Notice that in z_i, $k + 1$ registers are covered by p and the processes in P; however, process p is not necessarily hidden. We still need to find a run in which all the $k + 1$ covering processes are hidden.

Since the number of registers is assumed to be finite, by the pigeonhole principle, there must exist i and j where $i < j$ such that $w_i = w_j$.

Let *seq* be the suffix of y_j obtained by removing y_i from y_j ($seq = y_j - y_i$), and let z be the sequence obtained by extending z_i by *seq* (i.e., $z = z_i; seq$). We next argue that z is a run. As already pointed out, all writes by p in $(z_i - y_i)$ are to registers in W_i. The sequence *seq* begins with a series of writes to each of the registers in W_i and hence covers all possible writes of p. Thus, extending z_i by *seq* is possible, since no read event in *seq* ever accesses a register that was last written by p.

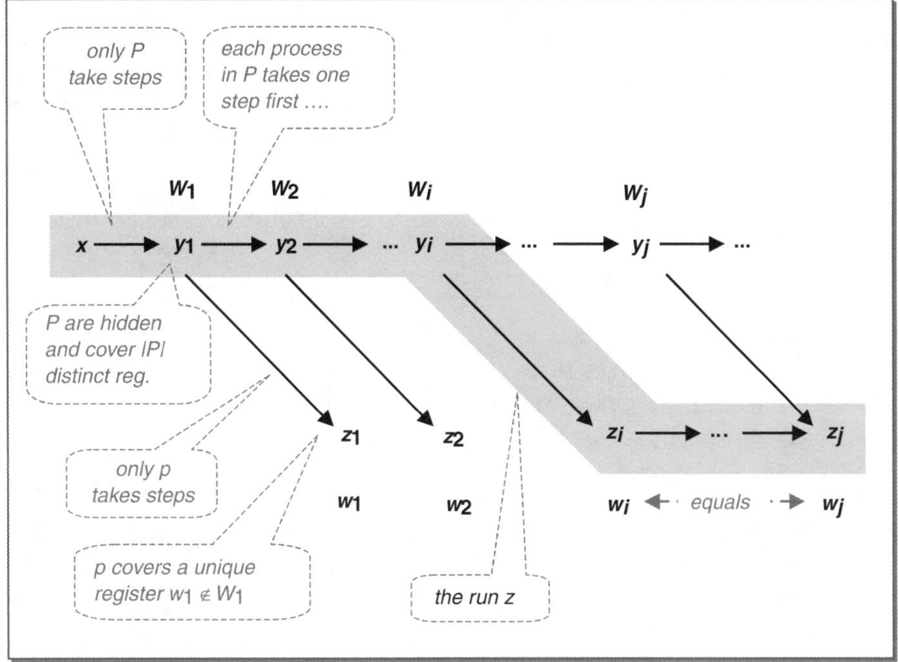

Figure 2.8 The run z constructed while proving the induction step. In z all the processes are hidden and the $k+1$ processes cover $k+1$ distinct registers.

Since p is not involved in extending z_i to z, it still covers w_i in z. Furthermore p is hidden in z since in the first k steps of *seq* processes in P have overwritten all the registers in W_i, and hence all the registers that p might have written in $(z_i - y_i)$.

Finally, from the fact that processes in P are hidden and cover the registers in W_j in run y_j, and the fact that each process in P has been in its remainder at least once during *seq*, it follows that the processes in P are hidden and cover the registers in W_j in z. Also we know that $w_i = w_j$ and since $w_j \notin W_j$ also $w_i \notin W_j$. Putting it all together, in the run z all the processes are hidden and p and the processes in P cover $k+1$ distinct registers. ∎

2.5.2 An Upper Bound: The One-bit Algorithm

Next we prove a theorem, which shows that the space lower bound of Theorem 2.16 is tight.

Theorem 2.22 *There is a deadlock-free mutual exclusion algorithm for n processes which uses n shared bits.*

To prove the theorem we present the One-bit algorithm which uses exactly n bits. The algorithm was developed independently by J. E. Burns (1981) and by L. Lamport (1986). The algorithm is interesting since it uses the minimum possible shared space. However, it has several disadvantages which we discuss later. As usual, it is assumed that there may be up to n processes potentially contending to enter the critical section, each has a unique identifier from the set $\{1, \ldots, n\}$. The algorithm makes use of a boolean array b, where, for every $1 \leq i \leq n$, all the processes can read the boolean registers $b[i]$, but only process i can write $b[i]$. The algorithm is defined formally below.

THE ONE-BIT ALGORITHM: `process i's program.`

Initially: all entries in b are *false*.

```
1   repeat
2       b[i] := true; j := 1;
3       while (b[i] = true) and (j < i) do
4           if b[j] = true then b[i] := false; await b[j] = false fi;
5           j := j + 1
6       od
7   until b[i] = true;
8   for j := i + 1 to n do await b[j] = false od;
9   critical section;
10  b[i] := false;
```

In lines 1–7, a process first indicates that it is contending for the critical section by setting its bit to *true* (line 2), and then it tries to read the bits of all the processes which have identifiers smaller than itself. If all these bits are *false* (while its bit is *true*) the process exits the loop. Otherwise, the process sets its bit to *false*, waits until the bit it is waiting on becomes *false* and starts all over again. In line 8, the process reads the bits of all the processes which have identifiers greater than itself. It exits this loop when it finds that each of the bits is *false* at least once since it entered this for loop. Then it can safely enter the critical section.

Properties of the One-bit Algorithm:

- Satisfies mutual exclusion and deadlock-freedom.
- Starvation of individual processes is possible.
- *It is not fast*: even in the absence of contention a process needs to access all the n (distinct) shared bits. Hence, also the system response time is of order n time units.
- *It is not symmetrical*: a process with a smaller identifier has higher priority. For example process 1 will never be locked out.
- It uses only n shared bits and hence it is space optimal.
- *Fault-tolerance*: the algorithm works correctly even when a finite number of processes fail. By a failure of process i, we mean that the process program counter is set to point to the beginning of its remainder code and that the value of $b[i]$ is set to *false* (i.e., the initial values). The process may then resume its execution; however, if a process keeps failing infinitely often, then it may prevent other processes from entering their critical section. For extensive discussion of the subject of fault tolerance see Section 3.3.

- *Non-atomic registers*: it is enough to assume that the registers are *safe* registers. That is, there is no need to assume that operations on the same memory location occur in some definite order; it works correctly even when it is allowed for reads which are concurrent with writes to return an arbitrary value.

Correctness Proof

We next prove the correctness of the One-bit algorithm. That is, we show that it satisfies both mutual exclusion and deadlock-freedom.

Theorem 2.23 *The One-bit algorithm satisfies mutual exclusion.*

Proof: Assume to the contrary that the algorithm does not satisfy mutual exclusion. This means that there is some run x and two processes i and j, such that both i and j are in their critical sections at x.

Let x^i be the shortest prefix of x such that for every z, $x^i \leq z \leq x$, $b_i = true$ at z. That is, in the last event of x^i process i set b_i to *true* (line 2) for the last time before entering its critical section. Clearly x^i is shorter than x. Let x^j be defined similarly for process j, and let us assume without loss of generality that $x^i < x^j$. This implies that for every z, $x^j \leq z \leq x$, $b_i = true$ at z. Thus, after changing its bit to *true*, process j succeeded in entering its critical section while process' i'th bit is continuously *true*. However, from the algorithm, another process, after changing its bit to *true* can enter its critical section, only if it finds that $b_i = true$ either in the while loop (line 4), or if it finds that $b_i = true$ in the for loop (line 8), a contradiction. ∎

Theorem 2.24 *The One-bit algorithm is deadlock-free.*

Proof: Assume to the contrary that it is not deadlock-free. This means that there is a run, say x, where:

1. each process is either in its remainder or in its entry code,
2. there is at least one process which is in its entry code, and
3. no process can change to another region in any extension of x.

Let k be the process with the smallest identifier, among all the processes which are in their entry code. Processor k is either executing the for loop (line 9), or if not then there must be an extension of x in which it reaches the for loop. This must happen, since at any extension of x, b_i is *false* for all $i < k$, and hence process k will eventually, at some extension of x, exit the while loop, and reach the for loop.

We conclude that there is an extension of x in which at least one process is executing the for loop. Since it is assumed that no process leaves its entry code (in any extension of x), any process that reaches the for loop in line 9 must stay there forever. Thus, there is an extension of x, say y, in which: each process that is in its entry code is either in the for loop, or it is busy-waiting in the while loop and its bit is *false*. The reason why its bit is *false* is since if the bit is not forever *false* the process has to scan all the bits of processes smaller then itself and (after maybe waiting) find that they are *false*. But this is not possible since the bit of process k stays always *true* once it reaches the for loop.

Thus, at y only the bits of the processes in the for loop are *true*. Let ℓ be the process with the largest identifier, among all the processes which are at line 9, at run y. When process ℓ executes the for loop, it must find that the bits of all the processes $\ell + 1$ through n are *false*, and hence it should move into its critical section. This contradicts the assumption that no process changes its region in any extension of x. Thus, the One-bit algorithm is deadlock-free. ∎

Remark: The tight space bounds are based on the fact that mutual exclusion is an on going activity. The situation changes when we look at the "one shot" mutual exclusion problem where it is only required that just one process eventually enters its critical section (also called the *leader election problem*). It is interesting to note that only $\lceil \log n \rceil + 1$ registers are necessary and sufficient for solving this problem (see Problems 3.51 and 3.52).

2.5.3 Computing with Infinitely Many Processes

Throughout the book we assume that the number of processes is finite (and is denoted by n). In this short subsection we explore the case where the number of processes is infinite. The motivation for assuming an infinite number of processes is mainly of theoretical interest. However, it may be of some practical value as well, since it covers the case where the number of processes is finite but is not known *a priori*.

Theorem 2.16 implies that when the number of processes is not finite (or finite but not known *a priori*), an unbounded number of registers are necessary for solving the mutual exclusion problem. This leads naturally to the question of whether an infinite number of registers suffice? We present a simple algorithm, due to M. Merritt and G. Taubenfeld (2000), that answers this question affirmatively.

Theorem 2.25 *There is a deadlock-free mutual exclusion algorithm for an infinite number of processes using an infinite number of bits.*

To prove the theorem we present a simple algorithm which uses an infinite number of shared bits. It is assumed that each process has a unique identifier from the set of natural numbers.

An Algorithm for Infinitely Many Processes: `process i's program.`

```
shared race.owner [1..∞, 1..∞], race.other [1..∞, 1..∞], win [1..∞,
    1..∞],lose [1..∞, 1..∞],control [1..∞]: arrays of boolean,
    initially all 0.
local index: integer, initially 0; level: integer, initially 1.

repeat
    repeat
        while control (level) = 1 do level := level + 1 od;
```

```
        race.owner [i, level] := 1;
        if race.other [i, level] = 0 then win [i, level] := 1
            else lose [i, level] := 1; await control(level) = 1 fi
    until win [i, level] = 1;
    repeat
        index := index + 1;
        race.other [index, level] := 1;
        if race.owner [index, level] = 1 then
            await (win [index, level] = 1 or lose [index, level] = 1) fi
    until win [index, level] = 1;
    if index ≠ i then await control(level) = 1 fi
until index = i;
critical section;
control(level) := 1;
```

Each level corresponds to one entry to a critical section, and it has a control bit which indicates whether this level is open (set to 0) or closed (set to 1). To enter the critical section, a process finds the minimum level with the control bit still open, contends there until it is the final winner or (if it isn't) spins until the control bit is set (to 1) on that level, then tries again on the next level.

For each level, there are four bits associated with each process i, which are: *race.owner*$[i, level]$, *race.other*$[i, level]$, *win*$[i, level]$, and *lose*$[i, level]$. The idea is that each process i uses the two bits *race.owner*$[i, level]$ and *race.other*$[i, level]$ to race against the other processes. The other two bits are used by the owner to signal whether it won or lost. For each *level*, the final winner is the minimum process i such that *win*$[i, level]$ is set, and that winner can enter its critical section.

Theorem 2.26 *The algorithm satisfies mutual exclusion and deadlock-freedom.*

Proof: To prove deadlock-freedom we first argue that each execution of the await statement in the second repeat loop eventually terminates. The first process i to perform the read of *race.owner*$[i, level]$ will eventually set *win*$[i, level]$. Every other process will either terminate before $index = i$, or see *race.owner*$[i, level]$ set, wait until *win*$[i, level]$ is set, and exit the repeat loop. In the other two cases of the await statements, a process waits at a given level, only if it can not win at that level. In that case, it will wait until the winner of that level exits its critical section and signals that this level is closed, by setting *control*$(level)$, and continues to the next level.

To prove mutual exclusion, notice that in an infinite run, for a given *level*, there is always a minimum i such that *win*$[i, level]$ is never set. Every other process j must see *race.owner*$[i, level]$ set, since process i reads *race.other*$[i, level] = 0$ immediately after setting *race.owner*$[i, level]$. Thus process j will lose at that level and not enter its critical section. Furthermore, j will wait until i exits its critical section and sets *control*$(level)$ to 1. So, only one process can enter its critical section at the same time. ∎

Self Review

1. Is it really necessary to construct an *infinite* run in the proof of Lemma 2.21?
2. The following is a weaker definition of a hidden process than the definition given on page 60.

   For process p and run z, let z′ be the longest prefix of z such that p is in its remainder in z′. Process p is hidden in run z if each event which p is involved in (z − z′) is either: a read event, a write event that is overwritten before any other process has read the value written, or ***a write event which does not change the value of a register*** *(i.e., the written value is the same as the previous value).*

   What breaks in the lower bound proof if we use the above definition instead of the original one?
3. Does the correctness of the One-bit algorithm depend on the order in which the bits are read in the two loops?
4. Consider the algorithm for infinitely many processes (on page 66). Is it necessary to assume that for each natural number i, there is a process with identifier i?

Answers: (1) The construction of the run can stop at the point where for some i and j where $i < j$, $w_i = w_j$. (2) Both Lemma 2.18 and Lemma 2.19 are incorrect with the above definition. In Lemma 2.18 the reason is that a process can hide itself by writing the same value twice in a row. In Lemma 2.19, consider a run in which: p_1 writes 1 to register r which initially has the value 0, then p_2 writes 1 to register r, and finally p_3 reads 1 from register r. With the original definition only p_1 is hidden in that run, while with the new definition both p_1 and p_2 are hidden. Removing any one of the write events results a run in which p_1 or p_2 is not hidden any more. (3) No. (4) No.

2.6 Automatic Discovery of Algorithms

A methodology for *automatic discovery* of synchronization algorithms for finite-state systems has been recently proposed by Y. Bar-David and G. Taubenfeld (2003). They built a tool and used it to automatically discover hundreds of new algorithms for mutual exclusion for two processes. The methodology is rather simple and the fact that it is computationally feasible is surprising. It works as follows: assume that you want to solve a specific problem P.

1. Write a model-checker M for P. That is, write a program (or use an existing one) that for any proposed algorithm (solution) A, decides whether A solves P.
2. For a given (restricted) programming language, write a program that will produce syntactically all possible (correct and incorrect) algorithms in that language, under certain user-defined parameters, such as: number of lines of code; number of processes; number, type, and size of shared variables; etc.
3. For each algorithm A generated in step 2, check if A solves P (using M).

The reason that automatic discovery has not been implemented before for synchronization algorithms is probably due to the fact that (automatic) verification is considered to be a time-consuming process, while the brute force approach suggested above may require (even for very short algorithms) trying to verify hundreds of millions of incorrect algorithms before finding a correct one.

The architecture of the tool which implements this methodology is as follows: Via a user-interface, the user can set the problem parameters: (1) number of processes (2) number of lines of code (3) number, size, and type of variables (4) type of conditions: simple or complex. Complex conditions are composed of two simple conditions (terms) related by *and*, *or*, or *x or*. The parameters are sent to the algorithm generator, which generates all the possible algorithms according to the given parameters. Each algorithm (which passes the optimization checks) is sent to verification. If an algorithm is verified as correct, it is sent back to the user-interface and displayed. Verification results are also returned to the algorithm generator for use in optimizations. A tool has been implemented in Java and C++, and has around 10,000 lines of code.

One of the challenges in building the tool was to be able to process enough algorithms in a reasonable time, so that interesting results can be found. To achieve this, many optimizations were implemented. As an example, consider mutual exclusion algorithms for two processes with three shared bits, complex conditions, four entry and one exit commands. For this setting there are over 10^{21} possible algorithms in the (high-level) generation language used in the implementation. Using all optimizations, less than $3 \cdot 10^7$ algorithms were generated and tested, of which 105 correct algorithms were found, one of which is the famous Peterson's algorithm which is described on page 32.

2.6.1 Three Algorithms

We list below three short algorithms for two processes, which were generated automatically by the tool discussed above. All the three algorithms satisfy mutual exclusion and deadlock-freedom. (In the self review questions you are asked to decide whether each of these algorithms also satisfies starvation-freedom.) Notice that while each condition in the await statements of Peterson's algorithm and Kessels' algorithm is composed of two terms, each condition in the three algorithms below has only one term.

Each algorithm makes use of only two (single-writer) bits, $b[0]$ and $b[1]$. Both processes can read them, but only process 0 can write $b[0]$ and only process 1 can write $b[1]$. The values of the two bits are initially 0. The symbol $i \in \{0, 1\}$ is used to designate the identifiers of the process executing the algorithm.

ALGORITHM #1: `process i's program.`

```
b[i] := 1;
while b[1 - i] = 1 do
        b[i] := 1 - i;
        await b[0] = 1 - i;
        b[i] := 1
```

```
od;
critical section;
b[i] := 0;
```

ALGORITHM #2: `process i's program.`

```
b[i] := 1;
        while b[1 − i] = 1 do
                while b[0] = i do b[i] := 0 od;
        b[i] := 1
od;
critical section;
b[i] := 0;
```

ALGORITHM #3: `process i's program.`

```
b[i] := i;
while b[0] = i do
        b[i] := 1;
        while b[1] = 1 − i do b[i] := 0 od
od;
critical section;
b[i] := 0;
```

Notice that in the third algorithm, process 0 does not set its flag bit to 1 in its first step.

2.6.2 More Results

The tool was run to find correct mutual exclusion algorithms for two processes using 2, 3, 4, 5, or 6 shared bits. A methodical search was conducted to find the shortest solutions: the number of commands was incrementally increased until a solution was found. The lengths of the shortest solutions are summarized in the table in Figure 2.9. The first column indicates the number of shared bits used; the second and third columns indicate the number of entry and exit commands. The fourth column indicates whether the use of complex conditions is allowed. The number of tested algorithms, and the number of correct algorithms found are displayed in the fifth and sixth columns. As a result of optimizations, not all generated algorithms were actually tested. The number of tested algorithms counts only those that were tested by the verifier. All correct algorithms that have been found are new (and shorter than previously known solutions), except for Peterson's algorithm. All the tests were performed on a Pentium 4/1.6 GHz PC. The full paper version includes: many new algorithms, more tests and results, details about the generator and the verifier (model-checker), and description of optimizations and techniques which dramatically improve the performance.

User-defined parameters				Result		
# of shared bits	# of entry comm-ands	# of exit comm-ands	complex condi-tions	tested algorithms	correct algo-rithms	appx. running hours
2	6	1	yes	7,196,536,269	0	216
2	7	1		846,712,059	66	39
3	4	1	yes	25,221,389	105	0.4
3	6	1		1,838,128,995	10	47
4	4	1	yes	129,542,873	480	1
4	5	1		129,190,403	56	1
4	6	1		[1] 900,000,000	80	12
5	5	1		[1] 22,000,000	106	0.4
6	5	1		[1] 70,000,000	96	1

Figure 2.9 The lengths of the shortest solutions that have been discovered.

[1]This run was stopped after few solutions were found. Not all possible algorithms were tested.

Self Review

1. In Section 2.6.1 we have presented three short algorithms for two processes. All the three algorithms satisfy mutual exclusion and deadlock-freedom. For each algorithm decide whether or not it also satisfies starvation-freedom. Justify your answer.

Answer: All the three algorithms do not satisfy starvation-freedom.

2.7 Bibliographic Notes

2.1

Dijkstra's quote from page 31 is taken from [107]. Peterson's algorithm (page 32) appeared in [282]. A more formal proof of its correctness can be found in [112]. Kessels' algorithm (page 35) appeared in [200].

Dekker's algorithm (page 77) is historically the first solution for the two-process mutual exclusion problem. Dekker's algorithm guarantees mutual exclusion and starvation-freedom. It is described and proved correct by Dijkstra in [107]. Two simple variants of Dekker's algorithm are presented in [118], and an even simpler version is given in [285]. Ghosh–Datta's algorithm (page 77) is taken from an unpublished manuscript, while Peterson–Fischer's algorithm (page 78) is from [287]. Hyman's incorrect solution (page 79) appeared in [182].

2.2

The first tournament algorithm for mutual exclusion was presented in [287]. The algorithm is based on the two process algorithm which is presented on page 78.

The tournament algorithm on page 38, which is based on Peterson's two process solution, was not published before. Kessels' algorithm (page 41) is from [200].

2.3

Dijkstra's algorithm (page 81) is historically the first solution for more than two processes. Dijkstra's algorithm is deadlock-free, but is not starvation-free [106].

Lamport's fast algorithm (page 42) is described in [224]. In his algorithm only five accesses to the shared memory are needed in order to enter a critical section in the absence of contention, and just two accesses are needed in the exit code. Lamport's algorithm was used in commercial applications, for example, when the TUXEDO system [328] was run on machines – like the MIPS 3000 series processors – that do not support an atomic test-and-set operation [247]. In [256], a performance optimization of Lamport's algorithm is described, which solves mutual exclusion efficiently in contexts in which process creation and destruction are rare.

2.4

Knuth presented the first starvation-free algorithm for n processes [204]. Knuth's algorithm (page 89) satisfies (2^{n-1})-fairness – a process will be able to enter its critical section before the other $n-1$ processes are able to execute their critical sections collectively 2^{n-1} times. A modified algorithm by de Bruijn (page 89) reduced this figure to $\frac{n(n+1)}{2}$ [105]. An improved algorithm was presented by Eisenberg and McGuire (page 90), which satisfies linear waiting (no process can execute its critical section twice while some other process is kept waiting) [125]. Peterson has presented in [282] a starvation-free algorithm for n processes (Problem 2.63, page 90). His algorithm does not satisfy bounded-waiting (Problem 2.64, page 91). In [294], it is incorrectly claimed that Peterson's algorithm satisfies that same fairness condition as de Bruijn's algorithm. An incorrect claim about the fairness of Peterson's algorithm is also made in [207]. Block and Woo have presented in [72] a starvation-free algorithm for n processes which is based on Peterson's algorithm (page 32) for two processes (Problem 2.65, page 91). The system response time of the algorithm is $O(n \times m)$ when m out of the n processes are competing for the critical section.

The Bakery algorithm (page 50) is described in [212]. The algorithm satisfies first-come-first-served fairness, and allows read errors to occur during writes. The fact that the algorithm uses only single-writer registers makes it suitable for use in message passing systems. Correctness proofs of the Bakery algorithm have appeared in [212, 216, 226], and a proof of a variant of it appeared in [218]. An improved version of the Bakery algorithm (page 86) appeared in [218]. A generalization of the Bakery algorithm is given in [213]. The observation that the correctness of the Bakery algorithm depends on an implicit assumption on the implementation of computing the maximum first appeared in [214]. The two examples of how to compute the maximum (page 51) are from [226]. The modified Bakery algorithm on page 54 is from [286].

The Black-White Bakery algorithm (page 55) is described in [323]. Few other attempts have been made to bound the space required by the Bakery algorithm. In [339], the integer arithmetic in the original Bakery algorithm is replaced with modulo arithmetic and the *maximum* function and the *less than* relation have been redefined. The resulting published algorithm is incorrect, since it does not satisfy deadlock-freedom. Also in [191], modulo arithmetic is used and the *maximum* function and the *less than* relation have been redefined. In addition, an additional integer register is used. Redefining and explaining these two notions in [191] requires over a full page and involves the details of another unbounded space algorithm. The Black-White Bakery algorithms use integer arithmetic, and do not require to redefine any of the notions used in the original algorithm.

Another attempt to bound the space required by the Bakery algorithm is described in [336]. The algorithm presented is incorrect when the number of processes n is too big; the registers size is bigger than 2^{15} values; and the algorithm is complicated. In [1], a variant of the Bakery algorithm is presented, which uses $3^n + 1$ values per register (the Black-White Bakery algorithm requires only $2n + 2$ values per register). Unlike the Bakery and the Black-White Bakery algorithms, the algorithm in [1] is not symmetric: process p_i only reads the values of the lower processes. It is possible to replace the unbounded timestamps of the Bakery algorithm (i.e., taking a number) with bounded timestamps, as defined in [184] and constructed in [116, 123, 146]; however, the resulting algorithm will be rather complex, when the price of implementing bounded timestamps is taken into account.

Several FIFO algorithms which are not based on the Bakery algorithm and use bounded size atomic registers have been published. These algorithms are more complex than the Black-White Bakery algorithm. We mention five interesting algorithms below. In [197], an algorithm that requires n (3-valued) shared registers plus two shared bits per process is presented. A modification of the algorithm in [197] is presented in [222] which uses n bits per process. In [240, 241], an algorithm that requires five shared bits per process is presented, which is based on the One-bit algorithm that was devised independently in [84, 86] and [222]. In [319], an algorithm that requires four shared bits per process is presented, which is based on a scheme similar to that of [270]. Finally, in [7] a first-in-first-enabled solution to the ℓ-exclusion problem is presented using bounded timestamps (1-exclusion means mutual exclusion).

2.5

The important lower bound which shows that any deadlock-free mutual exclusion algorithm for n processes must use at least n shared registers (Theorem 2.16, page 59) was proved by Burns and Lynch in [84, 86]. The One-bit algorithm (page 64), which uses n bits and hence provides a tight space upper bound, was developed independently by Burns [81] (also appeared in [86]), and by Lamport [222, 227].

The tight space bounds are based on the fact that mutual exclusion is an on going activity. The situation changes when we look at the “one shot” mutual exclusion problem where it is only required that just one process eventually enters its critical section (also called the *leader election problem*). It is interesting to note that only $\lceil \log n \rceil + 1$ registers are necessary and sufficient for solving this problem [316] (see Problems 3.51 and 3.52).

A lower and upper bound for the contention-free time complexity of solving the mutual exclusion problem as a function of the number of processes and the size of the biggest register that can be accessed in one atomic step is provided in [23] (see Problems 2.81 and 2.83). Lower bounds on the contention-free time complexity assuming limited write-contention are proven in [341] (see Problem 2.82). The deadlock-free algorithm for infinite number of processes using an infinite number of bits on page 66, as well as the algorithm on page 108, are from [259].

A formalism for reasoning about concurrent systems which does not assume that read and write are atomic operations is developed in [221, 222]. This formalism has been further developed in [223], where a very weak form of (non-atomic) shared register, called *safe* register (page 65), is defined. A safe register can be written and read concurrently, but read errors may occur during the writing of a shared register. Following Lamport's paper, many papers were published about implementing one type of shared register from another. In [166], a hierarchy of progressively stronger shared objects is defined. Objects at each level are able to perform tasks which are impossible for objects at the lower levels.

2.6

The three single-writer two-bit algorithms presented in Section 2.6.1 (page 69) appeared in [59]. These algorithms and many others were generated automatically using a methodology, called *automatic discovery*, which is presented in [59].

2.8 Problems

The problems are divided into several categories. See page 23 for a detailed explanation.

Problems based on Section 2.1

◦ 2.1 On page 34, there is an example of a run of Peterson's algorithm in which the system response time is (at least) five time units. Why can we not use the same run, as described below, to show that the system response time is six time units?

The run starts with both processes in their remainders and proceeds as follows

1. Process 0 executes $b[0] := true$;
2. Process 0 executes $turn := 0$;
3. Process 1 executes $b[1] := true$; process 0 performs the test $b[1] = false$;
4. Process 0 performs the test $turn = 1$; process 1 executes $turn := 1$;
5. Process 0 performs the test $b[1] = false$, while process 1 performs the test $b[0] = false$;

6. Process 0 performs the test *turn* = 1, while process 1 performs the test *turn* = 0;
7. At this point, after six time units have passed, process 0 which found that indeed *turn* = 1, is in its critical section.

○○ 2.2 Consider a variant of Peterson's algorithm (page 32), where the statement: **await** (b[1] = *false*) is added at the end of the code of process 0; and the statement: **await** (b[0] = *false*) is added at the end of the code of process 1. Does the modified algorithm satisfy deadlock-freedom and/or starvation-freedom? (Once you solve this problem, have a second look at Problem 1.20)

○○ 2.3 The await statement in Peterson's algorithm, **await** (b[1] = *false* **or** *turn* = 1); can be replaced by:

```
    while true do
            if b[1] = false then goto CS fi;
            if turn = 1 then goto CS fi
    od;
  CS:
```

Does it matter if we replace the order of the two if statements?

○○ 2.4 Modify Peterson's algorithm for two processes, without using additional registers, so that its contention-free time complexity is only *three* accesses to the shared memory (two accesses in the entry code and one in the exit code).

○○ 2.5 Prove that the following variant of Peterson's algorithm (page 32) satisfies mutual exclusion and starvation-freedom. What is the system response time?

A VARIANT OF PETERSON'S ALGORITHM FOR TWO PROCESSES:

Initially: b[0] = *false*, b[1] = *false*, the initial value of *turn* is immaterial.

PROGRAM FOR PROCESS 0:

```
b[0] := true;
if b[1] = true then
        turn := 0;
        await (b[1] = false or turn = 1) fi;
critical section;
b[0] := false;
```

PROGRAM FOR PROCESS 1:

```
b[1] := true;
if b[0] = true then
        turn := 1;
        await (b[0] = false or turn = 0) fi;
critical section;
b[1] := false;
```

(Notice that the contention-free time complexity is only three accesses to the shared memory – two accesses in the entry code and one in the exit code.)

◦ 2.6 Explain why algorithms that use only single-writer registers (such as Kessels' algorithm) can be easily implemented in a message passing network. That is, show how the read and write operations on single-writer registers are implemented in a message passing network.

◦• 2.7 Prove that Kessels' algorithm for two processes with single-writer bits, described on page 35, satisfies mutual exclusion. What is the system response time for this algorithm?

◦◦ 2.8 The await statement in Kessels' algorithm,
await ($b[1] = \mathit{false}$ **or** $\mathit{local}[0] \neq \mathit{turn}[1]$); can be replaced by:

```
while true do
        if b[1] = false then goto CS fi;
        if local[0] ≠ turn[1] then goto CS fi
od;
CS:
```

Does it matter if we replace the order of the two if statements? What is the system response time of Kessels' algorithm after such a replacement?

◦◦ 2.9 Does the following variant of Kessels' algorithm (page 35), satisfy mutual exclusion and/or starvation-freedom? What is the system response time?

A VARIANT OF KESSELS' ALGORITHM FOR TWO PROCESSES:

Initially: $b[0] = \mathit{false}$, $b[1] = \mathit{false}$, the initial values of $\mathit{turn}[0]$ and $\mathit{turn}[1]$ are immaterial.

PROGRAM FOR PROCESS 0:

```
b[0] := true;
if b[1] = true then
        local[0] := turn[1];
        turn[0] := local[0];
        await (b[1] = false or local[0] ≠ turn[1]) fi;
critical section;
b[0] := false;
```

PROGRAM FOR PROCESS 1:

```
b[1] := true;
if b[0] = true then
        local[1] := 1 − turn[0];
        turn[1] := local[1];
        await (b[0] = false or local[1] = turn[0]) fi;
critical section;
b[1] := false;
```

○• 2.10 The following algorithm, due to Dekker (1965), is historically the first solution for the mutual exclusion problem among two processes! Prove its correctness. The algorithm is for two processes and is a combination of the incorrect algorithms mentioned in the problems for Section 1.3.

Let $i \in \{0, 1\}$, and $j = i + 1 \pmod 2$ be the identifiers of the processes. It makes use of three shared bits *turn*, *flag*[0], and *flag*[1].

DEKKER'S ALGORITHM: `process i's program.`

Initially: $flag[i] = false$.

```
flag[i] := true;
while flag[j] do
        if turn = j then flag[i] := false;
                         await turn = i ;
                         flag[i] := true fi;
od;
critical section;
turn := j;
flag[i] := false;
```

Is starvation of individual processes possible?

○• 2.11 The following algorithm was developed by Sukumar Ghosh and Ajoy Kumar Datta (1991). The algorithm is for two processes 1 and 2, and it makes use of two registers: x which can hold three values 0, 1, and 2; and y which can hold two values 0 and 1. Both processes can read and write the registers x and y. The symbol $i \in \{1, 2\}$ is used to designate the identifiers of the process executing the algorithm.

GHOSH–DATTA'S ALGORITHM FOR TWO PROCESSES: `process i's program.`

Initially: $x = 0$ and $y = 0$.

```
start:  x := i;
        if y ≠ 0 then await y = 0;
                      goto start fi;
        y := 1;
        if x ≠ i then y := 0;
                      await x = 0;
                      goto start fi;
        critical section;
        y := 0;
        x := 0;
```

- Prove that it satisfies mutual exclusion and deadlock-freedom for two processes.
- Does it satisfy starvation-freedom for two processes?

- Does it satisfy deadlock-freedom for three processes? That is, $i \in \{1,2,3\}$.
- Does it satisfy mutual exclusion for three processes? That is, $i \in \{1,2,3\}$.

∘∘ 2.12 Prove that any starvation-free mutual exclusion algorithm for two processes must use at least two shared registers. The proof should be at most seven lines long. (In Section 2.5.1, we prove a much stronger result. Your proof here should be different and much simpler than the proof for the result of Section 2.5.1.)

∘∘ 2.13 The following starvation-free algorithm for two processes is due to Peterson and Fischer (1977). The algorithm uses only two registers, $c[1]$ and $c[2]$, each of which can hold three values. Furthermore, each register can be written by exactly one process. The algorithm makes use of two additional local registers, *temp*[1] and *temp*[2]. The general idea is for process 1 to set its register $c[1]$ the same as register $c[2]$, and wait for the two registers to be unequal before entering. Process 2 on the other hand sets its register unequal and waits for equality.

PETERSON–FISCHER'S ALGORITHM FOR TWO PROCESSES USING TWO 3-VALUED REGISTERS:

Initially: $c[1] = 0$ and $c[2] = 0$.

PROGRAM FOR PROCESS 1:

```
temp[1] := c[2];
if temp[1] ≠ 0 then c[1] := temp[1] else c[1] := 1;
temp[1] := c[2];
if temp[1] ≠ 0 then c[1] := temp[1];
repeat temp[1] := c[2] until temp[1] ≠ c[1];
critical section;
c[1] := 0;
```

PROGRAM FOR PROCESS 2:

```
temp[2] := c[1];
if temp[2] ≠ 0 then c[2] := 2 − temp[2] else c[2] := 1;
temp[2] := c[1];
if temp[2] ≠ 0 then c[2] := 2 − temp[2];
repeat temp[2] := c[1] until (temp[2] = 0 or temp[2] = c[2]);
critical section;
c[2] := 0;
```

Prove the correctness of the algorithm.

? 2.14 By now we know that there is a starvation-free algorithm which uses only two 3-valued registers (Problem 2.13), and that there is no starvation-free algorithm which uses only two *single-writer* bits (Problem 2.78). Is there a starvation-free algorithm which uses only two bits? Is there a starvation-free algorithm which uses only two registers: a 2-valued register (a bit) and a 3-valued register?

○○ 2.15 The following incorrect algorithm was published in the Communication of the ACM in January 1966. Explain why the algorithm is incorrect. The algorithm is for two processes; let $i \in \{0, 1\}$ be the identifiers of the processes. It makes use of three shared bits *turn*, *flag*[1], and *flag*[2].

HYMAN'S INCORRECT ALGORITHM: `process i's program.`

Initially: $flag[i] = false$ and the initial value of k is immaterial.

```
flag[i] := true;
while turn = 1 − i do
            await ¬flag[1 − i] ;
            turn := i
od;
critical section;
flag[i] := false
```

Problems based on Section 2.2

○○ 2.16 Does it matter if we replace the exit code in Kessels' tournament algorithm (lines 12–16, page 41) with the following exit code:

```
12  node := i + n;
13  while node ≥ 1 do
14        node := ⌊node/2⌋;
15        b[node, edge[node]] := false
16  od;
```

○○ 2.17 Replace the numbering scheme in the tournament algorithm from the first example with the numbering scheme in Kessels' algorithm, and replace the numbering scheme in Kessels' algorithm with that of the tournament algorithm from the first example.

○○ 2.18 Construct a starvation-free algorithm for n processes which uses only 3-valued registers. (Hint: Use the algorithm in Problem 2.13.)

○• 2.19 Construct a tournament algorithm, based on Kessels' algorithm for two processes (page 35), which uses only single-writer registers. (It is not required that the system response time be of order $\log n$.)

○• 2.20 Construct a tournament algorithm, based on the algorithm in Problem 2.13, which uses only n single-writer registers, each of which might assume $1+2\lceil \log n \rceil$ values.

Problems based on Section 2.3

○ 2.21 What is the value of register y, when process i is in its critical section?

○ 2.22 Is the following explanation correct? In line 7, of Lamport's fast algorithm, a process checks x. If process i finds out that $x = i$ it means that no other process is about to change y and hence process i can safely enter its critical section.

∘∘ 2.23 What is the maximum number of processes that can be in their critical sections *at the same time* if we change the order of the last two statements of Lamport's algorithm (lines 12 and 13)?

∘∘ 2.24 What is wrong with the following variant of Lamport's algorithm? Initially: $y = 0$, and $b[i] = false$.

```
start:  b[i] := true;
        x := i;
        if y ≠ 0 then b[i] := false;
                      await y = 0;
                      goto start fi;
        y := i;
        b[i] := false;
        if x ≠ i  then for j := 1 to n do await ¬b[j] od;
                      if y ≠ i then await y = 0; goto start fi
                  else y := i fi;
        critical section;
        y := 0;
```

∘• 2.25 What is wrong with the following variant of Lamport's algorithm? Initially: $y = 0$, $z = 0$, and $b[i] = false$.

```
start:  b[i] := true;
        x := i;
        if y ≠ 0 then b[i] := false;
                      await y = 0;
                      goto start fi;
        y := i;
        b[i] := false;
        if x ≠ i  then for j := 1 to n do await ¬b[j] od;
                      if y ≠ i then await y = 0; goto start fi;
                      await (z = 0)
                  else z := 1 fi;
        critical section;
        z := 0;
        if y = i  then y := 0 fi;
```

∘• 2.26 Below is a modification of Lamport's fast algorithm: Initially: $y = 0$, $z = 0$, and $b[i] = false$.

```
start:  b[i] := true;
        x := i;
        if y ≠ 0 then b[i] := false;
                      await y = 0;
                      goto start fi;
        y := i;
        if x ≠ i  then b[i] := false;
                      for j := 1 to n do await ¬b[j] od;
```

```
9                    if y ≠ i then await y = 0; goto start fi;
10                   await (z = 0)
11              else z := 1;
12                   b[i] := false
13        fi;
14        critical section;
15        b[i] := false;
16        z := 0;
17        if y = i then y := 0 fi;
18        b[i] := false;
```

Consider the following three variants of the above algorithm:

1. Remove lines 15 and 18 and keep line 12;
2. Remove lines 12 and 18 and keep line 15;
3. Remove lines 12 and 15 and keep line 18;

For each one of the above three variants decide if it is correct or not (and justify your answer).

What would be your answer when line 17 is replaced with the assignment "$y := 0$"?

∘• 2.27 The following algorithm, due to Dijkstra (1965), is historically the first solution for the mutual exclusion problem among n processes. Prove its correctness. The algorithm makes use of register k which is long enough to store a process identifier, and two boolean arrays each of n bits, named b and c. All the processes can read and write k, the processes can read the boolean registers $b[i]$ and $c[i]$, but only process i can write $b[i]$ and $c[i]$. (Each process also has a local register of type $1..n-1$.)

DIJKSTRA'S ALGORITHM: `process i's program.`

Initially: $b[i] = true$, $c[i] = true$, the initial value of k is immaterial.

```
   b[i] := false;
L: while k ≠ i do
           c[i] := true;
           if b[k] then k := i
   od;
   begin c[i] := false;
   for j := 1 to n do
           if j ≠ i and ¬c[j] then goto L fi
   od;
   critical section;
   c[i] := true;
   b[i] := true;
```

Is starvation of individual processes possible? What is the time complexity in the absence of contention? What is the system response time?

∘∘ 2.28 Modify the data structures and the control structures in Dijkstra's algorithm (Problem 2.27): (1) instead of using two boolean arrays use only one array with n entries, where each entry can hold three values; (2) instead of using the goto statement use iteration.

•• 2.29 In Lamport's algorithm, the number of times a process accesses shared registers before entering its critical section in the absence of contention is only five. However, four of the five accesses involve reading and writing registers of size $\log n$ bits. An interesting question is whether it is possible to reduce the number of times shared bits have to be accessed.

Prove that in any algorithm, the number of different bits a process needs to access before entering its critical section in the absence of contention is a function of n (and hence can not be a constant).

Remark: Notice that the above result implies that the contention-free complexity of any mutual exclusion algorithm that uses only *constant size* registers can not be constant.

? 2.30 Is there an algorithm, in which the contention-free time complexity is constant, which uses only one shared register that is not single-writer register (and possibly other single-writer registers).

Problems based on Section 2.4

∘ 2.31 Why is *linear-waiting* a weaker fairness requirement than *FIFO*?

∘ 2.32 Why is *bounded-waiting* a weaker fairness requirement than *r-bounded-waiting* for a fixed *r*?

∘∘ 2.33 In many algorithms which satisfy starvation-freedom but do not satisfy bounded-waiting, the only way *r*-bounded-waiting can be violated is for some processes to run much faster than others. One such example is the tournament algorithm based on Peterson's algorithm. Is this true for all starvation-free algorithms? That is, if we bound the number of steps that a process can take while some other process is waiting, so that no process can run too much faster than any other, does every starvation-free algorithm also satisfy bounded-waiting?

∘ 2.34 Below we show how to transform any deadlock-free mutual exclusion algorithm into a corresponding starvation-free mutual exclusion algorithm. The transformation was suggested by Yoah Bar-David (1998). *Is this transformation correct?*

Let *A* be a correct deadlock-free mutual exclusion algorithm. Using *A* we construct algorithm *B* as follows: In addition to the registers used in *A*, we use an atomic register called *turn* which is big enough to store a process identifier, and a boolean array called *flag*. All the processes can read and write the register *turn*, the processes can read the bit *flag*[*i*], but only process *i* can write *flag*[*i*]. The processes are numbered 1 through n.

Algorithm B: process i's program.

Initially: $flag[i] = false$, the initial value of $turn$ is immaterial.

```
                                   /* begin entry code */
flag[i] := true;
await (turn = i or flag[turn] = false);
entry code of A;
                                   /* end entry code */
critical section;
                                   /* begin exit code */
flag[i] := false;
if flag[turn] = false then turn := (turn mod n) + 1 fi;
exit code of A;
                                   /* end exit code */
```

Notice that evaluating the condition $flag[turn] = false$ requires *two* memory references; one to read $turn$ and the other to read the $flag$ bit. Also notice that if A is a fast algorithm then so is B. That is, in the absence of contention, the transformation adds three memory references to the entry code and four memory references to the exit code.

Is algorithm B a correct starvation-free mutual exclusion algorithm? Justify your answer.

∘∘ 2.35 Why is the following fast starvation-free mutual exclusion algorithm *incorrect*?

The new algorithm is composed of Lamport's fast deadlock-free algorithm (page 42), together with a mechanism which is designed to enforce the starvation-freedom property. The algorithm makes use of three registers x, y, and $turn$, which are long enough to store a process identifier, and two boolean arrays $b[1..n]$ and $waiting[1..n]$. In addition, each process uses a local register called $local$. All references to the register $turn$ and the array $waiting$ belong to a mechanism which is superimposed on Lamport's original algorithm. All the processes can read and write the registers x, y, $turn$ and the array $waiting$. The processes can read the boolean registers $b[i]$, but only process i can write $b[i]$.

An Incorrect Fast Starvation-free Algorithm: process i's program.

Initially: $y = 0$, $b[i] = false$, $waiting[i] = false$, the initial values of the other registers are immaterial.

```
start: waiting[i] := true;
b[i] := true;
x := i;
if y ≠ 0 then b[i] := false;
              await (y = 0 or waiting[i] = false);
```

```
            if waiting[i] = false then goto cs
            else goto start fi;
y := i;
if x ≠ i then b[i] := false;
            for j := 1 to n do await ¬b[j] od;
            if y ≠ i then await (y = 0 or waiting[i] := false);
                        if waiting[i] = false then goto cs
                        else goto start fi fi;
cs: critical section;
waiting[i] := false;
local := turn;
if local = i then local := (i + 1) mod n fi;
turn := (local + 1) mod n;
if waiting[local] = true then waiting[local] := false
else y = 0 fi;
b[i] := false;
```

Intuitively, the algorithm works as follows. When process i wants to enter its critical section, it first sets *waiting*[i] to *true*, and then starts to execute Lamport's original algorithm. It can enter its critical section in two ways: (1) it can become the winner as in Lamport's fast algorithm, or (2) the last winner, that is, the last process to enter the critical section, may grant permission to process i by resetting *waiting*[i] to *false*. When a process exits its critical section, it checks whether *waiting*[*turn*] = *true*. That is, it checks whether the process its identifier is equal to, the current value of the variable *turn*, wants to enter its critical section. If so, it grants that process permission to enter its critical section; otherwise, it increments *turn* and exits its critical section.

○○ 2.36 Prove that, in the Bakery algorithm, if process i is in its critical section then $(number[i], i) < (number[k], k)$ for any process $k \neq i$ with $number[k] \neq 0$.

○○ 2.37 Prove that the Bakery algorithm works using safe registers. i.e., it works correctly even when it is allowed for reads which are concurrent with writes to return an arbitrary value.

○○ 2.38 We have proved that the Bakery algorithm is starvation-free. Prove that it also satisfies the first-come-first-served property.

○○ 2.39 Does the Bakery algorithm satisfy mutual exclusion and/or starvation-freedom when the following implementation for computing the maximum is used?

COMPUTING THE MAXIMUM: `process i's program.`

```
local1 := i;
for local2 := 1 to n do
      if number[local1] ≤ number[local2] then local1 := local2 fi
```

```
od;
number[i] := 1 + number[local1];
```

○○ 2.40 Does the Bakery algorithm satisfy mutual exclusion and/or starvation-freedom when the following implementation for computing the maximum is used?

COMPUTING THE MAXIMUM: `process i's program.`

```
1 local1 := 0;
2 for local2 := 1 to n do
3    if local1 < number[local2] then local1 := number[local2] fi
4 od;
5 number[i] := 1 + local1;
```

What is the answer to this question, when "<" is replaced with "≤" in statement 3?

○○ 2.41 Consider the following variant of the Bakery algorithm (page 50), in which line 5 (only) is slightly modified. Is this algorithm correct? Justify your answer.

A VARIANT OF THE BAKERY ALGORITHM: `process i's program.`

Initially: all entries in *choosing* and *number* are *false* and 0, respectively.

```
1   choosing[i] := true;
2   number[i] := 1 + maximum(number[1], ..., number[n]);
3   choosing[i] := false;
4   for j = 1 to n do
5            [if i > j then] await choosing[j] = false fi;
6            await (number[j] = 0 or
                     (number[j], j) ≥ (number[i], i))
7   od;
8   critical section;
9   number[i] := 0;
```

○○ 2.42 Consider the following variant of the Bakery algorithm (page 50). (1) Is this algorithm correct? (2) What would be your answer if "$(number[j] \le 0)$" in line 5 below, is replaced with "$(number[j] = 0)$". Justify your answers.

A VARIANT OF THE BAKERY ALGORITHM: `process i's program.`

Initially: all entries in *number* are 0.

```
1   number[i] := −1;
2   number[i] := 1 + maximum(number[1], ..., number[n], 0);
3   for j = 1 to n do
4            if number[j] = −1 then await number[j] ≠ 1 fi;
```

```
            await (number[j] ≤ 0 or
                  (number[j], j) ≥ (number[i], i))
od;
critical section;
number[i] := 0;
```

∘∘ 2.43 This question refers to the Modified Bakery algorithm on page 54.

1. Prove that the algorithm is correct.
2. Would the algorithm be correct without assuming that all entries in *number* are initialized?
3. Does the Bakery algorithm satisfy mutual exclusion and/or starvation-freedom if the statement "*number*[*i*] := 0" is added at the end of the exit code of each process *i*?
4. Does the algorithm work using safe registers? i.e., it works correctly even when it is allowed for reads which are concurrent with writes to return an arbitrary value.
5. For each one of the four methods for computing the maximum mentioned so far (page 51, page 51, Problem 2.39, Problem 2.40), decide whether the algorithm satisfies mutual exclusion and/or starvation-freedom when using the methods.

∘• 2.44 The following algorithm, which is a variant of the Bakery algorithm, was developed by Lamport (1979). It is expressed in its most general form, in order to allow the widest possible choice of implementations. This requires introducing some new notation. We let ":>" mean "set to any value greater than". (Thus, $x :> y$ can be implemented, for example, by $x := y + 1$.) The statement

for all $j \in \{1, \ldots, n\}$ **do** S_j **od**

means that the statements $S_1, \ldots, S_n$ are to be executed concurrently (or in any order), where S_1 is the statement obtained by substituting 1 for j in S_j, etc. The shared registers consist of the array *number*[1..*n*] of non-negative integers. The algorithm is defined formally below.

A VARIANT OF THE BAKERY ALGORITHM: `process i's program.`

Initially: all entries in *number*[1..*n*] are 0.

```
number[i] :> 0;
number[i] :> maximum(number[1], ..., number[n]);
for all j ∈ {1, ..., n} do
   await (number[j] = 0 or (number[j], j) ≥ (number[i], i))
od;
critical section;
number[i] := 0;
```

Notice that the unboundedness of *number* [i] has nothing to do with the non-deterministic ":>" statement, but is inherent in the Bakery algorithm. Prove the correctness of the algorithm.

◦• 2.45 The Bakery algorithm satisfies FIFO, but uses unbounded size registers. Few attempts have been made in the past to bound the space required by the Bakery algorithm. In the following algorithm, which was published in 1990, the integer arithmetic in the original Bakery algorithm is replaced with modulo arithmetic and the *maximum* function and the *less than* relation have been redefined. Prove that the resulting published algorithm is incorrect, since it does not satisfy deadlock-freedom.

The algorithm lets the ticket numbers move around a ring of length $2n$, i.e., ranging from 0 to $2n-1$. To determine which of any two ticket numbers has precedence in entering its critical section, we compute the difference of these two ticket numbers. If the difference is greater than or equal to n, the process with the larger ticket number has precedence, otherwise the process with the smaller ticket number has precedence. More formally, to compute when expression a is less than expression b, denoted $a \prec b$, the logical expression that should be used is $(|a-b| \geq n) \otimes (a < b)$, where $\otimes$ is the logical operator exclusive or. The relation $A \succeq B$ holds when it is not the case that $a \prec b$. Finally, the relation $\prec$ used in the algorithm on ordered pairs of integers is defined by $(a,b) \prec (c,d)$ if $a \prec c$, or if $a = c$ and $b < d$. As in the Bakery algorithm this algorithm makes use of a boolean array *choosing*[1..n], and of an integer array *number*[1..n], where each entry ranges over $\{-1, 0, \ldots, 2n-1\}$.

AN INCORRECT BOUNDED-SPACE VERSION OF THE BAKERY ALGORITHM: `process` i`'s program`.

Initially: all entries in *choosing* and *number* are *false* and -1, respectively.

```
choosing[i] := true;
number[i] := (1 + modmax(number[1],...,number[n])) mod 2n;
choosing[i] := false;
for j = 1 to n do
    await choosing[j] = false;
    await (number[j] = −1 or (number[j], j) ⪰ (number[i], i))
od;
critical section;
number[i] := −1;
```

The function **modmax**, defined below, returns the ticket number which has the lowest precedence for entering its critical section.

```
function modmax (num: array of integers): integer;
ℓ := 1;
while num[l] = −1 do ℓ := ℓ + 1 od;
max := num[ℓ];
for k = ℓ + 1 to n do
    if ((|max-num[k]| ≥ n) ⊗ (max < num[k])) ∧ (num[k] > −1)
        then max := num[k] fi od;
return max;
end_function
```

◦ 2.46 In the Black-White Bakery algorithm, what should be the size of the entries of the *number* array if we replace line 3 with the following line: $number[i] := 1 + \text{maximum}(number[1], \ldots, number[n])$.

◦ 2.47 Would the Black-White Bakery algorithm be correct if line 12 is replaced with the following ($local_i$ is a local variable of process i):

```
local_i := color;
if local_i = mycolor_i then
   if local_i = black then color := white else color := black fi
fi
```

◦◦ 2.48 Explain why the Black-White Bakery algorithm is not deadlock-free if the third clause in the await statement in line 8 is removed.

◦◦ 2.49 Assume that we change the order of the last two statements (in the exit code) of the Black-White Bakery algorithm. Does this new version of the algorithm: (1) satisfy mutual exclusion for two processes? (2) satisfy mutual exclusion for three processes? (3) satisfy FIFO for two processes? (4) satisfy FIFO for three processes?

◦◦ 2.50 Explain why in the Black-White Bakery algorithm, unlike in the Bakery algorithm, we must assume that the registers are atomic registers and are not only safe registers.

◦◦ 2.51 Replace the multi-writer color bit in the Black-White Bakery algorithm with n single-writer atomic bits. Write the exact code and prove its correctness.

◦• 2.52 The following modification of Dijkstra's algorithm (page 81), due to D. E. Knuth (1966), is the first *starvation-free* solution for the mutual exclusion problem among n processes. Prove the correctness of Knuth's algorithm. The algorithm is for n processes each with unique identifier taken from the set $\{0, \ldots, n-1\}$. It makes use of register k which is long enough to store a process identifier ($k \in \{0, \ldots, n-1\}$), and an array *flag*. All the processes can read and write the register k, the processes can read the register *flag*[i], but only process i can write *flag*[i].

KNUTH'S ALGORITHM: `process i's program.`

Initially: *flag*[i] = 0; $k = 0$.

```
1  start: flag[i] := 1;
2         repeat
3             j = k;
4             while flag[j] = 0 do j := (j − 1) mod n od
5         until j = i;

6         flag[i] := 2;
7         for j := n − 1 downto 0 do
8             if j ≠ i and flag[j] = 2 then goto start fi
9         od;

10        k := i;
11        critical section;
12        k := (i − 1) mod n;
13        flag[i] := 0
```

○• 2.53 Show that, in Knuth's algorithm, a process may have to wait as many as $2^n - 1$ turns before it can enter its own critical section. The word *turn* refers to some process performing its critical section. (Hint: Notice that successive values of k are not always consecutive.)

○○ 2.54 Modify the the control structures in Knuth's algorithm: instead of using the goto statements use iterations.

○ 2.55 Does Knuth's algorithm remain correct if line 10 ($k := i$) is removed?

○ 2.56 Is it really necessary to assume that initially $k = 0$ in Knuth's algorithm?

○○ 2.57 Write a simplified version of Knuth's algorithm for two process mutual exclusion.

○• 2.58 The following algorithm, due to N. G. de Bruijn (1967), improves Knuth's algorithm by replacing lines 9–11, with:

```
critical section;
if flag[k] = 0 or k = i then k := (k − 1) mod n;
```

Show that, in de Bruijn's algorithm, a process may have to wait as many as $\frac{1}{2}n(n-1)$ turns before it can enter its own critical section.

○• 2.59 The following algorithm is due to M. A. Eisenberg and M. R. McGuire (1972). Prove its correctness, and show that it is linear-waiting (i.e., 1-bounded-waiting). The algorithm is for n processes each with unique identifier taken from the set $\{1, \ldots, n\}$. It make use of register k which is long enough to store a process identifier (i.e., $k \in \{1, \ldots, n\}$) and an array *flag*. All the processes can read and write the register k, the processes can read the register *flag*[i], but only process i can write *flag*[i].

Eisenberg–McGuire's Algorithm: `process i's program.`

Initially: $flag[i] = 0$, and the initial value of k is immaterial.

```
1  start: flag[i] := 1;
2         repeat
3              j = k;
4              while flag[j] = 0 do j := 1 + (j mod n) od
5         until j = i;
6         flag[i] := 2;
7         for j := 1 to n do
8              if j ≠ i and flag[j] = 2 then goto start fi
9         od;

10        if flag[k] ≠ 0 and k ≠ i then goto start fi;
11        k := i;
12        critical section;
13        j := k;
14        repeat
15             j := 1 + (j mod n);
16             if flag[j] ≠ 0 then k := j fi;
17        until flag[j] ≠ 0;
18        flag[i] := 0
```

Why does the algorithm not satisfy the FIFO requirement?

∘∘ 2.60 Modify the control structures in Eisenberg and McGuire's algorithm: instead of using the **goto** statements use iterations.

∘ 2.61 Does Eisenberg and McGuire's algorithm remain correct if line 11 ($k := i$) is removed?

∘∘ 2.62 Explain the idea behind the Eisenberg and McGuire improvement of the algorithms of Knuth and De Bruijn. (Recall that their algorithm is linear-waiting.)

∘• 2.63 The following starvation-free algorithm for n processes, due to Peterson, is a simple generalization of Peterson's algorithm for two processes presented on page 32. The two process solution is used repeatedly in $n-1$ levels to eliminate at least one process per level until only one remains. Prove its correctness.

The algorithm requires $2n-1$ shared registers, each of which can hold values in $\{1,\ldots,n-1\}$. It makes use of two arrays $b[1..n]$ and $turn[1..n-1]$ which are initially 0 and 1, respectively.

Peterson's Algorithm for n Processes: `process i's program.`

Initially: $b[1..n]$ all 0, $turn[1..n-1]$ all 1.

```
for j := 1 to n − 1 do
             b[i] := j;
```

```
            turn[j] := i;
            await ((∀k ≠ i : b[k] < j) or turn[j] ≠ i)
od;
critical section;
b[i] := 0;
```

(Recall that the boolean condition in the await statement is *not* evaluated atomically. When the evaluation of the condition requires to read more than one register, the registers are not read in one atomic step, but rather read sequentially one after the other.)

Remark: The system response time of the algorithm (and even its contention-free complexity) is $O(n^2)$. An improved algorithm where the system response time is $O(n \times m)$ when m out of the n processes are competing for the critical section is presented in Problem 2.65.

∘∘ 2.64 Consider Peterson's starvation-free algorithm for n processes from Problem 2.63. Show that this algorithm does not satisfy bounded-waiting. That is, one process can enter its critical section arbitrarily many times ahead of another process (that has already completed its first two assignments).

∘• 2.65 The following starvation-free algorithm for n processes, due to Block and Woo, is another generalization of Peterson's algorithm for two processes presented on page 32. The system response time of the algorithm is $O(n \times m)$ when m out of the n processes are competing for the critical section. This is better than the $O(n^2)$ contention-free complexity of Peterson's starvation-free algorithm for n processes presented in Problem 2.63. The two process solution is used repeatedly in m levels to eliminate at least one process per level until only one remains. Prove its correctness.

The algorithm requires $2n$ shared registers, n boolean and n integer registers each able to hold values in $\{1, \ldots, n\}$. The first array *flag*[1..*n*] states whether a process wants to enter its critical section. The second array *block*[1..*n*] specifies which process is to block at each level. In addition three local variables, called *level*, *counter*, and *j*, are used for each process.

BLOCK AND WOO ALGORITHM FOR *n* PROCESSES: `process i's program.`

Initially: *flag*[1..*n*] and *block*[1..*n*] all 0.

```
level := 0;
flag[i] := 1;
repeat
        level := level + 1;
        block[level] := i;
        repeat
```

```
                    counter := 0;
                    for j := 1 to n do
                        if flag[j] = 1 then counter := counter + 1 if
            until (block[level] ≠ i or counter ≤ level)
    until block[level] = i;
    critical section;
    flag[i] := 0;
```

? 2.66 Design a fast linear-waiting algorithm.

? 2.67 For deadlock-free solutions there is a tight bound of n bits. For starvation-free solutions there is a tight bound of n registers, on the number of registers. What are the space bounds on the *size* of registers for starvation-free solutions? Find tight bounds on the number and size of the registers needed to design algorithms which satisfy stronger fairness requirements such as linear-waiting and FIFO.

Problems based on Section 2.5

∘∘ 2.68 Give a very simple proof, without using Theorem 2.16, that there is no mutual exclusion algorithm for two processes using a single (read/write) shared register. The proof should be no longer then five lines.

∘ 2.69 In the run constructed in the proof of Lemma 2.21, are all the processes hidden in the run z_i?

∘∘ 2.70 In the proof of Lemma 2.21 an *infinite* run is constructed. Modify the proof of Lemma 2.21 so that only a finite run is constructed.

∘∘ 2.71 Does it follow from Theorem 2.16 (or its proof) that: Any deadlock-free mutual exclusion algorithm for n processes must use at least n *single-writer* registers? (Recall that a single-writer register is a register that only one process can write.)

∘∘ 2.72 The following is a definition of a hidden process which is different than the definition given on page 60. *For process p and run z, let z′ be the longest prefix of z such that p is in its remainder in z′. Process p is hidden in run z if each event which p is involved in (z − z′) is either: a read event, or a write event that is overwritten* ***by a write event of some other process*** *before any other process has read the value written.*

Is the lower bound proof still correct if we use the above definition instead of the original one?

∘∘ 2.73 Recall that the overwritten relation is transitive (i.e., if e_1 is overwritten by e_2 and e_2 is overwritten by e_3 then e_1 is overwritten by e_3).

The following is a weaker definition of a hidden process than the definition given on page 60. *For process p and run z, let z′ be the longest prefix of z such that p is in its remainder in z′. Process p is hidden in run z if each event which p is involved in (z − z′) is either: a read event, a write event that is overwritten* ***by a write event of some***

***other process** before any other process has read the value written, or **a write event which does not change the value of a register** (i.e., the written value is the same as the previous value).*

What breaks in the lower bound proof if we use the above definition instead of the original one? (*Hint*: the answer is different from the answer to the problem on page 68.)

•◦ 2.74 We have discussed shared memory systems which support atomic read and write operations (i.e., atomic registers). Here we focus attention on somewhat stronger systems in which it is possible to read or write several shared registers in one atomic step. We say that a system supports atomic m-register operations if it is possible for a process to read *or* write m registers in one atomic step.

Shown that the lower bound proof (Theorem 2.16) generalizes to the case of a system which supports atomic m-register operations for any $m \leq 1$.

? 2.75 Consider the following modified definition of deadlock-freedom:

k-deadlock-freedom: *If no more than k processes are trying to enter their critical sections, then some process (not necessarily one of these k processes) eventually enters its critical section.*

Notice that, for a system of n processes, the definition of deadlock-freedom is equivalent to that of n-deadlock-freedom, while it is stronger than k-deadlock-freedom for $k < n$.

What is the smallest k for which Theorem 2.16 holds, when replacing the requirement of deadlock-freedom with k-deadlock-freedom? (Notice that, it is easy to modify Lamport's fast algorithm to satisfy 1-deadlock-freedom with only two registers.)

◦ 2.76 Assume that we move line 8 of the One-bit algorithm (page 64) from its current position, and place it at the beginning of the code. Does the new algorithm satisfy mutual exclusion and/or deadlock-freedom?

◦◦ 2.77 Show that the One-bit algorithm violates the starvation-freedom property.

◦• 2.78 The One-bit algorithm uses only single-writer bits – bits that only one process is allowed to write. Prove that there is no starvation-free mutual exclusion algorithm for two processes which uses only two single-writer bits.

◦• 2.79 Below is a modification of the One-bit algorithm (page 64):

Initially: all entries in b are *false*; *flag* is a local variable.

```
repeat
    b[i] := true; j := 1;
    while (b[i] = true) and (j < i) do
        if b[j] = true then b[i] := false; await b[j] = false fi;
        j := j + 1
```

```
6          od
7      until b[i] = true;
8      j := i + 1;
9      repeat
10         flag := true;
11         b[i] := true;
12         j := i + 1;
13         while (flag = true) and (j ≤ n) do
14             if b[j] = true then
15                             flag := false;
16                             b[i] := false;
17                             await b[j] = false fi;
18             j := j + 1
19         od
20     until flag = true;
21     critical section;
22     b[i] := false;
```

Consider the following four variants of the above algorithm:

1. Remove lines 11, 12, 15, and 16;
2. Remove lines 8, 11, and 16;
3. Remove line 8;
4. Remove line 12.

For each one of the above variants decide if it satisfies deadlock-freedom and/or mutual exclusion. Justify your answer.

? 2.80 Recall that a w-writer r-reader register is a register which can be written by at most w processes and can be read by at most r processes. For a given w and r, how may registers must be used by any deadlock-free mutual exclusion algorithm for n processes, which uses only w-writer r-reader registers? Notice that the tight upper bound is proved only when each register can be read by all the processes (i.e., when $r = n$).

•• ? 2.81 Show that for every mutual exclusion algorithm for n processes;

1. $\frac{\log n}{\ell - 2 + 3\log\log n}$ is a lower bound on the contention-free time complexity, where ℓ is the size (in terms of bits) of the biggest register accessed by the algorithm in one atomic step;
2. even in the absence of contention, a process always needs to access $\sqrt{\frac{\log n}{\ell + \log\log n}}$ *different* shared registers before it enters its critical section.

The question of finding tight bounds is still open.

•• ? 2.82 Show that for every mutual exclusion algorithm for n processes:

1. $\Omega(\log_w n)$ is a lower bound on the contention-free time complexity, where w is the maximum number of processes that may simultaneously write the same register;

2. even in the absence of contention, a process always needs to access $\Omega(\sqrt{\log_w n})$ *different* shared registers before it enters its critical section;
3. even in the absence of contention, a process always needs to access $\Omega(\log_c n)$ *different* shared registers before it enters its critical section, where c is the maximum number of processes that may simultaneously access (i.e., read and write) the same register.

The question of finding tight bounds is still open.

∘∘ 2.83 Design an algorithm with contention-free time complexity $O(\lceil \frac{\log n}{\ell} \rceil)$, where ℓ is the size (in terms of bits) of the biggest register accessed by the algorithm in one atomic step.

∘∘ 2.84 Modify the deadlock-free algorithm for infinitely many processes (on page 66), so that it satisfies starvation-freedom.

∘∘ 2.85 An algorithm for solving the election problem for n processes is presented below. Recall that in the election problem, each correct process that starts participating eventually terminates and exactly one process is elected as a leader. We assume that processes are not required to participate in the algorithm; however, once a process starts participating it is guaranteed that it will never fail. (This assumption is exactly as in the mutual exclusion problem where a process may stay in the reminder section forever.) The model is an asynchronous shared memory that supports only single-writer and multi-reader shared registers.

A LEADER ELECTION ALGORITHM: process i's program ($1 \leq i \leq n$).

All registers are initialized to zero.

```
decide_i : 0..1;
wake_i : 0..n;                              /* # that wake up */
faulty_i : 0..n;               /* # that did not wake up +1 */

wake_i := 1;                       /* signals and counts itself */
decide_i := 1;

for j = 1 to n do                      /* counts # that wake up */
  if (wake_j ≠ 0) and (i ≠ j) then wake_i := wake_i + 1 fi od;
faulty_i := n − wake_i + 1;         /* # that may be faulty */
                                /* +1 to ensure faulty_i ≠ 0 */

for j = 1 to n do
  if wake_j ≠ 0 then                           /* j is correct */
    await faulty_j ≠ 0;
    if (faulty_j, j) > (faulty_i, i) then decide_i := 0 fi fi od
                                        /* lexicographic order */
```

if $decide_i = 0$ **then** "*I am not the leader*"
else "*I am the leader*" **fi.**

Below, we consider only single-writer registers. That is, all writes to a register are totally ordered. Lamport has defined three general classes of shared read/write registers – safe, regular, and atomic – depending on their properties when several reads and/or writes are executed concurrently. The weakest possibility is *safe* register, in which it is assumed only that a read not concurrent with any writes obtains the correct value (that is, the value of the last write or the initial value). A *regular* register is a safe register in which a read that overlaps a write obtains either the old or new value. An *atomic* register is a safe register in which the reads and writes behave as if they occur in some definite order.

The question about the above algorithm for solving the election problem is:

1. Does the algorithm solve the problem assuming the registers are atomic?
2. Does the algorithm solve the problem assuming the registers are regular?
3. Does the algorithm solve the problem assuming the registers are safe?

Mutual Exclusion Using Atomic Registers: Advanced Topics

3.1 Local Spinning Algorithms

All the mutual exclusion algorithms which use atomic registers, and many algorithms which use stronger synchronization primitives, include busy-waiting loops. The idea is that in order to wait, a process *spins* on a flag register, until some other process terminates the spin with a single write operation. Unfortunately, under contention, such spinning may generate lots of traffic on the interconnection network between the process and the memory. Hence, by consuming communication bandwidth spin-waiting by some process can slow other processes.

To address this problem, as already discussed in Section 1.4.3 (page 16), it is important to distinguish between *remote* access and *local* access to shared memory, and to try to reduce the number of remote accesses as much as possible.

We consider the following two machine architectures (which are illustrated in Figure 1.6 on page 16): (1) Cache coherent systems, where each process (or processor) has it own private cache. When a process accesses a shared memory location a copy of it migrates to a local cache line and becomes locally accessible until some other process updates this shared memory location and the local copy is invalidated. (2) Distributed shared memory systems, where instead of having the "shared memory" in one central location, each process "owns" part of the shared memory" and keeps it in its own local memory. A shared memory location is locally accessible to some process if it is in the part of the shared memory that physically resides on that process local memory. For algorithms designed for such systems, it is important to minimize the number of times a process has to access a shared memory location that is not locally accessible to that process.

We notice that spinning (busy-waiting) on a remote memory location while its value does not change is counted only as *one* remote operation that causes communication in a system with support for cache coherence (after one remote operation it migrates to a local cache line), while it is counted as *many* operations that cause communication in a distributed shared memory system.

3.1.1 Local Spinning

Assume that, for some distributed shared memory system, we need to choose between Peterson's algorithm (page 32) and Kessels' algorithm (page 35). Which one is better? Well, Kessels' algorithm is a much better choice. In Kessels' algorithm, we can let the registers *b*[0] and *turn*[0] physically reside on process 1 local memory, and let *b*[1] and *turn*[1] physically reside on process 0 local memory. The advantage of distributing the registers in such a way is that when a process waits in Kessels' algorithm (using an await statement) for a condition to become *true*, it is doing so by *spinning* (busy-waiting) only on *locally-accessible* registers.

An algorithm satisfies local spinning if the only type of spinning required is local spinning. Local spinning is the situation where a process is spinning on locally-accessible registers. Shared registers may be locally-accessible as a result of either coherent caching (CC) or when using distributed shared memory (DSM) where shared memory is physically distributed among the processors. Thus, we will define these two cases separately:

- An algorithm satisfies local spinning in the CC model, if in a system with support for cache coherence the only type of spinning required is local spinning (that is, if spinning only involves reading from local cache lines).
- An algorithm satisfies local spinning in the DSM model, if it is possible to physically distribute the shared memory among the processes in such a way that the only type of spinning required is local spinning.

We notice that an algorithm that satisfies local spinning in a distributed shared memory system is expected to perform well also when executed on a machine with no distributed shared memory even if that machine has no support for cache coherence. The reason is that each process busy-waits only on memory locations on which no other process spins, thus eliminating hot-spot contention caused by busy waiting.

We observe that: (1) an algorithm that has bounded time complexity in the CC model (resp. DSM model) satisfies local spinning in the CC model (resp. DSM model), and (2) an algorithm that does *not* satisfy local spinning in the DSM model has unbounded time complexity in the DSM model. (Time complexity is defined on page 16.)

As we have seen, Kessels' algorithm satisfies local spinning in the DSM model while Peterson's algorithm does not. In Peterson's algorithm, both processes need to spin on *turn*, and hence one of them (depending on the location of *turn*) will have to spin on a remote register and will generate an unbounded number of remote accesses. This leads us to the following simple observation: Any "reasonable" mutual exclusion algorithm for two processes that uses only single-writer registers satisfies local spinning in the DSM model.

It follows from the above observation that, in addition to Kessels' algorithm, the three algorithms that are described in Section 2.6 also satisfy local spinning (each one of these three algorithms uses only two single-writer bits). In the next section we describe local spinning algorithms for more than just two processes.

3.1.2 The Local Spinning Black-White Bakery Algorithm

In this section we modify the Black-White Bakery algorithm (page 55) so that the new algorithm: (1) satisfies local spinning in both the CC and the DSM models, (2) satisfies FIFO, and (3) uses bounded space. The algorithm is due to G. Taubenfeld (2004). We assume that the reader is familiar with the details of the Black-White Bakery algorithm.

In the Black-White Bakery algorithm, process i may need to wait for another process, say j, in one of two cases:

1. Process i might need to wait until the value of $choosing_j$ changes from *true* to *false*.
2. Process i has lower priority than process j and hence i has to wait until j exits its critical section.

The Black-White Bakery algorithm does not satisfy local spinning since in each one of these two cases process i waits by spinning on remote registers. To overcome this difficulty, in the new algorithm, process i uses two new single-reader shared bits, $spin.ch[i,j]$ and $spin.nu[i,j]$, which are both assumed to be locally accessible for process i.

1. In the first case, instead of spinning on $choosing_j$, process i spins locally on $spin.ch[i,j]$, waiting for j to notify it that the value of $choosing_j$ has been changed. Process j notifies i of such a change by writing into $spin.ch[i,j]$.
2. In the second case, instead of waiting for j to exit its critical section by spinning on the variables $number_j$, *color*, and $mycolor_j$, process i spins locally on $spin.nu[i,j]$, waiting for j to notify it that j has exited its critical section. Process j notifies i when it exits by writing into $spin.nu[i,j]$.

To implement all the (single-reader) spin bits, we use the two dimensional arrays $spin.ch[1..n, 1..n]$ and $spin.nu[1..n, 1..n]$ of bits. All these bits are used for spinning, and on a DSM machine they can be statically allocated, so that spinning is done only locally. That is, for each process i, the $2n$ bits $spin.ch[i, 1..n]$ and $spin.nu[i, 1..n]$ are locally accessible to process i and process i may spin (locally) only on those $2n$ bits.

We present the algorithm in two steps. First we use the above observations to transform the Bakery algorithm (page 50) into an algorithm that satisfies local spinning in both the CC and DSM models. Then we do the same for the

Black-White Bakery algorithm. The code of the *local spinning* Bakery algorithm is shown below.

THE LOCAL SPINNING BAKERY ALGORITHM: `process i's program.`

```
shared
    spin.ch[1..n, 1..n]: boolean array              /* spin on choosing */
    spin.nu[1..n, 1..n]: boolean array                /* spin on number */
    choosing[1..n]: boolean array
    number[1..n]: array of type {0,...,∞}
    Initially ∀i : 1 ≤ i ≤ n : choosing_i = false and number_i = 0,
    the initial values of all the other variables are immaterial.

choosing_i := true                              /* beginning of doorway */
number_i := 1 + max({number_j | 1 ≤ j ≤ n})
choosing_i := false
for j = 1 to n do spin.ch[j, i] := false od              /* notifyAll */
                                                    /* end of doorway */
for j = 1 to n do
    spin.ch[i, j] := true         /* waits until choosing_i = false */
    if choosing_j = true then await spin.ch[i, j] = false fi
    spin.nu[i, j] := true
    if (number_j = 0) ∨ ([number_j, j] ≥ [number_i, i])
    then skip else await spin.nu[i, j] = false fi
od
critical section
number_i := 0
for j = 1 to n do spin.nu[j, i] := false od              /* notifyAll */
```

The algorithm satisfies mutual exclusion, deadlock-freedom, FIFO fairness, and local spinning in both the CC and DSM models. The time complexity of the algorithm in both the CC and DSM models is $O(n)$. As in the original Bakery algorithm the algorithm uses unbounded size shared registers. This problem is resolved in the next algorithm. The code of the *local spinning* Black-White Bakery algorithm is shown below.

THE LOCAL SPINNING BLACK-WHITE BAKERY ALGORITHM:
`process i's program.`

```
shared
    spin.ch[1..n, 1..n]: boolean array              /* spin on choosing */
    spin.nu[1..n, 1..n]: boolean array                /* spin on number */
    color: a bit of type {black, white}
    choosing[1..n]: boolean array
    (mycolor,number)[1..n]: array of type {black, white} × {0,...,n}
    Initially ∀i : 1 ≤ i ≤ n : choosing_i = false and number_i = 0,
    the initial values of all the other variables are immaterial.
```

```
choosing_i := true                                  /* beginning of doorway */
mycolor_i := color
number_i := 1 + max({number_j | (1 ≤ j ≤ n) ∧ (mycolor_j = mycolor_i)})
choosing_i := false
for j = 1 to n do spin.ch[j,i] := false od                     /* notifyAll */
                                                         /* end of doorway */
for j = 1 to n do
     spin.ch[i,j] := true            /* waits until choosing_i = false */
     if choosing_j = true then await spin.ch[i,j] = false fi
     spin.nu[i,j] := true                              /* writes first to */
     if mycolor_j = mycolor_i                   /* avoid race condition */
     then if  (number_j = 0) ∨ ([number_j, j] ≥ [number_i, i]) ∨
              (mycolor_j ≠ mycolor_i)
          then skip else await spin.nu[i,j] = false fi
     else  if (number_j = 0) ∨ (mycolor_i ≠ color) ∨
              (mycolor_j = mycolor_i)
          then skip else await spin.nu[i,j] = false fi
     fi
od
critical section
if mycolor_i = black then color := white else color := black fi
number_i := 0
for j = 1 to n do spin.nu[j,i] := false od                     /* notifyAll */
```

Properties of the algorithm:

- Satisfies mutual exclusion, deadlock-freedom, and FIFO fairness.
- Satisfies local spinning in both the CC and DSM models. The time complexity in both the CC and DSM models is $O(n)$.
- $O(n^2)$ bounded size registers are used.

All the $O(n^2)$ spin bits are 2-writer single-reader bits. It is possible to reduce the number of registers used, by using n-writer registers; however, doing so will make the algorithm much more complicated because of the new possible race conditions.

The time complexity of the next (non-FIFO) local spinning algorithm we present is better than that of the local spinning Black-White Bakery algorithm. This seems to be the price to be paid for satisfying the FIFO property.

3.1.3 A Local Spinning Tournament Algorithm

The following tournament algorithm for n processes, due to J.-H. Yang and J. H. Anderson (1993), satisfies local spinning in both the CC and DSM models.

It is assumed that the number of processes n is a power of two (dummy processes may be added if n is not a power of two), and that the processes are numbered 0 through $n-1$. The tournament tree has $\log n$ levels numbered 0 through $\log n - 1$, and at each level the nodes are numbered from left to right starting from 0 (as shown in Figure 2.2, page 37).

Let *level* and *node* be the level and node numbers of some node v. For each node v, three shared registers are provided: $name[level, 2 \cdot node]$, $name[level, 2 \cdot node + 1]$, and $turn[level, node]$. In addition, for each level $0 \leq level \leq \log n - 1$ and process $0 \leq i \leq n - 1$, there is a shared register $flag[level, i]$. These flags are used for spinning, and on a DSM machine they can be statically allocated, so that spinning is done only locally. That is, for each process i, the $\log n$ registers $flag[*, i]$ are locally accessible to process i.

The registers *level, node*, and *id* are local to each process. The *level* and *node* registers, together, identify a specific node of the tree at which a process, say p, is currently competing, while the *id* register indicates the previous node which p had visited.

A Local Spinning Tournament Algorithm: `process i's program.`

Initially: the *name* registers are set to -1, the *flag* registers are set to 0, and the initial values of the other registers are immaterial.

```
1  id := i;
2  for level := 0 to log n − 1 do                        /* from leaf to root */
3       node := ⌊id/2⌋;                                   /* the current node */
4       name[level, id] := i;                            /* identify yourself */
5       turn[level, node] := i;                   /* update the tie-breaker */
           /* initiate the locally-accessible spin flag */
6       flag[level, i] := 0;
           /* deduce the process with which to compete */
7       if even(id) then rival := name[level, id + 1]        /* id is even */
                   else rival := name[level, id − 1] fi;
           /* has rival updated the tie-breaker first? */
8       if rival ≠ −1 and turn[level, node] = i then
                          /* release the rival from waiting */
9           if flag[level, rival] = 0 then flag[level, rival] := 1 fi;
           /* wait until rival updates the tie-breaker */
10          await flag[level, i] ≠ 0;
                                   /* re-examine tie-breaker */
11          if turn[level, node] = i then await flag[level, i] = 2 fi
12      fi;
13      id := node                                /* move to a higher level */
14 od;
15 critical section;
16 for level := log n − 1 downto 0 do                   /* begin exit code */
17      id := ⌊i/2^level⌋; node := ⌊id/2⌋;              /* set level and id */
18      name[level, id] := −1;                                /* erase id */
19      rival := turn[level, node];                         /* find rival */
20      if rival ≠ i then flag[level, rival] := 2 fi      /* notify rival */
21 od                                                   /* end exit code */
```

In line 1 process i starts with its own id. In line 3, i identifies the *node* at which it has to compete at the current level. It declares its intention to compete in line 4, and tries to get preference over its rival at line 5. The *turn* register is used as a tie-breaker between the two competing processes. The first process to update *turn* gets to enter its critical section first.

In line 6 process i resets *flag*[*level*, i], which is the register on which process i may spin at the current level if necessary. The *flag*[*level*, i] register is locally accessible to process i on a DSM machine. In line 7, process i deduces the identity of its rival (if any) for that level. If process i finds out that either its rival has not showed up (*rival* $= -1$, in line 8) or that its rival was the last to update the tie-breaker then process i wins and proceeds one level up.

Otherwise, process i has to figure out whether its rival has executed line 5 before process i, or if its rival has not executed line 5 yet. In the former case the rival wins and in the latter case process i wins. This question is resolved by executing lines 9–14. In line 9, i releases its rival from waiting in case the rival is waiting for i to update the tie-breaker. Then, in line 10 i waits until it is sure that its rival has updated the tie-breaker.

In line 11, i re-examines the tie-breaker to see if it is the first to update the tie-breaker. If it is not the first then it waits until its flag register equals 2 which means that its rival has finished its critical section and has executed its exit code. After executing its critical section process i informs all the processes that are waiting for it (on the pass from the leaf to the root) that it has finished, by setting their flag registers to 2.

Properties of the algorithm:

- Satisfies mutual exclusion and starvation-freedom.
- Satisfies local spinning in both the CC and DSM models. The time complexity in both the CC and DSM models is $O(\log n)$.
- $O(n \log n)$ shared registers are used.

The proofs of these properties are left as an exercise.

Self Review

1. Is it true that in local spinning algorithms for DSM systems, different processes must spin on different memory locations, while in local spinning algorithms for CC systems processes may share spin variables.
2. Is it the case that any mutual exclusion algorithm for two processes that satisfies local spinning in the DSM model must use only single-writer registers?
3. Explain why any "reasonable" mutual exclusion algorithm for two processes that uses only single-writer registers satisfies local spinning in the DSM model.
4. The Bakery algorithm is correct even when all the registers are assumed to be only safe (instead of atomic). Is it the same for the local spinning Bakery algorithm?
5. Would the local spinning Black-White Bakery algorithm still be correct if we replace the order between line 19 and line 20?
6. Would the tournament algorithm (page 102) be correct if line 16 is replaced with: "**for** *level* := 0 **to** $\log n - 1$ **do**"?

Answers: (1) Yes it is true. In CC systems processes can read different cached copies of the same memory location. (2) No. (3) Let A be a mutual exclusion algorithm for two processes that uses only single-writer registers. Let R_0 be the set of registers that process 0 can write, and let R_1 be the set of registers that process 1 can write. In "reasonable" algorithms a process never spins on a register that it can only write. Thus, if all the registers in R_0 physically reside on process 1 local memory, and all the registers in R_1 physically reside on process 0 local memory, only local spinning is possible. (4) Yes. (5) No. (6) No.

3.2 Adaptive Algorithms

3.2.1 Basic Definitions

Lamport's fast mutual exclusion algorithm, presented in Section 2.3, provides fast access in the absence of contention. However, in the presence of contention (of even just two processes), the winning process may have to check the status of all other n processes before it is allowed to enter its critical section. A natural question to ask is whether his algorithm can be improved for the case where there is contention of two or more processes?

Since the other contending processes are waiting for the winner, it is particularly important to speed their entry to the critical section, by the design of an *adaptive mutual exclusion* algorithm in which the time complexity is a function of the actual number of contending processes. That is, the time complexity is independent of the total number of processes and is governed only by the current degree of contention.

An adaptive algorithm: *An algorithm is adaptive with respect to time complexity measure ψ, if its time complexity ψ is a function of the actual number of contending processes.*

For example, an algorithm is adaptive w.r.t. system response time, if for any time interval, say T, where some process is in its entry code while no process is in its critical section (assuming there is an upper bound of one time unit for step time in the entry or exit code and no lower bound), the length of T is bounded by some function of the actual number of contending processes during T. We will consider adaptivity w.r.t. system response time, and other complexity measures such as time complexity in the CC and DSM models.

Two notions of contention can be considered: *interval contention* and *point contention*. The interval contention over time interval T is the number of processes that are active in T (i.e., the processes that are not in their remainder section). The point contention over time interval T is the maximum number of processes that are active at the *same time* in T. For example, as illustrated in Figure 3.1, assume that (1) processes p_1, p_2, and p_3 are active during the time intervals T_1, T_2, and T_3, respectively, and (2) T_1 overlaps with both T_2 and T_3, but T_2 and T_3 do not overlap. Then the point contention over T_1 is 2, while the interval contention is 3.

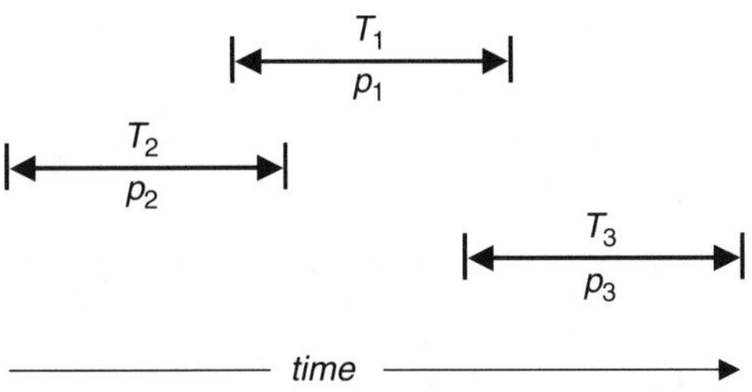

Figure 3.1 The point contention over T_1 is 2, while the interval contention over T_1 is 3.

We notice that point contention is always at most interval contention. All the adaptive algorithms presented in this section are adaptive w.r.t. both point and interval contention.

The *last* result presented in this section is an impossibility result which shows that there is *no* adaptive mutual exclusion algorithm w.r.t. process time complexity. That is, we show that for any mutual exclusion algorithm, whenever there is contention of two or more processes, there is no bound, not even as a function of the total number of processes, on the number of steps (which involve accessing the shared memory) taken by the winning process. Before presenting this negative result, we present three interesting adaptive algorithms.

3.2.2 A Simple Adaptive Algorithm

The first adaptive algorithm we present, due to M. Merritt and G. Taubenfeld (2000), is adaptive w.r.t. system response time. That is, the response time is independent of the total number of processes and is governed only by the current degree of contention. The algorithm is based on Lamport's fast algorithm (page 42). In the algorithm, the processes compete in levels, each of which is used to eliminate at least one competing process, until only one process remains. The winner enters its critical section, and in its exit code it publishes the index to the next empty level, so that each process can join the competition starting from that level. There are infinitely many such levels.

In addition to being adaptive, in the absence of contention, only eight accesses to the shared memory are needed in order to enter and exit the critical section. Furthermore, the algorithm works even when the number of processes are not known *a priori* (or even when the number of processes can grow without bound). The algorithm uses an infinite number of shared registers. This is unavoidable, as Theorem 2.16 implies that when the number of processes is not finite (or finite but not known *a priori*), an infinite number of registers are necessary. The algorithm is built out of simple building blocks called *splitters* which are introduced next.

Splitters

Lamport's fast algorithm (page 42) provides fast access in the absence of contention. As observed by Moir and Anderson (1995), Lamport's algorithm

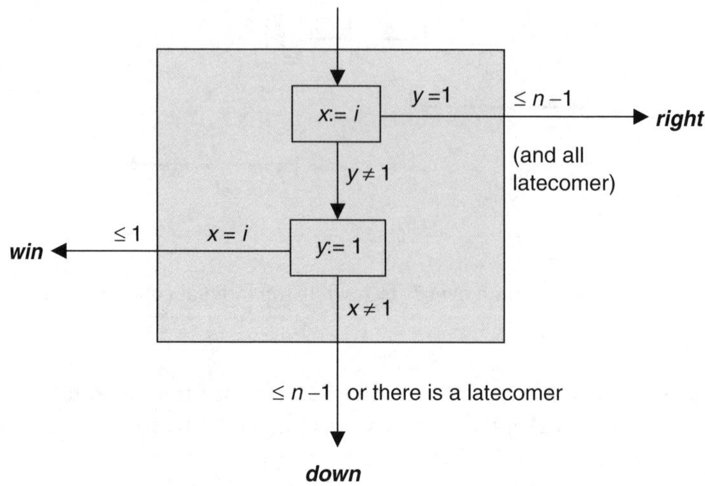

Figure 3.2 The MA-splitter.

implicitly uses a shared object called a *splitter*. This splitter, which we name the MA-splitter, is illustrated in Figure 3.2, and its code is given below.

THE MA-SPLITTER: `process i's program.`

> x: atomic register (the initial value is immaterial)
> y: atomic bit, initially 0
> $x := i$
> **if** $y = 1$ **then** *move right* **fi**
> $y := 1$
> **if** $x \neq i$ **then** *move down*
> **else** *win* **fi**

Each process that invokes the splitter moves either *down*, *right*, or *wins*. In any execution, define the *latecomers* to be the processes that invoke the splitter after the first process exits it. Let n be the number of *early* processes that invoke the splitter before this first process exits it. The properties of Lamport's splitter are listed below.

Lemma 3.1 *In any execution of the MA-splitter, the following properties hold:*

1. *At most $n-1$ early processes move right.*
2. *At most $n-1$ processes move down, or at least one latecomer moves right.*
3. *At most one process wins, and if $n = 1$ then exactly one process wins.*
4. *The latecomers all move right.*
5. *The splitter is wait-free.*

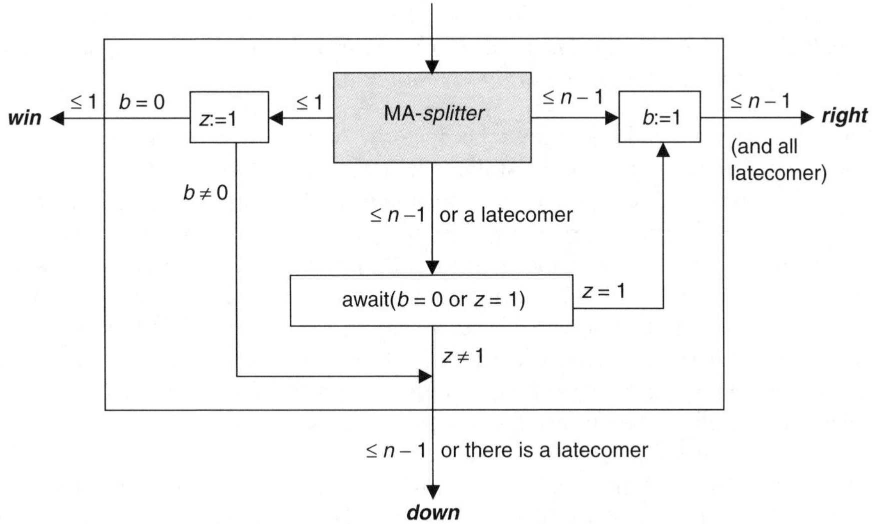

Figure 3.3 The MT-splitter.

Proof: To see, for example, why the third property holds, assume to the contrary that two processes i and j both *win*. Assume without loss of generality that process i tests the value of x at statement 4 after j does so. This implies that x is not written by any process between i's assignment $x := i$ in statement 1 and i's read of x in statement 4. Thus, j's read of x in statement 4 preceded i's assignment in statement 1, which in turn implies that j assigned 1 to y in statement 3 before i's read of y in statement 2. Thus, i must have read $y = 1$ at statement 2 and then "moved right", a contradiction. Similar arguments establish the other properties. ∎

Next, we present a modification of the MA-splitter, due to Merritt and Taubenfeld (2000), exchanging wait-freedom for starvation-freedom, but obtaining a new safety property. The new splitter which we name, the MT-splitter, is illustrated in Figure 3.3, and its code is given below.

THE MT-SPLITTER: `process i's program.`

```
x: atomic register (the initial value is immaterial)
b, y, z: atomic bits, initially 0
x := i
if y = 1  then   b := 1 move right fi
y := 1
if x ≠ i  then   await (b = 1) or (z = 1)
                 if z = 1 then move right
                 else move down fi
else      z := 1
          if b = 0 then win
          else move down fi fi
```

Lemma 3.2 *The MT-splitter satisfies the first four properties of the MA-splitter (as listed in Lemma 3.1), is starvation-free, and satisfies the following additional property: If a process wins then nobody moves down.*

Proof: Starvation-freedom follows because the MA-splitter is wait-free and the conditions satisfying the await statement are stable. The second property of Lemma 3.1 assures that some process must exit the MA-splitter to the *right* or by *winning*, and perform the assignment enabling all await statements to terminate. To see why the new safety property holds, observe that: (1) a process that reaches the await statement in line 4 (exiting Lamport's splitter going down) can move *down* in the new splitter only if b is set to 1 *before* z is set to 1, and (2) a process can *win* in the new splitter only if b is set to 1 *after* z is set to 1. Thus, if a process *wins* in the MT-splitter, every process that reaches the await statement in line 4 moves *right* in the MT-splitter. The winning process is also the (unique) process to *win* in the MA-splitter, and so nobody moves *down*.

The other four safety properties of the MA-splitter also hold for the new splitter. Notice first that any process that is an *early* process in the embedded MA-splitter is also an *early* process in the MT-splitter, and any process that is a *latecomer* in the MT-splitter is a *latecomer* in the embedded MA-splitter. The third and fourth safety properties follow immediately from the corresponding conditions in Lemma 3.1. To see that the first safety property holds, observe that one of the processes that are *early* in the MA-splitter exits it as a *winner* or *down*. In the first case, we are done, so assume no process *wins* in the MA-splitter. Then the processes exiting the MA-splitter *down* will continue and exit the new splitter going *down*.

Finally, we prove that the second safety property holds. If some process moves *right* in the MT-splitter (either an *early* process or a *latecomer*) then we are done. If no process moves *right* in the MT-splitter, then also no process moves *right* in the MA-splitter, and by the second safety property in Lemma 3.1, exactly one process (*early* in both splitters) *wins* in the MA-splitter, and then in the MT-splitter. (Since b is never set to 1.) ∎

The Algorithm

Using the properties of the MT-splitter, it is possible to solve mutual exclusion by interconnecting a collection of MT-splitters in an (infinite) chain, so that processes that move *down* enter the next splitter in the chain, as is illustrated in Figure 3.4. The complete code of the algorithm is given below.

AN ADAPTIVE DEADLOCK-FREE ALGORITHM: `process i's program.`

shared
    next: integer, initially 0
    $x[0..\infty]$: array of integers (the initial values are immaterial)
    $b[0..\infty]$, $y[0..\infty]$, $z[0..\infty]$: array of boolean, initially all 0
local
    level: integer, the initial value is immaterial
    win: boolean, initially 0

```
start: level := next              /* enter the chain of splitters */
  repeat
      x[level] := i
      if y[level]      then  b[level] := 1
                             await level < next
                             goto start fi
      y[level] := 1
      if x[level] ≠ i  then  await (b[level] = 1) ∨ (z[level] = 1)
                                                      /* move right */
                             if z[level] = 1 then  await level < next
                                                   goto start
                             else level := level + 1 fi    /* move down */
      else   z[level] := 1
             if b[level] = 0 then win := 1                  /* win */
             else level := level + 1 fi fi                  /* move down */
  until win = 1
  critical section
  next := level + 1                                         /* exit */
```

Properties of the adaptive algorithm:

- *Satisfies mutual exclusion and deadlock-freedom*: starvation of individual processes is possible, but the algorithm can be easily modified to avoid also starvation.
- In the absence of contention, only *eight* accesses to the shared memory are needed (seven in the entry code and one in the exit code).

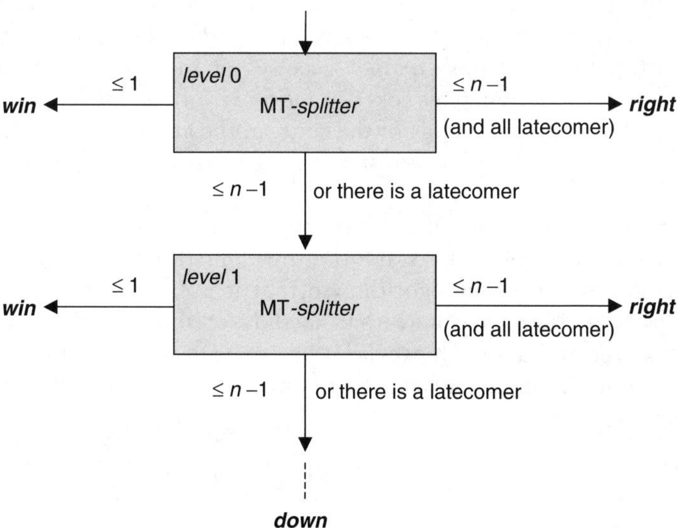

Figure 3.4 Adaptive mutual exclusion by interconnecting a collection of MT-splitters in an infinite chain.

- *It is adaptive w.r.t. system response time*: the system response time is of order k time units, where k is the point contention (the actual number of contending processes).
- *It works even when assuming unbounded concurrency*: the number of processes that are simultaneously active is finite but can grow without bound. Thus, the number of processes are not known *a priori*.
- *It is symmetric*: identifiers are only written, read, and compared for equality, but are not ordered or used to index shared registers. (Symmetry is defined on page 129.)
- *Drawback*: an infinite number of shared registers are used.

Theorem 3.3 *The algorithm is an adaptive, deadlock-free mutual exclusion algorithm for unbounded concurrency.*

Proof: In this solution, the processes compete in levels, where each level is implemented as a separate AT-splitter. Each level either has a *winner*, or eliminates at least one competing process (those that move *right*). Since all the *latecomers* move *right* at the first level, only finitely many processes can move *down* to subsequent levels. Hence, within finitely many levels, there is either a *winner* or a single process moves down–but this process will *win* this final level. The *winner* enters its critical section, and in its exit code it publishes the index of the next empty level, so that each process can join (or re-join) the competition starting from that level.

By the properties of the AT-splitter, when a process *wins* in a level, no process is active in any splitter with greater index. Every other active process will eventually move to the *right* in a splitter with equal or greater index, and wait for the global pointer *next* to be updated by the *winner*.

Measuring time complexity, exiting the critical section signals awaiting processes to proceed to a splitter at a new level. If n is the number of *early* processes at that splitter, then the next *winner* accesses at most $n+1$ splitters before entering the critical section. This takes at most $O(n)$ time. Hence, the algorithm is adaptive. Examining the details of the code, in the absence of contention, only eight accesses to shared atomic registers are needed before entering the critical section. ∎

The adaptive deadlock-free algorithm above is easily modified using standard "helping" techniques to satisfy starvation-freedom (Problem 3.19). It is much more difficult to modify the algorithm so that it uses only a *finite* number of registers (Problem 3.20). We note that a study of unbounded concurrency is mainly of theoretical interest; however, it has some practical value as well, since it covers the important case where the number of processes is finite but is not known *a priori*.

3.2.3 An Adaptive Tournament Algorithm

In a (non-adaptive) tournament algorithm each process enters the tournament tree through a designated leaf node, and in order to enter its critical section, a process has to traverse a path from a leaf to the root. There are at least $\log n$

nodes on some path from a leaf to the root, and hence the complexity of any such algorithm is $\Omega(\log n)$ under any reasonable definition of time complexity. Below we show how to overcome this limitation. The basic idea is rather simple; its implementation using bounded number of atomic registers is not.

The main idea

First, the performance of the tournament algorithm is slightly improved as follows: the processes are organized into a binary tree, where each (internal and leaf) node in the tree is "owned" by a single predetermined process. Each process, instead of entering the tournament tree through a designated leaf node, enters the tree through the unique node it "owns".

The decision which node is owned by which process is done as follows. The processes are numbered 1 through n, and the following numbering scheme is used for the nodes of the tree: the root is numbered 1, and for each node i, the left child of i is numbered $2 \cdot i$, while the right child is numbered $2 \cdot i + 1$ (see Figure 2.3, page 40). Using this numbering, each node $i \in \{1, \ldots, n\}$ is owned by process i.

To make it work, the binary tournament tree is defined by associating a *three-process* mutual exclusion algorithm with each node. A process i competes within the tournament tree by competing in each node on the pass from node i to the root. A node entry section may be invoked by the process that owns that node, and one process from the left and right subtrees beneath that node. This is why a three process algorithm is needed at each node. For later reference, we call such a tournament tree a *three-based tree*.

The above algorithm, although it improves on the original tournament algorithm, is not yet adaptive. Most of the processes own nodes that are far away from the root. So here is the basic idea of how to make this algorithm adaptive: Nodes in the *three-based tree* are not owned by a single *predetermined* process. Instead, each process that is interested in competing initially participates in an (adaptive) *renaming* algorithm in which it is assigned a new temporary name, from the range 1 through k where k is a constant multiple of the contention that the process experiences. The process then uses the new name as its entry point into the tree. That is, a process with a new name v enters the tree through node v. All this guarantees that the length of the path taken by a process is at most a constant multiple of the point contention that the process experiences and hence the resulting algorithm is adaptive. See Figure 3.5.

A description of the algorithm

Two groups have independently presented adaptive tournament algorithms based on the above idea. J. H. Anderson and Y.-H. Kim (2000) have presented an algorithm with $O(\min(k, \log n))$ time complexity in the DSM model where k is the point contention, while Y. Afek, G. Stupp, and D. Touitou (2002) independently devised an algorithm with very similar structure with $O(\min(k^2, k \log n))$ time complexity in the DSM model, where k is the interval contention. As the algorithm of Anderson and Kim is more efficient, we describe it next.

The main data structure used by the renaming algorithm is called the *renaming tree*. The renaming tree is built out of splitter elements. The splitter elements used are a modified version of the MA-splitters introduced on page 106 of the previous

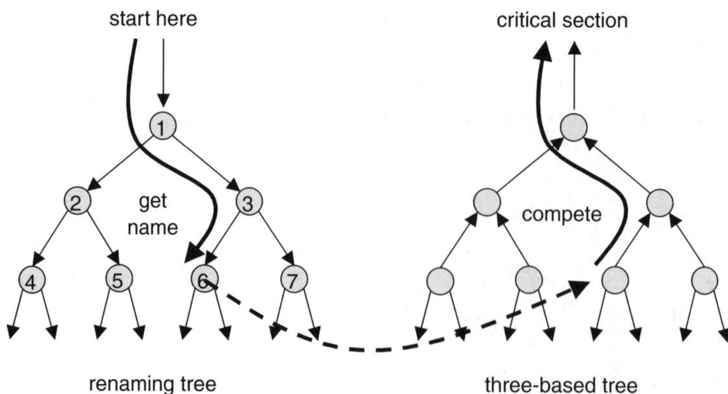

Figure 3.5 A renaming tree is constructed by assigning a splitter to each node of a binary tree. A three-based tree is constructed by assigning a 3-process mutex to each node of a binary tree. When a process wins at a node of the renaming tree, it enters the three-based tree at exactly the same position.

section (see Figure 3.2). These splitters, which have a slightly more complicated implementation than that of the MA-splitters, satisfy all the properties of the MA-splitters as stated in Lemma 3.1 (page 106), and in addition can be repeatedly acquired and released.

A process acquires a splitter when it *wins* at that splitter. A process releases a splitter that it has acquired by resetting some of the splitter's registers so that the splitter can be acquired again by some process. Both acquiring and releasing a splitter requires only O(1) memory accesses. The *renaming tree* is constructed by assigning a splitter to each node of a binary tree. For convenience, we will refer to the three directions associated with a splitter as *win*, *left*, and *right*, instead of the usual *win*, *down*, and *right*, respectively.

The numbering scheme that is used for the nodes of the renaming tree is similar to that of the three-based tree. (i.e., the root is numbered 1, and for each node i, the left child of i is numbered $2 \cdot i$, while the right child is numbered $2 \cdot i + 1$.)

We are now ready to describe the basic steps a process performs in the adaptive tournament algorithm. The algorithm uses three main data structures: (1) a *renaming tree*, (2) a *three-based tree*, and (3) a binary tournament tree called the *overflow tree*.

1. *Acquiring a name*: A process first acquires a new name by moving down from the root of the renaming tree, until it wins at some node. We notice that if contention is k, a process can descend at most $k - 1$ levels in the renaming tree, before it *wins* at some node. The number of that node at which the process wins is the process' new name.
2. *Competing in the three-based tree*: When a process wins at a node of the renaming tree, it enters the three-based tree at exactly the same position. A process with new name v competes within the three-based tree by competing in each node on the pass from node v to the root. See Figure 3.5.

3. *Critical section*: After a process wins at the root of the three-based tree, the process executes its critical section.
4. *Releasing a name*: Upon completing its critical section, the process executes its exit code. First, it releases its acquired name by releasing all of the splitters, in the renaming tree, on the path from the root to the node at which it has won.
5. *Exiting the three-based tree*: After releasing its name, the process executes each of the three-process exit sections, in the three-based tree, on the pass from the root to the node at which it has entered the tree.

We notice that in Step 1, a process wins at a node at a depth less than or equal to k, where k is the contention that the process experiences. In Step 2, the process uses the new name as its entry point into the three-based tree. All this guarantees that the length of the path taken by a process is at most a constant multiple of the point contention that the process experiences and hence the resulting algorithm has an $O(k)$ time complexity.

Unfortunately, the renaming tree may need n levels. In the worst case, all n processes may be active. However, with n levels, the tree will have $O(2^n)$ nodes which is obviously not acceptable. To reduce space complexity, we limit the height of the renaming tree to $\log n$. With a tree of this height, a process could "fall off" the end of the tree without acquiring a name. This can happen only if contention is at least $\log n$.

To handle the processes that "fall off" the end of the tree, an additional tournament tree with depth $\log n$ (and n leafs), called the *overflow tree*, is used. The overflow tree is implemented using the local spinning tournament algorithm which is described in Section 3.1.3 (page 101). (Any tournament algorithm, which is made of regular two-process mutual exclusion algorithms, will do if local spinning is not an issue.) If a process "falls off" the end of the renaming tree, it enters the overflow tree, through a designated *leaf* node using its original process id, and in order to enter its critical section, it traverses a path from the leaf to the root. The three-based tree and the overflow tree are combined by placing a two process mutual exclusion algorithm on top of each tree, as illustrated in Figure 3.6.

If contention is less than $\log n$, a process wins in some node of the renaming tree, and takes $O(k)$ time to reach the root and enter its critical section. If contention is higher than $\log n$, a process may go to the overflow tree, and in such a case it will take $O(\log n)$ time for it to enter its critical section. Thus the total number of remote memory references is $O(\min(k, \log n))$.

To preserve local spinning the two process algorithm that combines the two trees, and all the three process algorithms used in the construction of the three-based tree algorithm are all versions of the local spinning tournament algorithm from Section 3.1.3 (page 101) restricted for two and for three processes.

The Algorithm

We point out that the most challenging problem in implementing the algorithm has to do with the need to modify the MA-splitter so that it also supports a release operation. This problem is resolved by exploiting the fact that releasing can be done inside a critical section.

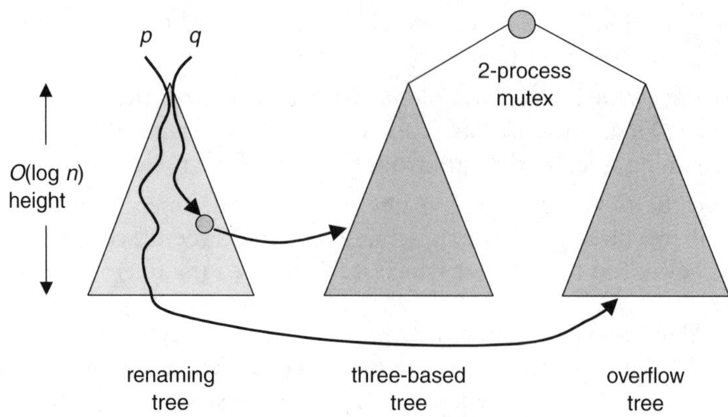

Figure 3.6 Process p fails to get a name and competes within the overflow tree. Process q get a name and competes within the three-based tree. The two trees are combined by a two process mutual exclusion algorithm.

Each (modified) splitter m supports three operations: (1) *AcquireNode*(m) which returns *win*, *left*, or *right*; (2) *ReleaseNode*(m, *dir*) which is invoked by process p in its exit code, only if p has invoked *AcquireNode*(m) in its entry section and the return value was *dir*; and (3) *ClearNode*(m) which is invoked by process p in its exit code, only if p has invoked *AcquireNode*(m) in its entry section and the return value was *win*. The complete code of the algorithm of Anderson and Kim is given below.

AN ADAPTIVE TOURNAMENT ALGORITHM: Process i's program, $0 \le i \le n$.

```
constants
    L = ⌊log n⌋                                  /* depth of the renaming tree */
    T = 2^(L+1) − 1                                 /* size of renaming tree */
type
    Ytype: record {free: boolean, rnd: 0..n − 1}                /* one word */
    Dtype: (left, right, win)                         /* splitter directions */
    Ptype: record {node: 1..2T + 1, dir: Dtype}             /* path info. */
shared
    X: array[1..T] of 0..N − 1
    Y,Reset: array[1..T] of Ytype, initially (true, 0)
    Round: array[1..T][0..n − 1] of boolean, initially false
    Obstacle: array[0..n − 1] of 0..T, initially 0
    Acquired: array[0..T] of boolean, initially false
local
    node: 1..2T + 1;  level,j: 0..L + 1;  dir: Dtype;  m : 1..T;  y : Ttype;
    path: array[0..L] of Ptype

node := 1; level := 0
repeat                                              /* searching for name */
```

```
    dir := AcquireNode(node)
    path[level] := (node, dir)
    if dir = left then level := level + 1; node := 2 · node
    elseif dir = right then level := level + 1; node := 2 · node + 1 fi
until (level > L) or (dir = win)
if level ≤ L then                                     /* got a name */
    for j := level downto 0 do          /* compete three-based tree */
        ENTRY_3(path[j].node,path[j].dir) od
    ENTRY_2(0)                      /* compete in 2-process mutex */
else                                           /* did not get a name */
    ENTRY_n(i)                          /* compete in overflow tree */
    ENTRY_2(1) fi                   /* compete in 2-process mutex */
fi                                            /* has reached the top */
critical section
for j := min(level,L) downto 0 do                  /* reset splitters */
    m := path[j].node, dir := path[j].dir
    ReleaseNode(m, dir) od
if level ≤ L then                        /* execute exit sections */
    EXIT_2(0)                            /* exit the 2-process mutex */
    for j := 0 downto level do           /* exit three-based tree */
        EXIT_3(path[j].node; path[j].dir) od
    ClearNode(node)
else
    EXIT_2(1)                            /* exit the 2-process mutex */
    EXIT_n(i)                              /* exit the overflow tree */
fi
```

```
function AcquireNode(m : 1..T): Dtype
X[m] := i
y := Y[m]
if y.free = false then return right fi
Y[m] := (false, 0)
Obstacle[i] := m
if X[m] ≠ i or Acquire[m] then return left fi
Round[m][y.rnd] := true
if Reset[m] ≠ y then Round[m][y.rnd] := false; return left fi
Acquired[m] := true
return win
```

```
procedure ReleaseNode(m: 1..T, dir: Dtype)
Obstacle[i] := 0
if dir = right then return fi
Y[m] := (false, 0)
X[m] := i
y := Reset[m]
Reset[m] := (false, y.rnd)
```

```
if (dir = win or Round[m][y.rnd] = false) and Obstacle[y.rnd] ≠ n
then Reset[m] := (true, y.rnd + 1 mod n);
        Y[m] := (true, y.rnd + 1 mod n) fi
if dir = win then Round[m][y.rnd] = false fi

procedure ReleaseNode(m : 1..T)
Acquired[m] := false
```

Each of the three-process entry sections of the nodes of the three-based tree is denoted $ENTRY_3(m, dir)$, where m is the corresponding node, and *dir* is direction returned when the process invoked *AcquireNode*(m), trying to acquire node m in the renaming tree.

The entry section of the overflow tree is denoted $ENTRY_n(i)$, where $i \in \{0, \ldots, n-1\}$ is the identity of the invoking process. The entry section of the two process algorithm which combines the three-based tree and the overflow tree is denoted $ENTRY_2(b)$, where $b \in \{0, 1\}$. The value of b is 0, when the invoking process arrives from the three-based tree, and it is 1 when the invoking process arrives from the overflow tree. The exit sections are specified similarly.

Properties of the algorithm:

- Satisfies mutual exclusion and starvation-freedom.
- It is adaptive w.r.t. time complexity in both the CC model and the DSM model.
- Its time complexity in both the CC model and the DSM model is $O(\min(k, \log n))$, where k is point contention.
- It uses $O(n^2)$ bounded size atomic registers, due to the *Round* array. The array can be replaced by an $O(n)$ linked list.

3.2.4 The Adaptive Black-White Bakery Algorithm

We present an adaptive version, due to G. Taubenfeld (2004), of the Black-White Bakery algorithm. To do so we use a general technique, invented by Y. Afek, G. Stupp, and D. Touitou (1999), and transform the Black-White Bakery algorithm (page 55) into its corresponding adaptive version. That is, the time complexity of the algorithm is a function of the actual number of contending processes rather than a function of the total number of processes.

An Active Set Object

The transformation makes use of a new shared object, called *active set*, which is defined as follows:

Active set: *An active set S object supports the following operations:*

- `join(S)`*: which adds the id of the executing process to the set S. That is, when process i executes this operation the effect is to execute,* $S := S \cup \{i\}$.
- `leave(S)`*: which removes the id of the executing process from the set S. That is, when process i executes this operation the effect is to execute,* $S := S - \{i\}$.

- `getset(S)`: *which returns the current set of active processes. More formally, the following two conditions must be satisfied,*
  - *the set returned includes all the processes that have finished their last* `join(S)` *before the current* `getset(S)` *has started, and did not start* `leave(S)` *in the time interval between their last* `join(S)` *and the end of the current* `getset(S)`.
  - *the set returned does not include all the processes that have finished their last* `leave(S)` *before the current* `getset(S)` *has started, and did not start* `join(S)` *in the time interval between their last* `leave(S)` *and the end of the current* `getset(S)`.

Afek *et al.* in 1999 have presented an implementation of the active set object which is wait-free, adaptive (in both the CC and the DSM models), and uses only a bounded number of bounded size atomic registers. Notice that wait-freedom implies local spinning, as a wait-free implementation must also be spinning-free. They have also shown how to transform the Bakery algorithm (page 50) into its corresponding adaptive version using the adaptive implementation of the active set object. We use below the same transformation to make the Black-White Bakery algorithms adaptive.

All the known adaptive wait-free implementations of an active set object are rather complicated and cumbersome. Hence, we avoid presenting an implementation of an active set object here, and hope that in the future a simple, short, and elegant implementation will be discovered. (See Problem 3.36.)

The Algorithm

Next, we transform the Black-White Bakery algorithm into its corresponding adaptive version. The basic idea is to use an active set object in order to identify the active processes and then to ignore the other processes. This keeps the time complexity a function of the number of active processes. The code of the algorithm is shown below.

THE ADAPTIVE BLACK-WHITE BAKERY ALGORITHM: `process` i`'s program.`

shared

S: adaptive active set, initially $S = \emptyset$
color: a bit of type $\{black, white\}$
choosing[1..*n*]: boolean array
(*mycolor*,*number*)[1..*n*]: array of type $\{black, white\} \times \{0, \ldots, n\}$
Initially $\forall i : 1 \leq i \leq n : choosing_i = false$ and $number_i = 0$,
the initial values of all the other variables are immaterial.

`/* beginning of doorway */`

$join(S)$ `/*` $S := S \cup \{i\}$ `*/`
$choosing_i := true$
$localS := getset(S) - \{i\}$ `/* reads S into local variable */`
$mycolor_i := color$

```
number_i := 1 + max({number_j | [(j ∈ localS)] ∧ (mycolor_j = mycolor_i)})
choosing_i := false
[localS := getset(S) − {i}]        /* reads S into local variable */
                                   /* end of doorway */
[for every j ∈ localS do]
    await choosing_j = false
    if mycolor_j = mycolor_i
    then await  (number_j = 0) ∨ ([number_j, j] ≥ [number_i, i]) ∨
                (mycolor_j ≠ mycolor_i)
    else await  (number_j = 0) ∨ (mycolor_i ≠ color) ∨
                (mycolor_j = mycolor_i) fi
od
critical section
if mycolor_i = black then color := white else color := black fi
number_i := 0
[leave(S)]                         /* S := S − {i} */
```

For computing the maximum, we assume that a process first reads into local memory *only* the tickets of processes in S, one at a time atomically, and then computes the maximum over numbers of the tickets with the same color as its own. The algorithm is adaptive w.r.t. time complexity in the CC model, where spinning on a variable while its value does not change is counted only as one operation (i.e., only remote un-cached accesses are counted).

Properties of the algorithm:

- Satisfies mutual exclusion, deadlock-freedom, and FIFO fairness.
- It is adaptive w.r.t. time complexity in the CC model, and it satisfies local spinning in the CC model.
- It is not adaptive w.r.t. time complexity in the DSM model, and it does not satisfy local spinning in the DSM model. This is due to the fact that two processes may spin on the same shared registers.
- Only a finite number of bounded size registers are used.

The above properties are easily proved, given the correctness of the original Black-White Bakery algorithm.

The time complexity of the algorithm in the CC model is dominated by the complexity of implementing the active set, and is $O(\max(k, comp.S))$, where k is the point contention and *comp.S* is the step complexity of the active set. The best known time complexity for implementing an active set is $O(k^2)$. Thus, using this implementation, the time complexity of the algorithm is $O(k^2)$ in the CC model, where k is the point contention.

Since the algorithm does not satisfy local spinning in the DSM model, its time complexity in the DSM model is unbounded. However, using the technique presented above, it is rather easy to transform the *local spinning* Black-White

Bakery algorithm (from page 100) into its corresponding local spinning *adaptive* version (Problem 3.24).

3.2.5 An Impossibility Result

The result presented in this section was proved by R. Alur and G. Taubenfeld (1992). As mentioned, a natural question to ask is whether Lamport's fast algorithm can be modified to provide a constant "process time complexity" also in the case where there is contention of only two processes? Here we give a negative answer to this question.

We show that for any mutual exclusion algorithm, whenever there is contention of two or more processes, there is no bound, not even as a function of the total number of processes, on the number of steps taken by the winning process. That is, in presence of contention the adversary can schedule the contending processes in such a way that each one of them will have to busy-wait. Recall that an *await* statement may lead to many accesses to the shared memory.

Theorem 3.4 *There is no two (or more) process mutual exclusion algorithm, with an upper bound on the number of times a winning process may need to access the shared memory in order to enter its critical section in presence of contention.*

Proof: Let M be an arbitrary two process mutual exclusion algorithm. Let the two processes be p_1 and p_2. The *execution tree* T_M of M is a binary tree whose nodes correspond to the global states of the algorithm. The tree is defined by the following rules:

- The root of T_M is the initial state where both processes are at the beginning of their entry code and have not taken any steps yet.
- The left child of a node is the state resulting from a step by p_1.
- The right child of a node is the state resulting from a step by p_2.
- A node is a leaf if and only if one of the processes is in its critical section at this node.

Thus, the tree T_M reflects all possible behaviors of the algorithm M up to the point where some process (for the first time) enters its critical section.

We label the nodes of T_M by either 1, 2 or both according to the following rules:

1. A leaf v is labeled by $i \in \{1,2\}$ if and only if p_i is in its critical section in v.
2. An internal node is labeled by the labels of both its children.

Thus an internal node v is labeled by $i \in \{1,2\}$ if and only if there is a path from v to a leaf labeled by i. Clearly, the root is labeled by both 1 and 2, and since we assume deadlock-freedom, every node is labeled by at least one identifier.

Notice that, by definition, if there is an infinite path where infinitely many nodes are labeled by $i \in \{1,2\}$ then all nodes in that path must be labeled by i (and possibly by the other identifier also).

Let v and v' be two nodes. We say that v and v' are *similar* with respect to process p_i, denoted by $v\langle p_i\rangle v'$, if and only if (1) the subsequence of events by p_i along the path from the root to v and the subsequence of events by p_i along the path from the root to v' are exactly the same, and (2) both v and v' assign the same values to all the shared registers and all the local registers of p_i.

In order to prove the theorem it suffices to show that for every $n > 0$ there exists a leaf v labeled by $i \in \{1,2\}$ such that the path from the root to v has more then n steps by process p_i.

Suppose that, for some $i \in \{1,2\}$, there is an infinite path, say ρ, containing infinitely many nodes labeled by i and containing infinitely many steps by p_i. Then, for any given n, we can find a prefix of ρ in which process p_i takes more than n steps, and extend this prefix to a leaf labeled by i. This gives a path that contains more then n steps by the winning process p_i, and we are done. So, let us assume that there is no such path ρ, and for later reference let us call this assumption, assumption A.

Assumption A, and the fact that not all the leaves are labeled the same, implies that:

> There is a node v such that (1) v is labeled by both 1 and 2, and (2) one of its children is labeled only by 1 and the other child is labeled only by 2.

Let v_1 be the left child of v, and let v_2 be the right child of v. There are two possible cases depending on which of v_1 and v_2 is labeled by 1 and which is labeled by 2. We now show that both cases lead to a contradiction and hence prove the theorem. We denote by e_i the event by p_i that leads from v to v_i. Let v_{12} be the right child of v_1, and let v_{21} be the left child of v_2.

Case 1: *The left child v_1 is labeled only by 1, and the right child v_2 is labeled only by 2:*

This situation is depicted in Figure 3.7. It follows from assumption A that: (1) The left most path starting from v_1, where only process p_1 takes steps, is finite, and ends with a leaf in which process p_1 is in its critical section; let ρ_1 be the sequence of events (edges) in this path. (2) The right most path starting from v_2, where only process p_2 takes steps, is finite, and ends with a node in which process p_2 is in its critical section; let ρ_2 be the sequence of events in this path.

We will consider several subcases depending on the nature of the events e_1 and e_2, and derive contradiction in each case.

- *e_1 is a read event*: The values of all the shared registers are the same in both v and v_1. Thus $v\langle p_2\rangle v_1$, and hence $v_2\langle p_2\rangle v_{12}$. Since ρ_2 involves events only by process p_2, and leads from v_2 to some leaf labeled by 2, ρ_2 also leads from v_{12} to some leaf labeled by 2. Hence v_{12} is labeled by 2, a contradiction to the assumption that v_1 is labeled only by 1.
- *e_2 is a read event*: Similar to above.
- *Both e_1 and e_2 are write events into different registers*: Then $v_{21}\langle p_2\rangle v_{12}$. Since ρ_2, leads from v_2 to some leaf which is labeled by 2, it also leads from v_{12} to

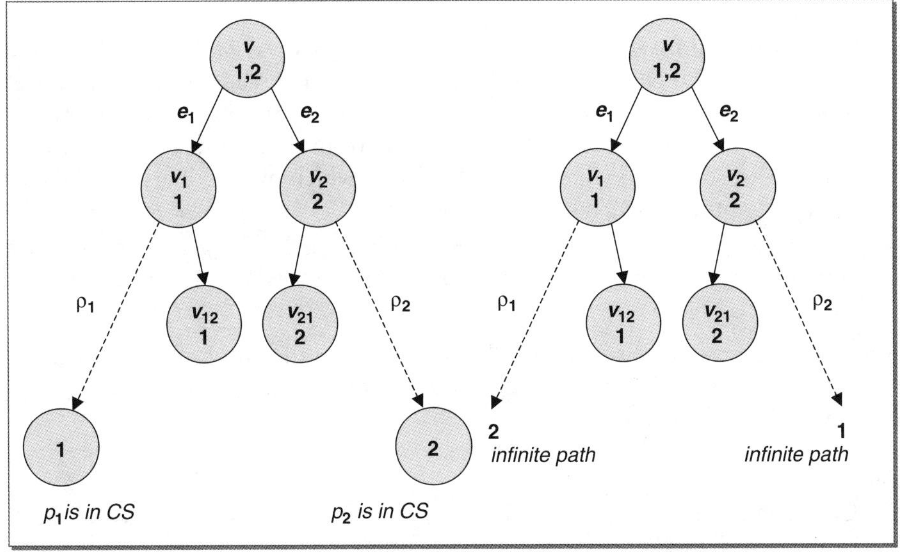

Figure 3.7 The left tree describes the situation in Case 1, while the right tree describes the situation in Case 2.

some leaf which is labeled by 2. Hence v_{12} is labeled by 2, and not just by 1, a contradiction.

- *Both e_1 and e_2 are write events into the same register*: We obtain a contradiction using exactly the same argument as for the case when e_1 is a read event.

Case 2: *The left child v_1 is labeled only by 2, and the right child v_2 is labeled only by 1:*

This situation is depicted in Figure 3.7. Since v is labeled by both 1 and 2, and e_1 is an event by process p_1, process p_2 is not in its critical section in v_1, and since v_1 is labeled only by 2, v_1 is not a leaf. Any path from v_1 to some leaf must involve an event by process p_2. Hence, the left most path starting from v_1, where only process p_1 takes steps, is infinite. Let ρ_1 be the sequence of events in this path. Using a similar argument (exchanging 1 and 2) we get that the right most path starting from v_2, where only process p_2 takes steps, is also infinite. Let ρ_2 be the sequence of events in this path.

Observe that v_{12} must be labeled only by 2, and v_{21} must be labeled only by 1. We obtain a contradiction by doing a case analysis on the nature of the events e_1 and e_2:

- *e_1 is a read event*: In this case, $v_2\langle p_2\rangle v_{12}$. Since ρ_2 involves events only by process p_2, and is executable from v_2, it is also executable from v_{12}. Since v_{12} is labeled only by 2, it means that there is an infinite path starting from v_{12} where all nodes are labeled by 2 and where only process p_2 takes steps; however, this contradicts assumption A.

- *e_2 is a read event*: Similar to above.
- *Both e_1 and e_2 are write events into different registers*: Then $v_{21}\langle p_2\rangle v_{12}$, and also $v_{21}\langle p_1\rangle v_{12}$. Let ρ_{21} be a sequence of events that leads from v_{21} to a leaf which is labeled by 1. Since v_{21} and v_{12} are similar for both processes and ρ_{21} is executable from v_{21}, it is also executable from v_{12}. Hence, there is a path from v_{12} to some leaf which is labeled by 1, which means that v_{12} is labeled by 1, and not just by 2, a contradiction.
- *Both e_1 and e_2 are write events into the same register*: We get a contradiction using exactly the same argument as for the case where e_1 is a read event. ∎

Remark: An important result that follows easily from the proof of Theorem 3.4 is that: *there is no wait-free election algorithm* (see Problem 3.27 and Problem 10.31 on pages 140 and 371).

Self Review

1. Consider the following statement: A deadlock-free mutual exclusion algorithm, say M, is *adaptive* with respect to time complexity measure ψ assuming *interval contention*, if and only if M is *adaptive* with respect to ψ assuming *point contention*. Is this statement correct assuming ψ is: (a) process time complexity; (b) system response time; (c) process response time. What would be the answer if M is starvation-free?
2. We have pointed out that the adaptive algorithm (on page 108) works even when assuming unbounded concurrency. Does the algorithm work assuming infinite concurrency? That is, does it work assuming that the number of processes that are *simultaneously* active can be infinite.
3. In the adaptive tournament algorithm the height of the renaming and three-based trees is $O(\log n)$. See Figure 3.6 (page 114). Let's assume that we change the height of these two trees to $O(\log n/\log\log n)$ (and keep the height of the overflow tree $O(\log n)$). Would this change improve the time complexity of the algorithm?
4. What properties would the adaptive Black-White Bakery algorithm not satisfy if we omit line 7.

Answers: (1) Yes, yes, no. Same when M is starvation-free. (2) No. (3) No. The time complexity would be $O(k)$ when k is at most $O(\log n/\log\log n)$ and $O(\log n)$ otherwise. (4) It would not satisfy mutual exclusion.

3.3 Fault-tolerant Algorithms

In this section we consider algorithms that are immune to some type of *process failures*, where a process may repeatedly fail and restart. Informally, a process fails by returning to the remainder code and resetting all the registers for which it has write access to their predefined default values. This means that registers which may be written by more than one process can not be used, since one of the processes that has the write permission may fail and "take the shared register with it". Thus, in this section we assume that only *single-writer* registers may be used. That is, each register has a process which "owns" it, and each process may write only the registers it owns, but may read registers owned by other processes.

The assumption that a failure involves setting the values of some registers is essential. Otherwise, since there is no way to distinguish between a process that failed and one that is running very slow, no fault-tolerant solution exists for completely asynchronous systems; a process can fail in its critical section leaving the system deadlocked. It is not so realistic to assume that when a process fails it will have time to reset its registers. However, there might be a way for one process to detect that some other process is faulty, and in such a case it does not have to try to actually read the other process' registers, but instead uses their default values.

As already mentioned, algorithms that use only single-writer registers can be easily implemented in a message passing network. A read can be implemented as a message sent from the process which is doing the read to the process which owns the register, which in turn replies with a message giving the value of its register or a message indicating that it has failed. If a process does not receive a response to a read request within some reasonable length of time, then it may assume that the other process has failed and may use the default value.

3.3.1 Defining Fault-tolerance

We define two types of process failures:

- An *immediate failure* of a process p means that the program counter of p is set to point to its remainder code, and the values of the registers it owns are immediately set to their default values.
- A *continuous failure* of a process p means that the program counter of p is set to point to its remainder code, and the values of the registers it owns may assume arbitrary values for a period of time, but eventually must be set to their default values (until p is restarted).

Thus, during a continuous failure of a process, reading its memory may yield any arbitrary values. However, eventually the process reaches a quiescent state in which its registers assume some default value.

A process may fail at any point in its program, and may resume its execution later. In the case of a continuous failure, a process may resume execution only after all its registers are set to their default values. For the rest of the section the default value of a register is going to be the same as its initial value. Next we define what it means for a process to tolerate faults.

Fault-tolerance: *An algorithm satisfies a given property in the presence of m failures, if the algorithm satisfies the property for all correct processes, as long as no more than m failures occur.*

The property may be mutual exclusion, deadlock-freedom, starvation-freedom, linear-waiting, etc. In particular, an algorithm satisfies mutual exclusion or deadlock-freedom in the presence of an infinite number of failures, if a process can not cause deadlock (of the correct processes) by repeatedly failing and restarting.

We have already pointed out that the One-bit algorithm (page 64) and the Bakery algorithm (page 50) can tolerate a finite number of failures. The One-bit algorithm satisfies mutual exclusion and deadlock-freedom in the presence of any *finite* number of continuous failures. The Bakery algorithm satisfies mutual exclusion, deadlock-freedom, and the first-come-first-served property in the presence of any *finite* number of continuous failures. However, both algorithms may deadlock in the case of an infinite number of immediate failures. For example, in the Bakery algorithm, if some process j continually fails and restarts, then all other processes could always find $choosing[j] = false$, and wait forever in statement 5.

It follows from Proposition 2.7 (page 46), that in any algorithm which can tolerate even one immediate failure, the number of different shared registers a process has to access in its entry code in order to enter its critical section in the absence of contention is at least n. This implies an $n+1$ lower bound on the contention-free time complexity of any such algorithm. We also make the following simple observation.

Proposition 3.5 *There does not exist a deadlock-free mutual exclusion algorithm which can tolerate an infinite number of continuous failures.*

Proof: If continuous failures are possible, a process that repeatedly fails and restarts can have a random value in the registers it owns, whenever some other process is reading them. These random values may always indicate to the reader that the (faulty) process is in its critical section preventing other processes from ever entering their critical sections. ∎

3.3.2 A Fault-tolerant Algorithm

The algorithm presented now, which is due to Howard P. Katseff (1978), satisfies the first-come-first-served property even in the presence of an infinite number of immediate failures. That is, there is a statement, called the doorway, in the entry code of each process such that whenever process i executes this statement, any process which later begin its entry code will execute its critical section after process i does (unless i fails). The algorithm uses only constant size registers.

The Basic Ideas

We start by describing a mechanism, due to Peterson and Fischer (1977), which ensures that the processes are served on a first-come-first-served basis. While it does not correctly solve the problem, it helps to introduce the key ideas of the actual solution.

When a process wishes to enter its critical section, it first examines the status of the other processes and makes a list, called the *behind-of list*, of those which already passed through their doorways. Before entering its critical section, a process waits until each process in its behind-of list either completes its critical section or fails. Consider the following (incorrect) attempt at solving the problem:

```
1 Build a behind-of list of those processes j with waiting[j] = 1;
2 waiting[i] := 1;
3 repeat
     Remove from the behind-of list those processes j with waiting[i] = 0
  until the list is empty;
4 critical section;
5 waiting[i] := 0;
```

Step 2 is the doorway. After process i passes through its doorway, all other processes will place it on their behind-of list and will be suspended until i executes its critical section. However, this solution satisfies neither mutual exclusion nor deadlock-freedom.

How can two processes be in their critical sections at the same time? Suppose we have a system with only two processes. These processes can simultaneously execute step 1. They will both have empty behind-of lists and thus can both proceed through steps 2 and 3 and enter their critical sections.

This problem can be corrected by placing the following code, adapted from Eisenberg–McGuire's algorithm (Problem 2.59), between steps 3 and 4.

```
L0: flag[i] := 1;
L1: for j := 1 to i − 1 do
         if flag[j] ≠ 0 then goto L1 fi od;
    flag[i] := 2;
    for j := 1 to n do
         if j ≠ i and flag[j] = 2 then goto L0 fi od;
```

The statement, *flag*[i] := 0; should also be added to step 5.

These lines of code guarantee that there is never more than one process in its critical section at any time. For example, consider the case where two processes simultaneously set their flag bits to 2. Each will notice that the other has done so, and will thus go back to *L0*. Now, only the lower numbered process will get past the loop at *L1* and go on through the second loop to its critical section.

We now look at the other problem: how can a deadlock occur? Suppose we have a two process system. The system can get in the following situation: Process 1 is in the loop of step 3 with process 2 in its behind-of list, and process 2 is executing its critical section. Now, process 2 can quickly exit its critical section and then start executing its entry code before process 1 has a chance to notice that process 2 has completed its critical section. Each process will be in the other's behind-of list, and hence both processes will not be able to proceed.

This problem can be corrected as follows. For every pair of processes i and j two 3-valued registers, called *count*[i, j] and *count*[j, i], are used. These registers are introduced to determine which process has last begun its entry code, and are initially set to 0. Values are assigned to these registers by inserting the following loop as the new first statement in the algorithm.

```
for j := 1 to n do count[i, j] := (count[j, i] mod 3) + 1 od;
```

Now, if $count[i, j] = (count[j, i] \bmod 3) + 1$ then process i entered its entry code after process j did. This is now used in step 3. Process i removes j from its behind-of list if $count[j, i] = (count[i, j] \bmod 3) + 1$ (or if $count[j, i] = 0$), because this means that j entered its code after i.

The Algorithm

Now that all the significant portions of the algorithm are explained, we get to put all the pieces together. The algorithm is for n processes each with unique identifier taken from the set $\{1, \ldots, n\}$. For every pair of processes i and j there is a 3-valued register, called $count[i, j]$, that i can write and j can read, and a register, called $count[j, i]$, that j can write and i can read. In addition for every process i, there are two bits, called *waiting*[i] and *flag*[i], which all the processes can read but only process i can write. All the registers are initialized to 0.

KATSEFF'S ALGORITHM: `process i's program.`

```
Initially: the values of all registers are 0.

    The first statement helps avoiding deadlock
    for j := 1 to n do count[i,j] := (count[j,i] mod 3) + 1 od;

    Build a behind-of list of processes that started
    earlier
    for j := 1 to n do local[j] := waiting[j] od;

    The last statement of the doorway
    waiting[i] := 1;

    Remove from the behind-of list processes that have
    been to their critical section, until the list is
    empty
    for j := 1 to n do
        if local[j] = 1 then
            await count[j,i] = 0 or count[j,i] = (count[i,j] mod 3) + 1
        fi
    od;
    The next few lines guarantee mutual exclusion
L0: flag[i] := 1;
L1: for j := 1 to i − 1 do
        if flag[j] ≠ 0 then goto L1 fi od;
    flag[i] := 2;
    for j := 1 to n do
        if j ≠ i and flag[j] = 2 then goto L0 fi od;
    critical section;
    flag[i] := 0; waiting := 0;
    for j := 1 to n do count[i,j] := 0 od;
```

We notice that the algorithm uses n^2 shared bits plus n 3-valued shared registers. The correctness of the algorithm has already been informally demonstrated through its development. We prove it formally.

Theorem 3.6 *Katseff's algorithm satisfies mutual exclusion, deadlock-freedom, and first-come-first-served in the presence of any (finite or infinite) number of immediate failures.*

Proof: First we prove that the algorithm satisfies the first-come-first-served property. The doorway statement (or the last statement of the doorway) is statement number 3. After process i passes through its doorway (that is, has set $waiting[i]$ to 1), any other process j that starts later will make the equality $count[j,i] = (count[i,j] \bmod 3) + 1$ *false* by executing statement 1, and will place process i on its behind-of list by executing statement 2. Thus, later process j will be suspended at statement 6, until i executes its critical section or fails.

Next we show that the algorithm is deadlock-free. If the algorithm is not deadlock-free, there must be an infinite run x in which from some point on some correct process is in its entry code and no process enters its critical section. Here, by correct process we mean a process that does not fail an infinite number of times in x. Since the registers of a faulty process are set to 0, x has a prefix where for some non-empty set of processes P, the processes in P are waiting for each other at statement 6. For this to happen it must be the case that for every $i \in P$ there is $j \in P$ such that $count[j,i] \neq (count[i,j] \bmod 3) + 1$. But this is clearly impossible.

Finally, we prove that the algorithm satisfies the mutual exclusion property. Assume that process i is in its critical section at run x. We need to show that no other process j can be in its critical section at x. Since process i is in its critical section in x, the last time i has checked $flag[j]$ (statement 14), it must have found that $flag[j] \neq 2$. At this point $flag[i] = 2$ and process j must have been before statement 12 (otherwise its flag would have been equal to 2). In order for j to enter its critical section, it must first check $flag[i]$. Hence, if j will check process i flag, it will find that $flag[i] = 2$, and will thus go back to *L0*. Now, process j will not be able to get past the loop at *L1*, until process i exits its critical section, and sets $flag[i]$ to 0. ∎

3.3.3 Self-stabilization

The concept of self-stabilization, due to E. W. Dijkstra (1974), refers to a system's ability to recover automatically from transient failures. A *transient failure* of a process means that the values of the shared registers it "owns" may assume arbitrary values for some time, while the process is faulty, but eventually the process recovers and resumes its normal behavior, starting in some arbitrary state. Notice that it is not required that a process which resumes its execution starts from its remainder, nor that its registers will be set to some default values.

After a transient failure, a process might resume its execution at a point where it is in its critical section, even though another process might be executing its critical section. Thus, after a transient failure has occurred, we can not expect that the system immediately resumes its normal behavior. The most we can hope for is that the system *eventually* resumes its normal behavior as long as no more failures occur.

No algorithm is deadlock-free in the presence of even one transient failure. A process may fail while in its critical section, and resume its execution in its remainder, staying there forever. Thus, the process will always appear to the other processes as if it is still in its critical section preventing other processes from entering their critical sections. In order to prevent such a deadlock situation, we will assume, for the rest of the section, that: every process executing its remainder code will eventually set its registers to their initial (default) values. We are now ready to introduce an important notion for fault-tolerance.

Self-stabilization: *An algorithm is self-stabilizing for a given property, if it guarantees that after any transient failure occurs, the property will eventually hold, assuming no more failures occur in the future.*

For properties like deadlock-freedom and starvation-freedom, requiring that these two properties eventually hold is the same as requiring that they hold now. Mutual exclusion and first-come-first-served properties eventually hold if they are violated only for a bounded length of time (i.e., bounded number of steps), after which they are required to hold forever.

None of the algorithms that we have presented so far is self-stabilizing for even deadlock-freedom. We now explain why the One-bit algorithm (page 64) is not self-stabilizing for mutual exclusion or deadlock-freedom. If all processes start at the await statement in line 4, with all the shared bits equal to *true* then the system is deadlocked. It is not self-stabilizing for mutual exclusion since some process, say i, could start in the for loop in line 8, with $b[i] = false$, execute there arbitrarily many steps, waiting as processes with higher identifiers repeatedly execute their critical sections, and then enter its critical section while another process is also in its critical section.

Lamport has showed that the One-bit algorithm can be made self-stabilizing for mutual exclusion or deadlock-freedom, by replacing the await statements (lines 4 and 8) with loops in which the value of $b[i]$ can be read and corrected if necessary. The modified algorithm, in which two statements are added to the original code of the One-bit algorithm, is given below.

THE MODIFIED ONE-BIT ALGORITHM: `process i's program.`

Initially: all entries in b are *false*.

```
repeat
     b[i] := true; j := 1;
     while (b[i] = true) and (j < i) do
          if b[j] = true then b[i] := false;
               repeat
                    if b[i] = true then b[i] := false fi
               until b[j] = false
```

```
            fi;
            j := j + 1
        od
until b[i] = true;
for j := i + 1 to n do
            repeat
                if b[i] = false then b[i] := true fi
            until b[j] = false
od;
critical section;
b[i] := false;
```

Theorem 3.7 *The modified version of the One-bit algorithm is self-stabilizing for mutual exclusion and deadlock-freedom.*

The reason why the original One-bit algorithm (page 64) is not self-stabilizing for mutual exclusion or deadlock-freedom is because, as a result of a fault, a process might be active with its bit set to the wrong value. The modified algorithm guarantees that every active process will always eventually check its bit and correct its value if necessary, and thus solves the problem.

Self Review

1. Is the following definition of self-stabilization equivalent to the one given on page 128? An algorithm is *self-stabilizing* for a given property, if the property eventually holds assuming that only a finite number of transient failures may occur.
2. Assume that you have built a tournament algorithm using the technique introduced in Section 2.2 (page 37) that is based on an algorithm for two processes which satisfies mutual exclusion and starvation-freedom in the presence of an infinite number of immediate failures. Does your tournament algorithm also satisfy mutual exclusion and starvation-freedom in the presence of an infinite number of immediate failures?

Answers: (1) No. (2) Yes.

3.4 Symmetric Algorithms

In the algorithms presented so far we have assumed that the identifiers of the processes are integers taken from the range $\{0, \ldots, n\}$. However, there may be situations when there are many more identifiers than processes. For example, there might be a small number of processes, say 100, but their identifiers can be taken from the range $\{0, \ldots, 2^{32}\}$. In such a case identifiers cannot be easily used to index registers, and hence it is better to use symmetric algorithms.

Symmetric algorithms: *A symmetric algorithm is an algorithm in which the only way of distinguishing processes is by comparing identifiers, which are unique.*

Identifiers can be written, read, and compared, but there is no way of looking inside any identifier. Thus, identifiers can not be used to index shared registers.

Two variants of symmetric algorithms can be defined depending on how much information can be derived from the comparison of two unequal identifiers.

- A *symmetric system with equality* can determine if two identifiers are the same or not, but if they are different then nothing else can be determined.
- A *symmetric system with arbitrary comparisons*, where a process can learn anything about identifiers if two unequal identifiers are compared. For example, comparisons can be defined that depend on a total order.

The symmetric algorithms presented in this section only use comparisons for equality. Furthermore, a process will only compare its own identifier with another. We point out that all the algorithms presented in previous sections, except for the adaptive algorithm for unknown number of processes from page 108, are not symmetric.

3.4.1 Symmetric Deadlock-free Algorithms

The following deadlock-free symmetric mutual exclusion algorithm was developed by E. Styer and G. L. Peterson (1989). The algorithm is for n processes each with unique identifier taken from some (possibly infinite) set which does not include 0. It make use of n shared registers which are long enough to store a process identifier.

Theorem 3.8 *There is a symmetric deadlock-free mutual exclusion algorithm for n processes which uses n atomic registers.*

The symmetric algorithm below matches the space lower bound (Theorem 2.16). Thus, n registers are necessary and sufficient for deadlock-free symmetric mutual exclusion. The algorithm uses a register called *turn* to indicate who has priority to enter the critical section, and $n - 1$ *lock* registers to ensure mutual exclusion. All the processes can read and write all the registers.

A SYMMETRIC DEADLOCK-FREE ALGORITHM: `process p's program.`

Initially: the values of all the registers are 0.

```
start: await(turn = 0);                 /* wait until cs is free */
       turn := p;
       repeat
           for j := 1 to n − 1 do        /* try to get all locks */
               if lock[j] = 0 then lock[j] := p fi od
           locked := true;
           for j := 1 to n − 1 do        /* do we have all locks? */
               if lock[j] ≠ p then locked := false fi od;
       until turn ≠ p or locked = true;
```

```
    if turn ≠ p then
        for j := 1 to n − 1 do           /* lost, release locks */
            if lock[j] = p then lock[j] := 0 fi od
        goto start fi;
    critical section;
    turn := 0;                             /* release all locks */
    for j := 1 to n − 1 do
        if lock[j] = p then lock[j] := 0 fi od;
```

A process, say p, initially waits until $turn = 0$. Then, process p takes priority by setting $turn$ to p, and attempts to obtain all the $n - 1$ locks by setting them to p. This prevents other processes that also saw $turn = 0$ and set $turn$ to themselves from entering. That is, if p is able to obtain all the locks before the other processes set $turn$, they will not be able to get any of the locks since they are not 0. Otherwise, if p sees $turn \neq p$, it will release the locks it holds, allowing some other process to proceed. On exiting the critical section, p sets $turn$ to 0, so the other processes can proceed, and releases all the locks it currently holds.

Properties of the algorithm:

- Satisfies mutual exclusion and deadlock-freedom.
- Starvation of individual processes is possible.
- It is symmetric with only comparisons for equality.
- n shared registers are used.

We now prove that the algorithm satisfies mutual exclusion and deadlock-freedom.

Theorem 3.9 *The algorithm satisfies mutual exclusion.*

Proof: Assume some process p is in its critical section. We show that no other process can enter its critical section before p exits. When process p last accessed $turn$ and the $n - 1$ locks, the value of each of these n shared registers was p. Any other process has to set all the $n - 1$ locks and see $turn$ set to its value for it to enter the critical section. But a process always checks a lock before writing it, and so can only change one lock which has been already set (and not released yet) by some other process. So if all the n shared registers have the value p, and each of the remaining $n - 1$ processes can overwrite at most one such register, at least one shared register must still hold the value p, preventing processes other than p from entering. ∎

Theorem 3.10 *The algorithm is deadlock-free.*

Proof: Assume to the contrary that at some point there is a deadlock. Since no process enters its critical section, $turn$ is not set to 0, and hence eventually $turn$ must have a non-zero value, say p, and this value will not change thereafter. Since the system is deadlock, every process other than p will eventually notice $turn = p$, it will release the locks it holds, will goto *start:* and not continue because *turn* is not zero. At this point, since process p always finds $turn = p$, nothing is preventing process p from getting all the locks and entering its critical section. Therefore the algorithm does not have a deadlock. ∎

3.4.2 Symmetric Starvation-free Algorithms

Next, we show how one can easily use the symmetric deadlock-free algorithm from the previous section to get a symmetric starvation-free algorithm.

The *symmetric process numbering* problem is to assign each of the n processes a number from 1 to n, given a symmetric initial state. (Once a process gets a number, it never attempts to get another number.) To solve the problem we can use the symmetric solution of the previous section. We assume that there is a shared register, called *counter*, which is initially 0. In order to get a number a process participates once in the symmetric deadlock-free algorithm; when it enters its critical section it increments the counter by 1, takes its value as its assigned number, and exits. The space complexity of this solution is n (not counting the counter). A more efficient solution, which uses only $2\lceil \log n \rceil + 1$ shared registers, is described in Problem 3.54, page 145. (The known lower bound is $\lceil \log n \rceil + 1$ registers, see Problem 3.52.)

Now we can easily construct a symmetric starvation-free mutual exclusion algorithm, by making a starvation-free mutual exclusion algorithm, say A, symmetric. Each process first participates in the symmetric process numbering algorithm to assign itself a number that will be used as its identifier from now on. Using this identifier the process can now participate in the (non-symmetric) algorithm A. Given that $2\lceil \log n \rceil + 1$ registers are sufficient for solving the symmetric process numbering problem, we get that:

Theorem 3.11 *There is a symmetric starvation-free mutual exclusion algorithm for n processes which uses $n + 2\lceil \log n \rceil + 1$ atomic registers.*

One disadvantage of the above solution is that it is not *memoryless*: a process has to have the ability to remember (also during the remainder region) a number from 1 to n (or to remember the knowledge that its process identifier remains constant). For memoryless systems, $2n + 1$ registers are necessary and sufficient for solving the symmetric starvation-free mutual exclusion problem (Problem 3.50).

3.4.3 Observations about Concurrency

In Section 2.5.1 it was shown that any deadlock-free mutual exclusion algorithm for n processes must use at least n shared registers. In proving this theorem we have used the fact that the n processes may all try to enter their critical sections simultaneously.

Now, let us assume that we know in advance that for some $k \leq n$, at any give time, at most k processes will ever try to enter their critical section simultaneously. What are the space bounds in such a case? From Theorem 2.16 it follows that k registers are necessary in such a case. Styer–Peterson's symmetric deadlock-free algorithm shows that k registers are also sufficient. This observation is formalized below.

We say that a mutual exclusion algorithm for n processes works assuming *k concurrency* if it is correct under the assumption that at most k processes may be outside their remainder sections at the same time. Notice that so far we have implicitly assumed that all algorithms for n processes work assuming n concurrency. The following lower bound follows immediately from Theorem 2.16.

Theorem 3.12 *Any algorithm for n processes assuming k concurrency that satisfies deadlock-freedom and mutual exclusion must use at least k shared registers.*

Next we observe that by the existence of Styer–Peterson's symmetric deadlock-free algorithm, this space bound is tight.

Theorem 3.13 *For any k, there is an algorithm for any number of processes assuming k concurrency that satisfies deadlock-freedom and mutual exclusion which uses k shared registers.*

Self Review

1. Can we replace statements 16 and 17 in the exit code of the symmetric algorithm (page 130) with the statement: **for** $j := 1$ **to** $n - 1$ **do** $lock[j] = 0$ **od**?
2. Can we move statement 15 in the exit code of the symmetric algorithm (page 130) to the end of the exit code (after statement 17)?

Answers: (1) No. (2) No.

3.5 Bibliographic Notes

3.1

Three important papers which have investigated local spinning are [39, 150, 254]. The various algorithms presented in these papers use strong synchronization primitives (i.e., stronger than atomic registers), and require only a constant number of remote accesses for each access to a critical section. Performance studies done in these papers have shown that local spinning algorithms scale well as contention increases. The algorithms from these three papers are presented in detail in Section 4.4 (page 160).

The first local spinning mutual exclusion algorithm using atomic registers was presented in [27]. The basic idea of Anderson's algorithm is described in Problem 3.12 (page 138). More efficient local spinning algorithms using only atomic registers are presented in [13, 27, 29, 323, 325, 340], and a local spinning algorithm using only non-atomic registers is presented in [31].

The local spinning Black-White Bakery algorithm (page 99), the first local spinning algorithm that satisfies FIFO fairness, is from [323]. The local spinning tournament algorithm presented on page 102 is from [340] (see also [32]). This tournament algorithm and a few other representative algorithms have been evaluated and compared in [345]. Another local spinning tournament algorithm is presented in [325]. The results about time complexity as stated in Problem 3.15 are from [31, 103] (see also [28, 340] for related issues). The results in Problems 3.16 and 3.31 are from [201].

3.2

The question whether there exists an adaptive mutual exclusion algorithm using atomic registers was first raised in [256], where an adaptive algorithm is presented for a given working system, which is useful provided process creation and deletions are rare. In [256], the term *contention sensitive* was used, but later the term *adaptive* become commonly used. In the literature, a local spinning and adaptive algorithm is sometimes called a *scalable* algorithm.

In [21], it is proven that the process time complexity of any deadlock-free mutual exclusion algorithm is unbounded (page 119). This result implies that no adaptive algorithm exists when time is measured by counting all accesses (local and remote) to shared registers.

The algorithm presented in Section 3.2.2 (page 108) which is adaptive w.r.t system response time is from [259]. The algorithm uses the MT-splitter as a building block, which in turn is based on the MA-splitter from [267]. Two papers have independently presented adaptive tournament algorithms. The adaptive algorithm presented in Section 3.2.3 (page 110) is from [29]. Another adaptive tournament algorithm with a very similar structure was independently devised in [13].

In [50, 97, 259] adaptive algorithms using atomic registers, which do not satisfy local spinning, are presented. In [13, 29], local spinning and adaptive algorithms are presented. None of these adaptive algorithms satisfies FIFO. In [323], a local spinning and adaptive algorithm which satisfies FIFO is presented.

In [12], the *active set* object is defined and an interesting technique for collecting information is introduced. This technique enables the transformation, in [12], of the Bakery algorithm [212] into its corresponding adaptive version. The resulting FIFO algorithm is adaptive but uses unbounded size registers. The adaptive Black-White Bakery algorithm (page 116), the first bounded-space adaptive algorithm that satisfies FIFO fairness, is from [323].

The step complexity of the wait-free implementation of the active set object from [12] is $O(k^4)$. A more efficient implementation exists which has only $O(k^2)$ step complexity [53, 183]. (This is an implementation of *collect* which is a stronger version of active set.) Thus, using this implementation, the time complexity of the adaptive Black-White Bakery algorithm is $O(k^2)$ for the CC model, where k is the point contention. The time complexity of the few known adaptive non-FIFO algorithms, and in particular the time complexity of [29], is better. This seems to be the price to be paid for satisfying the FIFO property.

The time complexity of the algorithm in [29] is $O(\min(k, \log n))$ for both the CC and DSM models, where k is point contention (this is also its system response time). The time complexity of the algorithm in [13] for both the CC and DSM models is $O(\min(k^2, k \log n))$; however, here k is interval contention (a weaker notion then point contention). The time complexity of the algorithm in [12] is $O(k^4)$ for the CC model, and since it does not satisfy local spinning its time complexity in the DSM model is unbounded. The time complexity of the algorithm in [97] for the CC model is $O(n)$; however, its system response time is $O(k)$. In [50], it is assumed that busy-waiting is counted as a single operation (even if the value of the lock changes several times while waiting). The step complexity of the algorithm in [50] is $O(k)$ and its system response time is $O(\log k)$. The system response time of the algorithm in [259] (which works for infinitely many processes) is $O(k)$.

The result stated in Problem 3.29 is from [31]. The results stated in Problems 3.30 and 3.24 are from [323]. The open problem mentioned in Problem 3.35 is from [32].

3.3

In fault-tolerant algorithms, processes are allowed to fail at any time, yet the algorithm must still function for the remaining processes. It is assumed that processes indicate their failure in a prescribed fashion, for example by setting some register to zero. See page 123 for the definition of immediate and continuous failures.

R. L. Rivest and V. R. Pratt have presented the first algorithm for n processes which can tolerate an infinite number of immediate failures. Their algorithm satisfies linear-waiting [299]. (The two process version of their algorithm is given on page 143.)

In [287], Peterson and Fischer presented an algorithm which is also immune to an infinite number of immediate failures and satisfies first-come-first-served. However, the doorway is not totally wait-free – a process may have to wait indefinitely before passing its doorway. (The two process version of their algorithm is given on page 78.)

Katseff's algorithm (page 126) is also immune to an infinite number of immediate failures. It serves processes on a first-come-first-served basis, and has a totally wait-free doorway. Katseff's algorithm uses n bits plus one 3-valued register per process [197].

Peterson has improved the space complexity of Katseff's algorithm, but his solution satisfies a weaker fairness requirement, and is more complicated. Peterson's algorithm uses just one 4-valued single-writer register per process, and satisfies 2-bounded-waiting [284]. It can be modified to use two bits per process. Peterson's fault-tolerant algorithm is presented on page 142. In [280], it is shown that there is no two process algorithm that is immune to an infinite number of failures which uses (a total of) two shared bits.

The One-bit algorithm (page 64) and the Bakery algorithm (page 50) are immune to any finite number of failures but can not tolerate an infinite number of failures. That is, a process which repeatedly fails and restarts may inhibit other processes from ever entering their critical sections.

The concept of self-stabilization is due to Dijkstra [110], where he has defined a system as self-stabilizing when "regardless of its initial state, it is guaranteed to arrive at a legitimate state in a finite number of steps." Our presentation of this notion (page 127) is adapted with some changes from [222]. The modified One-bit algorithm (page 128) is from [222]. There is an immense body of work on using self-stabilization as an approach for designing fault-tolerant systems. For a survey and a recent book on this topic see [304] and [117], respectively.

In [222], Lamport has studied fault-tolerant mutual exclusion algorithms and has defined the following notions. (See our definitions of immediate and continuous failures on page 123.) An algorithm is *shutdown-safe* for a property, if it satisfies that property as long as only immediate failures may occur, and after a process fails, it may not restart. An algorithm is *fail-safe* for a property, if it satisfies that property in the presence of a finite number of continuous failures. An algorithm is *abort-safe* for a property, if it satisfies that property in the presence of an infinite number of immediate failures. Notice that according to his terminology, Katseff's algorithm (page 126) is abort-safe for mutual exclusion and for first-come-first-served. Lamport has shown that the One-Bit Algorithm (page 64) is fail-safe for mutual exclusion and deadlock-freedom. He presented the Three-bit algorithm which is fail-safe and self-stabilizing (but not abort-safe) for mutual exclusion and starvation-freedom. He then presented a modification of Katseff's algorithm which works using safe registers, and further modified the algorithm so that it becomes also self-stabilizing (but requires $n!$ shared registers per process, and hence is of little practical interest).

3.4

The *symmetric* mutual exclusion problem adds the restriction that the only way of distinguishing processes is by comparing identifiers, which are unique (page 130). Burns proved that any symmetric solution is required to use at least one register which must be able to take on n values, and he also considered other possible definitions of symmetry [80].

In [316], Styer and Peterson have proved that n registers are necessary and sufficient for deadlock-free symmetric mutual exclusion (page 130), while $n + 2\lceil \log n \rceil + 1$ registers are sufficient for starvation-free symmetric mutual exclusion (page 132). In addition, they proved that $2n - 1$ registers are necessary and sufficient for *memoryless* starvation-free symmetric mutual exclusion [316] (Problem 3.50).

It is interesting to note that only $\lceil \log n \rceil + 1$ registers are necessary and sufficient for solving the "one-shot" mutual exclusion problem, also called the *election problem* [316] (Problems 3.51 and 3.52).

3.6 Problems

The problems are divided into several categories. See page 23 for a detailed explanation.

Problems based on Section 3.1

∘∘ 3.1 Explain why an algorithm that satisfies local spinning in the CC model (resp. DSM model) can have an unbounded time complexity in the CC model (resp. DSM model)?

∘∘ 3.2 What is the time complexity in the DSM model (see definition on page 16) of Kessels' single-writer algorithm for two processes (from page 35).

∘∘ 3.3 What is the time complexity in the DSM model (see definition on page 16) of each one of the three algorithms on page 69.

∘∘ 3.4 Consider a distributed shared memory machine which has support for cache coherence. Let *A* be an arbitrary algorithm that satisfies local spinning when executed on such a machine. Must *A* also satisfy local spinning in the DSM model or the CC model.

∘• 3.5 Reduce the space complexity of the local spinning Black-White Bakery algorithm (page 100), by letting each process spin on just two n-valued registers instead of using $2n$ spin bits per process.

∘ 3.6 Would the local spinning Black-White Bakery algorithm still be correct if we replace the order of line 4 and line 5?

∘∘ 3.7 In the tournament algorithm (page 102), at each level the nodes are numbered from left to right starting from 0. Assume that instead the following numbering scheme is used: the root is numbered 1, and for each node i, the left child of i is numbered $2 \cdot i$, while the right child is numbered $2 \cdot i + 1$ (see Figure 2.3, page 40). Modify the algorithm to reflect this change.

∘• 3.8 Modify Kessels' tournament algorithm from page 41 so that it satisfies local spinning in the DSM model.

∘• 3.9 Reduce the space complexity of the local spinning tournament algorithm (page 101) to $O(n)$ registers, by letting each process spin on the same flag register for all levels of the tree.

∘∘ 3.10 Systems with support for cache invalidation may perform significantly more remote memory references for some algorithms than systems with support for write-broadcast-update coherency, since write-broadcast-update coherency allows a process that releases a lock to update caches of other processes which are spinning locally *without* generating lots of traffic on the interconnection network between the processes and the memory. Explain how exactly the time complexity in the CC model of the local spinning Black-White Bakery algorithm (page 100) and the local spinning tournament algorithm (page 101) would be affected when these algorithms are executed on systems with support for write-broadcast-update coherency.

∘∘ 3.11 We have presented tournament algorithms, as a simple method that enables the construction of an algorithm for n processes from any given algorithm for two processes. Below we describe another such (much simpler but less efficient) method, which we name *global ordering*. The basic idea behind this method appears in some textbooks on operating systems and database systems and relates to the way a process can lock *several* resources before using them (see a detailed explanation in Section 7.2.2 (page 253).

The idea is for each process i to compete in order with every other process. First, using a mutual exclusion algorithm for two processes, i competes with process 1. If i wins (i.e., if i can enter its critical section in this two process algorithm) i continues and competes against process 2, and so on. If i wins against all the other processes, i may enter its critical section in the n-process algorithm. To exit its critical section, i executes all the $n-1$ exit codes in the two process mutual exclusion algorithms that it has participated in. The exact code follows.

In the algorithm below for n processes, each pair of processes i and j has a single two process mutual exclusion algorithm that only i and j may access which is called *mutex*(i,j) (which is the same as *mutex*(j,i)). We denote by *entry-mutex*(i,j) and *exit-mutex*(i,j) the entry code and the exit code of *mutex*(i,j), respectively. The processes are numbered 1 through n.

THE GLOBAL ORDERING ALGORITHM: `process i's program.`

```
for j = 1 to n do                              /* entry code */
      if j ≠ i then entry-mutex(i,j) fi
od;
critical section;
for j = n downto 1 do                          /* exit code */
      if j ≠ i then exit-mutex(i,j) fi
od;
```

We notice that in order to prevent deadlock, it is important that the underlying two process algorithms are executed in an increasing order.

Show that if Kessels' algorithm (page 35) is used as the underlying two process algorithm then the *Global Ordering algorithm* satisfies local spinning.

oo 3.12 Prove that the Global Ordering algorithm (from Problem 3.11) satisfies local spinning, if the underlying two process algorithm satisfies local spinning.

oo 3.13 What is the time complexity in the DSM model of the Global Ordering algorithm (Problem 3.11), assuming that the complexity of the underlying two process algorithm is O(1).

? 3.14 The definition of *remote access* is very delicate and depends on specific architectural details of a given system. For example, in machines with coherent caching, it might be appropriate to consider a read of a shared register x by a process p to be a remote access only if x has been written by another process since p's most recent access of x, or it is the first time p has accessed x. The intuition behind such a definition is that once process p has a copy of x in its cache, it can use it until somebody writes x, which will cause the cache coherence protocol to invalidate the copy of x which p has in its cache.

In such machines, it seems that any reasonable definition of remote access should satisfy at least the following requirement: the first access to a new shared register by a process is a remote access (since the process does not yet have a copy of that register in its cache). Thus, any lower bound on the number of different shared registers a process must access should imply a similar bound on the number of remote memory accesses, for such machines.

What is the maximum number of *different* shared registers a process may need to access in its entry code and exit code in order to enter and exit its critical section (in the presence of contention) since the last time some process released its critical section?

•• ? 3.15 The question of finding tight bounds for the time complexity in both the DSM model and CC model is still open. The best known upper bound is $O(\log n)$ (the tournament algorithm from page 101).

1. Show that for every mutual exclusion algorithm for n processes, $\Omega(\log\log n/\log\log\log n)$ is a lower bound on the time complexity in both the CC and DSM models.
2. The following result is stronger than the previous one. Show that for every mutual exclusion algorithm for n processes, $\Omega(\log n/\log\log n)$ is a lower bound on the time complexity in both the CC and DSM models.

•• 3.16 Prove the following result: For any k there exists some n such that for any n-process mutual exclusion algorithm based on atomic registers (or conditional objects), a run exists involving $\theta(k)$ processes in which some process performs $\Omega(k)$ remote memory accesses to enter and exit its critical section.

•◦ 3.17 Based on Lamport's fast algorithm (page 42) and on Yang and Anderson's algorithm (page 101), design a mutual exclusion algorithm using atomic registers, in which the time complexity in the DSM model is $O(1)$ in the absence of contention and $O(\log n)$ in the presence of contention.

Notice that the reason why it is not easy to come up with an efficient exit code by combining the above two algorithms is due to the fact that it is difficult to distinguish between a situation in which no process has a acquired the "fast path" and a situation in which some process is "about to" acquire the fast path.

Problems based on Section 3.2

◦ 3.18 Why must a mutual exclusion algorithm which is adaptive w.r.t. process response time satisfy starvation-freedom?

◦◦ 3.19 Modify the adaptive deadlock-free algorithm (on page 108), so that it satisfies starvation-freedom. Notice that because the number of processes is unbounded, an infinitely repeating enumeration is necessary (instead of round-robin schedule): a process helps others in the order given by the enumeration in which every process id appears infinitely often.

•• 3.20 Modify the adaptive deadlock-free algorithm (on page 108), so that it uses only a finite number of shared registers.

•◦ 3.21 The $O(n^2)$ space complexity of the adaptive tournament algorithm (page 114) is due to the *Round* array. Improve it, by replacing the array with an $O(n)$ linked list.

◦◦ 3.22 Would the adaptive Black-White Bakery algorithm still be correct if the order of line 1 and line 2 is replaced?

◦◦ 3.23 Would the adaptive Black-White Bakery algorithm still be correct if the order of line 16 and line 17 is replaced?

◦• 3.24 Modify the Black-White Bakery algorithm (from page 55) so that it: (1) is adaptive w.r.t. time complexity in both the CC model and the DSM model, and (2) satisfies local spinning in both the CC model and the DSM model.

◦◦ 3.25 Prove directly for each of the algorithms described so far, that they are not adaptive w.r.t. process time complexity, even when $n = 2$. (Do not use Theorem 3.4.)

◦◦ 3.26 In the proof of Theorem 3.4 (page 119), in the two places when we have considered the case where e_2 is a read event, we did not give a full argument, but rather said "similar to above". Complete the proof for these cases.

◦◦ 3.27 In Problem 3.51, we define the election problem (which is also called the "one shot" mutual exclusion problem). An election algorithm is *wait-free* if it solves the election problem and it guarantees that every participating process will terminate in a finite number of steps regardless of the behavior of other processes. That is, it is assumed that a process may fail/stop in its entry code and such a failure should not prevent other processes from terminating. (Wait-freedom is first discussed on page 48.) Explain why the following important theorem follows easily from the proof of Theorem 3.4 (page 119):

Theorem: *There is no wait-free election algorithm.*

◦◦ 3.28 Explain why it follows from the result mentioned in Problem 2.81 (page 94) that there is no adaptive mutual exclusion algorithm using only atomic bits (or only constant size registers).

◦• 3.29 Prove that there is no adaptive mutual exclusion algorithm, in both the CC and the DSM models, using only single-writer registers.

•◦ 3.30 Prove that there is no adaptive mutual exclusion algorithms, in both the CC and the DSM models, if registers accesses are non-atomic.

∘∘ 3.31 Use the result stated in Problem 3.16 (page 139), to establish a bound that precludes a deterministic algorithm with $O(\log k)$ time complexity in the DSM model, where k is the "point contention" (see definition on page 16).

∘• 3.32 Design a mutual exclusion algorithm (for n processes) with $O(\log k)$ system response time, where k is point contention. The algorithm may use an infinite number of shared registers.

•∘ 3.33 Design a mutual exclusion algorithm (for n processes) with $O(\log k)$ system response time, where k is point contention. The algorithm must use only a finite number of shared registers.

•• 3.34 Design a mutual exclusion algorithm that: (1) has $O(\log k)$ system response time where k is the point contention, (2) has $O(k^2)$ time complexity in the DSM model, and (3) uses only a finite number of shared registers.

? 3.35 Is there a mutual exclusion algorithm that: (1) has $O(\log k)$ system response time where k is the point contention, and (2) has $O(k)$ time complexity in the DSM model.

? 3.36 There are several known adaptive wait-free implementations of an active set object, but they are all rather cumbersome. Find an adaptive implementation of an active set object using only atomic registers which will be simple, short, and elegant. It is not required that the implementation be wait-free, as it is needed for the construction of an adaptive mutual exclusion algorithm. The definition of the active set object appears on page 116.

Problems based on Section 3.3

∘∘ 3.37 Show that if an algorithm satisfies a property in the presence of one continuous failure per process (each process may fail only once), then it will also satisfy the property in the presence of any number of finite continuous failures (assuming a process may resume execution only after all its registers are set to their default values).

∘∘ 3.38 Show that the One-bit algorithm satisfies mutual exclusion and deadlock-freedom in the presence of any *finite* number of continuous failures, and that the Bakery algorithm satisfies mutual exclusion, deadlock-freedom, and the first-come-first-served property in the presence of any *finite* number of continuous failures.

∘∘ 3.39 Does Kessels' algorithm for two processes (page 35) satisfy mutual exclusion and starvation-freedom in the presence of an infinite number of immediate failures?

∘∘ 3.40 Show that Peterson–Fischer's algorithm for two processes (page 78) satisfies mutual exclusion and starvation-freedom in the presence of an infinite number of immediate failures.

○○ 3.41 Does Katseff's algorithm satisfy mutual exclusion, deadlock-freedom, and first-come-first-served in the presence of any finite number of continuous failures?

○○ 3.42 Does Katseff's algorithm work correctly under the assumption that the shared registers are safe instead of atomic?

○○ 3.43 Does Katseff's algorithm work correctly, if we place statement 3 (i.e., *waiting*[*i*] := 1;) as the new first statement of the algorithm?

•○ 3.44 The following algorithm is due to Peterson (1983). Prove its correctness, and show that it satisfies 2-bounded waiting in the presence of *infinite* number of immediate failures. The algorithm is for n processes each with unique identifier taken from the set $\{1, \ldots, n\}$. It make use of an array C[1..n], its entries take on values from 0 to 3. All the processes can read C[i], but only process i can write it.

PETERSON'S FAULT-TOLERANT ALGORITHM: `process i's program.`

Initially: C[i] = 0.

```
function left(i);     % looking for process to left
  for j := i − 1 downto 1 do t := C[j];
      if t = 1 or t = 3 then return 1              /* normal */
      elseif t = 2 then return 2 fi fi od;
  for j := n downto i do t := C[j];
      if t = 1 or t = 3 then return 2            /* opposite */
      elseif t = 2 then return 1 fi fi od;
  return 1                          /* no side value seen */
end left;

procedure tick(i);
  waitloop: await C[i] ≠ left(i);
  for j := 1 to i − 1 do t := C[j];
      if t = C[i] or t = 3 then goto waitloop if od;
  C[i] := 3 − C[i]                                       /* tick */
end tick;
MAIN PROGRAM
C[i] := left(i);
tick(i); tick(i);
S := C[i];
reset: C[i] := S;
for j := i + 1 to n do await C[j] ≠ 3 od;
C[i] := 3;
for j := i + 1 to n do
  if C[j] = 3 then goto reset if od;
for j := 1 to i − 1 do await C[j] ≠ 3 od;
critical section;
C[i] := 0;
```

•∘ 3.45 The following algorithm is due to R. L. Rivest and V. R. Pratt (1976). Prove that the algorithm satisfies linear waiting in the presence of an infinite number of immediate failures.

The algorithm makes use of two shared registers: *shared*[1] and *shared*[2]. The registers are single-writer registers. That is process 1 can write *shared*[1] and read *shared*[2], while process 2 can write *shared*[2] and read *shared*[1]. Each of the shared registers is defined as a record with two fields named *one* and *two*. Field one may take on the values 0, 1, or 2 and when its value is 0 the corresponding process is either dead or uninterested in entering its critical section. Field two acts as a counter modulo 3; we assume from now on that all arithmetic performed on it will be performed modulo 3. The fields of each shared register may be changed simultaneously by making a single assignment. Even though each of the fields may assume one of three values, each of the registers will assume only seven distinct values since two of the combinations will not occur (which two combinations?). Notice that the programs for process 1 and process 2 are not symmetric.

RIVEST–PRATT'S ALGORITHM:

Initially: *shared*[1] = 0 and *shared*[2] = 0.

```
PROGRAM FOR PROCESS 1:
        local[1].one := 1; local[1].two := shared[2].two;
        shared[1] := local[1];     /* assign both fields */
        local[1].one := 2; local[1].two := shared[2].two;
        shared[1] := local[1];
  loop: local[1] := shared[2];
        if local[1].one ≠ 0 then
           if local[1].two ≠ shared[2].two + 1 then
              if local[1] ≠ shared[1] then goto loop fi fi fi;
        critical section;
        shared[1] := 0;
PROGRAM FOR PROCESS 2:
        local[2].one := 1; local[2].two := shared[1].two;
        shared[2] := local[2];
        local[2].one := 2; local[2].two := shared[1].two;
        shared[2] := local[2];
  loop: local[2] := shared[1];
        if local[2].one ≠ 0 then
           if local[2].two ≠ shared[1].two + 1 then goto loop fi fi;
        critical section;
        shared[2] := 0;
```

∘• 3.46 Modify the Bakery algorithm so that it becomes self-stabilizing for mutual exclusion and starvation-freedom.

•◦ 3.47 Prove that any symmetric deadlock-free mutual exclusion algorithm must use at least one shared register which can take on n different values.

? 3.48 Does a symmetric deadlock-free mutual exclusion algorithm, which uses only $n-1$ binary registers and one shared register which can take on n different values, exist?

•• 3.49 A *memoryless* algorithm is an algorithm in which a process that tries to enter its critical section does not use any information about its previous attempts to enter its critical section (like the fact that it entered its critical section five times so far, etc.). Put another way, in a memoryless algorithm, processes have only a single remainder state, and hence cannot retain any memory of prior executions of the algorithm. All the algorithms presented in this chapter are memoryless.

Prove that for any memoryless deadlock-free symmetric mutual exclusion algorithm, the number of different shared registers a process has to access in its entry code in order to enter its critical section in the absence of contention is at least n. (This implies a lower bound of $n+1$ on the *contention-free time complexity* of such algorithms.)

•• 3.50 Prove that $2n-1$ registers are necessary and sufficient for the design of any memoryless starvation-free symmetric mutual exclusion algorithm. Memoryless algorithms and symmetric algorithms are defined on pages 144 and 130, respectively. (Hint: use the solution to Problem 3.49.)

Remark: The sufficient condition holds even when comparisons for equality are assumed, while the necessary condition holds even for arbitrary comparisons.

•◦ 3.51 The tight space complexity of n registers (Section 2.5) is based on the fact that mutual exclusion is an on going activity. The situation changes when we look at the "one shot" mutual exclusion problem where it is only required that just one process eventually enters its critical section. This process is called the leader, and thus this variant of the problem is called the *leader election problem.*

More formally, in the leader election problem, each correct process that starts participating eventually terminates and exactly one of the participating processes is elected as a leader. We assume that processes are not required to participate in the algorithm; however, once a process starts participating it is guaranteed that it will never fail. (This assumption is exactly as in the mutual exclusion problem where a process may stay in the remainder section forever.) The number of processes n is assumed to be known.

An algorithm for solving the leader election problem for n processes using only $\lceil \log n \rceil + 2$ atomic registers is presented below.

1. Prove that the algorithm below correctly solves the leader election problem.
2. Modify the algorithm so that only $\lceil \log n \rceil + 1$ registers are used (i.e., the register *done* is removed).

The algorithm uses the shared registers *turn* and *done* and the array of shared registers V. All the shared registers are initially 0. Also, for each process, the local variables *level* and j are used.

Election Algorithm for n Processes: `process i's program` $(1 \le i \le n)$.

```
turn := i;
for level := 1 to ⌈log n⌉ do
        await ((V[level] = 0) or (done = 1));
        if done = 1 then "I am not the leader"; Halt fi;
        V[level] := i;
        if turn ≠ i then
                for j := 1 to level do
                        if V[j] = i then V[j] := 0 fi od;
                "I am not the leader"; Halt
        fi;
od;
done := 1;
Announce "I am the leader".
```

•• 3.52 Prove that the upper bound presented for the election problem in Problem 3.51 is tight. That is, any election algorithm for n processes must use at least $\lceil \log n \rceil + 1$ registers. (This lower bound holds even for non-symmetric algorithms.)

◦◦ 3.53 In the election problem considered in Problem 3.51, processes were free to either participate or not participate with no requirement to do either. Show that when each process is required to take at least one step (i.e., a process cannot delay indefinitely in its remainder section), three registers are sufficient for solving the symmetric election problem. (Notice that since we require the solution to be symmetric, the problem can not be solved by using "elect p_1".)

•◦ 3.54 The *symmetric process numbering* problem is to assign each of the n processes a number from 1 to n, given a symmetric initial state. Once a process gets a number, it never attempts to get another number. One simple way to solve the problem is to use the symmetric mutual exclusion algorithm from page 130. Assume that there is a shared register, called *counter*, which is initially 0. In order to get a number a process participates once in a symmetric deadlock-free algorithm; when it enters its critical section it increments the counter by 1, takes its value as its assigned number, and exits. By Theorem 2.16 (page 59), the space complexity of such a solution would be at least n (not counting the counter).

An algorithm for solving the process numbering problem for n processes using only $2\lceil \log n \rceil + 1$ atomic registers is presented below. Prove that the algorithm below correctly solves the problem.

The algorithm uses the shared registers *turn* and *counter* and the array of shared registers V. All the shared registers are initially 0. Also, for each process, the local variables *level* and j are used.

Symmetric Process Numbering Algorithm for n Processes: `process i's program` $(1 \leq i \leq n)$.

```
start:
for j := 1 to level do if V[j] = i then V[j] := 0 fi od;
await (turn = 0);
turn := i;
for level := 1 to 2⌈log n⌉ − 1 do
        while V[level] ≠ 0 do
                if turn ≠ i then goto start fi od;
        V[level] := i;
        if turn ≠ i then goto start fi od
(In critical section: take next number)
counter := counter +1; my_number := counter;
(Exit: let next process in)
for j := 1 to 2⌈log n⌉ − 1 do
        if V[j] = i then V[j] := 0 fi od;
if turn = i then turn := 0 fi.
```

? 3.55 Is the upper bound presented for the symmetric process numbering problem in Problem 3.54 tight? That is, must any (symmetric or non-symmetric) process numbering algorithm for n processes use at least $2\lceil \log n \rceil + 1$ registers?

Chapter 4

Blocking and Non-blocking Synchronization

4.1 Synchronization Primitives

We focus on an architecture in which n processes communicate asynchronously. Asynchrony means that there are no assumptions on the relative speeds of the processes. Each of the processes is considered to be a sequential program augmented with the ability to access shared memory. Processes communicate via a shared memory. From the point of view of the processes (or of the programmer) the memory is a collection of *registers* (also called variables), each of which consists of one or more bits. A register is *local* (also called private) if only one process can access it, a register is *shared* when two or more processes can access it. The shared memory is used for data sharing, information transfer, and in particular, for coordination and synchronization. To "get" information a process reads some shared memory location and to "send" information a process writes it in a shared memory so that other processes can read it later.

Various architectures differ in the level of *atomicity* that is supported. Atomic (or indivisible) operations are defined as operations whose execution is not interfered with by other concurrent activities. All the architectures support atomic reads and writes operations. That is, while a process reads or writes a register, say r, it can be assumed that no other process at the same time can access r. However, atomic reads and writes do not mean that a process in one atomic step can read a memory location and then write into it. Thus, for example, incrementing the value of some register by one, which involves both reading and writing, is not atomic in a system that supports only atomic reads and writes.

Most modern architectures support some form of atomicity which is stronger than simple reads and writes. Such stronger atomicity usually makes it possible, in one atomic step, to read a value v from a memory location r, and write back the value $f(v)$ into r, where f is a predefined function, and return v. There are many different such operations, depending on what is the function f that is applied during the operation. Common operations have special names and are defined below.

While most recent computers usually provide synchronization primitives that make it easy to achieve mutual exclusion, it is sometimes more efficient to use only atomic registers than the other more expensive (in terms of time) synchronization primitives. In the following, we will use the terms primitives and objects as synonyms.

4.1.1 Atomic Operations

Each of the operations below is defined as a function that gets as arguments one or more values and register names, updates the value of the registers, and returns a value. The execution of the function is assumed to be atomic. Call by reference is used when passing registers as arguments.

- *Read*: takes a register r and simply returns its value.

```
function read (r:register) return:value;
    return(r);
end-function
```

- *Write*: takes a shared register r and a value *val*. The value *val* is assigned to r.

```
function write (r:register, val:value);
    r := val;
end-function
```

- *Test-and-set*: takes a shared register r and a value *val*. The value *val* is assigned to r, and the old value of r is returned. (In some definitions *val* can take only the value 1.)

```
function test-and-set (r:register, val:value) return:value;
        temp := r;
        r := val;
        return(temp);
end-function
```

- *Swap*: takes a shared register r and a local register ℓ, and atomically exchanges their values.

```
function swap (r:register, l:local-register);
        temp := r;
        r := ℓ;
        l := temp;
end-function
```

A *swap* operation is also called *fetch-and-store* in the literature.

- *Fetch-and-add*: takes a register r and a value *val*. The value of r is incremented by *val*, and the old value of r is returned.

```
function fetch-and-add (r:register, val:value) return:value;
        r := r + val;
        return(r);
end-function
```

The *fetch-and-increment* operation is a special case where $val = 1$. That is, it is used to increment a value of a register by one.

- *Read-modify-write*: takes a register r and a function f. The value of $f(r)$ is assigned to r, and the old value of r is returned. Put another way, in one *read-modify-write* operation a process can atomically read a value of a shared register and then based on the value read, compute some new value and assign it back to the register.

```
function read-modify-write (r:register, f:function)
return:value;
        temp := r;
        r := f(r);
        return(temp);
end-function
```

All the operations mentioned so far are special cases of the *read-modify-write* operations. In fact, any memory access that consists of reading one shared memory location, performing an arbitrary local computation, than updating the memory location can be expressed as a *read-modify-write* operation of the above form.

- *Compare-and-swap*: takes a register r and two values: *new* and *old*. If the current value of the register r is equal to *old*, then the value of r is set to *new* and the value *true* is returned; otherwise r is left unchanged and the value *false* is returned.

```
function compare-and-swap (r:register, old:value, new:value)
return:value;
        if r=old then r := new; return(true)
        else return(false) fi;
end-function
```

- *Sticky-write:* takes a register r and a value *val*. It is assumed that the initial value of r is "undefined" (denoted by $\perp$). If the value of r is $\perp$ or *val*, then it is replaced by *val*, and returns "success"; otherwise r is left unchanged and it returns "fail". We denote "success" by 1 and "fail" by 0.
  The *sticky-bit-write* operation is a special case where it is only possible to write the values 0 and 1.
- *Move*: takes two shared registers r_1 and r_2 and atomically copies the value of r_2 to r_1. The *move* operation should not be confused with assignment (i.e., write); *move* copies values between two shared registers, while assignment copies values between shared and private (local) registers.

```
function move (r1:register, r2:register);
        r1 := r2;
end-function
```

- *Shared-swap:* takes two shared registers r_1 and r_2 and atomically exchanges their values.

```
function Shared-swap (r1:register, r2:register);
        temp := r1;
        r1 := r2;
        r2 := r1;
end-function
```

How do we implement these strong atomic operations? On a uni-processor, an operation will be atomic as long as a context switch does not occur in the middle of the operation. This can be achieved by disabling interrupts until after the atomic operation is done. Disabling interrupts, although very simple, is problematic for several reasons: There is a need to support synchronization operations in user-level applications. However, the operating system can not allow user code to disable interrupts as the user might never give the CPU back. In real time systems there is a need to guarantee how long it takes to respond to interrupts, and this can not be achieved when interrupts are disabled for an arbitrarily long time.

On a multi-processor, disabling interrupts does not provide atomicity. It stops context switches from occurring on a single CPU, but it does not stop other CPUs from accessing the shared memory. Instead, every modern multi-processor architecture provides hardware support for implementing some kind of a strong atomic synchronization primitive. The hardware is responsible for implementing this correctly on both uni-processors and multi-processors which usually requires special hooks in the multi-processor cache coherence strategy. Unlike disabling interrupts, this can be used on both uni-processors and multi-processors.

4.1.2 Objects

Objects are shared data structures. Each object has a *type* which defines the set of operations that the object supports. It is possible to access an object only by using one of the operations it supports. Each object also has *sequential specification* that specifies how the object behaves when these operations are applied sequentially. i.e., atomically, as defined in the previous subsection. Below we list some common objects.

- *Atomic register* – a shared register that supports (atomic) *read* and *write* operations.
- *Test-and-set object* – a shared register that supports *write* and *test-and-set* operations. The operation of writing 0 is called *reset*.
- *Test-and-set bit* – an object that supports a reset operation (i.e., write 0) and a restricted *test-and-set* operation where the value of *val* can only be 1. *Test-and-set* bits are implemented in hardware by most architectures.
- *Test-and-test-and-set object* – a shared register that like a *test-and-set* object supports *write* and *test-and-set* operations, where the operation of writing 0 is called *reset*. In addition, it also supports an atomic *read* operation.
- *Fetch-and-increment object* – a shared register that supports a *fetch-and-increment* operation.
- *Fetch-and-add object* – a shared register that supports a *fetch-and-add* operation.
- *Swap object* – consists of a shared register and supports a *swap* operation between the shared register and any local register. (Has been implemented in hardware in x86 architectures.)
- *Read-modify-write object* – a shared register that supports a *read-modify-write* operation.
- *Compare-and-swap object* – a shared register that supports a *compare-and-swap* operation. *Compare and swap* (CAS) has been implemented in hardware in Motorola 680x0, IBM 370, and SPARC architectures.
- *Sticky-bit* – supports *read* and *stick-bit-write* operations. Recall that such a “bit” can have three values, ⊥ (the initial value), 0, and 1. It is called a bit for historical reasons.
- *Move object* – consists of a collection of atomic registers and supports a *move* operation between any two registers (in this collection).
- *Shared-swap object* – consists of a collection of atomic registers and supports a *shared-swap* operation between any two atomic registers.
- *Queue*, *stack*, *tree*, etc. – all shared common data structures are objects. The difference is that as objects they can be accessed by many processes not just one as usually assumed in the study of data structures.
- *Load-link/store-conditional* – the object supports two operations, *load-link* which (atomically) reads the value of a shared register and *store-conditional* which tries to (atomically) write a value into the shared register. The *store-conditional* operation on register r by process p succeeds in writing a value, only if no other process has modified r since the last *load-link* operation on r by p. Otherwise, it returns a failure status. *Load-link/store-conditional* has been implemented in hardware in MIPS, PowerPC, and DECAlpha architectures.

- *Semaphore* – the operations that a semaphore supports are not atomic and involve waiting. The exact definition is given on page 176. Semaphores are one of the main synchronization primitives used in UNIX.
- *Monitor* – the operations that a monitor supports are also not atomic and involve waiting. The exact definition is given on page 181.

Java Concurrency Utilities (JSR-166) proposes a set of medium-level utilities that provide functionality commonly needed in concurrent programs. The contents of JSR-166 have been released as part of JDK1.5.0. It supports concurrent queues, compare&swap locks, readers and writers, semaphores, barriers, and more.

The fact that the operations supported by an object are atomic means that at any point in time the object is "processing" only one operation. However, this atomicity assumption is too restrictive, and it is safe to relax it in the following way: We may assume that processes can try to access the object at the same time; however, although operations of concurrent processes may overlap, each operation should appear to take effect instantaneously. In particular, operations that do not overlap should take effect in their "real time" order. This type of correctness requirement for shared objects, due to M. P. Herlihy and J. M. Wing (1990), is called *linearizability*.

An important consistency condition weaker than linearizability, called *sequential consistency*, was defined by L. Lamport (1979) as follows: The result of any execution is the same as if the operations of all the processes were executed in some sequential order, and the operations of each individual process appear in this sequence in the order specified by its program. Several weaker consistency conditions have been proposed in the literature, for example *casual consistency* and *relaxed consistency*.

In the literature, the notion of *synchronization primitives* is sometimes used to refer only to objects that are interesting in a concurrent environment and are meaningless in a sequential environment (such as test-and-set and compare-and-swap objects). The notion of *shared or concurrent data structures* is used to refer to objects that are also interesting in a sequential context (such as queues and stacks). We explore the relative computational power of the objects defined above in Section 9.6.

4.1.3 Non-atomic Registers

In the previous subsection, we have assumed that operations on the same memory location are atomic – they occur in some definite order. However, this assumption can be relaxed allowing the possibility of concurrent operations on the same register. For the case of single-writer and multi-readers shared registers (only one process can write a register but everyone can read it), Lamport has defined three general classes of shared registers which support read and write operations, called safe, regular, and atomic, depending on their properties when several reads and/or writes are executed concurrently.

The weakest possibility is a *safe* register (already discussed on page 65), in which it is assumed only that a read not concurrent with any writes obtains the correct value. That is, the read should return the value written by the most recent write, or the initial value if no write had yet occurred. In the case where a read from a register is concurrent with some write into that register, the read may return an arbitrary value.

A *regular* register is a safe register in which a read that overlaps a write obtains either the old or new value. An *atomic* register, which was already defined earlier, can be defined as a safe register in which the reads and writes behave as if they occur in some definite order.

Self Review

1. Define an object called *read-swap* as an object that supports both the *read* operation and the *swap* operation. What is the difference between a *read-swap* object and a *compare-and-swap* object? It is *impossible* to implement a *compare-and-swap* object from *read-swap* objects. Give an intuitive explanation why this is true.
2. Is a *load-link/store-conditional* object a "special case" of a *read-modify-write* object? i.e., is there a trivial implementation of a *load-link/store-conditional* object from *read-modify-write* objects?
3. Is a *shared-swap* object a "special case" of a *read-modify-write* object?

Answers: (1) In a *compare-and-swap* object, testing and then swapping are done as one atomic operation, while in the *read-swap* object they are two separate operations. (2) Yes. (3) No.

4.2 Collision Avoidance using Test-and-set Bits

In this subsection we study the mutual exclusion problem in a model which, in addition to supporting atomic registers, supports also test-and-set bits. Recall that a test-and-set bit supports two operations: a *test-and-set* operation which atomically reads the bit, sets it to 1 (*true*), and returns the value read; and a *reset* operation which assigns the value 0 (*false*). This model is more powerful than a model which supports only atomic registers. However, we notice that a test-and-set operation may be more expensive than a read and write operation in terms of the time it takes to complete such an operation.

A test-and-set bit is sometimes referred to as a *lock*, while the test-and-set and reset operations are called the lock and unlock operations, respectively. When a process finds that the lock is set by another process, a common technique is to let the process *spin* on the lock until it is unlocked. This is achieved by executing the loop: **while** *test-and-set(lock)* **do** skip **od** (i.e., **await** *test-and-set(lock)* $= 0$). For that reason, test-and-set bits that are used in this way are also called *spinlocks*.

4.2.1 A Trivial Deadlock-free Algorithm

The most simple mutual exclusion algorithm for that model uses only one test-and-set bit and is defined formally below. The algorithm uses a test-and-set bit called x. A process first keeps on accessing x until, in one atomic step, it succeeds in changing x from 0 to 1. Then, the process can safely enter its critical section. The exit code is simply to reset x to 0.

A DEADLOCK-FREE ALGORITHM: `process i's program.`

x: test-and-set bit, initially 0;

```
await (test-and-set(x) = 0);
critical section;
reset(x);
```

It is trivial to show that the algorithm satisfies mutual exclusion and is deadlock-free. Also, it is obvious that starvation of individual processes is possible. While a deadlock-free algorithm can be constructed using a single test-and-set bit, any starvation-free algorithm must use at least $\Omega(\sqrt{n})$ shared states, that is, $\Omega(\log n)$ bits (see Problem 4.16).

4.2.2 Using a Test-and-test-and-set Bit

In the previous algorithm a process, while it busy-waits, writes 1 into the bit x every time it tests x, even if the value of x does not change. From a practical point of view this leads to poor performance since each time x is written, the caches of all the processes which contain a copy of x need to be invalidated. To improve this situation a test-and-test-and-set bit can be used instead of a test-and-set bit. This enables the implementation of busy-waiting by first testing x until its value changes to 0, and only then to test-and-set x. The resulting algorithm is as follows:

A DEADLOCK-FREE ALGORITHM: `process i's program.`

x: test-and-test-and-set bit, initially 0;

```
1  await(x = 0);
2  while (test-and-set(x) = 1) do
3       await(x = 0) od;
4  critical section;
5  reset(x);
```

The algorithm satisfies mutual exclusion and is deadlock-free. However, as in the previous algorithm, starvation of individual processes is possible. We notice that even in this solution all waiting processes spin on the same bit, a fact which degrades performance.

The above algorithm is based on a *pessimistic* approach as it starts by testing the lock instead of attempting to acquire the lock. In the optimistic version of the algorithm line 1 is omitted and the algorithm starts with an attempt to acquire the lock. The pessimistic version is expected to perform better than the optimistic version under contention as it does not attempt unnecessarily to initially update the value of the lock. On a system with support for cache coherence, updating the value of the lock may cause many remote invalidations in the caches of other processes, even if the value of the lock is not changed by the test-and-set instruction. These invalidations generate lots of traffic on the interconnection network between the processes and the memory.

4.2.3 Collision Avoidance Locks

Collision avoidance is a technique where each contending process delays itself for a different amount of time before attempting to obtain the lock. This technique when implemented as part of the simple spinning locks presented in this section (or any other mutual exclusion algorithm) reduces the number of unsuccessful test-and-set or read operations, generates less traffic on the interconnection network between the processes and the memory, and hence improves the overall performance.

Simple locks, such as those presented earlier in this section, when implemented on systems with support for cache coherence are called *snoopy locks*. The main disadvantage of simple locks and snoopy locks is that each time the lock is released all the participating processes try to capture the lock, generating lots of traffic on the interconnection network. Collision avoidance locks have all the advantages of snooping locks and none of the disadvantages.

There are many variations of collision avoidance locks depending, for example, on whether the delay is fixed or dynamic. Various experimental results show that when dynamic delay is used, exponential increases are preferred over linear increases. The most popular method for exponential increases is called *exponential backoff* in which, after a failed attempt to obtain the lock, the delay time is doubled.

Another variation has to do with the decision of when exactly to increase the delay. There are two main options: (1) to increase after every separate access to the lock; or (2) not to increase when the lock is busy, but only when it is unlocked and a subsequent attempt to obtain it fails. Usually the second option is preferred.

Another variation has to do with the decision on what would be the initial delay and what is the maximum delay. For example, although using too large delays would reduce the number of collisions, it will favor newly arriving processes.

In the following algorithm exponential backoff is added to the algorithm from the previous subsection. The statement **pause**(*delay*) causes the executing process to wait for *delay* time unites.

A Deadlock-free Algorithm with Exponential Backoff: process *i*'s program.

```
shared x: test-and-test-and-set bit, initially 0
local delay: integer
constants base, cap    /* initial and maximum delays, resp. */

delay := base/2            /* set delay to the initial delay */
repeat
    delay := min(2 × delay, cap);     /* exponential backoff */
    while (x = 0) do pause(delay) od;
until (test-and-set(x) = 0);
critical section;
reset(x);
```

The constants *base* and *cap* and the *backoff factor* (which is set to 2 in the above algorithm) should be tuned for each individual machine architecture. Experimental results have shown that collision avoidance algorithms using exponential backoff adjust well to growing numbers of processes. Thus it is recommended that simple and snoopy locks that may encounter a high level of contention be protected with some form of collision avoidance.

4.2.4 A Fast Starvation-free Algorithm

We now present a simple solution to the mutual exclusion problem using a single test-and-set bit and atomic registers. The algorithm is fast even when there is contention – its worst-case time complexity is a constant. That is, regardless of the level of contention, the maximum number of steps of the process that enters its critical section in its entry code and exit code, since the last time some process exited its critical section, is a constant (assuming *test-and-set* takes constant time).

The algorithm employs a test-and-set bit *lock*, an array *waiting* of n atomic bits, and a shared atomic register *turn*. The algorithm follows.

A FAST STARVATION-FREE ALGORITHM: `process i's program.`

turn: atomic register ranges over $0..(n-1)$ (its initial value is immaterial);
lock: test-and-set bit, initially *false*;
waiting$[0..(n-1)]$: array of atomic bits, initially *false*;
lturn, *key*: local registers;

```
waiting[i] := true;
key := true;
while (waiting[i] and key) do
        key := test-and-set(lock) od;
critical section;
waiting[i] := false;
if turn = i then lturn := (turn + 1)mod n
             else lturn := turn fi;
if waiting[lturn] then turn := lturn; waiting[lturn] := false
             else turn := (lturn + 1)mod n; reset(lock) fi;
```

Intuitively, the algorithm works as follows. When process i wants to enter its critical section, it first sets *waiting*$[i]$ to *true*, and then repeatedly performs *test-and-set* operation on the bit *lock*. It can decide to enter its critical section in two ways. If *test-and-set* returns *false*, then the process has the lock, and can enter its critical section. On the other hand, the last winner (that is, the last process to enter the critical section) may grant permission to process i by resetting *waiting*$[i]$ to *false*. When some process exits its critical section, it checks if the process *turn* wants to enter the critical section, that is, if *waiting*[*turn*] is set. If so, it grants *turn* permission to enter the critical section; otherwise, it increments *turn* and resets *lock*.

Properties of the Fast Starvation-free Algorithm:

- Satisfies mutual exclusion and deadlock-freedom.
- *Satisfies n-fairness*: while a process is waiting to enter its critical section, all the remaining processes can enter their critical sections at most $n - 1$ times altogether.
- Process time complexity and system response time is a constant. That is, the algorithm provides fast access also in the presence of contention. (Recall that when using only atomic registers the time complexity is unbounded; see Theorem 3.4 on page 119.)
- $n + 1$ atomic registers and one *test-and-set* bit are used.

Theorem 4.1 *The algorithm satisfies mutual exclusion, n-fairness, and is deadlock-free.*

Proof: The proof that the algorithm satisfies mutual exclusion and deadlock-freedom is rather simple and is left as an exercise. To prove that it satisfies n-fairness, observe that each process i first sets *waiting*$[i]$ to *true*. When some process exits its critical section, if *waiting*$[turn]$ = *true* and $turn = i$ then process i gets the permission to enter its critical section, and in any case *turn* is incremented by one. Thus, for any i, during any time interval in which $n - 1$ processes have exited their critical section, there is a point at which $turn = i$. If process i is active when $turn = i$ (that is, *waiting*$[i]$ = *true*), then process i would get the permission to enter its critical section. ∎

Self Review

1. Would the deadlock-free algorithm with exponential backoff from page 155 be correct if we omit line 3?
2. Assume that, in the exponential backoff algorithm from page 155, three processes enter their critical sections while process i is in its entry code. What are all the possible values of the local *delay* variable of process i, after the three processes have exited their critical sections?
3. Would the fast starvation-free algorithm from page 156 still be correct if we replace lines 7 and 8 with the single statement: *lturn* := *turn*?

Answers: (1) The algorithm would be correct, but it will be an algorithm with a fixed delay, rather than an algorithm with exponential backoff. (2) $delay \in \{c/2, c, 2c, 4c, 6c\}$. (3) Yes, but it will be slightly less fair.

4.3 The Ticket Algorithm using RMW Objects

In this subsection our model of computation consists of a fully asynchronous collection of n identical anonymous deterministic processes that communicate via finite-sized shared registers. Access to the shared registers is via atomic "read-modify-write" (RMW) instructions which, in a single indivisible step, read the value in a register and then write to that register a new value that can depend on the value just read.

4.3.1 The Ticket Algorithm

Below we present a mutual exclusion algorithm which satisfies the FIFO requirement using a single n^2-valued register. The basic idea is as in the Bakery algorithm (see page 50). A process wishing to enter its critical section takes the next available ticket and waits until its ticket becomes valid, at which point it can safely enter its critical section. When it exits, it discards its ticket and validates the next invalid ticket in order (even if this ticket has not been taken yet).

The values of the shared read-modify-write register range over the set $N \times N$, where $N = \{0, 1, \ldots, n-1\}$. We use *ticket* and *valid* to designate the first and second components, respectively, of the ordered pair stored in the shared register. The brackets $\langle\ \rangle$ are used to explicitly mark the beginning and end of exclusive access to the shared read-modify-write register. An execution of a bracketed section is considered as an atomic action.

THE TICKET ALGORITHM: `process i's program.`

constant $N = \{0, 1, \ldots, n-1\}$
shared $(ticket, valid)$ a read-modify-write register ranges over $N \times N$;
  initially $ticket = valid$
local $(ticket_i, valid_i)$ ranges over $N \times N$

$\langle(ticket_i, valid_i) := (ticket, valid);$
  $ticket := (ticket + 1) \bmod n\rangle;$
while $ticket_i \neq valid_i$ **do**
    $\langle valid_i := valid\rangle$ **od**;
critical section;
$\langle valid := (valid + 1) \bmod n\rangle;$

Each process first reads the value of the shared register, stores its components in local memory, and increments *ticket* by one (modulo n). At any later point, a process becomes the first in the "waiting line" if it learns (by inspecting *valid*) that its ticket number $ticket_i$ equals *valid*, in which case it can safely enter its critical section.

Properties of the Ticket Algorithm:

- Satisfies mutual exclusion, deadlock-freedom and FIFO.
- Process time complexity and system response time is a constant.
- A single n^2-valued read-modify-write register is used.

The proof that the algorithm satisfies the above properties is very simple and is left as an exercise. The Ticket algorithm is optimal to within a constant factor in terms of the values of shared memory. That is, assuming very strong robustness and FIFO requirements, any algorithm for $n \geq 3$ processes that satisfies: mutual exclusion, deadlock-freedom and strong FIFO (also FIFO in the exit code) must use at least $\frac{n^2-3n+2}{2}$ shared states (Problem 4.19). It is interesting to note that relaxing the fairness requirement and not requiring that the exit code be wait-free (i.e., requirement 4 on page 12 may not be satisfied) enables the design of a linear-waiting algorithm for n processes which uses a single $(n+2)$-valued read-modify-write register (Problem 4.15).

4.3.2 A Simple Lower Bound

We consider now space lower bounds when using a single read-modify-write register. It is known that any starvation-free solution requires at least $\sqrt{2n}+\frac{1}{2}$ values. Requiring also that the algorithm be memoryless increases the lower bound to $\lfloor n/2 \rfloor + 2$ values. Achieving bounded-waiting requires at least $n+1$ values (bounded-waiting is defined on page 48). These bounds are nearly optimal, for algorithms are exhibited for the last two cases with $\lfloor n/2 \rfloor + 6$ values for the starvation-freedom case and $n+2$ values for 2-bounded waiting. However, in the algorithms which prove the above two upper bounds the exit code is *not* wait-free (i.e., requirement 4 on page 12 is not satisfied).

We now prove a slightly weaker lower bound than the result that bounded-waiting requires at least $n+1$ values. That is, we show that there is no algorithm that satisfies mutual exclusion, deadlock-freedom, and bounded-waiting which uses a single n-valued read-modify-write register.

Theorem 4.2 *Any algorithm for n processes that satisfies mutual exclusion, deadlock-freedom, and bounded-waiting must use at least n shared states.*

Proof: Let run_0 be a run in which all the processes are in their remainder codes. From run_0 we run process p_1 by itself until it enters its critical section. Call the resulting run run_1. Now we extend run_1 by letting each process $p_2, \ldots, p_n$ run in turn (by itself) until it enters its entry code. Let run_i $(2 \le i \le n)$ denote the run in which p_i first enters it entry code. That is, the run run_i extends the run run_{i-1} by steps of p_i only until p_i is in its entry code.

We denote by $V(run_i)$ the state (value of the shared registers) at run run_i. In order to prove the theorem we show that $V(run_i) \neq V(run_j)$ for all $1 \le i < j \le n$.

Assume to the contrary that $V(run_i) = V(run_j)$ for some $1 \le i < j \le n$. Then, run_i looks like run_j to processes $p_1, \ldots, p_i$. By the deadlock-freedom property, there is an (infinite) extension of run_i by processes $p_1, \ldots, p_i$ only, which causes some process $1 \le i, \le i$ to enter its critical section an infinite number of times. Since $V(run_i) = V(run_j)$, exactly the same extension is also applicable from run_j. But this violates the bounded-waiting property since p_j remains in its entry code during this extension of run_j. That is, it is possible to let process $i,$ enter its critical section as many times as needed before p_j is allowed to proceed and enter its critical section. ∎

Self Review

1. In the Ticket algorithm we use *ticket* and *valid* to designate the first and second components, respectively, of the ordered pair stored in the shared read-modify-write register. Would the algorithm still be correct if *ticket* and *valid* were two separate read-modify-write registers? That is, reading *valid* first and then reading and incrementing *ticket*. Justify your answer.

2. Assume that we delete the words "mod n" which appear in line 2 and in line 6 of the Ticket algorithm. What should be the size of the shared register for the algorithm to be correct?

Answers: (1) Yes, *valid* can even be atomic register. (2) Unbounded.

4.4 Local Spinning using Strong Primitives

In the Ticket algorithm from the previous section, all the processes busy-wait on the same (single) shared register. From a practical point of view this leads to poor performance in the presence of contention, since all processes spin on the same memory location. To improve this situation we present three local spinning mutual exclusion algorithms. All three algorithms implement queue-based locks, the first two satisfy local spinning only in the CC model, while the third algorithm satisfies local spinning in both the CC model and the DSM model. Several experimental results show that when many processes contend for a single lock, queue-based algorithms such as those presented in the following subsections usually give the best execution time since they are less sensitive to the number of processes.

Recall the definitions of time complexity in the CC model (Coherent Caching), and time complexity in the DSM model (Distributed Shared Memory) given on page 16, that is, time complexity when counting only remote memory accesses.

4.4.1 Anderson's Queue-based Algorithm

We slightly modify the Ticket algorithm to get a local spinning algorithm for the CC model. We use n additional atomic bits and arrange that no two processes spin on the same bit at the same time. The resulting algorithm, which was discovered by Thomas E. Anderson (1990), is described below.

The values of the *ticket* register range over the set $\{0, 1, \ldots, n-1\}$, and the entries of the array $valid[0..n-1]$ range over $\{0, 1\}$. As in the Ticket algorithm, when process i wishes to enter its critical section it takes the next available ticket and stores it in its local register $ticket_i$. Then it waits until its ticket becomes valid by spinning on $valid[ticket_i]$ until its value is 1. Since no two processes hold the same ticket at the same time, they will never spin on the same bit at the same time. The ticket numbers specify the order in which the processes will execute their critical sections. When process i exits its critical section, it signals the next waiting process to enter by setting $valid[ticket_i + 1]$ to 1, as illustrated in Figure 4.1.

The fact that process i directly enables the next process in line to enter its critical section with no further synchronization and minimal effect on other processes is the reason for the improved performance of Anderson's algorithm compared to simple spinning algorithms such as the Ticket algorithm (page 158) or the trivial algorithm using a single test-and-set bit (page 154). In these simple spinning algorithms, even on systems with support for cache coherence, each time the lock is released all the participating processes try to capture the lock, generating lots of traffic on the interconnection network between the processes and the memory.

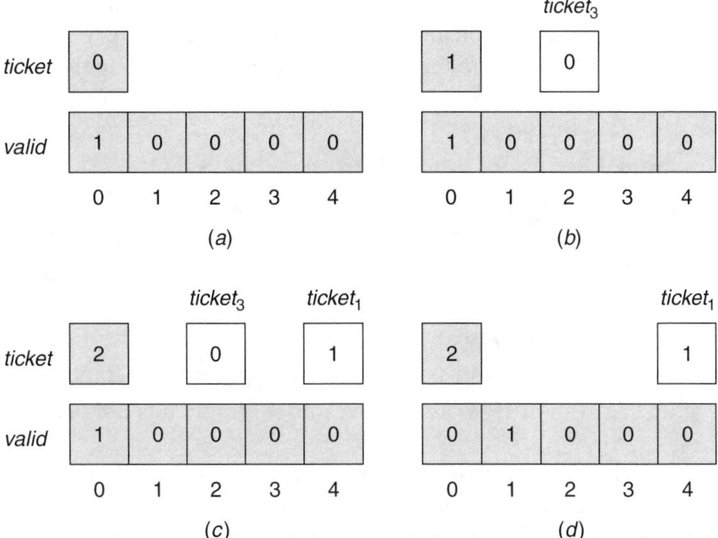

Figure 4.1 An execution of Anderson's algorithm. (*a*) The initial state. (*b*) After process 3 executes its entry section, $valid[ticket_3] = 1$. (*c*) After process 1 executes its entry section, $valid[ticket_1] = 0$. (*d*) After process 3 executes its exit section, $valid[ticket_1] = 1$.

As before, the brackets $\langle\ \rangle$ are used to explicitly mark the beginning and end of exclusive access to the shared read-modify-write register. An execution of a bracketed section is considered as an atomic action.

ANDERSON'S QUEUE-BASED ALGORITHM: `process i's program.`

shared
  ticket: read-modify-write register ranges over $\{0, 1, \ldots, n-1\}$;
    initially $ticket = 0$
  $valid[0..n-1]$: array of atomic bits ; initially $valid[0] = 1$ and
    $valid[i] = 0$, for $1 \leq i \leq n-1$
local $ticket_i$: ranges over $\{0, 1, \ldots, n-1\}$

```
⟨ticket_i := ticket;                          /* take a ticket /*
 ticket := (ticket + 1) mod n⟩; /* fetch-and-increment mod n /*
await valid[ticket_i] = 1;                    /* spin in cache /*
critical section;
valid[ticket_i] := 0;                               /* dequeue /*
valid[(ticket_i + 1) mod n] := 1           /* signal successor /*
```

Process i first reads the value of the shared register *ticket*, stores its value in local memory $ticket_i$, and increments *ticket* by one (modulo n). At any later point, process i becomes the first in the waiting queue when $valid[ticket_i] = 1$, and can safely enter its critical section.

Clearly, the spinning while executing the await statement in line 3 of the algorithm generates only a constant number of remote memory accesses in the CC model, and unbounded number of remote memory accesses in the DSM model.

Properties of the Algorithm:

- Satisfies mutual exclusion, deadlock-freedom, and FIFO.
- Different processes never spin on the same memory location at the *same* time. However, different processes may spin on the same memory location at *different* times.
- Time complexity in the CC model is a constant; however, time complexity in the DSM model is unbounded.
- Process time complexity and system response time are constants.
- An n-valued read-modify-write register and n atomic bits are used.

The proof that the algorithm satisfies the above properties is simple and is left as an exercise. We point out that several shared-memory machines support in hardware a basic fetch-and-increment operation (without counting modulo n). It is rather trivial to modify the previous algorithm to use such an operation on an unbounded size object. This is done as follows:

ANDERSON'S ORIGINAL QUEUE-BASED ALGORITHM: `process i's program.`

shared
ticket: fetch-and-increment object ranges over $\{0, 1, \ldots, \infty\}$;
initially $ticket = 0$
$valid[0..n-1]$: array of atomic bits ; initially $valid[0] = 1$ and
$valid[i] = 0$, for $1 \leq i \leq n-1$
local $ticket_i$: ranges over $\{0, 1, \ldots, \infty\}$

```
ticket_i := fetch-and-increment(ticket);          /* take a ticket /*
await valid[ticket_i mod n] = 1;                  /* spin in cache /*
critical section;
valid[ticket_i mod n] := 0;                       /* dequeue /*
valid[(ticket_i + 1) mod n] := 1                  /* signal successor /*
```

Queueing algorithms for mutual exclusion, such as Anderson's algorithm and the two algorithms presented in Sections 4.4.2 and 4.4.3, have several disadvantages: (1) Even when there is no contention, a process must take several steps in order to enter and exit its critical section (increment a counter, check a memory location, zero that location, set another location). Thus, when there is contention, queuing algorithms are better than simple busy-waiting algorithms such as the trivial algorithm using a test-and-set bit from page 154. When there is no contention simple busy-waiting might be better. (2) Preempting any busy-waiting process forces all the processes behind it to wait until it reaches the front of the queue before being rescheduled. One way to avoid this situation is to remove the process from the queue when the process is preempted.

Next we present another queue-based lock which uses a single swap object and atomic bits.

4.4.2 Graunke and Thakkar Queue-based Algorithm

The next algorithm, due to G. Graunke and S. Thakkar (1990), satisfies local spinning in the CC model but not in the DSM model.

The algorithm maintains a queue of processes which is implemented as a linked list. Each element in the linked list is an atomic bit. Each process i has its own atomic bit, called $node[i]$, which in a DSM machine can be assumed to be stored in process i's local memory.

In its entry code process i threads itself to the end of the linked list, by inserting $node[i]$ into the end of the list. Then process i spins on the atomic bit which *precedes* $node[i]$ in the list. That is, process i does *not* spin locally on its own bit. The process at the head of the queue can enter its critical section. In its exit code process i in one atomic step removes itself from the queue and signals to its successor to enter its critical section. This is achieved by flipping the value of the (single-writer) atomic bit $node[i]$.

In addition, a shared object called *tail*, which supports a swap operation, is used. The object *tail* has two fields: the first is a bit called *value*, and the second is a pointer called *node* which points to the end of the queue. The object *tail* is assumed to be stored in one word of memory, and hence both fields can be accessed in a single swap operation.

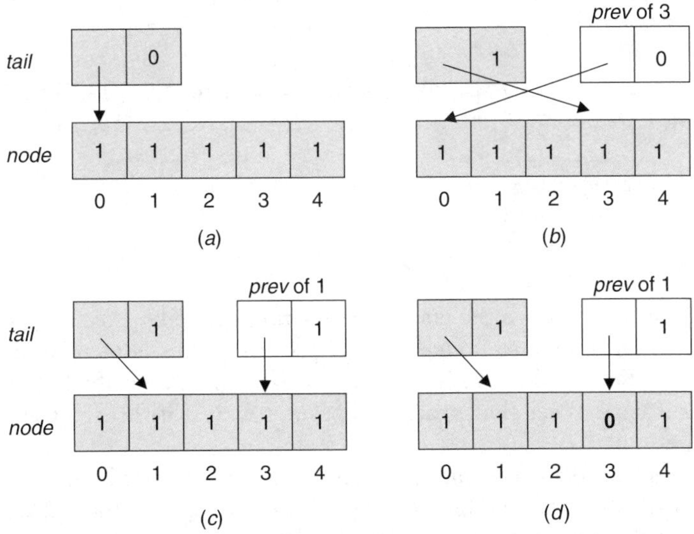

Figure 4.2 An execution of the Graunke and Thakkar algorithm. (*a*) The initial state. (*b*) After process 3 executes its entry section, $*prev.node \neq prev.value$ and process 3 can enter its critical section. (*c*) After process 1 executes its entry section, $*prev.node = prev.value = 1$ and process 1 has to wait. (*d*) After process 3 executes its exit section, $node[3] = 0$. Now, $*prev.node \neq prev.value$, and process 1 can enter its critical section.

Process i threads itself to the end of the linked list in one atomic swap operation. This is done by swapping the value of the shared *tail* object with a local register which contains the value and address of *node*[i]. After this atomic swap operation, *tail* contains the information about process i – the last process in the queue – while a local register of process i contains the information about process i's predecessor in the queue. An execution of the algorithm is illustrated in Figure 4.2.

As in the C programming language, the unary operator & gives the address of an object, so the statement $p = \&r$ assigns the address of r to p, and p is said to point to r. The unary operator $*$ is the *indirection* operator; when applied to a pointer, it accesses the object that the pointer points to. We use this style of implementation since in practice each atomic bit of the *node* array may reside in the local memory of a different process.

GRAUNKE AND THAKKAR ALGORITHM: `process i's program` ($0 \le i < n$).

```
shared
    node[0..n - 1]: array of atomic bits, initially all 1
    tail: record {value: boolean; node: pointer to atomic bit},
                        initially tail.value = 0 and tail.node = &node[0]
local
    prev: record {value: boolean; node: pointer to atomic bit}
    temp: bit

1   prev.value := node[i];        /* i prepares to thread itself */
2   prev.node := &node[i];        /* i prepares to thread itself */
3   swap(tail, prev);             /* tail.node points to node[i] */
                            /* prev.node points to predecessor */
                          /* prev.value = value of predecessor */
4   await *prev.node ≠ prev.value;          /* spin in cache until */
                                       /* the value is toggled */
5   critical section;
6   temp := 1 - node[i];
7   node[i] := temp                          /* signal successor */
```

Process i threads itself onto the end of the waiting queue by executing statement 3, after which *tail* points to *node*[i]. Then, process i spins (statement 4) waiting for its predecessor in the waiting queue to exit and to notify it that it may continue. It is easy to see that process i does not wait if it threads itself onto an empty queue.

In its exit code, process i notifies the next process in line that it may continue by flipping the value of its *node*[i] bit (statement 7). We notice that the exiting process, process i, does not need to know the identity of its successor. It is the responsibility of process i's successor to notice that the value of *node*[i] has been changed.

Properties of the Algorithm:

- Satisfies mutual exclusion, deadlock-freedom, and FIFO.
- Different processes never spin on the same memory location at the *same* time.

- *Satisfies local spinning in the* CC *model*: the time complexity in the CC model is a constant. However, since spinning is not done locally (i.e., a process spins on the bit of its predecessor in the queue), the time complexity in the DSM model is unbounded.
- Process time complexity and system response time are constants.
- A shared object (*tail*) which supports a swap operation is used together with atomic registers.

The proof that the algorithm satisfies the above properties is left as an exercise. When assuming that the shared memory is located in one central location (rather than distributed among the processes as in the case of distributed shared memory) the presentation of the algorithm can be simplified, avoiding the need to use the operators & and $*$. This can be done as follows:

GRAUNKE AND THAKKAR ALGORITHM: `process i's program` $(0 \le i < n)$.

```
shared
    node[0..n − 1]: array of atomic bits, initially all 1
    tail: record {value: boolean; node: ranges over 0..(n − 1)},
                              initially tail.value = 0 and tail.node = 0
local
    prev: record {value: boolean; node: ranges over 0..(n − 1)}
    temp: bit

prev.value := node[i];          /* i prepares to thread itself */
prev.node := i;                 /* i prepares to thread itself */
swap(tail, prev);               /* tail.node points to node[i] */
await node[prev.node] ≠ prev.value;      /* spin until toggled*/
critical section;
temp := 1 − node[i];
node[i] := temp                           /* signal successor */
```

In the next subsection, we present an algorithm where different processes never spin on the same memory location even at *different* times. Such an algorithm is expected to perform better than the previous two algorithms when used in distributed shared memory systems.

4.4.3 The MCS Queue-based Algorithm

The next algorithm, due to J. M. Mellor-Crummey and M. L. Scott (1991), satisfies *local spinning* in both the CC model and the DSM model since different processes never spin on the same memory location even at *different* times. Thus, the time complexity in both the CC and DSM models are constants.

The algorithm maintains a queue of processes which is implemented as a linked list. Each *element* in the linked list is an object with boolean field called *value* and pointer field called *next*. An element is an atomic register and is assumed to be stored in one word of memory. Each process *i* has its own element, called *node*[*i*], which in a DSM machine can be assumed to be stored in process *i*'s local memory. In addition, a shared object called *tail*, points to the end of the queue. The object *tail* is a special object which supports both swap and compare-and-swap operations.

In its entry code a process threads itself to the end of the linked list. Then, the process spins locally on its boolean *value* field until it is at the head of the queue. The process at the head of the queue can enter its critical section. In its exit code, a process removes itself from the head of the queue and signals to its successor to enter its critical section by setting its successor's *next* field to 1.

The main challenge is in implementing the part of the algorithm in which a process threads itself to the end of the linked list, as this can not be done in one atomic operation and requires three remote accesses to the shared memory. To prevent a race condition, the predecessor of the process that is being threaded is required in its exit code to wait until the threading is completed, and only then it may signal its successor and exit. As a result, the exit code is *not* wait-free. An execution of the algorithm is illustrated in Figure 4.3.

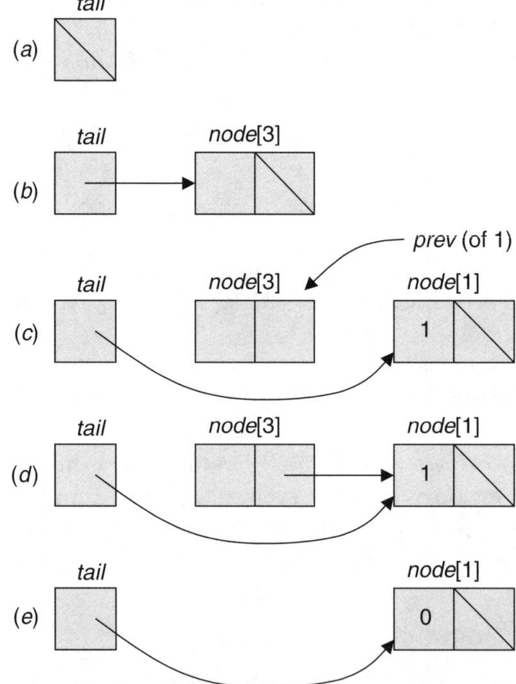

Figure 4.3 An execution of the MCS algorithm. (*a*) The initial state. (*b*) After process 3 executes its entry section, *prev* = *nil* and process 3 can enter its critical section. (*c*) After process 1 executes the compare-and-swap. (*d*) After process 1 executes its entry section, *node*[1].*value* = 1 and process 1 has to wait. (*e*) After process 3 executes its exit section, *node*[1].*value* = 0, and process 1 can enter its critical section.

As in the previous section, the unary operator & gives the address of an object and the unary operator ∗ is the *indirection* operator; when applied to a pointer, it accesses the object that the pointer points to. We use this style of implementation since in practice each element of the *node* array may reside in the local memory of a different process. However, we could have used a different style and avoid using the operators & and ∗ (see Problem 4.25).

THE MCS QUEUE-BASED ALGORITHM: process *i*'s program $(0 \le i < n)$.

```
type
      element: record {value: boolean; next: pointer to element}
shared
      node[0..n − 1]: array of records of type element
      tail: pointer to element, initially tail = nil
local
      mynode: pointer to element, initially mynode = &nodes[i]
      prev, successor: pointers to element

1   *mynode.next := nil; /* prepare to be last in the queue */
2   prev := mynode;                /* prepare to thread itself */
3   swap(tail, prev);                   /* tail points to mynode */
4   if prev ≠ nil then               /* mynode has predecessor */
5          *mynode.value := 1;                       /* must wait */
6          *prev.next := mynode;       /* pred. points to mynode */
7          await *mynode.value = 0     /* spin locally on pred */
8   fi;
9   critical section;
10  if *mynode.next = nil then          /* is there a successor? */
         /* if tail=mynode then tail:=nil return(true)*/
                                     /* else return(false) fi */
11         if compare-and-swap(tail, mynode, nil) = false then
      /* there is a successor; spin until next is update */
12                await *mynode.next ≠ nil;
13                successor := *mynode.next;
14                *successor.value := 0        /* signal successor */
15         fi
16  else                                         /* has successor */
17         successor := *mynode.next;
18         *successor.value := 0               /* signal successor */
19  fi
```

A process threads itself onto the end of the waiting queue by executing statements 3 to 6. After executing statement 3, *tail* points to *mynode* (of process *i*). In line 4 the process checks whether the list is empty or not, and if it is not empty the process links its node to that of its predecessor by executing statement 6.

Then, the process spins (statement 7) waiting for its predecessor in the waiting queue to exit and to notify it that it may continue.

The exit code of the algorithm is not wait-free (it does not satisfy requirement 4 on page 12). That is, the number of steps in the exit code (spinning in line 12) depends on the activity of another process (i.e., to execute the statement at line 7).

The reason for waiting in the exit code is the following: Since each process spins on its own dedicated shared register, a process that exits its critical section must notify its successor (assuming there is one) that it may continue. This is done by updating its successor spin register (lines 13–14 or lines 17–18). Thus the exiting process must know the identity of its successor. However, a process must execute more than one instruction in order to thread itself onto the end of the waiting queue (i.e., it needs to execute statements 3 to 6). Thus, the exiting process may notice that its successor has started threading itself onto the end of the waiting queue (that is its successor has executed statement 3) but has not finished yet. In such a case the exiting process must wait (line 12) for its successor to finish threading itself and reveal its identity.

Properties of the Algorithm:

- Satisfies mutual exclusion, deadlock-freedom, and FIFO.
- Satisfies local spinning (in the CC and DSM models), since different processes never spin on the same memory location even at *different* times.
- Because each process spins locally, the time complexity in the CC and DSM models is a constant.
- Process time complexity and system response time are constants.
- A shared object (*tail*) which supports swap and compare-and-swap operations is used together with atomic registers.

The proof that the algorithm satisfies the above properties is left as an exercise.

Several experimental tests have led to the following observations. Recall that simple locks on systems with support for cache coherence are called snoopy locks. With a large number of processes simple locks and snoopy locks are inefficient. The collision avoidance algorithms using exponential backoff (as defined on page 155) adjust well to growing number of processes. Tournament algorithms, although better than simple locks, do not adjust well to growing number of processes. The best performance is achieved by the queue lock algorithms which remain unaffected by the number of processes.

A few conclusions are that (1) it is recommended that locks that may encounter a high level of contention be protected with some form of collision avoidance; (2) simple and snoopy locks are adequate for a modest number of processes; and (3) queue locks are a good choice in the presence of contention for systems which support strong synchronization primitives such as fetch-and-increment, swap, and compare-and-swap.

Self Review

1. Can we replace the order of the two statements in the exit code of Anderson's algorithm (lines 5 and 6)?

2. Assume that $n > 5$ in Anderson's algorithm. Would the algorithm be correct if the initial value of *ticket* is 5, $valid[5] = 1$, and for all $i \neq 5$ the initial value of $valid[i]$ is 0?
3. Would the Graunke and Thakkar algorithm be correct if initially all the bits of the *node* array are set to 0 and *tail.value* is set to 1?
4. Is the initial value of *tail.node* in the Graunke and Thakkar algorithm really important?
5. Are the initial values of the $n-1$ bits $node[i]$, where $1 \leq i \leq n-1$, in the Graunke and Thakkar algorithm important?
6. Can we replace the order of lines 5 and 6 in the MCS algorithm? Justify your answer.
7. The exit code of the MCS Queue-based algorithm is not wait-free. Can we apply the transformation which is described in Problem 1.20 (page 27) and get a correct algorithm with a wait-free exit code?

Answers: (1) No, the modified algorithm would not be deadlock-free. (2) Yes. (3) Yes. (4) *tail.node* must point to one of the bits in the *node* array. (5) No. (6) No, as it will cause deadlock. (7) No. The new algorithm would not satisfy mutual exclusion.

4.5 Concurrent Data Structures

Concurrent access to a data structure shared among several processes must be synchronized in order to avoid interference between conflicting operations. Mutual exclusion locks are the de facto mechanism for concurrency control on concurrent data structures: a process accesses the data structure only inside a critical section code, within which the process is guaranteed exclusive access. The popularity of this approach is largely due to the apparently simple programming model of such locks and the availability of implementations which are efficient and scalable.

When using locks, the *granularity* of synchronization is important. Using a single lock to protect the whole data structure, allowing only one process at a time to access it, is an example of *coarse-grained* synchronization. In contrast, *fine-grained* synchronization enables "small pieces" of a data structure to be locked, allowing several processes with non-interfering operations to access it concurrently. Coarse-grained synchronization is easier to program but is less efficient and is not fault-tolerant compared to fine-grained synchronization.

Using mutual exclusion locks to protect the access to a shared data structure may degrade the performance of synchronized concurrent applications, as it forces processes to wait for a lock to be released. Moreover, slow or stopped processes may prevent other processes from ever accessing the data structure. In cases of concurrent updates of simple data structures such as queues, stacks, heaps, linked lists, and counters, locking may be avoided by using *lock-free* data structures. We will demonstrate the lock-free approach by presenting a lock-free implementation of a concurrent queue.

4.5.1 Non-blocking and Wait-free Synchronization

Several progress conditions have been proposed in the literature for lock-free concurrent data structures. The two most important conditions are non-blocking and wait-freedom.

- A data structure is *non-blocking* if it guarantees that *some* process will always be able to complete its pending operation in a finite number of its own steps regardless of the execution speed of other processes (admits starvation).
- A data structure is *wait-free* if it guarantees that *every* process will always be able to complete its pending operations in a finite number of its own steps regardless of the execution speed of other processes (does not admit starvation).

Notice that a *lock-based* data structure can not satisfy either property, since a process that fails inside its critical section can delay all other operations indefinitely.

The term non-blocking synchronization refers to algorithms that satisfy the non-blocking property. Advantages of using non-blocking algorithms are that they are not subject to deadlocks or priority inversion, they are resilient to process failures (no data corruption on process failure), and they do not suffer significant performance degradation from scheduling preemption, page faults, or cache misses. Non-blocking algorithms are still not used in many practical applications as such algorithms are often complex (each variant of a non-blocking queue is still a publishable result). However, there are results that indicate that the non-blocking synchronization paradigm can be suitable and beneficial to large scale parallel applications.

While non-blocking has the potential to significantly improve the performance of concurrent applications, wait-free synchronization (although desirable) imposes too much overhead upon the implementation. Wait-free algorithms are often very complex and memory consuming, and hence considered less practical than non-blocking algorithms. Furthermore, starvation can be efficiently handled by collision avoidance techniques such as exponential backoff (see page 155).

The term *lock-free* algorithms refers to algorithms that do not use locking in any way. Lock-free algorithms are designed under the assumption that synchronization conflicts are rare and should be handled only as exceptions; when a synchronization conflict is noticed the operation is simply restarted from the beginning. Non-blocking algorithms are, by definition, also lock-free, but lock-free algorithms are not necessarily non-blocking. In the literature, the terms lock-free and non-blocking are sometimes used as synonymous; however, as suggested by J. D. Valois (1994), it is useful to distinguish between algorithms that do not require locking and those that actually satisfy the non-blocking property.

General methodologies for implementing non-blocking algorithms have been proposed in the literature. Such implementations are usually less efficient compared to specialized algorithms. *Transactional memory* is one such methodology.

It was suggested by M. P. Herlihy and J. E. B. Moss (1993), and is based on the idea of transactions from databases. Transactional memory allows programmers to define customized read-modify-write operations and to apply them to multiple, independently-chosen words of memory as one indivisible step.

Various other progress conditions weaker than non-blocking have been proposed in the literature. For example, a data structure is *obstruction-free* if it guarantees that a process will be able to complete its pending operations in a finite number of its own steps, if all the other processes "hold still" long enough. Efficient lock-free algorithms usually require the use of powerful synchronization primitives such as compare and swap (CAS) or load linked/store conditional (LL/SC).

The correctness condition usually used for implementing concurrent data structures is *linearizability* (page 152). Recall, that linearizability implies that each operation should appear to take place instantaneously at some point in time, and that the relative order of non-concurrent operations is preserved.

4.5.2 A Non-blocking Concurrent Queue Algorithm

A concurrent queue is a linearizable data structure that supports enqueue and dequeue operations, by several processes, with the usual queue semantics. The enqueue operation inserts a value to the queue and the dequeue operation returns and deletes the oldest value in the queue.

Queues are among the most fundamental and highly studied concurrent data structures. One of the most effective dynamic-memory concurrent queue implementations is a non-blocking queue algorithm due to M. M. Michael and M. L. Scott (1996) which is included in the standard Java Concurrency Package. A key feature of this algorithm is that concurrent accesses to the head and the tail of the queue do not interfere with each other as long as the queue is not empty. In the sequel, we describe the Michael and Scott non-blocking queue algorithm.

The queue is implemented as a singly-linked list with *head* and *tail* pointers. Each node of the linked list is composed of records, each contains three fields, a pointer to the next node in the list, a *tag* field (explained below), and a *value* field. The *head* pointer always points to a dummy node used to simplify the algorithm, whose *value* field is meaningless, which is always the first node in the list. The *tail* points to the last node when there are no active operations or to the second to last node during an enqueue operation. When the queue becomes empty both head and tail point to the dummy node.

The algorithm uses CAS operations and is therefore susceptible to the ABA problem: Assume a process reads a value A from location x, computes a new value, and then attempts to use CAS in order to write the new value into x only if x has not been changed in the interim. If between the read and the CAS other processes changed A to B and then back to A, then the CAS will succeed when it should fail.

To avoid the ABA problem a tagging mechanism is used. A *tag* value is attached to each pointer, and every time the pointer is changed, the tag is incremented. In this way, even if the pointer changes and then changes back to its original value, the tag will have changed and the CAS operation will not succeed. This solution requires the use of a double-word compare-and-swap that operates on two adjacent words of memory simultaneously. Also, this solution does not guarantee that the ABA problem will not occur, but it makes it extremely unlikely. (Why? see Problem 4.29.)

The complete algorithm is given below. As explained on page 164, the unary operator & gives the address of an object, so the statement $p = \&r$ assigns the address of r to p, and p is said to point to r. The unary operator $*$ is the *indirection* operator; when applied to a pointer, it accesses the object that the pointer points to. In addition, the notation $a{\rightarrow}b$ is used as a shorthand for $(*a).b$, where a is a pointer to a record with component b.

MICHAEL AND SCOTT NON-BLOCKING QUEUE ALGORITHM: `program of a process.`

```
type
    pointer-rec: record {ptr: pointer to node; tag: unsigned integer}
    node: record {value: data type; next: record pointer-rec}
    queue: record {head: record pointer-rec; tail: record pointer-rec}
shared
    Q: pointer to queue
    elements of type node to be allocated from the free list
local
    lnode: pointer to node
    lhead, ltail, lnext: record pointer-rec
    lvalue: data type
    done: boolean
initially
    A (dummy) node with next.ptr field set to NULL is created,
    and both Q→head.ptr and Q→tail.ptr point to it.
    Q→head.tag = Q→tail.tag = 0

enqueue(Q: pointer to queue; val: data type)
    done := false                                   /* initialize done */
    lnode := new_node()                           /* allocate a new node */
    lnode→value := val                             /* set enqueued value */
    lnode→next.ptr := NULL                       /* last node in the queue */
    repeat                                     /* do until enqueue is done */
        ltail := Q→tail                          /* read tail ptr and tag */
        lnext := ltail.ptr→next                  /* read next ptr and tag */
        if ltail = Q→tail then                      /* check consistency */
            if lnext.ptr = NULL                            /* last node? */
            /* try to link lnode to the end of the queue               */
                if CAS( &ltail.ptr→next, lnext, ⟨lnode, lnext.tag + 1⟩)
                    then done := true                   /* enqueue done! */
                fi
            else
        /* enqueue failed; try to swing tail to a node                 */
                /* that was inserted by some other process             */
```

```
E13           CAS( &O→tail, ltail, ⟨lnext.ptr, ltail.tag + 1⟩)
E14       fi
E15     fi
E16 until done = true              /* do until enqueue is done */
/* enqueue done; try to swing tail to the inserted node */
E17 CAS( &O→tail, ltail, ⟨lnode, ltail.tag + 1⟩)
end_enqueue.

dequeue(Q: pointer to queue): return data type
D0  done := false                             /* initialize done */
D1  repeat                         /* do until enqueue is done */
D2      lhead := Q→head               /* read head ptr and tag */
D3      ltail := Q→tail               /* read tail ptr and tag */
D4      lnext := lhead→next        /* read next of dummy node */
D5      if lhead = Q→head then            /* check consistency */
D6        if lhead.ptr = ltail.ptr then /* empty or tail behind? */
D7          if lnext.ptr = NULL              /* is queue empty? */
D8            then return(NULL)     /* queue is empty! done */
D9          fi
        /* tail is falling behind; try to advance tail     */
D10         CAS( &Q→tail, ltail, ⟨lnext.ptr, ltail.tag + 1⟩)
D11       else                     /* no need to deal with tail */
D12         lvalue := lnext.ptr→value     /* save return value */
            /* try to swing head to the next node           */
            /* making it the new dummy node                 */
D13         if CAS( &O→head, lhead, ⟨lnext.ptr, lhead.tag + 1⟩)
D14           then done := true  /* dequeue done! exit loop */
D15         fi
D16       fi
D17     fi
D18 until done = true              /* do until dequeue is done */
D19 free(lhead.ptr)  /* add old dummy node to the free list */
D20 return(lvalue)
                  /* dequeue succeeded! queue was not empty */
end_dequeue.
```

The enqueue operation requires two successful CAS operations to complete, as illustrated in Figure 4.4, which are used to swing pointers. During an enqueue operation by process p, the first CAS operation (line E9) is used to link the new node of p onto the list, and the second (line E17) is used to update *tail*. The second CAS is not retried if the operation fails, since such a failure implies that some other process has already helped and successfully completed the second CAS operation instead of p (by executing the CAS operation at line E13 or at line D10). Such helping is necessary in order to guarantee non-blocking: As p may fail after completing the first CAS but before completing the second, every other process must be prepared to encounter a half-finished enqueue operation, and must help finishing it.

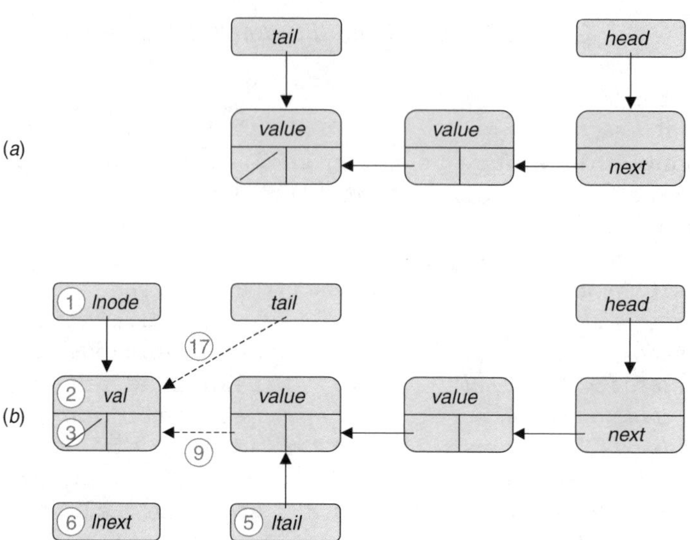

Figure 4.4 An execution of a successful enqueue operation. (*a*) The state before the enqueue; the first node is a dummy node. (*b*) The steps taken until enqueue is done; the numbers correspond to the statements executed.

The dequeue operation requires a single successful CAS operation to complete, as illustrated in Figure 4.5. During the dequeue operation a process uses a CAS operation (line D13) to advance the head pointer to the node immediately following the node currently at the front of the list. We notice that the dequeue operation ensures that *tail* does not point to the dequeued node nor to any of its predecessors, which allows the safe reuse of the dequeued nodes.

It is important to notice that rather than having *head* point to the node currently at the front of the queue, *head* always points at a *dummy node* which is the last node that was dequeued. This technique of having a dummy node at the front of the list, due to J. D. Valois (1994), helps avoid problems that occur when the queue is empty or contains only a single node, and eliminates contention between enqueue and dequeue operations. We observe that like most other queue algorithms, the Michael and Scott algorithm does not scale to a large number of concurrent operations. All concurrent enqueue and dequeue operations must synchronize on a few memory locations such as the *head* and *tail* registers. Thus, the algorithm can only allow one enqueue and one dequeue operation to complete in parallel.

Properties of the Non-blocking Concurrent Queue Algorithm:

- It is non-blocking.
- It is linearizable.
- The enqueue operation inserts a value to the queue and the dequeue operation returns and deletes the oldest value in the queue.
- The shared objects, *head*, *tail*, and the *nodes* of the linked list, all support compare-and-swap operations.

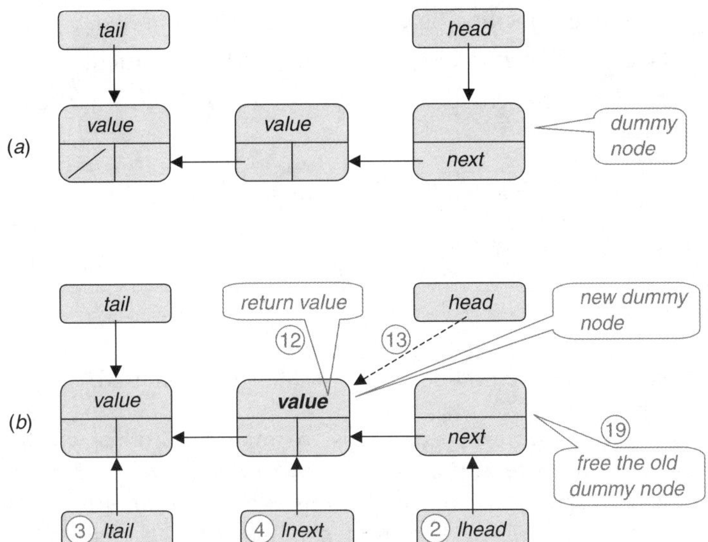

Figure 4.5 An execution of a successful dequeue operation. (*a*) The state before the dequeue; the first node is a dummy node. (*b*) The steps taken until dequeue is done; the numbers correspond to the statements executed.

To see that the algorithm is linearizable, assume that the enqueue operation takes effect when the new node is linked to the last node in the list, and the dequeue operation takes effect when *head* swings to the next node. It is not difficult to see that: the linked list is always connected; nodes are only inserted after the last node; nodes are only deleted from the beginning of the list; *head* always points to the first node; *tail* always points to a node in the list. Completing the details of the correctness proof is left as an exercise.

Finally, we notice that the classical *producer-consumer problem*, which is considered in detail in Section 8.1 (page 281), is basically the problem of implementing a *concurrent queue*, where the code for the producer implements the *enqueue* operation and the code for the consumer implements the *dequeue* operation. The solutions to the producer-consumer problem presented in Section 8.1 are blocking in the following sense: A consumer that tries to dequeue from an empty queue or a producer that tries to enqueue to a full queue (assuming a bounded size queue) is blocked until the queue state changes.

Self Review

1. Explain the relation between *non-blocking* and *deadlock-freedom*; explain the relation between *wait-freedom* and *starvation-freedom*.
2. Are algorithms that use load-link/store-conditional (LL/SC) operations susceptible to the ABA problem?
3. Is it true that in order to completely avoid the ABA problem when using CAS operations, the *tag* value (also called version number) must be carried with the object through memory deallocation and reallocation?

4. Would the *enqueue* method be correct if line E13 is omitted?
5. Would the *dequeue* method be correct if line D10 is omitted?
6. Would the *dequeue* method be correct if lines D14–D20 are replaced with the following code:

```
14                then free(lhead.ptr); return(lvalue)
15            fi
16        fi
17    fi
18 until false
```

7. Would the *enqueue* method be correct if line E17 is omitted?

Answers: (1) Non-blocking corresponds to implementations which are both fully-resilient (can tolerate any number of process failures) and deadlock-free. Wait-freedom corresponds to implementations which are both fully-resilient and starvation-free. (2) No. (3) Yes. The problem of memory reclamation for dynamic lock-free objects seems to be one of the reasons that has discouraged the wide use of lock-free data structures. (4) Because of the non-blocking requirement, the enqueue procedure would not be correct without line E13. (5) Because of the non-blocking requirement, the dequeue procedure would not be correct without line D10. (6) Yes. (7) Yes, but $Q \rightarrow tail.ptr$ would not always point to the last node of the list in states in which no process is accessing the queue.

4.6 Semaphores

Semaphores were introduced by E. W. Dijkstra as a synchronization mechanism which, among other things, enables *waiting* without the need to *busy-wait*. Dijkstra has explained it as follows:

> "Let us consider the period of time during which one of the processes is in its critical section. We all know, that during that period no other processes can enter their critical section and that, if they want to do so, they have to wait until the current critical section execution has been completed. For the remainder of that period hardly any activity is required from them: they have to wait anyhow, and as far as we are concerned *they could go to sleep*.
> Our solution [using atomic registers] does not reflect this at all: we keep the processes busy setting common variables all the time, as if no price has to be paid for this activity. But if our implementation – i.e. the ways in which or the means by which these processes are carried out – is such that *sleeping* is a less-expensive activity than this busy way of waiting, then we are fully justified (now also from an economic point of view) to call our solution misleading." (*E. W. Dijkstra*, 1968 [107])

A *general* semaphore *S* is a shared object that may take a non-negative integer value, denoted *value.S*, and support two special operations, called '*down*' and '*up*'.

- The initial value of the semaphore is assumed to be 1.

- When a process performs a down operation, if *value*.$S > 0$, then the value is decremented by 1; otherwise, the process is blocked until the value becomes greater than 0. Testing and decrementing the semaphore are executed atomically without interruption.
- When a process performs an up operation, the value is incremented by 1, in one atomic step.

A *binary semaphore* is a semaphore whose value is constrained to be either 0 or 1. The effect of a down operation on a binary semaphore is identical to that of a down operation on a general operation. However, to ensure that the value of a binary semaphore never exceeds 1, an up operation will simply set the binary semaphore value to 1. We notice that the execution of an up operation has no effect if the value of a binary semaphore is already 1. As in the case of test-and-set bits, discussed in the previous section, deadlock-free mutual exclusion can be implemented easily by enclosing each critical section between the operations down and up. That is: **down**(S); *critical section*; **up**(S); where S is a binary semaphore. In this section, whenever we use the word semaphore, we will mean a binary semaphore.

There are several types of semaphores which are distinguished by the way blocked processes are released.

- *Unfair semaphores*: No fairness assumption is made about the way blocked processes may proceed. In particular, even for two processes, infinite overtaking is possible. Unfair semaphore S can be trivially implemented using a test-and-set bit: assume that the initial value of S is 0; the down operation is implemented as **await** (*test-and-set*(S) $= 0$); and the up operation is *reset*(S). Unfair semaphores that are implemented in such a way, by continuously looping in the entry code, are called *spin locks*.
- *Weak semaphores*: A process that executes a strong up operation on a (weak) semaphore will not be the one to complete the next down operation on that semaphore, if another process has been blocked at that semaphore. Instead, one of the blocked processes is allowed to pass the semaphore.
- *Strong semaphores*: There is an upper bound on the number of times that a process may be prevented from passing that semaphore in favor of another process. Thus, infinite overtaking is impossible.

Let's consider once more the solution: **down**(S); *critical section*; **up**(S). We observe that, when S is an unfair semaphore the solution is not starvation-free even for two processes; if S is a weak semaphore then the solution is starvation-free for two processes but not for three, while with a strong semaphore it is starvation-free for any number of processes. Of course, one can define stronger types of semaphores which, for example, would guarantee FIFO scheduling.

As we have observed, an unfair semaphore can be implemented by a single test-and-set bit. Thus, it follows from the result stated in Problem 4.11 that any starvation-free mutual exclusion algorithm for n processes, using only atomic registers and unfair semaphores, must use at least n atomic registers and unfair semaphores. We now show that this is not the case for weak semaphores.

4.6.1 Constant Space Starvation-free Algorithm

We now present a solution to the mutual exclusion problem, due to S. A. Friedberg and G. L. Peterson (1987), using only two weak semaphores and two atomic bits. Recall that achieving constant space is not possible using unfair semaphores and atomic registers (see Problem 4.11). The algorithm is fast even when there is contention – its worst-case time complexity is a constant. We suggest that readers answer Problem 4.31, before they continue reading the description of the algorithm.

The first thing that a process does in its entry code is to check the value of a shared bit called *queue*, and to determine on which of two semaphores, S_0 or S_1, it should wait by executing a down operation. The first process in a group waiting on a semaphore, which succeeds to pass it, becomes the *doorkeeper* of that semaphore.

At any point, only one of the possible two doorkeepers (one for each semaphore) is active. To become active, the doorkeeper needs to get hold of both semaphores. The first thing that an active doorkeeper does is to switch the *queue* value so that all new processes will be directed to wait on the other semaphore.

An active doorkeeper is responsible that all the (finitely many) processes waiting on "its" semaphore will pass the semaphore and enter their critical sections. (The way this is implemented is explained in Problem 4.31.) Only then, the doorkeeper releases the other semaphore, enters its own critical section, and in its exit code it lets the doorkeeper of the other semaphore, if there is one, become an active doorkeeper.

FRIEDBERG AND PETERSON ALGORITHM: `program of a process.`

S_0 and S_1: weak semaphores, both are initially 1;
queue, empty: atomic bits initially 0 and *false*, respectively;
myqueue, otherqueue: local bits;

```
myqueue := queue;          /* remember semaphore to wait on */
down(S_myqueue)                      /* wait to be flushed */
if queue = myqueue                        /* first to enter? */
then                                /* become the doorkeeper */
    otherqueue := 1 - myqueue;
    down(S_otherqueue);           /* take the other semaphore */
    queue := otherqueue;                     /* change queue */
    repeat             /* flush out the processes waiting */
                                /* on the same semaphore */
        empty := true;
        up(S_myqueue);
        down(S_myqueue);
    until empty;
    Critical Section;
```

```
14      up(S_otherqueue);          /* give up the other semaphore */
15  else                                  /* not a doorkeeper */
16      empty := false;
17      Critical Section;
18  fi;
19  up(S_myqueue);             /* give up the original semaphore */
```

Notice that there might be a situation where some process, say p, checks the *queue* register and is then delayed for a long time before it starts to wait on the semaphore. In the meanwhile (while p is delayed) the doorkeeper might finish its work, without flushing off p. In such a case, p is allowed to enter its critical section without waiting for a doorkeeper.

Properties of the Friedberg and Peterson Algorithm:

- Satisfies mutual exclusion and deadlock-freedom.
- *Satisfies* 2-*bounded-waiting*: a process can enter its critical section ahead of another only twice: the first time if it starts on the other semaphore, and the second time if the other process just happened to pass the semaphore first. Thus, it satisfies only $2(n-1)$-fairness.
- Process time complexity and system response time is a constant.
- Two weak semaphores and two atomic bits are used.

4.6.2 Correctness Proof

We now prove that the algorithm satisfies mutual exclusion and starvation-freedom. The following definitions are used.

- An *active* process is a process that is in its entry code, critical section, or exit code.
- A *doorkeeper* is a process executing statements 4–14.
- A process *holds* a semaphore S, if it has passed but not released S.

Lemma 4.3 *Two processes that hold different semaphores at the same time can not both find the test in the 'if' statement in line 3 to be the same (i.e., both true or both false).*

Proof: Since the processes are holding different semaphores, the values of their local *myqueue* variables are different. Therefore, the value of *queue* must have been changed between the two tests. However, this is not possible since *queue* can be changed only by the doorkeeper while the doorkeeper is holding both semaphores. ∎

Theorem 4.4 *The algorithm satisfies mutual exclusion.*

Proof: Assume to the contrary that we have two processes in their critical section at the same time. Then, each one of them should hold at least one semaphore.

Neither of the two processes is a doorkeeper, since a doorkeeper must hold both semaphores while in its critical section. Thus, both processes have found the test in the if statement in line 3 to be *false*, which contradicts Lemma 4.3. ∎

Lemma 4.5 *If the doorkeeper is waiting on a semaphore (at either 6 or 11), then the number of the processes whose local myqueue value equals the semaphore index is decreasing.*

Proof: First we observe that there can not be two doorkeepers at the same time. This follows from the fact that a doorkeeper must hold at least one semaphore and must find the test in the if statement in line 3 to be *true*. By Lemma 4.3, this can not happen at the same time for two processes.

Let *sem* be the index of the semaphore that doorkeeper is waiting on. Since there are only a finite number of active processes at any time, the number of processes with *myqueue* equal to *sem* is finite. Also, we observe that the current value of *queue* must be different from *sem*, and hence no new active process will assign its *myqueue* to be *sem*.

The fact that a doorkeeper is waiting implies that some other process which is not a doorkeeper has the semaphore. But this process will eventually finish its critical section and be unable to restart and wait on the same semaphore. Thus, there will be one less active process waiting on *sem*. ∎

Lemma 4.6 *The doorkeeper will eventually enter its critical section.*

Proof: Since the number of active processes that are waiting on a semaphore that the doorkeeper is also waiting on is always decreasing, the doorkeeper will eventually succeed in passing every semaphore it is accessing. This means that the doorkeeper can be guaranteed of completing its *repeat* loop and entering its critical section. ∎

Theorem 4.7 *The algorithm is starvation-free.*

Proof: By Lemma 4.7, every doorkeeper eventually exits its critical section. Every process which is not a doorkeeper needs to hold only one semaphore, which it accesses at statement 2, before it can enter its critical section. Thus, every process that holds some semaphore eventually enters its critical section and releases the semaphore.

To prove the theorem, we need to show that no process can wait forever on a semaphore at statement 2. Assume to the contrary that some process p waits forever on a semaphore indexed *sem* at statement 2. Then, there must be an infinite cycle of processes taking and releasing the semaphore while p is waiting.

If one of these processes has $myqueue = queue = sem$, it will become the doorkeeper. The doorkeeper will force all processes waiting on the semaphore (indexed by *sem*) through the critical section. This is so because the doorkeeper can not execute the up, down pair consecutively if there is a waiting process and all waiting processes change *empty* to *false*.

There can not be an infinite cycle of processes that acquire the semaphore and have $myqueue \neq sem$, because every process that enters or reenters the protocol will wait on the other semaphore. ∎

Self Review

1. Let A be a mutual exclusion algorithm which uses semaphores. For each of the following two statements tell if it is correct or incorrect?
   (a) If A is deadlock-free with unfair semaphores, then A is starvation-free with strong semaphores;
   (b) If A is deadlock-free with weak semaphores, then A is starvation-free with strong semaphores.
2. Assume that in the Friedberg and Peterson algorithm, some process which is not a doorkeeper, say p, enters its critical section by executing the sequence of statements 1;2;3;16;17, and let S be the semaphore that p has to access in statement 2. Is it possible that while p is active (in its entry, critical section, and exit code) no other process is a doorkeeper of S?

Answers: (1a) No. (1b) No. (2) Yes!

4.7 Monitors

Monitors are program modules that are used to ensure exclusive access to resources, and for synchronization and communication among processes. Solving mutual exclusion using monitors is trivial, under any fairness assumption. The monitor concept, which is used in modern programming languages (such as Modula and Java), is reviewed below.

A monitor consists of a set of resources (data items) and a set of procedures that are the only way by which the resources can be manipulated. A process can access a resource only by calling one of the monitor's procedures. Mutual exclusion is enforced by ensuring that at most one process at a time may be executing any procedure in a monitor. That is, the monitor is locked when an execution of a procedure begins and the monitor is unblocked when it ends. If a process tries to invoke a procedure while the monitor is blocked, the process is suspended until the monitor becomes unblocked (i.e., the process is added to an "entry queue"). The syntax of a monitor is:

monitor *name*
    declarations of resources (i.e., variables)
    procedure $proc_1$ (parameters) body **end**;
    procedure $proc_2$ (parameters) body **end**;
    ...
end

In many cases, the mutual exclusion which is provided automatically by monitors is all that is needed. However, sometimes a process within a monitor needs to suspend its execution in order to enable another process to access the same monitor. For that purpose, monitors provide *conditional variables* with the associated operations '*signal*' and '*wait*'.

- When a process executes the statement wait(*c*), the process is delayed and is added to the rear of the queue of the conditional variable *c*. The monitor is then unlocked, which allows another process to use the monitor.
- Executing signal(*c*) awakens and removes the process at the front of *c*'s queue and adds it to the "run queue". This process executes at some future time when the monitor is unblocked. The process executing signal retains exclusive control of the monitor and can continue executing.

If a process executing in one monitor calls a procedure in another monitor, the first monitor is not unblocked. The operations signal and wait are similar to down and up operations on (general) semaphores. There are, however, a few differences between them.

1. Executing a down operation does not block a process if the semaphore value is greater than zero. In contrast, a wait operation always delays a process until a later signal is executed.
2. Executing an up operation on a semaphore either unblocks a waiting process or, if there is no waiting process, increments the semaphore value. In contrast, executing a signal on an empty queue has no effect.
3. A process awakened by an up operation can resume execution immediately. In contrast, a process awakened by a signal is restarted only when the monitor is unlocked.

When a monitor is unlocked, the next process to use the monitor is then chosen from one of a number of queues internal to the monitor (i.e., the *entry* queue and the *run* queue). In such a case it is not obvious which process should execute next, and depending on the kind of monitor, a particular choice is made. All other processes must wait until the monitor is again unlocked. The main difference among various types of monitors is the algorithm used by the implicit monitor scheduler to select the next process to be executed when the monitor is unblocked.

The signal operation, as described above, is non-preemptive since the signaling process continues executing. There are monitor types which support preemptive signaling, where the process executing signal is forced to delay, and the awakened process is the next to execute in the monitor. Finally, there exists also the notion of *automatic-signal* monitors, where conditional variables and signaling are eliminated by modifying the *wait* statement to use conditional expression.

There are several other operations on conditional variables that some monitors support. For example, to determine whether at least one process is delayed on a conditional variable *c*, a process in a monitor may invoke the function: **empty**(*c*), which is *true* if *c*'s queue is empty; otherwise it is *false*. The operation **signal**_*all*(*c*) awakens all processes delayed on *c* (i.e., moves them all to the "run queue"). Finally, when using a priority wait operation: **wait**(*c*, *rank*), the processes delayed on *c* are awakened in ascending order of *rank*.

In the following chapters we demonstrate how to solve several classical synchronization problems using monitors.

4.8 Fairness of Shared Objects

Fairness is a powerful abstraction that has led to fruitful results in the theory of concurrency. Various notions of fairness can be explained very briefly, but small differences have important consequences on the computability and complexity of concurrent systems.

Interprocess communication via shared objects generally requires some underlying fairness in their implementation. For example, when we previously considered solutions using various types of shared objects, we have always implicitly assumed that the objects are starvation-free. That is, if a process is trying to access an object then this process eventually succeeds. This motivates the question: What can be done when the primitive objects are assumed to satisfy other fairness assumptions.

4.8.1 Fairness Properties

In general, an object specification is a set of (finite or infinite) sequences of requests and responses, where the subsequence of each process alternates between requests and responses. Objects are discussed and defined in Section 4.1.2.

As already defined on page 44, a *state* of an algorithm (or a system) includes the local state of each process and the state of each shared object. An *event* is either: (1) an update of the internal state of a process, (2) a *request* by some process to access some shared object, (3) an update of the internal state of an object on behalf of a process with a pending access, or (4) a *response* by a shared object to a pending request. As in the standard interleaving semantics, a *run* α of a system is an alternating (finite or infinite) sequence $s_0 \stackrel{e_0}{\rightarrow} s_1 \stackrel{e_1}{\rightarrow} \cdots$ of configurations s_i and events e_i such that: (1) the initial configuration s_0 satisfies appropriate initial conditions, and (2) every configuration s_{i+1} is derived from the previous configuration s_i by executing a legal event e_i of a process or object.

Several of the fairness definitions below depend on the notion of a process *trying* to access an object. Let α be a run in which a process p issues a request R to a shared object o. We say that p is *trying to access* o during the interval beginning with the last response to p preceding R from any shared object, or beginning with the initial state if no such response exists, ending with the response to R, or the remainder of α if the response does not exist. That is, we include in the interval in which we consider p to be trying to access o, the local computation by p preceding the explicit request R, and any subsequent steps of the run up to the response. This definition relates local computation time with the time needed to access shared objects.[1] We say that a process p *succeeds* in accessing object o, when the object o responds to a pending request of p.

---

[1] Most models of concurrency assume that local computation time is negligible compared to the time it takes to access the shared memory. Although it is very convenient to assume that local computation takes zero time, in our framework it suffices to make this weaker assumption.

Some natural fairness properties for shared objects, o, are defined below. Each of these fairness properties restricts the set of runs of a system incorporating o to those satisfying the required condition. (Each property implies the preceding.)

- *deadlock-freedom*: If a process is trying to access an object o, then some process (not necessarily the same one) eventually succeeds in accessing o.
- *starvation-freedom*: If a process is trying to access an object o, then this process eventually succeeds. (Notice that one process can access o arbitrarily many times ahead of another.)
- *bounded-waiting*: o is deadlock-free, and in any run there is a bound r such that whenever a process, say p, is trying to access o then no other process successfully accesses o more than r times before p succeeds with its access.
- *r-bounded-waiting*: o is deadlock-free, and if a process is trying to access o then it will succeed before any of the other processes is able to access o a number of times equal to $r + 1$.

Notice that r-bounded-waiting imposes an *a priori* bound r on all runs, while bounded-waiting is much weaker, requiring that some bound r, not given *a priori*, must exist for any given run.

For a given object o, a fairness property F' is *weaker than* a fairness property F, if: o satisfies F implies o satisfies F'. We say that an object o satisfies *only* fairness property F, if any fairness property that o satisfies is weaker than F for o. When a given object o satisfies a fairness property F we call o an F object.

4.8.2 Basic Results

In this section, we make few observations about the various notions of fairness and the relations between them. The first observation implies that objects which satisfy only deadlock-freedom are much weaker than starvation-free objects.

Theorem 4.8 *There is no deadlock-free mutual exclusion algorithm using objects which satisfy only deadlock-freedom.*

Proof: The proof is based on the observation that deadlock-free objects are not sufficiently powerful to guarantee the transmission of even a single bit of information from a predefined sender process to a receiver process. Suppose we want to block transmission from process p to q. There is a run of p and q which is similar to a run in which q runs in isolation: at any object o (which satisfies only deadlock-freedom) touched by both p and q, one of two cases holds. Either q accesses o a finite number of times, all before p's first access to o, or q accesses o an infinite number of times, preventing p's first access from terminating. Now consider a mutual exclusion system in which process p holds the critical section and accesses shared object o to release it: by the above observation, there is a run in which p never succeeds in informing q that the critical section is available, so q can never enter it. ∎

We notice that there is a crucial distinction between a deadlock-free mutual exclusion *algorithm*, where some contending process must enter the critical section, and a deadlock-free mutual exclusion *object*. In the former case, a process is blocked until it enters the critical section (like a **down** operation on a semaphore), while in the latter case it may receive a "deny" answer (as in a test-and-set bit). In deadlock-free objects, infinitely many accesses by contenders (accesses which return but deny the contenders the critical section) can satisfy the deadlock-free constraint, while the holder of the critical section hangs forever in its attempt to release it.

As we have seen, there are many deadlock-free mutual exclusion algorithms using various starvation-free objects, such as, starvation-free registers, test-and-set, read-modify-write objects. Thus, such objects are stronger than similar objects which satisfy only deadlock-freedom.

Next, we make an observation which relates different fairness assumptions. It implies that in various cases, algorithms can be designed that perform well under fairness assumptions, but whose correctness is robust when those assumptions are violated.

As we have already observed on page 12, requirements or properties of algorithms are usually divided into two classes. The first are the *safety properties* which ensure that nothing bad will happen. The second are *liveness properties* which guarantee that something good eventually happens. Thus, in a mutual exclusion algorithm, mutual exclusion is a safety property, while deadlock-freedom and starvation-freedom are liveness properties. More formally, a property ϕ is a *safety* property if an infinite run satisfies ϕ if and only if all finite prefixes of the run satisfy ϕ.

Theorem 4.9 *An algorithm A satisfies a safety property ϕ (such as mutual exclusion) only if it does not matter whether the objects it uses are deadlock-free, starvation-free, or bounded-waiting.*

Proof: To show that it does not matter whether each of the objects being used is deadlock-free or starvation-free, it is enough to observe that the set of (legal) finite runs of A is the same whether each of the objects is deadlock-free or starvation-free. If A satisfies a safety property ϕ with starvation-free objects then, clearly, it satisfies ϕ with bounded objects. To prove the other direction, suppose A does not satisfy ϕ with starvation-free objects. If ϕ is a safety property then there is a finite run which violates ϕ. This run is also possible when using bounded-waiting objects since we can choose the bound to be as big as needed. Thus in turn A fails to satisfy ϕ with bounded objects. ∎

Bounded-waiting objects are arguably a better approximation of real shared objects compared to the (usually assumed) starvation-free objects. Furthermore, they sometimes enable us to design algorithms for problems that are unsolvable using objects which satisfy only starvation-freedom. In the case of registers which satisfy only starvation-freedom, any deadlock-free mutual exclusion algorithm for n processes must use at least n such registers (Theorem 2.16, page 59). A similar result holds also for bounded-waiting.

Theorem 4.10 *Any deadlock-free mutual exclusion algorithm for n processes using registers which satisfy only bounded-waiting must use at least n such registers.*

Proof: To prove the corresponding results for registers which satisfy only starvation-freedom (Theorem 2.16, page 59) we have shown how to construct a finite run which violates mutual exclusion, for any algorithm which uses fewer than n starvation-free registers. Since the constructed run is finite, this construction similarly constrains the number of registers which satisfy only bounded-waiting, needed. ∎

Theorem 4.10 seems to suggest that there is not much difference between starvation-free objects and bounded-waiting objects; however, this is not the case. While there is no wait-free election algorithm using registers which satisfies only starvation-freedom (Problem 3.27), there is a wait-free election algorithm using registers which satisfies only bounded-waiting (Problem 4.44).

4.8.3 Algorithms

Next we present several algorithms which make use of r-bounded-waiting objects. The algorithms demonstrate that r-bounded-waiting objects are much stronger than bounded-waiting objects. We start with a very simple observation about r-bounded-waiting registers.

Theorem 4.11 *For any positive integer r, there is a deadlock-free mutual exclusion algorithm using a single register which satisfies only r-bounded-waiting.*

Proof: The simple mutual exclusion algorithm uses a single r-bounded-waiting register and is based on Fischer's timing-based algorithm (page 345). The register, called x, is initially 0. A process first waits until $x = 0$ and then assigns its *id* to x. Then, it reads x exactly r times. The fact that x is an r-bounded-waiting register ensures that after a process finishes reading, the value of x remains unchanged until some process leaving its critical section sets x back to 0. If x hasn't been changed and hence equals the process id, the process can safely enter its critical section, otherwise it goes to the beginning of its code and repeats this procedure. A consensus algorithm is constructed in a similar way. ∎

Recall that a mutual exclusion algorithm is *fast* if in the absence of contention, a process can always enter its critical section and exit it in a constant number of steps. In particular, when using r-bounded waiting objects, the number of steps in this case does not depend on r.

Theorem 4.12 *For any positive integer r, there is a fast deadlock-free mutual exclusion algorithm using three registers which satisfy only r-bounded-waiting.*

Proof: An algorithm is presented in which, in the absence of contention, a process can always enter its critical section and exit it in a constant number of steps. The algorithm is a very simple adaption of the fast timing-based algorithm, which is presented on page 347.

A FAST ALGORITHM: `process i's program.`

x, y, z: r-bounded-waiting registers, initially $y = 0$ and $z = 0$.

```
1  start: x := i;
2         await (y = 0);
3         y := i;
4         if x ≠ i then for i = 1 to 2r do
                          dummy := x; dummy := y; dummy := z od;
5                         if y ≠ i then goto start fi;
6                         await (z = 0)
7                   else z := 1 fi;
8         critical section;
9         z := 0;
10        if y = i then y := 0 fi;
```

Process i first sets x to i, and then checks the value of y. When it finds $y = 0$, it sets y to i and then checks the value of x. Let us say that process i enters its critical section *along path* α if it finds $x = i$ at this step. It should be clear that at most one process can enter its critical section along path α. If a process finds $x \neq i$ then it starts looping (in line 4). The loop on line 4 is to suspend the executing process until each other process that is trying to access shared registers will have a chance to do so at least twice. This is possible only because the registers are r-bounded-waiting. The loop plays two roles:

1. Let us say that process i enters its critical section *along path* β if it finds $y = i$ after the loop at line 4. Then, looping in line 4 ensures that if process i finds $y = i$ after the loop, no other process can change the value of y until process i sets y to 0 in its exit code, and hence it follows that at most one process can enter along path β.
2. The loop at line 4 ensures that the process which enters its critical section along path α sets z to 1 *before* a process executing path β has a chance to test z. Thus, if process i entering along path β finds $y = i$ and $z = 0$, it can be sure that no other process is about to enter the critical section along path α.

The algorithm satisfies mutual exclusion and deadlock-freedom. A detailed correctness proof of the original timing-based algorithm appears on page 348. ∎

While achieving constant space for starvation-free mutual exclusion is not possible using registers and test-and-set bits which satisfy only bounded-waiting (Problem 4.43), it is possible when the objects satisfy r-bounded-waiting.

Theorem 4.13 *For any positive integer r, there is a starvation-free mutual exclusion algorithm, for an unspecified number of processes, using two test-and-set bits* *which satisfy only r-bounded-waiting and two bits which satisfy only starvation-freedom.*

Proof: The algorithm presented below is a very simple adaption of the Friedberg and Peterson algorithm (presented on page 178) which originally used weak semaphores. We give the code of the algorithm below, for more details see the original algorithm.

THE ALGORITHM: `program of a process.`

T_0 and T_1: r-bounded-waiting test-and-set bits, both are initially 0;
queue, empty: starvation-free bits initially 0 and *false*, respectively;
myqueue, otherqueue: local bits;
counter: local register;

```
myqueue := queue;                              /* remember where to wait */
await test-and-set(T_myqueue) = 0                  /* wait to be flushed */
if queue = myqueue                                   /* first to enter? */
then                                           /* become the doorkeeper */
    otherqueue := 1 - myqueue;
    await test-and-set(T_otherqueue) = 0;          /* take the other bit */
    queue := otherqueue;                                /* change queue */
    repeat                              /* flush out waiting processes */
        if empty := false then counter := 0
        else counter := counter + 1 fi;
        empty := true;
        release(T_myqueue);
        await test-and-set(T_myqueue) = 0;
    until counter = r;                         /* r-boundedness is used */
    Critical Section;
    release(T_otherqueue);                           /* give up the bit */
else                                               /* not a doorkeeper */
    empty := false;
    Critical Section;
fi;
release(T_myqueue);                         /* give up the original bit */
```

The algorithm satisfies mutual exclusion, deadlock-freedom, and 2-bounded-waiting (i.e., a process can enter its critical section ahead of another only twice). Process time complexity depends on r. ∎

Self Review
Consider the fast algorithm from page 187:

1. Does it matter if we change the order of the last two statements (lines 9 and 10)?
2. Does it matter if we change the order of the two statements at lines 5 and 6?

3. Will the algorithm still be correct if we replace the last statement (line 10), with the statement $y = 0$?
4. Is the algorithm correct if we replace the statement "**await**($y = 0$)" in line 2, with the statement: **if** $y \neq 0$ **then goto** *start* **fi**?
5. Is the algorithm correct if we replace the statement "**await**($z = 0$)" in line 6, with the statement: **if** $z \neq 0$ **then goto** *start* **fi**?

Answers: (1) Yes. (2) No. (3) No, it would not satisfy mutual exclusion. (4) Yes. (5) No, it would not satisfy deadlock-freedom.

4.9 Bibliographic Notes

4.1

Most modern processor architectures support some form of "read-modify-write" interprocess synchronization. There are interesting questions about the relative power of all these primitives. Suppose you have software that is written using the test-and-set primitive, and your hardware supports only fetch-and-add. How can you run the software on this hardware? Put another way, given two primitives A and B, is it possible to implement (in software) A by B? Are there problems that can be solved using A but can not be solved using B?

There are several results about the relative power of various objects [166]. Atomic registers are strictly weaker than most the other objects. That is, there is a problem, namely wait-free consensus for two processes, that can not be solved using only atomic registers but can be solved using most of the other objects, and any problem that can be solved using only atomic registers can also be solved using most of the other objects. In addition, it is known that test-and-set bits, swap, fetch-and-add, queues, stacks are strictly weaker than most other objects, except atomic registers. They can solve consensus for two processes but can not solve the wait-free consensus for three processes. Thus, we say that those objects have consensus number 2. The relative computational power of shared objects is explored in detail in Section 9.6.

As mentioned, Java Concurrency Utilities (JSR-166) proposes a set of medium-level utilities that provide functionality commonly needed in concurrent programs, and has been released as part of JDK1.5.0. It supports concurrent queues, compare&swap locks, readers and writers, semaphores, barriers, and more [231]; see also [230].

The notion of linearizability (page 152), which means that each operation should appear to take effect instantaneously, is due to M. P. Herlihy and J. M. Wing [173]. Non-atomic objects are discussed by Lamport in [223], where he defines the three general classes of shared registers which support read and write operations, called safe, regular, and atomic, depending on their properties when several reads and/or writes are executed concurrently.

Sequential consistency, as defined on page 152, is a consistency condition weaker than linearizability and is due to L. Lamport [217]. Based on the notion of sequential consistency, Lamport has defined the notion of *virtual* mutual exclusion: memory operations act as if all those in one critical section were performed either before or after all those in another. Virtual mutual exclusion says nothing about when the operations are really performed [217, 227]. A tutorial which describes many issues related to memory consistency models can be found in [2].

4.2

The trivial deadlock-free algorithm on page 154 is part of the folklore. The experimental results mentioned at the end of Section 4.2.3 regarding exponential backoff are based on experimental tests reported in [39, 150, 254]. The fast starvation-free algorithm on page 156 is from [22], and is based on a starvation-free algorithm by Burns [81] (see algorithm on page 195). In Burns' algorithm, the winning process, even in the absence of contention, executes $O(n)$ steps, where n is the total number of processes. In [281], it is proven that any starvation-free mutual exclusion algorithm for n processes using only atomic registers and test-and-set bits must use at least n atomic registers and test-and-set bits. All the lower bounds for the read-modify-write registers apply of course also to the weaker test-and-set registers. In [129] the above lower bound from [281] has been generalized to cover conditional objects. See also [69].

4.3

The Ticket algorithm on page 158 is from [132, 133], where a tight space bound of $\Theta(n^2)$ shared states is proved for the k-exclusion problem (for fixed k) assuming a strong FIFO and strong robustness properties. That is, FIFO in the exit code is also required, up to $k-1$ enabled processes can fail, and any number of other (not enabled) processes can fail anywhere else. Without the strong FIFO and strong robustness requirements (at most $k-1$ processes can fail), and not requiring that the exit code be wait-free, $O(n)$ shared states suffice [281]. In [83, 280], it is shown that any starvation-free solution requires at least $\sqrt{2n}+\frac{1}{2}$ values. Requiring also that the algorithm be memoryless increases the lower bound to $\lfloor n/2 \rfloor + 2$ values [280], while achieving bounded-waiting requires at least $n+1$ values [83, 280]. These bounds are shown in [83] to be nearly optimal, for algorithms are exhibited for the last two cases with $\lfloor n/2 \rfloor + 9$ values for starvation-freedom and $n+3$ values for linear-waiting. These last two upper bounds are improved in [281] to $\lfloor n/2 \rfloor + 6$ values for the starvation-freedom case and $n+2$ values for 2-bounded waiting. In the algorithms in [83, 281] the exit code is *not* wait-free (i.e., requirement 4 on page 12 is not satisfied.) The results in [83] build on earlier work reported in [101], in which a linear-waiting algorithm using a single $(2n-1)$-valued register is presented. Also, in the algorithm of [101] the exit code is not wait-free.

4.4

The queuing algorithm from page 161 is from [39]. In the original algorithm Anderson has used the fetch-and-increment operation. The other queuing algorithm (page 163) which uses swap objects is from [150]. In these two algorithms different processes may spin on the same memory location at different times. Their time complexity in the CC model is a constant, while their time complexity in the DSM model is unbounded. (See Section 4.1 for the definitions of these objects.)

The MCS algorithm (page 165) which uses both compare-and-swap and swap operations is from [254]. Unlike the previous two algorithms, the MCS algorithm satisfies local spinning in *both* the CC model and the DSM model. The MCS algorithm can be re-written to use only *swap*, but at the expense of not satisfying FIFO (newly arriving processes may be allowed to jump ahead of processes already in the queue). In [193], a simple correctness proof of the MCS lock is provided. An extension of the MCS algorithm that solves the reader and writers problem is presented in [255].

Another important queue-based lock was developed by Craig [100] and, independently by Magnusson, Landin, and Hagersten [248, 249]. As the MCS lock, the queue is implemented as a linked list, but with pointers from each process to its *predecessor*. The algorithm uses swap operations and may outperform the MCS lock on cache-coherent machines. Its time complexity in the CC model is a constant, while its time complexity in the DSM model is unbounded. A variant of the algorithm with constant time complexity in both the CC and the DSM models was presented in [100].

The experimental results mentioned at the end of the section are based on experimental tests reported in [39, 150, 254]. The principal conclusion from these empirical performance results (from the early nineties) is that "memory and interconnect contention due to busy-wait synchronization in shared-memory multi-processors need not be a problem" [254].

In [188, 305], queue-based algorithms are presented in which it is possible for a spinning process to "become impatient" and leave the queue before acquiring the lock. A recovery-based spin lock is presented in [298]. Guidelines for selecting different kinds of locks are given in [253]. Finally, a set of algorithms that perform well in the presence of multiprogramming while maintaining good performance on dedicated machines is presented in [205].

4.5

Algorithms for several concurrent data structures based on locking have been proposed since at least the 1970s [65, 126, 208, 232], and the benefits of avoiding locking have already been considered in [124]. In [173], the concept of a non-blocking data structure is introduced, and a non-blocking and linearizable implementation of a concurrent queue which uses an array of infinite length is presented. A comprehensive discussion of wait-free synchronization is given in [166]. Bounded wait-freedom is studied in [76]. The term lock-free was first used in [252]. The notion of obstruction-freedom was introduced in [169]. An evaluation of the performance of non-blocking implementations of queues, stacks, heaps, and counters is presented in [266].

General methodologies for generating non-blocking versions of sequential or concurrent lock-based algorithms were suggested in [5, 22, 64, 142, 167, 170,

171, 289, 307, 327]. The resulting implementations are less efficient compared to specialized algorithms. In [9, 34, 51, 185], a few more implementations of multi-objects are proposed.

The non-blocking queue algorithm presented on page 171 is from [265]. The algorithm is included in the standard Java Concurrency Package. The basic structure of the algorithm is similar to a queue algorithm from [331]. In [331], a technique called reference counting is proposed which guarantees to prevent the ABA problem without the need to use tags or double-word compare-and-swap; see [264] for a correction. The technique associates a reference count with each node of reusable memory, and a node is reused only when no process points to it. Other memory reclamation techniques for that enable elimination of the need for tags in (a variant of) the queue algorithm from [265], are proposed in [168, 261, 262]. In [268] the performance of the queue algorithm from [265] has been improved by using a scaling technique called elimination as a backoff technique for the algorithm from [265].

Non-blocking implementations of concurrent queues have appeared in many papers; a few examples are [15, 169, 173, 211, 219, 239, 317, 326, 331].Many other important papers have been published which include non-blocking implementations of other concurrent data structures such as stacks, double-ended queues, priority queues, heaps, linked lists, sets, search trees, dictionaries, hash tables, clocks, and counters; a few examples are [38, 46, 138, 153, 160, 225, 229, 260, 269, 306, 318, 332]. There are a few open-source libraries which provide implementations of lock-free and non-blocking data structures.

4.6

The notion of a (weak) semaphore was introduced by Dijkstra in [107]. Originally, the down and up operations were named by Dijkstra, *P* and *V*, respectively. The *P* operation is named after the Dutch word *passeren*, meaning "to pass", and the *V* operation is named after *vrygeven*, the Dutch word for "to release". In fact the concept of a semaphore is already discussed by Dijkstra in his manuscript EWD 51 from 1962, "Multiprogrammering en X8" (Multi-programming and X8) written in Dutch. See also [108].

It has been conjectured in [111] that no starvation-free solution to the problem exists for unknown number of processes and under the constraint of employing only a fixed number of weak semaphores and atomic registers. Morris has shown that it could be done with three semaphores and two n-valued atomic registers where n is the maximum number of processes [270] (page 201). (An incorrect claim is made in [42] that Morris' algorithm does not refute Dijkstra's conjecture.) Another solution using two semaphores (used together as a "split binary semaphore" [177]) and two n-valued atomic registers is presented in [251]. A variant of Morris' solution [270] is presented in [330].

Friedberg and Peterson have presented a new solution which improves the space complexity to two semaphores and two atomic bits (page 178). A variant of the Friedberg and Peterson algorithm (page 200) has appeared in [158].

As mentioned, weak semaphores were first introduced in [107]. According to this definition the group of blocked processes is modeled as a set, from which an up operation chooses at random a process to continue. Two stronger notions of semaphores (1) in which it is required that no process will be blocked indefinitely long and (2) where the group of blocked processes is modeled as a FIFO queue are mentioned in [109].

Many other varieties of semaphores were defined over the years. In [333] an extension of Dijkstra's (weak) semaphore is presented (dubbed PV-chunk in [235]) allowing the semaphores to be updated by "chuncks" that are arbitrary positive integers. In [278], a stronger type of semaphore, called PV-multiple, is defined, which allows several basic semaphores to be accessed in one step. The synchronization power of these and other types of semaphores, the relation between them and the way they can be used to solve various generalizations of the mutual exclusion problem are investigated in [162, 163, 186, 235, 274, 344].

Finally, the possibility of constructing a starvation-free solution using semaphores under various conditions is considered in [314], and a performance study is discussed in [273].

4.7

The concept of a monitor is due to Per Brinch-Hansen and C.A.R. Hoare. It is discussed in [74] and [176], and is explained in detail in [177], using many interesting examples. The idea of using automatic-signal monitors (rather than using conditional variables) is also from [177]. A comparison of various types of monitors can be found in [40, 78].

There are many other high level mechanisms for synchronization and communication which we have not covered. These include conditional critical regions [175] and path expressions [87].

4.8

All the results that are presented in Section 4.8 are taken from [258], where algorithmic issues that arise due to various fairness assumptions on how pending requests are served by shared objects are investigated. This paper includes also other results about fairness of shared objects.

In Section 10.1, a shared memory model, called the *known-delay* model, is considered where it is assumed that there is an upper bound on the time required for a single access to shared memory, and that the bound is known to all the processes. This timing-based model is related to a model, where all shared objects are assumed to satisfy r-bounded-waiting fairness for some known r. In Section 10.7, some of the work for the above timing-based model has been extended to the *unknown-delay* model, where an upper bound exists on the memory-access time, but is not known *a priori*.

The notion of *finitary fairness* was introduced in [19, 20]. Finitary fairness requires that for every run of a system there is an unknown bound k such that no enabled transition is postponed more than k consecutive times. Both systems that satisfy the finitary fairness assumption and unknown-delay timing-based systems are similar (but not the same) to a model where all shared objects satisfy bounded-waiting fairness.

The text [139], by N. Francez, brings together most of the known approaches for proving properties of programs and, in particular, focuses on proving the termination of programs under various fairness assumptions about the processes' behavior (such as unconditional, weak, and strong fairness). Our focus in Section 4.8 is less on formal verification issues and more on algorithmic issues that arise due to various fairness assumptions on how pending requests are served by shared objects.

Randomized Algorithms

As mentioned, it is proved in [83] that when using a single read-modify-write register, any *deterministic* starvation-free solution requires that the size of the register be at least $O(\log n)$ bits, and that this bound is tight. In [161], it is shown that all the lower bounds proved in [83] (for deterministic algorithms) are also required for probabilistic (randomized) algorithms of the same kind.

In [291], the first randomized algorithm was presented which uses only a single read-modify-write register of size $\Omega(\log \log n)$ bits, and it was claimed that the algorithm satisfies the following fairness property which is called *linear fairness*: In any round, any process competing for entrance to the critical section with m other processes succeeds with probability $\Omega(1/m)$. Here, a round is defined to be the time between two successive entrances to the critical section. Surprisingly, it was shown in [301] that the algorithm in [291] does not satisfy linear fairness. In [210] the randomized algorithm presented in [291] was modified using a shared register with the same number of bits (up to a constant) satisfying linear fairness. In [209], a tight lower bound of $\Omega(\log \log n)$ bits on the size of the shared register was proved.

4.10 Problems

The problems are divided into several categories. See page 23 for a detailed explanation.

Problems based on Section 4.2

∘ 4.1 Consider the deadlock-free algorithm using a test-and-test-and-set bit (page 154). Why do we need the first statement (**await**$(x = 0)$)?

∘ 4.2 Write an exponential backoff algorithm that uses a single test-and-set bit instead of using a test-and-test-and-set bit.

∘ 4.3 Write an optimistic version of the exponential backoff algorithm from page 155. (The notion "optimistic" is defined on page 154.)

∘∘ 4.4 Improve the performance of the fast starvation-free algorithm using a test-and-set bit (page 156), by using a test-and-test-and-set bit instead of a test-and-set bit.

∘ 4.5 What is the smallest k for which the starvation-free algorithm on page 156 satisfies k-bounded-waiting.

◦ 4.6 Write a fast starvation-free mutual exclusion algorithm with exponential backoff.

◦ 4.7 Write a fast starvation-free solution to the mutual exclusion problem using a single *swap* object (and atomic registers). (See page 151 for the definition of *swap*.)

◦ 4.8 Prove that there is no starvation-free mutual exclusion algorithm for two processes using a single test-and-set bit.

◦◦ 4.9 The following algorithm is a modified version of the fast starvation-free algorithm from page 156. (Notice that it does not use the shared register *Turn*.)

ANOTHER FAST ALGORITHM: `process i's program.`

```
lock: test-and-set bit, initially false;
wait[0..(n − 1)]: array of atomic bits, initially false;
lturn, Key: local registers ;

1   waiting[i] := true;
2   key := true;
3   while (waiting[i] and key) do
4           key := test-and-set(lock) od;
5   critical section;
6   waiting[i] := false;
7   if lturn = i − 1 then lturn := (lturn + 2)mod n
8                    else lturn := (lturn + 1)mod n fi;
9   if waiting[lturn] then waiting[lturn] := false
10                   else reset(lock) fi;
```

What kind of fairness properties does the algorithm satisfy?
Would the above algorithm still be correct if we replace lines 7 and 8 with the single statement: *Lturn := (Lturn +1) mod n* ?

◦◦ 4.10 We present below a starvation-free solution, due to James Burns (1978). The algorithm employs a test-and-set bit *lock*, and an array *waiting* of *n* atomic bits. The algorithm follows.

BURNS' STARVATION-FREE ALGORITHM: `process i's program.`

```
Initially: lock: test-and-set bit, initially false;
waiting[0..(n − 1)]: array of atomic bits, initially false;
key: local register;

waiting[i] := true;
key := true;
while (waiting[i] and key) do
        key := test-and-set(lock) od;
waiting[i] := false;
critical section;
j := (i + 1)mod n;
```

```
while (j ≠ i) and (not waiting[j]) do j := (j + 1)mod n;
if j = i then lock := false
        else waiting[j] := false;
```

What kind of fairness properties does the algorithm satisfy, and what is the process time complexity?

◦• 4.11 Prove that any starvation-free mutual exclusion algorithm for n processes using only atomic registers and test-and-set bits must use at least n atomic registers and test-and-set bits.

We observe that the above result implies that no starvation-free solution exists for unknown number of processes and under the constraint of employing only a fixed number of test-and-set bits and atomic bits. This observation also follows immediately from the result stated in Problem 4.16.

•◦ 4.12 A conditional operation is an operation that changes the value of an object only if the object has a particular value. A *conditional object* is an object that supports only conditional operations. Compare-and-swap and test-and-set are examples of conditional objects. A *write-conditional object* is an object that supports only a *write* operation *and* conditional operations.

- Prove that any starvation-free mutual exclusion algorithm for n processes using only atomic registers and conditional objects must use at least n atomic registers and conditional objects.
- Prove that any starvation-free mutual exclusion algorithm for n processes using only atomic registers and write-conditional objects must use at least $n/2$ atomic registers and write-conditional objects.

•• ? 4.13 Consider the definition of time complexity in the DSM model, as defined on page 16.

Show that for every mutual exclusion algorithm for n processes, $\Omega(\log\log n/\ \log\log\log n)$ is a lower bound on the time complexity in the DSM model, even under the assumption that any of the following objects can be used: atomic registers, test-and-set, compare-and-swap, load-link/store-conditional.

The problem of proving a tight bound is still open. The best known upper bound is $O(\log n)$.

Problems based on Section 4.3

•◦ 4.14 Design a starvation-free algorithm for n processes which uses a single $(n + c)$-valued read-modify-write register (where c is some constant). It is not required that the exit code be wait-free.

The best known algorithm whose exit code is not wait-free uses a single $(\lfloor n/2 \rfloor + 6)$-valued register and is *memoryless*. (Recall that in a memoryless algorithm, processes have only a single remainder state, and hence can not retain any memory of prior executions of the algorithm; see page 144.)

•◦ 4.15 Design a linear-waiting (i.e., 1-bounded-waiting) algorithm for n processes which uses a single $O(n)$-valued read-modify-write register. It is not required that the exit code be wait-free.

The best known linear-waiting algorithm whose exit code is not wait-free uses a single $(n+3)$-valued register and is *memoryless*. The best known 2-bounded-waiting algorithm uses a single $(n+2)$-valued register.

•• ? 4.16 Prove that:

1. any algorithm for n processes that satisfies mutual exclusion and starvation-freedom must use at least $\sqrt{2n} + \frac{1}{2}$ shared states. (That is, there is no algorithm that satisfies mutual exclusion and starvation-freedom which uses a single $\sqrt{2n}$-valued read-modify-write register.)
2. any *memoryless* algorithm for n processes that satisfies mutual exclusion and starvation-freedom must use at least $\lfloor n/2 \rfloor + 2$ shared states.

The best known upper bound for both cases, when the exit code is not required to be wait-free, is $\lfloor n/2 \rfloor + 6$ values (see Problem 4.14). Closing the gap is still an open problem.

◦• 4.17 Prove that any algorithm for two processes that satisfies mutual exclusion, deadlock-freedom, and bounded-waiting must use at least three shared states. (Bounded-waiting is defined on page 48.)

•• ? 4.18 Prove that any algorithm for n processes that satisfies mutual exclusion, deadlock-freedom, and bounded-waiting must use at least $n+1$ shared states.(Bounded-waiting is defined on page 48.)

That is, there is no algorithm that satisfies mutual exclusion, deadlock-freedom, and bounded-waiting which uses a single n-valued read-modify-write register.

The known upper bound, when the exit code is not required to be wait-free, is $n+2$ (see Problem 4.15). Finding a tight bound is still an open problem.

•• ? 4.19 Prove that any algorithm for $n \geq 3$ processes that satisfies mutual exclusion and strong FIFO (that is, FIFO in both the entry and exit code) must use at least $\frac{n^2-3n+2}{2}$ shared states.

The best known upper bound for this case is n^2 values (see algorithm on page 158). Closing the gap is still an open problem.

? 4.20 What bounds are obtainable for a model having several k-valued read-modify-write registers (instead of a single register as in Problems 4.14, 4.15, 4.16, 4.18, 4.19) assuming that the only indivisible access is on a single register.

Problems based on Section 4.4

◦ 4.21 Can we replace the order of lines 4 and 5 in Anderson's algorithm?

◦ 4.22 Is it true that in Anderson's algorithm, if *valid*[2] is at the queue, but is not at the end of the queue, then its immediate successor is *valid*[3]?

◦ 4.23 Is it true that in the Graunke and Thakkar algorithm (page 165), if *valid*[2] is at the queue, but is not at the end of the queue, then its immediate successor is *valid*[3]?

◦◦ 4.24 In the MCS algorithm (page 167), why can lines 13–14 or lines 17–18 not be omitted?

◦◦ 4.25 In the MCS algorithm, we are assuming that each process i has its own element *node*[*i*]. We have used & *node*[*i*] to denote the address of *node*[*i*], and the indirection $*$ to access the object that the pointer points to. We have used this style of implementation since in practice each element of the *node* array may reside in the local memory of a different process. However, we could have used a different style and avoided using the operators & and $*$. For example, the first statement at line 1 can be written as: *node*[*i*].*next* := *nil*. Rewrite the algorithm without using the operators & and $*$.

Problems based on Section 4.5

◦ 4.26 Write the code which initially creates a dummy node with *next.ptr* field set to NULL, and have both *Q*→*head.ptr* and *Q*→*tail.ptr* point to it.

◦◦ 4.27 Without changing the *enqueue* and *dequeue* methods write a *peek* method which returns the oldest value in the queue but does not delete it.

◦◦ 4.28 In solving the ABA problem (page 171) we have added a tag to each pointer. Do these tags need to be initialized? Justify your answer.

◦◦ 4.29 In solving the ABA problem (page 171) we have added a tag to each pointer, and mentioned that this solution does not guarantee that the ABA problem will not occur, but it makes it extremely unlikely. Explain why it does not guarantee that the ABA problem will not occur. (Hint: The root cause of the problem is that nodes are being recycled and reused while some processes are still looking at them.)

◦◦ 4.30 Assume that we prohibit the reuse of nodes (memory locations) that have been deleted from the queue during dequeue operations. In such a case, can the compare-and-swap primitive be used without worrying about the ABA problem? (The ABA problem is explained on page 171.)

Problems based on Section 4.6

◦ 4.31 Let S be a weak semaphore which is initially set to 0 (not to 1!), and let *empty* be a boolean register (its initial value is immaterial). Assume that there are some finite number of processes where all of them, except one, are executing the following code:

```
down(S);
empty := false;
up(S);
```

And, there is a special process, called *doorkeeper*, which executes the following code:

```
repeat
      empty := true;
      up(S);
      down(S)
until empty;
```

Explain why the doorkeeper loop cannot terminate while there are other processes waiting on semaphore S.

◦◦ 4.32 Let A be a mutual exclusion algorithm which uses semaphores. For each of the following statements tell if it is correct or incorrect?

1. If A is starvation-free with strong semaphores, then A is deadlock-free with weak semaphores.
2. If A is starvation-free with strong semaphores, then A is deadlock-free with unfair semaphores.
3. If A is starvation-free with weak semaphores, then A is deadlock-free with unfair semaphores.

◦• 4.33 Show that binary semaphores can simulate generalized semaphores. That is, any program using generalized semaphores can be translated to use only binary semaphores.

◦• 4.34 Show that, when assuming an infinite number of processes, the Friedberg and Peterson algorithm (page 178) does not satisfy starvation-freedom, but does satisfy deadlock-freedom.

◦◦ 4.35 Substituting lines 13–19 in the Friedberg and Peterson algorithm with the following code gives an algorithm with a more conventional appearance: the critical section appears in one place only (instead of two places).

```
13 else
14       empty := false
15 fi;
16 Critical Section;
17 if empty then up(S_otherqueue);
18 up(S_myqueue);
```

Is the algorithm correct? Justify your answer.

◦◦ 4.36 Let n be the total number of processes. It is suggested that it is possible to save one bit in the Friedberg and Peterson algorithm (page 178) by deleting line 16, and replacing lines 8–12 with:

```
for i = 1 to n − 1 do
      up(S);
```

```
        down(S)
od;
```

Is this new solution correct?

○• 4.37 In the Friedberg and Peterson algorithm (on page 178), the doorkeeper process ensures that all the processes that were waiting on the same semaphore as itself will have a chance to enter their critical section and only then the doorkeeper enters its critical section. In the following modification of the algorithm, the first process of a queue acts as a doorkeeper of the *other* queue. Hence it is "more fair" for the doorkeeper.

Prove that the algorithm satisfies mutual exclusion, starvation-freedom, 2-bounded-waiting; and that the algorithm does not satisfy 1-bounded-waiting.

HALDER AND SUBRAMANIAN ALGORITHM:

S_0 and S_1: weak semaphores, both are initially 1;
queue, empty: atomic bits initially 0 and *false*, respectively;
myqueue, otherqueue: local bits;

```
myqueue := queue;                 /* remember semaphore */
down(S_myqueue)                   /* wait to be flushed */
if queue = myqueue                    /* first to enter? */
then      /* become the doorkeeper */
     otherqueue := myqueue + 1 (mod 2);
     down(S_otherqueue)/* take the other semaphore */
     repeat                        /* flush out processes */
                             /* waiting on the other sem */
          empty := true;
          up(S_otherqueue);
          down(S_otherqueue);
     until empty;
     queue := otherqueue;                 /* change queue */
     up(S_otherqueue);       /* give up the other sem */
fi;
Critical Section;
empty := false;
up(S_myqueue);             /* give up the original sem */
```

•○ 4.38 In the following algorithm, due to J. M. Morris (1979), it is assumed that the number of processes is unknown but finite.

1. Prove that the algorithm satisfies 1-bounded-waiting (i.e., linear-waiting).
2. Does the algorithm satisfy starvation-freedom, if we change the order of **up**(b) and **up**(a) on line 5? (i.e., from **up**(b);**up**(a) to **up**(a);**up**(b).)
3. Show that, if it is assumed that a and b are *unfair* semaphores, the algorithm does not satisfy starvation-freedom.

4. Show that, when assuming unbounded infinite number of processes, the algorithm does not satisfy starvation-freedom. Does it satisfy deadlock-freedom in that case?

MORRIS' ALGORITHM: `program of a process.`

a, *b*, *m*: weak semaphores, initially 1;
count1 and *count2*: atomic registers initially 0;
local: local register;

```
down(b); local := count1; count1 := local + 1; up(b);
down(a); local := count2; count2 := local + 1;
    down(b); local := count1; count1 := local − 1;
        if count1 = 0 then up(b); up(m)
        else up(b); up(a) fi;
down(m); local := count2; count2 := local − 1;
Critical Section;
if count2 = 0 then up(a);
else up(m) fi;
```

oo 4.39 Prove that there is no starvation-free mutual exclusion algorithm for three processes using a single weak semaphore (and no atomic registers).

? 4.40 An obvious lower bound is that a starvation-free mutual exclusion algorithm for $n > 2$ processes must use at least one weak semaphore and one atomic bit. The Friedberg and Peterson algorithm (on page 178) uses two weak semaphores and two atomic bits. Finding a tight space bound is still an open problem.

Problems based on Section 4.7

oo 4.41 Emulate semaphores using monitors and conversely.

Problems based on Section 4.8

oo 4.42 In Problem 3.51, we have defined the election problem (which is also called the "one shot" mutual exclusion problem). Prove that there is no (fault-free) election algorithm using atomic registers which satisfy only deadlock-freedom. (Hint: use the result stated in Problem 3.27.)

o• 4.43 Prove that any starvation-free mutual exclusion algorithm for n processes using registers and test-and-set bits which satisfy only bounded-waiting must use at least n instances of these objects. (Hint: similar to the proof of Problem 4.11.)

o• 4.44 Below we present a wait-free election algorithm for two processes, using an unbounded number of registers which satisfy only bounded-waiting. (1) Prove that the algorithm is correct, and (2) use the algorithm for two processes to construct a wait-free election algorithm for n

processes using an unbounded number of registers which satisfy only bounded-waiting. (The election problem is defined in Problem 3.51.)

WAIT-FREE ELECTION: `program for process` $i \in \{0, 1\}$.

out: starvation-free register, initially ⊥
$x[1..\infty, 0..1]$ array of starvation-free registers, initially 0
$y[1..\infty]$ array of bounded-waiting registers, initially ⊥
round, *v*: local registers initially 1 and *i*, resp.

```
while out =⊥ do
    x[round, v] := 1;
    if y[round] =⊥ then y[round] := v fi;
    if x[round, v̄] = 0 then out := v
        else for j = 1 to round do dummy := y[round] od;
            v := y[round];
            round := round + 1 fi
od;
if out = i then "I am the leader"
    else "I am not the leader" fi.
```

○• 4.45 All the fairness definitions (on page 184) can be generalized to apply also to sets of objects as follows. Let O be a set of shared objects:

- *deadlock-freedom*: If a process is trying to access an object in O, then some process (not necessarily the same one) eventually succeeds in accessing some object in O.
- *starvation-freedom*: If a process is trying to access an object in O, then this process eventually succeeds.
- *bounded-waiting*: O is deadlock-free, and in any run there is a bound r such that whenever a process, say p, is trying to access an object in O then no other process successfully accesses objects in O more than r times before p succeeds with its access.
- *r-bounded-waiting*: O is deadlock-free, and if a process is trying to access an object in O then it will succeed before any of the other processes is able to access O a number of times equal to $r + 1$.

Prove that the following properties are correct:

1. If each object in O is deadlock-free then O is deadlock-free. The converse does not hold in general.
2. Each object in O is starvation-free if and only if O is starvation-free.
3. If O is bounded-waiting then each object in O is bounded-waiting. The converse does not hold in general.
4. If O is r-bounded-waiting then each object in O is r-bounded-waiting. The converse does not hold in general.

Barrier Synchronization

5.1 Barriers

It is sometimes convenient to design algorithms that are divided into phases such that no process may proceed into the next phase until all processes have finished the current phase and are ready to move into the next phase together. In such algorithms, each phase typically depends on the results of the previous phase. This type of behavior can be achieved by placing a *barrier* at the end of each phase, as illustrated in Figure 5.1, which ensures that all processes have reached a certain point in a computation before any of them proceed.

A barrier: *A barrier is a coordination mechanism (an algorithm) that forces processes which participate in a concurrent (or distributed) algorithm to wait until each one of them has reached a certain point in its program. The collection of these coordination points is called the barrier. Once all the processes have reached the barrier, they are all permitted to continue past the barrier.*

Using barriers enables, in various cases, significant simplification of the task of designing concurrent algorithms. The programmer may design an algorithm under the assumption that the algorithm should work correctly only when it executes in a *synchronous* environment (where the processes run at the same

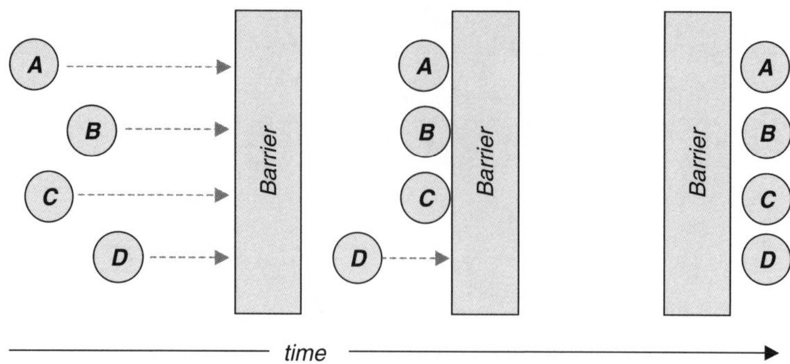

Figure 5.1 Barrier synchronization. The four processes approach the barrier; all except *D* arrive and have to wait; once all the processes (including *D*) have reached the barrier, they continue past the barrier.

speed or where the processes share a global clock). Then, by using barriers for synchronization, the algorithm can be adapted to work also in an *asynchronous* environment. Such an approach is particularly helpful for the design of numerical and scientific algorithms.

In the sequel, we present several implementations of barriers. Each one of these implementations is of a *reusable barrier*, which can be used over and over again to synchronize the processes and to divide the computation into many well defined phases. As with mutual exclusion, we would like barrier algorithms to employ local spinning in order to minimize interconnect traffic.

Recall that an algorithm which is implemented on a system with support for cache-coherence (the CC model) satisfies local spinning, if a process spins (busy-waits) only on locally-cached data, and a process' wait is over when the data on which it spins changes. Thus, local spinning produces no communication traffic while spinning. In distributed shared memory systems (the DSM model), an algorithm satisfies local spinning if a process may only spin on statically-assigned locations. This ensures that a process accesses only local memory while spinning and hence produces no communication traffic while spinning.

5.2 Atomic Counter

We presented several simple barriers which use an atomic counter. Recall that an atomic counter supports two atomic operations: incrementing the counter by 1, and decrementing the counter by 1.

5.2.1 A Simple Counter Barrier

Our first implementation uses an atomic counter which is initially set to 0. As soon as a process reaches the barrier it increments the counter by 1, and busy-waits. When the value of the counter reaches n, it means that all the n

processes have finished the current phase and have reached the barrier. The *last* process to increment the counter signals the other processes that they may continue to run past the barrier and it resets to 0 the value of the counter so that the barrier can be reused in the future. Waiting and signaling are done as follows: There is a single bit, called *go*, and all the waiting processes spin on this bit waiting for its value to be changed. The last process to reach the barrier terminates the spin with a single write operation which toggles the value of the *go* bit.

A Simple Barrier using an Atomic Counter (version #1): `program of a process.`

```
shared  counter: atomic counter ranges over {0,...,n}, initially 0
        go: atomic bit, initial value is immaterial
local   local.go: a bit, initial value is immaterial

local.go := go                       /* remembers current value */
counter := counter + 1
                               /* atomically increment the counter */
if counter = n then              /* last to arrive to the barrier */
   counter := 0                               /* reset the barrier */
   go := 1 − go                                      /* notify all */
else await(local.go ≠ go) fi            /* not the last to arrive */
```

One advantage of this simple barrier is that only the atomic *counter* must be initialized. When *all* the shared and local memory is initialized, the algorithm can be slightly simplified saving the first access to the *go* bit.

A Simple Barrier using an Atomic Counter (version #2): `program of a process.`

```
shared  counter: atomic counter ranges over {0,...,n}, initially 0
        go: atomic bit, initially 1
local   local.go: a bit, initially 1

local.go := 1 − local.go               /* toggles its local bit */
counter := counter + 1
                               /* atomically increment the counter */
if counter = n then              /* last to arrive to the barrier */
   counter := 0                               /* reset the barrier */
   go := local.go                                    /* notify all */
else await(local.go ≠ go) fi            /* not the last to arrive */
```

We notice that, in both versions of the simple barrier, the number of remote memory references per process is O(1) in the CC model and is unbounded in the DSM model. Our next solution improves on the performance of the simple barrier using additional atomic bits.

5.2.2 A Local Spinning Counter Barrier

In the previous algorithm, it is possible to replace the *go* bit, on which everyone may spin, with n bits $go[1], \ldots, go[n]$ such that process p_i may spin only on the bit $go[i]$. Doing so reduces memory contention since a process spins only on a locally accessible variable. This is implemented as follows:

LOCAL SPINNING BARRIER: `program of process` p_i, $i \in \{1, \ldots, n\}$.

```
shared  counter: atomic counter ranges over {0,...,n}, initially 0
        go[1..n]: array of atomic bits, initial values are immaterial
local   local.go: a bit, initial value is immaterial

local.go := go[i]                          /* remembers current value */
counter := counter + 1
                            /* atomically increment the counter */
if counter = n then            /* last to arrive to the barrier */
   counter := 0                                /* reset the barrier */
   for j = 1 to n do go[j] := 1 − go[j] od            /* notify all */
else await(local.go ≠ go[i]) fi            /* not the last to arrive */
```

We notice that the number of remote memory references per process in both the CC model and the DSM model is bounded. In the above algorithm, memory contention is reduced by letting each process spin only on a locally accessible variable. However, there is still memory contention when accessing the counter which is shared by all the processes. The solution in Section 5.4 will improve this aspect of the algorithm.

5.2.3 A Barrier without Shared Memory Initialization

In the previous two algorithms the counter is initialized to 0. It is easy to modify those algorithms so that the shared memory is not required to be initialized at all. Below, we demonstrate how this is done for the simple barrier. We assume that the counter can be atomically incremented modulo n (where n is the number of processes).

A BARRIER WITHOUT MEMORY INITIALIZATION: `program of a process.`

```
shared  counter: atomic counter ranges over {0,...,n − 1},
                                          initial value is immaterial
        go: atomic bit, initial value is immaterial
local   local.go: a bit, initial value is immaterial
        local.counter: atomic register, initial value is immaterial

local.go := go                             /* remembers current value */
local.counter := counter                   /* remembers current value */
counter := counter + 1 (mod n)             /* atomic increment mod n */
```

```
4 repeat
5    if   counter = local.counter /* all processes have arrived */
6    then go := 1 − go fi                            /* notify all */
7 until (local.go ≠ go)
```

In Section 5.7 we present a symmetric barrier algorithm that uses only three shared bits which are not required to be initialized. But first, we present in the next section a simple barrier algorithm that uses three shared bits two of which must be initialized.

Self Review

1. Is the following implementation of a reusable barrier correct? Justify your answer.

   A BARRIER USING AN ATOMIC COUNTER: program of a process.

   ```
   shared counter: atomic counter ranges over {0, ..., n}, initially 0

   1 counter := counter + 1          /* increment the counter */
   2 if counter = n then                      /* last to arrive */
   3    counter := 0                   /* reset and notify all */
   4 else await(counter = 0) fi          /* not the last to arrive */
   ```

2. Would the barrier synchronization algorithm using an atomic counter from page 205 be correct if we replace the order of lines 1 and 2?
3. Would the barrier synchronization algorithm using an atomic counter be correct if we replace the order of lines 4 and 5?

Answers: (1) No, after the counter is reset to 0, a fast process may increment it again before all the waiting processes get a chance to test it. This will result a deadlock. (2) No, because of a possible race condition. If all processes arrive, some process may flip the value of *go* (line 5) before the other process reads *go*. (3) No, because of a possible race condition. A fast process may finish the next phase and increment the counter before the counter is reset.

5.3 Test-and-set Bits

5.3.1 A Constant Space Barrier

Our next simple barrier algorithm uses two test-and-set bits, called *leader* and *counter*, and one atomic bit called *go*. A process first test-and-sets the *leader* bit trying to become the leader. Each process notifies the leader that it has arrived by setting the *counter* bit. Once the leader learns that all the processes have arrived it flips the *go* bit letting everybody know that they have all arrived and may continue past the barrier to the next phase.

A CONSTANT SPACE BARRIER: program of a process.


```
shared  leader, counter: test-and-set bits, both initially 0
        go: atomic bit, initial value is immaterial
local   local.go: a bit, initial value is immaterial
        local.counter: atomic register, initial value is immaterial

local.go := go                           /* remembers current value */
if test-and-set(leader) = 0 then                /* I am the leader */
   local.counter := 0                                /* start at 0 */
   repeat
      await (test-and-set(counter) = 1)        /* wait for process */
      local.counter = local.counter + 1
                                         /* a process has arrived */
      reset(counter)                              /* counter := 0 */
   until (local.counter = n − 1)
   reset(leader)                          /* prepare for next phase */
   go := 1 − go                                     /* notify all */
else                                         /* I am not the leader */
   await (test-and-set(counter) = 0)          /* notify the leader */
   await(local.go ≠ go)                     /* wait for all others */
fi
```

Although the algorithm uses constant space, spinning is done on a remote location even on machines with support for cache coherence. To improve performance a test-and-test-and-set bit can be used instead of a test-and-set bit, as done in Section 4.2.2 (page 154). This will enable implementation of busy-waiting by first testing the *counter* bit until its value changes to 0, and only then to test-and-set *counter*. Another way to improve performance is to use collision avoidance techniques, such as *exponential backoff*, which are discussed in Section 4.2.3 (page 155).

5.3.2 An Asymmetric Barrier without Memory Initialization

If one of the processes is *a priori* designated as a leader then one bit, the *leader* bit, can be saved. In fact, with an *a priori* designated leader we can design a barrier using one test-and-set bit and one atomic bit, where neither of these two bits needs to be initialized. This is done as follows.

The algorithm uses one test-and-set bit, called *counter*, and one atomic bit called *go*. Each process notifies the leader *twice* that it has arrived by setting the *counter* bit *twice*. The leader learns that all the processes have arrived when the counter bit is flipped $2n - 2$ times. Then the leader flips the *go* bit letting everybody know that they all have arrived and may continue past the barrier to the next phase. We assume that the designated leader is process number 1.

AN ASYMMETRIC CONSTANT SPACE BARRIER WITHOUT MEMORY INITIALIZATION: program of process i $(1 \leq i \leq n)$.

```
shared  counter: test-and-set bit, initial value is immaterial
        go: atomic bit, initial value is immaterial
local   local.go: a bit, initial value is immaterial
        local.counter: atomic register, initial value is immaterial

1   local.go := go                    /* remembers current value */
2   if i = 1 then                            /* I am the leader */
3     local.counter := 0                           /* start at 0 */
4     repeat
5       await (test-and-set(counter) = 1)     /* wait for process */
6       local.counter = local.counter + 1
                                          /* a process has arrived */
7       reset(counter)                          /* counter := 0 */
8     until (local.counter = 2n − 2)
10    go := 1 − go                                /* notify all */
11  else                                   /* I am not the leader */
12    await (test-and-set(counter) = 0)
                                         /* notify the leader once */
12    await (test-and-set(counter) = 0)
                                        /* notify the leader again */
13    await(local.go ≠ go)                   /* wait for all others */
14  fi
```

We notice that the value of the *counter* bit may initially be 1, and as a result the leader (process 1) may increment its *local.counter* once although no process has arrived yet. This will cause no problem as the leader waits to get *two* "signals" from each process.

A disadvantage of the above barrier is that it is *asymmetric*: one process, the leader, does more work than the others. In Section 5.7 we will present a *symmetric* barrier which only uses *three* shared bits *none* of which needs to be initialized.

Self Review

1. Explain why the constant space barrier from page 208 would be incorrect if the *counter* bit is initially set to 1.
2. Can the order of lines 5 and 6 in the constant space barrier be replaced? What about replacing lines 5 and 6 in the algorithm from page 209?
3. Can the order of lines 5 and 7 in the constant space barrier be replaced? What about replacing lines 5 and 7 in the algorithm from page 209?

Answers: (1) When the leader's *local.counter* equals n, only $n-1$ processes (including the leader) have arrived. (2) Yes for both. (3) No for both, since the first setting the counter by a non-leader (line 12) might be lost, leading to deadlock.

5.4 Combining Tree Barriers

A disadvantage of the barriers presented so far is that, in certain cases, all processes may try to access the same memory location at the same time (the shared *counter* for example) resulting in a high level of memory contention. This is why these algorithms are sometimes called *centralized* barriers, and the memory location which all processes access simultaneously is called a *hot-spot*. A simple way to reduce memory contention and improve "hot-spot contention" is to split a large barrier into many smaller barriers which are organized in a tree structure. Each small barrier corresponds to a node in the tree, and the number of subtrees of each node (the degree) equals the number of processes that may participate in each small barrier. This number should be tuned for each individual machine architecture.

The processes are divided into groups, with one group assigned to each leaf of the tree. Each process is trying to progress from a leaf to the root, where at each level of the tree it participates in a "small barrier" algorithm, in which it waits until one process arrives from each one of its neighbor's subtrees. In each internal node (i.e., "small barrier") one process *wins* and advances to the next level (the winner is usually the last to arrive). The process that *wins* at the root notifies the waiting processes that all the processes have arrived and that they all are permitted to continue past the barrier to the next phase of the computation. These type of barriers, called (software) combining tree barriers, have been first proposed by P.-C. Yew, N.-F. Tzeng, and D. H. Lawrie (1987).

We show below how to construct a combining tree barrier for n processes, by employing the *barrier using an atomic counter* (page 205) at each node of the tree. Let us denote the degree of the tree by the constant *degree*. That is, the number of processes that may participate at each instant of the simple barrier is *degree*. For simplicity, it is assumed that the number of processes n is a power of *degree*. When n is not a power of *degree*, it is always possible to add a few more "dummy" processes which never do anything. The processes are numbered 0 through $n - 1$.

A combining tree has $\log_{degree} n$ levels numbered starting from 0, and at each level the nodes are numbered from left to right starting from 0 as illustrated by the tree structure in Figure 2.2 (page 37). Thus, each node of the tree is uniquely identified by its level and node number. Let *level* and *node* be the level and node number of some node v.With each node v, we associate one atomic counter *counter*[*level*, *node*] and one atomic bit *go*[*level*, *node*]. These two objects are used to implement the barrier which is associated with this node. The registers *level*, *node*, and *local.go* are local to each process. The *level* and *node* registers, together, identify the node of the tree that the process is currently at.

A Combining Tree Barrier: `process i's program.`

Initially: the value of all the atomic *counters* is 0, and the values of the *go* bits and the local registers are immaterial.

```
node := i                                   /* initialized */
level := −1                                 /* initialized */
```

```
repeat
   node := ⌊node/degree⌋      /* access barrier number node */
   level := level + 1                       /* in level level */
                                             /* begin barrier */
   local.go := go[level,node]               /* remembers value */
   counter[level,node] := counter[level,node] + 1   /* atomic inc. */
   if counter[level,node] = degree then      /* last to arrive */
      counter[level,node] := 0            /* reset the barrier */
      if (level = log_degree n − 1) then               /* root */
         go[level,node] := 1 − go[level,node] fi  /* notify root */
   else await(local.go ≠ go[level,node]) fi       /* not the last */
                                               /* end barrier */
until (local.go ≠ go[level,node])

while (level ≠ 0) do       /* notify processes in your path */
   level := level − 1          /* access barrier number node */
   node := ⌊i/2^(level+1)⌋                  /* in level level */
   go[level,node] := 1 − go[level,node]
                                     /* and notify processes */
od
```

The combining tree barrier in which the nodes of the tree are implemented as simple barriers with atomic counters is more suitable for systems with support for cache coherence than for distributed shared memory systems, since processes may spin on locally-cached copies of data but not on statically-assigned locations. More precisely, the number of remote memory references per process is at most $O(\log n)$ in the CC model and is unbounded in the DSM model. However, there are no "big" hot-spots as in the centralized barriers.

A related barrier algorithm is the *tournament* barrier, which is very similar to the combining tree barrier. Processes start at the leaves of a binary tree. One process from each node continues up the tree to the next round of the tournament. However, unlike in the combining tree barrier, in the tournament barrier the *winner* at each node is *predetermined*. Thus, in a tournament barrier spin locations can be allocated statically allowing local spinning in both cache coherence and distributed shared memory systems. Next we described another tree-based barrier which seems to be more efficient than a tournament barrier.

Self Review

1. Explain why combining tree barriers (page 210) in which the nodes of the tree are implemented as local spinning counter barriers (page 206) are better for systems with support for cache coherence than for distributed shared memory systems.
2. As was pointed out, the number of remote memory references per process is at most $O(\log n)$ in the CC model. What is number of remote memory references of all the processes together?

3. What is the space complexity of the combining tree barrier?
4. What is the number of remote memory references per process of the tournament barrier? What is number of remote memory references of all the processes together?

Answer: (1) Since processes may spin on locally-cached copies of data and not on statically-assigned locations. (2) $O(n)$. (3) $O(n)$. (4) At most $O(\log n)$ per process for both the CC model and the DSM models, and $O(n)$ for all the processes together.

5.5 A Tree-based Barrier

In the following algorithm, due to J. M. Mellor-Crummey and M. L. Scott (1991), the processes are organized into a binary tree, where each node in the tree is owned by a single predetermined process. Each process waits until its two children arrive, *combines* the results and then passes them on to its parent. When the process at the root learns that its two children have arrived, it knows that all the processes have arrived and are waiting. At this point, the process at the root tells its children that they are permitted to continue past the barrier to the next phase, the children tell their children, the signal propagates down the tree until all the processes get the message.

The processes are numbered 1 through n, and for simplicity, it is assumed that n is a power of two minus 1. The algorithm uses the following numbering scheme for the nodes (processes) of the tree: the root is numbered 1, and for each node i, the left child of i is numbered $2 \cdot i$, while the right child is numbered $2 \cdot i + 1$ (see Figure 2.3, page 40). This numbering scheme allows a simple derivation of the number of the parent from the number of any child node. Each process i uses a shared bit called $arrive[i]$ to signal to its parent that it has arrived; and a bit called $go[i]$ on which it spins waiting for a signal from its parent.

A TREE-BASED BARRIER: program of process p_i, $i \in \{1, \ldots, n\}$.

```
shared  arrive[2..n]: array of atomic bits, initial values are all 0
        go[1..n]: array of atomic bits, initial values are all 0

if i = 1 then                                               /* root node */
   await(arrive[2] = 1); arrive[2] := 0                     /* left child */
   await(arrive[3] = 1); arrive[3] := 0                     /* right child */
   go[2] = 1; go[3] = 1                                     /* continue */
else if i ≤ (n − 1)/2 then                                  /* internal node */
   await(arrive[2i] = 1); arrive[2i] := 0                   /* left child */
   await(arrive[2i + 1] = 1); arrive[2i + 1] := 0           /* right child */
   arrive[i] := 1                                           /* signal parent */
   await(go[i] = 1); go[i] = 0                              /* wait for signal */
   go[2i] = 1; go[2i + 1] = 1                               /* continue */
else                                                        /* leaf node */
   arrive[i] := 1                                           /* signal parent */
```

```
    await(go[i] = 1); go[i] = 0 fi                    /* wait for signal */
fi
```

The algorithm is efficient for several reasons: the height of the tree is $\log n$ and hence information from the root propagates down faster than in the central counter-based barrier; each process spins only on a locally accessible bit (i.e., it spins on a statically-assigned location); and no bit is shared by more than two processes which helps to avoid memory contention (no hot-spots).

We notice that unlike the previous solutions which use an atomic counter or test-and-set bits, the tree-based barrier uses only atomic bits. The number of remote memory references per process is $O(1)$ for both the CC model and the DSM model. A possible disadvantage of the tree-based barrier is that it is *asymmetric*: *not* all the processes do the same amount of work.

Self Review

1. As was pointed out, the number of remote memory references per process is at most $O(1)$ for both the CC model and the DSM models. What is the number of remote memory references of all the processes together?
2. What is the space complexity of the tree-based barrier?

Answers: (1) $O(n)$. (2) $O(n)$.

5.6 The Dissemination Barrier

Next we present a *symmetric* barrier algorithm in which all the processes do the same amount of work. The barrier, due to D. Hensgen, R. Finkel, and U. Manber (1988), is based on algorithms for disseminating information among a group of processes and hence it is named the *Dissemination barrier*.

In the algorithm, processes can detect the presence of other processes directly or indirectly. The algorithm progresses in rounds, where in each round the number of processes detected is doubled. After $\log n$ rounds all the n processes are detected and they all may continue to the next phase of the computation (or terminate). The main idea is as follows:

> At round r (where $0 \leq r \leq \log n - 1$), every process i (where $0 \leq i \leq n - 1$) notifies process $i + 2^r \pmod n$ that it has arrived and waits for notification from process $i + 2^r \pmod n$. (See illustration in Figure 5.2.)

To implement the barrier we use, for each one of the n processes, a two dimensional array of size 2 by $\log n$ of (single-reader multi-writer) atomic bits. These bits are used by the processes to notify each other of their presence and for waiting. Each one of these n arrays of $2 \log n$ bits can be statically allocated, in such a way that spinning is done only locally. Thus, the algorithm satisfies local spinning even for distributed shared memory machines.

The two dimensional array which is allocated for process i is called *allflags*[i]. The values of two local variables, called *parity* (which ranges over {0,1}) and

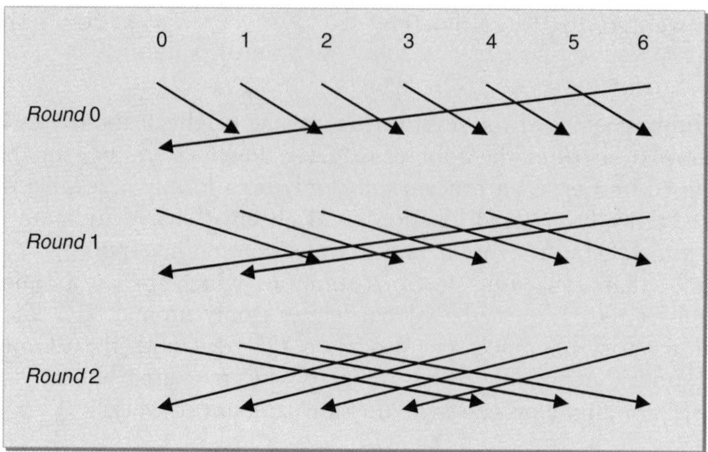

Figure 5.2 The Dissemination barrier. An execution of seven processes.

round (which ranges over $\{0, \ldots, \log n - 1\}$), are used for indexing into this array. During a single episode of the barrier, which takes $\log n$ rounds, the value of *round* is incremented by one when moving from one round to the other. The value of *parity* does not change during a single barrier episode. The value of the *parity* bit changes only between different *successive* episodes of the barrier, and is used to control the use of alternating sets of *flag* bits in successive barrier episodes. That is, in all *even* barrier episodes process i spins on the bits from $allflags[i][0,*]$ and in all *odd* barrier episodes process i spins on the bits from $allflags[i][1,*]$.

THE DISSEMINATION BARRIER: `program of process` p_i, $i \in \{0, \ldots, n-1\}$.

```
type     flags = two dimensional array[0..1, 0.. log n − 1] of atomic bits
         /* one such flags structure is used per process */
shared   allflags: array[1..n] of flags, initial values are all 0
         /* allflags[i] is locally accessible to process i */
local    parity, sense: bits, range over {0,1} initially both 0
         round: register, ranges over {0, ..., log n − 1}

1  for round := 0 to ⌈log n − 1⌉ do
2      allflags[i + 2^round (mod n)][parity, round] := sense
3      await (allflags[i][parity, round] = sense)
4  od
5  if parity = 1 then sense := 1 − sense fi
6  parity := 1 − parity
```

Line 1 indicates that each barrier episode is composed of exactly $\log n$ rounds. In line 2, process i in round *round* notifies process $i + 2^{round} \pmod{n}$ that it has arrived by toggling the $allflags[i + 2^{round} \pmod{n}][parity, round]$ bit. In line 3, process i waits for notification from process $i + 2^{round} \pmod{n}$ by spinning on the *allflags*[*i*][*parity*, *round*] bit. In lines 4 and 5 process *i* prepares for the next barrier episode by setting *sense* to a value different from the values in the spinning bits (line 4) and toggling the *parity* bit (line 5).

The algorithm is implemented using only shared atomic bits (no other stronger objects are needed), its space complexity is $O(n \log n)$, and the number of remote memory references per process is $O(\log n)$ for both the CC model and the DSM models. We point out that there is *no* need to assume that n, the number of processes, is a power of two.

Self Review

1. Would the Dissemination barrier (page 214) be correct if we change the initial value of all the local *parity* bits from 0 to 1?
2. Would the Dissemination barrier be correct if we change the initial value of all the local *sense* bits from 0 to 1?
3. Would the Dissemination barrier be correct if we replace the statement in line 2 with "$j := i + 2^{round} \pmod{n}$; *allflags*[*j*][*parity*, *round*] := 1 − *allflags*[*j*][*parity*, *round*]"?
4. As was pointed out, the number of remote memory references per process is at most $O(\log n)$ for both the CC model and the DSM models. What is the number of remote memory references of all the processes together?

Answers: (1) Yes. (2) No. (3) Yes. (4) $O(n \log n)$.

5.7 The See-Saw Barrier

We now present a barrier for n processes, called the *See-Saw* barrier, which has three desired properties, (1) the barrier is *symmetric*: no process is *a priori* designated as a leader; (2) the barrier uses only three bits: a 4-valued read-modify-write register (i.e., two bits) and one atomic bit; (3) it is not required to initialize the shared memory. A simple way to reduce the memory contention of the See-Saw barrier is to split the See-Saw barrier for n processes into many smaller barriers, and to organize the smaller barriers in a tree structure in order to get a *combining tree barrier* as explained in Section 5.4 (page 210). The See-Saw barrier presented below is based on a solution to the wakeup problem which was proposed by M. J. Fischer, S. Moran, S. Rudich, and G. Taubenfeld (1996).

5.7.1 The Algorithm

To understand the See-Saw barrier algorithm, the reader should imagine a playground with a see-saw in it. The processes will play the algorithm on the see-saw, adhering to strict rules. When each process enters the playground (arrives to the barrier), it sits on the up-side of the see-saw causing it to swing to the ground. Only a process on the ground (or down-side) can get off and when it does the see-saw must swing to the opposite orientation. These rules enforce a balance invariant which says that the number of processes on each side of the see-saw differs by at most one (the heavier side always being down).

Each process enters the playground with two tokens. The algorithm will force the processes on the bottom of the see-saw to give away tokens to the processes on the top of the see-saw. Thus, token flow will change direction depending on the orientation of the see-saw. Tokens can be neither created nor destroyed. The idea of the algorithm is to cause tokens to concentrate in the hands of a single process. Hence, eventually some process will see at least $2n$ tokens, and this process will notify everybody else that all the processes are at the barrier, by flipping the value of a shared atomic bit called *go*.

The following is the complete description of the See-Saw barrier algorithm. The 4-valued read-modify-write register is easily interpreted as two bits which we call the "*token* bit" and the "*see-saw*" bit. The two states of the *token* bit are called "token present" and "no token present". We think of a public *token slot* which either contains a token or is empty, according to the value of the *token* bit. The two states of the *see-saw* bit are called "left side down" and "right side down". The "*see-saw*" bit describes a virtual see-saw which has a left and a right side. The bit indicates which side is down (implying that the opposite side is up).

Each process remembers in local memory the number of tokens it currently possesses and which of four states it is currently in with respect to the see-saw: "never been on", "on left side", "on right side", and "got off". A process is said to be on the up-side of the see-saw if it is currently "on left side" and the *see-saw* bit is in state "right side down", or it is currently "on right side" and the *see-saw* bit is in state "left side down". A process initially possesses *two* tokens and is in state "never been on".

We define the algorithm by a list of rules. When a process is scheduled, it looks at one of the shared registers and at its own internal state and carries out the first applicable rule, if any. If no rule is applicable, it takes a null step which leaves its internal state and the value in the shared register unchanged.

Rule 1: (*Start of algorithm*) Applicable if the scheduled process is in state "never been on". The process reads the value of the *go* bit and saves it in a local bit called *local.go*. Then, the process gets on the up-side of the see-saw and flips the *see-saw* bit. By "get on", we mean that the process changes its state to "on left side" or "on right side" according to whichever side is up. Since flipping the *see-saw* bit causes that side to go down, the process ends up on the down-side of the see-saw.

Rule 2: (*Emitter*) Applicable if the scheduled process is on the down-side of the see-saw, has one or more tokens, and the token slot is empty. The process flips the *token* bit (to indicate that a token is present) and decrements by one the count of tokens it possesses. If its token count thereby becomes zero, the process flips the *see-saw* bit and gets off the see-saw by setting its state to "got off".

Rule 3: (*Absorber*) Applicable if the scheduled process is on the up-side of the see-saw and a token is present in the token slot. The process flips the *token* bit (to indicate that a token is no longer present) and increments by one the count of tokens it possesses.

Rule 4: (*Leader*) Applicable if the scheduled process is on the see-saw and sees at least $2n$ tokens. The process, called the *leader*, thus knows that all the n processes are at the barrier. The leader flips the shared *go* bit, notifying everybody that they are all permitted to continue past the barrier, and then gets off the see-saw by setting its state to "got off".

Rule 5: (*End of algorithm*) Applicable if the scheduled process is in state "got off". The process reads the value of the shared *go* bit and compares this value to the value of its *local.go* bit. If the two values are equal the process does nothing, otherwise the process knows that everybody has arrived and continues past the barrier.

The code of the See-Saw barrier is given below. We use *token* and *see-saw* to designate the first and second components, respectively, of the ordered pair stored in the 4-valued read-modify-write register.

THE SEE-SAW BARRIER: `program of a process.`

```
                                        /* there are n processes */
type    token.states = ranges over {token-present, no-token-present}
        see-saw.states = ranges over {left-side-down, right-side-down}
shared  (token, see-saw): rmw ranges over token.states × see-saw.states
        go: atomic bit ranges over {0, 1}
local   mystate: 4-valued register, ranges over
                   {never-been-on, on-left-side, on-right-side, got-off}
        mytokens: register, ranges over {0, ..., 2n + 1}
        local.go: bit, ranges over {0, 1}
R(·) is the reflection function on {left-side-down, right-side-down}

local.go := go                          /* remember current value */
mystate := never-been-on
mytokens := 2                           /* enters with two tokens */
repeat
        /* beginning of a read-modify-write operation */
if mystate = never-been-on then                 /* Rule 1: start */
   if see-saw = left-side-down then        /* gets on the up-side */
        mystate := on-right-side
   else mystate := on-left-side fi
   see-saw := R(see-saw)                 /* flips the See-Saw bit */
                                              /* Rule 2: Emitter */
elseif mystate = see-saw then               /* on the down-side? */
   if token = no-token-present then          /* token bit empty? */
        token := token-present                    /* emit a token */
        mytokens := mytokens − 1                /* one token less */
        if mytokens = 0 then                  /* no more tokens? */
            mystate := got-off             /* gets off the See-Saw */
            see-saw := R(see-saw) fi fi
                                         /* flips the see-saw bit */
```

```
                                                 /* Rule 3: Absorber */
17 elseif mystate ≠ see-saw then                 /* on the up-side? */
18    if token = token-present then              /* token bit full? */
19          token := no-token-present             /* absorb a token */
20          mytokens := mytokens + 1 fi           /* one token more */
21 fi             /* end of a read-modify-write operation */
                                                  /* Rule 4: Leader */
22 if mytokens ≥ 2n then                     /* all have arrived? */
23    mystate := got-off                  /* gets off the See-Saw */
24    go := 1 − go fi                             /* notifies all */
25 until (mystate = got-off)
26 await (go ≠ local.go)                         /* Rule 5: End */
```

We emphasize that accessing the 4-valued read-modify-write register in lines 5–21 is done in one atomic action. As in previous solutions, toggling the *go* bit prevents successive episodes of the barrier from interfering with each other.

The See-Saw barrier can also be used to solve the leader election problem (see page 144 for definition) by electing the process that sees $2n$ tokens. The leader can transmit an arbitrary message, for example a consensus value (consensus is defined in Chapter 9), and hence can solve also the consensus problem.

5.7.2 Correctness Proof

The two main ideas behind the algorithm can be stated as invariants.

Token invariant: *The number of tokens in the system is either* $2n$ *or* $2n + 1$ *and does not change at any time during the algorithm. (The number of tokens in the system is the total number of tokens possessed by all of the processes, plus 1 if a token is present in the token bit slot.)*

Proof: The number of tokens in the starting configuration is $2n$ with the possible addition of one token present in the *token* bit slot. The rules that affect tokens are rules 2 and 3 both of which maintain the token invariant. ∎

Balance invariant: *The number of processes on the left and right sides of the see-saw is either perfectly balanced or favors the down-side of the see-saw by one process.*

Proof: The see-saw starts empty, zero on either side. Rule 1 preserves the invariant because a process gets on the up-side and then flips the see-saw. If a process runs out of tokens, it must be on the down-side of the see-saw; hence, when rule 2 is applied the invariant is maintained. ∎

Theorem 5.1 *The See-Saw barrier is a correct barrier synchronization algorithm.*

Proof: By the token invariant, there are no more than $2n + 1$ tokens in the system. At most two come from each player; at most one comes from the initialized state of the *token* bit. Hence if a process "sees" $2k$ tokens, it has to be the case that at least $2k$ processes are awake.

Next, we argue that the algorithm comes to a state where everybody has reached the barrier and there is only one process remaining on the see-saw. We know there will be a time when everybody reached the barrier. Furthermore, for any number of processes $m \geq 2$ still active on the see-saw, there will be a future time when there are only $m - 1$ processes on the see-saw: By the balance invariant, there are some processes on both sides and hence eventually either rule 2 or rule 3 is applicable (i.e., there is no deadlock). Each process has arrived at the barrier, hence, rule 1 will no longer apply. Applying rules 2 and 3 will cause tokens to flow from the down-side to the up-side; eventually the token count of a down-side process will become zero and the process will get off the see-saw. Hence eventually there will be only one process remaining on the see-saw. This process will see $2n$ tokens and will know that all other processes are at the barrier. When this happens, this process will toggle the shared *go* bit notifying everybody they are all permitted to continue past the barrier. ∎

Self Review

1. Can the See-Saw barrier be implemented using two bits that can be "read-modify-write" only one at a time, instead of using a single 4-valued read-modify-write register?
2. It is assumed that a process initially possesses *two* tokens. Why is one token not enough?
3. Can we change the condition "$mytokens \geq 2n$" in line 22 of the See-Saw barrier algorithm (page 217) to "$mytokens = 2n$"?
4. How many times does the state of the shared memory change during one episode of the See-Saw barrier?

Answers: (1) No. (2) Given that the *token* bit can initially be empty or full, when a process sees n tokens it can not know for sure that all the processes have arrived. On the other hand it can not wait for $n + 1$ token as it may wait forever in case the *token* bit was initially empty. (3) Yes. (4) $O(n)$ times in the best case, and $O(n^2)$ times in the worst case.

5.8 Semaphores

It is relatively simple to implement barriers using semaphores. First, we implement a barrier for *two* processes using two binary semaphores, as follows:

A TRIVIAL BARRIER FOR TWO PROCESSES USING BINARY SEMAPHORES

shared *arrive*1, *arrive*2: binary semaphores, initially both 1

```
PROGRAM FOR PROCESS 1          PROGRAM FOR PROCESS 2
up(arrive1)                    up(arrive2)
down(arrive2)                  down(arrive1)
```

For n processes we use two binary semaphores, called *arrival* and *departure*, and an atomic register called *counter*. Each process initially tries to pass the *arrival* semaphore and increment the counter once. When the last process that increments the counter notices that the counter was incremented n times, it sets the *departure* semaphore to 1 enabling the other processes to decrement the counter. Each process decrements the counter once and continues past the barrier to the next phase.

A BARRIER FOR n PROCESSES USING BINARY SEMAPHORES: `program of a process.`

```
shared   arrival: binary semaphore, initially 1
         departure: binary semaphore, initially 0
         counter: atomic register ranges over {0, ..., n}, initially 0

down(arrival)
counter = counter + 1
if counter < n then up(arrival) else up(departure) fi
down(departure)
counter = counter - 1
if counter > 0 then up(departure) else up(arrival) fi
```

Only the last process to increment the counter will notice that all the processes have arrived and will release the *departure* semaphore letting everybody continue. Similarly, only the last process to decrement the counter will set the *arrival* semaphore back to 1, returning the algorithm to the original initial state, so that everything is ready for the next barrier episode.

Self Review

1. Would the barrier using binary semaphores be correct if a safe register is used instead of an atomic register for the *counter*?
2. Is the following barrier algorithm correct?

   A BARRIER FOR n PROCESSES USING BINARY SEMAPHORES: `program of a process.`

```
shared   arrival: binary semaphore, initially 1
         departure: binary semaphore, initially 0
         counter: atomic register ranges over {0, ..., n}, initially 0

down(arrival)
counter = counter + 1
if counter = n then up(departure) fi
up(arrival)
down(departure)
up(departure)
down(arrival)
counter = counter - 1
```

```
9 if counter = n then down(departure) fi
10 up(arrival)
```

Answers: (1) Yes, it would be correct. (2) No.

5.9 Bibliographic Notes

5.1

There dozens of important papers about barrier synchronization, and in the sequel we discuss only a few of these papers. The first paper on the subject is by Harry Jordan [194].

5.4

In [343], a (software) combining tree barrier based on the simple counter barrier (from page 210) was first proposed, and it was shown that a software combining tree can significantly decrease memory contention. Also, it was suggested that the counter barriers associated with the nodes of the tree be for four processes in order to achieve the best results. In [164] and in [238], a tournament barrier (page 211) was presented. An f-way tournament barrier is considered in [154].

5.5

In [254], a tree-based barrier was presented (page 212), which is based on the tournament barrier from [164]. The tree-based barrier from [254] is composed of two trees: the arrival tree with fan-in of 4 and a wakeup tree with fan-out of 2.

5.6

In [164], the Dissemination barrier (page 213) and a tournament barrier (page 211) were presented. The Dissemination barrier is an improvement of the *butterfly* barrier from [77], especially when the number of processes is not a power of two.

5.7

The See-Saw barrier is a simple adaptation of the See-Saw algorithm from [136] for solving the wakeup problem in the absence of faults.

More references

A Binomial spanning tree barrier was proposed in [329]. Barriers that allow disjoint subsets of processors to synchronize are considered in [128]. Techniques for nested barrier synchronization are presented in [292]. The notion of a fuzzy barrier, an extension of the barrier concept, is defined and studied in [155]. In [14], it is shown that for a small number of processes, exponential backoff can reduce the amount of network traffic required to achieve a barrier. In other situations adaptive backoff techniques result in a tradeoff between reduced network accesses and increased processor idle time.

5.10 Problems

The problems are divided into several categories. See page 23 for a detailed explanation.

Problems based on Section 5.2

∘∘ 5.1 Is the following variant of the simple barrier algorithm using an atomic counter from page 205 correct?

A BARRIER USING AN ATOMIC COUNTER: program of a process.

```
shared  counter: atomic counter ranges over {0,...,n}, initially 0
        go: atomic bit, initial value is immaterial
local   local.go: a bit, initial value is immaterial

go := 0                                        /* reset go */
counter := counter + 1                  /* atomic increment */
if counter = n then                       /* last to arrive */
   counter := 0                         /* reset the barrier */
   go := 1                                   /* notify all */
else await(go = 1) fi               /* not the last to arrive */
```

∘∘ 5.2 One advantage of the simple local spinning barrier from page 206 is that only the atomic *counter* must be initialized. Show that when *all* the shared and local memory can be initialized, the algorithm can be slightly simplified so that there is no need to access the shared bit (called $go[i]$) in line 1.

∘∘ 5.3 Modify the local spinning barrier using an atomic counter (page 206) so that there is no need to use the *local.go* bit at all. You may assume that the initial values of the *go* array entries are all 0.

∘∘ 5.4 Consider the following variant of the local spinning barrier algorithm from page 206. Is this algorithm correct?

LOCAL SPINNING BARRIER #2: program of process p_i, $i \in \{1,\ldots,n\}$.

```
shared  counter: atomic counter ranges over {0,...,n}, initially 0
        go[1..n]: array of atomic bits, initial values are immaterial
local   local.go: a bit, initial value is immaterial

local.go := go[i]
counter := counter + 1
j := (i + 1) mod (n + 1)
if counter = n then
   counter := 0
```

```
    go[j] := 1 − go[j]
    await(local.go ≠ go[i])
else await(local.go ≠ go[i])
    go[j] := 1 − go[j]
fi
```

Problems based on Section 5.3

∘∘ 5.5 Write a more efficient version of the constant space barrier algorithm from page 208, by using test-and-test-and-set bits instead of test-and-set bits.

∘∘ 5.6 Write a more efficient version of the constant space barrier algorithm from page 208, by using exponential backoff.

Problems based on Section 5.5

∘∘ 5.7 Modify the tree-based barrier algorithm from page 212 so that it works for any number, n, of processes.

∘∘ 5.8 Assume that in the tree-based barrier algorithm from page 212, instead of using the array of atomic bits $go[1..n]$, we use a single atomic bit, called go, on which all the waiting processes spin. Rewrite the algorithm and explain the pros and cons of such a modification.

∘∘ 5.9 Modify the tree-based barrier algorithm from page 212, so that instead of using one tree, two trees, called *up* and *down*, are used. In the *up* tree each process waits until all its children arrive and then notifies its parent. When the process at the root learns that its children have arrived, it sends a message which propagates down the *down* tree until all the processes get the message. The degree of the up tree should be 4 and the degree of the down tree should be 2.

Problems based on Section 5.6

∘ 5.10 In the Dissemination barrier (page 214), assume that we replace the statement in line 5 with, "**if** $parity = 0$ **then** $sense := 1 - sense$ **fi**". What should be the initial values of the shared and local registers for the algorithm to be correct?

∘∘ 5.11 In the Dissemination barrier (page 214) each process has $2 \log n$ single-reader bits on which it locally spins. In the following implementation, we have replaced each such $\log n$ bits with one register which can take $\log n + 1$ values. Explain why this implementation is wrong.

AN INCORRECT VERSION OF THE DISSEMINATION BARRIER: `program of process` p_i, $i \in \{0, \ldots, n-1\}$.

type *flags* = array[0..1] of atomic registers range over $\{0, \ldots, \log n\}$

```
shared  allflags: array[1..n] of flags, initial values are all 0
   /* allflags[i] is locally accessible to process i */
local   parity: bits, range over {0,1}, initially 0
        round: register, ranges over {0,...,log n − 1}

for round := 0 to log n − 1 do
   allflags[i + 2^round (mod n)][parity] := round + 1
   await (allflags[i][parity] > round)
od
parity := 1 − parity
```

Problems based on Section 5.7

∘∘ 5.12 In the See-Saw barrier algorithm, all the processes spin on the same *go* bit. Replace the *go* bit with n bits $go[1],\ldots,go[n]$ such that process p_i may spin only on the bit $go[i]$. Doing so will reduce memory contention since a process will spin only on a locally accessible variable.

∘∘ 5.13 Write the code of a combining tree barrier for n processes, which is based on small See-Saw barriers for four processes each?

•∘ 5.14 Modify the See-Saw barrier so that it uses only one 3-valued read-modify-bit register and one atomic bit.

Problems based on Section 5.8

∘∘ 5.15 Is the following barrier algorithm using binary semaphores correct?

A BARRIER FOR *n* PROCESSES USING BINARY SEMAPHORES: program of a process.

```
shared  arrival: binary semaphore, initially 1
        departure: binary semaphore, initially 0
        counter: atomic register ranges over {0,...,n}
   /* initial value of the counter is immaterial */
local   mycounter: integer, initial value is immaterial

down(arrival)
mycounter := counter
counter = counter + 1 (mod n)
if counter ≠ mycounter then
   up(arrival) else up(departure) fi
down(departure)
counter = counter + 1 (mod n)
if counter ≠ mycounter then
   up(departure) else up(arrival) fi
```

∘∘ 5.16 Is the following barrier algorithm using binary semaphores correct?

A BARRIER FOR n PROCESSES USING BINARY SEMAPHORES: `program of a process.`

```
shared   arrival, out: binary semaphores, both initially 1
         departure: binary semaphore, initially 0
         counter: atomic register ranges over {0, ..., n}, init. 0

down(arrival)
counter = counter + 1
if counter = n then down(out); up(departure) fi
up(arrival)

down(departure)
up(departure)

down(arrival)
counter = counter − 1
if counter = n then down(departure); up(out) fi
up(arrival)
down(out)
up(out)
```

Chapter 6

The ℓ-exclusion Problem

6.1 The Problem

The ℓ-*exclusion* problem, which is a natural generalization of the mutual exclusion problem, is to design an algorithm which guarantees that up to ℓ processes and no more may simultaneously access identical copies of the same non-sharable resource when there are several competing processes. That is, ℓ processes are permitted to be in their critical sections simultaneously. (Being in the critical section corresponds to allocation of one copy of the resource.) A solution is required to withstand the slow-down or even the crash (fail by stopping) of up to $\ell-1$ processes. For $\ell=1$, the 1-exclusion problem is exactly the mutual exclusion problem.

A process that fails by crashing simply stops executing more steps of its program, and hence, there is no way to distinguish a crashed process from a correct process that is running very slowly. The notion of a crash failure is different from the notion of immediate and continuous failures, discussed in Section 3.3, where a failed process announces that it has failed by setting its own (single-writer) shared registers to their default values.

To illustrate the ℓ-exclusion problem, consider the case of buying a ticket for a bus ride. Here a resource is a seat on the bus, and the parameter ℓ is the number of available seats. In the ℓ-exclusion problem, a passenger needs only to make sure that there is some free seat on the bus, but not to reserve a particular seat. A stronger version of the problem, called the ℓ-assignment problem (discussed on page 241), would require also to reserve a particular seat.

Another good example is that of a bank where people are waiting for a teller. Here the processes are the people, the resources are the tellers, and the parameter ℓ is the number of tellers. We notice that the usual bank solution, where people line up in a single queue, and the person at the head of the queue goes to any free teller, does *not* solve the ℓ-exclusion problem. If $\ell \geq 2$ tellers are free, a proper solution should enable the first ℓ people in line to move simultaneously to a teller. However, the bank solution, requires them to move past the head of the queue one at a time. Moreover, if the person at the front of the line "fails", then the people behind this person wait forever. Thus, a better solution is required which will not allow a single failure to tie up all the resources.

More formally, as with the mutual exclusion problem, it is assumed that each process is executing a sequence of instructions in an infinite loop. The instructions are divided into (the familiar) four continuous sections of code: the *remainder*, *entry*, *critical section*, and *exit* (see Figure 1.5, on page 11). The ℓ-exclusion problem is to write the code for the *entry code* and the *exit code* in such a way that the following basic requirements are satisfied.

ℓ-exclusion: *No more than ℓ processes are at their critical sections at the same time.*

ℓ-deadlock-freedom: *If strictly fewer than ℓ processes fail (are delayed forever) then if a process is trying to enter its critical section, then some process, not necessarily the same one, eventually enters its critical section.*

We notice that the ℓ-deadlock-freedom requirement is a (slightly) stronger property than only requiring that "if fewer than ℓ processes are in their critical sections, then it is possible for another process to enter its critical section, even though no process leaves its critical section in the meantime".

The ℓ-deadlock-freedom requirement may still allow "starvation" of individual processes. That is, a process that is trying to enter its critical section may never get to enter its critical section, and wait forever in its entry code. The following stronger requirement does not allow starvation.

ℓ-starvation-freedom: *If strictly fewer than ℓ processes fail (are delayed forever) then any correct process that is trying to enter its critical section must eventually enter its critical section.*

Notice that the ℓ-deadlock-freedom and ℓ-starvation-freedom requirements only require progress if there are fewer than ℓ failures. If ℓ processes fail while in the critical section then as far as the of the other processes can tell, these ℓ processes can be very slow and remain in their critical sections, which prevents any other process from entering its critical section.

While first-come-first-out (FIFO) is the strongest fairness condition for mutual exclusion, this notion should be slightly weakened for ℓ-exclusion since failures are possible and should be tolerated. As already mentioned, a single failure of a process at the head of the queue should not tie up all the resources. Below we define such a weaker notion of fairness called *FIFO-enabling*. Recall that on page 48, we have defined the notion of a *doorway*, which is the first part in the entry code in which its execution requires only bounded number of atomic steps and hence always terminates (i.e., the doorway is wait-free).

We say that a process is *enabled* to enter its critical section at some point in time, if sufficiently many steps of that process will carry it into the critical section, independently of the actions of the other processes. That is, an enabled process does not need to wait for an action by any other process in order to complete its entry section and to enter its critical section, nor can an action by any other process prevent it from doing so.

FIFO-enabling: *For any two processes p and q, if p completes its doorway before q starts its doorway, then p is enabled before q enters its critical section.*

Notice that FIFO-enabling does not imply deadlock-freedom. Finally, the usual assumptions that are made about the behavior of the processes in solving the mutual exclusion problem are also made here (see Section 1.3.1), and the same complexity measures are assumed (see Section 1.4).

Self Review

1. Does FIFO-enabling imply FIFO for 1-exclusion?
2. What is the maximum number of processes that can be simultaneously enabled, in a correct ℓ-exclusion algorithm?
3. Explain why the first-come-first-served property (page 49) and the ℓ-deadlock-freedom property cannot be mutually satisfied when ℓ is greater than one.

Answers: (1) Yes. (2) At most ℓ. (3) In an algorithm that satisfies FIFO, if the first process in line fails no other process can enter its critical section, and thus, ℓ-deadlock-freedom is not satisfied.

6.2 Algorithms Using Atomic Registers

We present two ℓ-exclusion algorithms for n processes. The first algorithm satisfies ℓ-starvation-freedom and uses only $O(n)$ registers, where each register can hold n values. The second algorithm satisfies the stronger FIFO-enabling requirement, but uses n unbounded size registers. Algorithms which satisfy FIFO-enabling using bounded size registers are mentioned in Section 6.5.

6.2.1 An ℓ-starvation-free Algorithm

The following ℓ-starvation-free algorithm for n processes using atomic registers, due to Gary Peterson (1990), is a simple generalization of Peterson's mutual exclusion algorithm for n processes presented in Problem 2.63 (page 90).

In the following algorithm $n - \ell$ levels are used to eliminate at least one process per level until only ℓ processes remain. The algorithm requires $2n - \ell$ shared registers, each able to hold values in the range $\{0, \ldots, n-1\}$. The first array $b[1..n]$ specifies the level which a process that wants to enter its critical section is at. The second array $turn[1..n-\ell]$ specifies which process is blocked at each level. In addition three local variables, called *level*, *counter*, and k, are used for each process, and ℓ is used as a constant.

AN ℓ-STARVATION-FREE ALGORITHM FOR n PROCESSES: `process i's program.`

Initially: $b[1..n]$ all 0, $turn[1..n-\ell]$ all 1.

```
1   for level := 1 to n − ℓ do
2         b[i] := level;
3         turn[level] := i;
4         repeat
5               counter := 0;
6               for k := 1 to n do
7                     if b[k] ≥ level then counter := counter +1 od
8         until (counter ≤ n − level or turn[level] ≠ i)
9   od;
10  critical section;
11  b[i] := 0;
```

We can describe the algorithm as a set of $n - \ell$ levels that a process needs to pass through, one level at a time, before it can enter its critical section. For a process to pass from some level, denoted *level*, to the next level (i.e., $level + 1$), one of the following two conditions should be satisfied:

1. another process arrived after it to that level; or
2. the number of processes in levels not smaller than *level* is at most $n - level$.

We notice that there is no way in this model for a process, say p, to count all other processes that are in levels not lower than itself in one atomic operation. During the counting loop (lines 4–8), processes that were already counted can change their status before the loop ends. If a process that was lower than p was not counted and then managed to climb to p's level before p's counting was completed, it will release p anyway by changing *turn*. On the other hand, if a process that was found to be higher than p got lower than p after the counting was completed (that process completed its critical section and exit code), then p will notice it in the next iteration.

Properties of the Algorithm:

- Satisfies ℓ-exclusion and ℓ-starvation-freedom.
- The contention-free time complexity is $O(n \times (n - \ell))$ accesses to the shared memory.
- $2n - \ell$ atomic registers, each able to hold n values, are used.

Theorem 6.1 *The algorithm satisfies ℓ-exclusion and ℓ-starvation freedom.*

Proof: Under maximum contention, exactly one process waits at each level, so having $n - \ell$ levels allows only ℓ processes into their critical sections. Once ℓ processes enter into their critical sections, any other active process must be waiting on any of the $n - \ell$ levels, and therefore no $\ell + 1$ processes can enter their critical sections at the same time. This explains (informally) why the algorithm satisfies ℓ-exclusion.

Next we prove that ℓ-deadlock-freedom is satisfied. Assume to the contrary that ℓ-deadlock-freedom is not satisfied. That is, there is a run in which strictly fewer than ℓ processes fail (are delayed forever), some correct process is trying to enter its critical section, and no correct process can enter its critical section. If there are processes in their critical sections we let them proceed and execute their exit code. Now consider the correct processes that are at the top-most non-empty level which has at least one correct process. If there are less than ℓ processes in that level then the algorithm will "allow" all of them to proceed and go up one level. If at that level there are more than ℓ processes, than at least two of them are correct, and therefore at least one of these two will find that *turn*[*level*] was changed and will be able to go up one level. Thus eventually some correct process will enter its critical section. This contradicts the assumption that progress is not possible.

The fact that the algorithm is ℓ-deadlock-free, together with the fact that at any level a new process always releases, by setting *turn*[*level*] to its value, all the other processes at the level that came before it to climb to the next level, ensures ℓ-starvation freedom. ∎

6.2.2 An Unbounded FIFO-enabling Algorithm

The next algorithm using atomic registers, due to Gary Peterson (1990), solves ℓ-exclusion and satisfies the strong FIFO-enabling fairness requirement. It uses single-writer registers of unbounded size. The algorithm is a generalization of a variant of Lamport's Bakery algorithm, presented on page 54. Recall that in this variant, for each process i, the *number*[i] register is never decreased, and thus the correctness proof is much simpler than that of the original Bakery algorithm (on page 50).

The algorithm makes use of two boolean arrays *trying*[1..n], *switch*[1..n], and an integer array *number*[1..n]. The entries *trying*[i], *switch*[i], and *number*[i] can be read by all the processes but can be written only by process i. (Thus, each such three registers can be implemented as one single-writer register.) Furthermore, the setting of *switch*[i] has to be done at the same time as process i sets *trying*[i] to *true*. Hence (*trying*, *switch*)[i] denotes a pair of boolean values encoded as a single four-valued register. In addition a local array *local_switch*[1..n] and two local variables *counter* and j are used for each process. The relation $<$ used in the algorithm on ordered pairs of integers is called the *lexicographic order* relation and is defined by $(a, b) < (c, d)$ if $a < c$, or if $a = c$ and $b < d$. The algorithm is defined formally below.

AN UNBOUNDED FIFO-ENABLING ℓ-EXCLUSION ALGORITHM: `process i's program.`

(trying, switch)[1..*n*]: type (boolean,boolean), initially *(false,false)*;
number[1..*n*]: type integer, initially 0;

```
       /* beginning of doorway */
 1     (trying,switch)[i] := (true, not switch[i]);
 2     number[i] := 1 + maximum(number[1], ..., number[n]);
 3     for j = 1 to n do local_switch[j] := switch[j] od;
       /* end of doorway */
 4     repeat
 5         counter := 0; /* counter is a local register */
 6         for j := 1 to n do
 7             if      trying[j] = true and
 8                     local_switch[j] = switch[j] and
 9                     (number[j], j) ≤ (number[i], i)
10             then    counter := counter + 1 fi od
11     until counter ≤ ℓ;
12     critical section;
13     trying[i] := false;
```

In line 1, process i indicates that it is contending for the critical section by setting its *trying* bit to *true* and flips its *switch* register. Then it takes a number which is greater than the numbers of all the other processes. After that, process i waits until it has one of the ℓ lowest numbers (i.e., has one of the ℓ highest priorities) among the active processes that have started before i has completed its doorway. If two active processes have the same number then (line 4 guarantees that) the process with the smaller identifier is assumed to hold a smaller number.

Next we explain why, for $\ell \geq 2$, the use of the *switch* registers is necessary for ensuring FIFO-enabling. Assume that we omit them. Consider the following run. Process p_1 runs first and completes its doorway (lines 1–3). Then, process p_2 starts and enters its critical section (this is possible since there are only two active processes). We now let ℓ processes with *numbers* lower than that of p_1 start, they set their trying bits and stop. Now, we let process p_1 continue, it can not enter its critical section since it sees ℓ trying processes with lower numbers. At that point p_1 is *not* enabled, although p_2, which has started after p_1 has completed its doorway, has entered its critical section. Thus, the algorithm does not satisfy FIFO-enabling if the *switch* registers are omitted.

Properties of the Algorithm:

- Satisfies ℓ-exclusion, ℓ-deadlock-freedom, and FIFO-enabling.
- The contention-free time complexity is $O(n)$ accesses to the shared memory.
- n unbounded (size) single-writer registers are used. (As already mentioned, the three single-writer registers of each process can be implemented as one such register.)

Theorem 6.2 *The algorithm satisfies ℓ-exclusion and ℓ-deadlock-freedom.*

Proof: Assume to the contrary that there is a group of processes, say Q, of $\ell + 1$ processes, such that all processes in Q are in their critical sections at the same time. Among these processes, let $p_i \in Q$ be the process with the lowest priority. For p_i to enter its critical section it must have seen at least one of the other processes in Q, say p_j, having lower priority than itself (line 9). This implies that p_j must have changed one of its single-writer shared registers between the time p_i last read it and the time p_j has entered its critical section. This can not be *number*[j] since this register is never decreased which will leave the priority of process j still lower than that of process i. Also, this can not be (*trying*, *switch*)[j], because this will force j to update *number*[j] before entering its critical section, setting it to a value greater than *number*[i], and hence having lower priority than i. Since we reach a contradiction, the algorithm satisfies ℓ-exclusion.

Let p be a process which has the highest priority among the correct processes that are trying to enter their critical sections. Assuming at most $\ell - 1$ processes have failed or are in their critical sections, p will be one of the ℓ highest priority processes and hence will be able to proceed and enter its critical section. Thus, the algorithm satisfies ℓ-deadlock-freedom. ∎

Theorem 6.3 *The algorithm satisfies FIFO-enabling.*

Proof: Assume to the contrary that process p_i has completed its doorway ahead of process p_j, process p_j has entered its critical section, but p_i is not enabled – it must wait for some process to do something before it can enter its critical section. Clearly p_i is not waiting for p_j since p_i has a higher priority (i.e., *number*[i] $<$ *number*[j]). Thus, there is a process, say p_k, that p_i must wait for, which process p_j did not have to wait for. The process p_k must be a process with a higher priority than p_i, its *trying*[k] bit must be set to *true*, and the value of *trying*[k] when process p_j last looked at it must have been *false*. Thus, p_k must have changed *trying*[k] from *false* to *true* between the last time p_j has tested it and the first time p_i has tested it. However, when setting *trying*[k] to *true*, *switch*[k] is also changed. So p_i will not have to wait for p_k, unless p_k has changed *switch*[k] an even number of times since p_j has last tested it. But, changing *switch*[k] even twice requires that p_k will enter its critical section in between, and hence p_k will have to set *number*[k] to be higher than the current value of *number*[i]. This will release p_i from the need to wait for p_k. A contradiction. ∎

Self Review

1. Would Peterson's algorithm (page 230) still be correct if we replace the first line with "**for** *level* := 1 **to** *n* – *l* **do**" (and assuming the *turn* array is of size $n - 1$)?
2. Would Peterson's algorithm (page 230) still be correct if we replace line 8 with "**until** (*counter* $\leq \ell$ **or** *turn[level]* $\neq i$)"?
3. Does Theorem 2.16 imply that a similar space lower bound holds also for any 2-deadlock-free 2-exclusion algorithm for n processes?

Answers: (1) Yes. (2) Yes. (3) No.

6.3 Using a Single Read-modify-write Register

In this subsection our model of computation consists of (a fully asynchronous collection of) n identical anonymous deterministic processes that communicate via a *single* finite-sized shared register. Access to the shared register is via atomic "read-modify-write" instructions which, in a single indivisible step, read the value in the register and then write a new value that can depend on the value just read. We first describe a trivial ℓ-exclusion ℓ-deadlock-free algorithm that uses a single register with only $\ell + 1$ shared states. However, this algorithm does not satisfy ℓ-starvation-freedom. The second algorithm is also very simple and satisfies FIFO-enabling; however, it uses an unbounded size register. The third algorithm is more complex, but satisfies FIFO-enabling using a bounded size register which has only $O(n^2)$ states. All the algorithms in this subsection are due to M. J. Fischer, N. A. Lynch, J. E. Burns, and A. Borodin (1979).

The basic idea in all the three algorithms is as in the Bakery algorithm (see page 50). A process wishing to enter its critical section takes the next available ticket and waits until its ticket becomes valid, at which point it can safely enter its critical section. When it exits, it discards its ticket and validates the next invalid ticket in order, even if this ticket has not been taken yet. Once a ticket becomes valid, it remains valid until discarded. Tickets are validated in the same order as they were issued, and at any time exactly ℓ (non-discarded) tickets are valid.

6.3.1 The Counter Algorithm

We first describe a trivial ℓ-deadlock-free algorithm that uses a single register with only $\ell + 1$ shared states, which does not satisfy ℓ-starvation-freedom. The algorithm generalizes the trivial deadlock-free mutual exclusion algorithm using a single test-and-set bit from page 154. In this algorithm, there are exactly ℓ tickets available and all of them are always valid. A process wishing to enter its critical section tries to get one of these ℓ tickets. If the process succeeds it can enter its critical section immediately, otherwise, it tries again (busy-waiting). When it exits, it returns its ticket so that somebody else can use it.

The brackets $\langle\ \rangle$ are used to explicitly mark the beginning and end of exclusive access to the shared read-modify-write register. An execution of a bracketed section is considered as an atomic action.

THE COUNTER ALGORITHM: `process i's program.`

shared *ticket* ranges over $\{0, 1, \ldots, \ell\}$; initially *ticket* $= 0$
local T ranges over $\{0, 1, \ldots, \ell\}$

repeat
    $\langle T := ticket;$
    if $T < \ell$ **then** $ticket := ticket + 1\rangle$
until $(T < \ell)$;
critical section;
$\langle ticket := ticket - 1\rangle$;

We notice that a process may never succeed in getting a ticket (i.e., busy-wait forever) and hence the algorithm is not ℓ-starvation-free.

Properties of the Counter Algorithm:

- Satisfies ℓ-exclusion and ℓ-deadlock-freedom, but does not satisfy ℓ-starvation-freedom.
- Process time complexity and system response time is a constant.
- Only a single read-modify-write register which has $\ell + 1$ values is used.

The proof that the algorithm satisfies the above properties is very simple and is left as an exercise.

6.3.2 The Numbered Ticket Algorithm

The next algorithm for ℓ-exclusion is a generalization of the Ticket algorithm for 1-exclusion which is described on page 158. The algorithm is very simple and it satisfies FIFO-enabling; however, it uses unbounded space. In the next subsection, this algorithm is modified to use only bounded space.

The values of the shared register range over the set $N \times N$, where $N = \{0, 1, \ldots, \infty\}$. We use *ticket* and *valid* to designate the first and second components, respectively, of the ordered pair stored in the shared register. As before, the brackets $\langle\ \rangle$ are used to explicitly mark the beginning and end of exclusive access to the shared read-modify-write register. An execution of a bracketed section is considered as an atomic action.

THE NUMBERED TICKET ALGORITHM: `process` i`'s program.`

```
constant N = {0, 1, ..., ∞}
shared (ticket,valid) ranges over N × N,
                    initially, ticket = 0 and valid = ℓ
local T ranges over N

    /* beginning of doorway */
    ⟨ticket := ticket + 1; T := ticket⟩;
    /* end of doorway */
    repeat
    until ⟨T ≤ valid⟩;
    critical section;
    ⟨valid := valid + 1⟩;
```

Each process first increments *ticket* by one, reads the new value of the *ticket* and stores it in local memory. At any later point, a process becomes one of the first ℓ processes in the "waiting line" if it learns (by inspecting *valid*) that its ticket number $ticket_i$ is less than or equals *valid*, in which case it can safely enter its critical section.

Properties of the Numbered Ticket Algorithm:

- Satisfies ℓ-exclusion, ℓ-deadlock-freedom, and FIFO-enabling.
- Process time complexity and system response time are constants.
- *ticket* and *valid* grow without bound.

The proof that the algorithm satisfies the above properties is very simple and is left as an exercise.

6.3.3 The Unbounded Colored Ticket Algorithm

We next present two *colored ticket* algorithms. The first is a very simple simulation of the Numbered Ticket algorithm and it still uses unbounded space. The second algorithm, which is the final Colored Ticket algorithm, is more complex, and satisfies FIFO-enabling using only $O(n^2)$ shared states, where n is the number of processes. We start with several observations about the previous algorithm.

Lemma 6.4 *In the Numbered Ticket algorithm:*

$$|ticket - valid| \geq \max(\ell, n - \ell).$$

Proof: It follows from the following two invariants that *ticket* and *valid* can not be too far apart:

1. $valid \geq ticket$ implies $valid - ticket \leq \ell$, and
2. $ticket \geq valid$ implies $ticket - valid \leq n - \ell$.

The result follows. ∎

Let $M \geq 1 + \max(\ell, n - \ell)$. Assume that we divide the tickets into blocks of size M. It is easy to see that either *ticket* and *valid* are in the same block, or they are in consecutive blocks.

Lemma 6.5 *In the Numbered Ticket algorithm:*

$$|\lfloor ticket/M \rfloor - \lfloor valid/M \rfloor| \leq 1.$$

Proof: By Lemma 6.4, $M > |ticket - valid|$. The result follows. ∎

Next we observe that the definition of M ensures that we can determine whether $ticket \leq valid$ (i.e., whether *ticket* is valid) simply by checking whether *ticket* and *valid* are in the same block and by comparing their relative positions within their respective blocks.

Lemma 6.6 *In the Numbered Ticket algorithm:*

$$ticket \leq valid$$

if and only if, either:

1. $(\lfloor ticket/M \rfloor = \lfloor valid/M \rfloor)$ *and* $(ticket \bmod M \leq valid \bmod M)$, *or*
2. $(\lfloor ticket/M \rfloor \neq \lfloor valid/M \rfloor)$ *and* $(ticket \bmod M > valid \bmod M)$.

Proof: Follows from Lemma 6.5, and the fact that $M > |ticket - valid|$. ∎

Lemma 6.6 reveals a slightly different way for doing validity testing, which the next two algorithms make use of. The colored ticket algorithms replace the numbered tickets by color tickets.

> A color ticket T is an order pair $(T.val, T.col)$, where $T.val$, the *value* of T, is a number in the set $\{0, \ldots, M-1\}$ indicating the position of the ticket within the block; and $T.col$, the color of T, is a non-negative integer indicating the block that contains the ticket T.

There is a one-to-one correspondence, denoted ϕ, between a numbered ticket i and a colored ticket $(i \bmod M, \lfloor i/M \rfloor)$. In the discussion below, when we refer to *ticket* and *valid*, we actually consider their corresponding colored versions, $(ticket \bmod M, \lfloor ticket/M \rfloor)$ and $(valid \bmod M, \lfloor valid/M \rfloor)$, respectively. Using this one-to-one correspondence, Lemma 6.6 enables the order of *ticket* and *valid* to be determined, without using an ordering on colors. Thus, a process can now determine if its (colored) ticket T is valid, as follows:

- T must be valid if its colors differ from the color of both *valid* and *ticket*, for then its color must be less than both.
- If T's color is the same as that of *valid*, then T is valid iff $T.val \leq valid.val$.
- If T's color differs from that of *valid*, but is the same as that of *ticket*, then T is valid only if $ticket.val > valid.val$. (That is, the corresponding "numbered ticket" is less than or equal to "numbered valid", which implies that T is less than "numbered valid".)

Below we give the complete code of the first Colored Ticket algorithm. As explained it simulates the Numbered Ticket algorithm using the one-to-one correspondence between numbered and colored tickets as discussed above. Thus the algorithm bounds the number of tickets *values*, but uses unbounded number of *colors*. The second algorithm will also bound the number of colors.

THE UNBOUNDED COLORED TICKET ALGORITHM: `process i's program.`

constants $N = \{0, 1, \ldots, \infty\}$, $M = 1 + \max(\ell, n - \ell)$, $\hat{M} = \{0, 1, \ldots, M-1\}$
shared $(ticket, valid)$ ranges over $(\hat{M} \times N) \times (\hat{M} \times N)$,
initially, $ticket = (0, 0)$ and $valid = (\ell, 0)$
local T ranges over $(\hat{M} \times N)$, B: boolean

```
                                        /* beginning of doorway */
⟨if ticket.val < M − 1                  /* take next ticket */
  then ticket.val := ticket.val + 1
```

```
  else ticket.val := 0; ticket.col := ticket.col + 1 fi;
  T := ticket⟩;
                                            /* end of doorway */
repeat                          /* validity testing:T ≤ valid?*/
     ⟨if T.col = valid.col
      then B := (T.val ≤ valid.val)         /* Lemma 6.6 part 1 */
      else  if T.col = ticket.col
            then B := (valid.val < ticket.val) fi      /* part 2 */
      else B := true fi⟩           /* T < valid and T < ticket */
until B;                                      /* until T is valid */
critical section;
⟨if valid.val < M − 1                     /* validate next ticket */
 then valid.val := valid.val + 1
 else valid.val := 0; valid.col := valid.col + 1 fi⟩;
```

6.3.4 The Bounded Colored Ticket Algorithm

Next we present the bounded version of the Colored Ticket algorithm. It is obtained by modifying the unbounded version so that only $\ell + 1$ different colors are used. To explain how this is done, we use the following definition:

Definition: *For two tickets, $T = (T.val, T.col)$ and $S = (S.val, S.col)$, T leads S, denoted $T \succeq S$, if and only if, either*

1. *$(T.col = S.col)$ and $(T.val \geq S.val)$, or*
2. *$(T.col \neq S.col)$ and $(T.val < S.val)$.*

We notice that, by Lemma 6.6, *ticket* $\succeq$ *valid* in the Colored Ticket algorithm if and only if $\phi^{-1}(ticket) \geq \phi^{-1}(valid)$ in the Numbered Ticket algorithm.

Reusing colors in the new (bounded space) algorithm is done by incrementing *ticket.col* or *valid.col* as follows:

- If *ticket.col* is being incremented, and *ticket* $\succeq$ *valid*, then a new color is chosen that is different from the color of any currently issued or valid ticket and is also different from *valid.col*.
- If *ticket.col* is being incremented, and it is *not* the case that *ticket* $\succeq$ *valid*, then *ticket.col* is set equal to *valid.col*.
- If *valid.col* is being incremented, and *valid* $\succeq$ *ticket*, then a new color is chosen that is different from the color of any currently issued or valid ticket and is also different from *ticket.col*.
- If *valid.col* is being incremented, and it is *not* the case that *valid* $\succeq$ *ticket*, then *ticket.col* is set equal to *ticket.col*.

The above technique ensures that no two processes ever simultaneously hold the same (colored) ticket. This follows from the fact that in the Numbered Ticket algorithm, $|ticket - valid \leq M|$.

The following observation shows how to apply the above technique with only $\ell + 1$ colors. We say that a color is *in use*, if it is the color of a valid or an issued ticket that has not been discarded, or it is equal to *ticket.col* or to *valid.col*.

Lemma 6.7 *Assume that in the Unbounded Colored Ticket algorithm, a new color is needed at time t. Then, at most ℓ colors are in use at time t.*

Proof: Since there are exactly ℓ valid tickets at any given time, it suffices to show that every color in use at time t is the same as the color of some valid ticket.

We notice that *valid.col* is always the color of the most recently validated ticket (which is one of the ℓ valid tickets), and hence it suffices to show that when a new color is needed, both *ticket.col* and the colors of all issued but not yet validated tickets are the same as *valid.col*. There are two possible cases when a new color is needed.

Case 1. A new color is needed because *valid* is about to be incremented. This can only happen when a process in its exit code is attempting to validate a new ticket, $valid.val = M - 1$ and $valid \succeq ticket$. Since in such a case $|\phi^{-1}(valid) - \phi^{-1}(ticket)| \leq \ell \leq M - 1$, it must be that $ticket.col = valid.col$. Moreover, since $valid \succeq ticket$, all issued tickets are valid, and thus the only colors in use are of the ℓ valid tickets.

Case 2. A new color is needed because *ticket* is about to be incremented. This happens when a process in its entry code is attempting to take a new ticket, $ticket.val = M - 1$ and $ticket \succeq valid$. In that case, it must be that $|\phi^{-1}(valid) - \phi^{-1}(ticket)| \leq n - \ell \leq M - 1$, which implies that $ticket.col = valid.col$. Moreover, since $ticket \succeq valid$, all issued tickets that are not yet valid must lie between *valid* and *ticket*, so they all must have color *valid.col*. Again, the only colors in use are of the ℓ valid tickets. ∎

Lemma 6.7 shows that as long as we use no less than $\ell + 1$ colors there will always be a free color when needed. Thus, $\ell + 1$ colors are sufficient instead of infinitely many colors. In order to be able to trace, at any given moment, which of these $\ell + 1$ colors are free, we introduce an array Q of length $\ell + 1$ into the shared register, where $Q(c) \in \{0, 1, \dots, \ell\}$ is the number of valid tickets of color c. To find a new free color a process simply scans for an entry $Q(c) = 0$ which indicates that the color c is free. The code of this function is as follows:

```
function NEW_COLOR returns: a free color in {0, 1, ..., ℓ};
 local variable: c ranges over {0, 1, ..., ℓ}

begin
        c := 0;
        while Q(c) > 0 do c := c + 1 od;
        return c;
end
```

The array Q is updated only in the exit code, whenever a ticket is discarded and a new one is validated. (It is never updated in the entry code when a process takes the next available ticket even if a new color is being used.) The complete code of the algorithm follows.

THE BOUNDED COLORED TICKET ALGORITHM: `process i's program.`

```
constants L = {0, 1, ..., ℓ}, M = 1 + max(ℓ, n − ℓ), M̂ = {0, 1, ..., M − 1},
                A = set of (ℓ + 1)-tuples of non-negative integers that sum to ℓ
shared (ticket,valid,Q) ranges over (M̂ × L) × (M̂ × L) × A,
      initially, ticket = (0,0), valid = (ℓ,0), Q[0] = ℓ and Q[i] = 0 for all i ≥ 1
local T ranges over (M̂ × L), B: boolean

                                                  /* beginning of doorway */
⟨if ticket.val < M − 1                                 /* take next ticket */
 then ticket.val := ticket.val + 1
 else   if ticket ⪰ valid                       /* if ticket leads valid */
        then ticket := New_Color                 /* finds unused color */
        else ticket.col := valid.col fi;
        ticket.val := 0 fi;
 T := ticket⟩;                                          /* end of doorway */
                                          /* validity testing is as before */
repeat                                      /* validity testing:T ≤ valid?*/
        ⟨if T.col = valid.col
         then B := (T.val ≤ valid.val)               /* Lemma 6.6 part 1 */
         else   if T.col = ticket.col
                then B := (valid.val < ticket.val) fi            /* part 2 */
         else B := true fi⟩                /* T < valid and T < ticket */
until B;                                              /* until T is valid */

critical section;
⟨if valid.val < M − 1                              /* validate next ticket */
 then valid.val := valid.val + 1
 else   if valid ⪰ ticket                       /* if valid leads ticket */
        then valid := New_Color                  /* finds unused color */
        else valid.col := ticket.col fi;
        valid.val := 0 fi;
 Q[valid.col] := Q[valid.col] + 1;
                                           /* update Quantity information */
 Q[T.col] := Q[T.col] − 1⟩;
```

The above algorithm simulates the Unbounded Colored Ticket algorithm. It is easy to see that any two issued or validated (and not discarded) tickets T and T' have the same color in the Bounded Colored Ticket algorithm, iff they have the same colors in the Unbounded Colored Ticket algorithm; hence the correctness of the bounded space algorithm follows from that of the unbounded space algorithm.

Properties of the Unbounded Colored Ticket Algorithm:

- Satisfies ℓ-exclusion, ℓ-deadlock-freedom, and FIFO-enabling.
- Process time complexity and system response time is a constant.
- For a fixed ℓ, $O(n^2)$ shared values are used.

We explain the above claim about the space complexity. The total number of shared values used by the algorithm is the product of the number of values used by Q, *ticket*, and *valid*. To compute the number of values needed to implement Q, we observe that at any given time, there are exactly ℓ valid tickets, so the total number of different values is the number of $(\ell + 1)$-tuples of non-negative integers that sum to ℓ. This number is the same as the number of partitions of ℓ identical elements into $\ell + 1$ buckets, which is exponential in ℓ, but is independent of n. Thus,

$$\textit{Total space is}: \binom{2\ell}{\ell}((\ell + 1)M)^2$$

Since, $M = O(n)$, for a fixed ℓ, the number of shared values used by the algorithm is $O(n^2)$.

Self Review

1. Would the Counter algorithm (page 234) still be correct if we replace the single statement in its exit code with the following two statements: $\langle ticket_i := ticket\rangle$; $\langle ticket := ticket_i - 1\rangle$?
2. Would the Counter algorithm (page 234) still be correct, if instead of executing the statements in lines 2 and 3 as one atomic action, they are executed separately?
3. In the Numbered Ticket algorithm (page 235), what is the maximum value of the following four expressions: $T - valid$, $valid - T$, $T - ticket$, $ticket - T$?
4. In the Unbounded Colored Ticket algorithm (page 237), can it be that $T.col \neq valid.col$ and $T.val < valid.col$?

Answers: (1) No. (2) No. It will not satisfy mutual exclusion, although it will still satisfy deadlock-freedom. (3) $n - \ell - 1$, infinite, 0, infinite. (4) Yes.

6.4 The ℓ-assignment Problem

A stronger version of the ℓ-exclusion problem is the *ℓ-assignment problem* (also called *slotted* ℓ-exclusion) which requires that ℓ *distinguishable* copies of a shared resource be shared among the n processes under the condition that up to k processes can fail.

The problem differs from the ℓ-exclusion problem in that an explicit assignment of resources must be made, that is, each process must be given a specific copy of the resource. As an example, consider again the case of buying a ticket for a bus ride or a flight. While in the ℓ-exclusion problem a passenger needs only to make sure that there is some free seat on the bus (but not to reserve a particular seat), in the ℓ-assignment problem, it is necessary to have a seat assignment before boarding the aircraft (although, when making the reservation, the passenger does not care which seat as long as she gets one).

We next show a simple way to solve the ℓ-assignment problem with up to k faults by composing any k-exclusion algorithm with a wait-free ℓ-naming algorithm.

The *wait-free ℓ-naming* problem is to assign unique names to initially identical processes. A required property of a solution is that the name space from which the names are assigned is $\{1, \ldots, \ell\}$. Once a process acquires a name it may release it. A process is *participating* in a naming algorithm as long as it tries to acquire a name, or if it has acquired a name and has not released it yet. It is assuming that at any point in time at most ℓ processes participate in the algorithm. A solution to the problem is required to be *wait-free*, that is, it should guarantee that every participating process will always be able to obtain a unique name or to release a name in a finite number of steps, regardless of the behavior of other processes (such as abnormal termination).

As an example, consider the following wait-free ℓ-naming algorithm. We use ℓ test-and-set bits with initial value 0, which are numbered 1 through ℓ. Each process scans the bits, in the same order, starting with the first bit. At each step, the process applies the test-and-set operation, and either moves to the next bit if the returned value is 1, or stops when the returned value is 0. The process is assigned the name equal to the bit on which its (last) test-and-set operation returned 0. To release a name, a process which has acquired the name j simply resets (to 0) the j'th test-and-set bit. The code of the ℓ-naming algorithm is defined below.

A WAIT-FREE ℓ-NAMING ALGORITHM: process p's program.

TS[1..ℓ]: array of shared test-and-set bits, initially all 0;

```
function request-a-name return:name;
    name := 1;
    while TS[name] = 1 do name := name + 1 od;
    return(name);
end-function

function release-a-name(name:integer);
    TS[name] := 0;
end-function
```

The above algorithm is wait-free as long as no more than ℓ processes are active simultaneously. To construct an ℓ-assignment algorithm with k faults from a k-exclusion algorithm and a wait-free ℓ-naming algorithm, we replace the critical section of the k-exclusion algorithm with the ℓ-naming algorithm. The code of the ℓ-assignment algorithm is defined below.

AN ℓ-ASSIGNMENT ALGORITHM: `process` p`'s program.`

```
loop forever
    remainder code (of ℓ-assignment);
    entry code of k-exclusion;
    entry code of ℓ-naming: request-a-name, return(name);
    critical section: accesses-resource(name);
    exit code of ℓ-naming: release-a-name(name);
    exit code of k-exclusion
end loop
```

Obviously, in the above algorithm we can assume $k = \ell$ and use the simple ℓ-naming algorithm using test-and-set bits.

An interesting result regarding the ℓ-assignment problem is that, when only atomic registers can be used, $\ell \geq 2k + 1$ is a necessary and sufficient condition for solving this problem (Problem 6.16, page 248). This result is in contrast to the fact that ℓ-exclusion is solvable so long as ℓ is greater than the maximal number of possible faults.

Since the processes usually already have unique names to start with, we can use a solution for *ℓ-renaming* instead of that for ℓ-naming. In the (long-lived) ℓ-renaming problem, each process starts with a name from some large name space (say, the integers), and it is required to choose a distinct name in the smaller range $\{1, \ldots, \ell\}$, assuming that at any point in time at most ℓ processes participate in the algorithm. Once a process acquires a name it may release it. It follows easily from the result mentioned above (Problem 6.16), that $\ell \geq 2n - 1$ is a necessary condition for solving the *wait-free ℓ-renaming* problem for n processes using atomic registers (Problem 6.17).

6.5 Bibliographic Notes

6.1

The ℓ-exclusion problem, which is an extension of the mutual exclusion problem (where $\ell = 1$), was first defined and solved (using read-modify-write registers) in [132, 133].

6.2

In [286], Peterson has proposed several ℓ-exclusion algorithms for solving the problem using read and write atomicity: (1) An ℓ-deadlock-free algorithm (Problem 6.3, page 246) which is based on a simple deadlock-free (mutual exclusion) algorithm which is contained within the Eisenberg and McGuire starvation-free algorithm [125] (Problem 2.59, page 89); (2) An ℓ-starvation-free algorithm (page 230), which is based on a (rather simple) generalization of Peterson's mutual exclusion algorithm [282] (Problem 2.63, page 90); (3) An unbounded FIFO-enabling algorithm (page 232) which is based on an interesting variant on Lamport's Bakery algorithm [212] (page 54); and (4) a complex FIFO-enabling algorithm with bounded size registers. The open problem mentioned in Problem 6.5 (page 246) is also from [286].

A (complex) FIFO-enabling solution using bounded size atomic registers is presented also in [7]. To illustrate the problem, the following example is given in [7]: Consider a system where each process controls some device which from time to time needs to enter a mode of high electrical power consumption. The main circuit breaker can withstand at most ℓ devices at high electric power consumption. By allowing each process to switch its device only when it is in its critical section, an ℓ-exclusion solution will protect the circuit breaker from burning out.

A long-lived and adaptive algorithm for collecting information using atomic registers is presented in [12] (see page 104 for definition of adaptivity). The authors employ these algorithms to transform algorithms, such as the Bakery algorithm [212] (see page 50), the ℓ-exclusion algorithm of [7], and the ℓ-assignment algorithm of [85], into their corresponding adaptive long-lived version.

An ℓ-starvation-free solution using safe registers alone is presented in [115]. (Safe registers are discussed on pages 65 and 152.) The ℓ-starvation-free algorithm presented in Problem 6.6 (on page 246) is a generalization of the starvation-free mutual exclusion algorithm from [72] (Problem 2.65, page 91).

In [63], the ℓ-exclusion problem (called in [63] the "identical-slot critical section" problem) is considered in a completely asynchronous distributed network. The fairness condition assumed is called *the transient priority rule*: Process p has higher priority than process q only if p entered its critical section less times than q, p tries to enter its critical section, and q *knows* this fact. (This is a stronger version of the global priority rule of [47].) The message complexity of the solutions is unbounded.

6.3

All the algorithms in Section 6.3 are taken from [132, 133]. The Numbered Ticket algorithm for ℓ-exclusion (page 235) is a generalization of the Ticket algorithm for 1-exclusion which is described on page 158. In [132, 133] a tight space bound of $\Theta(n^2)$ shared states is proved for the ℓ-exclusion problem *for fixed* ℓ assuming a strong FIFO and strong robustness properties. That is, also FIFO in the exit code is required, up to $\ell - 1$ enabled processes can fail, and any number of other (not enabled) processes can fail anywhere else. Without the strong FIFO and strong robustness requirements (at most $\ell - 1$ processes can fail), and not requiring that the exit code be wait-free, $O(n)$ shared states suffice for mutual exclusion [281]. There is still a large gap between the constants in the upper and lower bounds. Both depend on ℓ, but the constant in the upper bound is exponential in ℓ, while the constant in the lower bound is linear in ℓ. For more details see Problem 6.14.

Several algorithms for ℓ-exclusion which are based on strong primitives (fetch-and-increment, compare-and-swap) are considered in [35]. Time complexity is measured in terms of the number of remote accesses of shared memory required per critical section. (Remote accesses are defined on page 138.)

In [85], an interesting tight bound regarding the ℓ-assignment problem is proved, namely, that $\ell \geq 2k + 1$ is a necessary and sufficient condition for solving the ℓ-assignment problem using atomic registers (Problem 6.16, page 248).

In [47], a simpler version of the ℓ-assignment problem, called *distinct CS*, is considered. In this version all correct processes are required to repeatedly request resources (i.e., there is no remainder code). The fairness condition suggested in [47] is called *global priority*: Process p has higher priority than process q if p entered its critical section less times than q. It is mentioned in [85] that a lower bound similar to the one mentioned above (i.e., that $\ell \geq 2k + 1$ is also a necessary condition for solving the distinct CS problem) was proved by H. Attiya and M. Tuttle (Private communication).

We have explained how to construct an ℓ-assignment algorithm with k faults by composing a k-exclusion algorithm and a wait-free ℓ-naming or a wait-free ℓ-renaming algorithm (page 243). The naming algorithm we have described uses test-and-set bits (page 242). While it is not possible to construct a naming algorithm using only atomic registers, there are many papers on the construction of renaming algorithms using only atomic registers.

It is known that wait-free $(2n - 1)$-renaming is a problem that can be solved using atomic registers by n or fewer processes, but not by any larger number of processes. The renaming problem was first solved for message-passing systems [48], and then for shared memory systems using atomic registers [62]. Both these papers present one-shot algorithms (i.e., solutions that can be used only once). In [85] the first long-lived renaming algorithm was presented: The ℓ-assignment algorithm presented in [85] can be used as an optimal long-lived $(2n - 1)$-renaming algorithm with exponential step complexity. Several of the many papers on renaming using atomic registers are [4, 10, 12, 13, 52, 53, 144, 172, 183, 267]. A simple technique of implementing scalable shared objects by composing ℓ-exclusion and renaming is discussed in [33].

6.6 Problems

The problems are divided into several categories. See page 23 for a detailed explanation.

Problems based on Section 6.1

∘ 6.1 Explain why FIFO-enabling does not imply deadlock-freedom.

∘ 6.2
1. Why is the ℓ-deadlock-freedom requirement a stronger property than only requiring that "if fewer than ℓ processes are in their critical sections, then it is possible for another process to enter its critical section, even though no process leaves its critical section in the meantime"?
2. Why is the ℓ-starvation-freedom requirement a stronger property than only requiring that "if fewer than ℓ processes are in their critical sections, then any process that is trying to enter its critical section must eventually enter its critical section, even though no process leaves its critical section in the meantime"?

∘• 6.3 The following ℓ-deadlock-free algorithm, due to Gary Peterson (1990), is based on a simple deadlock-free (mutual exclusion) algorithm which is contained within the Eisenberg and McGuire starvation-free algorithm (Problem 2.59, page 89). Prove that the algorithm satisfies ℓ-deadlock-freedom and ℓ-exclusion, and that it does not satisfy ℓ-starvation-freedom. The algorithm requires a 3-valued single-writer register, called *trying*[*i*], per process which ranges over 0,1, and 2. In addition three local variables, called $count_1$, $count_2$, and j, are used for each process. ℓ is used as a constant.

PETERSON'S ℓ-DEADLOCK-FREE ALGORITHM: `process i's program.`

trying[1..*n*] range 0..2, intially 0.

```
start: trying[i] := 1;
repeat
   counter1 := 0; counter2 := 0;
   for j := 1 to n do
   if j < i and trying[j] = 1 then counter1 := counter1 + 1
   else if trying[j] = 2 then counter2 := counter2 + 1 fi fi
until counter1 + counter2 < ℓ
trying[i] := 2;
repeat
   counter1 := 0; counter2 := 0;
   for j := 1 to n do
   if j < i and trying[j] = 1 then counter1 := counter1 + 1
   else if trying[j] = 2 then counter2 := counter2 + 1 fi fi;
   if counter1 + counter2 > ℓ then goto start fi
until counter2 ≤ ℓ;
critical section;
trying[i] := 0;
```

•∘ 6.4 In Theorem 2.16 (page 59), it is proved that any deadlock-free 1-exclusion algorithm for n processes must use at least n shared registers. Is it true that, for any $\ell \geq 1$ and any $k \geq 1$, any ℓ-deadlock-free k-exclusion algorithm for n processes must use at least n shared registers?

? 6.5 For $\ell \geq 2$, design an algorithm for n processes which satisfies ℓ-exclusion and ℓ-deadlock-freedom and uses only n shared bits, or prove that this is not possible. This is an open problem even for $n = 3$ and $\ell = 2$.

Notice that the unbounded FIFO-enabling algorithm (page 232) uses only n single-writer registers; however, the registers are of unbounded size. Also there seems to be no obvious generalization of the One-bit algorithm from page 64 to ℓ-exclusion.

∘• 6.6 The following algorithm for n processes is a generalization of the starvation-free mutual exclusion algorithm presented in Problem 2.65 (on page 91). It is claimed that the algorithm satisfies ℓ-exclusion and ℓ-starvation-freedom. Is this claim correct?

The algorithm requires $2n$ shared registers, n boolean and n integer registers each able to hold values in $\{1, \ldots, n\}$. The first array, *flag*[1..*n*], states whether a process wants to enter its critical section. The second array, *block*[1..*n*], specifies which process is to block at each level. In addition three local variables, called *level*, *counter*, and *j*, are used for each process. ℓ is used as a constant.

AN ℓ-EXCLUSION ALGORITHM FOR n PROCESSES: `process i's program.`

Initially: *flag*[1..*n*] and *block*[1..*n*] all 0.

```
level := 0;
flag[i] := 1;
repeat
        level := level + 1;
        block[level] := i;
        repeat
                counter := 0;
                for j := 1 to n do
                if flag[j] = 1 then counter := counter + 1 if
        until (block[level] ≠ i or counter < level + ℓ)
until block[level] = i;
critical section;
flag[i] := 0;
```

•• 6.7 Modify the unbounded FIFO-enabling algorithm on page 232, so that it uses only bounded size atomic registers.

◦◦ 6.8 As we have explained, the unbounded FIFO-enabling algorithm on page 232 does not satisfy FIFO-enabling if the *switch* registers are omitted. What is the strongest fairness property that this algorithm does satisfy if the *switch* registers are omitted?

Problems based on Section 6.3

◦ 6.9 Implement the Counter algorithm (page 234) using ℓ test-and-set bits, instead of a single read-modify-write register which has $\ell + 1$ states.

◦ 6.10 Does the following variant of the Counter algorithm (page 234) satisfy ℓ-exclusion and ℓ-deadlock-freedom?

A VARIANT OF THE COUNTER ALGORITHM: `process i's program.`

shared *ticket* ranges over $\{0, 1, \ldots, \infty\}$; init. *ticket* $= 0$
local $ticket_i$ ranges over $\{0, 1, \ldots, \infty\}$

```
repeat
        ⟨ticket_i := ticket; ticket := ticket + 1⟩;
        if ticket_i > ℓ then ticket := ticket − 1⟩
until (ticket_i < ℓ);
```

```
critical section;
⟨ticket := ticket − 1⟩;
```

◦◦ 6.11 In the Numbered Ticket algorithm (page 235), we use *ticket* and *valid* to designate the first and second components, respectively, of the ordered pair stored in a single read-modify-write register. Thus, *ticket* and *valid* can be accessed together in a single atomic step. Would the Numbered Ticket algorithm still be correct under the assumption that *ticket* and *valid* are stored in two (different) read-modify-write registers?

◦• 6.12 Consider the Bounded Colored Ticket algorithm (page 240). Why is there no need to update Q in the entry code? Modify the algorithm so that Q is updated only in the entry code. Can it be that $T.col \neq valid.col$ and $T.val < valid.col$?

◦◦ 6.13 Consider the Bounded Colored Ticket algorithm (page 240). What are the properties of the algorithm if we replace the first seven statements with the following seven statements.

```
⟨if ticket.val < M − 1                    /* take next ticket */
then ticket.val := ticket.val + 1
else   while ticket ⪰ valid
         do skip od;
         ticket.col := valid.col fi;
         ticket.val := 0 fi;
T := ticket⟩;
```

? 6.14 When using a single read-modify-write object, a tight space bound of $\Theta(n^2)$ shared states is proved for the ℓ-exclusion problem *for fixed* ℓ. Even for a fixed ℓ, there is still a large gap between the constants in the upper and lower bounds. Both depend on ℓ, but the constant in the upper bound is exponential in ℓ, while the constant in the lower bound is linear in ℓ. If ℓ is allowed to be a function of n (the number of processes) then the bounds are not tight. For example, if $\ell = \log n$, then the colored ticket algorithm uses $O(n^4(\log n)^{3/2})$ values of shared memory, but the known lower bound is only $\Omega(n^2 \log n)$. If $\ell = O(n)$, then the gap is exponential. Closing the gap is an open problem.

Problems based on Section 6.4

◦ 6.15 Implement the ℓ-naming algorithm (page 242) using a single read-modify-write register which has $\ell + 1$ states, instead of the ℓ test-and-set bits.

•• 6.16 The ℓ-assignment problem is defined on page 241. Prove that a necessary and sufficient condition for solving the ℓ-assignment problem using atomic registers is that $\ell \geq 2k + 1$, where k is the maximal number of possible faults.

◦◦ 6.17 Explain why it follows from the result mentioned in Problem 6.16 that $\ell \geq 2n - 1$ is a necessary condition for solving the (long-lived) *wait-free* *ℓ-renaming* problem for n processes using atomic registers. (ℓ-renaming is defined on page 243.)

Multiple Resources

7.1 Deadlocks

In previous sections we have dealt with a deadlock that may occur in the context of acquiring a single resource. In the context of multiple resources, even when acquiring a single resource is done in deadlock-free manner, deadlocks are still possible.

Consider, for example, the problem of transferring money between two bank accounts. Assume that in order to transfer the money one has to (1) lock the two accounts, (2) transfer the money, (3) release the locks. If two clerks need to transfer money between the same two accounts, and they try to lock the two accounts not in the same order, then the system may deadlock, having each clerk locking one account and waiting for the other. This deadlock situation is illustrated in Figure 7.1(a). How would you "program the clerks" in order to prevent possible deadlocks assuming that there are millions of bank accounts, not just two? There is a simple answer to this question that follows from one of the results which is described in Section 7.2 (i.e., Theorem 7.1).

Another example where "a deadlock" may occur is *bridge crossing*, as illustrated in Figure 7.1(b), where cars heading in the same direction can cross the bridge at the same time, but cars heading in opposite directions can not. Thus, two cars coming from opposite direction can be stuck on the bridge if both try to cross the bridge at the same time.

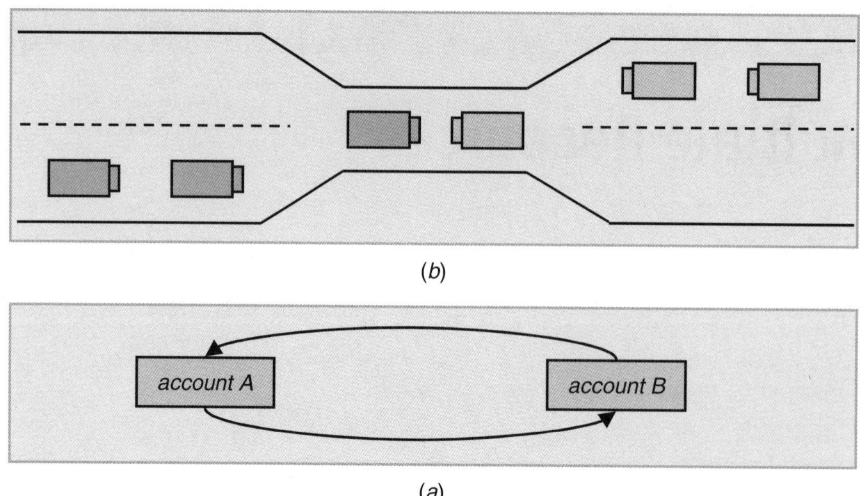

Figure 7.1 Examples of deadlocks. (*a*) Transferring money between two accounts. (*b*) Bridge crossing: the resources are the two entrances.

Basic Concepts

We define the notion of a deadlock in the context of multiple resources and explain a few concepts that are used later in this chapter.

Deadlock: *A set of processes is deadlocked if each process in the set is waiting for an event that only another process in the set can cause.*

The event in the above definition is usually a release of a currently held resource. Thus, in a deadlock situation, there is a set of blocked processes each holding one or more resources and waiting to acquire a resource held by another process in the set. A system with multiple resources is *deadlock-free* if it can never deadlock. There are four different ways for handling deadlocks:

- *Ignore the problem*: This is the approach taken in the Unix and Windows operating systems. The justifications for taking this approach are that deadlocks occur very rarely and that the cost of prevention is high. As operating systems become more complex, deadlocks probably will not be completely ignored in such systems in the future.
- *Deadlock detection and recovery*: Here, it is assumed that a system (or a program) can enter a deadlock state because of a bad design. The goal is to write a *deadlock detection* algorithm that will detect the existence of a deadlock and will resolve it.
- *Deadlock avoidance*: As in the previous case, also in this case, it is assumed that the system can enter a deadlock state, if available resources are allocated immediately whenever they are requested. The goal is to design an algorithm that will be responsible for allocating the resources, and that will ensure that

by careful allocation of the available resources the system will never enter a deadlock state.

- *Deadlock prevention*: It is the responsibility of the programmer (or the system designer) to write a program (design a system) that will never deadlock. This is done by negating *one* of the following four necessary conditions for a deadlock to occur.

Deadlock can arise only if the following four conditions hold *simultaneously*:

- *Mutual exclusion*: Only one process at a time can use a resource.
- *Hold and wait*: A process can request a resource while holding another resource.
- *No preemption*: A resource can be released only voluntarily by the process holding it.
- *Circular wait*: There must be a cycle involving several processes, each waiting for a resource held by the next one.

Deadlock prevention is the best approach for handling deadlocks and is discussed in the next section. The deadlock prevention techniques presented in Section 7.2 are later used in Section 7.4, where the design of a deadlock-free solution to the dining philosophers problem is presented.

Deadlock avoidance algorithms are discussed in Section 7.3, where a *centralized* algorithm is presented. The results from Section 7.3 are not used elsewhere in the book and hence, at first reading, the reader may skip Section 7.3 without loss of continuity.

Self Review

1. How can a deadlock be resolved after it has been detected?
2. Consider a system with r identical resources. The system has 15 processes each needing a maximum of 15 resources. What is the smallest value for r, which makes the system deadlock-free, without a need to use a deadlock avoidance algorithm? Justify your answer.
3. Two processes, p_1 and p_2, each need to hold five records, 1, 2, 3, 4, and 5, in a database to complete. If p_1 asks for them in the order 1, 2, 3, 4, 5 and p_2 asks for them in the same order, deadlock is not possible. However, if p_2 asks for them in the order 5, 4, 3, 2, 1 then deadlock is possible. With five resources, there are 5! or 120 possible combinations each process can request the resources. Hence there are $5! \times 5!$ different algorithms. What is the exact number of algorithms (out of $5! \times 5!$) that is guaranteed to be deadlock-free?

Answers: (1) There are various ways to resolve a deadlock: to abort all deadlocked processes; to abort one process at a time until the deadlock is resolved; to take a resource (or more) from some process; etc. (2) 211. Let p be the number of processes and m the maximal number of resources a process may need. Then the answer in general is $r \geq p(m-1)+1$ (3) $(120 \times 120)/5$. This is based on the fact that an algorithm is deadlock-free if and only if at their first resource both processes try to access the same resource.

7.2 Deadlock Prevention

The best approach for handling deadlocks is to prevent them from happening. In Sections 7.2.1 and 7.2.2, we present several simple design principles which, when applied properly, prevent the occurrence of deadlocks. Deadlock prevention is done by attacking *one* of the four necessary conditions for a deadlock discussed on page 251.

Attacking the *mutual exclusion condition* is done by allowing some of the resources, such as printers, to be spooled. That is, only the printer daemon uses printer resource and thus deadlock for a printer is eliminated. However, only a few types of resources can be spooled and hence this type of attack is not so useful in general. Also attacking the *no preemption condition* is not a good option in general. Think for example of taking the printer from a process that has not finished printing yet.

7.2.1 Two Phase Locking and Timestamping-ordering

Attacking the *hold and wait condition* is done by requiring processes to request all the resources they need in advance; this way a process never has to wait for what it needs. The problem with this approach is that in many systems a process is not required to know in advance all the resources it may need. Furthermore, this approach will tie up resources other processes could be using.

Two Phase Locking. A variation of the above approach is implemented in the *two phase locking* algorithm, which works as follows:

1. *Phase one*: The process tries to lock all the resources it currently needs, one at a time–if the needed resource is not available, the process releases all the resources it has already managed to lock, and starts over;
2. *Phase two*: If phase one succeeds, the process uses the resources to perform the work needed and then releases all the resources it had locked in phase one.

We notice that processes may never finish phase one and hence some kind of a deadlock, called *livelock*, is possible.

Timestamping-ordering. A related method that prevents deadlock and even starvation is to select an ordering among the processes and, whenever there is a conflict, let the smaller process win. The most common algorithm that uses this method is the *timestamping algorithm*. Before a process starts to lock the resources it needs, a unique new timestamp is associated with that process. It is required that if a process has been assigned timestamp T_i and later a new process is assigned timestamp T_j then $T_i < T_j$. To implement this method, we associate with each resource a timestamp value, which is the timestamp of the process that is currently holding that resource.

1. *Phase one*: The process tries to lock all the resources it currently needs, one at a time. If a needed resource is not available and the timestamp value is smaller than that of the process, the process releases all the resources it has already managed to lock, waits until the resource with the smaller timestamp is released, and starts over. Otherwise, if the timestamp value of the resource is not smaller, the process does not release resources, it simply waits until the resource is released and locks it.
2. *Phase two*: If phase one succeeds, the process uses the resources to perform the work needed and then releases all the resources it had locked in phase one.

Timestamps can be implemented, for example, using the system clock value. Another approach would be to use a logical counter that is incremented every time a new timestamp is assigned.

7.2.2 The Total Order Theorem

The most effective prevention technique is achieved by attacking the *circular wait condition*. We present below a simple trick that always prevents deadlocks from occurring. The idea is to impose a total ordering of all the resources, and to require that each process requests the resources in an increasing order.

Theorem 7.1 (The Total Order Theorem) *Assume that all the resources are numbered, and that there is a total order between the numbers of the different resources. If each process requests resources in an increasing order of enumeration, then deadlock is not possible.*

Proof: This design is attacking the *circular wait condition*, as it guarantees that there is no cycle involving several processes, where each is waiting for a resource held by the next one in the cycle. ∎

This approach, as illustrated in Figure 7.2, can be used for example to solve the problem of transferring money between two bank accounts. There is a total order between account numbers. The account numbers are used as the resource numbers, and the locking of the two accounts is done in an increasing order. Theorem 7.1 guarantees that this solution is indeed deadlock-free.

Next, we make a simple observation which relates the notion of a deadlock and the notion of starvation. As in the case of a deadlock, in previous sections we have dealt with starvation that may occur in the context of a single

Figure 7.2 The total order technique: Each process requests resources in an increasing order of enumeration.

resource. In the context of multiple resources, even when acquiring a single resource is done in starvation-free manner, a deadlock (and hence also starvation) is still possible, simply because a process may never be able to acquire all the resources it needs and hence may *never* release a resource that it has already locked.

Starvation: *Starvation is a situation where some process may never be able to acquire (i.e., lock) all the resources it needs.*

A system with multiple resources is *starvation-free* if starvation is not possible in the system. Notice that by saying that acquiring a single resource R is starvation-free, we mean that every process that is trying to lock R eventually succeeds, under the assumption that every process that locks R eventually releases it. In the following, we assume that a process releases the resources it has locked only after it has managed to lock all the resources it has needed.

Theorem 7.2 *Assume that in a system with multiple resources the algorithm to acquire a single resource is starvation-free. Then the system is deadlock-free if and only if it is starvation-free.*

Proof: The *if* direction is trivial. To prove the *only if* direction, assume that the system is deadlock-free but not starvation-free. Then there must be a process p and a resource R such that p tries to acquire R but never succeeds, although R is released infinitely often. However, this contradicts the assumption that the algorithm to acquire R is starvation-free. ▮

An immediate corollary of Theorems 7.1 and 7.2 is:

Corollary 7.3 *Assume that (1) all the resources are numbered, and that there is a total order between the numbers of the different resources, and (2) the algorithm to acquire a single resource is starvation-free. Then, if each process requests resources in an increasing order of enumeration, then starvation is not possible.*

Next, we will consider a classical synchronization problem which involves multiple resources. We will present several solutions to the problem, and will make use of the *Total Order Theorem* in order to prove that the solutions are deadlock-free (i.e., the theorem is used in the proofs of Theorems 7.6 and 7.10).

Self Review

1. Does livelock imply deadlock?
2. Is livelock possible when using two phase locking?
3. Are livelock or deadlock possible when using timestamping-ordering?

Answers: (1) No, although in both cases nobody makes *real* progress. (2) Yes. (3) No (assuming, of course, that the algorithm for acquiring a single resource is starvation-free).

The following problem, which arises when processes have to share multiple resources, was proposed by Dijkstra in 1968. It has to do with deadlock avoidance. As already explained in Section 7.1, in deadlock avoidance the goal is to design an algorithm that will be responsible for allocating resources to processes, and that will ensure that by careful allocation of the available resources the system will never enter a deadlock state. It is important to notice that, in the context of our discussion here, the algorithm presented for allocating the resources is a *centralized* algorithm. The reader may skip this subsection without loss of continuity.

7.3.1 The Problem

We assume that there is a known number of identical resources (i.e., all resources are of the same type), and for each process (1) the maximum number of resources the process may need is *known in advance*; and (2) once a process gets all the resources it needs, it uses the resources to perform the work needed and then releases them. Although the maximum number of resources a process may need is known *a priori*, a process does not necessarily need them all at once. In such a setting, let us examine a few strategies for the design of an allocation algorithm that avoids deadlock.

The simplest allocation algorithm would be to let the processes run one after the other, and thus never to allocate resources to two or more processes simultaneously. This strategy is guaranteed to avoid deadlock, as long as the maximum demand of each process does not exceed the number of available resources. Of course, this is a rather inefficient strategy as it prevents concurrency.

Another safe strategy, which enables a limited amount of concurrency, is to allocate resources to processes simultaneously as long as the sum of their maximum demands does not exceed the total number of resources. This approach seems to be too restrictive, as it effectively reserves each process its maximum demand during the complete time of its execution.

Consider the following situation: There are 100 resources and two processes. Each process maximum demand is 52 resources, and currently each process is holding 48 resources and needs one more in order to continue its operation. A well-designed allocation algorithm will avoid allocating each one of the processes one more resource, because such a state where each process is holding 49 resources is *unsafe* as it unavoidably leads to a deadlock state. As Dijkstra has written (1968):

> "This situation, when one process can continue only provided the other one is killed first, is called *The Deadly Embrace*. The problem to be solved is: how can we avoid the danger of the Deadly Embrace without being unnecessarily restrictive."

Next, we show how to design such a deadlock avoidance algorithm. In particular, in the above example, the allocation algorithm described below would allocate the additional resource requested to one of the processes (but not to the other process), wait until this process requests an additional three resources, allocate them, and only after the process terminates and releases the 52 resources it holds, the algorithm will allocate more resources to the other process.

7.3.2 The Banker's Algorithm

In Dijkstra's presentation, he had considered a banker (the allocation algorithm) who has finite capital expressed in florins (the identical resources). The banker is willing to accept customers (the processes) that may borrow florins from him under a few condition discussed below. We describe below an allocation algorithm, to be called the *Banker's algorithm*. However, in the presentation we refer directly to processes and resources rather than customers and florins. It is assumed that the resources are allocated to the processes on the following conditions:

- Each process must *a priori* declare its maximum demand for resources, which must be less than the total number of resources;
- As long as the number of resources allocated to a process does not exceed its maximum demand, it may ask to get more resources;
- When a process requests resources, it may have to wait;
- When the number of resources a process gets reaches its maximum demand, it must return the resources in a finite amount of time.

The problem is to design an algorithm that can be used to decide whether resources can be allocated to a requesting process without running into the danger of *the deadly embrace* – i.e., without reaching an unsafe state which will unavoidably lead to a deadlock situation where it will not be possible to allocate each process its maximum demand.

When a process requests resources, the Banker's algorithm must decide if immediately allocating the resources leaves the system in a *safe* state. Inspection whether a state is safe amounts to inspecting whether all processes will be able to get their maximum demand, and later release them (obviously, this should not happen simultaneously). In other words, a safe state means that the banker sees a way of getting all his money back.

Safe state: *A state is safe if there exists a sequence* $p_1, p_2, \ldots, p_n$ *of processes such that for each process* p_i*, the number of resources that* p_i *needs (i.e., its maximum demand minus the resources it already has) can be satisfied by the available resources (i.e., those that have not been allocated yet) plus the resources already allocated to all processes* p_j *where* $j < i$*. Such a sequence of processes is called a safe sequence.*

To see why a safe state guarantees that all processes will be able to get their maximum demand and release the resources, we observe that when a safe sequence exists:

- If p_i's maximum demand is not immediately available, then p_i can wait until all p_j where $j < i$ have released their resources.

- When p_{i-1} is finished, p_i can be allocated its maximum demand, and later release the resources in a finite amount of time.
- When p_i finishes, p_{i+1} can get its maximum demand, and so on.

The original Banker's algorithm has been developed by Dijkstra for a single type of resource (i.e., some finite number of *florins*). The version of the algorithm presented below extends the original algorithm to multiple resources types (i.e., a customer may ask to borrow both florins, dollars, euros, and shekels). We assume the processes are numbered 1 through n, and we let m denote the number of different types of resources. The m resource types are R_1 through R_m. The data structures that are maintained by the Banker's algorithm are discussed next.

- An array of length m, called *Available*. It is used to keep track of the number of resources available at any point. For $1 \leq j \leq m$, $Available[j]$ resources of type R_j are currently available.
- A two dimensional array of size $n \times m$, called *Maximum*. It is used to record the maximum demand as announced by each process. Thus, at most $Maximum[i, j]$ resources of type R_j may be requested by process p_i. We use the notation $Maximum_i[1..m]$ to denote the vector of maximum demands for each one of the m resources of process p_i.
- A two dimensional array of size $n \times m$, called *Allocation*. It is used to record the number of currently allocated resources. Thus, at most $Allocation[i, j]$ resources of type R_j are currently allocated process p_i. We use the notation $Allocation_i[1..m]$ to denote the vector of resources currently allocated to process p_i.
- A two dimensional array of size $n \times m$, called *Need*. It is used to record the resources each process may still request. Thus, at most $Need[i, j]$ resources of type R_j may still be requested by process p_i to complete its work. We use the notation $Need_i[1..m]$ to denote the vector of additional resources that process p_i may still request. We notice that:

$$Maximum[i, j] = Allocation[i, j] + Need[i, j].$$

We are now ready to present the Banker's algorithm. The algorithm uses a function which inspects whether a state is safe or not. This function is specified *after* the code of the Banker's algorithm. For two vectors $A[1..m]$ and $B[1..m]$, the condition $A[1..m] < B[1..m]$ is *true* if $A[j] < B[j]$ for all $1 \leq j \leq m$, and the assignment $A[1..m] := B[1..m]$ means $A[j] := B[j]$ for all $1 \leq j \leq m$.

THE BANKER'S ALGORITHM

with input vector $\ell_1, \ldots, \ell_m$, which means that process p_i requests ℓ_j more resources of type R_j, for every $1 \leq j \leq m$

additional variables

R_i: array[1..m] of integers, initially $R_i[j] = \ell_j$ for $1 \leq j \leq m$

/* p_i requests $R[j]$ more resources of type R_j */

```
if R_i[1..m] > Need_i[1..m] then throw an exception fi
                        /* p_i has exceeded its maximum demand */
else  if R_i[1..m] > Available[1..m] then p_i must wait fi
                        /* resources are not available */
      else  pretend to allocate requested resources to p_i
            by modifying the state as follows:
                Available[1..m] := Available[1..m] − Request_i[1..m]
                Allocation_i[1..m] := Allocation_i[1..m] + Request_i[1..m]
                Need_i[1..m] := Need_i[1..m] − Request_i[1..m]
            if new state is not safe then p_i must wait
                        /* and the previous state is restored */
            else new state is safe and the resources are allocated to p_i fi
      fi
fi
```

Below we describe the algorithm which inspects whether a state is safe or unsafe. The significance of the concept of a safe state lies in the fact that starting from a safe state there is at least one way to allocate the claimed resources to each process even when each process asks for its maximum demand and does not release any resource until it has been allocated its maximum demand.

Algorithm for Testing whether a State is Safe

```
additional variables
   free: array[1..m] of integers                 /* free resources */
   done: array[1..m] of bits, initially done[i] = false for 1 ≤ i ≤ m
   safe: a bit, initially true

free[1..m] := Available[1..m]
i := 1
for i := 1 to n do
      if (done[i] = false) and (Need_i[1..m] ≤ free[1..m]) then
            free[1..m] := free[1..m] + Allocation_i[1..m]
            done[i] := true
            i := 1
      else i := 1 + 1 fi
od
for i := 1 to n do
      if done[i] = false then safe := false fi
od
if safe = true then the state is safe
else the state is not safe fi
```

A simple optimization for shortening the testing time of the above algorithm is as follows. Suppose the current state is safe, a request has been made by process p_i, and we want to determine if the state after satisfying the request is also safe. If at any point during the execution of the above algorithm the available resources (as recorded in the array *free*) are sufficient to complete process p_i then we may terminate the algorithm with the result that the state is safe.

We point out that if the scheduler (the banker) is restricted, for example by imposing a FIFO discipline on the order in which resources are allocated, then we must not consider any state to be safe if its safety was predicated on sequences of allocation and releasing of resources which are not possible under the new discipline.

Self Review

1. Explain why the optimization of the *algorithm for testing whether a state is safe*, as described on page 258, is correct.
2. The Banker's algorithm ensures that a system will never enter an unsafe state. In order to implement it, the algorithm (choose one answer):
   (a) Checks that the maximum request of every process does not exceed the amount of the systems' available resources.
   (b) Checks that in every order that we schedule the processes, there will never be a deadlock.
   (c) Checks that there is at least one order in which we can schedule the processes, in which there is no deadlock.
   (d) Checks that the maximum request of at least one process does not exceed the amount of the systems' available resources.
   (e) None of the above.

Answers: (1) Answer: The reason is that if p_i, the process that made the request, can complete and release all the resources it holds, all other processes can also terminate, since the state previous to the request was safe and they could therefore have been completed before the request was made. (2) The third statement is the correct one.

7.4 The Dining Philosophers Problem

The dining philosophers problem is a classical synchronization problem which models the allocation of multiple resource in a distributed system. The problem was first posted by E. W. Dijkstra in 1971.

7.4.1 The Problem

In the dining philosophers problem, as illustrated in Figure 7.3, n philosophers (resp. n processes) are seated around a table (resp. placed at vertices of an undirected ring) and half-way between each pair of adjacent philosophers there is a single fork (resp. a fork is associated with each edge). The life cycle of a philosopher consists of thinking, becoming hungry and trying to eat, eating, and then back to thinking, ad infinitum. Thus, a philosopher is at any time in one of the following three possible states: thinking, hungry, or eating.

A philosopher may transit from a thinking state to a hungry state spontaneously, at any time. In order to move from the hungry state to the eating state a philosopher needs to get the two forks associated with its incident edges. Hence neighboring

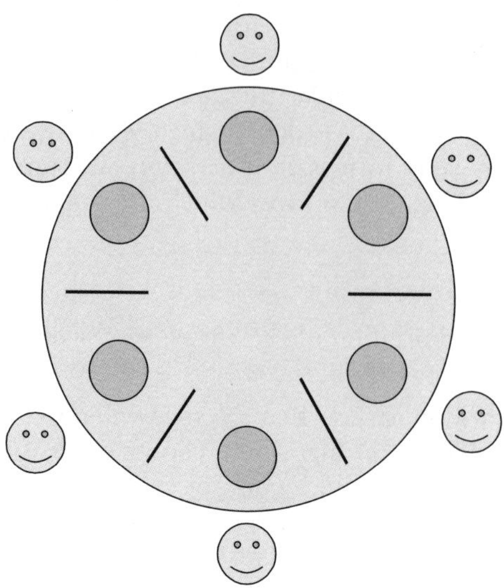

Figure 7.3 The dining philosophers problem. There is a fork (or a chopstick) between any two philosophers. A philosopher needs to get the two forks in order to eat. The problem is to design a strategy for each one of the philosophers so that each hungry philosopher eventually gets to eat.

philosophers cannot eat at the same time. It is assumed that eating times are finite. That is, a philosopher eats only for finite amount of time and after eating releases the two forks and resumes thinking.

The problem is to design a strategy for each one of the philosophers which enjoys a few desirable properties. One such property is *starvation-freedom* which means that each hungry philosopher eventually gets to eat as long as no other philosopher dies (or eats forever). Sometime, the starvation-free property is relaxed and it is asked that the strategy satisfies only *deadlock-freedom*. That is, if at any time there is a hungry philosopher then at a later time some philosopher will eat.

Two other desirable properties are: *high concurrency* and *fault-tolerance*. Concurrency is a measure of how many philosophers are able to eat simultaneously when all the philosophers are hungry. It is obvious that if a philosopher dies while eating, the neighbors will never be able to eat. In several existing algorithms it is the case that a death of a philosopher may prevent all other philosophers from eating. In light of this, it seems natural to design *fault-tolerant* algorithms. Informally, an algorithm is fault-tolerant (also called *robust*) if a philosopher does not depend on other "distant" philosophers.

7.4.2 Preliminaries

We assume the following:

1. The algorithms must be *fully distributed*: Communication is only between neighboring philosophers either by sending messages or by using registers

that are shared only by two neighboring philosophers. In particular, there is no central shared memory (that can be accessed by all philosophers) or an additional person that coordinates between the philosophers.

2. The control of each fork is *isolated* from the other forks: The philosophers may acquire and release forks only one at a time. We avoid referring to the specific details of the implementation of how a single fork is acquired, and only assume that the implementation is starvation-free.
3. *Crash failures* are the only allowable faulty behavior: Faulty philosophers either never start or after some point they stop never to be started again.
4. Philosophers are *fully asynchronous*: No assumptions are made about the relative speeds of the philosophers. For example, if a philosopher is waiting for a neighbor to finish eating and release the forks, he can not tell whether the neighbor has crashed while eating, or if the neighbor is just running very slowly.
5. Eating period is *finite* but not bounded: A philosopher can not use any kind of timeout test to detect a crash failure.

In order to formally define various concepts, we first need to give a high-level abstract description of a dining philosophers algorithm. In the description we are only concerned with the state of a philosopher after taking a step. We identify an algorithm with a set of possible *runs*, where a run is an *infinite* sequence of *events* that happens over time. We will use the term *finite* run for a prefix of an (infinite) run.

An event is of the form $thinking_p$, $hungry_p$, or $eating_p$, where p is some philosopher which is *involved* in the event. The description of an event abstracts all details except what is the state of p after the event. We say that at some prefix of a run, philosopher p is in a thinking state (resp. hungry, eating) if the last event which involves p at that prefix is $thinking_p$ (resp. $hungry_p, eating_p$).

The set of runs is assumed to satisfy several properties. We do not give a complete list here, but point out that these properties capture the facts mentioned in the introduction: a philosopher is in exactly one of three possible states: thinking, hungry, or eating. A philosopher may remain in a thinking state forever, and can transit from thinking state to hungry state spontaneously. A philosopher can transit to an eating state only after acquiring the two forks. A philosopher in an eating state eventually releases both forks and goes to thinking state again.

- A philosopher is *correct* in an (infinite) run if he is involved in infinitely many events in the run, and he is *faulty* otherwise.
- A correct philosopher p is *starving* at a given (infinite) run if the event $hungry_p$ appears infinitely many times and the event $eating_p$ appears only a finite number of times in that run. Notice that a faulty philosopher never starves.
- An algorithm is *deadlock-free* if for any run r, at least one philosopher is not starving in r. (Notice that this definition covers also the case of no *livelock* as discussed on page 252.)
- An algorithm is *starvation-free* if for any run r, the fact that all philosophers are correct in r implies that no philosopher is starving in r.

7.4.3 Concurrency and Robustness

Concurrency is a measure of how many philosophers are able to eat simultaneously out of a set of hungry philosophers. That is, if all philosophers are hungry, how many of them should be able to eat simultaneously. Having high concurrency is a most desirable property.

In order to define concurrency, we need to introduce the notion of a *maximal finite run*. We say that a finite run r is *maximal* if, except for all the philosophers that are in an eating state in r, no philosopher is able to eat in any extension of r unless one of the eating philosophers transits from eating to thinking (and thereby releases the forks).

m-concurrent: *An algorithm is m-concurrent if for any maximal finite run r, at least m philosophers are eating in r.*

In an m-concurrent algorithm, whenever all philosophers are hungry, and no philosopher releases the forks after eating, at least m of the philosophers will eventually eat. Notice that an algorithm is deadlock-free only if it is (at least) 1-concurrent, but not vice versa.

Theorem 7.4 *Any algorithm that solves the dining philosophers problem is at most $\lceil n/3 \rceil$-concurrent.*

Proof: Consider a finite run in which each philosopher i, where $i \equiv 0 \bmod 3$, becomes hungry, picks up both forks and eats simultaneously. If $i \not\equiv 0 \bmod 3$ then we also let philosopher 1 eat. This is possible since these philosophers do not share forks. Clearly, this run is maximal since no other philosopher can eat. Thus, we have shown that for any algorithm that solves the dining philosophers problem, there exists a maximal finite run in which at most $\lceil n/3 \rceil$ can eat simultaneously. ∎

Intuitively, a dining philosophers algorithm is *k-robust*, if all philosophers except for some k consecutive philosophers fail, then it will still be the case that one of the k philosophers will not starve.

k-robust: *An algorithm is k-robust if for any run r and for any sequence S of at least k consecutive philosophers, if all the philosophers except those of S are faulty in r then at least one philosopher of S is not starving at r.*

The concept of k-robust is the natural generalization of the deadlock-free concept. An algorithm (for n philosophers) is deadlock-free only if it is n-robust, but not vice versa. It is important to notice that in the above definition all but the k consecutive philosophers are assumed to be faulty. As we shall show later there is a (randomized) algorithm which is 3-robust, but has a run that, with probability 1, starves $n-1$ philosophers and lets one philosopher eat infinitely often.

Theorem 7.5 *Any algorithm that solves the dining philosophers problem is at most 3-robust.*

Proof: Consider the philosophers p_1 and p_2, and assume that the left neighbor of p_1 and the right neighbor of p_2 had failed while eating. Since the left fork of p_1 and the right fork of p_2 can never be obtained by p_1 and p_2 respectively, p_1 and p_2 will then never eat. Thus, no algorithm is 2-robust, and we have an immediate lower bound of $k = 3$ for any dining philosophers algorithm. ∎

k-chain: *In what follows, we call a sequence of k consecutive philosophers a k-chain and refer to the philosophers in this chain as $p_1p_2 \ldots p_k$. The fork to the right of p_i will be called f_i; fork f_i is shared by p_i and p_{i+1}. We will always assume that when p_0 (p_1's left neighbor) and p_{k+1} (p_k's right neighbor) fail, they fail while eating; this is the worst possible case because if this happens, f_0 and f_k can never be obtained by p_1 and p_k respectively.*

Self Review

1. Is the following claim correct? In an m-concurrent algorithm whenever all philosophers are hungry, at least m of them will eventually eat.
2. Consider the following alternative definition for k-robustness: A dining philosophers algorithm is k-robust if for any (infinite) run r and for any maximal sequence S of k consecutive non-faulty philosophers, there exists a philosopher p in S such that p does not starve in r. What is the relation between the above definition and the original definition of k-robust on page 262?

Answers: (1) No, one might eat infinitely often blocking everybody else. (2) The definitions are not equivalent.

7.5 Hold and Wait Strategy

In this section we consider algorithms in which a hungry philosopher acquires his forks in some specified order. If a fork is not available when requested, the philosopher waits until it is released by his neighbor and then takes it. If the philosopher acquires one fork and the other fork is not immediately available, he holds the acquired fork until the other fork is released. According to this, each philosopher is either a *L-type* philosopher or a *R-type* philosopher:

- *L-type*: The philosopher first obtains his left fork and then his right fork.
- *R-type*: The philosopher first obtains his right fork and then his left fork.

7.5.1 The LR Algorithm

In the first algorithm we assume that the philosophers are numbered consecutively around the ring from 1 to n. (This numbering is used only for the purpose of assigning a strategy to each philosopher.)

The LR algorithm: *In the LR algorithm, the philosophers are assigned acquisition strategies as follows: philosopher i is R-type if i is even, L-type if i is odd.*

Theorem 7.6 *The LR algorithm is starvation-free.*

Proof: We start by numbering all the forks as follows: We pick at random a fork and number it 0. Let f be a fork at distance i (counting clockwise) from the 0 fork. If i is even then we number f with the number $i - 1$, otherwise, we number f with the number $i + 1$. Notice that there is a total order between the numbers of the different forks (i.e., no two forks get the same number). The resulting numbering is illustrated in Figure 7.4. With respect to this numbering, the algorithm where each philosopher tries to lock its two forks in an increasing order of enumeration is exactly the LR algorithm. Hence, by Theorem 7.1 the algorithm is deadlock-free. Assuming that acquiring a single fork is done in a starvation-free manner, by Corollary 7.3 the *LR* algorithm is also starvation-free. ∎

It follows from Theorem 7.4 that the LR algorithm is at most $\lceil n/3 \rceil$-concurrent; however, the LR algorithm does not match this lower bound.

Theorem 7.7 *The LR algorithm is at most* $\lceil n/4 \rceil$*-concurrent.*

Proof: Consider a finite run in which:

1. Each R-type philosopher i, where $i \equiv 0 \bmod 4$, becomes hungry, picks up both forks and eats. If $n \not\equiv 0 \bmod 4$ then we let also philosopher 1 eat. (This is possible since these philosophers do not share forks.)

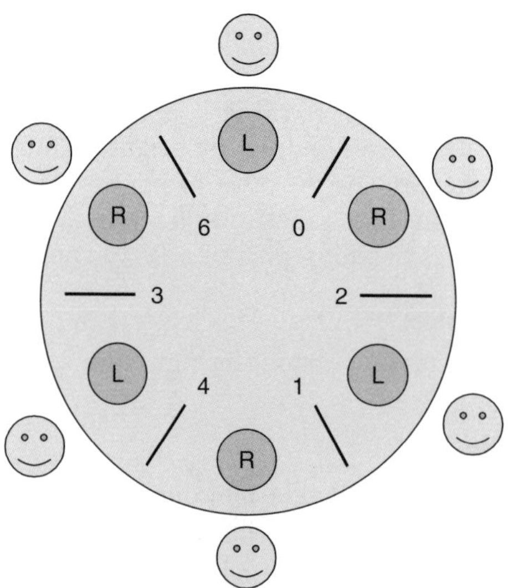

Figure 7.4 The LR algorithm. With respect to the numbering of the forks, the algorithm where each philosopher tries to lock its two forks in an increasing order of enumeration is the LR algorithm.

2. Each L-type philosopher i, where $i \equiv (0 \bmod 4) + 1$, becomes hungry and waits for its left fork to be released (except maybe philosopher 1, when $n \not\equiv 0 \bmod 4$).
3. Each L-type philosopher i, where $i \equiv (0 \bmod 4) + 3$, becomes hungry picks up its left fork and then waits for its right fork to be released.
4. Each R-type philosopher i, where $i \equiv (0 \bmod 4) + 2$, becomes hungry and waits for its right fork to be released.

Clearly, this run is maximal. Thus, we have shown that for the LR algorithm there exists a finite run in which at most $\lceil n/4 \rceil$ philosophers can eat simultaneously. ▮

Although the upper bound on the concurrency of the LR algorithm is $\lceil n/4 \rceil$, in the next subsection we present an algorithm, called the LLR algorithm, which is $\lfloor n/3 \rfloor$-concurrent. Next, we examine the robustness of the LR algorithm.

Theorem 7.8 *The LR algorithm is not 4-robust.*

Proof: Consider the 4-chain RLRL of philosophers $p_1, \ldots, p_4$. We schedule p_1 until he obtains f_1. Next schedule p_4 until he obtains f_3. After this sequence of events, no philosopher can eat; p_1 and p_4 will never obtain their second forks, if we assume that their neighbors died while eating, and p_2 and p_3 can never obtain a fork since their neighbors do not release forks until after eating. ▮

Theorem 7.9 *The LR algorithm is 5-robust if and only if n is even.*

Proof: If n is even, there are two possible 5-chains, but they are reflections of each other. Without loss of generality, we will consider the 5-chain LRLRL of processes $p_1, \ldots, p_5$. We will show that if p_2, p_3, and p_4 are hungry infinitely often, then one of them must eat infinitely often.

If p_2 eats infinitely often we are done, so suppose that p_2 eats only a finite number of times. If so, then p_3 must hold f_2 infinitely often. Assume that p_3 only eats finitely often. This means that f_3 is held by p_4 infinitely often. Since p_4 is R-type, it follows that f_3 and f_4 are simultaneously held infinitely often. Because the eating periods are finite, p_4 must eat infinitely often.

If n is odd, then the ring contains the 5-chain RLRLL. First schedule p_1 until he obtains f_1. Next schedule p_4 until he obtains f_3. Finally schedule p_5 until he obtains f_4. After this point, no philosopher in the chain can eat: p_1 waits forever for f_0, so p_2 will never obtain f_1; similarly, p_5 waits forever for f_5, which implies that p_4 never gets f_4, which in turn implies that p_3 never gets f_3. ▮

7.5.2 The LLR Algorithm

The next algorithm, due to S. P. Rana and D. K. Banerji (1986), is better than the LR algorithm in terms of concurrency; the concurrency measure used here is the number of philosophers who are able to eat simultaneously if all of them are hungry.

The LLR algorithm: *In the LLR algorithm, the philosophers are assigned acquisition strategies as follows: philosopher i is R-type if i is divisible by 3, L-type otherwise.*

Theorem 7.10 *The LLR algorithm is starvation-free.*

Proof: We start by numbering all the forks as follows: We pick at random a fork and number it 0. Let f be a fork at distance i (counting clockwise) from the 0 fork. If $(i \bmod 3) = 1$ then we number f with the number $i + 2$; if $(i \bmod 3) = 2$ then we number f with the number i; if $(i \bmod 3) = 0$ then we number f with the number $i - 2$. Notice that there is a total order between the numbers of the different forks (i.e., no two forks get the same number). The resulting numbering is illustrated in Figure 7.5. With respect to this numbering, the algorithm where each philosopher tries to lock its two forks in an increasing order of enumeration is exactly the LLR algorithm. Hence, by Theorem 7.1 the algorithm is deadlock-free. Assuming that acquiring a single fork is done in a starvation-free manner, by Corollary 7.3 the LLR algorithm is also starvation-free. ∎

It follows from Theorem 7.4 that the LR algorithm is at most $\lceil n/3 \rceil$-concurrent. We show that the LR algorithm almost matches this lower bound.

Theorem 7.11 *The LLR algorithm is* $\lfloor n/3 \rfloor$*-concurrent.*

Proof: We show that when all the philosophers want to eat, in the 3-chain LLR at least one of the three philosophers will be able eat. Since the 3-chain LLR repeats $\lfloor n/3 \rfloor$ times, the result will follow.

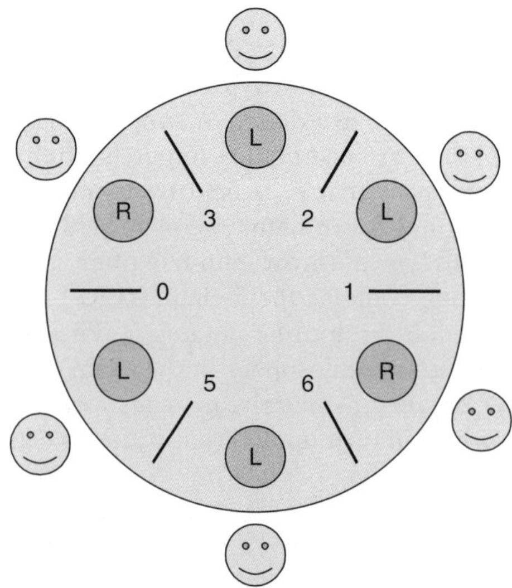

Figure 7.5 The LLR algorithm. With respect to the numbering of the forks, the algorithm where each philosopher tries to lock its two forks in an increasing order of enumeration is the LLR algorithm.

Consider the 3-chain LLR of philosophers p_1, p_2, and p_3. If p_1 acquires both forks, the proof is completed. So, assume that p_1 is waiting for a fork. There are two possible cases: (1) p_1 is waiting for f_0 (its left fork); or (2) p_1 is waiting for f_1 (its right fork).

Case 1: In this case, p_2 can always get f_1 and then compete for f_2. If p_3 is not competing for f_2 then p_2 will get f_2, and we are done. However, if p_3 is also competing for f_2, then both p_2 and p_3 are competing for their second fork, and the one to succeed in this competition will have both forks and will be able to eat.

Case 2: In this case, p_1 already holds f_0 and is waiting for f_1. If p_2 is not competing then p_1 will get its second fork and we are done. So let's assume that p_2 is competing and succeeds in getting f_1. We now continue as in case 1. If p_3 is not competing for f_2 then p_2 will get f_2 and we are done. However, if p_3 is also competing for f_2, then both p_2 and p_3 are competing for their second fork, and the one to succeed in this competition will have both forks and will be able to eat. ∎

Theorem 7.12 *The LLR algorithm is not 4-robust.*

Proof: Consider the 4-chain LRLL of philosophers $p_1, \ldots, p_4$. First schedule p_3 until he obtains f_2. Next schedule p_4 so that he takes f_3. Now no philosopher can eat; p_4 waits forever for f_4, p_3 must then wait forever for f_3, and p_1 and p_2 never obtain any forks. ∎

Theorem 7.13 *The LLR algorithm is 5-robust if and only if* $n \equiv 0 \bmod 3$.

Proof: When $n \equiv 0 \bmod 3$, there are three possible 5-chains to consider:

1. LLRLL. If p_2 and p_3 are hungry infinitely often, then one of them must eat infinitely often. If p_2 does not, then f_2 is held infinitely often by p_3, and since p_3 is R-type, f_2 and f_3 must be simultaneously held infinitely often. The eating periods are finite, so p_3 must eat infinitely often.
2. RLLRL. One of p_2, p_3, p_4 eats infinitely often.
3. LRLLR. One of p_2, p_3, p_4 eats infinitely often.

If $n \not\equiv 0 \bmod 3$, then the ring contains the 5-chain LRLLL. First schedule p_1 until he takes f_1. Now schedule p_3, p_4, and p_5 in order to obtain f_2, f_3, and f_4 respectively. After this, no philosopher can eat. ∎

7.5.3 A Lower Bound

At this point we have presented two algorithms which are 5-robust, for certain values of n. Since there are many possible assignments of L-type and R-type to the philosophers in the ring, it seems natural to wonder if we can do better than 5-robust, perhaps by using a complicated assignment of L-type and R-type which may even depend on n. We will now show that this is not the case.

Theorem 7.14 *There is no 4-robust algorithm that solves the dining philosophers problem using a hold and wait strategy.*

Proof: We prove the theorem by showing that in any algorithm using the hold and wait strategy, there exists a 4-chain that can deadlock. The proof is by enumeration. We consider the 16 possible 4-chains; some of them are actually isomorphic under reflection, but for the sake of clarity we will consider all. First we show that of the 16 possible 4-chains, eight lead to deadlock. We can not use this reasoning directly on the remaining eight, but we can show that each of these remaining 4-chains must be part of some larger configuration which *does* contain a "bad" 4-chain (we assume that $n \geq 8$). For example, consider the 4-chain LLLR. This chain does not deadlock, but consider p_0, p_1's left neighbor. p_0 must be either L-type or R-type. If we now look at the 4-chain $p_0p_1p_2p_3$, we have either LLLL or RLLL. However, both of these 4-chains can deadlock. We proceed in a similar manner with each of the remaining seven chains to eventually obtain a 4-chain which deadlocks.

For the following eight 4-chains, we briefly list a sequence of scheduled events which will lead the system to a deadlocked state.

1. LLLL. p_2 takes f_1, p_3 takes f_2, p_4 takes f_3.
2. LRLL. p_3 takes f_2, p_4 takes f_3.
3. RLLL. p_1 takes f_1, p_3 takes f_2, p_4 takes f_3.
4. RLRL. p_1 takes f_1, p_4 takes f_3.
5. RRLL. p_1 takes f_1, p_2 takes f_2, p_4 takes f_3.
6. RRLR. p_1 takes f_1, p_2 takes f_2.
7. RRRL. p_1 takes f_1, p_2 takes f_2, p_4 takes f_3.
8. RRRR. p_1 takes f_1, p_2 takes f_2, p_3 takes f_3.

We now show that each of the eight remaining 4-chains is part of a configuration containing one of the above 4-chains. This is done by *sliding* the 4-chain "window" one step to the left and obtaining a bad 4-chain. Some of these require several steps in order to reach one of the above 4-chains, but when we reach a 4-chain that has previously been shown to lead to a bad 4-chain, we can stop at that point. We present the remaining cases in a particular order so that we only have to consider the chains that result from a one-step slide.

9. LLLR. If we slide the window to the left, we obtain either LLLL (case 1 above) or RLLL (case 3).
10. RLLR. Sliding left leads to LRLL (case 2) or RRLL (case 5).
11. LLRL. Sliding left leads to LLLR (case 9) or RLLR (case 10).
12. LLRR. Sliding left leads to LLLR (case 9) or RLLR (case 10).
13. LRLR. Sliding left leads to LLRL (case 11) or RLRL (case 4).
14. RLRR. Sliding left leads to LRLR (case 13) or RRLR (case 6).
15. LRRL. Sliding left leads to LLRR (case 12) or RLRR (case 14).
16. LRRR. Sliding left leads to LLRR (case 12) or RLRR (case 14).

We have shown that in any assignment of L-type or R-type to the philosophers in the ring, there exists a 4-chain that can deadlock. ∎

We notice that Theorem 7.14 holds even if the algorithm is not required to be starvation-free. Theorems 7.8 and 7.12 now follow immediately from Theorem 7.14.

7.5.4 Relating Concurrency and Robustness

We now relate concurrency and robustness by showing that when using the hold-and-wait strategy, a certain level of robustness will guarantee a certain level of concurrency.

Theorem 7.15 *If a hold-and-wait dining philosophers algorithm is k-robust, then it is $\lceil n/k \rceil$-concurrent.*

Proof: The proof is by contradiction. Suppose that for some maximal run all the philosophers want to eat, and less than $\lceil n/k \rceil$ can eat simultaneously. Then there exists a chain S of at least k consecutive hungry philosophers, none of which can eat until one of the philosophers finishes eating. Because hold-and-wait strategy is assumed, no philosopher of S can know whether any of the other philosophers are faulty or not. Thus, there must exist a run where indeed all philosophers in S are hungry, and all the other philosophers have failed. However, this contradicts the fact that the algorithm is k-robust. ∎

We point out that that converse does not hold. Rana and Banerji's LLR algorithm is $n/3$-concurrent, but not even 3-robust. Also Theorem 7.15 is not necessarily correct for other strategies, for example the (randomized) Free Philosophers algorithm discussed later (on page 272) is 3-robust but only 1-concurrent.

Self Review

1. Is the following claim correct: Any algorithm where (1) each philosopher is either an L-type or an R-type, (2) at least one philosopher is an L-type, and (3) at least one philosopher is an R-type, is deadlock-free.
2. Consider the proof of Theorem 7.6, which shows the the LR algorithm is starvation-free, and find another numbering for the forks that can be used instead of the numbering used in this proof.

Answers: (1) Yes. (2) If i is even then we number f with the number $i/2$, otherwise, we number f with the number $\lfloor (i+n-1)/2 \rfloor$.

7.6 Wait and Release Strategy

We now consider algorithms in which a philosopher may release a held fork before eating. In particular, if a philosopher obtains one fork and the other fork is not free, the held fork is released and the philosopher starts over. Recall that we assume that the philosophers are ordered around the ring from 1 to n. We define $\mathcal{L}$-type and $\mathcal{R}$-type philosophers as follows:

- $\mathcal{L}$-type: The philosopher waits until the left fork is free, and then takes it. If the right fork is free, he takes it and then eats, otherwise he releases the left fork and begins again.
- $\mathcal{R}$-type: The philosopher waits until the right fork is free, and then takes it. If the left fork is free, he takes it and then eats, otherwise he releases the right fork and begins again.

The $\mathcal{LR}$ wait/release algorithm: *Philosopher i is $\mathcal{R}$-type if i is even, $\mathcal{L}$-type if i is odd.*

Recall that we have made the following assumption: The forks that the philosophers wait for are allocated in a starvation-free manner; that is, if a philosopher does not hold any fork and is waiting for a fork that is being held by his neighbor, the neighbor will not be able to release and acquire the fork infinitely often without giving the waiting philosopher a chance to hold it. This starvation-free allocation can be implemented with shared variables as we have shown in previous chapters and we will not go into the details again here.

Lemma 7.16 *In the $\mathcal{LR}$ wait/release algorithm, every starved philosopher has a neighbor who does not starve.*

Proof: Suppose without loss of generality that an $\mathcal{L}$-type philosopher p is starved. By the assumption that the allocation of a single fork is starvation-free, p will acquire its left fork infinitely often. This means that, since he is starved, his right fork is always in use when he tries to take it. However, since his right neighbor p' is $\mathcal{R}$-type, p' must be holding both forks whenever p tries to take the fork between them. Since p fails to obtain his forks infinitely often, p' must eat infinitely often; in other words, every starved philosopher has a neighbor who does not starve. ∎

Theorem 7.17 *The $\mathcal{LR}$ wait/release algorithm is deadlock-free, but it is not starvation-free.*

Proof: By Theorem 7.16, every starved philosopher has a neighbor who does not starve, which implies that the algorithm is deadlock-free. To see that it is not starvation-free consider the 2-chain $\mathcal{LR}$. We consider a run in which p_1 is scheduled so that he eats infinitely often, and thus holds f_1 infinitely often. Now, we arrange that whenever p_2 tries to acquire f_1 (while holding f_2) he finds that f_1 is held by p_1. Thus, p_2 never gets to eat. ∎

Theorem 7.18 *The $\mathcal{LR}$ wait/release algorithm is $\lfloor n/3 \rfloor$-concurrent.*

Proof: By 7.16, every starved philosopher has a neighbor who does not starve. This implies that, when there are no faults, in any 3-chain at least one philosopher can eat. Hence, if all the philosophers want to eat, at least $\lceil n/3 \rceil$ philosophers will be able to eat. ∎

We now show that the algorithm exhibits the best possible robustness.

Theorem 7.19 *The $\mathcal{LR}$ wait/release algorithm is 3-robust if and only if n is even.*

Proof: Assume n is even. Consider the 3-chain $\mathcal{LRL}$. We show that p_2 can always eat. p_2 first waits for f_2. If it is not free, it is held by p_3, and p_3 must eventually release it because p_3 will fail to obtain f_3. Because the forks are acquired in a starvation-free manner, p_2 is guaranteed to eventually get f_2 after it is released by p_3. Once p_2 holds f_2, he looks to see if f_1 is free. Since p_1 waits forever for f_0, f_1 is always available for p_2. p_2 can then pick up f_1 and proceed to the eating state. Similarly, in the 3-chain $\mathcal{RTR}$, p_2 can always eat.

When n is odd, either the 3-chain $\mathcal{RRT}$ or the 3-chain $\mathcal{RLL}$ are possible, and in these cases it is easy to show that the scheduler can prevent all the three philosophers from eating. ∎

Recall that the lower bound for the hold and wait strategy is that there is no 4-robust algorithm. We have just shown that the wait and release strategy can attain a level of robustness that the hold and wait strategy can not.

Self Review

1. Is it true that an algorithm where all the philosophers are $\mathcal{L}$-type is not livelock-free?
2. We have seen that the $\mathcal{LR}$ wait/release algorithm is not starvation-free. Prove that there is no *wait and release* algorithm which is starvation-free.

Answers: (1) Yes. (2) Same proof as in the proof of the $\mathcal{LR}$ wait/release algorithm.

7.7 Randomized Algorithms

We now present two symmetric algorithms: Each philosopher begins the algorithm in the same state, and the code for all the philosophers is identical. We notice that the LR, LLR, and $\mathcal{LR}$ algorithms shown earlier do not satisfy this constraint; in those algorithms, the actions carried out by a philosopher depend on the philosopher's position in a global ordering of the ring.

It is easy to prove that there is no deterministic and symmetric algorithm to the dining philosopher problem, which is also deadlock-free (Problem 7.24). To overcome this difficulty, *randomization* is used to break symmetry. In a randomized algorithm a philosopher can use coin tossing, and use its outcome to decide what to do next. We will often say that a randomized algorithm is deadlock-free, starvation-free, or k-robust *with probability 1*. Intuitively, this means that in the course of an infinite time period, the chances of a deadlock, starvation, or "not k-robust" occurring are zero.

In addition to using randomization, we also apply the *wait and release* strategy, that is, if a philosopher obtains one fork and the other fork is not free, the held fork is released and the philosopher starts over.

7.7.1 The Free Philosophers Algorithm

The following algorithm, due to D. Lehmann and M. O. Rabin (1981), is deadlock-free with probability 1, it is not starvation-free, and it is 3-robust. In this algorithm, a philosopher first flips a fair coin and according to the outcome, decides whether it is an $\mathcal{L}$-type or an $\mathcal{R}$-type. Then it continues as in the deterministic $\mathcal{LR}$ wait/release algorithm of the previous subsection. As before, fork access may be implemented by test-and-set variables or semaphores which are shared by adjacent philosophers.

LEHMANN-RABIN FREE PHILOSOPHERS ALGORITHM:

```
/* R(·) is the reflection function on {right, left} */

repeat forever
    think
    become hungry
    repeat
        s := a random element from {right, left}
        await (s fork is free) and then take it   /* one step */
        if R(s) fork is free then take R(s) else release s fork fi
    until (holding both forks)
    eat
    release both forks
end
```

The Free Philosophers algorithm is deadlock-free with probability 1. However, it is not starvation-free and is not 2-concurrent, since there is a schedule that, with probability 1, starves $n-1$ philosophers. (See the chapter's bibliographic notes for a paper which proves that the algorithm is deadlock-free with probability 1.)

Theorem 7.20 *The Free Philosophers algorithm is 3-robust with probability 1.*

Proof: It is easy to see that p_2 can eat infinitely often. If p_1 becomes hungry, p_1 will eventually, with probability 1, choose *left* as his random direction, and will then wait forever for f_0; since p_1 will now never take f_1, this will allow p_2 to use f_1 as often he wants. If p_3 becomes hungry, p_3 will eventually, with probability 1, choose *right* as his random direction, and will then wait forever for f_3; since p_3 will now never take f_2, this will allow p_2 to use f_2 as often he wants and thus, p_1 to eat as often as he pleases. ∎

7.7.2 The Courteous Philosophers Algorithm

Lehmann and Rabin have also presented a second algorithm which is starvation-free but is not even $n-1$-robust. The algorithm uses shared variables to ensure that a philosopher does not eat an infinite number of times while his neighbor is hungry. A philosopher uses two single-writer variables *left-signal* and *right-signal* to let his neighbors know that he is hungry. The *left-last* and *right-last* multi-writer shared variables are written and read by neighbors; there is one such variable for each fork, and the value it holds indicates which philosopher ate last with that fork.

LEHMANN-RABIN COURTEOUS PHILOSOPHERS ALGORITHM:

```
shared
left-signal, right-signal: {on,off}, initially both are off
        /* Neighbors can read but not write */
left-neighbor-signal, right-neighbor-signal: {on,off}, initially both are off
        /* left-neighbor-signal is the left neighbor's right-signal */
left-last, right-last: {left,neutral,right}, initially both are neutral
        /* left-last is the left neighbor's right-last */

        /* R(·) is the reflection function on {right,left} */
repeat forever
    think
    become hungry
    left-signal := on; right-signal := on
    repeat
        s := a random element from {right,left}
        await (s fork is free
                        and (s-neighbor-signal = off
                             or s-last = neutral
                             or s-last = s))
            and then take s fork
        if R(s) fork is free then take R(s) else release s fork fi
    until (holding both forks)
    eat
    left-signal := off; right-signal := off
    left-last := right; right-last := left
    release both forks
end
```

Although the Courteous Philosophers algorithm is starvation-free with probability 1, it is not 2-concurrent and does not tolerate even a single failure. We assume a completely adversarial scheduler which can schedule failures as well as steps taken.

Theorem 7.21 *The Courteous Philosophers algorithm is not 2-concurrent and is not $(n-1)$-robust.*

Proof: We show that in the Courteous Philosophers algorithm, there exists a schedule such that, with probability 1, after the failure of one philosopher (or if an eating philosopher does not releases the forks) the remaining philosophers can eat only a finite number of times before reaching a deadlocked state.

We first schedule a single philosopher, say p_0, until he is eating (has both forks), and then we have p_0 crash at that point (i.e., let him eat forever). Consider the $(n-1)$-chain $p_1p_2 \ldots p_{n-1}$, where $p_0 = p_n$ is the philosopher which crashed. Now schedule p_1 until it randomly chooses *left*; p_1 now waits forever for f_0. We now move on to p_2; at this point, its *left-last* and *right-last* variables are set to *neutral*, since none of its forks have been used. We first schedule p_2 until it eats once; this will change its *left-last* and *right-last* variables, and in particular *left-last* = *right*. Continue scheduling p_2 until *left* is chosen randomly; we may have to loop through several times before this occurs, but with probability 1 he will only eat a finite number of times before choosing *left*. At this point p_2 is stuck at the wait statement, because *left-neighbor-signal* = *on* and *left-last* = *right*. Now move on to p_3; *left-last* = *left*, so we schedule until he has eaten once (so that *left-last* = *right*), and then continue as above until *left* is randomly chosen and p_3 now waits forever. We continue in order through p_{n-2}. We now schedule p_{n-1} until *right* is chosen, and he will wait forever for the fork held by $p_n = p_0$. At this point we have reached a deadlocked state; p_1 and p_{n-1} wait for forks which are never released, and the remaining philosopher waits for variables which are never changed. ∎

In Problem 7.25, we present a randomized starvation-free algorithm which is 5-robust for all n. The advantage of using a completely symmetric randomized algorithm over the hold and wait algorithms is that every philosopher follows the same code, and we need not assign different strategies based on a global ordering of the philosophers.

Self Review

1. Can we replace the order of lines 6 and line 7 in the Free Philosophers algorithm?
2. Can we replace the order of line 12 and the await statement at lines 7–11 in the Courteous Philosophers algorithm?

Answers: (1) No. With such a change deadlock is possible. (2) No.

7.8 Bibliographic Notes

7.1 & 7.2

Several books on operating systems have a section about deadlocks which covers the basic concepts [57, 145, 308, 310, 313, 321]. The two-phase locking algorithm was introduced in [127]. Timestamp-based concurrency-control algorithms are discussed in [68, 297].

7.3

In [107] the problem of avoiding deadlock, called by Dijkstra the problem of Deadly Embrace, and the Banker's algorithm were presented. In fact they first appeared in Dijkstra's manuscript EWD 108, 'En algorithme ter voorkoming van de dodelijke omarming' (An algorithm to prevent the deadly embrace) written in Dutch. The original Banker's algorithm is a centralized algorithm and was developed for a single type of resource. It was later extended to multiple resource types by Habermann (a former PhD student of Dijkstra) in [156]. See [180, 277] for a few more comments about Habermann's algorithm. It was also extended to allow each process to make resource allocation decisions independently and concurrently, see for example [271]. An extension of the Banker's algorithm which allows processes to acquire either exclusive or *shared* access to resources using read and write locks is presented in [165].

7.4

The dining philosophers problem, a classical synchronization problem, was first presented by Dijkstra in 1971 [109]. Early algorithms usually made use of some sort of centralized mechanism [75, 109, 178, 179]. However, it seems more reasonable to require an algorithm to be distributed; that is, philosophers interact only with nearby philosophers when acquiring resources. A distributed algorithm decreases the likelihood that an action of one philosopher will affect other distant philosophers. Various algorithms which satisfied this constraint have been proposed [79, 88, 140, 233, 244, 293, 309].

The notion of concurrency, defined on page 262, is from [293]. As discussed in [293], high concurrency is a most desirable property of a dining philosophers algorithm. In [175], Hoare proposes a measure of efficiency for a dining philosophers protocol: the length of the longest sequence of consecutive hungry philosophers, none of which can eat until some other philosopher finishes eating. The measure of robustness, called k-robust, which is defined on page 262, is a variant on Hoare's efficiency measure and is taken from [141]. Most of the results about robustness in this chapter are from [141].

7.5

The LR algorithm (page 263) seems to be folklore and has appeared in various papers [79, 88, 244]. The observation that the LR algorithm is at most $n/4$-concurrent is from [88]. The LLR algorithm (page 266) was proposed by Rana and Banerji [293], where it is also shown that the LLR algorithm is better than the LR algorithm in terms of concurrency (see Theorems 7.7 and 7.11, on pages 264 and 266 respectively). The lower bound on robustness (Theorem 7.14, page 268) is from [141].

7.6

The few results about the wait and release strategy (page 269) are from [141].

7.7

A *fully symmetric* algorithm means that the strategies for all philosophers are identical. There is a simple argument which proves that there does not exist a *deterministic* fully distributed, fully symmetric algorithm to the problem which is deadlock-free [243, 233]. However, there does exist a symmetric *randomized* algorithm which is starvation-free (and hence also deadlock-free) [233]. The randomized algorithm in Problem 7.25 is a variant of an algorithm from [141], and is based on algorithms from [233, 315]. In [120], a deadlock free variant of Lehmann-Rabin's randomized algorithm from [233] is presented. A starvation-free randomized algorithm is presented in [93]. A formal correctness proof that the Free Philosophers algorithm (page 272) is deadlock-free with probability 1 appeared in [242].

Generalizations

Lynch [244] has shown how the dining philosophers problem can be extended to an arbitrary graph network, in which a philosopher needs to acquire the forks on all incident edges in order to eat. Chandy and Misra [92] generalize this further by introducing the drinking philosophers problem, in which a philosopher needs some non-empty subset of its resources; this subset of resources may change over time. In [337], a variant of the algorithm from [92] is described and proved correct in a modular way. All the above papers assume a fault-free model.

It is interesting to look at an analogous measure of k-robust for a general graph structure and to determine the fault-tolerance for the algorithms to these extensions. It seem that the algorithms in [92, 148] are not robust while the algorithms in [315] seem to exhibit a good level of fault-tolerance when used in general graph structures.

Few papers on the *dining philosophers* problem in asynchronous message passing systems have considered the notion of *failure locality* (also called crash locality) [56, 94, 95, 288, 315]. Failure locality of an algorithm is defined as the smallest m such that any process, for which there are no failures within a distance of m in the conflict graph, is free from starvation. All these papers achieve a constant failure locality, while trying to minimize response time and message complexity. We notice that failure locality does not imply short "waiting chains".

In [60], a few algorithms for the dining/drinking philosophers problem are presented in various models. In [149, 181], self-stabilizing dining philosophers algorithms are presented. A recent algorithm is described in [272].

7.9 Problems

Problems based on Section 7.1

∘∘ 7.1 Two processes, p_1 and p_2, each need to hold six records, 1, 2, 3, 4, 5, and 6 in a database, to complete. If p_1 asks for them in the order 1, 2, 3, 4, 5, 6 and p_2 asks them in the same order, deadlock is not possible. However, if p_2 asks for them in the order 6, 5, 4, 3, 2, 1 then deadlock is possible. With five resources, there are 6! possible combinations each process can request the resources. Hence there are 6! × 6! different algorithms. What is the exact number of algorithms (out of 6! × 6!) that is guaranteed to be deadlock free?

Problems based on Section 7.2

∘ 7.2 Show that the timestamping algorithm is starvation-free.

∘∘ 7.3 Can the assumption in Theorem 7.1, that there is a total order between the numbers of the different resources, be relaxed?

∘∘ 7.4 Assume that all the resources are numbered, and that there is a total order between the numbers of the different resources. Requiring that each process requests resources in an increasing order of enumeration is an example of (choose one answer):

1. Deadlock avoidance where the system remains in safe state.
2. Deadlock prevention where circular waits cannot occur.
3. Deadlock avoidance where the hold and wait condition cannot occur.
4. Deadlock avoidance where circular waits are unlikely.
5. None of the above.

Problems based on Section 7.3

∘∘ 7.5 This question is taken from an operating systems course exam given at Berkeley University (2004). The question is about deadlock avoidance. A restaurant would like to serve four dinner parties: P1, P2, P3, and P4. The restaurant has a total of eight plates and 12 bowls. The restaurant is using the Banker's algorithm as it is a deadlock avoidance algorithm. Assume that each group of diners will stop eating and wait for the waiter to bring a requested item (plate or bowl) to the table when it is required. Assume that the diners do not mind waiting.

The maximum requests of the four parties are: P1 requests seven plates and seven bowls, P2 requests six plates and 10 bowls, P3 requests one plate and two bowls, P4 requests two plates and four bowls.

The current allocations of the four parties are: P1 has two plates and three bowls, P2 has three plates and five bowls, P3 has zero plates and one bowl, P4 has one plate and two bowls.

Answer the following two questions:

1. Will the restaurant be able to feed all the four parties successfully? Prove your answer.
2. Assume a new dinner party, P5, comes to the restaurant at this time. Their maximum needs are five plates and three bowls. Initially the waiter brings two plates to them. In order to be able to feed all five parties successfully, what is the minimum number of additional bowls and plates the restaurant needs to buy. Justify your answer.

∘∘ 7.6 Suppose five processes p_0, p_1, p_2 p_3, and p_4, each of which has declared its maximum use of tape drives, scanners, printers, and CDs prior to execution, as shown in the table *Maximum* below. At some point during execution, resources are allocated as shown in the table *Allocation* below.

The maximum requests of the five processes are as follows:

Maximum	*tapes*	*scanners*	*printers*	*CDs*
Process p_0	2	1	0	2
Process p_1	1	1	2	0
Process p_2	2	0	2	1
Process p_3	1	2	0	1
Process p_4	3	2	1	1

The current allocations of the five processes are as follows:

Allocation	*tapes*	*scanners*	*printers*	*CDs*
Process p_0	0	0	0	1
Process p_1	0	1	0	0
Process p_2	1	0	1	1
Process p_3	1	1	0	0
Process p_4	2	0	1	1

Suppose that total resources existing in the system are four tape drives, four scanners, two printers, and four CDs.

1. Find a (safe) sequence of processes that shows that the system is in a safe state. Hint: Construct any additional tables necessary to find the sequence.
2. Suppose now that p_0 requests to get the second CD (in addition to the one it already got). Will the request of p_0 be granted or refused if the Banker's algorithm is being used to avoid deadlock? Justify your answer.

◦◦ 7.7 A system has four processes and five different types of allocatable resources. The number of available resources, the current allocation, and maximum needs are as follows:

	Allocated	*Maximum*	*Available*
Process p_1	10212	11914	00x11
Process p_2	20011	22911	
Process p_3	11210	21710	
Process p_4	11110	11221	

What is the smallest value for x for which this is a safe state? Justify your answer.

◦• 7.8 In the Banker's algorithm processes may only ask for an exclusive access to a resource. Extend the Banker's algorithm to allow processes to acquire either exclusive or *shared* access to resources.

•◦ 7.9 The Banker's algorithm is a centralized algorithm. Extend it to allow resource allocation decisions to be made concurrently.

Problems based on Section 7.4

◦ 7.10 Let A be an algorithm that solves the dining philosophers problem for n philosophers. Explain why:

1. A is deadlock-free implies that A is 1-concurrent;
2. A is 1-concurrent does not imply that A is deadlock-free;
3. A is deadlock-free implies that A is n-robust;
4. A is n-robust does not imply that A is deadlock-free.

∘∘ 7.11 Is it necessary to assume in the proofs of Theorems 7.4 and 7.5 that the philosophers are *selfish*? That is, if a philosopher is hungry and the two forks are free he will always pick them and eat regardless of what other philosophers do.

Problems based on Section 7.5

∘ 7.12 Implement the LR algorithm and the LLR algorithm using weak semaphores.

∘ 7.13 Prove the following claim: An algorithm where all the philosophers are L-type is not deadlock-free.

∘∘ 7.14 Consider the proof of Theorem 7.10, which shows that the LLR algorithm is starvation-free, and find another numbering for the forks that can be used instead of the numbering used in this proof.

∘ 7.15 Show that in the LR algorithm, a failure of a single philosopher does not affect another philosopher more than two neighbors distant.

∘• 7.16 Is the LR algorithm $\lfloor n/4 \rfloor$-concurrent?

∘ 7.17 For each one of the following two claims decide if it is correct or not. Justify your answer.

1. The LLR algorithm is 6-robust iff $n \equiv 0 \bmod 3$ or $n \equiv 1 \bmod 3$.
2. The LLR algorithm is 7-robust for any n.

∘∘ 7.18 In the RRL algorithm, the philosophers are assigned acquisition strategies as follows: Philosopher i is L-type if i is divisible by 3, R-type otherwise. Compare the properties of the LLR algorithm and the RRL algorithm.

? 7.19 Is there an algorithm, using the "Hold and Wait Strategy", which is 5-robust for any n?

Problems based on Section 7.6

∘ 7.20 Prove the following claim: Any algorithm where (1) each philosopher is either an $\mathcal{L}$-type or an $\mathcal{R}$-type, (2) at least one philosopher is an $\mathcal{L}$-type, and (3) at least one philosopher is an $\mathcal{R}$-type, is deadlock-free (i.e., livelock-free).

∘∘ 7.21 Is the $\mathcal{LR}$ wait/release algorithm 4-robust when n is odd?

∘∘ 7.22 In the $\mathcal{LLR}$ wait/release algorithm, the philosophers are assigned acquisition strategies as follows: Philosopher i is $\mathcal{R}$-type if i is divisible by 3, $\mathcal{L}$-type otherwise. What are the concurrency and robustness properties of this algorithm?

∘• 7.23 There are may ways to combine the "Hold and Wait" Strategy and the "Wait and Release" Strategy. For example, in the $\mathcal{LR}$ LR algorithm, the philosophers are assigned acquisition strategies as follows:

1. philosopher i is $\mathcal{L}$-type if $i \equiv 1 \bmod 4$;
2. philosopher i is $\mathcal{R}$-type if $i \equiv 2 \bmod 4$;
3. philosopher i is L-type if $i \equiv 3 \bmod 4$;
4. philosopher i is R-type otherwise.

What are the concurrency and robustness properties of this algorithm?

Problems based on Section 7.7

∘ 7.24 Prove that there is no deterministic and symmetric algorithm that solves the dining philosopher problem, which is also deadlock-free.

∘• 7.25 We present a randomized starvation-free algorithm which is fault-tolerant. As in the Courteous Philosophers algorithm, a philosopher uses two single-writer variables *left-signal* and *right-signal* to let his neighbors know that he is hungry.

A FAULT-TOLERANT RANDOMIZED ALGORITHM:

```
shared
left-signal, right-signal: {on, off}, initially both are off
    /* Neighbors can read but not write */
left-neighbor-signal, right-neighbor-signal: {on, off}, initially both are off
    /* left-neighbor-signal is the left neighbor's right-signal */
    /* R(·) is the reflection function on {right, left} */
repeat forever
   think
   become hungry
   await(left-neighbor-signal = off)
   await(right-neighbor-signal = off)
   left-signal := on; right-signal := on
   repeat      /* free philosopher starts here */
      s := a random element from {right, left}
      await (s fork is free) and then take it
      if R(s) fork is free then take R(s) else release s fork fi
   until (holding both forks)
   eat
   left-signal := off; right-signal := off
end
```

Which of the following claims is correct? Justify your answer.

1. The algorithm is starvation-free.
2. The algorithm is not 4-robust.
3. The algorithm is 5-robust.

Classical Synchronization Problems

8.1 The Producer-Consumer Problem

The *producer-consumer* problem, which is a classical cooperation problem, was proposed by E. W. Dijkstra in 1968. The problem can be described as follows. Assume that there are two groups of processes:

Producers: *Processes in this group produce data items which are delivered to the consumers.*

Consumers: *Processes in this group consume data items which are produced by the producers.*

Communication between these two groups is achieved by using a shared *buffer*, which is used to implement a queue. The producers add data items to the end of the buffer while the consumers remove (consume) data items from the beginning of the buffer. We assume the processes are always participating and trying to either produce or consume data items. That is, there is *no* remainder section as in the mutual exclusion problem.

The producer-consumer problem is to write (1) the code for the producers that is used to access the buffer in order to add new produced data items, and (2) the code for the consumers that is used to access the buffer in order to consume data items. The code must satisfy the following requirement:

Every data item that is produced is eventually consumed; and there is no deadlock.

An inefficient solution to the producer-consumer problem would be to use a mutual exclusion algorithm and to require that all accesses to the shared buffer are done in the critical section. However, this will cause unnecessary delays as producers will have to wait for consumers and vice versa. Thus, although this is not a necessary requirement, it is preferred that:

Producers wait for consumers only when the buffer is full; and consumers wait for producers only when the buffer is empty.

Two versions of the problem exist: (1) *Unbounded-buffer*, which places no limit on the size of the buffer; (2) *Bounded-buffer*, which assumes that there is a fixed buffer size. We will consider only the more interesting case where the buffer size is assumed to be bounded.

For simplicity, we will assume that there is only one producer and only one consumer; the generalization to multiple producers and consumers when using blocking synchronization (i.e., mutual exclusion locks) is straightforward and is left as an exercise. Also, it is assumed that a function called *produce_item* is used to produce new data items, and a procedure *consume_item* [*item*] is used to consume data items. Finally, we assume that the system is asynchronous, that is, no assumption is made about the relative speed of the processes.

It is important to notice that a producer-consumer problem is basically the problem of implementing a *concurrent queue*, where the code for the producer implements the *enqueue* operation and the code for the consumer implements the *dequeue* operation. Thus, the non-blocking concurrent queue algorithm presented in Section 4.5.2 (page 171) solves the producer-consumer problem for any number of processes.

8.1.1 Atomic Registers

In this solution, the bounded buffer is implemented as a shared array of size n, and two pointers *in* and *out* are used to mark the end and beginning of the buffer, respectively. These two pointers are also used to check whether the buffer is full

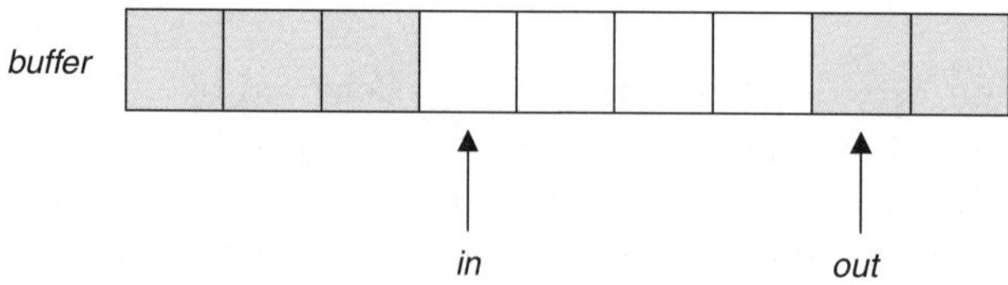

Figure 8.1 Bounded buffer of size nine using atomic registers. The condition $in = out$ indicates that the buffer is empty, while the condition $(in + 1) \bmod n = out$ indicates that the buffer is full.

or empty. The condition $in = out$ indicates that the buffer is empty, while the condition $(in + 1) \bmod n = out$ indicates that the buffer is full. This is illustrated in Figure 8.1. We notice that the buffer is considered as full when it includes $n - 1$ data items (and not n); this waste of one location is necessary in order to be able to distinguish between the cases when the buffer is empty and the case when it is full. The algorithm is given below.

A PRODUCER-CONSUMER ALGORITHM USING ATOMIC REGISTERS

```
shared  buffer: array[0..n − 1] of integers
        in, out: atomic registers range over {0, . . . , n − 1}, initially both 0
local   local_item: of type integer
```

PROGRAM FOR THE PRODUCER

```
loop
   local_item := produce_item
   await((in + 1) mod n ≠ out)
   buffer[in] := local_item
   in := (in + 1) mod n
end_loop
```

PROGRAM FOR THE CONSUMER

```
loop
   await (in ≠ out)
   item :=buffer[out]
   out := (out + 1) mod n
   consume_item[local_item]
end_loop
```

The algorithms in this section are rather simple and hence no formal correctness proofs will be given.

8.1.2 Atomic Counter

An atomic counter is a shared object that can be incremented and decremented atomically. An atomic counter can be trivially implemented using a single fetch-and-add object. Using an atomic counter, it is easy to update the previous solution so that the buffer is full when all the n locations (and not only $n - 1$ locations as in the previous algorithm) are used. Each time a data item is inserted the counter is atomically incremented by 1, and similarly the counter is decremented when a data item is removed. In this solution, the condition $counter = 0$ indicates that the buffer is empty, while the condition $counter = n$ indicates that the buffer is full. The algorithm is given below.

A PRODUCER-CONSUMER ALGORITHM USING AN ATOMIC COUNTER

```
shared  buffer: array[0..n − 1] of integers
        counter: atomic counter ranges over {0, . . . , n}, initially 0
local   local_item: of type integer
        in, out: registers range over {0, . . . , n − 1}, initially both 0
```

PROGRAM FOR THE PRODUCER

```
loop
   local_item := produce_item
   await(counter ≠ n)
   buffer[in] := local_item
```

PROGRAM FOR THE CONSUMER

```
loop
   await (counter ≠ 0)
   item :=buffer[out]
   out := (out + 1) mod n
```

```
5   in := (in + 1) mod n
6   counter := counter + 1
7 end_loop
```

```
5   counter := counter − 1
6   consume_item(local_item)
7 end_loop
```

We remind the reader that incrementing and decrementing the counter (in line 6 and line 5, respectively) are atomic operations.

8.1.3 General Semaphores

The next algorithm makes use of two general semaphores (the exact definition of a semaphore is given on page 176). The use of semaphores enables us to present algorithms with no busy-waiting. The semaphore *full* is used for counting the number of data items currently in the buffer and is initially 0; the semaphore *empty* is used for counting the number of free locations in the buffer and is initially n.

A PRODUCER-CONSUMER ALGORITHM USING GENERAL SEMAPHORES

```
shared  buffer: array[0..n − 1] of integers
        empty: semaphore ranges over {0, . . . , n}, initially n
        full: semaphore ranges over {0, . . . , n}, initially 0
local   local_item: of type integer
        in, out: registers range over {0, . . . , n − 1}, initially both 0
```

PROGRAM FOR THE PRODUCER

```
loop
  down(empty)
  local_item := produce_item
  buffer[in] := local_item
  in := (in + 1) mod n
  up(full)
end_loop
```

PROGRAM FOR THE CONSUMER

```
loop
  down(full)
  local_item :=buffer[out]
  out := (out + 1) mod n
  consume_item(local_item)
  up(empty)
end_loop
```

The producer first decrements the *empty* semaphore indicating that there is one free location less. If *empty* = 0 before the decrement, the producer is blocked until at least one data item is consumed. After the producer inserts a data item to the buffer the producer increments the *full* semaphore. The consumer first decrements the *full* semaphore indicating that there is one more free location. If *full* = 0 before the decrement, the producer is blocked until at least one data item is inserted. After the consumer removes a data item from the buffer the consumer increments the *empty* semaphore.

8.1.4 Binary Semaphores

We now modify the previous algorithm so that instead of using the general semaphores *full* and *empty*, which are used for counting the number of items in the buffer, we use only binary semaphores. We use three binary semaphores and an atomic register called *counter*. (Notice that the register *counter* is not required to be an atomic counter.) The counter is used to count the number of items in the buffer. One of the semaphores, called *mutex*, is used to guarantee that the producer and the consumer do not access the counter at the same time. As in the algorithm which uses an atomic counter (page 283), each time a new data item is inserted into the buffer the counter is atomically incremented by 1, and similarly it is decremented when a data item is removed. The condition $counter = 0$ indicates that the buffer is empty, and when this happens the consumer waits on the *empty* semaphore. The condition $counter = n$ indicates that the buffer is full, and when this happens the producer waits on the *full* semaphore. A register *local_counter* is used by a process for remembering the value of the counter the last time the process has changed it.

A Producer-Consumer Algorithm using Binary Semaphores

```
shared  buffer: array [0..n − 1] of integers
        counter: register ranges over {0,...,n}, initially 0
        empty: binary semaphore ranges over {0,1}, initially 0
        full: binary semaphore ranges over {0,1}, initially 0
        mutex: binary semaphore ranges over {0,1}, initially 1
local   local_item: of type integer
        local_counter: register ranges over {0,...,n}, initially 0
        in, out: registers range over {0,...,n − 1}, initially both 0
```

PROGRAM FOR THE PRODUCER

```
1  loop
2     if local_counter = n then
3          down(full) fi
4     local_item := produce_item
5     buffer[in] := local_item
6     down(mutex)
7     counter := counter + 1
8     local_counter := counter
9     up(mutex)
10    if local_counter = 1 then
11         up(empty) fi
12    in := (in + 1) mod n
13 end_loop
```

PROGRAM FOR THE CONSUMER

```
1  loop
2     if local_counter = 0 then
3          down(empty) fi
4     local_item :=buffer[out]
5     out := (out + 1) mod n
6     down(mutex)
7     counter := counter − 1
8     local_counter := counter
9     up(mutex)
10    if local_counter = n − 1 then
11         up(full) fi
12    consume_item(local_item)
13 end_loop
```

When the producer, after inserting a date item, finds out that there is exactly one item in the buffer (line 10), it notifies a possibly waiting consumer that it can continue (line 11). Similarly, when the consumer, after removing a data item, finds out that there are exactly $n - 1$ items in the buffer (line 10), it notifies a possibly waiting producer that it can continue (line 11).

8.1.5 Monitors

Next we present a simple solution using monitors. Recall that at most one process can be inside the monitor at any given time (see page 181). Thus this is a rather inefficient solution which does not allow for both the producer and the consumer to access the buffer at the same time. Two conditional variables, called *full* and *empty*, are used: *full* is used by the consumer to suspend itself when the buffer is full, and *empty* is used by the consumer to suspend itself when the buffer is empty.

A PRODUCER-CONSUMER ALGORITHM USING A MONITOR

```
local     local_item: of type integer

PROGRAM FOR THE PRODUCER

loop
  local_item := produce_item
  producerConsumer.producer(local_item)
end_loop

PROGRAM FOR THE CONSUMER

loop
  local_item := producerConsumer.consumer
  consume_item(local_item)
end_loop

monitor producerConsumer

  full, empty: conditional variables
  buffer: array[0..n − 1] of integers
  in, out: range over {0, . . . , n − 1}, initially all 0
  counter: ranges over {0, . . . , n}, initially 0

procedure producer(item: integer)
  if(counter = n) then wait(full) fi
  buffer[in] := item
  in := (in + 1) mod n
  counter := counter + 1
  if (counter = 1) then signal(empty) fi
end producer

function consumer: integer
  if (counter = 0) then wait(empty) fi
  consumer :=buffer[out]                 /* return this value */
  out := (out + 1) mod n
  counter := counter − 1
  if (counter = n − 1) then signal(full) fi
end consumer
end_monitor
```

8.1.6 Sleep and Wakeup

Explain why the following algorithm is incorrect. In the algorithm we use a *sleep* operation, which blocks the caller until another process wakes it up, and a *wakeup* operation which accepts as a parameter the identifier of the process to be awakened. When the producer finds out that the buffer is full it goes to sleep (instead of busy-waiting) until the consumer wakes it up, and when the consumer finds out that the buffer is empty it goes to sleep (instead of busy-waiting) until the producer wakes it up.

An Incorrect Algorithm using Sleep and Wakeup

```
shared  buffer: array[0..n − 1] of integers
        counter: atomic counter ranges over {0,...,n}, initially 0
local   local_item: of type integer
        in, out: registers range over {0,...,n − 1}, initially both 0
```

PROGRAM FOR THE PRODUCER

```
loop
   local_item := produce_item
   if(counter = n) then sleep fi
   buffer[in] := local_item
   in := (in + 1) mod n
   counter := counter + 1
   if (counter = 1) then
         wakeup(consumer) fi
end_loop
```

PROGRAM FOR THE CONSUMER

```
loop
   if (counter = 0) then sleep fi
   item :=buffer[out]
   out := (out + 1) mod n
   counter := counter − 1
   if (counter = n − 1) then
         wakeup(producer) fi
   consume_item(local_item)
end_loop
```

Answer: The algorithm is incorrect for the following reason. Consider the following scenarios: the consumer finds out that the buffer is empty; now, before the consumer has a chance to execute the *sleep* operation, the producer adds one data item to the buffer and executes the *wakeup*(*consumer*) operation. Since the consumer is not yet asleep the wakeup signal is lost. Now the consumer executes the *sleep* operation, and sleeps forever.

Self Review

1. Does it follow from the requirement that "every data item that is produced is eventually consumed" that "there is no deadlock"?
2. Would the producer-consumer algorithm using general semaphores (page 284) be correct if *unfair* semaphores are used? What about binary semaphores?
3. Would the producer-consumer algorithm using binary semaphores (page 285) be correct if we omit line 8, and substitute *counter* for *local_counter* in all the if statements (line 2 and line 10)?
4. Consider the algorithm using a monitor from page 286. Assume that we replace the second if statement in the producer's code (line 6) with: signal(*empty*), and replace the second if statement in the consumer's code (line 6) with: signal(*full*). Would the algorithm still be correct?

Answers: (1) No, since there might be a deadlock when the buffer is empty. (2) Yes. (3) No. (4) Yes, but less efficient.

8.2 Readers and Writers

Consider the example of an *airline reservation system* where multiple processes can *read* the database at the same time, but if one process is *writing*, no other process is allowed to access the database. One simple way to implement such a system is to use a mutual exclusion algorithm and to require that an access to the database is done only while in a critical section. Such a solution would be very inefficient as it prevents readers from accessing the database at the same time. This issue is addressed by the next problem, which is due to P. L. Courtois, F. Heyman, and D. L. Parnas (1971).

The readers and writers problem: In this problem it is assumed that there are two groups of processes, the *readers* and the *writers*. As in the mutual exclusion problem (Section 1.3), it is assumed that each process, a reader or a writer, is executing a sequence of instructions in an infinite loop. The instructions are divided into four continuous sections of code: the *remainder*, *entry*, *critical section*, and *exit*.

A process starts by executing the remainder code. At some point the process might need to execute some code in its the critical section. In order to access its critical section a process has to go through an entry code which guarantees that the following (safety) condition always holds:

> There is no limit on the number of readers that can be in their critical sections simultaneously, that is, the readers may share the critical section with each other. However, the writers must have exclusive access, that is, a writer can be in its critical section only when no other process (a reader or another writer) is in its critical section.

Once a process finishes its critical section, the process executes its exit code in which it notifies other processes that it is no longer in its critical section. After executing the exit code the process returns to the remainder (see Figure 1.5, page 11). There are two approaches for solving the problem:

- *Priority to readers*: If a reader arrives while another reader is in its critical section, then the new reader is allowed to enter its critical section, even if a writer is waiting. This approach may starve writers.
- *Priority to writers*: If a reader arrives while a writer is waiting then the reader must wait until all the writers exit their critical sections, one at a time. This approach may starve readers.

In the first approach a reader is waiting only if a writer has already obtained permission to access its critical section. In particular, a reader never waits for other readers to exit. In the second approach, the writer enters its critical section as soon as possible. Other variants of the problems, with no starvation of either readers or writers, have also been considered in the literature.

To simplify the presentation, when the code for the readers and writers algorithm is presented, only the entry code and exit code are described, and the remainder code and the infinite loop within which this code resides are omitted.

8.2.1 Semaphores

Below we present two algorithms. The first is simple and gives priority to readers, while the second, which is more complex, gives priority to writers. Both algorithms were discovered by Courtois, Heymans, and Parnas.

Priority to Readers

In the following algorithm we wish minimum delay for the readers. Thus, the algorithm may starve the writers while a stream of readers arrives. The algorithm uses two weak semaphores and one atomic register.

READERS AND WRITERS USING BINARY SEMAPHORES

```
shared  countR: atomic register, initially 0
        mutex, w: binary (weak) semaphores, initially both 1
```

PROGRAM FOR A READER

```
down(mutex)
countR := countR + 1
if countR = 1 then down(w) fi
up(mutex)
critical section
down(mutex)
countR := countR − 1
if countR = 0 then up(w) fi
up(mutex)
```

PROGRAM FOR A WRITER

```
down(w)
critical section
up(w)
```

A reader first tries to pass the *mutex* semaphore and to get exclusive access to *countR*. Then it indicates that there is one more reader by incrementing *countR*. If a reader finds out that it is the first reader, it tries to pass the *w* semaphore in order to get exclusive access to its critical section. Once it succeeds, it releases the *mutex* semaphore, allowing more readers to move in. In its exit code the reader tries to get exclusive access to *countR*. Then it indicates that there is one less reader by decrementing *countR*. At that point it checks whether there are other active readers. If there are no more readers it releases the *w* semaphore allowing a writer to move in. The writer simply tries to get exclusive access to its critical section by passing the *w* semaphore; in its exit code it simply releases the *w* semaphore.

Priority to Writers
In the following algorithm we wish writing to take place as early as possible. Thus, the algorithm may starve the readers, while a stream of writers arrives. A reader which arrives after a writer has announced that it is ready to write must wait even if the writer is also waiting. The algorithm uses five semaphores (weak or even unfair) and two atomic registers.

READERS AND WRITERS USING BINARY SEMAPHORES

```
shared  countR, countW: registers, initially both 0
        mutexR, mutexW, mutex, w, r: binary semaphores, initially all 1

PROGRAM FOR A READER
1  down(mutex)
2    down(r)
3      down(mutexR)
4      countR := countR + 1
5      if countR = 1 then down(w) fi
6      up(mutex)
7    up(r)
8  up(mutex)
9  critical section
10 down(mutexR)
11 countR := countR - 1
12 if countR = 0 then up(w) fi
13 up(mutexR)

PROGRAM FOR A WRITER
1  down(mutexW)
2  countW := countW + 1
3  if countW = 1 then down(r) fi
4  up(mutexW)
5  down(w)
6  critical section
7  up(w)
8  down(mutexW)
9  countW := countW - 1
10 if countW = 0 then up(r) fi
11 up(mutexW)
```

We notice that lines 3–6 and lines 9–13 in the reader's program are the same as the reader's program in the previous solution. Similarly, lines 5–7 in the writer's program are the same as the writer's program in the previous solution. The semaphore r is used to protect access by readers to the critical section while a writer is waiting. That is, the first reader to pass the semaphore r in line 3, will block new readers. The *mutex* semaphore guarantees that writers will get priority over any possible reader. Without *mutex*, it is possible that a writer and one or more readers will be waiting simultaneously for a reader to release the semaphore r, and in such a case it is not possible to give priority to a writer which is waiting on r.

8.2.2 Monitors

Below we give a solution using a monitor. In this solution, it is assumed that to determine whether at least one process is delayed on a conditional variable c, a process in a monitor may invoke the function *empty*(c), which returns 1 (*true*) if c's queue is empty; otherwise it returns 0 (*false*). The solution gives priority to the first waiting writer over waiting readers, and it never starves readers or writers.

The following variables are used. A counter, called *countR*, which counts the number of the readers that are in their critical sections; a bit, called *writing*, which is set to 1 when a writer is in its critical section. In addition two conditional variables are used, *waitR* on which readers wait for their turn, and *waitW* on which writers wait for their turn. The code is given below.

Readers and Writers using a Monitor

PROGRAM FOR A READER	PROGRAM FOR A WRITER
1 *ReaderWriter.enterReader*	1 *ReaderWriter.enterWriter*
2 *critical section*	2 *critical section*
3 *ReaderWriter.exitReader*	3 *ReaderWriter.exitWriter*

```
monitor ReadersWriters
   waitR, waitW: conditional variables
   countR: integer, initially 0
   writing: bit ranges over {0,1}, initially 0

1 procedure enterReader
2    if(writing ≠ 0) or empty(waitW) ≠ 0 then wait(waitR) fi
3    countR := countR + 1
4    signal(waitR)
5 end enterReader

1 procedure exitReader
2    countR := countR − 1
3    if (countR = 0) then signal(waitW) fi
4 end enterReader

1 procedure enterWriter
2    if(countR ≠ 0) or (writing ≠ 0) then wait(waitW) fi
3    writing := 1
4 end enterWriter

1 procedure exitWriter
2    writing := 0
3    if empty(waitR) ≠ 0 then signal(waitR) else signal(waitW) fi
4 end exitWriter
end_monitor
```

Notice that when there are waiting writers, one of the waiting writers will have a chance to enter its critical section before *new* readers get their chance to move. Once the writer exits, *all* the waiting readers enter their critical sections before the next writer enters its critical section. To see that, let's focus on the statement **signal**(*waitR*) in line 4 of the *enterReader* procedure. Using this statement a reader before entering its critical section enables another waiting reader to move on, and so on. While this is happening, no new reader will be able to enter the monitor; new readers may enter the monitor only after the last **signal**(*waitR*) is executed (and lost).

Self Review

1. Explain why a readers and writers algorithm also solves the mutual exclusion problem, but not vice versa.
2. Would the first readers and writers algorithm using semaphores (page 289) be correct if *unfair* semaphores are used?
3. Consider the first readers and writers algorithm using semaphores (page 289). Assume that a *writer* is in its critical section, and another *writer* and a *reader* are waiting. Which of them will go first once the *writer* exits?

Answers: (1) When you let each process behave like a writer, you solve the mutual exclusion problem. (2) Yes. (3) If weak semaphores are used then one of them will be chosen arbitrarily. If the semaphores guarantee FIFO scheduling then the first to do a down operation on the mutex semaphore will go first.

8.3 The Sleeping Barber

The following synchronization problem was proposed by Dijkstra in 1968. A barber shop has one barber, one barber chair, and *n* customers chairs, as illustrated in Figure 8.2. The problem is to write a program to coordinate the barber and the customers such that every waiting customer is eventually served, under the following assumptions:

- When there are no customers, the barber always falls asleep;
- If a customer arrives while the barber is asleep, the customer wakes up the barber and sits in the barber chair;

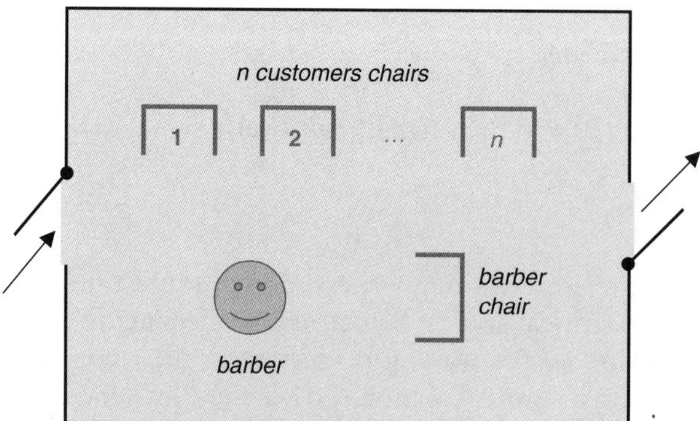

Figure 8.2 The sleeping barber. The barber shop has one barber, one barber chair, and *n* customers chairs.

- If a customer arrives while the barber is busy and there is a free chair, the customer sits in a free chair and waits;
- If a customer arrives while the barber is busy and all chairs are occupied, the customer leaves the shop;
- When the barber finishes cutting a customer's hair, this customer leaves and one of the waiting customers moves to the barber chair.

A solution to the problem is presented below using semaphores. We use four semaphores and one atomic register. The atomic register *waiting* is used to count the number of waiting customers, not including the customer that is currently being served. When a new customer finds out that $waiting = n$ the customer immediately leaves the shop. The *mutex* semaphore is used to provide exclusive access to *waiting*. The semaphore *customer* is used to count the number of waiting customers (again, not including the customer that is currently being served). When the barber finds out that $customer = 0$, the barber waits (sleeps) on the *customer* semaphore. Finally, the *barbers* semaphore counts the number of idle barbers (which is either 0 or 1). When a customer finds out that $barber = 0$, the customer waits on the *barbers* semaphore. Finally, the *sync* semaphore guarantees that the barber will not ask a new customer to sit on the barber chair until the previous customer leaves.

SLEEPING BARBER USING SEMAPHORES

```
shared  waiting: atomic register ranges over {0,...,n}, initially 0
        customers: general semaphore ranges over {0,...,n}, initially 0
        mutex: binary semaphore, initially 1
        sync: binary semaphore, initially 0
```

PROGRAM FOR THE BARBER

```
1 loop
2    down(customers)
3    down(mutex)
4    waiting := waiting - 1
5    up(barbers)
6    up(mutex)
7    cut customer's hair
8    down(sync)
9 end_loop
```

PROGRAM FOR A CUSTOMER

```
1 down(mutex)
2 if waiting < n then
3    waiting := waiting + 1
4    up(customers)
5    up(mutex)
6    down(barbers)
7    get haircut
8    up(sync)
9 else up(mutex) fi
```

The barber first checks the *customer* semaphore (line 2), and if there are no customers, it goes to sleep until the first customer shows up. When a customer arrives it first tries to get exclusive access to *waiting* and *customers*, by acquiring the *mutex* semaphore (line 1). When it succeeds, it first checks to see whether all chairs are occupied (line 2). If so, the customer immediately leaves the shop (line 9). Otherwise, the customer increments the counters *waiting* and *customers* (lines 3 and 4) and releases *mutex* (line 5). Then, it waits on the semaphore *barbers* for the barber to wake up (line 6). We notice that, in line 4, the customer wakes up a possibly sleeping barber by incrementing *customers*. Once that barber succeeds in acquiring *mutex* (line 3) it decrements *waiting* (line 4), and lets one customer proceed (line 5). When the haircut is over the barber waits for the customer to leave (line 8) and starts over.

Self Review

1. In the Sleeping Barber algorithm (page 293) why do we need both *waiting* and *customers* to count the number of waiting customers?
2. Consider the Sleeping Barber algorithm. Assume that we replace the statement **down**(*sync*) in line 8 of the Barber's program with **up**(*sync*), and replace the statement **up**(*sync*) in line 8 of the Customer's program with **down**(*sync*). Would the algorithm still be correct?
3. Do we need to assume that the semaphores used are weak or is it enough to assume that the semaphores are unfair?
4. Consider the Sleeping Barber algorithm. Which of the following changes will leave the algorithm correct?
   (a) Replacing the order of lines 2 and 3 in the Barber's program;
   (b) Replacing the order of lines 5 and 6 in the Barber's program;
   (c) Replacing the order of lines 4 and 5 in the Customer's program;
   (d) Replacing the order of lines 5 and 6 in the Customer's program.
5. Is the Sleeping Barber algorithm still correct if we assume that n, the number of chairs, is unbounded (i.e., $n = \infty$)?

Answers: (1) Because there is no way to read the value of a semaphore without the risk of being suspended on the semaphore. Thus, we need *waiting* to enable a new customer to leave without waiting, and we need *customers* to enable the barber to wait when there are no customers. (2) No. In such a case the barber may ask a new customer to sit on the barber chair while the previous customer has not left yet. (3) Unfair semaphores are also fine. (4) No (deadlock). Yes. Yes. No (deadlock). (5) No. The barber may never succeed in locking *mutex*, and hence, in such a case, nobody will get haircut.

8.4 The Cigarette Smoker's Problem

The cigarette smoker's problem is a synchronization problem that was proposed by S. S. Patil in 1971. Assume that there is a group of four people which consists of three *smokers* and one *agent*. To roll and smoke a cigarette three ingredients are needed: paper, tobacco, and matches. One of the smokers has an infinite supply of paper, another has an infinite supply of tobacco, and another has an infinite supply of matches. The agent has an infinite supply of all the three ingredients. The four participants repeatedly perform the following:

The agent puts two ingredients on the table; the smoker who has the remaining ingredient takes the two ingredients, rolls a cigarette, smokes it, and notifies the agent on completion. Then the agent puts another two ingredients on the table, and so on.

The problem is to write a program to synchronize the agent and the smokers. The code of the agent is considered to be an unchangeable part of the problem definition and is given below. The agent uses four semaphores named $S[1], S[2], S[3]$, and *agent*. The first three semaphores indicate which ingredients are currently available on the table. $S[1] = 1$ indicates that a paper is available, $S[2] = 1$ indicates that tobacco is available, $S[3] = 1$ indicates that a match is available. The *agent* semaphore is used by the agent to decide when she should wait and when she can put more ingredients on the table.

The Cigarette Smoker's Algorithm using Binary Semaphores

```
shared  S: array [1..3] of binary semaphores, initially all 0
        agent: binary semaphore, initially 1
local   i, j: range over {1, 2, 3}
```

PROGRAM FOR THE AGENT

```
1 loop
2    Set i and j (at random) to two different values from {1, 2, 3}
3    down(agent)
4    up(S[i])
5    up(S[j])
6 end_loop
```

As mentioned, the code of the agent is part of the *problem* definition. The agent puts the two ingredients on the table by performing *up* operations on two semaphores, and she does not directly signal to the smoker that should smoke next. We first observe that the following simple implementation of the smokers is *not* correct:

Smoker with paper

```
loop
   down(S[2])
   down(S[3])
   "smoke"
   up(agent)
end_loop
```

Smoker with tobacco

```
loop
   down(S[3])
   down(S[1])
   "smoke"
   up(agent)
end_loop
```

Smoker with matches

```
loop
   down(S[1])
   down(S[2])
   "smoke"
   up(agent)
end_loop
```

The above solution is incorrect since it may deadlock. To see that, assume that the agent in line 2 sets i to 1 and j to 2, which means that after she finishes executing lines 3, 4, and 5, the ingredients *paper* and *tobacco* are available on the table. Now, if the smoker with papers takes the tobacco (by executing **down**($S[2]$)), and the smoker with matches takes the paper (by executing **down**($S[1]$)), the algorithm is deadlocked.

Next we present a correct algorithm due to Parnas (1975). In addition to the three smokers, three other processes, called *helpers*, are used. The helpers identify which are the two available ingredients, and signal the appropriate smoker. The code for each one of the three helpers is as follows:

THE CIGARETTE SMOKER'S ALGORITHM (CONT.)

```
shared (in addition to the semaphores used by the agent)
        R: array [1..6] of binary semaphores, initially all 0
        mutex: binary semaphore, initially 1
        t: atomic register, initially 0
```

HELPER #1 (PAPER AVAILABLE)

```
1 loop
2    down(S[1])
3    down(mutex)
4    t := t + 1
5    if t ≠ 1 then
6       up(R[t]) fi
5    up(mutex)
6 end_loop
```

HELPER #2 (TOBACCO AVAILABLE)

```
1 loop
2    down(S[2])
3    down(mutex)
4    t := t + 2
5    if t ≠ 2 then
6       up(R[t]) fi
5    up(mutex)
6 end_loop
```

HELPER #3 (MATCHES AVAILABLE)

```
1 loop
2    down(S[3])
3    down(mutex)
4    t := t + 4
5    if t ≠ 4 then
6       up(R[t]) fi
5    up(mutex)
6 end_loop
```

The smokers simply wait for a signal from the helpers. Their code is as follows:

SMOKER WITH PAPER

```
loop
   down(R[6])
   t := 0
   "smoke"
   up(agent)
end_loop
```

SMOKER WITH TOBACCO

```
loop
   down(R[5])
   t := 0
   "smoke"
   up(agent)
end_loop
```

SMOKER WITH MATCHES

```
loop
   down(R[3])
   t := 0
   "smoke"
   up(agent)
end_loop
```

Patil (1971) has shown that there is no solution to the problem if conditional statements and an array of semaphores are not allowed to be used. (Patil has defined the agent by six processes and without using an array of semaphores.) Parnas (1975) has shown that a solution is possible using either conditional statements or an array of semaphores. To get Parnas' solution, which avoids using conditional statements, simply replace the if statement in the code of each one of the helpers (lines 5 and 6) by the statement "**up**($R[t]$)". (If one worries about semaphore overflow then three more helper processes can be added which spin on $R[1]$, $R[2]$, and $R[3]$.)

8.5 More Synchronization Problems

We discuss below a few additional synchronization problems, without presenting their solutions. There readers are encouraged to try, as an exercise, to solve a few of these problems themselves.

8.5.1 Group Mutual Exclusion and Room Synchronization

The *group mutual exclusion* problem, due to Yuh-Jzer Joung (1998), generalizes the classical mutual exclusion and readers and writers problems. In this problem n processes repeatedly attend m "sessions" labelled from $\{1, \ldots ,m\}$. Processes that have requested to attend the same session may do it concurrently. However, processes that have requested to attend different sessions may not attend their sessions at the same time.

Exactly the same problem was also considered by G. E. Blelloch, P. Cheng, and P. B. Gibbons (2001), under the name the *room synchronization* problem. The room synchronization problem involves supporting a set of m mutually exclusive "rooms" where any number of users can execute code simultaneously in any one of the rooms, but no two users can simultaneously execute code in separate rooms.

As an example, consider a system with a shared CD jukebox. By assigning a session number to each CD, a group mutual exclusion algorithm would allow multiple processes to read the current loaded CD concurrently, while forcing processes that require different CDs to wait. Allowing concurrent requests for the same CD to read it at the same time reduces the frequency of CD switches and improves the utilization of the CD jukebox.

Another example has to do with the design of concurrent queue (or concurrent stack). Using a group mutual exclusion algorithm, we can guarantee that no two users will ever simultaneously be in the *enqueue.session* or *dequeue.sesson*, so the enqueue and dequeue operations will never be interleaved. However, it will allow any number of users to be in either the enqueue or dequeue session simultaneously. Doing so, simplifies the design of an efficient concurrent queue as our only concern now is to implement concurrent enqueue operations and concurrent dequeue operations.

More formally, the problem is defined as follows: as in the mutual exclusion problem, it is assumed that each process is executing a sequence of instructions in an infinite loop. The instructions are divided into four continuous sections of code: the *remainder*, *entry*, *critical section*, and *exit*. Thus, the structure of a group mutual exclusion solution looks as follows:

```
loop forever
        remainder code;
        entry code (for session s);
```

critical section (attending session s);
exit code
end loop

A process starts by executing the remainder code. At some point it might need to attend some session, say *s*. In order to attend session *s*, a process has to go through an entry code which guarantees that while it is attending this session, no other process is allowed to attend another session. In addition, once a process finishes attending a session, the process executes its exit code in which it notifies other processes that it is no longer attending the session. After executing the exit code the process returns to the remainder.

The group mutual exclusion problem is to write the code for the *entry code* and the *exit code* in such a way that the following three basic requirements are satisfied.

Mutual exclusion: *No two processes are attending different sessions at the same time.*

Concurrent entering: *If some process, say p, is trying to attend a session s while no process is requesting a conflicting session, then p completes its entry code in a bounded number of its own steps.*

Starvation-freedom: *If a process is trying to attend a session (enter its critical section), then this process must eventually attend the session (enter its critical section).*

The *concurrent entering* requirement precludes the direct application of a solution to the mutual exclusion problem, since it requires that processes can attend the same session concurrently. Also, always admitting a process that wants to attend the current session could lead to starvation of processes that are waiting for different sessions. Thus, in such a case, there is a need for a mechanism for "closing" a session.

It is possible to replace the starvation-freedom requirement with a weaker deadlock-freedom requirement: If a process is trying to attend a session *s*, then some process, not necessarily the same one, eventually attends session *s*. Also, it is possible to define stronger fairness requirements, similar to those defined for the mutual exclusion problem. The usual assumptions made about the behavior of the processes in the mutual exclusion problem (see page 10), such as the assumption that the exit code is wait-free, also apply to this problem.

8.5.2 Concurrent Reading and Writing of Clocks

Consider a finite clock that is updated by one process and read by one or more other processes in an asynchronous multi-process system. The clock is represented as a fixed-length sequence of digits. We assume that the entire clock is updated in one atomic operation, but reading each digit is a separate (atomic) operation. Each update increments the clock value until the clock reaches its maximum value. The next update causes the clock to wrap around to zero.

The problem, due to L. Lamport (1990), is to design an algorithm for reading the clock that always returns a "correct" clock value, even if the clock is being updated while the read is being performed. A value is considered correct if it is actually assumed by the clock during the time interval while the clock is being read.

For example, assume a conventional 24-hour clock in which times in hours and minutes are represented by four digits in the form *hh:mm*. A read that occurs while the clock is being changed from 11:57 to 12:04 is allowed to return any value between 11:57 and 12:04. However, it is not allowed to return values such as 11:04, 12:07, or 12:57. Similarly, a read that occurs while the clock is being changed from 23:58 to 00:12 can return 23:59 or 00:05. A read that is so slow that the clock makes a complete cycle before it finishes can return any clock value.

It is not difficult to show that the clock problem can not be solved simply by reading the digits from left to right (most significant digit to least significant digit) twice. That is, it is not possible to design a procedure to output a correct time based on those digits read.

The problem is to design a procedure that reads the digits in any order and as many times as needed and outputs a correct time. When solving the problem it is also allowable to decide exactly how to update the clock.

8.5.3 The Choice Coordination Problem

A central issue in distributed and concurrent systems is how to coordinate the actions of asynchronous processes. Coordination becomes even more difficult if as many as $n - 1$ of the n processes can fail. The choice coordination problem with k alternatives (k-CCP), introduced by M. O. Rabin (1982), highlights many of the difficulties inherent in such *wait-free* situations. Solutions to the k-CCP thus lend insight into how to coordinate asynchronous actions.

In the k-CCP, n asynchronous processes must choose between k alternatives. The agreement on a single choice is complicated by the fact that there is *no a priori* agreement on names for the alternatives. That is, each process has its own naming convention for the alternatives. A solution to the k-CCP is a wait-free algorithm which guarantees that all correct processes terminate having chosen the same alternative.

A slightly more concrete version of the k-CCP associates a shared register with each alternative. All inter-process communication must be accomplished by writing in and reading from these registers. However, the registers do not have global names; the first register examined and the subsequent order in which registers are scanned may be different for each process. That is, a single register may be considered the fifth register by one process and the eighth by another. Even the order of the names may be different. Thus one process may scan four alternatives in order 3, 2, 1, 4 while another scans 2, 4, 1, 3.

A wait-free algorithm is a solution to the general k-CCP if, for all possible orderings and initial registers assigned to the asynchronous processes, eventually a special symbol, say e, is written in exactly one register and all correct processes terminate with a pointer to the register containing the symbol *e*. An algorithm is a solution to the unidirectional (bidirectional) *k*-CCP if the algorithm solves the *k*-CCP when all processes are assigned the same ordering (or its inverse). The efficiency of the algorithm is defined by the number of different symbols which may be written in the registers; thus, algorithms requiring the least number of values in the shared registers are considered optimal.

8.5.4 The H_2O Problem

The problem is to write a variant of a barrier that only allows processes to pass in certain combinations, in order to help with the chemical reaction to form water. The goal is to get two *H* atoms and one *O* atom all together at the same time so that a complete molecule can be produced. The atoms are simulated by processes which need to be synchronized. Each *H* atom invokes a procedure called *H.ready* when it is ready to react, and each *O* atom invokes a procedure called *O.ready* when it is ready.

The H_2O problem is to write the code for *H.ready* and *O.ready* (using some given synchronization primitives such as atomic registers, semaphores, etc.) so that:

- The atoms (processes) are delayed until there are at least two *H* atoms and one *O* atom present, and then one of the atoms must call a procedure named *makeWater*.
- After the *makeWater* call, two instances of *H.ready* and one instance of *O.ready* should return from their calls. That is two processes which simulate *H* atoms and one process which simulates an *O* atom continue past the barrier.

The algorithm is required to be starvation-free.

8.5.5 The Roller Coaster Problem

The roller coaster problem, due to J. S. Herman (1989), also has to do with writing a variant of a barrier that only allows processes to pass in certain combinations. There are *n* passenger and *m* cars. Each passenger repeatedly waits to take a ride in a car. Each car can hold *c* passengers, where $c < n$. A car can go around the track only when it is full. Once a car is full, it goes around the track and when it stops all the passengers get off the car.

The passengers and the cars are simulated by processes which need to be synchronized. When a car arrives, *c* passengers should invoke a procedure called *get-on-car*, then one waiting car should invoke a procedure called *depart*, then the (same) *c* passengers should invoke a procedure called *get-off-car*. The problem is to write the code for the passengers and the cars. The solution is required to be:

- *Starvation-free*: Every waiting passenger eventually gets to take a ride in a car.
- *Efficient*: The cars should be utilized to enable each passenger to take as many rides as possible.

It is assumed that there is only one track, and cars can not pass each other. That is, the cars finish going around the track in the order in which they started.

Self Review

1. Explain why a solution to the group mutual exclusion problem also solves the mutual exclusion problem.
2. Explain why a solution to the group mutual exclusion problem also solves the readers and writers problem.
3. Does a solution to the group mutual exclusion problem also solve the ℓ-exclusion problem?

Answers: (1) Each process uses its unique id as a session number. (2) Each writer requests a different session, and the readers all request the same special session. This allows readers to attend the session concurrently while ensuring that the writers attend in isolation. (3) No. The group mutual exclusion problem has some similarity to the ℓ-exclusion problem, in that it allows processes which access the same session to be in their critical sections concurrently. However, unlike ℓ-exclusion, it does not impose any bound on the number of processes that may attend the same session concurrently, and distinguish between processes from different sessions.

8.6 Bibliographic Notes

8.1

The producer-consumer problem (page 281) was first presented by Dijkstra in [107, 109]. The variant of the producer-consumer problem presented in Problem 8.8 (page 303) is also from [107]. The non-blocking concurrent queue algorithm presented in Section 4.5.2 (page 171), which solves the producer-consumer problem for any number of processes, is from [265].

8.2

The readers and writers problem was suggested by Courtois, Heyman, and Parnas [99]. The readers and writers algorithms using semaphores that are presented on page 289 and page 290 are from [99]. A scalable (local-spinning) solution to the readers and writers problem is presented in [255]. A related but *different* problem is the *concurrent reading while writing* (CRWW) problem. In the CRWW problem, which was first considered by L. Lamport in [215] (under the name concurrent reading *and* writing), a process may read shared data while the data is being modified by another process. The writer is not allowed to wait (it must be wait-free), but readers may starve. A bounded space algorithm that solves the CRWW problem with neither the readers nor the writer ever waiting using atomic bits only, is presented in [283]. See also [334].

The sleeping barber problem (page 292) was presented by Dijkstra in [107, 109], as a variant of the producer-consumer problem.

8.4

The cigarette smoker's problem (page 294) was presented by Patil in [278]. Patil has shown that there is no solution to the problem if conditional statements and an array of semaphores are not allowed to be used. (Patil has defined the agent by six processes and without using an array of semaphores.) Parnas has shown that a solution is possible using either conditional statements or an array of semaphores [276]. See also [206].

8.5

8.5.1

The group mutual exclusion problem was first stated and solved by Yuh-Jzer Joung in [195, 196], using atomic registers. The problem is a generalization of the mutual exclusion problem [106] and of the readers and writers problem [99], and can be seen as a special case of the drinking philosophers problem [92]. Group mutual exclusion is the same as room synchronization [71]. In [71], the room synchronization problem is defined, a solution is presented, and it is shown how it can be used to efficiently implement concurrent queues and stacks using a fetch-and-add operation. See also [70].

In [198, 199], a technique of converting any solution for the mutual exclusion problem to solve the group mutual exclusion problem was introduced. The algorithm from [198, 199] satisfies a much weaker concurrent entering property compared to the one considered in [195] and its exit code is not wait-free. In [157], another algorithm is presented that satisfies the stronger concurrent entering property. Efficient local spinning group mutual exclusion algorithms are presented in [104]. In [190], a reduction is presented that transforms any abortable FCFS mutual exclusion algorithm into a group mutual exclusion algorithm. A combined problem of ℓ-exclusion and group mutual exclusion, called the group ℓ-exclusion problem, is considered in [320, 335].

8.5.2

The problem of concurrent reading and writing of clocks, presented on page 298, is from [225]. The problem is related to the concurrent reading while writing (CRWW) problem, mentioned on page 301.

8.5.3

The choice coordination problem with k alternatives (k-CCP) was introduced by M. O. Rabin in [290]. For the case of $k = 2$ and $t = n - 1$ (t is the possible number of faults), Rabin has presented a deterministic algorithm using $m = n + 2$ symbols (for each register), proved a lower bound of $m \geq (n/8)^{1/3}$ for deterministic algorithms, and contrasted these results with a randomized algorithm which, for

m symbols, terminates correctly with probability $1 - 1/2^{m/2}$. In [61] deterministic and randomized algorithms were presented for the 2-CCP which both use $O(t^2)$ symbols, and various results for the 3-CCP were presented. In [152] the k-CCP was solved for any number k of alternatives. The two main questions that the authors have addressed and resolved are: (1) Assuming that there is no limitation on the size of each register, under what circumstances is the k-CCP solvable? (2) How many symbols for each of the k registers are necessary and sufficient to solve the k-CCP, as a function of k and n?

8.5.4 & 8.5.5

The H_2O problem appears as an exercise in a book by G. R. Andrews [41] (under the name, *the water molecule problem*), and also appears in several exams in operating systems courses at U.C. Berkely. The roller coaster problem is from [174]. Our presentation of this problem is based on an exercise from [40]. Solutions to various synchronization problems using semaphores appear in [119].

8.7 Problems

The problems are divided into several categories. See page 23 for a detailed explanation.

Problems based on Section 8.1

- ◦ 8.1 Can the producer-consumer algorithm using atomic registers (page 283) be modified, using atomic registers only, so that all the n buffer locations are used?
- ◦ 8.2 The producer-consumer algorithm using an atomic counter (page 283) would not be correct if the counter is not atomic. Explain why.
- ◦ 8.3 Assume that only one process (the producer or the consumer) is allowed to access the buffer at any give time. Using one additional binary semaphore, modify the algorithm using general semaphores (page 284) so that it satisfies this requirement.
- ◦ 8.4 In the producer-consumer algorithm using binary semaphores (page 285), explain why in the code of the producer it is important that the data item be inserted (line 5) before the counter is incremented (line 7).
- ◦ 8.5 Does the *counter* in the producer-consumer algorithm using binary semaphores (page 285) need to be an *atomic* counter?
- ◦◦ 8.6 Fix the incorrect algorithm, from page 287, which uses *sleep* and *wakeup*.
- ◦◦ 8.7 We have assumed that there is only one producer and only one consumer. Choose three of the algorithms and modify them so that they work with multiple producers and multiple consumers.
- ◦◦ 8.8 Solve the following variant of the producer-consumer problem, which was also proposed by Dijkstra. In this problem producers can offer data items of different sizes, and the size of an item is expressed in the

number of locations in the buffer that are needed to store the item. The consumers consume successive items from the buffer without knowing *a priori* what is the size of the next item. The question whether the buffer will be able to accommodate the next item produced depends on the size of this data item and the number of available locations. Furthermore, there are several producers and it is required that a producer wishing to offer the larger item gets priority over a producer wishing to offer a smaller item to the buffer. (When two or more producers are offering items that happen to be of the same size we just do not care.)

Problems based on Section 8.2

○• 8.9 Consider the two readers and writers algorithms using semaphores (page 289 and page 290). Both algorithms do not guarantee a FIFO discipline for the writers. Modify the algorithms so that they do guarantee a FIFO discipline for the writers, by using an additional array of n semaphores where n is the number of writers.

○○ 8.10 What are the fairness properties of the following algorithm? It is assumed that there are n readers and a single writer. The algorithm uses a semaphore and $n + 1$ atomic bits, and allows processes to busy-wait.

READERS AND WRITERS USING A SEMAPHORE AND REGISTERS

```
shared  reading[1..n]: array of atomic bits, initially false
        writing: atomic bit, initially false
        mutex: binary semaphore, initially 1
```

PROGRAM FOR THE *i*th READER

```
down(mutex)
await (writing = false)
reading[i] := true
up(mutex)
critical section
reading[i] := false
```

PROGRAM FOR THE WRITER

```
down(mutex)
for j := 1 to n do
    await (reading[i] = false) od
writing := true
up(mutex)
critical section
writing := false
```

? 8.11 What is the minimum number of semaphores needed in order to solve (each one of the two versions of) the readers and writers problem assuming only a constant number of additional atomic registers can be used?

○○ 8.12 Consider the readers and writers algorithm using a monitor from page 291. Write three versions of this algorithm: the first always gives priority to readers; the second always gives priority to writers; and in the third at most three readers may bypass a waiting writer and at most three writers may bypass a waiting reader.

○• 8.13 Write a readers and writers algorithm that satisfies local spinning.

○• 8.14 Write a readers and writers algorithm using atomic registers only.

Problems based on Section 8.3

∘∘ 8.15 Modify the Sleeping Barber algorithm (page 293) so that it works also when there is more than one barber.

∘• 8.16 Solve the sleeping barber problem using atomic registers only. Your solution should be as simple and efficient as possible.

Problems based on Section 8.4

∘∘ 8.17 Replace the array of semaphores $R[1..6]$ in the Cigarette Smoker's algorithm by three semaphores called *paper*, *tobacco*, and *matches*.

∘• 8.18 Assume that line 3 in the code of the agent (**down**(*agent*)) is deleted. That is the agent might put several instances of the same ingredient on the table. Modify the solution to deal with this case.

∘∘ 8.19 Can the algorithm deadlock if the following code is used by the agent:

PROGRAM FOR THE AGENT

```
loop
   down(agent)
   up(S[1])
   up(S[2])
   up(S[3])
end_loop
```

Problems based on Section 8.5

∘• 8.20 This problem refers to the *concurrent reading and writing of clocks* problem from page 298.

- Show that we can not solve the clock problem by reading the digits from left to right (most significant digit to least significant digit) twice. That is, it is not possible to design a procedure to output a correct time based on those digits read.
- Design a procedure that reads the digits in any order and as many times as you want and outputs a correct time. You can decide also how exactly to update the clock.

∘• 8.21 Solve two of the four problems mentioned in Section 8.5 using:(1) atomic registers only, (2) registers and semaphores, and (3) registers and your favorite synchronization primitive.

Consensus

9.1 The Problem

The *consensus problem* is to design an algorithm in which all correct processes reach a common decision based on their initial opinions. A consensus algorithm is an algorithm that produces such an agreement. While various decision rules can be considered such as "majority consensus", the problem is interesting even where the decision value is constrained only when all processes are unanimous in their opinions, in which case the decision value must be the common opinion. More formally the problem is defined as follows. There are n processes $p_1, p_2, \ldots, p_n$. Each process p_i has an input value $x_i \in \{0, 1\}$. It *decides* on a value v if it writes v to its output register. It may decide at most once. The requirements of the consensus problem are that there exists a *decision value* v such that:

- *Agreement*: Each non-faulty process eventually decides on v.
- *Validity*: $v \in \{x_1, x_2, \ldots, x_n\}$.

In particular, if all input values are the same, then that value must be the decision value. We point out that the first requirement has two parts. The first (the agreement part) is that all processes that decide choose the same value, and the second (the termination part) is that all non-faulty processes eventually decide.

The consensus problem defined above is also called *binary* consensus as the input value x_i is either 0 or 1. A generalization of the problem where the input value is taken from a set of size k is called the k-consensus problem. In the following we will consider only binary consensus.

The problem is a fundamental coordination problem and is at the core of many algorithms for fault-tolerant distributed applications. Achieving consensus is straightforward in the absence of faults, for all processes can share their initial values and then all apply a uniform decision rule to the resulting vector of initial values. However, such a simple algorithm cannot tolerate even a single process crash, for its correctness depends on all processes obtaining the same initial value vector.

Most of the published algorithms for solving this problem assume that communication is done by sending and receiving messages. Since our focus is on concurrent computing, we will consider only algorithms in which processes communicate via shared memory. Much is known about the consensus problem in various models. For example, it is known that no (deterministic) consensus algorithm can tolerate even a single crash failure in an asynchronous shared memory model in which only atomic read/write registers are used (see Section 9.5). Before proving this important impossibility result, we present several consensus algorithms in various shared memory models.

9.2 Three Simple Consensus Algorithms

We present three very simple consensus algorithms, due to M. C. Loui and H. Abu-Amara (1987). The first is a trivial n-process algorithm which uses a single 3-valued read-modify-write register. The second is a two process algorithm which uses two read-modify-write bits. The third algorithm is an n-process algorithm which uses n read-modify-write bits.

As in previous chapters, the brackets $\langle$ and $\rangle$ are used to explicitly mark the beginning and end of exclusive access to a shared read-modify-write register. An execution of a bracketed section is considered as an atomic action. Furthermore, a process can not fail while executing the code between the bracket $\langle$ and the next bracket $\rangle$. This corresponds to the assumption in our underlying model that a read-modify-write operation is atomic, so a process is assumed not to crash in the middle of such an operation.

9.2.1 A Single 3-valued Read-modify-write Register

In the following algorithm the first process to access the shared register sets the register's value to its own input value, and all the other processes adopt this value as the decision value.

A TRIVIAL CONSENSUS ALGORITHM: program for process with input $v \in \{0, 1\}$.

```
shared
x read-modify-write register ranges over {⊥, 0, 1}, initially x = ⊥

⟨ if x = ⊥ then x := v fi
  decide(x) ⟩
```

The algorithm is *wait-free*, one process can not prevent another process from reaching a decision, and thus the algorithm can tolerate an arbitrary number of process (crash) failures.

We notice that the read-modify-write register can be replaced by a *compare-and-swap* object which is initially set to ⊥. Each process attempts to replace ⊥ with its input; and the final decision value is the input value of the process that succeeds.

9.2.2 Two Processes, Two Read-modify-write Bits

It is easy to design a consensus algorithm for two processes using *three* read-modify-write bits. Assume that the initial values of all the three bits are 0. Each process uses one bit to announce its input, and then each of the processes tries to set the last bit from 1. The decision value is the input of the process that was the first to access the third bit, changing it from 0 to 1.

The following algorithm for *two* processes uses only *two* read-modify-write bits, called x and y, which are both initially set to 0.

A CONSENSUS ALGORITHM FOR TWO PROCESSES: program for process p_i with input $in_i \in \{0, 1\}$.

```
shared
x, y read-modify-write bits range over {0, 1}, initially both 0

1 ⟨ if x = 1 then decide(1)
2   else    x = in_i ⟩
3           ⟨ if y = 0 then y := 1; decide(in_i) ⟩
4             else   if x = 0 then decide(0) else decide(1 − in_i) fi
5             fi
6   fi
```

Process p_i checks x first, then y and then x again. In each one of these checks p_i makes the following decisions:

1. Check x (line 1). If $x = 1$ then p_i decides 1 and halts, otherwise it sets x to in_i and continues.
2. Check y (line 3). If $y = 0$ then p_i sets y to 1, decides on in_i and halts, otherwise p_2 continues.
3. Check x (line 4). If $x = 0$ then p_i decides 0 and halts, otherwise it decides on the complement of in_i and halts.

Properties of the Algorithm:

- *The algorithm is wait-free*: a failure of one process can not prevent another process from reaching a decision (the algorithm can tolerate single crash failures).
- Two atomic read-modify-write bits are used.
- The number of participating processes is at most two.

Theorem 9.1 *The algorithm for two processes satisfies the properties of validity, agreement, and wait-freedom (i.e., the algorithm can tolerate a single crash failure).*

Proof: Assume without loss of generality that p_1 is the first process to check x. There are three possible cases:

- *Case 1*: $in_1 = 1$. Since p_1 sets x to 1, process p_2 later finds that $x = 1$, decides 1 and halts without accessing y. Thus when p_1 finds that $y = 0$ it also decides 1.
- *Case 2*: $in_1 = 0$ and p_1 sets y to 1 first. In this case p_1 decides 0. Once p_2 finds that $y = 1$, it checks x again. At this point $x = in_2$. If $x = 0$ then p_2 decides 0, agreeing with p_1. If $x = 1$ (which implies that also $in_2 = 1$) then p_2 decides on $1 - in_2$ (i.e., on 0), again agreeing with p_1.
- *Case 3*: $in_1 = 0$ and p_2 sets y to 1 first. In this case p_2 decides on in_2. Once p_1 finds that $y = 1$, it checks x again. At this point $x = in_2$. If $x = 0$ then p_1 decides 0, agreeing with p_2. If $x = 1$ (which implies that also $in_2 = 1$) then p_2 decides on $1 - in_1$ (i.e., on 1), again agreeing with p_2. ∎

9.2.3 Many Processes, Four Read-modify-write Bits

It is known that there is no consensus algorithm for three or more processes using (any number of) atomic read-modify-write bits that can tolerate *two* crash failures (Problem 9.5). Below we present a consensus algorithm for n processes, using four read-modify-write bits only, that can tolerate a *single* crash failure.

The four bits, called x, y, *decision*, and *finish*, are all initially set to 0. Process 1 and process 2 execute the previous algorithm for two processes using x and y. Then they write the decision value into the *decision* bit and set the *finish* bit to 1. Each process busy-waits until it notices that the *finish* bit is set to 1, and then decides on the value of the *decision* bit.

A CONSENSUS ALGORITHM FOR MANY PROCESSES: `program for process` p_i `with input` $in_i \in \{0, 1\}$.

> **shared**
> x, y read-modify-write bits range over $\{0, 1\}$, initially both 0
> *decision* read-modify-write bits range over $\{0, 1\}$, initially 0
> *finish* read-modify-write bits range over $\{0, 1\}$, initially 0
> **local**
> $decision_1$ atomic bit, local to process p_1
> $decision_2$ atomic bit, local to process p_2

```
1  if i ∈ {1,2} then
2     ⟨ if x = 1 then decision_i := 1
3       else    x = in_i ⟩
4             ⟨ if y = 0 then y := 1 ; decision_i := in_i ⟩
5               else   if x = 0 then decision_i := 0 else decision_i := 1 − in_i fi
6               fi
7       fi
8       decision := decision_i; finish := 1
9  else await(finish = 1) fi                                  /* i ∉ {1,2} */
10 decide(decision)
```

Notice that lines 2–7 are essentially the code of the previous algorithm for two processes.

Properties of the Algorithm:

- The algorithm can tolerate a single crash failure.
- Four atomic read-modify-write bits are used.
- The number of participating processes is unbounded.

Theorem 9.2 *The algorithm for any number of processes satisfies the properties of validity, agreement, and can tolerate a single crash failure.*

Proof: Since lines 2–8 are essentially the code of the previous algorithm for two processes, by the correctness of the previous algorithm, both process 1 and process 2 will agree on the same value. Since there is at most one failure, either process 1 or process 2 will write the decision value into the *decision* bit and set the *finish* bit to 1. Once the value of *finish* is set to 1, the value of the *decision* bit will not change. Eventually all the correct processes will notice that the value of the *finish* bit is 1, and decide on the value of the *decision* bit. ∎

Self Review

1. Consider the consensus algorithm for two processes from page 309. Is it important that the two bits are *both* initially 0.
2. Consider the consensus algorithm for many processes from page 310. Is it important that *all* the four bits are initially 0.

Answers: (1) Yes. (2) No, the initial value of the decision bit is immaterial.

9.3 Consensus without Memory Initialization

We present a solution to the consensus problem, due to M. J. Fischer, S. Moran, and G. Taubenfeld (1993), where all processes are programmed alike, there is no global synchronization (i.e., the model is asynchronous), it is not possible to simultaneously reset the shared memory to a known initial state, and processes may be faulty. The consensus algorithm for n processes which is presented can tolerate up to $\lceil n/2 \rceil - 1$ failures and uses a single $(2\lceil 1.5n - 1 \rceil)$-valued shared register.

Our model of computation consists of a fully asynchronous collection of n identical anonymous deterministic processes that communicate via a *single* finite-sized register. Access to the register is via atomic "read-modify-write" instructions which, in a single indivisible step, read the value in the register and then write a new value that can depend on the value just read.

The shared register is subject to *initialization failure* in which an arbitrary unknown value is placed in the shared register before the algorithm begins. That is, nothing is assumed about the initial value of the shared register. Processes are subject to *crash failures* in which a process at an arbitrary time simply ceases to participate further in the algorithm. We assume that a majority of the processes are non-faulty.

As in previous chapters, the brackets $\langle$ and $\rangle$ are used to explicitly mark the beginning and end of exclusive access to a shared read-modify-write register. An execution of a bracketed section is considered as an atomic action. Furthermore, a process can not fail while executing the code between the bracket $\langle$ and the next bracket $\rangle$.

9.3.1 The Algorithm

The algorithm uses a shared register whose values range over the set $B \times C$, where $B = \{0, 1\}$ and $C = \{0, \ldots, \lceil 1.5n \rceil - 2\}$. We use b and c to designate the first and second components, respectively, of the ordered pair stored in the shared register. Thus, b ranges over B, c ranges over C, $|B| = 2$, and $|C| = \lceil 1.5n \rceil - 1$. Let $k = \lceil n/2 \rceil$. We call the the interval $[0, k-1]$ the 0-*interval* and the interval $[k, 2k-1]$ the 1-*interval*. These two intervals are disjoint subsets of C since $2k \leq |C|$.

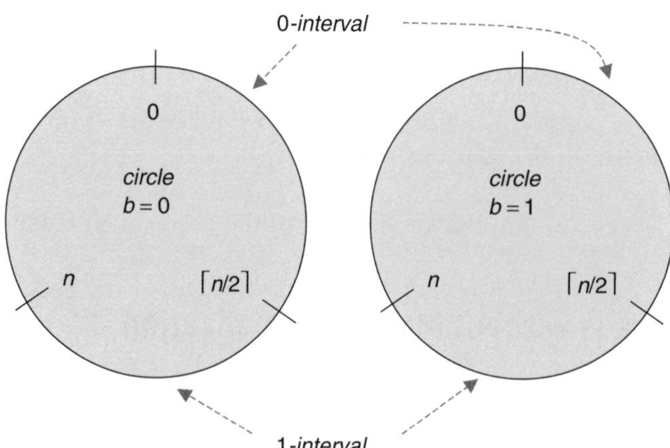

Figure 9.1 Viewing the $3n$ values of the shared register as numbers that are being arranged clockwise in two circles.

The algorithm uses the function $d(a_1, a_2) = 1 + ((a_2 - a_1 - 1) \bmod |C|)$, defined for $a_1, a_2 \in C$. If we think of the numbers in C as being arranged clockwise in a circle, as illustrated in Figure 9.1, then $d(a_1, a_2)$ is the distance one must travel clockwise around the circle starting from a_1 before reaching a_2. (In the special case that $a_1 = a_2$, one must travel all the way around the circle.) Thus, $1 \leq d(a_1, a_2) \leq |C|$, and $a_1 + d(a_1, a_2) \equiv a_2 \pmod{|C|}$.

CONSENSUS FOR n PROCESSES USING $2\lceil 1.5n - 1 \rceil$ VALUES: program for process p_i with input x_i.

```
constant B = {0, 1}
constant C = {0, ..., ⌈1.5n⌉ − 2}
constant k = ⌈n/2⌉
shared (b, c) ranges over B × C
local (b_i, c_i) ranges over B × C
output v_i ranges over {0, 1, ⊥}, initially ⊥

⟨ (b_i, c_i) := (b, c)
  c := (c + 1) mod |C| ⟩
while v_i = ⊥ do
    ⟨ case b of
      b_i:
      if d(c_i, c) > n then
           v_i := ⌊c/k⌋                          /* make decision */
      else if d(c_i, c) > n/2 then
           v_i := x_i; b := 1 − b; c := v_i * k  /* become master */
      1 − b_i:
           v_i := ⌊c/k⌋ ⟩                        /* make decision */
end-while
repeat forever
    ⟨ c := v_i * k ⟩
end-repeat
```

Each process, when it starts to operate, reads the value of the shared register, stores its components in local memory, and increments c by one (modulo $|C|$). At any later point, a process becomes the *master* if it learns (by inspecting c) that more than half of the processes have wakened up but the value of b has still not changed. The master decides on its own input value, and this value v will eventually become everyone's decision value. If the master chooses zero, it sets c to the beginning of the 0-interval; otherwise it sets c to the beginning of the 1-interval. Simultaneously, it changes the value of b, thereby indicating to processes that are already awake that a decision has been made. When any other process first learns that the decision has been made, it makes its own decision according to the interval in which c lies. A process can learn that a decision has been made either by seeing b change value, or by seeing that c appears to have been incremented by more than n (modulo $|C|$). Every process, after making its decision, continues forever setting c to the beginning of the interval corresponding to its decision.

Properties of the Algorithm:

- It is not required to initialize the shared memory.
- A single $(2\lceil 1.5n - 1\rceil)$-valued read-modify-write register is used.
- The algorithm can tolerate up to $\lceil n/2\rceil - 1$ crash failures.

9.3.2 Correctness Proof

Next we prove that the algorithm satisfies all the properties as claimed.

Theorem 9.3 *The consensus algorithm for n processes which uses a single $(2\lceil 1.5n - 1\rceil)$-valued read-modify-write register can tolerate arbitrary initialization failures and as many as $\lceil n/2\rceil - 1$ process crash failures.*

Proof: The case $n = 1$ is trivial. Assume now $n \geq 2$. We show that the algorithm satisfies all of the conditions of the theorem.

We consider separately the cases $n = 2$ and $n > 2$. If $n = 2$, then both b and c are binary registers and we assume no failures. Then for all $a_1, a_2 \in C$, $d(a_1, a_2) = 1$ if $a_1 \neq a_2$ and $d(a_1, a_2) = 2$ if $a_1 = a_2$. By inspection of the algorithm, the first process p_i to wake up will make $c_i \neq c$ and will wait until $c_i = c$. This will become true when the second process, p_j, wakes up and increments c. On p_i's next step, it will become master and decide on its value x_i, and it will set $b := 1 - b$ and $c := x_i$. When p_j next takes a step, it will notice that $b = 1 - b_j$ and will decide on $c = x_i$.

Assume now that $n \geq 3$. We use the notation $[a_1, a_2]$ to denote the set of values in C that lie on the circle between a_1 and a_2, inclusive, i.e.,

$$[a_1, a_2] = \{a_1, a_2\} \cup \{a : d(a_1, a) + d(a, a_2) < |C|\}.$$

We extend this notation to arbitrary integers by first reducing a_1 and a_2 modulo $|C|$, i.e., $[a_1, a_2] = [(a_1 \bmod |C|), (a_2 \bmod |C|)]$.

To see that this algorithm works, one must verify several properties. In every run with fewer than $n/2$ faulty processes, there is exactly one master. The value of b is changed exactly once during the run, and that change is made by the master. The step at which b is changed is called the *decision step*. Before the decision step, no process decides on an output value, $b = \overline{b}$ and $c = (\overline{c} + w) \bmod |C|$, where $(\overline{b}, \overline{c})$ is the initial value of the shared register and w is the number of processes that have wakened up so far. After the decision step, $b = 1 - \overline{b}$ and $vk \leq c \leq vk + w' \leq vk + k - 1$, where v is the master's decision value and w' is the number of processes that have wakened up since the decision step. Every process that decides after the decision step chooses v as its decision value, and every non-failing process eventually decides. This implies the correctness of the algorithm.

We now substantiate these claims. A formal proof would verify them by simultaneous induction on the length of the run. We instead argue informally for their correctness.

Any process p_i that wakes up before the decision step will have $b_i = \overline{b}$ and $c_i \in [\overline{c}, \overline{c} + n - 1]$. Thereafter, until the the decision step, p_i will see $b = b_i$ and

$c \in [c_i + 1, \bar{c} + n]$, so $d(c_i, c) \leq n$. Thus, no process p_i will decide before the decision step.

Some process will become master, and hence there will be a decision step. Suppose not. At least $\lfloor n/2 \rfloor + 1 > n/2$ processes are non-failing and eventually wake up. Let p_i be the first non-failing process to wake up. Then eventually $c = c_i + \lfloor n/2 \rfloor + 1$ will become *true*. Thereafter, it will always be true that $n/2 < d(c_i, c) \leq n$. But then p_i becomes master on its next step, a contradiction.

We next show that after the decision step, no process becomes master or changes the value of b, and c always lies in the v-interval, where v is the decision value of the master. Hence, any process that makes a decision chooses v.

The master sets c to vk, the start of the v-interval, when it makes its decision. Thereafter c is incremented as new processes wake up and is reset to vk by processes that have already decided on v. Since at most $k - 1$ processes wake up after the decision step, c is confined to the v-interval $[vk, (v + 1)k - 1]$. Therefore, any process that makes its decision during this time on the basis of the interval in which c lies will decide on the master's value v.

Any process p_i that wakes up before the decision step has $b_i = \overline{b}$, so the next time that it takes a step after the decision step, it will see $b = 1 - \overline{b} = 1 - b_i$ and will decide on v. In particular, it will not itself become a master. Any process p_j that wakes up after the decision step will set c_j to a value in the interval $[vk, (v + 1)k - 2]$. This is because c is confined to the v-interval, as noted above, and $c_j \neq (v + 1)k - 1$ since at most $k - 2$ *other* processes wakened up and incremented c after the decision step and before p_j wakes up. Thereafter, p_j will always see a value of c in the v-interval. It follows that either $d(c_j, c) \leq n/2$, in which case p_j does nothing, or $d(c_j, c) > n$, in which case p_j decides on v. To see this, we consider three cases. If $c_j = c$, then $d(c_j, c) = |C| > n$. If $c_j \neq c$ and $c \in [c_j, (v + 1)k - 1]$, then $d(c_j, c) \leq d(vk, (v + 1)k - 1) = k - 1 < n/2$. If $c_j \neq c$ and $c \in [vk, c_j]$, then $d(c_j, c) \geq d((v + 1)k - 2, vk) = |C| + vk - ((v + 1)k - 2) = (\lceil 1.5n \rceil - 1) - k + 2 = n + 1 > n$.

It remains to show that every non-failing process eventually makes a decision. First, at most $k - 1$ processes are faulty, and at least $\lfloor n/2 \rfloor + 1 > n/2 > k - 1$ processes wake up before or at the decision step. Hence, at least one of these is non-faulty and is either the master or will make its decision on the first step it takes after the decision step. Forever after, it repeatedly resets c to vk, so c will eventually stabilize to vk. Any process p_j that has not already decided by that time will decide on v at its next step, either because it sees $b \neq b_j$ or because it sees $d(c_j, c) > n$. Thus, all non-failing processes decide on v, the value chosen by the master. ∎

Self Review

1. In the algorithm in Section 9.3, we use b and c to designate the first and second components, respectively, of the ordered pair stored in the shared register. Would the algorithm still be correct if b and c were two separate read-modify-write registers? Justify your answer.

Answer: No. In such a case, more than one process can become a master.

9.4 Reaching Consensus Using a Shared Queue

A concurrent FIFO queue is a linearizable data structure that supports *enqueue* and *dequeue* operations, by several processes, with the usual queue semantics. The enqueue operation inserts a value to the queue and the dequeue operation returns and removes the oldest value in the queue. That is, the values are dequeued in the order in which they were enqueued. If the queue is empty the dequeue operation returns a special symbol. A *peek* operation, of reading the oldest value in the queue without removing it, is *not* supported.

Our goal is to solve the consensus problem for *two* processes only using a single shared queue which is initially *empty*, and (any number of) atomic registers. The solution should be wait-free, that is, it should tolerate the crash (fail-stop) failure of any number of processes. We point out that solving the problem for two processes is the best we can hope for. It is known that there is no wait-free solution to the consensus problem for *three* processes using queues and atomic registers.

Solving the problem with an initialized queue (and two bits) is very simple. Assume the queue initially contains two elements called *winner* and *loser*, where the *winner* element is at the head of the queue. Each process initially writes its input (i.e., its preference) in an atomic bit. Then, it dequeues an element from the queue. If the dequeued element is *winner* the process decides on its own input, otherwise it decides on the input of the other process.

We also point out that consensus has a trivial wait-free implementation for any number of processes using an initially empty queue which supports a peek operation (called augmented queue). Each process inserts its input value into the queue using an enqueue operation, and then uses a peek operation to find out what is the value at the front of the queue and decides on it.

The problem is deceptive and at first glance it seems very simple to solve. The only way to understand its tricky nature, when the queue is initially empty, is by trying to solve it. For that reason we suggest that readers stop at this point and try to solve the problem by themselves.

We present below two solutions. The first algorithm, due to P. Jayanti and S. Toueg (1992), is asymmetric. The algorithm uses one queue and three atomic bits.

CONSENSUS ALGORITHM #1:

shared
  Q: queue, initially empty
  R: atomic bit, initially 0
  input: array [0..1] of bits, initial values are immaterial
local
  val: bit

PROGRAM FOR PROCESS 0
input[0] := input of process 0
enqueue(*Q*, `lose`)

PROGRAM FOR PROCESS 1
input[1] := input of process 1
R := 1

```
val := R
if val = 1 then
    if dequeue(Q) = empty
    then decide(input[0])
    else decide(input[1]) fi
else decide(input[0]) fi
```

```
if dequeue(Q) = empty
then decide(input[1])
else decide(input[0]) fi
```

When process 0 finds that $R = 0$ or when process 1 finds that the queue is empty, each concludes that there is no contention and decides on its own input. Otherwise, they both perform a dequeue operation, and the decision value is the input of the last (second) process to dequeue.

The second consensus algorithm, due to Roy Ramon (2005), is symmetric. The algorithm uses one queue and one atomic bit.

CONSENSUS ALGORITHM #2: `Program for process` i `with input` $in_i \in \{0, 1\}$.

```
shared
    Q: queue, initially empty
    R: atomic bit, initially 0

if in_i = 0 then                                    /* in_i=0 */
    enqueue(Q, 0)                        /* announce arrival */
    if R = 0 then decide(0)                      /* no rival */
    else                                            /* R=1 */
        if dequeue(Q) = empty
        then decide(0)                       /* dequeue last */
        else decide(1) fi                   /* dequeue first */
    fi
else                                                /* in_i=1 */
    R := 1                               /* announce arrival */
    if dequeue(Q) = empty
    then decide(1)                /* no rival or dequeue last */
    else decide(0) fi                       /* dequeue first */
fi
```

If both processes have the same input value then clearly they will decide on that value as either Q or R is not updated. When there are conflicting input values, either (1) one process is faster and decides without noticing that the other process "is around" and in this case the decision value is that of the fast process, or (2) as in the previous algorithm, they both perform a dequeue operation, and the decision value is the input of the last (second) process to dequeue.

Self Review

1. Does the consensus algorithm #1 work correctly if the atomic bit R is replaced with a safe bit?
2. Does the consensus algorithm #1 work correctly if all the three atomic bits are replaced with safe bits?

3. Does the consensus algorithm #2 work correctly if the atomic bit R is replaced with a safe bit?
4. Do any of the consensus algorithms work correctly if the empty queue is replaced with an empty *stack*, every enqueue operation is replaced with a *push* operation and every dequeue operation is replaced with a *pop* operation? Assume the push and pop operations have the usual stack semantics.

Answers: (1) Yes. (2) No. (3) Yes. (4) Yes for both algorithms.

9.5 Impossibility of Consensus with One Faulty Process

In this section we prove one of the most fundamental results in the area of distributed and concurrent computing: There is no consensus algorithm that can tolerate even a single crash failure in an asynchronous shared memory model in which only atomic read/write registers are used. This result was first proved for the message passing model by Fischer, Lynch, and Paterson (1985) and later extended by Loui and Abu-Amara (1987) for the (stronger) shared memory model in which only atomic read/write registers are used.

The proof is by contradiction. We show that any such consensus algorithm must have an infinite run in which each process participates infinitely often (hence all processes are correct) and where no decision is made, thus, violating the requirement that each correct process must eventually reach a decision. The construction of this infinite run is done in two steps:

- First we show that there must exist an empty run (that is, an initial state) in which the final decision value is not yet determined (that is, both 0 and 1 are possible decision values).
- Then, we show that for any finite run x in which the final decision value is not yet determined, and for any process p, there is an extension y of x which includes one step of p and maybe also steps of other processes, so that in y the final decision value is not yet determined.

Starting from the empty run found in step 1, we can now repeatedly apply step 2, to construct the desired infinite run.

9.5.1 A Formal Model

We characterize asynchronous shared memory systems which support only atomic read/write registers by stating several properties that any algorithm operating in such systems must satisfy. The properties do not give a complete characterization of these systems; only those properties are stated that are needed to prove the impossibility result.

We assume a set of *object names* $\{o_0, o_1, \ldots\}$, a set of *process names* $\{p_0, p_1, \ldots, p_{n-1}\}$, and a set of *object states* $\{s_0, s_1, \ldots\}$. An *event* corresponds to an atomic step performed by a process. Events are classified into two types: read events and write events. A read event may not change the state of an object, while a write event updates the state of an object and does not return a value. We use the notation e_p to denote an instance of an arbitrary event at a process p.

A *run* is a pair (f, S) where f is a function which assigns initial states (values) to the objects and S is a finite or infinite sequence of events. When S is finite, we say that the run is finite. An algorithm $Alg = (C, N, O)$ consists of a non-empty set C of runs, a set N of processes, and a set of shared objects O. (We consider only atomic registers in this section.) For any event e_p at a process p in any run in C, the object accessed in e_p must be in O. Let $x = (f, S)$ and $x' = (f', S')$ be runs. Run x' is a *prefix* of x (and x is an *extension* of x'), denoted $x' \leq x$, if S' is a prefix of S and $f = f'$. When $x' \leq x$, $(x - x')$ denotes the suffix of S obtained by removing S' from S. Let $S; S'$ be the sequence obtained by concatenating the finite sequence S and the sequence S'. Then $x; S'$ is an abbreviation for $(f, S; S')$.

The *value* (state) of an object at a finite run is the last value that was written into that object, or its initial value (determined by f) if no process updated the object. We say that process p is *enabled* at run x if there exists an event e_p such that $x; e_p$ is a run. Also, we say that an event e_p is enabled at run x if $x; e_p$ is a run. For simplicity, we write xp to denote either $x; e_p$ when p is enabled in x, or x when p is not enabled in x.

We say that r is a *local* register of p if only p can access r. For any sequence S, let S_p be the subsequence of S containing all events in S which involve p. Runs (f, S) and (f', S') are *indistinguishable* for a set of processes P, denoted by $(f, S)[P](f', S')$, iff for all $p \in P$, $S_p = S'_p$ and $f(r) = f'(r)$ for every local register r of p.[1] When $P = \{p\}$ we write $[p]$ instead of $[P]$, and by $\overline{p}$ we denote the set of all processes excluding p. It is assumed that x is a run of an algorithm if and only if all finite prefixes of x are runs. Without loss of generality, it is assumed that the processes are deterministic. That is, if $x; e_p$ and $x; e'_p$ are runs then $e_p = e'_p$.

The runs of an asynchronous algorithm must satisfy the following properties:

1. If a *write* event which involves p is enabled at run x, then the same event is enabled at any finite run that is indistinguishable to p from x.
2. If a *read* event which involves p is enabled at run x, then some read event of the same object is enabled at any finite run that is indistinguishable to p from x. That is, if p is "ready to read" some value from an object then an event on some other process cannot prevent p from reading from this object although p may read a different value.
3. It is possible to read only the last value that was written into an object or its initial value if the object has not been written yet. A read event has no effect on the state.

It follows from the above properties that if an event e_p is enabled at a run x, then e_p is enabled at any run y (1) that is indistinguishable to p from x, and (2) in which the state of the object accessed during e_p is the same in x and y.

[1] The *indistinguishability* relation is similar to the *looks like* relation as defined on page 59.

9.5.2 Basic Observations

The following lemmas, easy consequences of the properties and definitions, are used in the proofs that follow.

Lemma 9.4 *Let w, x, and y be runs of an algorithm and P a set of processes such that (see Figure 9.3(a)),*

- *$w \leq x$ and $w[P]y$,*
- *the state of all the objects (local and shared) that the processes in P can access are the same in w and y, and $(x - w)$ contains only events of processes in P.*

Then, $z = y; (x - w)$ is a run of the algorithm and $x[P]z$.

Proof: By induction on the length of $(x - w)$. ∎

In order to discuss important properties of asynchronous algorithms, we need the concept of a fair run. Process p is *correct* in a run y if for each run $x \leq y$, if p is enabled at x then some event in $(y - x)$ involves p. A process has *crashed* or is *faulty* in a run if it is not correct in that run. A run is P-fair if all processes in P are correct in it.

Lemma 9.5 *Let x be a P-fair run of an algorithm and let y be a run such that $x[P]y$. Then y is P-fair.*

Proof: Suppose $p \in P$ and let y' be a finite run such that $y' \leq y$. If y' contains no events at p, let x' be *null* (*null* is an empty run). Otherwise, let e'_p be the last event at p in y'. Then there is a corresponding event e_p in x. Let x' be the prefix of x ending in e_p. In either case, since $x[P]y$, it follows that $x'[p]y'$. Thus, if p is enabled in y' then p is enabled in x'. In such a case, it follows that $(x - x')$ and hence $(y - y')$ contain an event involving p. The lemma follows. ∎

Recall that xp denotes either $x; e_p$ when p is enabled in x, or x when p is not enabled in x.

Lemma 9.6 *For every finite run x of an algorithm and every set of processes P there is a P-fair extension y of x such that $x[\overline{P}]y$.*

Proof: For a set of processes $P = \{p_1, \ldots, p_k\}$ we write xP instead of $xp_1 \ldots p_k$.[2] Hence, $xP^2 = xPP = xp_1 \ldots p_k p_1 \ldots p_k$, and $xP^\infty = xPP \ldots = xp_1 \ldots p_k p_1 \ldots p_k \ldots$. Clearly the run xP^∞ is a P-fair extension of x such that $x[\overline{P}]xP^\infty$. ∎

We next define binary consensus algorithms in the context of the formal model we have defined at the previous subsection. For the rest of the section, consensus always means binary consensus.

---

[2] The definition of xP implicitly assumes an order on the process names in P that is respected in the order of events in $\langle xp_1 \ldots p_k \rangle$.

Consensus: A consensus algorithm $Cons = (C, N, O)$ that can tolerate one crash failure is an algorithm for n processes, where each process has a local, binary, read-only *input* register and a local, binary, write-once *output* register. The possible values of the input registers are 0 and 1.[3] The consensus algorithm *Cons* must satisfy the following conditions:

- For every set P of $n-1$ processes, every P-fair run has a finite prefix in which all the correct processes decide on either 0 or 1 (i.e., each correct process writes 0 or 1 into its local output register), the decisions of all processes are the same, and this decision value is equal to the input value of some process.
- The set of runs C includes 2^n empty runs, each with a different boolean combination as initial values in the input registers, and with identical initial values in the remaining objects.
- The set C is limit-closed: if every finite prefix of a run x is in C, then x is in C. Furthermore, for every finite run x in C, and every process p, xp is in C.

9.5.3 The Impossibility Theorem

The impossibility result can now be stated formally as follows:

Theorem 9.7 *There is no consensus algorithm using atomic registers that can tolerate even a single crash failure.*

The proof of Theorem 9.7 uses the following notions, abbreviations, and lemmas. A finite run x is *v-valent* if in all extensions of x where a decision is made, the decision value is v ($v \in \{0, 1\}$). A run is *univalent* if it is either 0-valent or 1-valent, otherwise it is *bivalent*. We say that two univalent runs are *compatible* if they have the same valency, that is, either both runs are 0-valent or both are 1-valent. The notions of univalent and bivalent runs are illustrated in Figure 9.2. Using Lemmas 9.4, 9.5, and 9.6, we can prove the following simple lemma.

Lemma 9.8 *In any consensus algorithm that can tolerate one crash failure, if two univalent runs are indistinguishable for a set P of $n-1$ processes, and the state of all the objects that the processes in P can access are the same at these runs, then these runs must be compatible.*

Proof: Let w and y be univalent runs and P a set of $n-1$ processes, such that $w[P]y$ and the state of all the objects (local and shared) that the processes in P can access are the same at w and y. By Lemma 9.6, w has a P-fair extension, x, in which $x - w$ contains only events of processes in P. (See Figure 9.3(a).) Let w be v-valent, for $v \in \{0, 1\}$. Then by the definition of a consensus algorithm that can tolerate one crash failure, the processes in P decide v in x (i.e., the members of P write v to their output registers). By Lemma 9.4, $z = y; (x - w)$ is a run of the

[3] Formally, the runs in C include only read events, by the associated process, for each input register, and at most one write event, again by the associated process, for each output register.

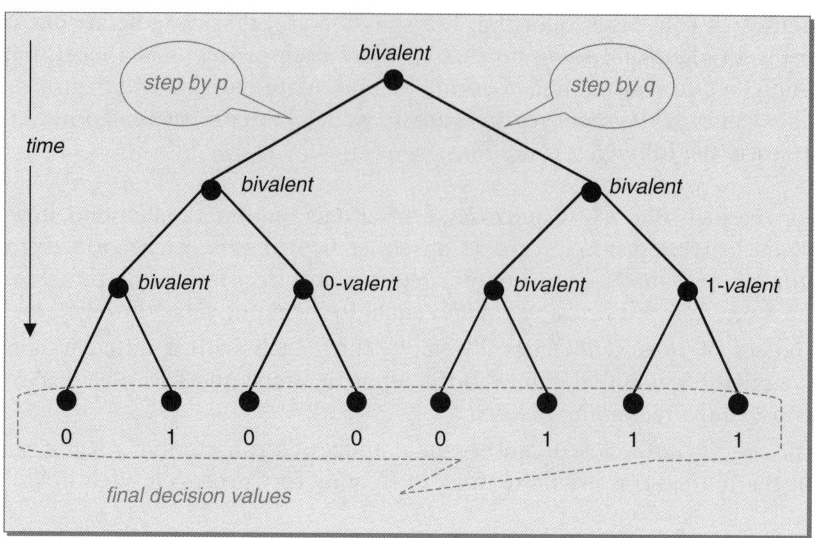

Figure 9.2 Univalent and bivalent runs. The figure shows the runs of an algorithm for two processes. Each edge represents a step by a process, and each path that starts at the root corresponds to a run.

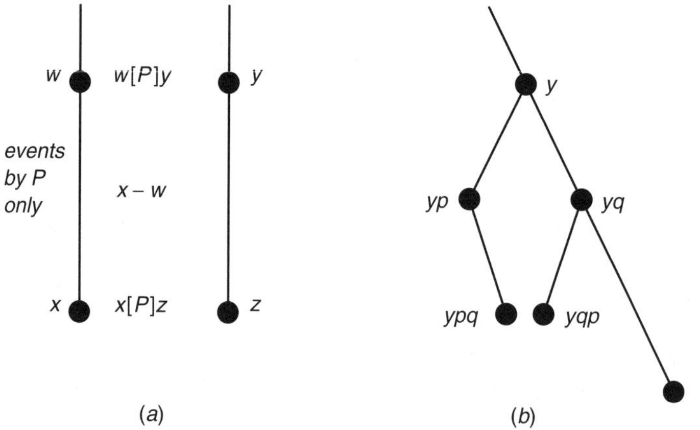

Figure 9.3 Illustration of runs in the proofs of Lemmas 9.4, 9.8, and 9.9.

algorithm such that $z[P]x$, and by Lemma 9.5, z is P-fair. Since the members of P write v to their output registers in z, z is v-valent. Hence, since $y \leq z$, y must also be v-valent. ∎

Lemma 9.9 *Let y be a run of a consensus algorithm that can tolerate one crash failure and let p and q be two different processes such that (1) $y \neq yp$ and $y \neq yq$, and (2) the runs yp and yqp are univalent. Then, the runs yp and yqp must be compatible.*

Proof: We consider the following three possible cases, and show that each one of them leads to the conclusion that the runs yp and yqp are compatible. (See Figure 9.3(b).) Recall that each event is either a read or a write event. We will assume that in the last event in yp process p is accessing some register, say o, and in the last event in yq process q is accessing some register, say o'.

Case 1: In yp the last event is a *read* event by p. Thus, $ypq[\overline{p}]yqp$, and the values of all the objects, which are not local to p, are the same in both ypq and yqp. Hence by Lemma 9.8, ypq and yqp are compatible. Since ypq is an extension of yp, it must be that yp and yqp are also compatible.

Case 2: $o \neq o'$. Since the two next events from y of p and q are independent, $ypq[N]yqp$, and the values of all objects are the same in both ypq and yqp. (Recall that N is the set of all the processes.) As in the previous case, by Lemma 9.8, ypq and yqp are compatible; since ypq is an extension of yp, it must be that yp and yqp are also compatible.

Case 3: $o = o'$ and in yp the last event is a *write* event by p to o. Since p *writes* to o in its next operation from y, the value of o must be the same in yp and yqp. (Here we use the fact that the write by p overwrites the possible changes of o made by q.) Hence, $yp[\overline{q}]yqp$ and the values of all the objects, which are not local to q, are the same in yp and yqp. By Lemma 9.8, yp and yqp are compatible. ∎

Lemma 9.10 *Any consensus algorithm that can tolerate one crash failure has a bivalent empty run.*

Proof: We show that a bivalent empty run must exist. Assume to the contrary that every empty run is univalent. The empty run with all 0 inputs must be 0-valent, and similarly the empty run with all 1 inputs must be 1-valent. Thus, by Lemma 9.8, all the empty runs with all but one 0 inputs are 0-valent, and similarly all the empty runs with all but one 1 inputs are 1-valent. By repeatedly applying this argument i times we get that all the empty runs with all but i 0 inputs are 0-valent, and similarly all the empty runs with all but i 1 inputs are 1-valent. Thus, when i is half the number of processes, we get that there are two empty runs x_0 and x_1 that differ only at the value of a single input, for process p, such that x_0 is 0-valent and x_1 is 1-valent. However, this contradicts Lemma 9.8. Hence, an empty bivalent run exists. ∎

We are now ready to finish the proof of Theorem 9.7.

Proof of Theorem 9.7: We assume to the contrary that *Cons* is a consensus algorithm that can tolerate a single crash failure, and show that this leads to a contradiction. By Lemma 9.10, *Cons* has an empty bivalent run x_0. We begin with x_0 and pursue the following round-robin *bivalence-preserving scheduling* discipline (recall that P denotes a set of processes, x and y denote runs, and yp is an extension of the run y by one event of process p):

```
x := x0; P := ∅; i := 0                         /* initialization */
repeat
      if x has a bivalent extension ypi       /* which involves pi */
      then x := ypi                        /* bivalent extension of x */
```

```
        else P := p_i                 /* no such bivalent extension */
        i := i + 1(mod n)                         /* round-robin */
until |P| = 1.
```

If the above procedure does not terminate, then there is an N-fair run with only bivalent finite prefixes. However, the existence of such a run contradicts the definition of a consensus algorithm that can tolerate one crash failure. Hence, the procedure will terminate with some bivalent finite run x, and a singleton set $P = \{p\}$ for some process p, such that: *for every extension y of x, the run yp is univalent.*

Let $\overline{v} = 1 - v$. Suppose that the run xp is v-valent. Since x is bivalent, there is a (shortest) extension z of x which is $\overline{v}$-valent. (See Figure 9.4(a).)

Let z' be the longest prefix of z such that $x[p]z'$ (notice that either $z' = z$ or $z = z'p$). From the assumption about z', it follows that $z'p$ is $\overline{v}$-valent. (See Figure 9.4(b).)

Consider the extensions of x which are also prefixes of z'. Since $x[p]z'$, it follows that for every y such that $x \leq y \leq z'$, $y \neq yp$. Since xp and $z'p$ are not compatible, there must exist *different* runs y and yq such that (1) $x \leq y < yq \leq z'$, (2) $p \neq q$, and (3) yp and yqp are univalent but not compatible. (See Figure 9.4(c).) However, by Lemma 9.9 the runs yp and yqp must be compatible. A contradiction. ▮

Self Review

1. The validity requirement is that the common decision value must be the input value of some process. A weaker requirement, called the *non-triviality* requirement, is that a consensus algorithm must have different runs that produce different decision values (the values 0 and 1 in the case of binary consensus). Is the non-triviality requirement enough to prove the impossibility of consensus with one faulty process?

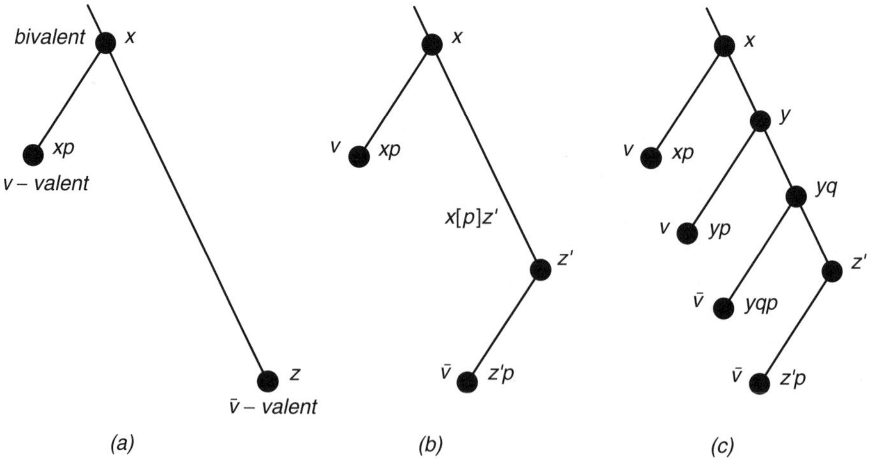

Figure 9.4 Illustration of runs in the proofs of Theorem 9.7.

2. Show that the impossibility result, for asynchronous shared memory systems which support atomic registers, as stated in Theorem 9.7 (page 321), implies a similar result for asynchronous message passing systems.

Answers: (1) Yes, there is a need to modify the proof of Lemma 9.10. (2) We observe that a shared memory system which supports atomic read/write registers can simulate a message passing system which supports send, receive, and even broadcast operations. Hence the impossibility result proved in this subsection holds also for such a message passing system. The simulation is as follows. With each process p we associate an unbounded array of shared registers which all processes can read from but only p can write into. To simulate a broadcast (or sending) of a message, p writes to the next unused register in its associated array. When p has to receive a message, it reads from each process all the new messages.

9.6 The Relative Power of Synchronization Primitives

In previous chapters we have presented and used many different types of objects. In this section we address the following questions: What is the relative power of these objects? Are there problems that can be solved using one type of objects and can not be solved using another type? Obviously, if objects of type o_1 can be implemented by objects of type o_2, then "o_2 can do whatever o_1 can do".

Let us consider the following example. In Section 9.2.2 we have seen that there is a wait-free implementation of consensus for two processes using read-modify-write bits. On the other hand, in Section 9.5, we have proved that there is *no* wait-free implementation of consensus for two processes using atomic registers. It follows easily from these two results that there is no wait-free implementation of read-modify-write bits using only atomic registers, and thus, atomic registers are not "stronger" than read-modify-write bits. To prove that read-modify-write bits are strictly stronger than atomic registers we would need to provide a specific wait-free implementation.[4]

Generalizing from this example, the ability to solve consensus would be our main tool for answering the following type of questions: Given two objects o_1 and o_2, is there a wait-free implementation of a single object of type o_1 from objects of type o_2 and atomic registers? It turns out that the answer depends on whether the consensus problem can be solved using these two objects.

Consensus number: *The consensus number of an object of type o, denoted CN(o), is the largest n for which it is possible to solve consensus for n processes using any number of objects of type o and any number of atomic registers. If no largest n exists, the consensus number of o is infinite.*

The notion of a consensus number was first introduced by M. P. Herlihy (1991) as a measure for the computational power of shared objects. The importance of

[4] Recall that a wait-free implementation of a concurrent object is one that guarantees that any process can complete any operation in a finite number of steps, regardless of the speed of the other processes.

this notion as a tool for exploring the relative power of different shared objects is captured in the following theorems.

Theorem 9.11 *Let o_1 and o_2 be two objects such that $CN(o_1) < CN(o_2)$. Then, in a system with $CN(o_2)$ processes:*

- There is no wait-free implementation of an object of type o_2 from objects of type o_1 and atomic registers;
- There is a wait-free implementation of an object of type o_1 from objects of type o_2 and atomic registers.

Proof: From the definition of a consensus number it follows that it is not possible to implement consensus using objects of type o_1 and registers; however, it is possible to implement consensus using objects of type o_2 and registers. Thus, it is not possible to implement objects of type o_2 from objects of type o_1 and registers.

In the next section we prove that if the consensus number of an object o is n, then in a system with at most n processes, any object which has sequential specification has wait-free linearizable implementation using atomic registers and objects of type o. This result implies that there is a wait-free implementation of an object of type o_1 from objects of type o_2 and atomic registers. ∎

Theorem 9.11 addresses the relative power of objects with different consensus numbers. The next theorem is about objects with the same consensus number.

Theorem 9.12 *Let o_1 and o_2 be two objects with consensus number n. Then, using any number of additional atomic registers:*

- The objects o_1 and o_2 can wait-free implement each other when the number of processes is less than or equal to n;
- The objects o_1 and o_2 do not necessarily wait-free implement each other when the number of processes is more than n.

Proof: As mentioned in the proof of Theorem 9.11, in the next section we prove that if the consensus number of an object o is n, then in a system with n or less processes, any object which has sequential specification has wait-free linearizable implementation using atomic registers and objects of type o. This result implies that there is a wait-free implementation of an object of type o_1 from objects of type o_2 and atomic registers, and vice versa. As for the second part, there are examples of objects with the same consensus number which do not (wait-free) implement each other when the number of processes is large (Problem 9.24). ∎

From the results presented so far in this chapter it follows that:

1. CN(atomic-register) $= 1$ (Section 9.5)
2. CN(read-modify-write bit) ≥ 2 (Section 9.2.2)
3. CN(queue) ≥ 2 (Section 9.4)

Consensus Number	Object
1	atomic-register, atomic-snapshot, safe^m, regular^m
2	test-and-set, fetch-and-increment, fetch-and-add, swap, queue, stack, read-modify-write bit, fetch-and-increment^m, fetch-and-add^m
$\Theta(\sqrt{m})$	swap^m
$2m-2$	m-register assignment, atomic-register^m ($m > 1$)
∞	compare-and-swap, LL/SC, sticky-bit, queue^2 3-valued read-modify-write, augmented-queue

Figure 9.5 The consensus hierarchy. Objects are classified by their consensus number: the maximum number of processes that can reach consensus using multiple instances of the object and atomic registers.

4. CN(3-valued read-modify-write register) $= \infty$ (Section 9.2.1)
5. CN(compare-and-swap) $= \infty$ (Page 309)

These results imply, for example, that we can not construct a wait-free FIFO queue using only atomic registers. Many important results are known about the consensus number of specific objects. The exact consensus numbers of several interesting objects are summarized in the table in Figure 9.5.

In the table we refer also to *multi-objects* in which processes may simultaneously access several objects in one atomic operation. That is, given a shared memory system with a set of component objects O, and a parameter m, the multi-object O^m is an object in which a process is allowed to simultaneously (and atomically) execute operations on up to m of the component objects of type O. Examples are a *register^m* multi-object which allows processes to read and write up to m registers in a single atomic operation; and a *queue^2* multi-object which allows processes to enqueue and dequeue up to two queues in a single atomic operation.

The *register^m* object generalizes the *m-register assignment*, proposed by M. P. Herlihy (1991), which supports writes to m registers in a single atomic operation, and the *atomic-snapshot* object, which supports reads of multiple registers in a single atomic operation. An *augmented queue* is a queue that in addition to the usual enqueue and dequeue operations, also supports a *peek* operation which returns the oldest value in the queue but does not remove it from the queue.

The consensus hierarchy: *The consensus hierarchy (also called the wait-free hierarchy) is an infinite hierarchy of objects such that the objects at level i of the hierarchy are exactly those objects with consensus number i.*

In the consensus hierarchy (1) no object at one level together with registers can implement any object at a higher level, and (2) each object at one level together with registers can implement any object at a lower level.

Classifying objects by their consensus numbers is a powerful technique for understanding the relative power of shared objects. Modern multi-processor (and also uni-processor) architectures support powerful synchronization primitives. The observations made in this section can help in deciding whether these primitives are sufficient for efficiently implementing important non-blocking objects and data structures.

Self Review

1. Is there an object with consensus number less than 1?
2. Let o_1, o_2, and o_3 be three objects such that $CN(o_1) < CN(o_3)$ and $CN(o_2) < CN(o_3)$. Is it true that it must be the case that in a system with $CN(o_3)$ processes, there is no wait-free implementation of an object of type o_3 from objects of types o_1 and o_2, and atomic registers?
3. Does the fact that $CN(\text{fetch-and-increment}) = CN(\text{queue}) = 2$ imply that there is a wait-free implementation of a queue object from fetch-and-increment objects and atomic registers, for $n = 3$?
4. Does the fact that $CN(\text{fetch-and-increment}^2) < CN(\text{queue}^2)$ imply that there is *no* wait-free implementation of a queue object from fetch-and-increment objects and atomic registers, for $n \geq 2$?

Answers: (1) No. (2) No, there are examples which show that the claim is incorrect. (3) No. (4) No, in fact it is an interesting open problem whether such an implementation exists! See Problem 9.29.

9.7 The Universality of Consensus

An object o is *universal* if any object which has sequential specification has wait-free linearizable implementation using atomic registers and objects of type o. In 1991, M. P. Herlihy proved that consensus is universal. This result immediately implies that in a system of n processes, objects with consensus number at least n, such as compare-and-swap and LL/SC, are universal objects. In what follows we prove the universality of consensus.

9.7.1 Basic Definitions

As usual, our model of computation consists of an asynchronous collection of n processes, numbered 1 through n, that communicate via shared objects. To simplify the presentation in this section, it is convenient to use the notion of a consensus object instead of a consensus algorithm (the two notions are essentially the same).

Consensus. A consensus object o supports one operation: $o.propose(v)$, satisfying:

- *Agreement*: In any run, the $o.propose()$ operation returns the same value, called the *consensus value*, to every process that invokes it.

- *Validity*: In any run, if the consensus value is v, then some process invoked $o.propose(v)$.

When the value $v \in \{0, 1\}$ the object is called binary consensus object, and when the value $v \in \{0, \ldots, k\}$ the object is called k-consensus object.

Specifying Wait-free Objects. We assume any wait-free object, o, is specified by two relations:

$$apply \subset \text{INVOKE} \times \text{STATE} \times \text{STATE},$$

$$\text{and } reply \subset \text{INVOKE} \times \text{STATE} \times \text{RESPONSE},$$

where INVOKE is the object's domain of invocations, STATE is its domain of states (with a designated set of start states), and RESPONSE is its domain of responses.

- The *apply* relation denotes a state change based on the pending invocation and the current state. Invocations do not block: it is required that for every invocation and current state there is a target state.
- The *reply* relation determines the calculated response, based on the pending invocation and the updated state. It is required that for any pair INVOKE × STATE there is a target state and a response.

Intuitively, an object o begins in a start state and pending invocations enable the later occurrence of an *apply* event, which updates the state. A *reply* event does not update the object state, but enables the later response. In what follows, we assume that basic objects used to implement other objects are wait-free.

Observation 9.13 *A k-consensus object has a wait-free implementation from binary consensus objects and atomic bits, for any $k \geq 2$.*

Proof: To implement a singe k-consensus object, we use $\lceil \log k \rceil + 1$ binary consensus objects, which are numbered 0 through $\lceil \log k \rceil$, and k atomic bits which are numbered 1 through k and are initialized to 0. To propose a value $v \in \{0, \ldots, k\}$, a process p does the following: (1) it sets the atomic bit number v to 1; (2) it proposes the binary encoding of v, bit by bit, to the binary consensus objects in an increasing order starting from object number 0. If at some point during the second step the bit p has proposed is not accepted as the consensus value at the corresponding binary consensus object, p stops proposing v, scans the atomic bits and chooses one of the bits that are set to 1, say v', and starts proposing the value v'. This procedure repeats itself until p succeeds in proposing some value from $\{0, \ldots, k\}$ to all the $\lceil \log k \rceil + 1$ binary consensus objects. This value is the final consensus value. ∎

For the purpose of the universal construction below, we resolve any nondeterminism, and assume that there is a single start state. Given these restrictions, we may assume, without loss of generality, that the object's domain of states is the set of strings of invocations, and that the function from INVOKE × STATE to STATE simply appends the pending invocation to the current state.

Theorem 9.14 *Binary consensus (n-consensus) object is universal in a system with n processes, for any positive n. That is, any wait-free object can be implemented using atomic registers and binary consensus (n-consensus) objects, in a system with n processes.*

Proof: Let o be an an arbitrary wait-free object which can be specified as described earlier. We present a (universal) construction that implements o from (wait-free) consensus objects and atomic registers. Since, by Observation 9.13, wait-free n-consensus objects can be implemented from wait-free binary consensus objects and atomic bits, we will use in the construction below only n-consensus objects.

The basic idea behind the construction is as follows: the object o is implemented as a linked list which is represented as an unbounded array. The entries of the array represent a sequence of invocations applied to the object. A process invokes an operation by threading a new invocation onto the end of the list. The current state of the objects corresponds to applying the sequence of invocations (in order, one at a time) to the object.

In the actual implementation there are two principal data structures:

1. For each process i there is an unbounded array, $Announce[i][1..\infty]$, each element of which is a *cell* which can hold a single invocation. The $Announce[i][j]$ entry describes the j-th invocation (operation name and arguments) by process i on o. Only i can write the entries of this array and everybody else can read them.
2. The object itself is represented as an unbounded array $Sequence[1..\infty]$ of process-id's, where each $Sequence[k]$ is an n-consensus object. Intuitively, if $Sequence[k] = i$ and $Sequence[1], \ldots, Sequence[k-1]$ contains the value i in exactly $j-1$ positions, then the k-th invocation on o is described by $Announce[i][j]$. In this case, we say that $Announce[i][j]$ has been *threaded.*

The universal construction of object o is described below as the code process i executes to implement an operation on o with invocation *invoke*. In outline, the construction works as follows: process i first announces its next invocation, and then threads unthreaded, announced invocations onto the end of *Sequence*. It continues until it sees that its own operation has been threaded, computes a response, and returns. To ensure that each announced invocation is eventually threaded, the correct processes first try to thread any announced, unthreaded cell of process ℓ into entry $Sequence[k]$, where $\ell = k \pmod n + 1$. This "helping" technique guarantees that once process ℓ announces an operation, at most n other operations can be threaded before the operation of process ℓ is threaded.

A UNIVERSAL CONSTRUCTION: `program for process` $i \in \{1,\ldots,n\}$ `with invocation` *invoke*

```
shared
   Announce[1..n][1..∞] array of cells which range over INVOKE ∪ {⊥},
       initially all cells are set to ⊥
   Sequence[1..∞] array of n-consensus objects
local to process i
   MyNextAnnounce integer, initially 1         /* next vacant cell */
   NextAnnounce[1..n] array of integers, initially 1
                                                /* next operation */
   CurrentState ∈ STATE, initially the initial state of o   /* i's view */
   NextSeq integer, initially 1            /* next entry in Sequence */
   Winner range over {1, ... ,n}          /* last process threaded */
   ℓ range over {1, ... ,n}                   /* process to help */

          /* write invoke to a vacant cell in Announce[i] */
1  Announce[i][MyNextAnnounce] := the invocation invoke
2  MyNextAnnounce := MyNextAnnounce + 1
3  while ((NextAnnounce[i] < MyNextAnnounce) do
                        /* continue until invoke is threaded */
                   /* each iteration threads one operation */
4       ℓ := NextSeq (mod n) + 1      /* select process to help */
5       while Announce[ℓ][NextAnnounce[ℓ]] = ⊥          /* valid? */
7       do
6            ℓ := ℓ + 1     /* not valid; help next process */
7       od
9       Winner := Sequence[NextSeq].propose(ℓ)       /* propose ℓ */
                   /* a new cell has been threaded by Winner */
                                        /* update CurrentState */
10      CurrentState :=
            apply(Announce[Winner][NextAnnounce[Winner]], CurrentState)
11      NextAnnounce[Winner] := NextAnnounce[Winner] + 1
12      NextSeq := NextSeq + 1
13 od
14 return(reply(invoke, CurrentState))
```

Process i keeps track of the first index of *Announce*[i] that is vacant in a local variable denoted *MyNextAnnounce*, and first (line 1) writes the invocation into *Announce*[i][*MyNextAnnounce*], and (line 2) increments *MyNextAnnounce* by 1. To keep track of which cells it has seen threaded (including its own), process i keeps n counters in an array *NextAnnounce*[1..n], where each *NextAnnounce*[j] is one plus the number of times i has read cells of j in *Sequence*. Hence *NextAnnounce*[j] is the index of *Announce*[j] where i looks to find the next operation announced by j. We notice that, having incremented *MyNextAnnounce* (line 2):

> *NextAnnounce*[i] = *MyNextAnnounce* − 1 until the current operation of process i has been threaded.

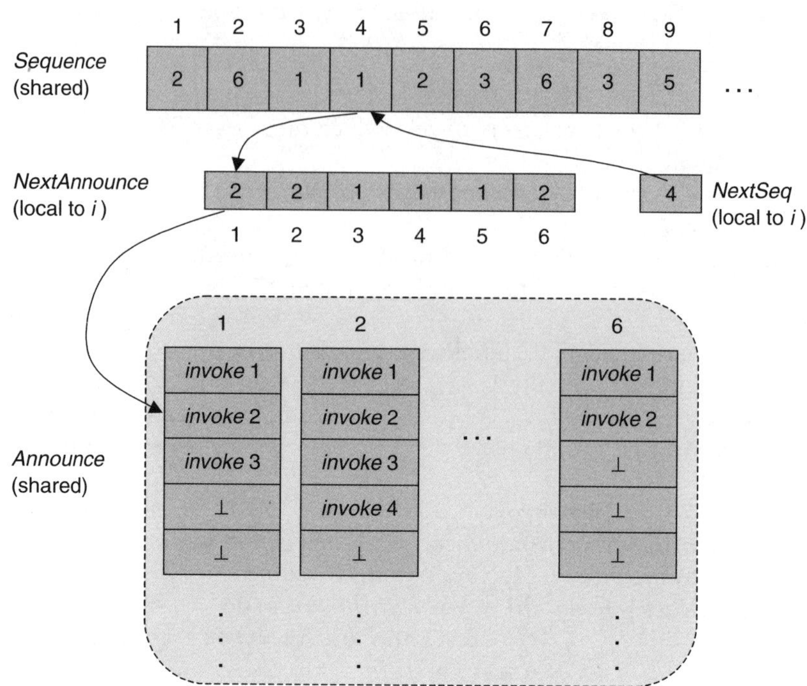

Figure 9.6 Partial state of a run of the universal construction. (See text.)

This inequality is thus the condition (line 3) in the while loop (lines 3–13) in which process i threads cells. Once process i's invocation is threaded (and $NextAnnounce[i] = MyNextAnnounce$), it exits the loop and returns the associated response value (line 14). Process i keeps an index *NextSeq* which points to the next entry in $Sequence[1..\infty]$ whose element it has not yet accessed.

Figure 9.6 illustrates the shared data structures and some structures local to process i, at a point when processes $1, 2, 3$, and 6 have each threaded two operations, and process 5 has threaded one operation. From process i's point of view, only three operations have been threaded so far, and a 4th operation is in the process of being threaded.

To thread cells, process i proposes (line 9) the id of process ℓ to the consensus object $Sequence[NextSeq]$, and after a decision is made, records the consensus value for $Sequence[NextSeq]$ in the local variable *Winner* (line 9). The value in $Sequence[NextSeq]$ is the identity of the process whose cell has just been threaded.

After choosing to help process ℓ (line 4), process i checks (line 5) that $Announce[\ell][NextAnnounce[\ell]]$ contains a valid operation invocation. As discussed above, process i gives preference (line 4) to a different process for each cell in *Sequence*. Thus, all active processes will eventually agree to give preference to any pending invocation, ensuring it will eventually be threaded.

Once process i knows the id of the process whose cell has just been threaded, as recorded in *Winner*, it can update (line 10) its view of the object's state with the winner invocation, and increment its records of process *Winner*'s successfully threaded cells (line 11) and the next unread cell in *Sequence* (line 12). Having successfully threaded a cell, process i returns to the top of the while loop (line 3).

Eventually, the invocation of process i will be threaded and the condition at the while loop (line 3) will be *false*. At this point, the value of the variable *CurrentState* is the state of the object after process i's invocation has been applied to the object. Based on this state, process i can return the appropriate response. ∎

An immediate implication of Theorem 9.14 relates the notions of *universality* with the notion of *consensus number*.

Theorem 9.15 *An object o is universal in a system with n processes if and only if the consensus number of o is at least n.*

Proof: Assume that o is *universal* in a system with n processes. Then, by definition, any object has a wait-free implementation using atomic registers and objects of type o. Thus, also consensus for n processes has a wait-free implementation using atomic registers and objects of type o, which implies that the consensus number of o is at least n.

Assume that the consensus number of o is n. Since consensus is universal in a system with n processes, any object which can implement consensus must also be universal in a system with n processes. Since the consensus number of o is at least n then, by definition, consensus has wait-free implementation using atomic registers and objects of type o. Thus o is universal in a system with n processes. ∎

The universality result provides a way to identify those objects that are most powerful for a given system. This knowledge can help in deciding which basic objects to use when building a new system or designing a new algorithm. The universal construction does not provide a practical method for constructing wait-free objects using universal objects. We have tried to keep the universal construction as simple as possible. It is possible to modify the construction so that it uses only bounded space; however, such general constructions should not be used to implement specific objects as they are less efficient compared to specialized implementations.

Self Review

1. Let o be a universal object in a system of 100 processes. Is it the case that o must also be universal in a system of 101 processes?
2. Does it follow from Theorem 9.14 that atomic registers can be implemented using binary consensus objects?
3. In Figure 9.6, the number of processes is six. List the names of all the processes that process i can be (out of these six processes).
4. Consider Figure 9.6. What are the possible values of *MyNextAnnounce* of process i?

5. Does the fact that CN(fetch-and-increment) $= CN$(queue) $= 2$ imply that there is a wait-free implementation of a queue object from fetch-and-increment objects and atomic registers, for $n = 2$?

Answers: (1) No. (2) No. (3) Process i can be process 4, process 5, or process 6, but it can not be any one of the other three processes. (4) The value of *MyNextAnnounce* of process i is either 2 or 3. (5) Yes, by Theorem 9.15, since a fetch-and-increment object is universal for $n = 2$.

9.8 Bibliographic Notes

9.1

The *consensus problem* is to design an algorithm in which all correct processes reach a common decision based on their initial opinions. The problem was formally defined by M. Pease, R. Shostak, and L. Lamport in [279]. The original requirement given in [279] (called interactive consistency) is slightly stronger than the agreement requirement we use, and requires that all non-faulty processes decide on a vector which includes the inputs of all non-faulty processes. The definition of the consensus problem as we have defined it is the one that is generally accepted today. Dozens of papers have been published on solving the consensus problem in various models. A few examples are [114, 122, 131, 134, 135, 228, 237, 279].

9.2

The consensus algorithms using read-modify-write bits have appeared in [237]. In [237], it is proved that there is no consensus algorithm for three or more processes using (any number of) atomic read-modify-write bits and atomic registers that can tolerate *two* crash failures (Problem 9.5).

9.3

The consensus algorithm that works without shared memory initialization is from [137]. Initialization failures relates to the notion of self-stabilizing systems defined by Dijkstra [110]. However, Dijkstra considers only non-terminating control problems such as the mutual exclusion problem, whereas in this section it is shown how to solve the consensus problem in which a process makes an irrevocable decision after a finite number of steps.

In [136] the *wakeup problem* is defined and solved in a similar model to ours (assuming that the shared memory is not initialized) and it is shown that there are reductions between the wakeup problem and the consensus problem. By using these reductions, it is possible to show that the following results follow from those presented in [136]: (1) In the absence of faults, it is possible to reach consensus on one of k values using a single 5-valued shared register; (2) There is no consensus algorithm that can tolerate $\lceil n/2 \rceil$ failures; (3) Let P be a consensus algorithm that can tolerate $\lceil n/2 \rceil - 1$ failures, and let V be the set of shared memory values used by P. Then $|V| = \Omega(n^{0.63})$; and (4) There is a consensus algorithm that can tolerate $\lceil n/2 \rceil - 1$ failures, which uses a single $8n$-valued register. The result presented in Section 9.3 improves this upper bound.

9.4

The solution to consensus using initialized queue is from [166]. Two solutions to consensus using initially empty queue were presented in Section 9.4. Algorithm #1 is from [192]. Algorithm #2 was proposed by Roy Ramon as an answer to a question that I gave in a take home final exam in a distributed computing course (2005).

9.5

The impossibility result that there is no consensus algorithm that can tolerate even a single crash failure in an asynchronous shared memory model was first proved for the message passing model by Fischer, Lynch, and Paterson [135], and has later been extended by Loui and Abu-Amara for the (stronger) shared memory model in which only atomic read/write registers are used [237]. The underlying ideas and much of the terminology of Section 9.5 are adapted from [135, 237].

Systems where it is possible to access *several* shared registers in one atomic step are investigated [166, 257], see Problem 9.16 (page 339) for a few of the results. Two other celebrated impossibility results in distributed computing are that it is impossible to solve wait-free set-consensus (see Problem 9.17), and wait-free$(2n-2)$-renaming using atomic read/write registers (see Problem 9.18). The first of these two results was proved in [73, 172, 302], while the second result was proved in [172].

9.6

Most of the results in this section and the next one are based on Herlihy's work on wait-free synchronization [166]. In [166], Herlihy classified shared objects by their consensus number: the maximum number of processes that can reach consensus using multiple instances of the object and atomic registers, and found the consensus number of many important objects. For additional results regarding the consensus hierarchy see [187, 236]. A recent survey which covers many related impossibility results can be found in [130].

The notion of multi-objects and most of the results mentioned in Figure 9.5 regarding multi-objects are from [11, 257]. In [257], the properties of the *register*^{m} multi-object which allows processes to read and write up to m registers in a single atomic operation are studied. The *register*^{m} object generalizes the *m-register assignment*, proposed in [166], which supports writes to m registers in a single atomic operation; and the *snapshot* objects, which support reads of multiple registers in a single atomic operation. The first constructions of an atomic snapshot object from atomic registers were proposed independently in [26] and [3]. The result stated in Problem 9.30 (page 340) is from [300].

The ability to access multiple memory locations in one atomic step is useful in implementing concurrent lock-free data structures. For that reason, lock-free implementations of atomic multi-word operations from strong (universal) single-word operations were proposed in several papers; see for example [9, 34, 51, 171, 185, 307]. See also the discussion on page 191. There are many constructions of an atomic multi-writer register from weaker types of registers; see for example [234].

9.7

The power of various shared objects has been studied extensively in shared memory environments where processes may fail benignly, and where every operation is wait-free. Objects that can be used, together with atomic registers, to build wait-free implementations of any other object are called *universal objects*. Previous work on shared objects provided methods, called universal constructions, to transform sequential specifications of arbitrary shared objects into wait-free concurrent implementations that use universal objects [166, 289]. In particular, Plotkin showed that sticky bits are universal [289], and independently, Herlihy proved that consensus objects are universal [166]. See also the discussion on page 191 regarding other general constructions. In [16, 250], the universality of consensus in the presence of Byzantine process failures (as opposed to crash failures) is proved when less than a third of the processes are faulty.

The universal construction presented on page 331 conceptually mimics the original construction from [166], and is a modified version of the construction from [250]. A bounded space version of the universal construction from [166] appears in [192].

Additional References

Two more approaches for solving consensus are the use of randomization and failure detectors. A good survey paper on randomized asynchronous consensus algorithms using atomic registers is [45]. Solving consensus using unreliable failure detectors is considered in [90, 91, 295]. Solving consensus (and other problems) in the presence of memory faults (as opposed to process faults) has been investigated in [8, 189].

9.9 Problems

The problems are divided into several categories. See page 23 for a detailed explanation.

Problems based on Section 9.2

∘ 9.1 Design a (very simple) consensus algorithm for two processes using *three* test-and-set bits.

∘ 9.2 Consider the consensus algorithm for two processes from page 309. Is the following modification of the algorithm correct or not?

The algorithm uses only *two* read-modify-write bits, called x and y, which are both initially set to 0.

ANOTHER CONSENSUS ALGORITHM FOR TWO PROCESSES: `program for process` p_i `with input` $in_i \in \{0,1\}$.

```
shared
x, y read-modify-write bits range over {0, 1}, initially both 0

⟨ x = in_i; if x = 1 then decide(1) ⟩
else
        ⟨ if y = 0 then y := 1; decide(in_i) ⟩
        else  if x = 0 then decide(0) else decide(1 − in_i) fi
        fi
fi
```

◦ 9.3 Consider the consensus algorithm for many processes from page 310. Explain why this algorithm can not tolerate two crash failures.

◦◦ 9.4 Prove that there is no consensus algorithm for *two* (or more) processes using *one* atomic read-modify-write bit, even if the processes never fail.

•• 9.5 Prove that there is no consensus algorithm for *three* or more processes using (any number of) atomic read-modify-write bits that can tolerate *two* crash failures.

Problems based on Section 9.3

◦ 9.6 Assume a model similar to that of Section 9.3 where a single uninitialized read-modify-write register is used. Show that in such a model, there is no consensus algorithm that can tolerate $\lceil n/2 \rceil$ failures.

◦◦ 9.7 Consider the consensus problem in an *uninitialized* shared register model where the (single) shared register is accessed via atomic read-modify-write operations. We have presented a consensus algorithm for n processes which can tolerate up to $\lceil n/2 \rceil - 1$ failures and which uses a single $(2\lceil 1.5n - 1 \rceil)$-valued read-modify-write register.

Assume that instead of $\lceil n/2 \rceil - 1$ failures there are only t failures, where $0 \le t \le \lceil n/2 \rceil - 1$. Modify the algorithm so that it uses as little space as possible. What is the size of the shared register needed in your modified algorithm as a function of t and n?

•◦ 9.8 Assume a model similar to that of Section 9.3 where a single uninitialized read-modify-write register is used. Show that, *in the absence of faults*, it is possible to reach consensus on one of k values using a single 5-valued shared register.

•• 9.9 Assume a model similar to that of Section 9.3 where a single uninitialized read-modify-write register is used. Prove the following: Let P be a consensus algorithm that can tolerate $\lceil n/2 \rceil - 1$ failures, and let V be the set of shared memory values used by P. Then $|V| = \Omega(n^{0.63})$.

Problems based on Section 9.4

◦ 9.10 Modify algorithm #1 in such a way that the two atomic bits *input*[0] and *input*[1] are not needed.

◦◦ 9.11 We have given a very simple wait-free solution to the consensus problem from two processes using an *initialized* queue and two bits (page 316). Give a simple wait-free solution to the consensus problem from two processes using a single *initialized* queue, without using any additional objects.

◦• 9.12 The following algorithm is based on Peterson's mutual exclusion algorithm from page 32. Is the algorithm correct? Justify your answer.

CONSENSUS ALGORITHM FOR TWO PROCESSES:

```
shared
    Q: queue, initially empty
    input: array [0..1] of bits, initial values are immaterial
    b: array [0..1] of bits, initial values are false
    turn: atomic bit, initial values is immaterial
```

PROGRAM FOR PROCESS 0:

```
input[0] := input of process 0
enqueue(Q, win)
b[0] := true
turn := 1
if (b[1] = true and turn = 1)
then decide(input[1])
else   if dequeue(Q) = win
       then decide(input[0])
       else decide(input[1]) fi
fi
```

PROGRAM FOR PROCESS 1:

```
input[1] := input of process 1
b[1] := true
turn := 0
if (b[0] = true and turn = 0)
       if dequeue(Q) = win
       then decide(input[1])
       else decide(input[0]) fi
else decide(input[1]) fi
```

Problems based on Section 9.5

◦◦ 9.13 Consider Lemmas 9.4, 9.5, and 9.6. Which of the three properties that an asynchronous algorithm must satisfy (see page 319) is used in the proof of each lemma?

○• 9.14 Show that the impossibility result from Section 3.2, as stated in Theorem 3.4 (page 119), follows from Theorem 9.7 (page 321).

○• 9.15 Recall that in the election problem, each correct process that starts participating eventually terminates and exactly one process is elected as a leader.

We have shown that in asynchronous systems, there is no consensus algorithm that can tolerate even a single process fault, when using only atomic read/write registers. Prove that a similar result holds also for leader election. (You may use the known impossibility result for consensus or prove it directly.)

•○ 9.16 We have discussed shared memory systems which support atomic read and write operations (i.e., atomic registers). Here we focus attention on somewhat stronger systems in which it is possible to read or write several shared registers in one atomic step. We say that a system supports atomic m-register operations (or register^m objects) if it is possible for a process to read *and* write m registers in one atomic step (allows mixing both read and write in the same atomic step).

The register^m object is of particular theoretical interest: Each successive value of m provides a quantum increase in the synchronization power of the primitive. Hence, these primitives populate an infinite hierarchy between test-and-set bits (which can be used to solve wait-free consensus for exactly two processes), and read-modify-write objects (which can be used to solve wait-free consensus for any number of processes).

1. Show that in a system that supports atomic m-register operations it is possible to solve wait-free consensus for up to $2m - 2$ processes ($m > 1$).
2. Show that in a system that supports atomic m-register operations it is not possible to solve wait-free consensus for more than $2m - 2$ processes ($m > 1$).

Would the above result hold if mixing both read and write in the same atomic step is not allowed.

•• 9.17 The *(n, k)-set consensus problem* is to find a solution for n processes, where each process starts with an input value from some domain, and must choose some participating process' input as its output. All n processes together may choose no more than k distinct output values. An (n, k)-set consensus object (or algorithm) is an object which solves the (n, k)-set consensus problem. We notice that the $(n, 1)$-set consensus problem is the familiar consensus problem for n processes.

Prove the following result: For any $2 \leq k \leq n$, a wait-free (n, k)-set consensus object can not be implemented using any number of wait-free $(n, k - 1)$-set consensus objects and atomic registers.

•• 9.18 The *(n, k)-renaming problem* is to find a solution for n processes, where each process starts with a *unique* (integer) id and must choose a *unique* value in the range $1, \ldots, k$. An (n, k)-renaming object (or algorithm) is an object which solves the (n, k)-renaming problem.

It is known that for $n > 1$ it is possible to implement a wait-free $(n, 2n-1)$-renaming object using atomic registers only. Prove that for $n > 1$ it is *not* possible to implement a wait-free $(n, 2n-2)$-renaming object using atomic registers only.

∘• 9.19 Prove that while it is easy to implement a wait-free $(n, 2n-2)$-renaming object using wait-free $(n, 1)$-set consensus objects and atomic registers, it is *not* possible to implement a wait-free $(n, 1)$-set consensus object using wait-free $(n, 2n-2)$-renaming objects and atomic registers. Hint: Use the result from Problem 9.5.

Problems based on Section 9.6

∘ 9.20 Show that $CN(\text{augmented-queue}) = \infty$.

∘• 9.21 Show that $CN(\text{queue}^2) = \infty$.

∘• 9.22 Show that for every positive integer m, there is an object with consensus number m.

∘∘ 9.23 Explain what exactly it means for a set of objects to *implement* an object. Defining formally the notion of *implementation* is rather tricky.

∘• 9.24 Give an example of two objects with the same consensus number which do not wait-free implement each other when the number of processes is too large.

∘• 9.25 A shared memory object O is *commutative* if the relative order of any two operations can not be determined by the non-participating processes. Examples of commutative objects include test-and-set, fetch-and-add, fetch-and-complement. Prove that: If O is a commutative object then $CN(O^m) \leq 2$, for any $m \geq 1$.

•∘ 9.26 Show that $CN(\text{test-and-set}) = CN(\text{swap}) = CN(\text{fetch-and-add}) = 2$.

∘• 9.27 What is the consensus number of test-and-test-and-set bit?

∘• 9.28 A concurrent stack is a linearizable data structure that supports push and pop operations, by several processes, with the usual stack semantics. The push operation pushes a value onto the top of the stack and the pop operation returns and deletes the most recent value in the stack. Prove that $CN(\text{stack}) = 2$.

? 9.29 Is there a wait-free (linearizable) implementation of a queue object from a set of test-and-set objects, fetch-and-add objects, swap objects, and atomic registers, for $n \geq 3$?

•• 9.30 Prove that, if O is an object with consensus number $c > 2$, then $CN(O^m) = \Omega(c\sqrt{m})$, and if in addition O supports a read operation, then $CN(O^m) = \Omega(cm)$. (Neither of these lower bounds can be improved.) The notion of multi-object is defined on page 327.

•∘ 9.31 Implement: (1) a regular register from safe registers; (2) a single-writer single-reader atomic register from regular registers; (3) an atomic multi-writer multi-reader atomic register from atomic single-writer single-reader registers.

∘• 9.32 Implement an atomic snapshot object from atomic registers.

Problems based on Section 9.7

∘∘ 9.33 Assume that in the universal construction (page 331) we replace lines 4–7 with the statement "$\ell := i$" . Would the universal construction satisfy wait-freedom? Would it satisfy non-blocking? Justify your answer.

∘• 9.34 Let o_1 be a universal object in a system of n processes, and assume that o_2 is not universal in a system of n processes. Prove that there is no non-blocking implementation of o_1 from any number of atomic registers and objects of type o_2 in a system of n processes.

∘• 9.35 Prove that consensus is universal by providing a *bound space* universal construction.

Chapter 10

Timing-based Algorithms

10.1 Timing-based Systems

The complexity of synchronization in a concurrent environment may depend on timing assumptions. In an asynchronous system, no timing assumptions are made about the relative speeds of the processes, while timing-based systems assume the existence of bounds on the speeds of the processes.

We focus in this chapter on a timing-based system which provides an interesting abstraction of the timing details of concurrent systems. We assume that there is an upper bound on memory access time. This assumption is inherently different from the asynchronous model where no such bound exists. The appeal of such a system lies in the fact that while it abstracts from implementation details, it is sometimes a better approximation of the real concurrent systems compared to the asynchronous model, and enables more efficient solutions to be obtained.

We will assume that the basic atomic operations are reads and writes; however, we add some assumptions about the speed of the processes as follows.

- *Timing assumption*: There is an upper bound δ_i on the time it takes for a single access to the shared memory by process i.
  For the rest of this section we assume that $\Delta = \max\{\delta_i\}$. That is, Δ is an upper bound on the time it takes for the slowest process in the system to execute a statement which involves an access to the shared memory.
- *Explicit delay statements*: Each process can delay itself by executing the statement:

  delay (d), for some constant d.

  A *delay* statement *delay*(d) by a process p delays p for at least d time units before it can continue.

We need to slightly modify the definition of time complexity for timing-based systems. In addition to the number of accesses to the shared memory, we now also count (separately) the total amount of explicit delay executed in the entry and exit codes.

Before we proceed, we distinguish between two inherently different models. One assumes that the upper bound on the speed of the processes is *known a priori*, and the other assumes that such a bound exists but is *unknown*.

- In the *known-delay* model, it is assumed that individual processes *know* the upper bound Δ. Consequently, *delay* statements can refer directly to this value, and a process can force every other (non-faulty) process to take at least one step by executing the statement *delay*(Δ).
- In the *unknown-delay* model, it is assumed that some upper bound exists, but it is *not* known to individual processes *a priori*. Consequently, *delay* statements can not refer to Δ directly. In this model we want a single algorithm that works for all possible values of Δ without referring to its actual value. The term *time-adaptive* algorithms is sometimes used in the literature for algorithms that are designed for the unknown-delay model.

For the known-delay model:

1. In Section 10.3, we present a mutual exclusion algorithm that, in the absence of contention, grants access to a critical section after only five accesses to shared memory, and in the presence of contention, delays the winning process for only $2 \cdot \Delta$ time units. But first, in Section 10.2, we present another interesting mutual exclusion algorithm for that model.
2. In Section 10.5, we present a consensus algorithm where, in the absence of contention, a process decides after five accesses to shared memory. In the presence of contention, a process needs to take five steps, and has to explicitly delay itself once for Δ time units. The algorithm is also *wait-free*, which means that it can tolerate any number of crash failures.

For the unknown-delay model:

1. In Section 10.6, we present a wait-free consensus algorithm where, in the absence of contention, a process decides after a *constant* number of its own steps.
2. In Section 10.7, we present a mutual exclusion algorithm where, in the presence of contention, a process needs to delay itself for $2 \cdot \Delta$ time units before entering its critical section. The algorithm has a "warm-up" period during which a process might have to access n registers before entering the critical section. The algorithm always provides fast access in the absence of contention.

All the algorithms in this chapter use atomic registers only.

10.2 Mutual Exclusion with Known Delays

The first and most simple mutual exclusion algorithm for the known-delay model, in which there is a known bound on the speed of the processes, is due to M. J. Fischer (1987). The algorithm is defined formally below and is illustrated in Figure 10.1. The algorithm uses only one shared register named x. A process first waits until $x = 0$ and then assigns its *id* to x, delays itself and then checks x. If x has not been changed the process can safely enter its critical section, otherwise it repeats this procedure. The processes are numbered 1 through n.

FISCHER'S TIMING-BASED MUTUAL EXCLUSION ALGORITHM: `process i's program.`

Initially: $x = 0$.

```
repeat  await (x = 0);
        x := i;
        delay(Δ);
until   x = i;
critical section;
x := 0;
```

In this algorithm the *delay* statement plays the role of ensuring that after a process finishes the *delay* statement, the value of x remains unchanged until some process leaving its critical section sets it to 0.

Properties of Fischer's Timing-based Algorithm:

- Satisfies mutual exclusion and deadlock-freedom.
- Starvation of individual processes is possible.
- *Does not guarantee fast access*: Even in absence of contention the winning process must delay itself. That is, the algorithm does not distinguish between

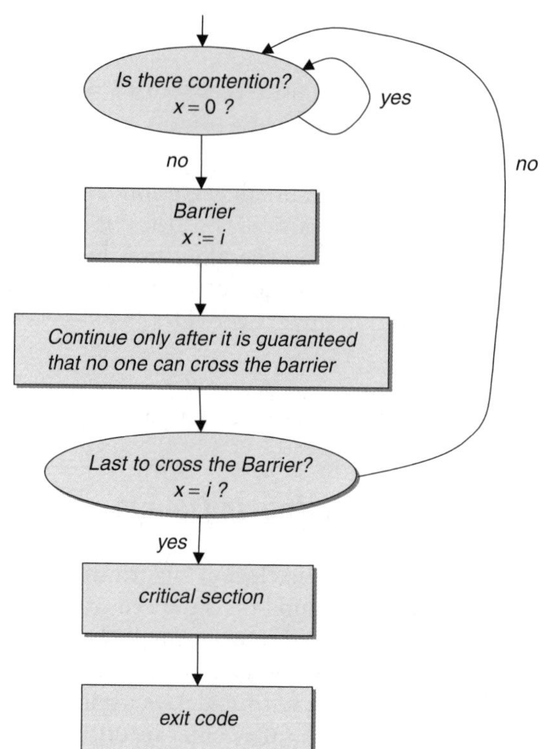

Figure 10.1 Schematic for Fischer's timing-based algorithm. The last process to cross the Barrier is the one which gets to enter the critical section.

the cases where there is contention and the case where there is no contention, and behaves the same in both cases.

- *Low process time complexity*: In the case when there is contention (of even n processes), the winner accesses the shared memory at most four times and has to delay itself for Δ time units before it can enter its critical section. (Why four and not just three?) Hence, also the system response time is a constant.
- Only one shared register is used.

The arguments for proving all the above properties are not difficult and are left as an exercise for the reader. The disadvantage of this solution is that even in the absence of contention a process needs to delay itself. Fischer's algorithm, and also Lamport's algorithm (page 42), raise the question whether there is an algorithm where:

1. In the absence of contention, as in Lamport's algorithm, a process can always enter its critical section and exit it fast without having to delay itself; and
2. In the presence of contention, as in Fischer's algorithm, a process does not have to check the status of all other n processes before it can enter its critical section, but may need to delay itself for some time.

One way to do it is to design an adaptive algorithm as discussed in Section 3.2.2 (page 105). However, for a timing-based system it is possible to design even more efficient algorithms. In the next section we present an algorithm which has these two desired properties.

Self Review

1. Is Fischer's algorithm correct when the processes are numbered 0 through $n - 1$?
2. Assume that we delete line 3 ($delay(\Delta)$) from Fischer's algorithm. Is the resulting algorithm deadlock-free?
3. Does it matter if we change the order of the two statements at lines 2 and 3 of Fischer's algorithm?

Answers: (1) No. (2) Yes. (3) Yes, the algorithm would not satisfy mutual exclusion.

10.3 Fast Mutual Exclusion with Known Delays

In this section we combine ideas from Lamport's algorithm (page 42) and Fischer's algorithm (page 345) to obtain a timing-based based mutual exclusion algorithm that performs well in the absence of contention. The algorithm was developed by R. Alur and G. Taubenfeld (1992). Only five accesses to the shared memory are needed to enter a critical section in the absence of contention, and in the presence of contention, the winning process may need to delay itself for $2 \cdot \Delta$ time units. Also, at most three accesses to the shared memory are needed to execute the exit code.

10.3.1 The Algorithm

The algorithm is defined formally below and is illustrated in Figure 2.4 (page 43). The processes are numbered 1 through n.

ALUR–TAUBENFELD'S FAST TIMING-BASED ALGORITHM: process i's program.

Initially: $y = 0$, $z = 0$.

```
start: x := i;
       await (y = 0);
       y := i;
       if x ≠ i then delay(2·Δ);
                     if y ≠ i then goto start fi;
                     await (z = 0)
                else z := 1 fi;
       critical section;
       z := 0;
       if y = i then y := 0 fi;
```

The mutual exclusion property crucially depends on the assumption about the speeds of the processes. We recall that it is assumed that the value of Δ is at least the time taken by the slowest process to complete an access to a shared register. In a time-sharing environment this is actually an assumption about the fairness of the scheduler.

Properties of the Fast Timing-based Algorithm:

- Satisfies mutual exclusion and deadlock-freedom.
- Starvation of individual processes is possible.
- *Fast access*: In the absence of contention a process executes only a constant number of steps (namely, five) from the location *start* to its critical section, and only a constant number of steps (at most three) to execute the exit code.
- *Process time complexity*: In the case when there is contention, the winner may need to access the shared memory at most seven times and has to delay itself for $2 \cdot \Delta$ time units before it can enter its critical section. (Why seven accesses and not just six?) Hence, also system response time is a constant.
- Only three shared registers are used.

The property of fast access in the absence of contention is obvious: in the absence of contention, process i executes three write statements and two read statements before entering its critical section, and executes at most two write statements and one read statement in its exit code. Similarly, it is easy to check that the process time complexity is as mentioned above.

Remark: The timing-based algorithm fails to guarantee mutual exclusion if the timing constraints are not met. That is, if we remove all the *delay* statements from the algorithm, the resulting algorithm does not satisfy the mutual exclusion property. By using a simple technique, due to Lynch and Shavit (1992), it is possible to modify the algorithm so that it will guarantee mutual exclusion (but not deadlock-freedom) even when the timing constraints on the speed of the processes are not met. This is done by simply replacing the critical section of the algorithm with the following code:

```
c and d are shared registers, initially d = 0.
   c := i;
   if d ≠ 0 then goto start fi;
   d := 1;
   if c ≠ i then goto start fi;
   critical section;
   d := 0;
```

We leave the proof that this modification actually works for the reader.

10.3.2 Correctness Proof

We next prove the mutual exclusion and deadlock-freedom properties, but first we introduce the notion of fair timing-based transition systems which will help us present the proof in a more formal way. This definition is similar to the definition given in the correctness proof of the fast algorithm of Section 2.3, adapted to reflect the timing assumption.

Fair timing-based transition systems: The behavior of our algorithm can be formalized using the model of fair timing-based transition systems. A *state* of the algorithm is completely described by the values of the shared registers x, y, and z, and the values of the location counters of all the processes. We will use ℓ_i to denote the location counter of process i. Thus, ℓ_i ranges over the set 0..10 (0 is the remainder code). A *run* of the algorithm is a finite or an infinite sequence

$$\sigma = s_0 \xrightarrow{e_1} s_1 \xrightarrow{e_2} \cdots$$

of states s_i and process indices e_i satisfying

1. *Initialization*: In the initial state s_0, all the registers, except for x, have the value 0.
2. *Consecution*: For $i \geq 0$, state s_{i+1} is the state resulting from executing a single transition of process e_i in state s_i.
3. *Fairness*: For every process i, in any infinite run, either process i takes infinitely many steps, or there is some $k \geq 0$ such that it is in its remainder code (ℓ_i equals 0) in all states $s_{k'}$ with $k' \geq k$.
4. *Timing constraint*: For process i, let j and $k > j$ be indices such that (i) $e_j = e_k = i$, (ii) $e_{j'} \neq i$ for $j < j' < k$, and (iii) process i is about to execute a *delay* statement in state s_j. Then for every process $i' \neq i$, it can not be the case that $\ell_{i'}$ is in $\{3, 4, 7, 10\}$ in state s_j, and $e_{j'} \neq i'$ for all $j \leq j' < k$.

While defining the consecution relation, the *delay* statement is treated like a skip statement: its only effect is to change the value of the location counter. A process is in its critical section when its location counter is 8; the location counter changes to 10, after it executes the assignment $z := 0$. Also note that when the control of process i is at location 5, it moves to location 1 if $y \neq i$.

The timing constraint captures the crucial aspect of the real time assumptions about the speeds of various processes needed for the correctness proof. It says that by the time process i executes one of the *delay* statements, every other process i' at one of the locations 3, 4, 7, or 10 executes at least one statement. The assumption that the parameter Δ for the *delay* statement is at least the time taken by the slowest process to complete an access to a shared register clearly implies the timing constraint. We are now ready to prove the correctness of the algorithm.

Theorem 10.1 *The fast timing-based algorithm satisfies mutual exclusion.*

Proof: As in Lamport's fast mutual exclusion algorithm, process i first sets x to i, and then checks the value of y. When it finds $y = 0$, it sets y to i and then checks the value of x. Let us say that process i enters its critical section along path α if it finds $x = i$ at this step. It should be clear that at most one process can enter its critical section along path α. If a process finds $x \neq i$ then it delays itself. The *delay* statement plays two roles:

1. Let us say that process i enters its critical section along path β if it finds $y = i$ after the *delay* statement. The delay ensures that if process i finds $y = i$ after the *delay* statement, no other process can change the value of y until process i sets y to zero in its exit code, and hence it follows that at most one process can enter along path β. To see this we observe that, as in Fischer's protocol, the *delay* statement ensures that, while process i delays itself, every other process j that got past the **await**($y = 0$) statement finishes the assignment $y := j$. Furthermore, while process i delays itself, a process j, in the exit code, that got past the condition in the if statement finishes the assignment $y := 0$.

2. Recall that in Lamport's protocol, the *delay* statement is replaced by a loop that checks n registers, one for every possible contender. However, unlike in Lamport's case, a process entering its critical section along path β does not know whether or not some other process entered its critical section along path α. An additional binary register z is used for this purpose. A process entering its critical section along path α sets z to 1, and a process entering its critical section along path β must wait until z is 0 before entering. Here the second role of the *delay* statement becomes important. It ensures that the process which enters its critical section along path α sets z to 1 *before* a process executing path β gets a chance to test z. To see this observe that a process j entering its critical section along path α executes three steps between the **await**($y = 0$) statement and the entry to its critical section. If process j is before the assignment $y := j$ when process i reaches its *delay* statement, then process i will find $y \neq i$ after it finishes the delay. If process j is after the assignment $y := j$ when process i reaches its *delay* statement, then since process i delays itself by time $2 \cdot \Delta$, it will find $z = 1$ after the delay, unless process j leaves its critical section in the meantime. Thus, if process i entering along path β finds $y = i$ and $z = 0$, it can be sure that no other process is about to enter the critical section along path α. (Notice that in the description of the roles of the *delay*, we implicitly used the timing constraint.)

The exit code needs to reset both the locks y and z to ensure progress. This is tricky: there may be a process waiting at **await**($z = 0$) which can enter its critical section immediately after z is reset, and there may be a process waiting at **await**($y = 0$) which can enter its critical section along path α immediately after y is reset. It seems that doing the two reset actions in any order leads to a possible violation of the mutual exclusion requirement. However, observe that if process i is in its critical section and $y \neq i$ then process i must have entered along path α, and there is some other contending process which will eventually win along path β, so in this case there is no need to reset y. On the other hand, if $y = i$ then there is no process waiting at the **await**($z = 0$) statement, and hence a process waiting at **await**($y = 0$) can be safely released. ∎

Theorem 10.2 *The fast timing-based algorithm is deadlock-free.*

Proof: We want to prove that if some process starts executing its algorithm then some process eventually enters its critical section.

Consider a run $\sigma = s_0, s_1, \ldots$ of the algorithm. We will prove that the deadlock-freedom property holds for this run. The proof is by contradiction. Suppose it does not. The following sequence of assertions leads to the desired contradiction. In the following sequence, each assertion is followed by a brief justification.

1. *If $z = 1$ then some process is in its critical section.*
   A process can set z to 1 only before entering its critical section, and it always sets z to 0 when it exits its critical section. Hence if $z = 1$ then somebody has entered its critical section and has not exited it yet.
2. *There exists k such that $\ell_i \in 1..7$ in s_k for some i, and $\ell_j \neq 8$ for all j in all states $s_{k'}$ with $k' \geq k$.*
   This is because the run σ violates deadlock-freedom by assumption.
3. *There exists m such that $\ell_i \in 1..7$ in s_m for some process i, and in all states $s_{m'}$ with $m' \geq m$, $z = 0$ and $\ell_j \notin 8..10$ for all processes j.*
   Since the run is fair, starting from state s_k (assertion 2) every process eventually leaves the locations 9..10, and from this, and from assertion 1, assertion 3 follows.
4. *If process j is in its entry code in state $s_{m'}$ (i.e., $\ell_j \in 1..7$) for $m' \geq m$, then eventually $\ell_j = 1$.*
   This follows from the facts that process j keeps taking steps, it never enters its critical section, and by assertion 3, can not get blocked at location 7 (since z stays 0).
5. *There is some state s_p, $p \geq m$, with $y \neq 0$.*
   Process i of assertion 3 (which is in its entry code) will eventually reach location 1 according to assertion 4, and then, if y stays 0 it will eventually execute the assignment at location 2.
6. *In all states $s_{p'}$ with $p' \geq p$, y is non-zero.*
   Following the state s_p, no process is ever at location 10, which is the only place where y is reset.
7. *There is $q \geq p$ and process j such that $y = j$ in all states $s_{q'}$ with $q' \geq q$.*
   From assertion 6, it follows that for process j, if $\ell_j \neq 3$ in s_p, then in all the following states also $\ell_j \neq 3$ (no process can get past the await statement at location 1). Thus, after all the processes at location 2 in state s_p execute the assignment, the value of y cannot change.
8. *For every process i, it is always the case that $y = i$ implies $l_i \notin 0..1$. (0 is the remainder code.)*
   As long as $y = i$ process i can return to location $l_i \in 0..1$ only after entering the critical section and exiting it. Upon exiting either it sets $y = 0$ or it finds $y \neq i$.
9. From assertions 6 and 3, there exists $r \geq q$ such that $y = j$ and $\ell_j = 1$ in the state s_r. This is a contradiction to assertion 8. ∎

Self Review

1. Does it matter if we change the order of the last two statements of the fast algorithm (lines 9 and 10)?

2. Does it matter if we change the order of the two statements at lines 5 and 6 of the fast algorithm?
3. Is the fast algorithm still correct if we replace the last statement (line 10), with the statement $y = 0$?
4. Is the algorithm correct if we replace the statement "**await**($y = 0$)" in line 2, with the statement: **if** $y \neq 0$ **then goto start fi**?
5. Is the algorithm correct if we replace the statement "**await**($z = 0$)" in line 6, with the statement: **if** $z \neq 0$ **then goto start fi**?

Answers: (1) Yes. (2) No. (3) No, it would not satisfy mutual exclusion. (4) Yes. (5) No, it would not satisfy deadlock-freedom.

10.4 Consensus with Known Delays

In this section we present a very simple consensus algorithm that works in the *known-delay* model using only one atomic register. As we have already mentioned, such a model where there is a known upper bound on memory access time is inherently different from an asynchronous model where no such bound exists. This model is stronger than the asynchronous model enabling us to design fault-tolerant algorithms for problems, such as consensus, that are unsolvable in the asynchronous model.

The algorithm presented below is *wait-free*, no process takes infinitely many steps without deciding. The requirement of wait-freedom means that one process can not prevent another process from reaching a decision, and thus the algorithm must tolerate an arbitrary number of process failures.

Let Δ denote the *known* upper bound on memory access time. The algorithm has a register called x which is initially set to $\perp$, and which will eventually contain the decision value. The code to be executed by a process with input v is shown below.

A TIMING-BASED CONSENSUS ALGORITHM: `program for process with input` $v \in \{0, 1\}$.

shared x ranges over $\{\perp, 0, 1\}$, initially $x = \perp$

1 **if** $x = \perp$ **then** $x := v$ **fi**
2 *delay*(Δ)
3 *decide*(x)

A process with input v first checks the value of x and if there is no current decision value, it sets x to v (line 1). The *delay* statement (line 2) ensures, as in the case of Fischer's mutual exclusion algorithm (page 345), that the value of x will stay unchanged after some process finishes the delay. After the delay the process can safely decide on the value of x (line 3).

Properties of the Algorithm:

- The algorithm is *wait-free*, which means that it can tolerate any number of crash failures.

- Before deciding, a process needs to take two or three steps, and has to explicitly delay itself once for Δ time units.
- One 3-valued atomic register is used.
- The number of participating processes is unbounded.

The proofs of these properties are simple and are left as an exercise.

Self Review
1. What is wrong with the algorithm if line 2 (*delay*(Δ)) is deleted?

Answer: Processes may decide on conflicting values.

10.5 Fast Consensus with Known Delays

In this section we present a *fast* consensus algorithm that works in the *known-delay* model using only atomic registers. That is, in the absence of contention, a process decides after a *constant* number of its own steps without using a *delay* statement. The algorithm is also *wait-free*, no process takes infinitely many steps without deciding. The algorithm was discovered by R. Alur and G. Taubenfeld (1992).

10.5.1 The Algorithm

Let Δ denote the *known* upper bound on memory access time. The algorithm uses the following data structures: For each input $v \in \{0, 1\}$, there is a flag $x[v]$, initially *false*. We use $\overline{v}$ to denote the complement of v. The register y is initially $\perp$, and contains the current decision value. The code to be executed by a process with input v is shown below.

A FAST TIMING-BASED CONSENSUS ALGORITHM: `program for process with input` $v \in \{0, 1\}$.

shared
  y ranges over $\{\perp, 0, 1\}$, initially $y = \perp$
  $x[0..1]$: array of boolean, initially $x[0] = x[1] = false$

$x[v] := true$
if $y = \perp$ **then** $y := v$ **fi**
if $x[1 - v]$ **then** *delay*(Δ) **fi**
decide(y)

A process with input v sets the flag $x[v]$, and if there is no current decision value, then it executes $y := v$. The current decision value changes only if two processes with different inputs read $y = \perp$ before any assignment to y finishes. But in this case, both the flags $x[0]$ and $x[1]$ will be set, and every process is forced to execute the *delay* statement before deciding. The *delay* statement ensures, as in the case of Fischer's mutual exclusion algorithm, that the value of y will stay unchanged after some process finishes the delay.

Properties of the Algorithm:

- The algorithm is *fast*, which means that in absence of contention, a process decides after five steps without using a *delay* statement. (This is computed simply by counting the number of steps.)
- The algorithm is *wait-free*, which means that it can tolerate any number of crash failures.
- In the worst case, a process needs to take five steps, and has to explicitly delay itself once for Δ time units.
- Two atomic bits and one 3-valued atomic register are used.
- The number of participating processes is unbounded.

10.5.2 Correctness Proof

We now present the correctness proof of the algorithm. Recall that an *execution* α of the system is an alternating sequence $s_0 \stackrel{e_0}{\rightarrow} s_1 \stackrel{e_1}{\rightarrow} \cdots$ of configurations s_i and events e_i such that (1) the initial configuration s_0 satisfies some initial conditions, and (2) every configuration s_{i+1} is derived from the previous configuration s_i by executing the event e_i. Define the *explicit delay* of an event e, denoted by $d(e)$, to be m if e is the *delay* statement *delay*(m), and 0 otherwise. A *time assignment* τ for an execution α is a mapping that assigns a real-valued occurrence time τ_i *to* each event e_i in α such that:

1. the occurrence times are non-decreasing;
2. if α is infinite then the sequence of occurrence times is unbounded;
3. whenever two events e_i and e_j are consecutive steps of the same process, then the difference $\tau_j - \tau_i$ is greater than $d(e_i)$.

The last requirement captures the assumption regarding the lower bounds on execution speeds.

The assumption about the time needed to access shared memory is reflected in the following notion of admissibility. Let Δ be a positive real number. A timing assignment τ for an execution α is said to be Δ-*admissible* iff whenever two events e_i and e_j are consecutive steps of the same process, $\tau_j - \tau_i \leq \Delta + d(e_i)$. An execution α is Δ-*admissible* if there exists a Δ-admissible time assignment for α. Finally, a *timed execution* is a pair (α, τ) such that τ is a Δ-admissible time assignment for α.

Theorem 10.3 *The algorithm satisfies the properties of validity, agreement, and wait-freedom in the known-delay model.*

Proof: Observe that no process ever writes $\perp$ to y, and writes its input to y if it finds $y = \perp$. It follows that when a process decides, the value of y is in $\{0, 1\}$. To show validity, suppose all processes start with the same input, say, 0. Then $y \in \{\perp, 0\}$ is an invariant of the execution. It follows that no process ever decides on 1 in this case.

To prove agreement, consider a timed execution (α, τ). Suppose that two processes decide on conflicting values in α. This implies that there exists a process with input 0 that writes to y, as well as a process with input 1 that writes to y. Let i_0 be the least index such that a process with input 0 finds $y = \perp$ at step i_0, and i_1 be the least index such that a process with input 1 finds $y = \perp$ at step i_1. Since the flags $x[v]$ are set at the beginning, it follows that $x[0]$ is set in all states following s_{i_0} and $x[1]$ is set in all states following s_{i_1}. Consequently, in state s_i, with $i = max(i_0, i_1)$, both $x[0]$ and $x[1]$ are set, and $y = \perp$.

Let j be the smallest index such that some process writes to y at step j. Clearly, $y \neq \perp$ holds in all states $s_{j'}$ for $j' > j$. Hence, $j > i$, and every process that decides executes the *delay* statement. Let p be the first process to decide, say, at step k.

We want to show that no process changes the value of y after step k, and this implies agreement. Assume to the contrary. Suppose q writes to y at step $k' > k$. Suppose that p checks the if clause of the *delay* statement at step m. It follows that $m > j$, and in state s_m, $y \neq \perp$. This means that q checks the value of y at some step $m' < m$. Since p executes the *delay* statement, $t_k - t_m > \Delta$. This implies $t_{k'} - t_{m'} \geq t_k - t_m > \Delta$, a contradiction to the upper bound Δ on the speed of q.

Each process executes a bounded number of steps, and there is no waiting. Wait-freedom follows trivially. ∎

Self Review

1. Assume that we delete line 3 from the consensus algorithm. What is the problem with the modified algorithm?
2. Does it matter if we change the order of the two statements at lines 2 and 3 of the consensus algorithm?

Answers: (1) Processes may decide on conflicting values. (2) Yes.

10.6 Fast Consensus with Unknown Delays

In this section we present a consensus algorithm that works in the unknown-delay model using only atomic registers, which was discovered by R. Alur, H. Attiya, and G. Taubenfeld (1994). This algorithm is an adaptation of the consensus algorithm for the known-delay model from Section 10.5. The algorithm presented below is *wait-free*, no process takes infinitely many steps without deciding. Furthermore, the algorithm is *fast*; in the absence of contention, a process decides after a *constant* number of its own steps, without using a *delay* statement.

10.6.1 The Algorithm

Let Δ denote the unknown upper bound on memory access time. Initially, each process starts with some estimate, say 1, for Δ. The algorithm proceeds in rounds. Each process has a preference for the decision value in each round; initially this preference is the input value of the process. In each round r, processes execute a timing-based consensus algorithm with their current estimate of Δ, using their preferences for this round as inputs. The algorithm guarantees that once processes have the same preference in some round, they will remain in agreement and will eventually decide. The timing-based algorithm used in each round avoids conflicting decisions even if the current estimate for Δ is wrong. If no decision is made in a round then the processes advance to the next round, using a larger estimate for the time bound Δ. Eventually, processes either decide, or they end up using the correct estimate, in which case, the timing-based algorithm guarantees that they will decide.

The algorithm uses the following shared data structures: an infinite array $x[1..\infty, 0..1]$ of bits, and an infinite array $y[1..\infty]$ where the possible values of each $y[i]$ are $\{\perp, 0, 1\}$. The decision value is written to the shared register *out*. In addition, each process p_i has a local register v_i, containing its current preference and a local register r_i, containing its current round number. The estimate d_r used in round r is $r!$. The reason for choosing this estimate is that the sequence $d_r = r!$ provides optimal time complexity.

In round r, process p_i first flags its preference v by writing 1 to $x[r, v]$. Then, the process checks the lock on this round by reading $y[r]$, and writes its preference to $y[r]$, if $y[r]$ still has its initial value $\perp$. Process p_i then reads the flag for the other preference (denoted by $\overline{v}$). If $x[r, \overline{v}]$ is not set, then every process that reaches round r with the conflicting preference $\overline{v}$ will find $y[r]$ set to v. Consequently, process p_i can safely decide on v, and it writes the decision value to *out*. Otherwise, it waits for d_r (the estimate of Δ for the current round), and then sets its preference for the next round by reading $y[r]$.

FAST CONSENSUS WITH UNKNOWN DELAYS: `program for process` p_i `with input` in_i.

```
constants d_r = r! for all r
shared
        x[1..∞, 0..1] infinite array of bits, initially all 0
        y[1..∞] infinite array, ranges over {⊥, 0, 1}, initially all ⊥
local
        r_i integer, initially 1
        v_i bit, initially in_i
output out ranges over {⊥, 0, 1}, initially ⊥

while out =⊥ do
      x[r_i, v_i] := 1
      if y[r_i] =⊥ then y[r_i] := v_i fi
      if x[r_i, v̄_i] = 0   then out := v_i
                             else delay(d_{r_i})
                                  v_i := y[r_i]
                                  r_i := r_i + 1 fi
od
decide(out)
```

Two processes with conflicting preferences for round r will not resolve the conflict only if both of them find $y[r] =\perp$ first, and one of them proceeds and chooses its preference for the next round before the other one finishes the assignment to $y[r]$.

However, if each process is required to finish the assignment within time Δ, and the value of d_r exceeds Δ, then this can not happen. Also notice that if all processes in a round have the same preference, then a decision is reached in that round. These observations, together with the fact that the sequence $d_1, d_2, \ldots$ increases without a bound, ensure termination. The next section includes a complete proof of correctness for this algorithm.

Properties of the Algorithm:

- The algorithm is *wait-free*, which means that it can tolerate any number of crash failures.
- The algorithm is *fast*: in the absence of contention, a process decides after a *constant* number of its own steps (Problem 10.23, page 370).
- If every step finishes within time Δ, the algorithm guarantees that a process decides within time $O(\Delta \cdot fac^{-1}(\Delta))$ irrespective of the failures of other processes, where fac^{-1} is the inverse of the factorial function;[1] notice that $fac^{-1}(r) = \Theta(\frac{\log r}{\log\log r})$ (Problem 10.26, page 370).
- Infinitely many atomic registers are used.
- The number of participating processes is unbounded.

10.6.2 Correctness Proof

We now present the correctness proof of the algorithm. We assume that a process keeps taking idling steps after it has decided. Thus an infinite execution contains infinitely many steps by every non-faulty process.

Lemma 10.4 *If p_i decides on a value v then $in_j = v$ for some p_j.*

Proof: If there are two processes that have different inputs then the lemma holds trivially. Suppose all processes start with the same input *in*. Consider the following formula ϕ:

$$\forall i.\, v_i = in \wedge \forall r.\, y[r] \in \{\bot, in\} \wedge out \in \{\bot, in\}\ .$$

Initially ϕ holds. It is easy to check that each transition of the algorithm preserves ϕ. Thus ϕ is an invariant of the algorithm. The lemma follows immediately. ∎

Let $r \geq 1$ and $v \in \{0,1\}$. Formally, a process p_i *reaches* round r, if it executes statement 2 with $r_i = r$. A process p_i *prefers* the value v in round r, if $v_i = v$ when p_i reaches round r. A process p_i *commits* to the value v in round r, if it executes the assignment $out := v$ with $r_i = r$.

Lemma 10.5 *If all processes reaching round r have the same preference v for round r, then all non-faulty processes reaching round r commit to v in round r.*

---

[1] For a real number $d > 0$, $fac^{-1}(d)$ is the smallest r such that $r! \geq d$.

Proof: Suppose all processes reaching round r have the same preference v for round r. Thus, whenever some process p_i sets the bit $x[r, v_i]$ to 1, v_i equals v. Consequently, $x[r, \overline{v}] = 0$ is an invariant. Now consider a process p reaching round r. Assuming that p continues to take steps in round r, p will find $x[r, \overline{v}]$ unset at statement 4, and commit to the value v. ∎

Lemma 10.6 *If some process commits to v in round r then all processes reaching round $r+1$ prefer v in round $r+1$.*

Proof: Suppose some process p commits to v in round r. Since p finds $x[r, \overline{v}]$ unset at statement 4, it follows that every process with preference $\overline{v}$ for round r finds $y[r] \neq \perp$ at statement 3. This implies that for a committed value v, $y[r] \neq \overline{v}$ is an invariant of the program. Since a process decides on its preference for round $r+1$ by reading $y[r]$, the lemma follows. ∎

Lemma 10.7 *No two processes decide on conflicting values.*

Proof: Suppose two processes decide on conflicting values. This means that there exist non-faulty processes p_0 and p_1 such that p_0 commits to 0 in round r and p_1 commits to 1 in round r'. We will obtain a contradiction.

First suppose that $r \neq r'$. Without loss of generality, let $r < r'$. Since p_0 commits to 0 in round r, from Lemma 10.6 all processes reaching round $r+1$ prefer 0 in round $r+1$, and consequently, from Lemma 10.5, if non-faulty, commit to 0 in round $r+1$. Since p_1 reaches round $r+1$, and is non-faulty, it follows that p_1 commits to 0 in round $r+1$; a contradiction.

Now suppose that $r = r'$. In round r, process p_0 prefers 0, and process p_1 prefers 1. If process p_0 finds $x[r, 1]$ unset at statement 4, then process p_1 must find $x[r, 0]$ set at statement 4, and vice versa. Consequently, it is not possible that both commit in round r. ∎

Next, we prove that every correct process eventually chooses a number and terminates. Using the notion of admissibility, defined on page 354, we can now state and prove the following lemma which guarantees termination.

Lemma 10.8 *In a Δ-admissible execution, if $d_r \geq \Delta$ then all processes reaching round $r+1$ have the same preference in round $r+1$.*

Proof: Assume $d_r \geq \Delta$. Consider a Δ-admissible execution α, and a Δ-admissible time assignment τ for it. Let k be the smallest index such that the event e_k is the assignment $v_i := y[r]$ (at statement 6) by some process p_i that reaches round $r+1$. Let the event e_l correspond to the *delay* statement *delay*(d_r) (at statement 5) by process p_i. We know that $\tau_k - \tau_l > d_r$, and hence, $\tau_k - \tau_l > \Delta$.

Process p_i, before it reaches the *delay* statement, either finds $y[r] \neq \perp$, or assigns its preference for round r to $y[r]$. Hence, in states s_m, for $m \geq l$, $y[r] \neq \perp$. Let $y[r] = v$ in state s_k. We want to prove that $y[r] = v$ in all states s_m for $m \geq k$. Suppose not. Let p_j, $j \neq i$, be a process that writes to $y[r]$ (at statement 3) at step $k' > k$. Let $e_{l'}$ be the event that p_j tests the condition $y[r] = \perp$ (at statement 3). Since $y[r] \neq \perp$ in all states s_m for $m \geq l$, we have $l' < l$. This implies

$\tau_{k'} - \tau_{l'} \geq \tau_k - \tau_l > \Delta$. Since l' and k' are consecutive steps of p_j, this contradicts Δ-admissibility of τ. Thus $y[r] = v$ in all states s_m for $m \geq k$.

Since every process reaching round $r+1$ chooses its preference for round $r+1$ by reading $y[r]$ at some step $m \geq k$, the lemma follows. ▮

If $d_r \geq \Delta$ then Lemma 10.8 and Lemma 10.5 imply that in a Δ-admissible execution, no process can reach round $r+2$, and every nonfaulty process decides in round $r+1$ or lower. If the sequence $d_1, d_2, \ldots$ is unbounded, then for every Δ, there is some r such that $d_r \geq \Delta$. Consequently, we get termination in each Δ-admissible execution. This implies the following theorem.

Theorem 10.9 *The algorithm satisfies the properties of validity, agreement, and wait-freedom in the unknown-delay model.*

Self Review

1. Can processes decide on conflicting values if the *delay* statement (at line 5) is deleted.
2. Does it matter if we change the order of the two statements at lines 2 and 3 of the consensus algorithm?
3. Does it matter if we change the order of the two statements at lines 6 and 7 of the consensus algorithm?
4. Does it matter if we replace the statement $r_i := r_i + 1$ at line 7, with the statement $r_i := r_i + i$.
5. Does it matter if we replace the statement $r_i := r_i + 1$ at line 7, with the statement $r_i := r_i + 3$.

Answers: (1) No. (2) Yes. (3) No. (4) Yes. (5) No.

10.7 Fast Mutual Exclusion with Unknown Delays

We now present a fast mutual exclusion algorithm for the unknown-delay model which was discovered by R. Alur, H. Attiya, and G. Taubenfeld (1994).

Since in this model a time bound on the speed exists but is not known, the processes keep an estimate of this time (stored in a shared register), and update it when it is noticed that the estimate is not accurate. An entry to the critical section which involves an update (of the estimate) is going to be much slower than an entry without an update. However, the algorithm has the property that at most Δ updates are necessary.

10.7.1 The Algorithm

The precise code for the algorithm is given below. The algorithm is composed of two basic algorithms. The first is Alur and Taubenfeld's algorithm from Section 10.3 (abbv. AT). Statements 1–10 are the entry code of AT and statements 29–31 are its exit code. We point out that in the original AT algorithm the register *bound* is initially set to Δ (which is assumed to be known). Furthermore, while the AT algorithm satisfies mutual exclusion only when $bound \geq \Delta$, the proof of deadlock-freedom does not depend in any way on the value of *bound*. We will exploit this property in the construction. The critical section of AT is now replaced by Lamport's fast algorithm: statements 11–28. (Lamport's original algorithm appears on page 42.) These two algorithms are combined, together with a mechanism for estimating and updating the current bound. All references to the register *update* and the array *trying* belong to this mechanism, and are not part of the original AT and Lamport's algorithms.

Intuitively, the algorithm works as follows. First, each process executes the AT algorithm, using the current estimate *bound*. If the estimate is correct, or if there is no contention, only one process will proceed to the next stage (i.e., get to statement 11). However, it is possible that the current estimate used by the processes is incorrect. In this case, more than one process may proceed to the next stage, and therefore, to guarantee mutual exclusion, Lamport's algorithm is embedded at this point. If a process discovers contention while executing Lamport's algorithm, it "knows" that the current estimate used is incorrect, and has to be increased. (Contention is discovered when either of the conditions in statements 14 and 18 is evaluated to *true*.)

FAST MUTUAL EXCLUSION WITH UNKNOWN DELAYS: `process i's program.`

Initially: $y = 0$, $yy = 0$, $z = 0$, $bound = 1$, $update = 0$, $trying[i] = 0$ and $b[i] = 0$ for all i.

```
1   start1: repeat
2               if update = 1 then trying[i] := 0; await update = 0 fi;
3               trying[i] := 1;
4               x := i;
5           until (y = 0);
6           y := i;
7           if x ≠ i then delay(2 · bound);
8                         if y ≠ i then goto start1 fi;
9                         await (z = 0) or (update = 1)
10          else z := 1;

11  start2: if update = 1 then goto start1 fi;
12          b[i] := 1;
13          xx := i;
14          if yy ≠ 0 then b[i] := 0;
15                         await (yy = 0) or (update = 1);
16                         goto start2 fi;
17          yy := i;
18          if xx ≠ i then b[i] := 0;
19                         for j := 1 to n do await (b[j] = 0) or (update = 1) od;
20                         if yy ≠ i then await (yy = 0) or (update = 1);
21                                        goto start2
22                         else update := 1 fi fi;     /* set lock */
```

```
23      critical section;
24      trying[i] := 0;
25      if update = 1 then for j := 1 to n do await trying[j] = 0 od;
26                      bound := bound + 1 fi;
                                              /* increment bound */
27      yy := 0;
28      b[i] := 0;

29      z := 0;
30      if update = 1 then y := 0; update := 0
31                      else if y = i then y := 0 fi fi;
```

To avoid complications only a process that enters its critical section (statement 23) is allowed to update the register *bound*. This guarantees that no two processes try to update the estimate at the same time, and thus the value of *bound* never decreases.

The update is done as follows: First the process sets *update* to 1, signaling that it wants to make an update (statement 22). Then, it waits until each active process returns to the beginning of its trying code and waits for *update* to become 0 (statement 2). It is easy to check that once *update* is 1, eventually every process will test it. Once process *i* finds that *update* is 1, it returns to the beginning of its code, signals to the updating process that it is at the beginning by setting *trying*[*i*] to 0, and waits (statement 2). Once the updating process gets acknowledgements from all active processes, it safely increments *bound* (statement 26), executes the exit code of both the algorithms, and releases the lock (Statement 30), which leaves the system in its initial configuration (except for *bound*).

The fact that the processes return to the beginning of their code before *bound* is incremented guarantees that the value of *bound* will never be greater than Δ.

Once *bound* equals Δ, the entry code of AT (statements 1–10) ensures that no two processes execute Lamport's algorithm (statements 11–28) at the same time. Hence, from that point on, processes will always enter their critical section along the fast path of Lamport's algorithm.

In summary, each process starts by checking if an update of *bound* is taking place in which case it waits until the update is finished. Then the process performs the entry code for the timing-based mutual exclusion algorithm using the current estimate. If it gains access to the critical section (of AT), the process executes Lamport's fast mutual exclusion algorithm. However, in the algorithm, if a process enter its critical section via the slow path, it "knows" that the current estimate in use is incorrect, and should be increased. It does so by first signaling other processes to go to the beginning of their code and, after they all do so, it increments the register *bound*.

10.7.2 Correctness Proof

The proofs of both mutual exclusion and deadlock-freedom do not depend in any way on the assumption that there exists a bound on the speed of the processes, and hence these properties hold also in asynchronous systems. The design of the algorithm and its correctness proof are based on the following straightforward general observation.

Lemma 10.10 *Let A and B be mutual exclusion algorithms (with disjoint sets of shared registers), and let C be the algorithm obtained by replacing the critical section of A with the algorithm B. (If the critical section of A has a label, then in C this label is associated with the first statement of B.)*

1. *If both A and B are deadlock-free then C is deadlock-free.*
2. *If either A or B satisfies mutual exclusion then C satisfies mutual exclusion.*

Proof: The entry code of C is composed from the entry code of A, denoted by C_A, followed by that of B, denoted by C_B. Assume that both A and B are deadlock-free. If some process starts executing algorithm C, then, since A is deadlock-free, eventually some process will finish C_A and will proceed to C_B. Since B is deadlock-free, eventually some process will finish C_B and will enter its critical section. Thus, C is deadlock-free.

If A satisfies mutual exclusion, then no two processes can be at their C_B code at the same time. If B satisfies mutual exclusion, then no two processes can finish their C_B code at the same time. In either case, it implies that no two processes are in their critical section at the same time. ∎

The correctness of the algorithm is based on Lemma 10.10 and the properties of AT and Lamport's algorithms. The algorithm satisfies the correctness requirements also in the asynchronous model.

As already explained, the algorithm is obtained by replacing the critical section of Alur and Taubenfeld's algorithm with Lamport's algorithm (statements 11–28). These two algorithms are combined, together with a mechanism for estimating and updating the current time bound. All references to the register *update* and the array *trying* belong to this mechanism, and are not part of the original AT and Lamport's algorithms.

It is known that Lamport's algorithm satisfies mutual exclusion and deadlock-freedom, and that the AT algorithm satisfies deadlock-freedom regardless of the value of *bound*.

Theorem 10.11 *The algorithm satisfies deadlock-freedom.*

Proof: As long as the value of *update* is 0, executing statements 1–10 or statements 11–22, is the same as executing the entry code of the AT algorithm or the entry code of Lamport's algorithm, respectively. Since both AT and Lamport's algorithms are deadlock-free (regardless of the value of *bound*), Lemma 10.10 implies that the algorithm can not be deadlocked while the value of *update* is continuously 0.

We observe that if the value of *update* is 1, then there must be some process (called the *winner*) which is either in its critical section or in its exit code. It is easy to check that once *update* is 1, eventually every process (other than the winner) will test it. Once process i finds that *update* is 1, it returns to the beginning of its code, and signals to the winner that it is at the beginning by setting *trying*[i] to 0. Thus, eventually the winner gets acknowledgements from all active processes, which implies that the winner can not be blocked forever in the for loop of statement 25, and will eventually set *update* back to 0. This implies that the system can not be deadlocked, while the value of *update* is continuously 1.

Thus, a deadlock can occur in an infinite execution only if *update* changes values an infinite number of times. However, each time *update* changes its value, some process either enters or exits its critical section. Therefore, in an execution where *update* changes values an infinite number of times, no deadlock can occur. ∎

Theorem 10.12 *The algorithm satisfies mutual exclusion.*

Proof: As long as the value of *update* is 0, executing statements 11–28, is the same as executing Lamport's algorithm. Since Lamport's algorithm satisfies mutual exclusion, by Lemma 10.10, the new algorithm must also satisfy mutual exclusion when the value of *update* is 0.

If the value of *update* is 1, then there must be some process (the *winner*) which is either in its critical section or in its exit code. Once the winner sets update to 1, no other process can enter the critical section until *update* is set back to 0. To see that, observe that once *update* is 1, eventually every process will test it, and once a process finds that *update* is 1, it returns to the beginning of its code, signals to the updating process that it is at the beginning by setting *trying*[i] to 0, and waits (statement 2) until *update* is set to 0. The winner sets *update* to 0 in its exit code, only after it gets acknowledgements from all active processes. The fact that the processes return to the beginning of their code before *update* is reset guarantees that no process executes Lamport's (embedded) algorithm, which in turn guarantees that no two processes can enter their critical section as long as the value of update is not changed. ∎

10.7.3 Time Complexity

Next we show that the register *bound* is updated at most Δ times.

Lemma 10.13 *bound* $\leq \Delta$ *is an invariant of the algorithm.*

Proof: Once *bound* reaches the correct Δ, the delay in statement 7 is going to be greater than $2 \cdot \Delta$. Thus, from that point on, this code (statements 1–10) behaves exactly as the original AT algorithm. This means that from now on only one process can be in Lamport's algorithm (statements 11–28), and hence no more updates will occur. Thus, the number of times a winning process has to update *bound* after executing its critical section is bounded by Δ. ∎

The next theorem shows that the algorithm is time-efficient. In the theorem, the time it takes for a process to enter its critical section is measured from the last time some process exited its critical section.

Theorem 10.14 *The algorithm has the following properties:*

1. *Fast access: In the absence of contention a process executes only a constant number of steps (13) from the location start1 to its critical section, and only a constant number of steps (8) to execute the exit code. No delays are necessary.*
2. *In the presence of contention, a winning process which does not update the register bound executes a constant number of steps (14) and may need to delay itself for at most $2 \cdot \Delta$ time units, before entering its critical section.*
3. *In the presence of contention, a winning process which needs to update the register bound may execute $O(n)$ steps and may need to delay itself for at most $2 \cdot \Delta$ time units, before entering its critical section. (This may happen at most Δ times.)*

Proof: The first part is straightforward. By Lemma 10.13, *bound* $\leq \Delta$. Thus, executing the delay in statement 7 takes at most $2 \cdot \Delta$ time units. Note that a winning process updates *bound*, if and only if it finds the condition in statement 18 (i.e., $xx \neq i$), to be *true*. The second part of the theorem is easily verified by counting steps in the algorithm.

It is only when a process finds the condition in statement 18 to be *true* that it executes the for statement at statement 19, in which it may need to execute $O(n)$ steps. This implies the third part of the theorem, and explains why the term $O(n)$ is added. ∎

Observe that there is a tradeoff between the number of updates of the register *bound* and its maximum value. Incrementing by 1 is the best strategy, since it gives the best amortized time complexity when the number of entries to the critical section is much bigger than Δ.

In the algorithm the value of the register *bound* can only be increased, and after it is updated Δ times, it will reach its maximum value Δ. In a dynamic system where processes are created and destroyed, the upper bound on the speed of the processes may change over time. The algorithm adapts to an increase in Δ (that may be caused by adding slow processes). However, when Δ decreases (a slow process is destroyed) the value of *bound* may be too high leading to inefficient utilization. This may be resolved by periodically resetting *bound* to zero, and letting it adjust to reflect the current speed.

Self Review

1. What would be the maximum value of the variable *bound*, if instead of incrementing the register *bound* by 1, we double its value when it is updated?

Answer: The variable *bound* is updated at most $\log \Delta$ times, and *bound* $\leq 2 \cdot \Delta - 1$.

10.2

Fischer's timing-based mutual exclusion algorithm (page 345) has appeared in a paper written by Lamport [224]. Lamport's paper contains also a fast timing-based algorithm (page 367); however, as Lamport has pointed out, his algorithm works correctly only when some bound is assumed on the time needed to execute the critical section [224]. Formal proofs of Fischer's algorithm can be found in [89, 303].

10.3

Alur–Taubenfeld's mutual exclusion algorithm, presented on page 347, appeared in [21, 25]. Most recent shared-memory systems support access to a word of memory at different granularities. Thus, a few registers can be packed into one word of memory, and doing that makes it possible to read or write more than one register in one atomic step. This is demonstrated by Michael–Scott's timing-based algorithm (page 368) [263], and the new algorithm from Problem 10.18 (page 369), where the performance of Lamport's fast algorithm and Alur–Taubenfeld's algorithm is improved by more than 25%, by exploiting the ability to read and write atomically at both full- and half-word granularities.

A fast starvation-free timing-based algorithm, in which a failure of a process in its critical section does not block any other process, is presented in [22]. This algorithm is used as a basis of a general method for transforming a given sequential implementation of a data structure into a wait-free concurrent implementation.

In [246], the simple idea mentioned in the remark on page 348, is used to design a timing-based algorithm where only the property of deadlock-freedom depends on the timing assumptions, and mutual exclusion is guaranteed even in presence of timing faults; however, unlike the algorithm on page 347, this algorithm does not provide fast access in the absence of contention. A mutual exclusion algorithm which is resilient to timing failures is presented in [324]. Timing-based mutual exclusion with local spinning is considered in [203].

Less related is the work in [54], where a variant of the mutual exclusion problem is studied in a message passing model with inaccurate clocks, where some bounds on the speeds of the processes and the time to deliver a message are known.

10.4 & 10.5

Despite the impossibility result presented in Section 9.5 (page 318), consensus can be achieved using atomic registers by adding timing assumptions. The fast timing-based consensus algorithm, which is presented on page 353, has appeared in [25]. A consensus algorithm which is resilient to timing failures is presented in [324]. Timing-based systems allow consensus to be solved by (indirectly) imposing constraints on the scheduler (i.e., the adversary's control is restricted). Another way to restrict the scheduler is explored in [36], where it is shown how to solve consensus assuming priority-based scheduling and quantum-based scheduling. In particular, in [37] it is shown that in a priority-scheduled uni-processor system, consensus is solvable in constant time using atomic registers. Several related results for message-passing systems are presented in [114, 122].

10.6

The design of algorithms for the unknown-delay model using only atomic registers was investigated in [18]. The consensus algorithm for the unknown-delay model, presented on page 356 has appeared in [18]. This consensus algorithm is an adaptation of the consensus algorithm for the known-delay model from Section 10.5. A similar approach is taken in constructing the randomized consensus algorithm from [44] with the delays removed from the algorithm in [18].

10.7

The mutual exclusion algorithm for the unknown-delay model (page 360), which works under the assumption that a time bound on the memory access time exists but is not known, appeared in [17, 18].

10.9 Problems

The problems are divided into several categories. See page 23 for a detailed explanation.

Problems based on Section 10.2

∘∘ 10.1 Prove the correctness of Fischer's algorithm. That is, prove the list of properties on page 345.

Problems based on Section 10.3

∘∘ 10.2 Why is the fast algorithm incorrect if we use *delay*(Δ) instead of *delay*($2 \cdot \Delta$) in line 4.

∘∘ 10.3 Prove that the statement *delay*($2 \cdot \Delta$) can be replaced by two *delay*(Δ) statements; the first is placed at the same place as before and the second is placed before the **await**($z = 0$) statement.

∘∘ 10.4 Is the algorithm correct if we replace the statement "**await**($z = 0$)" in line 6, with the statement: **if** $z \neq 0$ **then if** $y = i$ **then** $y = 0$ **fi**; **goto** *start* **fi**?

∘ 10.5 What is the value of register y when process i is in its critical section?

∘∘ 10.6 We have pointed out how to modify the timing-based algorithms so that they guarantee mutual exclusion even when the timing constraints are not met (see page 348). Prove that this modification actually does it.

○○ **10.7** We have pointed out how to modify timing-based mutual exclusion algorithms, using *two* additional registers, so that they guarantee mutual exclusion even when the timing constraints are not met (page 348). Show that only *one* additional register is needed for modifying Fischer's algorithm. That is, there exists a correct timing-based mutual exclusion algorithm that guarantees mutual exclusion even when the timing constraints are not met, which uses only *two* atomic registers.

○○ **10.8** What is wrong with the following fast timing-based solution?

Initially: $y = 0$.

```
start: x := i;
       await (y = 0);
       y := i;
       if x ≠ i then delay(2·Δ);
                 if y ≠ i then goto start fi fi;
       y := i;
       critical section;
       y := 0;
```

○○ **10.9** What is wrong with the following fast timing-based solution?

Initially: $y = 0$, $z = 0$.

```
start: x := i;
       await (y = 0);
       y := i;
       if x ≠ i  then delay(2·Δ);
                 await (z = 0);
                 if y ≠ i then goto start fi
             else z := 1 fi;
       critical section;
       y := i; z := 0; y := 0;
```

○○ **10.10** The following algorithm is due to Lamport (1987). Prove that the algorithm is correct only when there is a bound on the time needed to execute the critical section. What is the minimal such bound?

LAMPORT'S FAST TIMING-BASED ALGORITHM: `process` *i*`'s program.`

Initially: $y = 0$.

```
start: x := i;
       if y ≠ 0 then goto start fi;
       y := i;
       if x ≠ i then delay(Δ);
                 if y ≠ i then goto start fi fi;
       critical section;
       y := 0;
```

◦◦ 10.11 Let A and B be two deadlock-free timing-based mutual exclusion algorithms. Let C be the algorithm which results from replacing the critical section of A with algorithm B and removing all the *delay* statements (from both A and B). It is obvious that C might no longer satisfy mutual exclusion. Is C deadlock-free?

◦• 10.12 Design a *fast starvation-free* timing-based solution, where in the presence of contention, the winner may need to access the shared memory a constant number of times and has to delay itself for only $c \cdot \Delta$ time units, for some constant c, before it can enter its critical section.

•• 10.13 Design a fast timing-based algorithm, where the exit code includes just one assignment statement.

•◦ 10.14 Recall that: (1) in Lamport's fast mutual exclusion algorithm (page 42) the contention-free step complexity is 7; (2) in Alur–Taubenfeld's fast timing-based mutual exclusion algorithm (page 347) the contention-free step complexity is 8.

In some shared memory systems it is possible to read and write atomically at both full and half-word granularities. For such systems, design an optimization of Alur and Taubenfeld's algorithm, in which the contention-free step complexity is only 6.

Hint: assume that registers y and z occupy adjacent half-words in memory, where they can be read or written either separately or together, atomically.

◦• 10.15 In some shared memory systems it is possible to read and write atomically at both full and half-word granularities. For such systems, the following optimization of Alur and Taubenfeld's algorithm, observed by M. M. Michael and M. L. Scott (June 1993), is possible. Prove its correctness.

Registers y and z are assumed to occupy adjacent half-words in memory, where they can be read or written either separately or together, atomically.

MICHAEL–SCOTT'S FAST TIMING-BASED ALGORITHM: `process i's program.`

Initially: $y = 0$, $z = 0$.

```
1 start: x := i;
2        if y ≠ 0 then goto start fi;
3        y := i;
4        if x ≠ i then delay(2·Δ);
5                 if (y, z) ≠ (i, 0) then goto start fi fi;
6        z := 1;
7        critical section;
8        (y, z) := (0, 0);
```

◦ 10.16 In the following, we list two possibilities for replacing statement 2 in Michael–Scott's fast timing-based algorithm in Problem 10.15 (i.e., the statement: **if** $y \neq 0$ **then goto** *start* **fi**.) Which of these changes preserves the correctness of the algorithm?

Case 1: **await** $(y = 0)$;

Case 2: **if** $(y, z) \neq (0, 0)$ **then goto** *start* **fi**;

○○ 10.17 In the following, we list four possibilities for replacing statement 5 in Michael–Scott's fast timing-based algorithm in Problem 10.15 (i.e., the statement: **if** $(y, z) \neq (i, 0)$ **then goto** *start* **fi**). Which of these changes preserves the correctness of the algorithm?

Case 1: **if** $y \neq i$ **then goto** *start* **fi**;
if $z \neq 0$ **then goto** *start* **fi**;

Case 2: **if** $z \neq 0$ **then goto** *start* **fi**;
if $y \neq i$ **then goto** *start* **fi**;

Case 3: **if** $y \neq i$ **then goto** *start* **fi**;
await $(z = 0)$;

Case 4: **await** $(z = 0)$;
if $y \neq i$ **then goto** *start* **fi**;

○• 10.18 As already mentioned in Problem 10.15, at some shared memory systems it is possible to read and write atomically at both full and half-word granularities. Prove that the following algorithm is correct and compare it with the algorithm in Problem 10.15.

Registers y and z are assumed to occupy adjacent half-words in memory, where they can be read or written either separately or together, atomically.

A FAST TIMING-BASED MUTUAL EXCLUSION ALGORITHM: process i's program.

Initially: $y = 0$, $z = 0$.

```
start: x := i;
       await (y, z) = (0, 0);
       y := i;
       if x ≠ i then delay(2·Δ);
                 if y ≠ i then goto start fi;
                 await z = 0 fi;
       (y, z) := (0, 1);
       critical section;
       z := 0;
```

? 10.19 Is it possible to design a *fast* timing-based solution, where in the presence of contention, the winner may need to access the shared memory a constant number of times and has to delay itself for *only* $1 \cdot \Delta$ time units before it can enter its critical section.

Problems based on Sections 10.4 & 10.5

○○ 10.20 Prove the correctness of the simple timing-based consensus algorithm from page 352.

∘∘ 10.21 Below is another fast timing-based consensus algorithm. Prove that the algorithm is correct and compare it to the fast timing-based consensus algorithm from page 353.

A FAST TIMING-BASED CONSENSUS ALGORITHM: `program for process` i `with input` $in_i \in \{0, 1\}$.

```
shared registers
   x, y, z ranges over {⊥, 0, 1}, initially y = ⊥ and y = ⊥

         if z ≠ ⊥ then decide(z) ; goto end fi;
         x := i;
         if y ≠ ⊥ then goto wait fi;
         y := in_i;
         if x ≠ i then
  wait:          delay(3·Δ);
                 if z ≠ ⊥ then decide(z) else decide(y) fi
         else z := in_i ; decide(z) fi;
  end.
```

? 10.22 What is the minimum number of atomic registers needed for a *fast* wait-free timing-based consensus algorithm?

Problems based on Section 10.6

∘ 10.23 Explain why the consensus algorithm with unknown delays (page 356) is *fast*. That is, in absence of contention, a process decides after a *constant* number of its own steps.

∘∘ 10.24 How many steps will it take for a process to decide, if the statement $delay(d_{r_i})$ at line 5 is replaced with the statement $delay(2r)$?

∘∘ 10.25 How many steps will it take for a process to decide, if the statement $delay(d_{r_i})$ at line 5 is replaced with the statement $delay(2^r)$?

•∘ 10.26 Prove that if every step of the algorithm finishes within time Δ then a process decides within time $O(\Delta \cdot fac^{-1}(\Delta))$ irrespective of the failures of other processes, where fac^{-1} is the inverse of the factorial function. For a real number $d > 0$, $fac^{-1}(d)$ is the smallest r such that $r! \geq d$. Notice that $fac^{-1}(r) = \Theta(\frac{\log r}{\log \log r})$.

•• 10.27 Show that the worst-case time complexity of any two process algorithm for consensus in the unknown-delay model is $\Omega(\Delta \cdot fac^{-1}(\Delta))$. Notice that this bound implies that the algorithm presented in Section 10.6.1 is time-optimal. The lower bound implies that not knowing Δ multiplies the time complexity by a factor of $fac^{-1}(\Delta)$.

? 10.28 Is there a wait-free consensus algorithm for the unknown-delay model which uses only finitely many atomic registers?

◦ 10.29 Replace the arrays b and *trying*, each of n bits, with one array of n 3-valued registers.

◦• 10.30 Adapt the proof of Theorem 2.16 (page 59) to show that, in the unknown-delay model, any deadlock-free mutual exclusion algorithm for n processes must use at least n shared registers.

•◦ 10.31 In Problem 3.27, it is claimed that, when using only atomic registers, there is no wait-free election algorithm. Show that for the unknown-delay model, this claim does not hold. That is, develop a wait-free election algorithm for the unknown-delay model.

Bibliography

[1] U. Abraham. Bakery algorithms. In *Proc. Concurrency, Specification and Programming Workshop*, pages 7–40, October 1993.

A variant of the Bakery algorithm is presented, which uses $3^n + 1$ values per registers. Unlike the Bakery algorithm the algorithm is not symmetric: process p_i only reads the values of the lower processes.

[2] S. V. Adve and K. Gharachorloo. Shared memory consistency models: A tutorial. *IEEE Computer*, **29**(12):66–76, 1996.

This tutorial describes many issues related to memory consistency models with a focus on consistency models proposed for hardware-based shared memory systems.

[3] Y. Afek, H. Attiya, D. Dolev, E. Gafni, M. Merritt, and N. Shavit. Atomic snapshots of shared memory. *Journal of the ACM*, **40**(4):873–890, 1993.

A shared data object, called atomic snapshot, is introduced that can be implemented from atomic registers. An atomic snapshot, which is the same as a composite register from [26], is partitioned into words that can be written by individual processes, and can be instantaneously read (scanned) in its entirety.

[4] Y. Afek, H. Attiya, A. Fouren, G. Stupp, and D. Touitou. Long-lived renaming made adaptive. In *Proc. 18th ACM Symp. on Principles of Distributed Computing*, pages 91–103, May 1999.

Includes the first sieve algorithm which is used as a building block from renaming [10, 53, 183]. The journal version of some of the results is [53].

[5] Y. Afek, D. Dauber, and D. Touitou. Wait-free made fast. In *Proc. 27th ACM Symp. on Theory of Computing*, pages 538–547, May–June 1995.

Two wait-free universal methods are presented whose time complexity is a function of the actual number of processes that access the object concurrently with an operation.

[6] Y. Afek, D. Dolev, E. Gafni, M. Merritt, and N. Shavit. A bounded first-in, first-enabled solution to the ℓ-exclusion problem. *Lecture Notes in Computer Science*, **486**:422–431, 1991.

Older version of [7].

[7] Y. Afek, D. Dolev, E. Gafni, M. Merritt, and N. Shavit. A bounded first-in, first-enabled solution to the ℓ-exclusion problem. *ACM Trans. on Programming Languages and Systems*, **16**(3):939–953, 1994.

A (complex) FIFO-enabling solution to the ℓ-exclusion problem is presented, which is achieved using read and write atomicity. The algorithm makes use of concurrent timestamps for solving the problem within bounded size memory. (FIFO-enabling is defined on page 229.) Journal version of [6]. See [286] for many results concerning the ℓ-exclusion problem.

[8] Y. Afek, D. S. Greenberg, M. Merritt, and G. Taubenfeld. Computing with faulty shared objects. *Journal of the ACM*, **42**(6):1231–1274, 1995.

The effects of the failure of shared objects on distributed systems investigated. Several constructions of non-faulty wait-free shared objects from a set of shared objects, some of which may suffer any number of faults, are presented. See also [189].

[9] Y. Afek, M. Merrit, G. Taubenfeld, and D. Touitou. Disentangling multi-object operations (extended abstract). In *Proc. 16th ACM Symp. on Principles of Distributed Computing*, pages 111–120, August 1997.

The authors implement an atomic operation on multiple shared memory objects, in systems which directly support only a RMW operation on a single location. The implementation exhibits low contention between concurrent operations and a high level of concurrency.

[10] Y. Afek and M. Merritt. Fast, wait-free $(2k-1)$-renaming. In *Proc. 18th ACM Symp. on Principles of Distributed Computing*, pages 105–112, May 1999.

An adaptive one-shot optimal-name-space $(2k-1)$-renaming object is presented, whose step complexity is $O(k^2)$. The algorithm is based on the sieve building block from [4].

[11] Y. Afek, M. Merritt, and G. Taubenfeld. The power of multiobjects. *Information and Computation*, **153**(1):117–138, 1999.

Shared memory systems that support multi-object operations are considered in which processes may simultaneously access several objects in one atomic operation, and bounds on the synchronization power (consensus number) of multi-object systems are provided.

[12] Y. Afek, G. Stupp, and D. Touitou. Long-lived adaptive collect with applications. In *Proc. 40th IEEE Symp. on Foundations of Computer Science*, pages 262–272, October 1999.

Long-lived and adaptive algorithms for collecting information using atomic registers are presented. The authors employ these algorithms to transform algorithms, such as the Bakery algorithm [212] (see page 50) and ℓ-exclusion, into their corresponding adaptive long-lived version.

[13] Y. Afek, G. Stupp, and D. Touitou. Long lived adaptive splitter and applications. *Distributed Computing*, **30**:67–86, 2002.

Long-lived and adaptive implementations of mutual exclusion and (wait-free) renaming using atomic registers are presented. The system response time and worst case number of operations per process of the adaptive mutual exclusion algorithm is $O(k^2)$, where k is the number of processes that take steps concurrently. Both algorithms rely on the basic building block of a long-lived and adaptive splitter.

[14] A. Agarwal and M. Cherian. Adaptive backoff synchronization techniques. In *Proc. 16th Annual International Symp. on Computer Architecture (ISCA)*, pages 396–406, June 1989.

A class of adaptive back-off methods is proposed that do not use any extra hardware and can significantly reduce the memory traffic to synchronization variables. The simulations show that when the number of processors participating in a barrier synchronization is small compared to the time of arrival of the processors, reductions of 20 percent to over 95 percent in synchronization traffic can be achieved at no extra cost.

[15] O. Agesen, D. Detlefs, C. H. Flood, A. T. Garthwaite, P. A. Martin, M. Moir, N. Shavit, and G. L. Steele Jr. DCAS-based concurrent deques. *Theory of Computing Systems*, **35**(3):349–386, 2002.

Two linearizable non-blocking implementations of concurrent deques using the DCAS operation are presented.

[16] N. Alon, M. Merritt, O. Reingold, G. Taubenfeld, and R. N. Wright. Tight bounds for shared memory systems accessed by Byzantine processes. *Distributed Computing*, **18**(2):99–109, 2005.

The authors provide efficient constructions and tight bounds for shared memory systems in which processes may exhibit Byzantine faults, in a model previously explored in [250].

[17] R. Alur, H. Attiya, and G. Taubenfeld. Time-adaptive algorithms for synchronization. In *Proc. 26th ACM Symp. on Theory of Computing*, pages 800–809, May 1994.

Concurrent systems in which there is an unknown upper bound on memory access time are considered. Two basic synchronization problems, consensus and mutual exclusion, are investigated in a shared memory environment that supports atomic registers. See [18] for the journal version.

[18] R. Alur, H. Attiya, and G. Taubenfeld. Time-adaptive algorithms for synchronization. *SIAM Journal on Computing*, **26**(2):539–556, 1997.

Journal version of [17].

[19] R. Alur and T. Henzinger. Finitary fairness. In *Proc. 9th IEEE Symp. on Logic in Computer Science*, pages 52–61, July 1994. See [20] for the journal version.

Finitary fairness requires that for every run there is an unknown bound k such that no enabled transition is postponed more than k consecutive times. It is shown that under finitary fairness formal verification can be simplified and that fully-resilient consensus is solvable since finitary fairness can replace the timing assumption for the fully-resilient consensus algorithm in [18].

[20] R. Alur and T. Henzinger. Finitary fairness. *ACM Transactions on Programming Languages and Systems*, **20**(6):1171–1194, November 1998.

Journal version of [19].

[21] R. Alur and G. Taubenfeld. Results about fast mutual exclusion. In *Proc. 13th IEEE Real-Time Systems Symp.*, pages 12–21, December 1992.

A fast timing-based algorithm is presented, where only five accesses to the shared memory are needed in order to enter a critical section in the absence of contention. In the presence of contention, the winning process may need to delay itself for $2 \cdot \Delta$ time units, where Δ is an upper bound on the time taken by the slowest process to access the shared memory (page 347). Also, it is proven that there is no algorithm with an upper bound on the number of times a winning process needs to access atomic registers in order to enter its critical section in presence of contention (page 119). See also [25].

[22] R. Alur and G. Taubenfeld. How to share an object: A fast timing-based solution. In *Proc. 5th IEEE Symp. on Parallel and Distributed Processing*, pages 470–477, December 1993.

A fast starvation-free timing-based mutual exclusion algorithm is presented. The algorithm is also wait-free–a failure of a process in its critical section does not block any other process. This algorithm is used as a basis of a general method for transforming a given bounded sequential implementation of a data structure into a wait-free concurrent implementation.

[23] R. Alur and G. Taubenfeld. Contention-free complexity of shared memory algorithms. In *Proc. 13th ACM Symp. on Principles of Distributed Computing*, pages 61–70, August 1994.

Lower and upper bounds for the contention-free time complexity of solving the mutual exclusion and naming problems are given. For example, it is shown that the contention-free step complexity of every mutual exclusion algorithm for n processes is greater than $\frac{\log n}{\ell-2+3\log\log n}$, where ℓ is the size (in terms of bits) of the biggest atomic register accessed by the algorithm in one atomic step. See [24] for the journal version.

[24] R. Alur and G. Taubenfeld. Contention-free complexity of shared memory algorithms. *Information and Computation*, **126**(1):62–73, 1996.

Journal version of [23].

[25] R. Alur and G. Taubenfeld. Fast timing-based algorithms. *Distributed Computing*, **10**(1):1–10, 1996.

Journal version of some of the results from [21] (does not include the impossibility result).

[26] J. H. Anderson. Composite registers. *Distributed Computing*, **6**(3):141–154, 1993.

A shared data object, called a composite register, is introduced that can be implemented from atomic registers. A composite register, which is the same as an atomic snapshot from [3], is an array-like variable that is partitioned into a number of components. An operation of such a register either writes a value to one of the components or reads the values of all of the components.

[27] J. H. Anderson. A fine-grained solution to the mutual exclusion problem. *Acta Informatica*, **30**(3):249–265, May 1993.

The main result is the observation stated in Problem 3.12 (page 138).

[28] J. Anderson and Y.-J. Kim, Fast and scalable mutual exclusion. In *Proc. 13th International Symp. on Distributed Computing*, LNCS 1693. Springer-Verlag, 1999, 180–194.

A mutual exclusion algorithm using atomic register is presented, in which the time complexity in the DSM model (see definition on page 16) is O(1) in the absence of contention and O($\log n$) in the presence of contention. The algorithm is based on Lamport's fast algorithm (page 42) and on Yang and Anderson's algorithm (page 102). (See Problem 3.17, page 139). See [29].

[29] J. H. Anderson and Y.-J. Kim. Adaptive mutual exclusion with local spinning. In *Proc. 14th International Symp. on Distributed Computing. LNCS*, 1914. Springer-Verlag, 29–43, 2000.

The paper presents an adaptive mutual exclusion algorithm using atomic register, in which the time complexity in the DSM model (see definition on page 16) is $\theta(\min(k, \log n))$ where k is the maximum *point contention*. The space complexity is $\theta(n)$.

[30] J. H. Anderson and Y.-J. Kim. An improved lower bound for the time complexity of mutual exclusion. In *Proc. 20th ACM Symp. on Principles of Distributed Computing*, pages 90–99, August 2001.

See [31] for the journal version.

[31] J. H. Anderson and Y.-J. Kim. An improved lower bound for the time complexity of mutual exclusion. *Distributed Computing*, **15**(4):221–253, 2002.

It is proved that $\Omega(\log n/\log\log n)$ is a lower bound on the time complexity in both the CC and DSM models (see definition on page 16). This result holds assuming any of the following objects can be used: atomic registers, together with any set of comparison objects. This result improves the result in [103] See Problem 3.15.

[32] J. H. Anderson, Y.-J. Kim, and T. Herman. Shared-memory mutual exclusion: Major research trends since 1986. *Distributed Computing*, **16**:75–110, 2003.

Special issue celebrating the 20th anniversary of PODC. The paper mainly focuses on discussing results about adaptive mutual exclusion and local spinning; see also [29].

[33] J. H. Anderson and M. Moir. Using k-exclusion to implement resilient, scalable shared objects. In *Proc. 14th ACM Symp. on Principles of Distributed Computing*, pages 141–150, August 1994.

It is suggested that the object is first protected by k-exclusion algorithm; processes that passed the k-exclusion rename themselves before accessing the object. This enables the usage of an object that was designed only for up to k processes, rather than a less efficient object designed for n processes. The implementation uses test-and-set objects.

[34] J. H. Anderson and M. Moir. Universal constructions for multi-object operations. In *Proc. 14th ACM Symp. on Principles of Distributed Computing*, pages 184–193, August 1995.

The authors present wait-free and non-blocking universal constructions that allow operations to access multiple objects atomically.

[35] J. H. Anderson and M. Moir. Using local-spin k-exclusion algorithms to improve wait-free object implementations. *Distributed Computing*, **11**:1–20, 1997.

Several algorithms for ℓ-exclusion which are based on strong primitives (fetch-and-increment, compare-and-swap) are considered. Time complexity is measured in terms of the number of remote accesses of shared memory required per critical section. (Remote accesses are defined on page 138.) The ℓ-assignment problem is also discussed.

[36] J. H. Anderson and M. Moir. Wait-free synchronization in multiprogrammed systems: Integrating priority-based and quantum-based scheduling. In *Proc. 18th ACM Symp. on Principles of Distributed Computing*, pages 123–132, May 1999.

Shows how to solve consensus assuming priority-based scheduling and quantum-based scheduling.

[37] J. H. Anderson, M. Moir, and S. Ramamurthy. A simple proof technique for priority-scheduled systems. *Information Processing Letters*, 77(2–4):63–70, 2001.

It is shown that in a priority-scheduled uni-processor system, consensus is solvable in constant time using atomic registers.

[38] R. J. Anderson and H. Woll. Wait-free parallel algorithms for the union-find problem. In *Proc. 23rd ACM Symp. on Theory of Computing*, pages 370–380, May 1991.

The authors give a wait-free implementation of an algorithm for Union-Find using compare-and-swap primitives.

[39] T. E. Anderson. The performance of spin lock alternatives for shared-memory multiprocessor. *IEEE Trans. on Parallel and Distributed Systems*, **1**(1):6–16, January 1990.

Spin-waiting can slow other processors by consuming communication bandwidth. This important paper examines the question: are there efficient algorithms for software spin-waiting given hardware support for atomic instruction, or are more complex kinds of hardware support needed for performance? The performance of several software spin-waiting alternatives and several hardware solutions are considered. See Section 4.4.1, page 160.

[40] G. R. Andrews. *Concurrent Programming: Principles and Practice*. The Benjamin/Cumming Publishing Company, Inc., 1991.

The book offers comprehensive coverage of concurrent programming theory and implementation issues. An older version of [41].

[41] G. R. Andrews. *Multithreaded, Parallel, and Distributed Programming*. Addison-Wesley, 2000.

Covers the core concepts that programmers using concurrency and multithreading should know, and presents different methods of implementing concurrent systems at both low and high levels. Uses many simple synchronization algorithms to demonstrate these concepts and implementations. A modified version of [40].

[42] J. K. Annot, M. D. Janssens, and A. J. Van De Goor. Comments on Morris's starvation-free solution to the mutual exclusion problem. *Information Processing Letters*, **23**(2):91–97, August 1986.

An incorrect claim is made that Morris' algorithm [270] does not refute Dijkstra's conjecture [111]. Also, Morris' algorithm for an unknown number of processors, using three weak binary semaphores [270], is modified to an algorithm for a known number of processors, using two weaker binary semaphores and n atomic bits. We note that when the number of processes is known this can be done without using semaphores at all (page 47).

[43] K. R. Apt. Edsger Wybe Dijkstra (1930–2002): A portrait of a genius. *Formal Aspects of Computing*, **14**:92–98, 2002.

Sections included: Scientific career, Scientific contributions, Working style, His opinions, Life in Austin, Lifestyle, Legacy.

[44] J. Aspnes. Fast deterministic consensus in a noisy environment. In *Proc. 19th ACM Symp. on Principles of Distributed Computing*, pages 299–308, July 2000.

Shows that randomness in the environment can be substitute for randomness in the algorithm. The consensus algorithm presented is similar to the algorithm from [18] with the delays removed.

[45] J. Aspnes. Randomized protocols for asynchronous consensus. *Distributed Computing*, **16**(2–3):165–175, 2003.

A survey paper that illustrates the history and structure of randomized asynchronous consensus algorithms using atomic registers by giving detailed descriptions of several such algorithms.

[46] J. Aspnes, M. P. Herlihy, and N. Shavit. Counting networks. *Journal of the ACM*, **41**(5):1020–1048, 1994.

The authors introduce counting networks, a new class of networks that can be used to count, and give two counting network constructions. Counting networks avoid the sequential bottlenecks inherent to earlier solutions and substantially lower the memory contention.

[47] H. Attiya, A. Bar-Noy, D. Dolev, D. Koller, D. Peleg, and R. Reischuk. Achievable cases in an asynchronous environment. In *Proc. 28th IEEE Symp. on Foundations of Computer Science*, pages 337–346, October 1987.

A simpler version of the ℓ-assignment problem (page 241), called *distinct CS*, is considered. In this version all correct processes are required to repeatedly request resources (i.e., there is no remainder code). The fairness condition suggested in [47] is called *global priority*: process p has higher priority than process q if p entered its critical section less times than q. It is mentioned in [85] that a lower bound, similar to the one proven in [85] for ℓ-assignment, was proved by H. Attiya and M. Tuttle (Private communication) for the distinct-CS problem (i.e., that $\ell \geq 2k + 1$ is also a necessary condition for solving the distinct CS problem).

[48] H. Attiya, A. Bar-Noy, D. Dolev, D. Koller, D. Peleg, and R. Reischuk. Renaming in an asynchronous environment. *Journal of the Association for Computing Machinery*, **37**(3):524–548, 1990.

Presents the first one-shot $(n + t)$-renaming algorithm, where t is a bound on the number of faults, for the message passing model. The algorithm has exponential message complexity.

[49] H. Attiya and V. Bortnikov. Adaptive and efficient mutual exclusion. In *Proc. 19th ACM Symp. on Principles of Distributed Computing*, pages 91–100, July 2000.

An adaptive algorithm for mutual exclusion is presented using atomic registers. The system response time of the algorithm is $O(\log k)$, and the process response time, under the assumption that busy waiting is counted as just one step, is $O(k)$, where k denotes the contention level. The space complexity is $O(nN)$, where N is the range of processes' names. See [50] for the journal version.

[50] H. Attiya and V. Bortnikov. Adaptive and efficient mutual exclusion. *Distributed Computing*, **15**(3):177–189, 2002.

Journal version of [49].

[51] H. Attiya and E. Dagan. Improved implementations of binary universal operations. *Journal of the ACM*, **48**(5):1013–1037, 2001.

An efficient algorithm for implementing binary operations (of any type) from unary LL/SC operations is presented.

[52] H. Attiya and A. Fouren. Polynomial and adaptive long-lived $(2k-1)$-renaming. In *Proc. 14th International Symp. on Distributed Computing, LNCS 1914*. Springer-Verlag, 2000, 149–163.

The authors improve some of their results from [53].

[53] H. Attiya and A. Fouren. Algorithms adapting to point contention. *Journal of the ACM*, **50**(4):444–468, 2003.

Presents adaptive algorithms for renaming, timestamping and collecting information. The adaptive collect object has $O(k^2)$ step complexity when using results from [183] as building blocks. The $(2k-1)$-renaming has exponential step complexity. Journal version of some of the results from [4].

[54] H. Attiya and N. A. Lynch. Time bounds for real-time process control in the presence of timing uncertainty. *Information and Computation*, **110**:183–232, 1994.

A timing-based variant of the mutual exclusion problem is considered. It is assumed that there is a known upper bound on the time it takes to release the resource, and that only an inaccurate clock can be used to measure time.

[55] H. Attiya and J. Welch. *Distributed Computing: Fundamentals, Simulations and Advanced Topics (Second Edition)*. Wiley, 2004.

The book contains lots of significant algorithms and impossibility results in the area of distributed algorithms.

[56] B. Awerbuch and M. Saks. A dining philosophers algorithm with polynomial response time. In *Proc. 31st IEEE Symp. on Foundations of Computer Science*, pages 65–74, 1990.

The authors define a general dynamic job scheduling problem, which includes drinking philosophers as a special case.

[57] J. Bacon and T. Harris. *Operating Systems, Concurrent and Distributed Software Design*. Harlow: Addison-Wesley, 2003.

Presents fundamental operating system concepts and algorithms, including a chapter about low-level synchronization algorithms.

[58] B. S. Baker and E. G. Coffman, Jr. Mutual exclusion scheduling. *Theoretical Computer Science*, **162**(2):225–243, 1996.

Mutual exclusion scheduling is the problem of scheduling unit-time tasks non-preemptively on m processors subject to constraints, represented by a graph G, so that tasks represented by adjacent vertices in G must run in disjoint time intervals. Minimizing the completion time is NP-hard; however, polynomial time is sufficient to produce optimal schedules for forests, and simple heuristics perform well on certain classes of graphs.

[59] Y. Bar-David and G. Taubenfeld. Automatic discovery of mutual exclusion algorithms. In *Proc. 17th International Symp. on Distributed Computing*, LNCS 2648. Springer-Verlag, 2003, 136–150.

A methodology for automatic discovery of synchronization algorithms is presented. The authors built a tool and used it to automatically discover hundreds of new mutual exclusion algorithms for two processes. The methodology is rather simple and the fact that it is computationally feasible is surprising. The brute force approach may require (even for very short algorithms) the mechanical verification of hundreds of millions of incorrect algorithms before a correct algorithm is found.

The the main contribution is in demonstrating that the approach suggested is feasible. See discussion on page 74.

[60] J. Bar-Ilan and D. Peleg. Distributed resource allocation algorithms. In *Proc. International Workshop on Distributed Algorithms*, LNCS 647, Springer-Verlag, 1992, 277–291.

A few algorithms for the dining/drinking philosophers problem are presented in different models of computation and communication in a distributed system.

[61] A. Bar-Noy, M. Ben-Or, and D. Dolev. Choice coordination with limited failure. *Distributed Computing*, **3**:61–72, 1989.

The authors extend the analysis from [291] for choice coordination with two alternatives and $n-1$ faults to arbitrary number of faults, examine the local storage requirements, and study a semi-synchronous model. See Section 8.5.3 (page 299) for more details.

[62] A. Bar-Noy and D. Dolev. Shared memory versus message-passing in an asynchronous distributed environment. In *Proc. 8th ACM Symp. on Principles of Distributed Computing*, pages 307–318, August 1989.

Presents the first wait-free one-shot $(2n-1)$-renaming algorithm using atomic registers. The algorithm has an exponential step complexity.

[63] A. Bar-Noy, D. Dolev, D. Koller, and D. Peleg. Fault-tolerant critical section management in asynchronous environments. *Information and Computation*, **95**(1):1–20, 1991.

The ℓ-exclusion problem (called in the paper the "identical-slot critical section" problem) is considered in a completely asynchronous distributed network. The fairness condition assumed is called *the transient priority rule*: process p has higher priority than process q only if p entered its critical section less times than q, p tries to enter its critical section, and q *knows* this fact. (This is a stronger version of the global priority rule of [47].) The message complexity of the solutions is unbounded.

[64] G. Barnes. A method for implementing lock-free shared-data structures. In *Proc. 15th Annual ACM Symp. on Parallel Algorithms and Architectures*, pages 261–270, June–July 1993.

A general approach for implementing lock-free algorithms is suggested.

[65] R. Bayer and M. Schkolnick. Concurrency of operations on B-trees. *Acta Informatica*, **9**:1–21, 1977.

B-trees are highly useful for storing large amounts of information. The authors study concurrent access to B-trees.

[66] M. Ben Ari. *Principles of Concurrent and Distributed Programming*. Prentice-Hall, Inc., 1990.

The book provides an introduction to concurrent progamming focusing on general principles.

[67] A. J. Bernstein and P. M. Lewis. *Concurrency in Programming and Database Systems*. Jones and Bartlett Publishers, 1993.

The book is addressed to both practitioners, who want an introduction to the mathematical design theory, and practitioners, who want to use that theory in the implementation of real-world systems.

[68] P. A. Bernstein and N. Goodman. Timestamp-based algorithms for concurrency control in distributed database systems. In *Proc. International Conference on Very Large Databases*, pages 285–300, October 1980.

Several timestamp-based concurrency-control algorithms are discussed.

[69] B. N. Bershad, D. D. Redell, and J. R. Ellis. Fast mutual exclusion for uniprocessors. *Sigplan Notices*, **27**(9):223–233, 1992.

Restartable atomic sequences, an optimistic mechanism for implementing simple atomic operations such as test-and-set on a uniprocessor, are described. It is shown that improving the performance of low-level atomic operations, and therefore mutual exclusion mechanisms, improves application performance.

[70] G. E. Blelloch, P. Cheng, and P. B. Gibbons. Scalable room synchronization. *Theory of Computing Systems*, **36**:397–430, 2003.

A scalable solution to the group mutual exclusion problem is presented, with applications to linearizable stacks and queues, and related problems. See also [71].

[71] G. E. Blelloch, P. Cheng, and P. B. Gibbons. Room synchronization. In *Proc. 13th Annual Symp. on Parallel Algorithms and Architectures*, pages 122–133, July 2001.

Room synchronization is the same as group mutual exclusion [195]. The authors define room synchronization, present a solution, and show how it can be used to efficiently implement concurrent queues and stacks using a fetch-and-add operation. See also [70].

[72] K. Block and T. K. Woo. A more efficient generalization of Peterson's mutual exclusion algorithm. *Information Processing Letters*, **35**(5):219–222, 1990.

A starvation-free algorithm for n processes is presented. The algorithm is described in Problem 2.65 (on page 91). The algorithm is a generalization of Peterson's algorithm for two processes presented on page 32. The system response time of the algorithm is $O(n \times m)$ when m out of the n processes are competing for the critical section. This is better than the $O(n^2)$ contention-free complexity of Peterson's starvation-free algorithm for n processes presented in Problem 2.63 (page 90). (Peterson's algorithms are from [282].) See also Problem 6.6 (page 246).

[73] E. Borowsky and E. Gafni. Generalized FLP impossibility result for t-resilient asynchronous computations. In *Proc. 25th ACM Symp. on Theory of Computing*, pages 91–100, May 1993.

Among other results, the authors prove the impossibility result for set-consensus as stated in Problem 9.17 (page 339).

[74] P. Brinch Hansen. *Operating Systems Principles*. Prentice-Hall, Inc., 1973.

An introduction to operating systems. Introduces a programming language notation for monitors based on the class concept of Simula 67.

[75] P. Brinch Hansen. Distributed processes: A concurrent programming concept. *Communications of the ACM*, **21**:934–941, 1978.

Among other things, the paper includes a centralized solution to the dining philosophers problem.

[76] H. Brit and S. Moran. Wait-freedom vs. bounded wait-freedom in public data structures (extended abstract). In *Proc. 13th ACM Symp. on Principles of Distributed Computing*, pages 52–60, August 1994.

Studies the relation between wait-freedom and bounded wait-freedom. While wait-freedom requires only that every operation (process) always terminates within a finite number of steps, bounded wait-freedom requires that it terminates within a fixed and pre-determined number of steps.

[77] E. D. Brooks, III. The butterfly barrier. *International Journal of Parallel Programming*, **15**(4):295–307, 1986.

Introduced the butterfly barrier. The butterfly barrier requires that the number of processes be a power of two. This was later improved by the introduction of the Dissemination barrier (see [164]).

[78] P. A. Buhr, M. Fortier, and M. H. Coffin. Monitor classification. *ACM Computing Surveys*, **27**(1):63–107, 1995.

A taxonomy of monitors is presented that encompasses all the extant monitors and suggests others not found in the literature or in existing programing languages.

[79] J. E. Burns. Complexity of communication among asynchronous parallel processes. Technical Report GIT-ICS-81/01, Georgia Institute of Technology, 1981.

The Ph.D. dissertation of Jim Burns. Among many other results Burns had also presented the LR algorithm to the dining philosophers problem (see page 263).

[80] J. E. Burns. Symmetry in systems of asynchronous processes. In *Proc. 22nd IEEE Symp. on Foundations of Computer Science*, pages 169–174, October 1981.

Two definitions of symmetry are developed. It is shown that strong symmetry does not allow any solution to the problem of deadlock-free mutual exclusion using atomic registers, while weak symmetry requires the use of n registers, at least one of which must be able to take on n values.

[81] J. E. Burns. Mutual exclusion with linear waiting using binary shared variables. *SIGACT News*, **10**(2):42–47 (summer 1978).

Upper and lower bound are proved for solving the mutual exclusion with shared bits and test-and-set bits. See algorithm on page 195.

[82] J. E. Burns, M. J. Fischer, P. Jackson, N. A. Lynch, and G. L. Peterson. Shared data requirements for implementation of mutual exclusion using a test-and-set primitive. In *Proc. International Conference on Parallel Processing*, pages 79–87, August 1978.

Older version of [83].

[83] J. E. Burns, P. Jackson, N. A. Lynch, M. J. Fischer, and G. L. Peterson. Data requirements for implementation of N-process mutual exclusion using a single shared variable. *Journal of the Association for Computing Machinery*, **29**(1):183–205, 1982.

Bounds are presented for n-process mutual exclusion in a model which supports a read-modify-write operation (or the slightly weaker generalized test-and-set operation). It is shown that any starvation-free solution requires at least $\sqrt{2n} + \frac{1}{2}$ values. A technical restriction increases the lower bound to $\lfloor n/2 \rfloor$ values, ($\lfloor n/2 \rfloor + 2$ in [280]) while achieving bounded waiting requires at least $n + 1$ values. These bounds are shown to be nearly optimal, for algorithms are exhibited for the last two cases with $\lfloor n/2 \rfloor + 9$ and $n + 3$ values (for linear-waiting), respectively. In the algorithms the exit code is not wait-free (i.e., requirement 4 on page 12 is not satisfied). For improved upper bounds see [281]. See also [161] and read page 194 for more details.

[84] J. E. Burns and A. N. Lynch. Mutual exclusion using indivisible reads and writes. In *Proc. 18th Annual Allerton Conference on Communication, Control and Computing*, pages 833–842, October 1980.

Older version of [86].

[85] J. E. Burns and G. L. Peterson. The ambiguity of choosing. In *Proc. 8th ACM Symp. on Principles of Distributed Computing*, pages 145–158, August 1989.

Among other results, the authors show that a necessary and sufficient condition for solving the ℓ-assignment problem using atomic registers is that $\ell \geq 2k+1$, where k is the maximal number of possible faults. The ℓ-assignment problem is defined on page 241. Also, this paper introduces the first long-lived renaming algorithm, since the ℓ-assignment algorithm presented in the paper can be used as an optimal long-lived $(2n-1)$-renaming algorithm with exponential step complexity. See also [47].

[86] J. E. Burns and N. A. Lynch. Bounds on shared-memory for mutual exclusion. *Information and Computation*, **107**(2):171–184, December 1993.

It is shown that n atomic bits are necessary and sufficient to solve the problem of deadlock-free mutual exclusion for n processes using only atomic registers (page 59).

[87] R. H. Campbell and A. N. Habermann. The specification of process synchronization by path expressions. *Lecture Notes in Computer Science*, **16**:89–102, 1974.

The notion of *path expressions* is introduced. In path expression, the operands are procedure names and the operators specify whether the procedures are to be executed exclusively, concurrently, or sequentially.

[88] T. A. Cargill. A robust distributed solution to the dining philosophers problem. *Software–Practice and Experience*, **12**:965–969, 1982.

The LR algorithm (page 263), which seems to be folklore, is studied. The author makes the observation (Theorem 7.7, page 264) that the LR algorithm is at most $n/4$-concurrent; no proof is given; see also [80, 244].

[89] J. A. Carruth and J. Misra. Proof of a real-time mutual-exclusion algorithm. Notes on UNITY: 32–92. Also in: *Parallel Processing Letters*, **6**(2):251–257, 1996.

Fischer's algorithm (page 345) is proved using the technique of establishing an appropriate invariant.

[90] T. D. Chandra, V. Hadzilacos, and S. Toueg. The weakest failure detector for solving consensus. *Journal of the ACM*, **43**(4):685–722, 1996.

The authors determine what information about failures is necessary and sufficient to solve consensus in asynchronous distributed systems subject to crash failures. See also [91].

[91] T. D. Chandra and S. Toueg. Unreliable failure detectors for reliable distributed systems. *Journal of the ACM*, **43**(2):225–267, 1996.

The authors introduce the concept of unreliable failure detectors and study how they can be used to solve consensus in asynchronous systems with crash failures. See also [90].

[92] K. M. Chandy and J. Misra. The drinking philosophers problem. *ACM Trans. on Programming Languages and Systems*, **6**:632–646, 1984.

The paper extends the dining philosophers problem to an arbitrary graph network, in which a philosopher needs to acquire the resources on some non-empty subset of its incident edges in order to eat; this subset of resources may change over time (see also [337]).

[93] C. Chang. Bidding against competitors. *IEEE Trans. on Software Engineering*, **16**(1):100–104, 1990.

Two economical bidding schemes are discussed, which can be used to construct randomized solutions to the mutual exclusion and the dining philosophers problems.

[94] M. Choy and A. K. Singh. Efficient fault-tolerant algorithms for distributed resource allocation. *ACM Trans. on Programming Languages and Systems*, **17**(3):535–559, 1995.

The authors have defined a new metric for evaluating resource allocation algorithms called failure locality (see page 276) which measures the robustness of an algorithm in the presence of process failures, and presented a few efficient algorithms. See also [95].

[95] M. Choy and A. K. Singh. Localizing failures in distributed synchronization. *IEEE Trans. on Parallel and Distributed Systems*, 7(7):705–716, 1996.

Uses failure locality from [94] as a measure of the fault-tolerance of distributed algorithms. This measure captures the general idea of allowing part of a system to continue to function despite the failure of other parts of the system. The authors concentrate on two problems, the dining philosophers problem and the committee coordination problem, and present algorithms for them.

[96] M. Choy and A. K. Singh. Adaptive solutions to the mutual exclusion problem. In *Proc. 12th ACM Symp. on Principles of Distributed Computing*, pages 183–194, August 1993.

See [97] for the journal version.

[97] M. Choy and A. K. Singh. Adaptive solutions to the mutual exclusion problem. *Distributed Computing*, 8(1):1–17, 1994.

Algorithms are developed for which the system response time is a function of the actual number of contending processes. That is, the response time is independent of the total number of processes and is governed only by the current degree of contention. Journal version of [96].

[98] G. Coulouris, J. Dollimore, and T. Kindberg. *Distributed Systems, Concepts and Design, 3rd edition.* Addison-Wesley, 2001.

The book aims to convey insight into, and knowledge of, the principles and practice underlying the design of distributed systems, both Internet-based and otherwise. Includes a chapter about coordination and agreement.

[99] P. L. Courtois, F. Heyman, and D. L. Parnas. Concurrent control with Readers and Writers. *Communications of the ACM*, **14**(10):667–668, 1971.

The first paper to discuss the readers and writers problem (see page 288). Two solutions are presented: one for the case where we wish minimum delay for the readers (see page 289); the other for the case where we wish writing to take place as early as possible (see page 290).

[100] T. S. Craig. Building FIFO and priority-queuing spin locks from atomic swap. Technical Report TR-93-02-02, Dept. of Computer Science, Univ. of Washington, February 1993.

Different versions of queuing spin locks are designed for machines with and without coherent-cache. These locks include extensions to provide nested lock acquisition, conditional locking, timeout of lock requests, and preemption of waiters. These locks apply to both real-time and non-real-time parallel systems.

[101] A. B. Cremers and T. N. Hibbard. Mutual exclusion of n processes using an $O(n)$-valued message variable. *Lecture Notes in Computer Science*, 62:165–176, 1978.

(5th ICALP, Italy.) An n-process solution is developed which uses a single $(2n-1)$-valued read-modify-write register and satisfies linear waiting. However, the exit code is not wait-free (i.e., does not satisfy the 4*th* requirement on page 12).

[102] J. M. Crichlow. *The Essence of Distributed Systems.* Prentice-Hall, Inc., 2000.

A short high-level description of core issues in the design and construction of distributed systems.

[103] R. Cypher. The communication requirements of mutual exclusion. In *Proc. Seventh Annual Symp. on Parallel Algorithms and Architectures*, pages 147–156, July 1995.

It is proved that $\Omega(\log\log n/\log\log\log n)$ is a lower bound on the time complexity in both the CC and DSM models. This result holds assuming any of the following objects can be used: atomic registers, together with any set of comparison objects (such as test-and-set, compare-and-swap, and load-link/store-conditional). This result is improved in [30]. See Problem 3.15 (page 139).

[104] R. Danek and V. Hadzilacos. Local-spin group mutual exclusion algorithms. In *Proc. 18th International Symp. on Distributed Computing*, LNCS 3274. Springer-Verlag, 2004, 71–85.

Efficient local spinning group mutual exclusion algorithms are presented.

[105] N. G. deBruijn. Additional comments on a problem in concurrent programming control. *Communications of the ACM*, **10**(3):137–138, 1967.

Knuth algorithm [204] is modified to obtain $(\frac{n(n+1)}{2})$-bounded-waiting (page 89).

[106] E. W. Dijkstra. Solution of a problem in concurrent programming control. *Communications of the ACM*, **8**(9):569, 1965.

A classical paper in which the mutual exclusion problem was first stated. The paper presents the first solution to the mutual exclusion problem for n processes. It is deadlock-free, but is not starvation-free.

[107] E. W. Dijkstra. Co-operating sequential processes. In F. Genuys, ed., *Programming Languages*, pages 43–112. New York: Academic Press, 1968. Reprinted from: Technical Report EWD-123, Technological University, Eindhoven, the Netherlands, 1965.

A classical paper by Dijkstra which also discusses Dekker's algorithm–the first solution to the mutual exclusion problem for two processes using atomic registers. Also introduces the important notion of a *semaphore*.

[108] E. W. Dijkstra. The structure of the "THE"-multiprogramming system. *Communications of the ACM*, **11**(5):341–346, 1968.

Describes the design of a multiprogramming operating system, and introduces many new important concepts. Besides introducing semaphores, this paper also laid the groundwork for virtual memory systems, processor allocation, and hierarchical design using layers of abstraction.

[109] E. W. Dijkstra. Hierarchical ordering of sequential processes. *Acta Informatica*, **1**:115–138, 1971.

Also in *Operating Systems Techniques*, C. A. R. Hoare and R. H. Perrott, eds, Academic Press, 1972. Various principles of synchronizing sequential processes are discussed, including: the mutual exclusion problem, semaphores and the dining philosophers problem.

[110] E. W. Dijkstra. Self-stabilizing systems in spite of distributed control. *Communications of the ACM*, **17**:643–644, 1974.

The notion of self-stabilization is introduced, and three algorithms are presented. (The correctness proof of one of them is given in [113].) A system is defined to be self-stabilizing if regardless of its initial state, it is guaranteed to arrive at a legitimate state in a finite number of steps.

[111] E. W. Dijkstra. A strong P/V-implementation of n-process implementation of conditional critical regions. Technical Report EWD 651, Burroughs Corp., 1978.

Includes a conjecture that no starvation-free solution to the mutual exclusion problem exists for unknown number of processes and under the constraint of employing only a fixed number of weak semaphores. This conjecture is refuted in [270].

[112] E. W. Dijkstra. An assertional proof of a program by G. L. Peterson. Technical Report EWD 779, Burroughs Corp., 1981.

Gives a formal proof of Peterson's algorithm [282].

[113] E. W. Dijkstra. A belated proof of self-stabilization. *Distributed Computing*, **1**:5–6, 1986.

A correctness proof is given for the solution with three-state machine presented in [110].

[114] D. Dolev, C. Dwork, and L. Stockmeyer. On the minimal synchronism needed for distributed consensus. *Journal of the ACM*, **34**(1):77–97, 1987.

The results reported in [135] are extended: Several critical system parameters, including various synchrony conditions, are identified and how varying these affects the number of faults that can be tolerated is examined.

[115] D. Dolev, E. Gafni, and N. Shavit. Toward a non-atomic era: ℓ-exclusion as a test case. In *Proc. 20th ACM Symp. on Theory of Computing*, pages 78–92, May 1988.

A (complex) ℓ-starvation-free solution to the ℓ-exclusion problem using safe registers alone is presented.

[116] D. Dolev and N. Shavit. Bounded concurrent time-stamping. *SIAM Journal on Computing*, **26**(2):418–455, 1997.

Bounded timestamps are defined in [184]. This paper introduces concurrent time-stamping, a paradigm that allows processes to temporally order concurrent events in an asynchronous shared-memory system. Concurrent time-stamp can be used as the basis for solutions to problems such as mutual exclusion, ℓ-exclusion, randomized consensus, and multi-writer multi-reader atomic registers. The constructions are complex. For an n-process system the construction requires n registers of $O(n)$ bits each, the time complexity is $O(n)$ operations for an update and $O(n^2 \log n)$ for a scan.

[117] S. Dolev. *Self-Stabilization*. The MIT Press, March 2000.

Self-stabilization refers to a system's ability to recover automatically from unexpected faults. The author presents the fundamentals of self-stabilization and demonstrates the process of designing self-stabilizing distributed systems.

[118] R. W. Doran and L. K. Thomas. Variants of the software solution to mutual exclusion. *Information Processing Letters*, **10**(4–5):206–208, 1980.

Two simple variants of Dekker's algorithm [107] for two processes which eliminate the nested loops are presented.

[119] A. B. Downey. *The Little Book of Semaphores*. Published by the author (for free), 2003.

Includes many solutions to classical and not-so-classical synchronization problems using semaphores.

[120] M. Duflot, L. Fribourg, and C. Picaronny. Randomized dining philosophers without fairness assumption. *Distributed Computing*, **17**(1):65–76, 2004.

Lehmann-Rabin's randomized algorithm from [233] requires a fairness assumption on the scheduling mechanism: if a philosopher is continuously hungry then he must eventually be scheduled. The authors modify the algorithm in order to get rid of the fairness assumption.

[121] C. Dwork, M. P. Herlihy, and O. Waarts. Contention in shared memory algorithms. In *Proc. 25th ACM Symp. on Theory of Computing*, pages 174–183, May 1993.

Suggests modeling contention at a shared object with the help of stall operations. In the case of simultaneous accesses to a single memory location, only one operation succeeds, and other pending operations must stall. The measure of contention is simply the worst-case number of stalls that can be induced by an adversary scheduler. The authors used this model to prove bounds on contention of counting networks, mutual exclusion, and agreement.

[122] C. Dwork, N. Lynch, and L. Stockmeyer. Consensus in the presence of partial synchrony. *Journal of the ACM*, **35**(2):288–323, 1988.

Partial synchrony lies between the cases of a synchronous system and an asynchronous system. Fault-tolerant consensus algorithms are given for various cases of partial synchrony and various fault models. Lower bounds which show in most cases that the algorithms are optimal with respect to the number of faults tolerated are also given.

[123] C. Dwork and O. Waarts. Simple and efficient bounded concurrent timestamping or bounded concurrent timestamp systems are comprehensible. In *Proc. 24th ACM Symp. on Theory of Computing*, pages 655–666, May 1992.

A better solution than that of [116]. See also [146, 184].

[124] W. B. Easton. Process synchronization without long-term interlock. In *Proc. 3rd ACM Symp. on Operating Systems Principles*, pages 95–100, October 1971.

A technique is presented for avoiding long-term interlocking of shared data. Four principles of OS architecture are presented; implementation of a system adhering to these principles requires that long-term lockout be avoided.

[125] M. A. Eisenberg and M. R. McGuire. Further comments on Dijkstra's concurrent programming control problem. *Communications of the ACM*, **15**(11):999, 1972.

deBruijn's algorithm [105] is modified to obtain linear-waiting: no process can execute its critical section twice while some other process is kept waiting (page 90).

[126] C. S. Ellis. Extendible hashing for concurrent operations and distributed data. In *Proc. 2nd ACM Symp. on Principles of Database Systems*, pages 106–116, March 1983.

The extendible hash file is a dynamic data structure that is an alternative to B-trees for use as a database index. A locking-based solution to allow for concurrency is presented.

[127] K. P. Eswaran, J. N. Gary, A. Lorie, and I. L. Traiger. The notion of consistency and predicate locks in database systems. *Communications of the ACM*, **19**(11):624–633, 1976.

Introduces the two-phase locking algorithm.

[128] A. Feldmann, T. Gross, D. O'Hallaron, and T. M. Stricker. Subset barrier synchronization on a private-memory parallel system. In *Proc. 4th ACM Symp. on Parallel Algorithms and Architectures*, pages 209–218, June–July 1992.

The paper investigates algorithms that allow disjoint subsets of processors to synchronize independently and in parallel.

[129] F. E. Fich, D. Hendler, and N. Shavit. On the inherent weakness of conditional synchronization primitives. In *Proc. 23rd ACM Symp. on Principles of Distributed Computing*, pages 80–87, July 2004.

Among other results, the authors have proved the result stated in Problem 4.12 (page 196).

[130] F. E. Fich and E. Ruppert. Hundreds of impossibility results for distributed computing. *Distributed Computing*, **16**(2–3):121–163, 2003.

The authors survey results from distributed computing that show problems to be impossible, either outright or within given resource bounds, in various models.

[131] M. J. Fischer. The consensus problem in unreliable distributed systems (a brief survey). In *Proc. 1983 International FCT-Conference on Fundamentals of Computation Theory*, LNCS 158. Springer-Verlag, 1983, 127–140.

A short survey of a few results.

[132] M. J. Fischer, N. A. Lynch, J. E. Burns, and A. Borodin. Distributed FIFO allocation of identical resources using small shared space. *ACM Trans. on Programming Languages and Systems*, **11**(1):90–114, 1989.

A simple and efficient algorithm for the FIFO allocation of ℓ identical resources is presented, together with a lower bound on fault-tolerant ℓ-exclusion. Journal version of some of the results in [133]. Assumes strong FIFO and robustness requirements. That is, FIFO in the exit code is also required, up to $\ell - 1$ enabled processes can fail, and any number of other (not enabled) processes can fail anywhere else.

[133] M. J. Fischer, N. A. Lynch, J. E. Burns, and A. Borodin. Resource allocation with immunity to limited process failure. In *Proc. 20th IEEE Symp. on Foundations of Computer Science*, pages 234–254, October 1979.

The bounds of [82, 83] for mutual exclusion are extended to the case of fault-tolerant ℓ-exclusion. Older version of [132].

[134] M. J. Fischer, N. A. Lynch, and M. Merritt. Easy impossibility proofs for distributed consensus problems. *Distributed Computing*, **1**(1):26–39, 1986.

Easy proofs are given, of the impossibility of solving several consensus problems, namely Byzantine agreement, weak agreement, Byzantine firing squad, approximate agreement and clock synchronization, in certain communication graphs.

[135] M. J. Fischer, N. A. Lynch, and M. S. Paterson. Impossibility of distributed consensus with one faulty process. *Journal of the ACM*, **32**(2):374–382, 1985.

It is proved that there is no consensus algorithm that can tolerate even a single crash failure in a message-passing system. This is one of the most interesting results in the area of distributed computing. See also [237].

[136] M. J. Fischer, S. Moran, S. Rudich, and G. Taubenfeld. The wakeup problem. *SIAM Journal on Computing*, **25**(6):1332–1357, 1996.

A new problem – the wakeup problem – is presented. The authors present efficient solutions to the problem and show how these solutions can be used to solve the consensus problem, the leader-election problem, and other related problems. See also [137].

[137] M. J. Fischer, S. Moran, and G. Taubenfeld. Space-efficient asynchronous consensus without shared memory initialization. *Information Processing Letters*, **45**(2):101–105, 1993.

A solution to the consensus problem is presented; where all processes are programmed alike, there is no global synchronization (i.e., the model is asynchronous), it is not possible to simultaneously reset the shared memory to a known initial state, and processes may be faulty. The algorithm is presented in Section 9.3 (page 311). See also [136].

[138] M. Fomitchev and E. Ruppert. Lock-free linked lists and skip lists. In *Proc. 23rd ACM Symp. on Principles of Distributed Computing*, pages 50–59, July 2004.

A lock-free implementation of a singly-linked list is presented, and is used to implement a lock-free skip list dictionary data structure. The algorithms use a single-word compare-and-swap.

[139] N. Francez. *Fairness*. Springer-Verlag, 1986.

The book brings together most of the known approaches for proving properties of programs and, in particular, focuses on proving the termination of programs under various fairness assumptions about the processes' behavior (such as unconditional, weak, and strong fairness).

[140] N. Francez and M. Rodeh. A distributed abstract data type implemented by a probabilistic communication scheme. In *Proc. 21st IEEE Symp. on Foundations of Computer Science*, pages 373–379, 1980.

A fully distributed algorithm which solves the dining philosophers problem, expressed as a CSP program, is presented.

[141] D. A. Franciskovich and G. Taubenfeld. Fault tolerance in distributed dining philosophers algorithms. *Unpublished manuscript*, 1990.

A measure of fault tolerance in a dining philosophers algorithm is considered. The fault tolerance of some known algorithms is determined. Most of the robustness results presented in Chapter 7 (page 249) are from this paper.

[142] K. Fraser and T. Harris. Concurrent programming without locks.

The authors present three abstractions which make it easier to develop non-blocking data structures: multi-word compare-and-swap, word-based software transactional memory, and object-based software transactional memory. Implementations are presented. July 2004.

[143] S. A. Friedberg and G. L. Peterson. An efficient solution to the mutual exclusion problem using weak semaphores. *Information Processing Letters*, **25**(5):343–347, 1987.

A starvation-free solution to the mutual exclusion problem that uses two weak semaphores and two shared bits is presented (see page 178). The algorithm satisfies 2-bounded waiting and is correct even if the number of processes is unbounded but only a finite number of them are attempting to enter their critical section at the same time.

[144] E. Gafni, M. Merritt, and G. Taubenfeld. The concurrency hierarchy, and algorithms for unbounded concurrency. In *Proc. 20th ACM Symp. on Principles of Distributed Computing*, pages 161–169, August 2001.

It is demonstrated that many interesting problems, such as collect, snapshot, and renaming, have (adaptive) wait-free solutions even when the number of processes is not *a priori* known or even when it is infinite. Furthermore, it is shown that the unbounded concurrency is strictly weaker than bounded *concurrency*.

[145] D. L. Galli. *Distributed Operating Systems*. Prentice-Hall, Inc., 2000.

Covers several distributed operating system concepts, including chapters about concurrency control and distributed synchronization.

[146] R. Gawlick, N. A. Lynch, and N. Shavit. Concurrent timestamping made simple. In *Israel Symp. on Theory of Computing Systems*, pages 171–183, 1992.

Provides more easily verifiable CTSS constructions than that of [116]. See also [123, 184].

[147] P. B. Gibbons, Y. Matias, and V. Ramachandran. The QRQW PRAM: Accounting for contention in parallel algorithms. In *Proc. Fifth Annual ACM-SIAM Symp. on Discrete Algorithms*, pages 638–648, January 1994.

The authors proposed the Queue-Read Queue-Write PRAM model, in which the time to execute a read or a write on a shared register is a linear function of the number of processes accessing the same register concurrently.

[148] D. Ginat, A. U. Shankar, and A. K. Agrawala. An efficient solution to the drinking philosophers problem and its extensions. *Lecture Notes in Computer Science*, **392**:83–93, 1989. In: *Proc. 3rd International Workshop on Distributed Algorithms*.

A drinking philosophers algorithm is proposed that solves the problem directly without using a dining philosophers subroutine. As a result, it is more message efficient, but requires unbounded counters.

[149] M. G. Gouda. The stabilizing philosopher: asymmetry by memory and by action. *Tech. Rep.* CS-TR-12, University of Texas at Austin, 1987.

A class of systems of dining philosophers is discussed, where each system in the class is both asymmetric by memory and self-stabilizing at the same time.

[150] G. Graunke and S. Thakkar. Synchronization algorithms for shared-memory multiprocessors. *IEEE Computers*, **23**(6):60–69, 1990.

Several new software synchronization mechanisms are developed and evaluated. The mechanisms remain valuable even when changes are made to the hardware synchronization mechanism to improve support for highly contested locks. See Section 4.4.2 (page 163) for some of the results.

[151] J. Gray. Notes on data base operating systems. *Operating Systems, An Advanced Course*, Lecture Notes in Computer Science, **60**:393–481, 1978. Also appeared as IBM Research Report RJ2188.

Among many other issues, the coordinated attack problem is introduced (see page 8).

[152] D. S. Greenberg, G. Taubenfeld, and Da-Wei Wang. Choice coordination with multiple alternatives (preliminary version). In *Proc. 6th International Workshop on Distributed Algorithms*, LNCS 647. Springer-Verlag, 1992, 54–68.

The authors characterize when the choice coordination problem with k alternatives can be solved deterministically, prove upper and lower space bounds for deterministic solutions, and provide a randomized algorithm which is significantly better than the deterministic lower bound. See Section 8.5.3 (page 299) for more details.

[153] M. Greenwald. Two-handed emulation: how to build non-blocking implementations of complex data-structures using dcas. In *Proc. 21st ACM Symp. on Principles of Distributed Computing*, pages 260–269, July 2002. Also appeared as IBM Research Report RJ2188.

A technique which yields efficient implementations of a class of non-blocking data structures is presented including a doubly-linked list and a dynamically resizable hash-table.

[154] D. Grunwald and S. Vajracharya. Efficient barriers for distributed shared memory computers. In *Proc. 8th International Symposium on Parallel Processing*, pages 604–608, April 1994.

The authors present two new barrier algorithms, and discuss the tradeoffs and the performance of seven algorithms on two architectures.

[155] R. Gupta. The fuzzy barrier: a mechanism for high speed synchronization of processors. In *Proc. Third International Conference on Architectural Support for Programming Languages and Operating Systems*, pages 54–63, April 1989.

Processes that are stalled waiting for other processors to reach the barrier are essentially idling and can not do any useful work. To address this problem the barrier concept is extended to include a region of statements that can be executed by a process while it awaits synchronization.

[156] A. N. Habermann. Prevention of system deadlocks. *Communications of the ACM*, **12**(7):373–377, 1969.

Dijkstra's original banker's algorithm was developed for a single type of resource [107]. This paper (by a former PhD student of Dijkstra) extends it to multiple resource types (see Section 7.3, page 255). See also [180, 277].

[157] V. Hadzilacos. A note on group mutual exclusion. In *Proc. 20th Symp. on Principles of Distributed Computing*, pages 100–106, August 2001.

Proposes a simple formulation of "concurrent entering" that is similar to the one considered in [195], and is stronger then the one from [198]. Also presents another algorithm that satisfies this stronger property.

[158] S. Haldar and D. K. Subramanian. An efficient solution to the mutual exclusion problem using unfair and weak semaphore. *Operating Systems Review (ACM)*, **22**(2):60–66, 1988.

A simple variant of the algorithm from [143] is presented (see page 200) which also solves the problem with two weak binary semaphores and two atomic bits. As the solution in [143], this version also satisfies 2-bounded waiting.

[159] J. Y. Halpern and Y. Moses. Knowledge and common knowledge in a distributed environment. *Journal of the ACM*, **37**(3):549–587, 1990.

A general framework for formalizing and reasoning about knowledge in distributed systems is presented. Includes an impossibility proof for the coordinated attack problem (see page 8).

[160] T. L. Harris. A pragmatic implementation of non-blocking linked-lists. In *Proc. 15th International Symp. on Distributed Computing*, LNCS 2180. Springer-Verlag, 2003, 300–314.

A non-blocking implementation of concurrent linked-lists is presented supporting linearizable insertion and deletion operations.

[161] S. Hart, M. Sharir, and A. Pnueli. Termination of probabilistic concurrent programs. In *Proc. ACM Symp. on Principles of Programming Languages*, pages 1–6, January 1982.

The asynchronous behavior of several concurrent processes, which may use randomization, is studied. Among other results, it is shown that the use of randomization is, in certain cases, no more powerful than using deterministic algorithms. In proving this result, it is also shown that: Rabin's algorithm in [291] is not lockout-free if general fair schedules are allowed, and that the lower bounds given in [82] are also required for probabilistic algorithms of the same kind. See page 194 for more details.

[162] P. B. Henderson and Y. Zalcstein. A graph-theoretic characterization of the PV-chunk class of synchronizing primitives. *SIAM Journal on Computing*, **6**(1):88–108, 1977.

A characterization is provided, of the class of graphs which correspond to the system of synchronizing primitives PV-chunk [235, 333] in terms of a normal form representation, and an efficient algorithm for determining whether an arbitrary graph is in the class is presented. See also [163, 274].

[163] P. B. Henderson and Y. Zalcstein. Synchronization problems solvable by generalized PV systems. *Journal of the ACM*, **27**(1):60–71, 1980.

A characterization is provided, of those synchronization problems solvable by Dijkstra's PV system of primitives and its various generalizations including PV-general, PV-chunk, Vector Addition, and Loopless Petri Net systems. See also [162, 274].

[164] D. Hensgen, R. Finkel, and U. Manber. Two algorithms for barrier synchronization. *International Journal of Parallel Programming*, **17**(1):1–17, 1988.

Introduced the Dissemination barrier (page 213) and a tournament barrier (page 211).

[165] D. A. Hensgen, D. L. Sims, and D. Charley. Fair banker algorithm for read and write locks. *Information Processing Letters*, **48**(3):131–137, 1993.

An extension of the banker's algorithm (Section 7.3, page 255) is presented which allows processes to acquire either exclusive or shared access to resources using read and write locks.

[166] M. P. Herlihy. Wait-free synchronization. *ACM Trans. on Programming Languages and Systems*, **13**(1):124–149, 1991.

A hierarchy of objects such that no object at one level has a wait-free implementation in terms of objects at lower levels is introduced, and the universality of consensus is proved.

[167] M. P. Herlihy. A methodology for implementing highly concurrent data objects. *ACM Trans. on Programming Languages and Systems*, **15**(5):745–770, 1993.

A methodology is proposed for constructing lock-free and wait-free implementations of concurrent objects, for machines with support for load-linked/store-conditional operations.

[168] M. P. Herlihy, V. Luchangco, P. Martin, and M. Moir. Nonblocking memory management support for dynamic-sized data structures. *ACM Trans. on Computer Systems*, **23**(2):146–196, 2005.

A technique is introduced that allows lock-free data structures to allocate and free memory dynamically using any thread-safe memory management library.

[169] M. P. Herlihy, V. Luchangco, and M. Moir. Obstruction-free synchronization: Double-ended queues as an example. In *Proc. 23rd International Conference on Distributed Computing Systems*, page 522, May 2003.

The authors introduce obstruction-freedom, a progress condition weaker than non-blocking. To illustrate the benefits of obstruction-freedom, they present two obstruction-free CAS-based implementations of double-ended queues.

[170] M. P. Herlihy, V. Luchangco, M. Moir, and W. N. Scherer, III. Software transactional memory for dynamic-sized data structures. In *Proc. 22nd ACM Symp. on Principles of Distributed Computing*, pages 92–101, July 2003.

The authors propose a new form of software transactional memory designed to support dynamic-sized data structures, and describe an obstruction-free implementation.

[171] M. P. Herlihy and J. E. B. Moss. Transactional memory: architectural support for lock-free data structures. In *Proc. 20th Annual International Symp. on Computer architecture*, pages 289–300, May 1993.

Transactional memory, a new multiprocessor architecture intended to make lock-free synchronization as efficient as conventional techniques based on mutual exclusion, is introduced. Transactional memory allows programmers to define customized read-modify-write operations that apply to multiple, independently-chosen words of memory.

[172] M. P. Herlihy and N. Shavit. The topological structure of asynchronous computability. *Journal of the ACM*, **46**(6):858–923, 1999.

Proves, among other results, that $\ell \geq 2n - 1$ is a necessary condition for solving the one-shot wait-free ℓ-renaming problem for n processes using atomic registers. (ℓ-renaming is defined on page 243.) The weaker result for long-lived renaming was already proved in [85] (Problem 6.17). See also Problems 9.17 and 9.18.

[173] M. P. Herlihy and J. M. Wing. Linearizability: a correctness condition for concurrent objects. *ACM Trans on Programming Languages and Systems*, **12**(3):463–492, 1990.

Linearizability is a correctness condition for concurrent objects, which provides the illusion that each operation applied by concurrent processes takes effect instantaneously at some point between its invocation and its response. This paper defines linearizability, and shows how to reason about concurrent objects, given they are linearizable.

[174] J. S. Herman. A comparison of synchronization mechanisms for concurrent programing. CSE-89-26, University of California at Davis, 1989.

Among other things, introduces the roller-coaster problems (page 300).

[175] C. A. R. Hoare. Towards a theory of parallel programming. In C. A. R. Hoare and R. H. Perrott, eds, *Operating System Techniques*. Academic Press, 1972.

The notion of *conditional critical regions* is presented: shared registers that need to be accessed with mutual exclusion are declared within the same resource; such registers are accessed only in *region* statements that name the resource. Mutual exclusion is implicit and is supported by guaranteeing that execution of region statements that name the same resource is not interleaved.

[176] C. A. R. Hoare. A structured paging system. *Computer Journal*, **16**(3):209–215, 1973.

Introducing the *monitor* synchronization concept. See also [177].

[177] C. A. R. Hoare. Monitors: An operating system structuring concept. *Communications of the ACM*, **12**(10):548–557, 1974.

The most influential paper on monitors. Contains many examples, including a bounded buffer, interval timer, and disk head scheduler. Also, the notion of a split binary semaphore is presented. See also [176].

[178] C. A. R. Hoare. Communicating sequential processes. *Communications of the ACM*, **21**:666–677, 1978.

Presents a programing language, called CSP, for concurrent programming. Includes examples of synchronization algorithms.

[179] R. C. Holt, G. S. Graham, E. D. Lazowska, and M. A. Scott. *Structured Concurrent Programming with Operating Systems Applications*. Addison-Wesley, 1978.

Among other things, the paper includes a centralized solution to the dining philosophers problem.

[180] R. C. Holt. Comments on prevention of system deadlocks. *Communications of the ACM*, **14**(1):37–38, 1971.

Makes the simple observation that the algorithm from [156] is correct only if the scheduler (banker) is not restricted in the way it may allocate resources. See also [277].

[181] D. Hoover and J. Poole. Distributed self-stabilizing solution to the dining philosophers problem. *Information Processing Letters*, **41**(4):209–213, 1992.

A distributed dining philosophers algorithm which is self-stabilizing is presented. The algorithm is not efficient as only one philosopher at a time may change its state.

[182] H. Hyman. Comments on a problem in concurrent programming control. *Communications of the ACM*, **9**(1):45, 1966.

A solution is presented which, as pointed out by Knuth [204], is wrong (page 79).

[183] M. Inoue, S. Umetani, T. Masuzawa, and H. Fujiwara. Adaptive long-lived $O(k^2)$-renaming with $O(k^2)$ steps. In *Proc. 15th International Symp. on Distributed Computing*, LNCS 2180. Springer-Verlag, 2001, 123–135.

A long-lived adaptive renaming algorithm is presented, using a finite number of bounded size atomic registers. An implementation of the sieve object is also presented which has $O(k)$ step complexity, where k is the point contention.

[184] A. Israeli and M. Li. Bounded time-stamps. *Distributed Computing*, **6**(4):205–209, 1993.

The first to isolate the notion of bounded timestamping (timestamping using bounded size memory) as an independent concept, developing an elegant theory of bounded sequential timestamp systems. See also [116, 123, 146].

[185] A. Israeli and L. Rappoport. Disjoint-access-parallel implementations of strong shared memory primitives. In *Proc. 13th ACM Symp. on Principles of Distributed Computing*, pages 151–160, August 1994.

Efficient implementation of atomic multi-word operations from single word operations is proposed.

[186] R. T. Jacob and I. P. Page. Synthesis of mutual exclusion solutions based on binary semaphores. *IEEE Trans. on Software Engineering*, **15**(5):560–568, 1989.

A graphical form of the problem is considered in which each vertex represents a process and each edge represents a mutual exclusion constraint between its endpoints. An *edge semaphore* solution for mutual exclusion problems is defined, and those graphs which are edge solvable are characterized.

[187] P. Jayanti. Robust wait-free hierarchies. *Journal of the ACM*, **44**(4):592–614, 1997.

A hierarchy is robust if each type is stronger than any combination of lower level types. The author studies two specific hierarchies which are based on the ability to solve consensus.

[188] P. Jayanti. Adaptive and efficient abortable mutual exclusion. In *Proc. 22nd ACM Symp. on Principles of Distributed Computing*, pages 295–304, July 2003.

The paper presents an adaptive and abortable algorithm using objects that can support four operations: load-link, store-conditional, read, and write. The algorithm uses unbounded size objects.

[189] P. Jayanti, T. D. Chandra, and S. Toueg. Fault-tolerant wait-free shared objects. *Journal of the ACM*, **45**(3):451–500, 1998.

The authors consider the problem of implementing shared objects that tolerate the failure of both processes and base objects. See also [8].

[190] P. Jayanti, S. Petrovic, and K. Tan. Adaptive and efficient abortable mutual exclusion. In *Proc. 22nd ACM Symp. on Principles of Distributed Computing*, pages 275–284, July 2003.

The authors present a FCFS group mutual exclusion algorithm that uses only $O(N)$ bounded shared registers, and describe a reduction that transforms any abortable FCFS mutual exclusion algorithm into a group mutual exclusion algorithm.

[191] P. Jayanti, K. Tan, G. Friedland, and A. Katz. Bounding Lamport's Bakery algorithm. In *Proc. 28th Annual Conference on Current Trends in Theory and Practice of Informatics*, LNCS 2234. Springer-Verlag, 2001, 261–270.

Bounds the space required by the Bakery algorithm [212]. The integer arithmetic in the original Bakery algorithm is replaced with modulo arithmetic. The algorithm makes use of an additional integer register, and the *maximum* function and the *less than* relation are redefined.

[192] P. Jayanti and S. Toueg. Some results on the impossibility, universality, and decidability of consensus. In *Proc. 6th International Workshop on Distributed Algorithms*, LNCS 674. Springer-Verlag, pages 69–84.

Includes, bounded space universal construction; solution to consensus using initially empty queue; and more.

[193] T. Johnson and K. Harathi. A simple correctness proof of the MCS contention-free lock. *Information Processing Letters*, **48**(5):215–220, 1993.

The authors provide a correctness proof of the MCS lock from [254].

[194] H. Jordan. A special purpose architecture for finite element analysis. In *Proc. International Conference on Parallel Processing*, pages 263–266, August 1978.

Considers barrier synchronization in paralled algorithms.

[195] Yuh-Jzer Joung. Asynchronous group mutual exclusion. In *Proc. 17th ACM Symp. on Principles of Distributed Computing*, pages 51–60, August 1998.

The group mutual exclusion problem was first stated and solved. The problem is a generalization of the mutual exclusion problem [106] and of the readers/writers problem [99]. The problem is exactly the same as the room synchronization problem from [71]. See [196] for the journal version.

[196] Yuh-Jzer Joung. Asynchronous group mutual exclusion. *Distributed Computing*, **13**(4):189–206, 2000.

Journal version of [195].

[197] H. P. Katseff. A new solution to the critical section problem. In *Proc. 10th ACM Symp. on Theory of Computing*, pages 86–88, May 1978.

A mutual exclusion algorithm which can tolerate an *infinite* number of immediate failures is presented. The algorithm serves processes on a first-come-first-served basis, and (unlike [287]) has a wait-free doorway–the doorway can be reached independently of the actions of the other processes, i.e., without waiting. The algorithm uses $n+1$ single-writer registers per process. (The algorithm is presented on page 126.)

[198] P. Keane and M. Moir. A simple local-spin group mutual exclusion algorithm. In *Proc. 18th ACM Symp. on Principles of Distributed Computing*, pages 23–32, May 1999.

A solution to the group mutual exclusion problem ([195]) is presented. The algorithm uses known solutions to the mutual exclusion problem, and its properties depend on the mutual exclusion algorithm used. The exit code in this solution is not wait-free.

[199] P. Keane and M. Moir. A simple local-spin group mutual exclusion algorithm. *IEEE Trans. on Parallel and Distributed Systems*, **12**(7):673–685, 2001.

Journal version of [198].

[200] J. L. W. Kessels. Arbitration without common modifiable variables. *Acta Informatica*, **17**(2):135–141, 1982.

First, a two-process mutual exclusion algorithm, based on Peterson's algorithm [282], is presented which uses only single-writer atomic registers (page 35). Then, the algorithm is generalized for any arbitrary number of competitors by applying the binary solution in a binary arbitration tree. i.e., tournament tree (page 41).

[201] Y.-J. Kim and J. Anderson. A time complexity bound for adaptive mutual exclusion, *Proc. 15th International Symp. on Distributed Computing*, LNCS 2180. Springer-Verlag, 2001, 1–15.

Establishes a bound that precludes a deterministic algorithm with $O(\log k)$ time complexity in the DSM model, where k is the "point contention". See Problem 3.16.

[202] Y.-J. Kim and J. H. Anderson. A space- and time-efficient local-spin spin lock. *Information Processing Letters*, **84**(1):47–55, 2002.

The paper presents a (non-adaptive) mutual exclusion algorithm using an atomic register, in which the time complexity in both the CC and DSM models is $\theta(\log n)$ and the space complexity is $\theta(n)$. The algorithm is a simple modification of the algorithm from [340].

[203] Y.-J. Kim and J. H. Anderson. Timing-based mutual exclusion with local spinning. In *Proc. 17th International Symp. on Distributed Computing*, LNCS 2848, Springer-Verlag, 2003, 30–44.

The paper considers the time complexity of timing-based mutual exclusion when counting only remote memory reference (RMR) and delay statements. The main conclusion is that in systems in which delay statements are supported, substantially smaller RMR time complexity is possible than in asynchronous systems.

[204] D. E. Knuth. Additional comments on a problem in concurrent programming control. *Communications of the ACM*, **9**(5):321–322, 1966.

The first starvation-free mutual exclusion algorithm for n processes is presented (page 89). A process will be able to enter its critical section before the other $n-1$ processes are able to execute their critical sections (collectively) 2^{n-1} times.

[205] L. I. Kontothanassis, R. W. Wisniewski, and M. L. Scott. Scheduler-conscious synchronization. *ACM Trans. on Computer Systems*, **15**(1):3–40, 1997.

In the presence of multiprogramming, problems arise when running processes block or, worse, busy-wait for action on the part of a process that the scheduler has chosen not to run. The authors describe and evaluate a set of algorithms that perform well in the presence of multiprogramming while maintaining good performance on dedicated machines.

[206] S. Kosaraju. Limitations of Dijkstra's semaphore primitives and petri nets. *Operating Systems Review (ACM)*, 7(4):122–126, 1973.

A follow up of [278].

[207] T. Kowaltowski and A. Palma. Another solution of the mutual exclusion problem. *Information Processing Letters*, **19**(3):145–146, 1984.

A simple solution using atomic registers is proposed, where a process need wait no more than $n-1$ turns, at the cost of having an additional scheduler process. The authors incorrectly observe that in Peterson's algorithm [282], the delay of a process is at most $n-1$ turns. As is pointed out in [312], there exist previous solutions

([125, 212]) which satisfy the same or stronger fairness condition. Moreover, the other solutions do not need to use an additional scheduler process.

[208] H. T. Kung and P. L. Lehman. Concurrent manipulation of binary search trees. *ACM Trans. on Database Systems*, 5(3):354–382, 1980.

The systems presented can support any number of concurrent processes which perform searching, insertion, deletion, and rotation (reorganization) on the tree, but allow any process to lock only a constant number of nodes at any time. Searches are essentially never blocked.

[209] E. Kushilevitz, Y. Mansoure, M. O. Rabin, and D. Zuckerman. Lower bounds for randomized mutual exclusion. In *Proc. 25th ACM Symp. on Theory of Computing*, pages 154–163, May 1993.

The main result is that a constant size read-modify-write register can not guarantee strong fairness, even if randomization is allowed. More imprecisely, a lower bound of $\Omega(\log\log n)$ bits on the size of the register is proved, which is tight, since it matches the upper bound of [210]. See page 194 for more details.

[210] E. Kushilevitz and M. O. Rabin. Randomized mutual exclusion algorithms revisited. In *Proc. 11th ACM Symp. on Principles of Distributed Computing*, pages 275–283, August 1992.

In [301] it is reported that the properties of the randomized algorithm in [291] are not as claimed. In the present paper, the algorithm in [291] is modified, so as to overcome the difficulty which was pointed out in [301]. See page 194 for more details.

[211] E. Ladan-Mozes and N. Shavit. An optimistic approach to lock-free fifo queues. In *Proc. 18th International Symp. on Distributed Computing*, LNCS 3274. Springer-Verlag, 2004, 117–131.

A lock-free queue algorithm is implemented by first constructing an "optimistic" doubly-linked list whose pointers are updated using a simple store, yet can be "fixed" if a bad ordering of events causes them to be inconsistent.

[212] L. Lamport. A new solution of Dijkstra's concurrent programming problem. *Communications of the ACM*, **17**(8):453–455, 1974.

A simple solution to the mutual exclusion problem, called the Bakery algorithm, is presented (see page 50). The solution serves processes on a first-come-first-served basis, it allows the system to continue to operate despite the failure of any individual component and uses only safe registers.

[213] L. Lamport. The synchronization of independent processes. *Acta Informatica*, 7:15–34, 1976.

A generalized version of the Bakery algorithm is used to implement a powerful synchronizing primitive.

[214] L. Lamport. A bug in the Bakery algorithm. Technical Report CA–7704–0611, Massachusetts Computer Associates, Inc., April 1977.

It is shown that the correctness of the Bakery algorithm depends on an implicit assumption on the implementation of computing the maximum.

[215] L. Lamport. Concurrent reading and writing. *Communications of the ACM*, **20**(11):806–811, 1977.

The first paper to consider the problem of asynchronous processes reading shared data while the data are being modified by another process. The writer is not allowed to wait (it must be wait-free), but readers may starve. The solution presented requires an unbounded number of shared variables. This problem is different from the readers and writers problem as defined in Section 8.2 (page 288). See also [283, 334].

[216] L. Lamport. Proving the correctness of multiprocess programs. *IEEE Trans. on Software Engineering SE–3*, 2:125–143, 1977.

The inductive assertion method is generalized to permit formal correctness proofs for multiprocess programs. The correctness proof of the Bakery algorithm is used to illustrate the method.

[217] L. Lamport. How to make a multiprocessor computer that correctly executes multiprocess programs. *IEEE Trans. on Computers*, **28**(9):690–691, 1979.

Defines sequential consistency–the atomicity condition traditionally assumed for multiprocess programs (see page 152).

[218] L. Lamport. A new approach to proving the correctness of multiprocess programs. *ACM Trans. on Programming Languages and Systems*, **1**(1):84–97, 1979.

A non-assertional approach to proving multi-process correctness is described by proving the correctness of an improved version of the Bakery algorithm.

[219] L. Lamport. Specifying concurrent program modules. *ACM Trans. on Programming Languages and Systems*, **5**(2):190–222, 1983.

An approach and formalism is developed for the specification of concurrent systems.

[220] L. Lamport. Solved problems, unsolved problems and non-problems in concurrency. In *Proc. 3rd ACM Symp. on Principles of Distributed Computing*, pages 1–11, August 1984.

An edited transcript of an invited talk given at the 2nd ACM Symp. on Principles of Distributed Computing. Includes, among other topics, an interesting description of the mutual exclusion problem.

[221] L. Lamport. The mutual exclusion problem: Part I–a theory of interprocess communication. *Journal of the ACM*, **33**:313–326, 1986.

A formalism for reasoning about concurrent systems which does not assume that read and write are atomic operations is developed.

[222] L. Lamport. The mutual exclusion problem: Part II–statement and solutions. *Journal of the ACM*, **33**:327–348, 1986.

Four solutions are given, ranging from the One-bit algorithm (page 64) which requires only one shared safe bit per process and permits individual starvation, to one requiring about n safe bits per process that satisfies strong fairness and fault-tolerance requirements.

[223] L. Lamport. On interprocess communication, parts I and II. *Distributed Computing*, **1**(2):77–101, 1986.

A formalism for specifying and reasoning about a concurrent system, which is not based on atomic actions, is described. In part II, the formalism is used to specify several classes of interprocess communication mechanism and to prove the correctness of algorithms for implementing them.

[224] L. Lamport. A fast mutual exclusion algorithm. *ACM Trans. on Computer Systems*, **5**(1):1–11, 1987.

A deadlock-free solution to the mutual exclusion problem is presented that, in the absence of contention, requires only seven memory accesses (page 42). A timing-based algorithm is also presented (page 367).

[225] L. Lamport. Concurrent reading and writing of clocks. *ACM Trans. on Computer Systems*, 8(4):305–310, 1990.

As an exercise in synchronization *without* mutual exclusion. Lock-free algorithms are developed to implement both a monotonic and a cyclic multiple-word clock that is updated by one process and read by one or more other processes.

[226] L. Lamport. *win* and *sin*: Predicate transformers for concurrency. *ACM Trans. on Programming Languages and Systems*, **12**(3):396–428, 1990.

The weakest liberal precondition and strongest postcondition predicate transformers are generalized to allow reasoning about concurrent programs. A proof of the Bakery algorithm is included.

[227] L. Lamport, S. Perl, and William Weihl. When does correct mutual exclusion algorithm guarantee mutual exclusion? *Information Processing Letters*, **76**(3):131–134, 2000.

The notions of *true* mutual exclusion, and the weaker *virtual* mutual exclusion are discussed. It is shown that mutual exclusion algorithms designed assuming sequentially consistent memory may not guarantee true mutual exclusion in practice; they only guarantee virtual mutual exclusion. (See page 190.)

[228] L. Lamport, R. Shostak, and M. Pease. The byzantine generals problem. *ACM Trans. on Programming Languages and Systems*, **4**(3):382–401, 1982.

Explains the consensus problem that was first introduced in [279] as follows: "A group of generals of the Byzantine army camped with their troops around an enemy city. Communicating only by messenger, the generals must agree upon a common battle plan. However, one or more of them may be traitors who will try to confuse the others. The problem is to find an algorithm to ensure that the loyal generals will reach agreement." The results are related to those from [279].

[229] V. Lanin and D. Shasha. Concurrent set manipulation without locking. In *Proc. 17th ACM Symp. on Principles of Database Systems*, pages 211–220, August 1988.

Set manipulation consists of the actions insert, delete, and member on keys. A concurrent set manipulation algorithm is proposed that uses no locking and relies on atomic read-modify-write operations.

[230] D. Lea. *Concurrent Programming in Java*. Addison-Wesley, 1999.

Many design patterns for concurrent programming in Java are presented.

[231] D. Lea. The Java concurrency package JSR-166. *http://gee.cs.oswego.edu/dl/concurrency-interest/index.html*, 2004.

Java Concurrency Utilities is a set of medium-level utilities that provide functionality needed in concurrent programs. The contents of JSR-166 have been released as part of JDK1.5.0. It supports concurrent queues, compare-and-swap locks, reader and writers, semaphores, barriers, and more.

[232] P. L. Lehman and S. B. Yao. Efficient locking for concurrent operations on B-trees. *ACM Trans. on Database Systems*, **6**(4):650–670, 1981.

The B-tree and its variants have been found to be highly useful for storing large amounts of information. A simple locking-based solution is presented, where no read-locks are used and only a small constant number of nodes are locked by any update process at any given time.

[233] D. Lehmann and M. O. Rabin. On the advantages of free choice: A symmetric and fully distributed solution to the dining philosophers problem. In *Proc. 8th ACM Symp: on Principles of Programming Languages*, pages 133–138, January 1981.

Two algorithms in which randomization is used to break symmetry are presented. The first algorithm, called the Free Philosophers Algorithm (page 272), satisfies deadlock-freedom while the second, called the Courteous Philosophers Algorithm (page 273), satisfies starvation-freedom.

[234] M. Li, J. Tromp, and P. M. B. Vitányi. How to share concurrent wait-free variables. *Journal of the ACM*, **43**(4):723–746, 1996.

The main construction presented is of an efficient multi-writer multi-reader atomic register directly from single-writer, single-reader atomic registers using $O(n)$ control bits.

[235] R. J. Lipton. Limitations of synchronization primitives with conditional branching and global variables. In *Proc. 6th ACM Symp. on Theory of Computing*, pages 230–241, April 1974.

Four synchronization primitives are compared, and it is shown that their relative power is not the same. The primitives are: PV (Dijkstra semaphore [107]), PV-chunk [333], PV-multiple [278], and up/down [338].

[236] Wai-Kau Lo and Vassos Hadzilacos. All of us are smarter than any of us: Nondeterministic wait-free hierarchies are not robust. *SIAM Journal on Computing*, **30**(3):689–728, 2000.

It is shown that if non-deterministic object types are allowed, the consensus hierarchy is not robust. See [187] for the definition of robustness.

[237] M. C. Loui and H. Abu-Amara. Memory requirements for agreement among unreliable asynchronous processes. *Advances in Computing Research*, **4**:163–183, 1987.

Among other results, it is proved that there is no consensus algorithm that can tolerate even a single crash failure in a shared memory system in which only atomic read/write registers are used. See also [135].

[238] B. D. Lubachevsky. Synchronization barrier and related tools for shared memory parallel programming. *International Journal of Parallel Programming*, **19**(3):225–250, 1990.

Among other results, a tournament barrier (page 211) is presented.

[239] S. S. Lumetta and D. E. Culler. Managing concurrent access for shared memory active messages. In *Proc. International Parallel Processing Symp.*, pages 272–278, March–April 1998.

The authors present a lock-free concurrent queue algorithm and demonstrate performance superior to several locking alternatives.

[240] E. A. Lycklama. A first-come-first-served solution to the critical section problem using five bits. M.Sc. Thesis, University of Toronto.

Older version of [241], October 1987.

[241] E. A. Lycklama and V. Hadzilacos. A first-come-first-served mutual exclusion algorithm with small communication variables. *ACM Trans. on Programming Languages and Systems*, **13**(4):558–576, 1991.

An algorithm that satisfies the "first-come-first-served" property and requires only five shared bits per participant is presented. The algorithm works in a model of concurrency that does not assume atomic operations.

[242] N. A. Lynch, I. Saias, and R. Segala. Proving time bounds for randomized distributed algorithms. In *Proc. 13th ACM Symp. on Principles of Distributed Computing*, pages 314–323, August 1994.

A method of analyzing time bounds for randomized distributed algorithms is presented. The power of the method is illustrated by its use in proving a constant upper bound on the expected time for some process to reach its critical region in Lehmann and Rabin's Dining Philosophers algorithm [233].

[243] N. A. Lynch. Fast allocation of nearby resources in a distributed system. In *Proc. 12th ACM Symp. on Theory of Computing*, pages 70–81, April 1980.

The dining philosophers problem is extended to an arbitrary graph network. See [244].

[244] N. A. Lynch. Upper bounds for static resource allocation in a distributed system. *Journal of Computer and System Science*, **23**:254–278, 1981.

The dining philosophers problem is extended to an arbitrary graph network, in which a philosopher needs to acquire resources on all incident edges in order to eat, and a solution is presented and analyzed.

[245] N. A. Lynch. *Distributed Algorithms*. Morgan Kaufmann Publishers, Inc., 1996.

The book contains lots of significant algorithms and impossibility results in the area of distributed algorithms, presented in an automata-theoretic setting.

[246] N. A. Lynch and N. Shavit. Timing-based mutual exclusion. In *Proc. 13th IEEE Real-Time Systems Symp.*, pages 2–11, December 1992.

A timing-based algorithm is presented where only the property of deadlock-freedom depends on the timing assumptions, and mutual exclusion is guaranteed even in presence of timing faults. Unlike the algorithms in [21, 224], this algorithm does not provide fast access in the absence of contention.

[247] M. R. MacBlane. Source level atomic test-and-set for the tuxedo system source product. Technical report, UNIX System Laboratories, May 1991.

Explains how Lamport's algorithm [224] is used to implement a test-and-set operation when TUXEDO [328] is run on machines–like the MIPS 3000 series processors–that do not support an atomic test-and-set operation.

[248] P. S. Magnusson, A. Landin, and E. Hagersten. Efficient software synchronization on large cache coherent multiprocessors. Technical Report T94:07, Swedish Institute of Computer Science, February 1994.

Expanded version of [249].

[249] P. S. Magnusson, A. Landin, and E. Hagersten. Queue locks on cache coherent multiprocessors. In *Proc. 8th International Symp. on Parallel Processing*, pages 165–171, April 1994.

Two queue-based lock algorithms are presented. The authors have compared these new algorithms to previously published queue-based algorithms in terms of performance, memory requirements, code size, and required hardware support. They concluded that one of the two new algorithms is the best overall queue-based lock algorithm for the class of architecture studied. See also [248].

[250] D. Malkhi, M. Merritt, M. K. Reiter, and G. Taubenfeld. Objects shared by Byzantine processes. *Distributed Computing*, **16**(1):37–48, 2003.

This work explores situations in which processes accessing shared objects can fail arbitrarily (Byzantine faults). Shows that sticky bits are universal in the Byzantine failure model. See also [16].

[251] A. J. Martin and J. R. Burch. Fair mutual exclusion with unfair *P* and *V* operations. *Information Processing Letters*, **21**(2):97–100, 1985.

The authors slightly improve on the space complexity of the solution in [270]. A starvation-free (1-bounded waiting) solution using two weak binary semaphores (used together as a "split binary semaphore") and two *n*-valued atomic registers is presented, which works for an unknown but finite number of processors.

[252] H. Massalin and C. Pu. A lock-free multiprocessor OS kernel. Technical Report CUCS-005-91, Columbia University, 1991.

The authors have implemented a multi-processor OS kernel using only lock-free synchronization methods based on double-word compare-and-swap.

[253] P. E. McKenney. Selecting locking primitives for parallel programming. *Communications of the ACM*, **39**(10):75–82, 1996.

The paper presents a pattern language to assist in selecting synchronization primitives for parallel programs. This pattern language assumes that the locking design has already been chosen.

[254] J. M. Mellor-Crummey and M. L. Scott. Algorithms for scalable synchronization on shared-memory multiprocessors. *ACM Trans. on Computer Systems*, **9**(1):21–65, 1991.

It is shown that one can construct busy-wait synchronization algorithms that induce no memory or interconnect contention. The idea is to spin on locally-accessible flag variables, until some processor terminates the spin with a single remote write operation. The algorithms use swap and compare-and-swap operations. See Section 4.4.3 (page 165), and Section 5.5 (page 212) for some of the results.

[255] J. M. Mellor-Crummey and M. L. Scott. Scalable reader-writer synchronization for shared-memory multiprocessors. *ACM SIGPLAN Notices*, **26**(7):106–113, 1991.

In [254] the authors have presented scalable spin-locks and barriers. In this work they extend their previous work and present reader-writer locks that exploit locality in the memory hierarchies of shared-memory multi-processors to eliminate contention.

[256] M. Merritt and G. Taubenfeld. Speeding Lamport's fast mutual exclusion algorithm. *Information Processing Letters*, **45**:137–142, 1993. (Published as an AT&T technical memorandum, May 1991.)

A linked list is used to speed up a mutual exclusion algorithm. This optimization permits additional concurrency by allowing scans of the list to be concurrent with insertions and deletions of list entries.

[257] M. Merritt and G. Taubenfeld. Atomic *m*-register operations. *Distributed Computing*, 7(4):213–221, 1994.

The authors investigate systems where it is possible to access several registers in one atomic step, characterize those systems in which the consensus can be solved in the presence of faults, give bounds on the space required, and describe a fast mutual exclusion algorithm using atomic *m*-register operations.

[258] M. Merritt and G. Taubenfeld. Fairness of shared objects. In *Proc. 12th International Symp. on Distributed Computing*, LNCS 1499. Springer-Verlag, 1998, 303–317.

All the results that are presented in Section 4.8 are taken from [258], where algorithmic issues that arise due to various fairness assumptions on how pending requests are served by shared objects are investigated. The paper includes also several other results about fairness of shared objects.

[259] M. Merritt and G. Taubenfeld. Computing with infinitely many processes. In *Proc. 14th International Symp. on Distributed Computing*, LNCS 1914. Springer-Verlag, 2000, 164–178.

Several classic problems in concurrent computing are explored assuming the number of processes which may participate is infinite. In particular, a new adaptive algorithm for starvation-free mutual exclusion is presented. See the algorithms on pages 66 and 108.

[260] M. M. Michael. High performance dynamic lock-free hash tables and list-based sets. In *Proc. 14th ACM Symp. on Parallel Algorithms and Architectures*, pages 73–82, August 2002.

A CAS-based lock-free list-based set algorithm is presented, and is used as a building block of an algorithm for lock-free hash tables.

[261] M. M. Michael. Safe memory reclamation for dynamic lock-free objects using atomic reads and writes. In *Proc. 21st ACM Symp. on Principles of Distributed Computing*, pages 21–30, July 2002.

A lock-free memory management method for dynamic lock-free objects is presented that allows arbitrary memory reuse. It can be used to prevent the ABA problem for pointers to dynamic nodes in most algorithms, without requiring extra space per pointer or per node. See [262].

[262] M. M. Michael. Hazard pointers: Safe memory reclamation for lock-free objects. *IEEE Trans. on Parallel and Distributed Systems*, **15**(6):491–504, 2004.

This paper presents hazard pointers, a memory management methodology that allows memory reclamation for arbitrary reuse. Journal version of [261].

[263] M. M. Michael and M. Scott. Fast mutual exclusion, even with contention. Technical Report 460, Department of Computer Science, University of Rochester, June 1993.

A fast timing-based mutual exclusion algorithm is presented which capitalized on the ability of memory systems to read and write at both full- and half-word granularities. The authors have tested their algorithm (page 368), Lamport's algorithm [224] (page 367), and Alur–Taubenfeld algorithm [21] (page 347), and found that, with backoff in place, all work extremely well, outperforming the naive hardware locks of the Silicon Graphics Iris multi-processor, even with heavy contention.

[264] M. M. Michael and M. L. Scott. Correction of a memory management method for lock-free data structures. Technical Report 599, University of Rochester, 1995.

In [331], a memory management method is proposed for link-based data structures that addresses the ABA problem. The authors report and correct possible race conditions in the above method.

[265] M. M. Michael and M. L. Scott. Simple, fast, and practical non-blocking and blocking concurrent queue algorithms. In *Proc. 15th ACM Symp. on Principles of Distributed Computing*, pages 267–275, 1996.

A non-blocking concurrent queue algorithm using compare-and-swap, and a two-lock queue algorithm using simple locks (i.e., test-and-set) are presented and evaluated.

[266] M. M. Michael and M. L. Scott. Nonblocking algorithms and preemption-safe locking on multiprogrammed shared memory multiprocessors. *Journal of Parallel and Distributed Computing*, **51**(1):1–26, 1998.

The results reported indicate that simple data structure non-blocking algorithms, which exist for queues, stacks, and counters, can work extremely well.

[267] M. Moir and J. H. Anderson. Wait-free algorithms for fast, long-lived renaming. *Science of Computer Programming*, **25**(1):1–39, 1995.

Presents a long-lived renaming algorithm by which is implemented connecting splitters in a grid. The splitter construct is contained within Lamport's fast mutual exclusion algorithm (page 42) [224].

[268] M. Moir, D. Nussbaum, O. Shalev, and N. Shavit. Using elimination to implement scalable and lock-free fifo queues. In *Proc. 17th ACM Symp. on Parallelism in Algorithms and Architectures*, pages 253–262, July 2005.

By using a scaling technique called elimination as a backoff technique for the queue algorithm from [265], the authors have demonstrated that elimination can be applied to improve the performance of linearizable FIFO queues.

[269] S. Moran, G. Taubenfeld, and I. Yadin. Concurrent counting. *Journal of Computer and System Sciences*, **53**(1):61–78, 1996.

The authors study implementations of wait-free counters, which count modulo some given number, using only small size objects.

[270] J. M. Morris. A starvation-free solution to the mutual exclusion problem. *Information Processing Letters*, **8**(2):76–80, 1979.

A starvation-free solution using three weak binary semaphores and two n-valued atomic registers is presented, which works for an unknown but finite number of processors and satisfies 1-bounded waiting (page 201). Refutes Dijkstra's conjecture [111].

[271] L. E. Moser and P. M. Melliar-Smith. The world banker's algorithm. *Journal of Parallel and Distributed Computing*, **9**:369–373, 1990.

A version of Dijkstra's banker's algorithm [107] that allows each process to make resource allocation decisions independently and concurrently is presented. The algorithm is for a single resource type and assumes synchronous model with broadcast.

[272] M. Nesterenko and A. Arora. Dining philosophers that tolerate malicious crashes. In *Proc. 22nd International Conference on Distributed Computing Systems* pages 191–198, July 2002.

A solution to the problem of dining philosophers is presented that tolerates malicious crashes. In a malicious crash the failed process behaves arbitrarily for a finite time and then ceases all operation undetectably to other processes. The tolerance of the solution is achieved by the combination of stabilization and crash failure locality.

[273] E. P. Ogrady and R. Lozano. A performance study of mutual exclusion/synchronization mechanisms in an IEEE 796 bus multiprocessor. *IEEE Micro*, **5**(4):32–47, 1985.

Of three mechanisms evaluated, the FIFO semaphore tied up the system bus the least. The FIFO semaphore mechanism should produce faster operation and less bus activity than a single lock implementation.

[274] E. T. Ordman. Minimal threshold separators and memory requirements for synchronization. *SIAM Journal on Computing*, **18**(1):152–165, 1989.

Suppose each vertex of a graph represents a process, and two vertices are connected by an edge iff the two corresponding processes cannot be executing their critical sections simultaneously. If this graph is a threshold graph, then mutual exclusion can be easily solved using PV-chunk operations on a single register which can take $t + 1$ values, where t is the minimal threshold separator number of the graph [162]. In this paper it is proved that the above upper bound is tight. The bounds hold even for read-modify-write registers (as used in [83]), which is considerably less restrictive than PV-chunk.

[275] C. Papadimitriou. *The Theory of Database Concurrency Control.* Computer Science Press, 1986.

Concurrency control is the problem of synchronizing access of many users to the same database so as to avoid inconsistencies. This book explains, analyzes, and compares the known techniques for concurrency control in a uniform, clear framework.

[276] D. L. Parnas. On a solution to the cigarette smokers' problem (without conditional statements). *Communications of the ACM*, **18**(3):181–183, 1975.

See page 294 for the definition of the cigarette smokers' problem. A follow up of [278].

[277] D. L. Parnas and A. N. Habermann. Comment on deadlock prevention method. *Communications of the ACM*, **15**(9):840–841, 1972.

Refers to a comment from [180] about the algorithm in [156].

[278] S. S. Patil. Limitations of capabilities of Dijkstra's semaphore primitives for coordination among processes. In *Project MAC computational structures group, MIT, memo 57*, 1971.

The author defines a strong type of semaphore, called a PV-multiple, which makes it possible to access several basic semaphores in one step, and introduces the cigarette smoker's problem.

[279] M. Pease, R. Shostak, and L. Lamport. Reaching agreement in the presence of faults. *Journal of the ACM*, **27**(2):228–234, 1980.

The first paper that defines the consensus problem (see page 307). The communication model is asynchronous message-passing systems. Correct processors always communicate honestly, whereas faulty processors may lie. It is shown that the problem is solvable for, and only for, $n \geq 3m + 1$, where m is the number of faulty processors and n is the total number. It is also shown that if faulty processors can refuse to pass on information but can not falsely relay information, the problem is solvable for arbitrary $n \geq m \geq 0$ (see also [228]).

[280] G. L. Peterson. Concurrency and complexity. Technical Report TR59, University of Rochester, August 1979.

The thesis of Gary Peterson. The lower bounds are mentioned in [281] and similar, but not as good, lower bounds are in [83]. Includes, among many other results, a result that there is no two process mutual exclusion algorithm that is immune to infinite number of failures, which uses only two shared bits.

[281] G. L. Peterson. New bounds on mutual exclusion problems. Technical Report TR68, University of Rochester, February 1980 (Corrected, Nov. 1994).

Upper bounds are presented for n-process mutual exclusion in a model which supports a read-modify-write operation. It is shown that a memory-less starvation-free solution can be achieved with $\lfloor n/2 \rfloor + 2$ values, 2-bounded waiting can be achieved with $n + 2$ values, while (normal) FIFO can be achieved with $n + 6$ values. These upper bounds improve the bounds presented in [83]. In the algorithms the exit code is not wait-free (i.e., requirement 4 on page 12 is not satisfied). Also several algorithms are presented using various types of semaphores (unfair, weak, and strong), and it is proved that any starvation-free mutual exclusion algorithm for n processes using only atomic registers and test-and-set bits must use at least n atomic registers and test-and-set bits (Problem 4.11).

[282] G. L. Peterson. Myths about the mutual exclusion problem. *Information Processing Letters*, **12**(3):115–116, 1981.

A simple two-process solution to the mutual exclusion problem is presented (page 32). The solution is also modified to solve the n-process case (page 90).

[283] G. L. Peterson. Concurrent reading while writing. *ACM Trans. on Programming Languages and Systems*, 5(1):46–55, 1983.

The problem of asynchronous processes reading shared data while the data are being modified by another process (CRWW) is considered. The main algorithm presented solves the problem with neither the readers nor the writer ever waiting. Actually, it presents the first wait-free implementation of a single-writer atomic register from single-writer atomic bits. The CRWW problem is different from the readers and writers problem as defined in Section 8.2 (page 288). See also [215, 334].

[284] G. L. Peterson. A new solution to Lamport's concurrent programming problem using small shared variables. *ACM Trans. on Programming Languages and Systems*, 5(1):56–65, 1983.

A mutual exclusion algorithm which can tolerate an *infinite* number of immediate failures is presented. In the algorithm, no process can be passed by another more than two times total. It uses one 4-valued single-writer register per process. Peterson's fault-tolerant algorithm is given on page 142.

[285] G. L. Peterson. The essential Dekker's algorithm. Technical report, Georgia Institute of Technology, June 1986.

A simple algorithm is presented that is the essential Dekker's algorithm for two process mutual exclusion. The algorithm is a little more complex than the two process solution given in [282] but is far simpler than the original Dekker's algorithm [107] and the variants of Dekker's algorithm in [118].

[286] G. L. Peterson. Observations on ℓ-exclusion. In *Proc. 28th Annual Allerton Conference on Communication, Control and Computing*, pages 568–577, October 1990.

Several algorithms for solving the ℓ-exclusion problem using read and write atomicity are presented: an ℓ-deadlock-free algorithm (Problem 6.3, page 246), an ℓ-starvation-free algorithm (page 230), an unbounded FIFO-enabling algorithm (page 232) which is based on an interesting variant of Lamport's Bakery algorithm (page 54), and a complex bounded FIFO-enabling algorithm. (FIFO-enabling is defined on page 229.) The open problem mentioned in Problem 6.5 (page 246) is from this paper. See [7], for another (complex) FIFO-enabling solution.

[287] G. L. Peterson and M. J. Fischer. Economical solutions for the critical section problem in a distributed system. In *Proc. 9th ACM Symp. on Theory of Computing*, pages 91–97, May 1977.

Several mutual exclusion algorithms which can tolerate an infinite number of immediate failures are presented. One of the algorithms uses bounded size shared registers, and satisfies the first-come-first-served policy. However, its doorway is not wait-free – a process may have to busy-wait before passing its doorway. The paper is the first to present tournament algorithms. (The two process algorithm is presented on page 78.)

[288] S. M. Pike and P. A. G. Sivilotti. Dining philosophers with crash locality 1. In *Proc. 24th IEEE International Conference on Distributed Computing Systems*, pages 22–29, March 2004.

Using an eventually perfect failure detector, the authors construct an algorithm with crash locality 1 under partial synchrony.

[289] S. A. Plotkin. Sticky bits and universality of consensus. In *Proc. 8th ACM Symp. on Principles of Distributed Computing*, pages 159–175, August 1989.

Shows that Sticky bits are universal: they can be used to transform sequential specifications of arbitrary objects into wait-free concurrent implementations.

[290] M. O. Rabin. The choice coordination problem. *Acta Informatica*, **17**:121–134, 1982.

The choice coordination problem with k alternatives is introduced. The paper focuses mainly on the case of $k = 2$. See Section 8.5.3 (page 299) for more details.

[291] M. O. Rabin. N-process mutual exclusion with bounded waiting by $4\log_2 N$-valued shared variable. *Journal of Computer and System Science*, **25**(1):66–75, August 1982.

A randomized mutual exclusion algorithm is presented. In [301] it is proved that the properties of the randomized algorithm from [291] are not as claimed. In [210], the algorithm has been modified, so as to overcome the difficulties which were pointed out in [301]. See page 194 for more details.

[292] V. Ramakrishnan, I. D. Scherson, and R. Subramanian. Efficient techniques for fast nested barrier synchronization. In *Proc. 7th Annual ACM Symp. on Parallel Algorithms and Architectures*, pages 157–164, July 1995.

Two hardware barrier synchronization schemes are presented which can support deep levels of control nesting in data parallel programs.

[293] S. P. Rana and D. K. Banerji. An optimal distributed solution to the dining philosophers problem. *International Journal of Parallel Programming*, **15**:327–335, 1986.

The LLR algorithm is introduced (page 266), and it is shown that this algorithm allows the maximum achievable concurrency (Theorem 7.11, page 266).

[294] M. Raynal. *Algorithms for Mutual Exclusion.* MIT Press, 1986. Translation of: *Algorithmique du Parallélisme*, 1984.

A collection of some early algorithms for mutual exclusion.

[295] M. Raynal. A short introduction to failure detectors for asynchronous distributed systems. *ACM SIGACT News Distributed Computing Column 17*, **36**(1), 2005.

An introductory survey to the failure detector concept.

[296] M. Raynal and J. Helary. *Synchronization and Control of Distributed Systems and Programs.* Wiley, 1990. Translation: *Synchronisation et contrôle des systèmes et des programmes répartis*, 1988.

The focus is on algorithms for message passing systems.

[297] D. P. Reed. Implementing atomic actions on decentralized data. *ACM Trans. on Computer Systems*, **1**(1):3–233, 1983.

Presents a timestamp-based concurrency-control approach.

[298] I. Rhee and C-Y Lee. An efficient recovery-based spin lock protocol for preemptive shared memory multiprocessors. In *Proc. 15th Annual ACM Symp. on the Principles of Distributed Computing*, pages 77–86, May 1996.

The authors propose a recovery-based spin lock protocol in which preemptions are allowed to happen at any time, and when an inopportune preemption that causes delay occurs, the preempted process is immediately recovered from the preemption. The experimental study shows that queue-based spin locks with either a prevention-based or a recovery-based preemption handling scheme are also suitable for real-time computing.

[299] R. L. Rivest and V. R. Pratt. The mutual exclusion problem for unreliable processes: preliminary report. In *Proc. 17th IEEE Symp. on Foundations of Computer Science*, pages 1–8, 1976.

The first mutual exclusion algorithm which can tolerate an *infinite* number of immediate failures is presented. The algorithm satisfies linear waiting, and uses bounded size registers. (The two process version of the algorithm is presented on page 143.)

[300] E. Ruppert. Consensus numbers of multi-objects. In *Proc. 17th ACM Symp. on Principles of Distributed Computing*, pages 211–217, June–July 1998.

See Problem 9.30 (page 340) for main result.

[301] I. Saias. Proving probabilistic correctness statements: The case of Rabin's algorithm for mutual exclusion. In *Proc. 11th ACM Symp. on Principles of Distributed Computing*, pages 263–274, August 1992.

A general methodology to prove correctness of randomized algorithms is presented. The methodology is used to show that the properties of Rabin's mutual exclusion algorithm [291] are not as claimed. That is, it is shown that there is a schedule under which a set of processes can suffer lockout for arbitrary long periods. See page 194 for more details.

[302] M. Saks and F. Zaharoglou. Wait-free k-set agreement is impossible: The topology of public knowledge. *SIAM Journal on Computing*, **29**(5):1449–1483, 2000.

The authors prove the impossibility result for set-consensus as stated in Problem 9.17 (page 339).

[303] F. B. Schneider, B. Bloom, and K. Marzullo. Putting time into proof outlines. *Lecture Notes in Computer Science*, **600**:618–639, 1992.

A logic for reasoning about timing properties of concurrent programs is presented. The correctness proof for Fischer's timing-based mutual exclusion algorithm (page 345) is used to illustrate the logic in action.

[304] M. Schneider. Self-stabilization. *ACM Computing Surveys*, **25**(1):45–67, 1993.

A survey on the topic of self-stabilization. Includes a good list of references.

[305] M. L. Scott. Non-blocking timeout in scalable queue-based spin locks. In *Proc. 21st ACM Symp. on Principles of Distributed Computing*, pages 31–40, July 2002.

A queue-based lock is presented in which the timeout code is non-blocking. The algorithm uses compare-and-swap and swap (i.e., fetch-and-store) objects, and has unbounded space and time complexities.

[306] O. Shalev and N. Shavit. Split-ordered lists: lock-free extensible hash tables. In *Proc. 22nd ACM Symp. on Principles of Distributed Computing*, pages 102–111, July 2003.

A lock-free implementation of an extensible hash table using compare-and-swap operations is presented which provides concurrent insert, delete, and search operations with an expected O(1) cost.

[307] N. Shavit and D. Touitou. Software transactional memory. In *Proc. 14th ACM Symp. on Principles of Distributed Computing*, pages 204–213, August 1995.

Building on the hardware-based transactional synchronization methodology from [171], the authors offer a software method for supporting flexible transactional programming of synchronization operations. The method uses load linked/store conditional operations.

[308] A. Silberschatz, P. B. Gagne, and P. Galvin. *Operating System Concepts, 6th edition.* Wiley, 2001.

Presents fundamental operating system concepts and algorithms, including a chapter about process coordination.

[309] A. K. Singh and M. G. Gouda. Rankers: A classification of synchronization problems. *Science of Computer Programming*, **21**(3):191–223, 1993.

A methodology for solving synchronization problems is developed. This methodology is illustrated by solving a number of synchronization problems such as mutual exclusion, producer-consumer, dining philosophers, etc.

[310] M. Singhal and N. G. Shivaratri. *Advanced Concepts in Operating Systems: Distributed, Database and Multiprocessor Operating Systems.* McGraw-Hill, Inc., 1994.

The book offers comprehensive coverage of many topics including: process synchronization, distributed mutual exclusion, deadlock, agreement, security, cryptography, and scheduling.

[311] C. R. Snow. *Concurrent Programming.* Cambridge University Press, 1992.

An introduction to concurrent progamming for undergraduates. Uses a few (early) synchronization algorithms to demonstrate the basic ideas.

[312] P. K. Srimani. Another solution of the mutual exclusion problem–comments. *Information Processing Letters*, **20**(3):165, 1985.

Points out that there exist earlier and much better solutions than the one in [207].

[313] W. Stallings. *Operating Systems, Internals and Design Principles, 4th edition.* Prentice-Hall, Inc., 2001.

Presents fundamental operating system concepts and algorithms, including a chapter about mutual exclusion and synchronization.

[314] E. W. Stark. Semaphore primitives and starvation-free mutual exclusion. *Journal of the Association for Computing Machinery*, **29**(4):1049–1072, 1982.

Definitions of several types of semaphore primitives are given. It is then shown that under certain conditions, although it is possible to implement starvation-free mutual exclusion with one type, it is not possible to do so with some other type.

[315] E. Styer and G. L. Peterson. Improved algorithms for distributed resource allocation. In *Proc. 7th ACM Symp. on Principles of Distributed Computing*, pages 105–116, August 1988.

Styer and Peterson are perhaps the first to consider the issue of failure locality for general resource allocation problems. They measure the locality of an algorithm by the length of the longest waiting chain of processes that may be formed in the system. Obtain an algorithm with failure locality of 3 and exponential response times.

[316] E. Styer and G. L. Peterson. Tight bounds for shared memory symmetric mutual exclusion problems. In *Proc. 8th ACM Symp. on Principles of Distributed Computing*, pages 177–191, August 1989.

The *symmetric* mutual exclusion problem adds the restriction that the only way of distinguishing processes is by comparing identifiers, which are unique. It is proved that n registers are necessary and sufficient for deadlock-free symmetric mutual exclusion, while $2n - 1$ registers are necessary and sufficient for memoryless starvation-free symmetric mutual exclusion. (See page 136.)

[317] H. Sundell and P. Tsigas. Lock-free and practical deques using single-word compare-and-swap. In *Proc. 8th International Conference on Principles of Distributed Systems*, 2004.

The authors present a lock-free implementation of concurrent deque that supports parallelism for disjoint accesses. The algorithm is based on a general lock-free doubly linked list.

[318] H. Sundell and P. Tsigas. Scalable and lock-free concurrent dictionaries. In *Proc. 2004 ACM Symp. on Applied Computing*, pages 1438–1445, March 2004.

A lock-free implementation of a concurrent dictionary which is based on a randomized sequential list structure called skiplist is presented.

[319] B. K. Szymanski. Mutual exclusion revisited. In *Proc. 5th Jerusalem Conf. on Information Technology*, pages 110–117, October 1990.

Four mutual exclusion algorithms, based on Morris' algorithm [270], are presented. They include an algorithm that satisfies the "first-come-first-served" property and requires only four shared bits per participant; and an algorithm that satisfies the "linear-waiting" property and requires only three shared bits per participant. The algorithms also satisfy some strong fault-tolerance properties.

[320] M. Takamura, T. Altman, and Y. Igarashi. Speedup of Vidyasankar's algorithm for the group k-exclusion problem. *Information Processing Letters*, **91**(2):85–91, 2004.

An improvement to the algorithm from [335] is proposed.

[321] A. S. Tanenbaum. *Modern Operating Systems, 2nd edition.* Prentice-Hall, Inc., 2001.

Presents fundamental operating system concepts and algorithms, including a chapter about processes and threads.

[322] A. S. Tanenbaum and M. V. Steen. *Distributed Systems, Principles and Paradigms.* Prentice-Hall, Inc., 2002.

Covers the principles and technologies of distributed systems, including: communication, replication, fault tolerance, and security. Includes one chapter about synchronization.

[323] G. Taubenfeld. The black-white bakery algorithm. In *Proc. 18th International Symp. on Distributed Computing*, LNCS 3274. Springer-Verlag, 2004, 56–70.

A mutual exclusion algorithm is presented that has four desired properties: (1) it satisfies FIFO fairness, (2) it satisfies local-spinning, (3) it is adaptive, and (4) it uses a finite number of bounded size atomic registers. It is the first algorithm (using only atomic registers) which satisfies both FIFO and local-spinning, and it is the first bounded space algorithm which satisfies both FIFO and adaptivity.

[324] G. Taubenfeld. Computing in the presence of timing failures. In Proc. 26th *International Conference on Distributed Computing Systems*, July 2006.

Timing failures refer to a situation where the environment in which a system operates does not behave as expected regarding the timing assumptions, that is, the timing constraints are not met. The author investigates the ability to recover automatically from transient timing failures, and presents time-resilient solutions to the mutual exclusion and consensus problems.

[325] Y.-K Tsay. Deriving a scalable algorithm for mutual exclusion. In *Proc. 12th International Symp. on Distributed Computing*, September 1998. *LNCS 1499* Springer Verlag 1998, 393–407.

A local spinning tournament algorithm is presented which is based on variants of the algorithms of Peterson (page 32) and Kessels (page 35) for two processes.

[326] P. Tsigas and Y. Zhang. A simple, fast and scalable non-blocking concurrent fifo queue for shared memory multiprocessor systems. In *Proc. 13th ACM Symp. on Parallel Algorithms and Architectures*, pages 134–143, July 2001.

A non-blocking queue algorithm using compare-and-swap is presented and analyzed.

[327] J. Turek, D. Shasha, and S. Prakash. Locking without blocking: making lock based concurrent data structure algorithms nonblocking. In *Proc. 11th ACM Symp. on Principles of Database Systems*, pages 212–222, August 1992.

A technique is proposed that can convert existing lock-based algorithms into non-blocking algorithms with the same functionality.

[328] *TUXEDO System Release 4.0–Product Overview*, 1990.

The TUXEDO Transaction Processing System provides applications designers and programmers with a framework for building on-line transaction processing application in a distributed computing environment.

[329] N.-F. Tzeng and A. Kongmunvattana. Distributed shared memory systems with improved barrier synchronization and data transfer. In *Proc. 11th International Conference on Supercomputing*, pages 148–155, July 1997.

Introduces new barrier synchronization algorithms.

[330] J. T. Udding. Absence of individual starvation using weak semaphores. *Information Processing Letters*, **23**(3):159–162, October 1986.

Another variant of Morris' solution [270] is presented, by massaging a partially correct but obvious program into a less obvious but correct one.

[331] J. D. Valois. Implementing lock-free queues. In *Proc. 7th International Conference on Parallel and Distributed Computing Systems*, pages 212–222, October 1994.

Two algorithms based on linked lists and arrays are presented and evaluated. Also, a technique called reference counting is proposed which guarantees to prevent the ABA problem without the need to use tags or double-word compare-and-swap.

[332] J. D. Valois. Lock-free linked lists using compare-and-swap. In *Proc. 14th ACM Symp. on Principles of Distributed Computing*, pages 214–222, August 1995.

The author implements non-blocking singly-linked lists, allowing concurrent traversal, insertion, and deletion by any number of processes, and uses it as a building block for implementing a concurrent dictionary object.

[333] H. Vantilborgh and A. van Lamsweerde. On an extension of Dijkstra's semaphore primitives. *Information Processing Letters*, **1**:181–186, 1972.

Discusses a possible generalization of the semaphore primitives which allows distinguishing in various cases amongst different processes waiting at the same semaphore. In this extension (dubbed PV-chunk in [235]) the semaphores is allowed to be updated by "chunck" that are arbitrary positive integers.

[334] K. Vidyasankar. Concurrent control with Readers and Writers revisited. *Information Processing Letters*, **4**:81–85, 1990.

A modification is proposed to Peterson's construction, see [283], of single-writer multi-reader multi-valued atomic register using multi-valued safe registers atomic bits. The resulting construction is simple and short.

[335] K. Vidyasankar. A simple group mutual ℓ-exclusion algorithm. *Information Processing Letters*, **85**(2):79–85, 2003.

A combined problem of ℓ-exclusion and group mutual exclusion, called the group ℓ-exclusion problem, is introduced and solved.

[336] S. Vijayaraghavan. A variant of the Bakery algorithm with bounded values as a solution to Abraham's concurrent programming problem. In *Proc. Design, Analysis and Simulation of Distributed Systems*, March–April 2003.

The algorithm is incorrect when the number of processes n is too big. It is complicated (one of the conditions includes seven terms).

[337] J. L. Welch and N. A. Lynch. A modular drinking philosophers algorithm. *Distributed Computing*, **6**(4):233–244, 1993.

A variant of the Drinking Philosophers algorithm from [92] is described and proved correct in a modular way. The algorithm in [92] is based on a particular dining philosophers algorithm and relies on certain properties of its implementation. The Drinking Philosophers algorithm presented is able to use an arbitrary dining philosophers algorithm as a subroutine.

[338] P. Wodon. Still another tool for controlling cooperating algorithms. In *Carnegie-Mellon University Report*, 1972.

Defines the *up/down* synchronization primitive (see also [235]).

[339] T. Woo. A note on Lamport's mutual exclusion algorithm. *Operating Systems Review (ACM)*, **24**(4):78–80, 1990.

In Lamport's Bakery algorithm, the ticket numbers are not bounded. This paper "resolves" this problem by allowing the ticket numbers to move around a ring of length $2N$, where N is the number of processes. It is easy to show that the resulting published algorithm is incorrect.

[340] J.-H. Yang and J. H. Anderson. Fast, scalable synchronization with minimal hardware support. In *Proc. 12th ACM Symp. on Principles of Distributed Computing*, pages 171–182, August 1993.

See [342] for the journal version. The paper presents a local-spinning tournament algorithm with process time complexity of $O(\log_2 n)$, when only remote accesses are counted (page 102). Also a local-spinning algorithm is presented in which the time complexity in the DSM model is $O(1)$ in the absence of contention and $O(n)$ in the presence of contention. See also [28, 29, 202].

[341] J.-H. Yang and J. H. Anderson. Time bounds for mutual exclusion and related problems. In *Proc. 26th ACM Symp. on Theory of Computing*, pages 224–233, May 1994.

Tradeoffs are established between time complexity and write-contention for solutions to the mutual exclusion problem. One of the results implies an $\Omega(\log_w n)$ lower bound on the contention-free time complexity of any algorithm that uses atomic registers, where w is the maximum number of processes that may simultaneously write the same register.

[342] J-H. Yang and J. H. Anderson. A fast, scalable mutual exclusion algorithm. *Distributed Computing*, **9**(1):51–60, 1995.

Journal version of [340]. See [28, 29] for stronger results.

[343] P.-C. Yew, N.-F. Tzeng, and D. H. Lawrie. Distributing hot-spot addressing in large-scale multiprocessors. *IEEE Trans. on Computers*, **C-36**(4):388–395, 1987.

Introduced the (software) combining tree barrier (page 210).

[344] K. Yue and R. T. Jacob. An efficient starvation-free semaphore solution for the graphical mutual exclusion problem. *Computer Journal*, **34**(4):345–349, 1991.

A method for constructing starvation-free solutions for graphical mutual exclusion problems based on semaphores associated with processes is described. The number of semaphores used is equal to the number of processes.

[345] X. Zhang, Y. Yan, and R. Castaneda. Evaluating and designing software mutual exclusion algorithms on shared-memory multiprocessors. *IEEE Parallel and Distributed Technology*, **4**(1):25–42, 1996.

The authors have implemented, evaluated and compared the scalabilities of several representative mutual exclusion algorithms which use atomic registers. They also proposed three new mutual exclusion algorithms that combine features of existing algorithms. Their results show that the performance of software-based algorithms is highly architecture-dependent.

Index

A

B

C

D

E

F

G

H

I

J

K

L

M

N

P

Q

R

S

Y